D1528490

MERLIN'S SECRET

*The African and Near Eastern
Presence in the Ancient British Isles*

Robert N. List

University Press of America,® Inc.
Lanham • New York • Oxford

Copyright © 1999 by
University Press of America,® Inc.
4720 Boston Way
Lanham, Maryland 20706

12 Hid's Copse Rd.
Cumnor Hill, Oxford OX2 9JJ

Library of Congress Cataloging-in-Publication Data

List, Robert N.
Merlin's secret : the African and Near Eastern presence in the
ancient British Isles / Robert N. List.
p.   cm.
Includes bibliographical references and index.
1. Prehistoric peoples—Great Britain. 2. Ethnology—Great Britain.
3. Great Britain—Civilization—Middle Eastern influences. 4.
Great Britain—Civilization—African influences. I. Title.
GN805.L56 1999 936.1—dc21   99—21550 CIP

ISBN 0-7618-1395-0 (cloth: alk. ppr.)
ISBN 0-7618-1396-9 (pbk: alk. ppr.)

Contents

Acknowledgments

Grateful acknowledgments are made to Dover Publications. Family crests reproduced on p. 377 of *Merlin's Secret* are reproduced with permission from Dover Publications' *Heraldic Crests: A Pictoral Archive of 4, 424 Designs fror Artists and Crafts People* by James Fairbairn.

Also, I wish to thank Prof. Doris E. Saunders for her encouragement and inspiration.

Dedication

To Suwandi O. and to Prof. Doris Saunders, who
introduced me to giants.

Chapter 1

~~~~~~

Big Lies: An Introduction

Who were the ancient colonists who crossed the open sea and helped to populate the land mass which would later be called the British Isles? From where did they come? Were some of them non-Aryan in extraction? From the eclipse of the Aurignacian Age [c. 40,000 B.P.] to the Neolithic and Bronze Ages to the Roman Conquest and even into post-Roman times, strangers from various points of departure migrated into what are today known as Ireland, Wales, Scotland and England. When examining the Neolithic Age in Britain, most historians who specialize in these matters are still unable to identify the ethnicity of the megalith-builders whose handiwork dots the weathered landscapes of the western peripheries of the British Isles. Nor can they speak with certainty regarding the identity of the masons of Stonehenge I, or of the makers of the stepped pyramid called Silbury Hill, or of the builders of the eerie underworld chambers of New Grange. Equally baffling are the ancient place-names of towns, mountains, lakes and rivers which lie scattered across the British Isles, titles which often echo exotic and forgotten origins. And more baffling still are the human sacrifices once conducted by the star-struck Druids, ritual slaughters which often involved the burning alive of scores of men, women and children lashed to towering wicker men. Who were these Druids? From what lands did they migrate? And what demons were they trying to appease?

Many historians argue that these so-called mysteries are by no means impenetrable. Advancing the generally unpopular assertion that many early Britons were *people of color* who originated from areas as remote as the Mediterranean, Black, and Red Sea littorals, they pose and attempt to answer several questions in an effort to clear up these and other lingering enigmas regarding the origins of many early Britons. Here is a sampling.

Did Africoid *negritos*, later called Grimaldi Man, penetrate Europe from Spain to the very edge of the Arctic ice fields during the recession of the glaciers which marked the Aurignacian Age? Did later waves of colonists from the Mediterranean, Black, and Red Sea basins trek across continental European land routes and sail the Western Atlantic seaway to populate the British Isles during the Neolithic, Bronze, and the early La Tene Iron Ages?

Did highly-skilled artisans from the Nile Valley or their descendants construct Stonehenge I and the nearby stepped pyramid called Silbury Hill? Did Ethiopian-Greek and Libyan-Greek incense entrepreneurs and Eastern Mediterranean Phoenician tin, copper and gold prospectors populate Cornwall and portions of coastal Ireland and Wales for centuries prior to the Roman occupation of Britain? Did a contingent of the Roman occupation force include a North African commander and various Numidian mercenaries? Did certain swarthy Britons, who dyed their skin bluish-purple and tattooed themselves with Abyssinian serpent designs, wage war against invading Roman legions? Were pre-Christian and early Christian Irish royal families and Scottish Picts practicing kingship election rituals and matrifocally-based inheritance customs that originated in Ethiopia and Upper Egypt? Did the titles and the religious beliefs of the Bronze Age kings and priesthoods of the Mediterranean and Red Sea basins reappear in pre-Christian Ireland and in its Scottish colony of Dal Riada? Can traces of North African Berber syntax be found in the Gaelic language? Can many English and Gaelic words and place-names be derived not only from Indo-European but also from ancient Egyptian, Ethiopian and Coptic roots and cognates? Did substantial numbers of seafaring Moors from North Africa and Spain assert naval hegemony over the Western Atlantic seaway in post-Roman times? Did Moorish pirates descend upon coastal Ireland, Wales and Scotland during the early medieval period? Did Byzantine, Coptic Egyptian/Ethiopian, and North African heresies, rampant in the early centuries of the first millennium c.e., become transplanted in pre-Patrician, Christian Ireland and in its Scottish colony? Did the stylistic motifs of Coptic art overwhelmingly influence the Insular illuminated manuscript style of seventh century c.e. Ireland and Scotland? Did families of mixed European and Moorish descent accompany William the Conqueror during his invasion of Southern England in 1066 and migrate to England during the subsequent Norman resettlement of the region? Did various returning Crusaders and Knights bring love-children of mixed English and Muslim descent to the British Isles? Did members of well-heeled, continental Moorish families, after fleeing the horrors of the Reconquista and the Inquisition in Spain, intermarry with various members of the British upper crust? And does a dash of Moorish ancestry inform the pedigree of the current royal family itself?

This study will attempt to answer these questions and many more as it attacks two lingering 'big lies' regarding the origins and the religious persuasion of many early Britons. For it is now apparent that race-based distortions have been passed on from generation to generation by historians swimming in the academic mainstream.

And what are those twin 'big lies' that continue to be spun? The first deception would have us believe that pre-Hellenic, island-dwelling Greeks, whose descendants may well have been the ancestors of many living Britons, were Aryan invaders from the North who spoke an Indo-Aryan tongue. Egyptians, Ethiopians, Semites and Phoenicians of various hues exerted only marginal impact on this pre-Hellenic civilization, the lie continues. The second big lie echoes the first. For its proponents would have us believe that during the Mesolithic, Neolithic, Bronze and Iron Ages the inhabitants of the British Isles were exclusively Aryan, Caucasoid, Anglo-Saxon, Nordic or whatever similar adjectives can be mustered. Dusky Merlin of King Arthur's Camelot would likely have dismissed that misconception with a good belly laugh, as would the generations of *merlins* who preceded him.

Willy-nilly, the Aryan-based, pre-Hellenic Greek paradigm was modified slightly by various chroniclers and applied with equal gusto to the history of the British Isles. This application attempted both to guarantee the Aryan origins of the early Britons and to devalue any contradicting ancient testimonies of folklore, classical historians, and theories of the much-derided diffusionist school. Early Britain was devoid of people of African and Semitic origin, those adhering to the British version of the Aryan paradigm insist. No Egyptians, Ethiopian-Greeks, Berbers, or Semites from the Eastern and Southern Mediterranean, and the Black and Red Sea littorals need apply. Assuming that Egypt, especially, was a closed, stay-at-home society that had virtually no interest in colonizing Greece, and even less in penetrating the British Isles and Scandinavia, they court illogic. As a result, they assume that just as Indo-Aryan word roots overwhelmingly informed the language of pre-Hellenic Greece, these roots exclusively undergirded the vocabulary of the Romance languages of Europe as well. Therefore, any attempt to go hunting for Egyptian, Semitic, Abyssinian, Coptic or North African Berber word roots or syntax in these predominantly Caucasoid areas of the world would be a fool's errand.

To better understand this controversy, the two conflicting models used to account for the origins of pre-Hellenic Greeks need to be examined. These are the Ancient Model and the Aryan Model, paradigms which Martin

Bernal explores in his series entitled *Black Athena*.

Briefly, architects of the Ancient Model argue that primitive tribes inhabiting pre-Hellenic Greece such as the Pelasgians, were finally civilized by Egyptian and Phoenician colonists who enjoyed a hegemony in much of coastal Greece during the heroic age. But the proponents of the Aryan Model, in opposition to those of the Ancient Model, suppose that pre-Hellenic, Indo-Aryan invaders from the north mixed with the surviving coastal and inland Caucasoid indigenes to eventually create the Greek civilization of that heroic age (Bernal 1991, 1).

The theories of pre-Hellenic Greek origins posed by adherents of the Ancient Model are critical to this study, for *Lebor Gabala Erinn,* or the "book of the taking of Ireland," [hereafter referred to as *Lebor Gabala*] traces the origins and itineraries of its last five invader groups which entered Ireland to none other than these pre-Hellenic Greek Isles which classical sources argue were initially populated by Africans and Semites. Consequently, then, a number of the pre-Hellenic peoples noted by Bernal were likely ancestral to many of those colonists included in the waves of invader groups which entered the British Isles well beforeRoman times.

Bernal calls for a revised Ancient Model that would stress the prominence of Egypto-Ethiopian and Phoenician culture and language diffusion into pre-Hellenic Greece without denying some Indo-Aryan influences as well. In doing so, he reveals that the shift away from the Ancient Model which posits Egypt as an intellectual ancestor of Greece occurred in the last quarter of the eighteenth century. That displacement resulted from the racially charged atmosphere of the period which felt more comfortable with the concept of an Indo-European or Aryan race in the family tree rather than the duskier Egyptian prototypes (Bernal 1987, 224-25). Bernal cites Sir William Jones' contention made in 1786 that Sanskrit is closely related to Greek and Latin. Jones argues that Sanskrit, Gothic and Celtic share so many of the same verb roots and other grammatical forms that they must have derived from the same, albeit defunct, Indo-European mother tongue (Bernal 1987, 229-30).

Bernal satirically presents additional arguments for honoring Sanskrit, or the so-called lost mother tongue, as the sole ancestor of the Romance languages. He notes that since the Brahmins of India traced their ancestry back to Aryan invaders who originated from the central Asian highlands, German Romantics were content to argue that the Caucasian race and even mankind itself could trace their origins to the mountainous regions of Central Asia as well (1987, 229).

With similar tongue in cheek, Bernal reveals that two decades later, Friedrich Schlegel boasts: "Everything, absolutely everything, is of Indian origin" (1987, 230). Schlegel goes so far as to reverse the diffusion process out of Egypt, arguing, like Godfrey Higgins before him, that Egypt's greatness resulted from Indian colonization in ancient times. Bernal indicates that although Schlegel also praises Arabic and Hebraic languages, Schlegel, nonetheless, devalues the Egyptian influence. For Schlegel argues that although Egyptian civilization influenced Jewish culture, such an influence was really no sign of Egyptian accomplishments, given, in Schlegel's view, that Egypt's high civilization had been inherited from the Indian subcontinent (Bernal 1987, 231).

Bernal goes on to cite the ambivalent attitudes held about Egypt which characterized much of the thinking of nineteenth century German linguists in general. For they torpedoed the assertion of classical historians that ancient Egyptian word roots also found their way into pre-Hellenic Greek, Old English and Gaelic languages as well (Bernal 1987, 230ff.). For Bernal, this pseudo-scholarly ambivalence toward Egypt in the nineteenth century amounted to an intellectual game of approach-avoidance that helped to manufacture the 'Egyptian problem':

> *If it had been scientifically 'proved' that Blacks were biologically incapable of civilization, how could one explain Ancient Egypt-- which was inconveniently placed on the African continent? There were two, or rather, three solutions. The first was to deny that the Ancient Egyptians were black; the second was to deny that the Ancient Egyptians had created a 'true' civilization; the third was to make doubly sure by denying both. The last has been preferred by most 19th- and 20th-century historians.* (1987, 241)

Noting his belief that dark skin pigmentation was pervasive in both the Old and Middle Kingdoms prior to the invasion of the Hyksos when it began to lighten through intermarriage, Bernal spoofs J. A. Gobineau's mental gymnastics. In accordance with biblical tradition, Gobineau categorizes the Egyptians as black Hamites. And to get around the problem of blacks being synonymous with high culture, Gobineau accepts Schlegel's argument that Egypt's dawn culture resulted from Indian colonization. In response, Bernal argues that to solve the so-called Egyptian problem, the blackness of the Egyptians was turned on its ear. Hence the illogical conclusion was reached that in the dawn period of Egypt, Caucasians from India constituted the pure Egyptian race. It was these Caucasians, it was argued, who built the Old Kingdom pyramids. Furthermore, the decline of Egypt resulted from miscegenation with black Africans, a blending which reached its climax during Egypt's sunset period (1987, 245).

Bernal cites another would-be impediment that prevented a more rational acceptance of Egyptian, and not merely Sanskrit, as a proto-language. The Egyptians, it was erroneously believed, were not monotheists. As a result, Christianity could not be the debris of Egyptian religion as the maverick Gerald Massey, and the translator of the *Book of the Dead*, Sir Peter le Page Renouf, insisted. And to add insult to injury, anthropologists of the mainstream proposed that the Egyptian language failed to possess the *spiritual* elements needed to be one of the precursors of Greek and Latin. Bernal reveals that in 1904 Egyptologist Wallace Budge drove this illogic home in a statement of such extraordinary lameness that it is quoted at length:

> The Egyptians, being fundamentally an African people, possessed all the virtues and vices which characterized the North African races generally, and it is not to be held for a moment that any African people could become metaphysicians in the modern sense of the word. In the first place, no African language is suitable for giving expression to theological and philosophical speculations, and even an Egyptian priest of the highest intellectual attainments would have been unable to render a treatise of Aristotle into language which his brother priests, without teaching, could understand. The mere construction of the language would make such a thing impossible, to say nothing of the ideas of the great Greek philosopher, which belong to the domain of thought and culture wholly foreign to the Egyptian. (Budge 1904, I, 143; Bernal 1987, 261)

Dredging up another example of Budge's illogic, Bernal cites Budge's specious attack on H. Brugsch's argument that the Egyptian for 'divine', *ntr* was the root of the Greek and Latin word 'nature':

> It is difficult to see how the eminent Egyptologist could attempt to compare the conception of God formed by a half-civilized African people with those of such cultivated nations as the Greeks and Romans." (Budge 1904, I, 68; Bernal 1987, 261)

This same myopia is shared by Egyptologist Adolph Ermann, who grudgingly admits in another extraordinarily specious quote that Egyptian could, in fact, have provided the roots for many Greek words. Debating whether or not the Egyptian *br* could be the root word for 'small boat' in Greek, Ermann sputters:

> I do not doubt that broad-minded colleagues could find substantially more [Egyptian loan words in Greek], as I could have. I must in this case remind

them that in a script in which the vowels are unmarked, and with a vocabulary in which the meanings are very precarious, with some good will, one can find an Egyptian origin for every Greek word . . . this is a sport that I happily leave to others. (1883, 336; Bernal 1987, 263)

Bernal identifies another irony regarding the study of Egyptian language, noting that even though scholars of the Renaissance and the Enlightenment wished to pursue comparative studies with Egyptian, no Rosetta Stone had yet emerged. But, he goes on, in the mid- and late-nineteenth century, post-Rosetta Stone scholars also exploring Coptic, the ritual language used by the Coptic priests that virtually preserves dynastic Egyptian intact, were dissuaded from pursuing comparative studies because of their Aryan bias. This bias led them to mistakenly believe that language of the Egyptians was inferior to those of the ancient Indians, Greeks and Romans (1987, 257).

For Bernal, racism and imperialism are great impediments to the scientific method, and these blights continue to wreak havoc well into the twentieth century. He recalls that Egypt's status declined with the onslaught of racism in the 1820s. And as racial anti-Semitism reared it head in the 1880s and again between 1917 and 1939, the status of the Phoenicians experienced a similar decline among scholars. As a result, by World War II, Greece, mainstream scholars argued, inherited virtually no cultural legacy from Egypt and Phoenicia, classical legends of Phoenician and Egyptian colonization of pre-Hellenic Greece to the contrary. This devaluation of Egyptian and Phoenician influences on Greece, he goes on, continues to our day, despite the decline of anti-Semitism after the Second World War (1987, 442).

And the same myopia washed up on British shores. For if *Lebor Gabala* is to be believed, these largely coastal-dwelling, pre-Hellenic Greeks, to whom the Ancient Model attributes Ethiopian, Egyptian and Phoenician origins, were the ancestors of the earliest invader groups which, after circuitous wanderings through North Africa and Spain, finally descended upon Ireland in the Neolithic and Bronze Ages.

Such myopia must be challenged. By serving as a clearing-house for various scholarly studies arguing the case for African and Semitic colonization of early Britain, *Merlin's Secret* will forge a new synthesis of evidence in regard to the African and Near Eastern etiology of much of the culture, language and racial stock found in the early British Isles.

As early as 1858 George and Henry Rawlinson, decipherers of Mesopotamia's cuneiform scripts, write:

Recent linguistic discovery tends to show that a Cushite or Ethiopian race did in the earliest times extend itself along the shores of the Southern ocean from Abyssinia to India. The whole peninsula of India was peopled by a race of this character before the influx of Aryans; it extended from the Indus along the seacoast through the modern Belochistan and Kerman, which was the proper country of Asiatic Ethiopians; the cities on the northern shores of the Persian Gulf are shown by the brick inscriptions found among their ruins to have belonged to this race; it was dominant in Susiana and Babylonia, until overpowered in one country by the Aryan, in the other by Semitic intrusion; it can be traced, both by dialect and tradition, throughout the whole south coast of the Arabian peninsula; and it still exists in Abyssinia, where the language of the principal tribe (the Galla) furnishes, it is thought, a clue to the cuneiform inscriptions of Susiana and Elymais, which date from a period probably a thousand years before our era. (1858, 360)

Brunson (1985) argues for a powerful Egyptian presence in seventh century B.C.E. Palestine. He cites an excavation at Lakish resulting in the discovery of 695 skulls which were transported to London: "the relationships found suggest that the population of the town of 700 B.C.E. was entirely, or almost entirely, of Egyptian origin" (Ussiskhin 1982, 56-57). Ancient chroniclers such as Pliny, who wrote that Cepheus, an Ethiopian king, ruled Syria, and Tacitus, who noted the Roman belief that the Jews migrated from Ethiopia, reinforce this archeological record (Rogers 1967, 92). That Ethiopians known as Adites, Thamudites, and Himyars [meaning dusky] were early inhabitants of Southern Arabia is confirmed by the *Encyclopedia Britannica*, according to Wayne Chandler, who quotes a key passage:

The inhabitants of Yemen, Hadramaut, Omat and the adjoining districts, in the shape of the head, color, length and slenderness of limbs and scantiness of hair, point to an African origin . . . The first dawning gleams that deserve to be called history find Arabia under the rule of a southern race. They claimed descent from Khatan. They were divided anciently into several aristocratic monarchies. These Yemenite kings, descendants whose rulers were called 'Tobba,' of Hamitic etymology, reigned with a few dynastic interruptions for about 2500 years. They demanded the obedience of the entire southern half of the peninsula and the northern by tribute collectors. The general characteristics of the institutions of Yemen bore considerable resemblance to the neighboring ones of the Nile Valley. (1995, 271)

As will be argued in subsequent chapters, Sabaean colonists and prospectors appear to have been commonplace in Neolithic and Bronze Age Britain.

In the act of modifying the Aryan Model for British climes, generally astute anthropologists such as Carelton Coon are guilty of an obfuscation that muddles pre-Hellenic Greek origins. A case in point can be found in the often brilliant *Races of Europe*. At one point Coon ponders the language of the Basques, a mountain people living in Northern Spain who, like various living North African, Irish and Welsh populations, have in their blood the highest incidence of the type O gene in Europe [using the standard ABO system]. Ignoring the evidence of the blood specialists, he argues that Basque derives either from a Neolithic tongue brought into ancient Iberia from the Mediterranean, or from a language derived from pre-Phoenician Western Asia, or from a blend from both imported tongues (1939, 501-502). The adjective of currency at the time-- Hamitic-- is conspicuous by its absence.

This study applies many of Bernal's observations regarding the scholarly myopia which denies or devalues the influence of Afroasiatic languages on the formation of early Greek to a similar blurring of reality operative when tracing the Egyptian, Greek, and North African origins of various words and syntactical structures found in the languages spoken in the early British Isles. Bernal's insistence that numerous Egyptian roots inform many Greek word etymologies echoes Gerald Massey's assertions a century earlier regarding the Egyptian and Coptic word cognates which Massey believed he discovered not only in certain English and Gaelic words but also in various ancient place-names that dot the map of contemporary Britain.

In their attempts to counteract the second lie, several ethnologists over the past three centuries have argued that a substantial influx of colonists of various hues and ethnicities, derived from the Mediterranean, Black, and Red Sea basins, entered the British Isles from pre-history to historical times. Both qualitative and quantitative evidence undergirds their hypotheses regarding these numerous migrations to the western peripheries of the British Isles. These propositions range from the testimony of Greek and Roman classical writers and indigenous folklore to hard data derived from the areas of comparative linguistics and blood type analysis, cranial studies, and archeological anomalies.

Nonetheless, most contemporary historians have largely ignored or dismissed such claims of substantial African and Semitic origins for many an early Briton. This denial has led to numerous historical misreadings which prevent living Britons and their cousins around the globe from gaining a true understanding of the multi-ethnic heritage of countless individuals of British descent.

For at least three centuries, mainstream anthropologists, historians and linguists engaged in unraveling the pedigrees of Neolithic and Bronze Age

Britons have been spin-doctoring this sometimes specious Aryan Model. Largely ignoring Classical Greek and Roman testimonies, and dodging medieval and Renaissance histories such as *Lebor Gabala*, certain sections of Geoffrey of Monmouth's *The History of the Kings of Britain* and Rafael Holinshed's *Chronicles*, to name a few, they extend the pale of the Aryan Model to the north. And whenever the possibility that dark-skinned, pre-Hellenic, Ethiopian-Greeks or Libyan-Greeks, or olive-skinned, curly-haired Phoenicians may have played a significant or even a minor role in the peopling of the early British Isles raises its swarthy head, red lights begin to flash in the brains of otherwise competent and even brilliant researchers, and seemingly indissoluble problems emerge.

In 1899 linguist J. Morris Jones discovered a bizarre parallel. Syntactical anomalies [syntax being the order of words in sentences] in both Indo-European-derived Welsh and Irish result from the vestiges of a pre-Aryan language system, which is today called Afroasiatic. This syntax identifiable in Welsh and Irish is derived by Morris Jones from an identical syntax found in Coptic and Berber languages. But when faced with his own conclusion that Africans must have been a major component in the population of the British Isles in the Neolithic Age, the Bronze Age and even in the Iron Age, Morris Jones found it necessary to categorize these likely itinerants as full-fledged members of the so-called North African White Race (1899, 618).

And anthropologist Francis Rodd, after weighing his evidence and proposing that descendants of the Tuareg Berber tribes account for many a nomad in the migrations from North Africa to the British Isles in Neolithic and Bronze Age times, decided in 1926 that the Tuareg are, with few exceptions, a Caucasian tribal complex and *have been so since at least 2500 B.C.E.* (1926, 46). Rodd either did not consider or did not care to consider that the lightening process which occurred in the broad expanses of North Africa was a relatively recent phenomenon accompanying the Moorish takeover of the region. Although a Caucasoid people called the Tamahu did inhabit Libya, as the western borders of Pharaonic Egypt were called, from at least 2500 B.C.E., the results of the mixing process that Rodd observes in the much broader expanse of contemporary North Africa resulted largely from extramarital sexual activities between Arabs and Moors of varying complexions with a select portion of the hundreds of thousands of white female slaves filched by Muslim slave traders largely from the Slavic regions of Eastern Europe and from Galicia in Northern Spain. Seeing the large white component in the North African of his day, Rodd and others drew a color curtain across Africa which appeared to separate the blacks of the sub-Saharan region from the so-called North African White Race. And to make matters worse, that curtain was pushed back well before the Muslim conquest.

This color curtain has proven to be quite pernicious. Laboring under the belief that the Moors of Spain were exclusively tawny or white Moors derived from olive-skinned Arabs, historian John Crow as late as 1965 argues in *Spain: The Root and the Flower* that:

> One must be careful here to specify that the Africa here referred to is not the lower part of the dark continent peopled by black men. It is Northern Africa, the ancient homeland of the Iberians, of the Carthaginians, a Semitic race, of the Jews themselves, and of the Moors, composed of many Arab-speaking groups. (1965, 6)

But largely through the efforts of archeologists such as S. Gsell, pre-Muslim North Africans are having their dark pigmentation restored to them. For Gsell reported that the vast majority of skeletons he exhumed at Carthage dating to the time of Hannibal revealed the predominance of Negroid characteristics as will be demonstrated later.

Cultural diffusion, it seems, was a supportable proposition as long as it could be shown that it was Caucasians who were on the move northward from Africa, instead of transplanted Ethiopian-Greeks, Libyan-Greeks, Near Eastern Semites, sea-roving Phoenicians and the like.

And if still more convincing evidence of African and Near Eastern migrations into the British Isles and other heavily Caucasoid European areas surfaces, yet another strategy is introduced. Generally astute anthropologists such as Colin Renfrew can always save the day by espousing variations of the independent invention theory. If Old Kingdom, black Africans were constructing the stepped pyramid of Saqqara, and unidentified Britons were constructing the stepped pyramid called Silbury Hill, simultaneously and using the same mathematics, it is just a coincidence. Somehow, he would have us believe, both of these highly complex architectural projects blossomed in complete isolation from one another.

This study brings together a body of evidence provided by scores of anthropologists, historians, literary critics, and linguists mainly of nineteenth and twentieth century vintage who listened to a different drummer. The diffusionist and hyper-diffusionist theories of some of the more notable scholars, many not so affectionately labeled old cranks in their day, are critically examined for strengths and weaknesses. The diffusionist theory *par excellence* of Gerald Massey, who was convinced that many English and Gaelic words could be derived from Egyptian rather than Sanskrit loan words, is scrutinized in depth. Given similar examination are observations posited by linguists such as J. Morris Jones and Heinrich Wagner, who argue that although Celtic tongues are largely Indo-European in origin, certain syntactical anomalies in Insular Celtic, nonetheless, derive from the syntax of the non-Aryan Berber and Coptic speaking invaders [nervously labeled Caucasoid by Morris Jones]. Quantitative data provided by craniologists such as G. M. Morant, T. L. Woo, and Brenda N. Stoessiger, who match the cranial features of mainly dolichocephalic [long-headed] skulls excavated in the British Isles at Neolithic sites with skulls originating in the Nile Valley, lower East Africa and North Africa in matching time frames, is also weighed and sifted. Likewise, additional quantitative data from British and Welsh blood specialists such as W. E. R. Hackett, I. Morgan Watkin and A. E. Mourant, who note similar ABO blood antigen frequencies in various living populations along the western periphery of Spain and the British Isles, the Nile Valley, East Africa and the Berber band extending across North Africa to the Canary Islands, is scrutinized. And diffusionist propositions from historians such as David Mac Ritchie, Walter Simson and William Skene, who upset the Victorian world by arguing that a considerable number of dark-skinned Moors and Gypsies populated transmarine and Northeastern Scotland beginning in early medieval times, are cited to corroborate much of the quantitative data provided by the craniologists and blood specialists. Then too, observations regarding African and Near Eastern cultural diffusion proposed by students of myth and literature such James Bonwick, George Lawrence Gomme, and Charles Squire, who were fascinated by the enduring legends of the dark fairies, brownies and black giants that peopled the early folklore of the British Isles, are presented. And numerous reformulations and modifications of earlier diffusionist theory proposed by twentieth century scholars such as Joel Augustus Rogers, Edward Scobie, Cheikh Anta Diop, Winthrop Palmer Boswell, Bob Quinn, Alice E. Lasater, Jim Bailey, Ivan van Sertima, Martin Bernal, J. P. Cohane, John Ivimy and others are reviewed, and their observations corroborated with earlier evidence. Given the unearned obscurity of a small group of these authors and their works-- such as Massey's *A Book of the Beginnings* and *Ancient Egypt, the Light of the World*; David Mac Ritchie's *Ancient and Modern Britons*; Morris Jones' "Pre-Aryan Syntax in Insular Celtic," which appears in the Appendix B of John Rhy's *The Welsh People*; and Winthrop Palmer Boswell's *The Snake in the Grove* and *Irish Wizards in the Woods of Ethiopia*-- substantial discussions of their works will be offered in subsequent chapters in the hope of bringing the key arguments posed by these much ignored pioneers of Afrocentrism to the light of day.

The proposition that Africans and Semites of various complexions played a central role in the peopling of the British Isles and in the evolution of its religion and culture has accumulated over the years and has finally reached a critical mass. As a result, there is a need for a comprehensive overview on the entire subject. This study provides that overview.

The impact of this on-going revision of the history of the British Isles should not be underestimated. It cries out for serious genealogical reexaminations of the pedigrees and family trees of numerous British, Scottish, Welsh and Irish families bearing North African and Moorish surnames as well as heraldic crests replete with Moors' heads. Prominent surnames such as Campbell, Douglas, Duff, Dun, McLeod, MacAlpin, Moore, More, Macrae, Morris and scores of others should not be immune to this process. This historical revision also challenges students of the etymology and syntax of the English and Gaelic languages to re-examine Egyptian, Coptic and Berber word roots and attribute to them a prestige formerly reserved for Indo-European cognates. It should also provoke a reassessment of the status of women in the pre-Christian British Isles and facilitate comparisons with the elevated position of women in the Mediterranean and Red Sea basins. The studies cited should likewise facilitate a clearer understanding of the etiology of the lingering pre-Aryan rituals, customs and folklore of the British Isles. They should also stimulate a reassessment of medieval Moorish contributions to the British Isles in the areas of the chivalric codes of knighthood, literature, scientific and medical advancements and the like. For one of the little told stories of European history is that of the Moors who flocked into central Europe and the British Isles by the thousands during the Moorish occupation of Spain and its aftermath, the bloody *Reconquista*.

But another piece of the puzzle regarding African and Near Eastern influences in the British Isles is still missing. For to fully comprehend the enormity of this diffusion process in northern climes, the importation of a bizarre, cometary religion needs to be examined. Likely carried to Ireland by the invader groups described in *Lebor Gabala* and by Phoenician prospectors during the Late Bronze Age, this religion was birthed in Ethiopia, Egypt and the Sabaean deserts bordering the Red Sea. Centuries later it infiltrated Celtic druidic ritual and formed the substructure of Insular, pre-Patrician Christianity. In the sixth century C.E., the religion was given renewed vigor when the night sky revealed its horrors.

Merlin, or shall we say, the various *merlins* who continued the tradition of the Hebrew prophets of doom, knew these horrors well. For as the prophecies of Arthur's Merlin reveal, the grim memory of these sky-gods, once dubbed Osiris, Set, Horus, Yahweh, Asmodeus, Hercules, Zeus,

Dionysius, Apollo, Python, Typhon and the like in southern climes, was imported to Britain. And in the fifth and sixth centuries c.e. a new set of sky-gods reappeared over Europe. In the British Isles they were called Gargantua, Cuchulain, Balor, Lugh and Midir. In response to their visitations the druidic merlins frantically cast their spells and made their sacrifices to keep the sky from falling.

And what did these various deities represent? Comet fragments and their respective trains of meteorites which wreaked havoc across the Earth in the form of devastating meteor showers, according to Victor Clube and William Napier, two leading astrophysicists at England's Oxford University. Initially, meteor strikes plagued the Neolithic and Bronze Ages, and again, on a smaller scale, they reoccurred in the fifth, sixth and twelfth centuries c.e., Clube and Napier argue (1990, 43). As a result, the nascent, Insular Christianity of Ireland and Scotland largely maintained the deities and rituals of the so-called Pagan faiths which preceded it. Thus, the heretical Insular Christianity that was sweeping across Merlin's fifth and sixth century homeland of Scotland was quite simply new wine in a very old bottle.

Substantial evidence derived from sources as diverse as the testimonies of classical writers to data gleaned from modern-day astrophysics supports the argument that catastrophic meteor showers, some on a world-wide scale, periodically raked the planet from at least the fourth millennium b.c.e. through the collapse of the Late Bronze Age, with an encore again in the fifth and sixth centuries c.e. The sixth century event appears to have abruptly curtailed the age of Camelot and destroyed much of the vegetation of the British Isles.

Centuries later, a less brutal celestial encore marked the eve of the first Crusade. Sifting through many classical and medieval accounts, Clube and Napier develop the hypothesis that the major deities worshiped in the pantheons of the ancient religions of the Mediterranean and Red Sea basins and in those of pre-Christian Britain and Ireland were based upon these naturalistic events.

This study incorporates Clube's and Napier's hypothesis and proposes *that the African and Near Eastern religion imported to the British Isles in pre-Christian and early Christian times and its local refinements were largely based upon the worship of two primal dragon-pairs of cometary deities, the Osiris-Set and the Horus-Set dyads.* These dragon or serpent pairs, the first of which preceded the second, were comprised of the fragments of a disintegrating, short-period, super-comet which Clube and Napier identify, a comet that became locked in a periodic Earth grazing orbit. During each subsequent fly-by the respective dragon-pair appeared to engage in a terrifying series of celestial combats in the skies overhead, often pummeling the Earth with lethal meteor showers in the process. The cometary faces of Osiris and Set and Horus and Set were barely disguised in countless myths of the Mediterranean and Red Sea littorals, and these twin comets, this study proposes, were symbolized on earth by a series of god-kings, earthy representatives, who were sequestered in the scores of *nemetons,* or sacred groves, which dotted the shores and the inland mountaintops along these two sea littorals. This study holds, then, that as a result of these near misses, a series of cometary religions sprang up in the Mediterranean and Red Sea basins and in the adjacent Near East, creeds that led to the bizarre rituals of the murder of the ailing kings of the sacred groves [tanistry], the perpetuation of royal incest, and the ubiquitous animal and human sacrifice that was designed to propitiate these cometary deities. Each god-king, elected as he was through the vicissitudes of matrifocal tanistry, was regarded as a sacred hermaphrodite, for he was bonded, often in a pre-sexual relationship, either with his mother, daughter or sister according to the tenets of royal incest, and his very life was subject to the whim of his female consort. For his role in life was to preserve order both in the heavens and on Earth: To thwart the much-feared Doomsday, manifested as a catastrophic meteor shower, by magically serving as an emblem of the virile, pre-fallen, protector-comet Osiris which once ruled the heavens during the Golden Age before being driven from the sky by its adversary Set. But when old age began to creep up on the aging god-king, or when the reappearance of the Set comet or one of Set's later avatars proved particularly menacing, his consort could order his execution by goading the tanist supplanter to strangle or behead the aging king and bury his remains in the sacred grove.

For a time, Arthur's Merlin likely presided over these cometary, kingship rituals which formed the cornerstone of druidic ritual in Scotland. Imported to the British Isles from the third through the second millennium B.C.E. by the six invader groups described in *Lebor Gabala,* or the *Book of the Invasions,* a history composed by Coptic-influenced monks at Clonmacnoise Abbey in Ireland, these rituals flourished on fresh soil. In Ireland and in its Scottish colony of Dal Riada, the cometary theology which incorporated the primal 'murder' of comet Osiris by comet Set or Seth, flourished up to the sixth century C.E. and influenced not only Druidism, but the renegade, heretical theology of pre-Patrician, Insular Christianity, and the equally heretical Insular and Continental Grail legends as well.

Spectacular cometary reappearances, more benign than previous visits, occurred again in the twelfth century C.E., and as this study will demonstrate, accounted for the frenetic activity which resulted in the erection of Gothic cathedrals such as St. Denis and Chartres. Robert Payne's tribute to Abbot Suger, the master mason of Saint Denis, prototype of Europe's Gothic cathedrals, nearly hits the target:

> Almost single-handedly, Abbot Suger, the son of a serf, brought Gothic art into existence. He it was who filled the churches with light and sent the slender columns spinning so high they seemed to be reaching to the foothills of heaven. He shattered the walls to let the light in, and gilded the altar so that it would shine like the sun. For him all light was heavenly, being God's breath made visible, and the radiance of the angels. So he built a church like a cascade of jewels, a fountain of emeralds and rubies, a lake of silver and gold, to bring people closer to the heart of the glowing mystery of the light. He built a church in the form of a treasure casket of jewels flashing in God's holy fire. (1963, 161)

This study will demonstrate that "the glowing mystery of light" and "God's holy fire," which the Gothic imagination hoped to enshrine in its towering cathedrals, emanated from the terrifying pyrotechnics of a comet's passing in the twelfth century C.E., a dazzling light show evoking in the spectators the twin emotions of terror and ecstasy which led not only to an orgy of stone-cutting but to considerable blood-letting as well.

But centuries before the strange birth of Arthur's Merlin and the Gothic industry of the Middle Ages nearly a half a millennium later, a more ghastly show of celestial pyrotechnics occurred in the twin sea basins to the south, according to Clube and Napier (1990, 41ff.). So ghastly was it that the memory of its unearthly light became frozen in a persistent religious iconography that developed a life of its own. For shortly after the death of Ramesses II in 1232 B.C.E., the mysterious ten plagues of Egypt commenced. Exodus 10-12 reveals that these plagues created general consternation in Egypt, allowing for the escape of the Israelites amid a hail of stones and a rain of blood that fell from cloud-blackened skies. Although many argue that the ten plagues resulted from the side effects of the Thera eruption, Bernal proposes a 1628 B.C.E. date for the Thera event, thus making the catastrophes of the thirteenth century B.C.E. yet another travail which had to be endured (1991, 274ff.). Clearly, during this time the Eastern Mediterranean basin was a good place to leave. And it was propitious to leave because, as this study proposes, the hail of stones and the rain of blood and the vast cloud canopy that obscured the sun resulted not from volcanism, but from a climactic meteor shower, one of several that raked the twin sea basins over the centuries.

An excerpt from the Ipuwer Papyrus of the late thirteenth century B.C.E., discovered in Memphis and purchased by the Museum of Leiden in the Netherlands, gives some idea of the horrors of the period: "Nay, but the land turneth around as doth a potter's wheel . . . gates, columns and walls are consumed with fire . . . the southern ship [Upper Egypt] is adrift. The towns are destroyed . . . great and small say, 'I wish I were dead!'" And the Ermitage Papyrus housed in St. Petersburg provides insight into the valley of the shadow of death imagery of Isaiah 9, for "None can live when the sun is veiled by clouds" (Ermann 1927, 95,108; Velikovsky 1977b, 140).

Named Phaeton, Sekhmet, Anat, or Typhon, the comet fragment appears to have either brushed the earth's atmosphere or ripped through it during the fifth year of the reign of Pharaoh Merneptah (1232-1222 B.C.E.). In the texts of Sethos II (circa 1215 B.C.E.) the threatening Sekmet comet is described prior to its descent: "Sekmet was a circling star, which spread out his fire in flames, a fire-flame in his storm" (Breasted 1903, III, 117). Confirmation of the devastation caused by meteor showers also comes from Ras Shamra prior to that city's collapse near the end of the thirteenth century: "The star Anat has fallen from heaven; he slew the people of the Syrian land, and confused the two twilights and the seats of the constellations" (Bellamy 1938, 69). And in the Carnac inscription it is written that in the fatal fifth year of Pharaoh Merneptah's reign: "Libya has become a barren desert; the Libyans come to Egypt to seek sustenance for their bodies" (Spanuth 1979, 193; See Holscher 1937, 61ff.). And in the Medinet Habu texts, Ramesses III laments: "Libya has become a desert; a terrible torch hurled flame from heaven to destroy their souls and lay waste their land . . . their bones burn and roast within their limbs" (Spanuth 1979, 147). Centuries later, Pliny reflects on the event in his *Natural History*: "A terrible comet was seen by the people of Ethiopia and Egypt, to which Typhon, the King of that period [of Ethiopia] gave his name; it had a fiery appearance and was twisted like a coil, and it was very grim to behold: it was really not a star so much as what might be called a ball of fire" (1962, 223).

The focus of this study will be two-fold. First, it will follow the lead of the numerous scientists, anthropologists, and other historians, poets and ethnologists, who argue for the case for the African and Near Eastern origins of many inhabitants of the British Isles dating from the Aurignacian Age to eve of the European slave trade. Second, it will examine the emergence of cometary religion in southern climes, and then trace the evolution of this bizarre creed in the north. By serving as a clearing-house for the scholars cited in this study, *Merlin's Secret* will forge a new synthesis of evidence in regard to the African and Near Eastern origins of much of the racial stock, language, religion and culture that flourished in the early British Isles.

Chapter 2

~~~~~~

Preliminary observations of the early diffusionists

In the nineteenth and early twentieth centuries, the Aryan Model, as defined in Bernal's *Black Athena*, had won the hearts and minds of the mainstream scholars of European ethnohistory. To revive the outlawed Ancient Model quickly earned many a scholar the unenviable title of old crank. Despite this cloning of Aryan thought, a few intrepid scholars were willing to subject themselves to ridicule.

Using qualitative approaches, these nineteenth and early twentieth century mavericks propose that a substantial African Diaspora not only arrived on the shores of the British Isles, but also become inextricably woven into the islands' ethnic fabric during prehistoric and early historic times. These colonists, identified euphemistically by some scholars as "pre-Aryans," or "brown Mediterraneans," and more specifically by other, crankier scholars as Africans and Semites, or the direct descendants of such, are said to have migrated to Britain, Ireland, Wales and Scotland during the Aurignacian, Neolithic, Bronze and Iron Ages. And centuries later, some scholars argue, additional waves of Andalusian colonists and traders migrated to the British Isles not only during the Moorish occupation of Spain but also shortly after the ensuing expulsions of the Moors from that war- ravaged country.

After years of neglect, the bolder of these old cranks, along with some of their more reticent colleagues, are being rediscovered in this and other treatments of the issue of race in the history of the British Isles and the Continent. Many of the more prominent members of this dead anthropologists' society referred to in this and later chapters include Gerald Massey, David Mac Ritchie, Arthur Clive, James Bonwick, George Gomme, Charles Squire, John Rhys, and V. Gordon Childe.

Using a variety of qualitative approaches which include the study of folklore and early and late medieval literature, the investigation of classical Greek and Roman source material, the search for Afroasiatic loan words in the English language, the examination of curious pre-Aryan place-names throughout the Isles, and the study of early archeological sites and related inscriptions, they attempted, often without what today would be called a quantitative methodology, to prove that the British Isles had, since the Aurignacian Age, been visited and colonized by various African and Eastern Mediterranean invaders of myriad complexions.

These misnamed old cranks should not be ignored for at least two reasons. First, many were privy to a dying oral history, and to fading Celtic dialects such as Manx that had become extinct by the twentieth century. And second, numerous anthropologists using quantitative methodologies to examine the African and Near Eastern presence issue in the later years of the twentieth century came to nearly identical conclusions regarding that alleged presence in the British Isles. As a result, it will be necessary in subsequent chapters to indicate those areas of common agreement between the observations of these pioneering scholars and the propositions of their later quantitative cousins. To invoke legalese, accretion of the evidence adds to its weight, and the accumulated bulk that will be cited in this study may allow the much-ignored old cranks a few posthumous last laughs.

The supposition that non-Aryans once inhabited the British Isles resulted from several archeological anomalies that were being discovered throughout Britain.   And these anomalies attracted the attention of various ethnohistorians. In 1851 D. Wilson reported in *The Archeology of Scotland* that Sudanic ring money, long ago used as tribute paid to the Pharaohs by Sudanese Negroes, had been unearthed in Scotland (1851, 309). Added to that glitch were caches of blue beads found at the archeological district of Stonehenge dating from 1500 B.C.E. to 1200 B.C.E., beads identical in composition to others ubiquitous in ancient Egyptian sites (Rogers 1967, I, 196). And why was a black goddess once worshiped in Scotland? D. A. MacKenzie in *Ancient Man in Britain* asked that question when he wrote: "In Scotland, a black goddess (the Nigra Dea) in Adomnan's *Life of Columba* is associated with Loch Lorchy" (Rogers 1967, I, 197). And if these anomalies were not enough, in 1911 A. Bulleid and H. Gray asserted in *The Glastonbury Lake Village* report that Grimaldi skeletons had been unearthed at the site (Rogers 1967, I, 196).

One candidate for old crank status was John Rhys. He was well aware of such anomalies when he occupied the seat of Professor of Celtic at the University of Edinburgh for several years. In 1891 he published a comprehensive study of Welsh and Manx legends entitled *Celtic Folklore* in which he raises the ultimate question regarding the population substratum of the pre-Cesarian British Isles: "The neo-Celtic nations of these islands consist, speaking roughly, of a mixture of the invading Celts with the earlier inhabitants whom the Celts found in possession" (1891, 663). Speaking of an indigenous group called the "lake fairies," he goes on to propose that "we seem to have a trace of a non-Aryan race, that is to say, probably some of the early inhabitants of this island" (1891, 663). And from where might this non-Aryan race have come? He tries to provide an answer:

> Now the students of ethnology . . . tell us that we have among us, notably in Wales and Ireland, living representatives of a dark-skinned, long-skulled race of the same description as one of the types which occur . . . among the Basque populations of the Pyrenees. (1891,664-65).[1]

George Gomme, a rather timid crank of the same period, echoes more imprecise suspicions about the Celtic substratum of the British Isles in *Folklore as an Historic Science*. Gomme was puzzled by the the word Celt. Although it implied a white-skinned person who was, nevertheless, non-Aryan, the term was vague because what, in fact, was an Aryan? Gomme tries to untie the semantic and racial knots by arguing somewhat euphemistically that the original inhabitants of the British Isles were non-Celtic, non-Teutonic and conversant in a non-Aryan language (1908, 209). The adjective, 'African,' is carefully avoided.

In *Celtic Myth and Legend*, Charles Squire is a bit bolder when he attempts to deconstruct the vague term 'Aryan':

> The ancient inhabitants of Britain-- the Gaelic and British Celts-- have been already described as forming a branch of what are roughly called 'Aryans.' This name, however, has little reference to race, and really signifies the speakers of a group of languages which can be all shown to be connected, and to descend remotely from a single source-- a hypothetical mother-tongue spoken by a hypothetical people which we term 'Aryan,' or, more correctly, 'Indo-European.' (1975, 31)

He goes on to reveal the imprecision of the term in regard to delineating the race of the speakers of these language derivatives:

Not very long ago, it was supposed that this common descent of language involved a common descent of blood. A real brotherhood was enthusiastically claimed for all the principal European nations, who were also invited to recognize Hindus and Persians as their long-lost cousins. Since then, it has been conceded that, while the Aryan speech survived, though greatly modified, the Aryan blood might well have disappeared, diluted beyond recognition by crossing with the other races whom the Aryans conquered, or among whom they more or less peacefully settled. As a matter of fact, there are no European nations-- perhaps no people at all except a few remote savage tribes-- which are not made up of the most diverse elements. Aryan and non-Aryan long ago blended inextricably, to form by their fusion new peoples. (1975, 31-32)

Earlier in *Celtic Myth and Legend*, Squire attempts to track the ethnohistory of the elusive Celt, a people he believes to be a "mixed race" (1975, 19). Mixed with whom, one must ask? Squire provides his spin on the aboriginal race of the British Isles:

It was the people who built the 'long barrows'; and which is variously called by ethnologists the Iberian, Mediterranean, Berber, Basque, or Euskarian race. In physique it was short, swarthy, dark-haired, dark-eyed, and long-skulled; its language belonged to a class called 'Hamitic,' the surviving types of which are found among the Gallas, Abyssinians, Berbers, and other North African tribes; and its seems to have come originally from some part either of Eastern, Northern, or Central Africa. Spreading thence it was probably the first people to inhabit the Valley of the Nile, and it sent offshoots into Syria, and Asia Minor. The earliest Hellenes found it in Greece under the name of 'Pelasgoi'; the earliest Latins in Italy as the 'Etruscans'; and the Hebrews in Palestine, as the 'Hittites.' It spread northward into Europe as far as the Baltic, and westward along the Atlas chain, to Spain, France, and our own islands. (1975, 19-20)[2]

Suddenly, Squire finds himself standing on some very alien territory. And he goes into greater detail regarding the Silures, inhabitants of South Wales during the period of the Roman invasion, whom he describes, paraphrasing Tacitus' *Agricolae et Germanae,* as "an entirely different race from any other in Britain": "The dark complexions and curly hair of these Iberians seemed to Tacitus to prove them immigrants from Spain" (Squire 1975, 22). Was the black cat poking its head out of the proverbial bag?

T. H. Huxley proposes as much when he joins the fray during the mid-nineteenth century. David Mac Richie notes his observations: "Probably at the time of Caesar, and certainly in that of Tacitus, there existed in these islands two distinct types of populations: the one of tall stature, with fair skin, yellow hair, and blue eyes; the other of short stature, with dark skin, dark hair, and black eyes" (Mac Ritchie 1991, I, 185). Huxley goes on to argue that "this dark population, represented by the Silures, bore considerable physical resemblance to the people of Aquitania and Iberia; while the fair population . . . resembled the Belgae who inhabited the northeast of France and that country now called Belgium" (Mac Ritchie 1991, I, 186). For Huxley, who greatly influenced David Mac Ritchie's thinking, the early inhabitants of the British Isles include two great types: the *Xanthochroi* and the *Melanochroi*. The Xanthochroi, or "fair whites," were tall, with eyes of blue or gray; their hair ranged from straw-colored to red or chestnut; and they had considerable body-hair, according to Huxley. Their skull shapes, he goes on, covered the gamut of extreme dolichocephaly to pronounced brachycephaly. Of the Melanochroi, or "dark whites," Huxley proposes:

> Under its best form this type is exhibited by many Irishmen, Welshmen, and Bretons; by Spaniards, South Italians, Greeks, Armenians, Arabs, and high-caste Brahmins. A man of this group may, in point of physical beauty and intellectual energy, be the equal of the best of the Xanthochroi: but he presents a great contrast, in other respects, to the latter type, for the skin, though clear and transparent, is of a more or less brown hue, deepening to olive, the hair fine and wavy, is black, and the eyes are of a like hue. (Mac Ritchie 1991, I, 4-5)

In 1926, Druscilla Houston paints the nascent Arabs of whom Huxley speaks a shade darker when she argues that Arabia was the earliest Ethiopian colony.

Mac Ritchie, perhaps the least known and crankiest of the bunch, proposes in one of great ethnohistorical sleepers of all time entitled *Ancient and Modern Britons* that many of the swarthy ancestors of this darker population were exterminated [as was the case with the American Indians], but that ancient bloodbath did not completely eradicate the native Britons:

> Whether the whites of Britain were always in the majority may be questioned. A mere handful of successful invaders-- being successful-- might kill off the earlier races in great numbers: at first, in open warfare, and latterly by passing laws which awarded death to all those practicing the religion and customs of the conquered people. Thus, although the British Islands, at the present day, contain many millions of fair-whites, and not a single pure black (of British descent), this fact does not predicate a similar distribution of color at-- say-- the date of the Norman Conquest. (1991, II,

101-02)

And what about those elusive Druids? Could some of them been of a swarthy hue? Writing from a similar nineteenth century diffusionist perspective, Arthur Clive argues that Druidism had little in common with the Celtic imagination, but arose from a darker race in Ireland. James Bonwick cites one of Clive's more extreme contentions "that all of what was noble and good contained in the institution was some way derived from the Southern and Euskarian [Basque] sources" (Bonwick 1986, 20). In *Irish Druids and Old Irish Religions* Bonwich recalls that Ptolemy, who knew Ireland as Little Britain, believed that the druid lore practiced there was of Egyptian origin (1986, 21). And Bonwick cites another observation from the early Christian Boetius: "Cratilinth, the Scottish King, B.C. 277 was very earnest in the over throw of Druidism in the Isle of Mon [Man] and elsewhere; and upon the occasion of Diocletian's persecution, when many Christians fled to him for refuge, he gave them the Isle of Mon for their residence." There Mannanan Beg "was the establisher and cultivator of religion after the manner of the Egyptians.-- He caused great stones to be placed in a circle" (Bonwick 1986, 44). W. W. Atkinson in *Reincarnation and the Law of Karma* walks further out on a limb, declaring that druidic philosophy resembled the Inner Doctrine of the Egyptians and the Greek mystics who succeeded them, and arguing that vestiges of Hermeticism and Pythagoreanism were obviously prevalent in Greek mysticism. And he cites traditions that the earliest druidic priests migrated to Gaul and areas further north from Egypt or Greece (Ivimy 1974, 180).

Speaking of Tara, the ancient seat of Irish kings, Bonwick argues that the location was named after the Semitic place-name Terah, the city to which Jeremiah allegedly fled with the ark of David (1986, 259). He goes on to cite the tradition that Jeremiah, and Princess Scota, daughter of Pharaoh, escaped to Britain following the siege of Jerusalem, carrying David's ark to Ireland. (1986, 259). Charles Squire reinforces Bonwick when referring to the same post-Christian Irish chroniclers [whose itinerary for Scota duplicates the route ascribed by Geoffrey of Monmouth for Brutus]. Regarding the wanderings of Scota [identified in *Lebor Gabala* with the sixth invader group], Squire asserts the tradition laid out in Holinshed's *Chronicles* that:

> the first Irishman was a Scythian called Fenius Farsa. Deprived of his old
> throne, he had settled in Egypt, where his son Niul married a daughter of the
> reigning Pharaoh. Her name was Scota, and she had a son called Goidel,
> whose great-grandson was named Eber Scot, the whole genealogy being

probably invented to explain the three names by which the Gaels called themselves-- Finn, Scot and Goidel. Fenius and his family and clan were turned out of Egypt for refusing to join in the persecution of the children of Israel, and sojourned in Africa for forty-two years. Their wanderings took them to 'the altars of the Philistines, by the Lake of Osiers'; then, passing between Rusicada and the hilly country of Syria, they traveled through Mauretania as far as the Pillars of Hercules; and thence landed in Spain, where they lived many years, greatly increasing and multiplying. (Squire 1975, 120-21)

The Irish Tuatha de Danaan, who become the dark elves and faeries of a hundred tales told in front of roaring peat fires; the dark, Iberian, non-Aryan Firbolgs of Ireland [who Squire in *Celtic Myth and Legend* argues bore several tribal names-- *Corca-Oidce,* or "People of Darkness," *Corca-Duibhne,* or "People of the Night," and *Hi-Dorchiade,* or "People of the Night"]; the Druids who arrived in clouds of gun-powder-like smoke; the Picts [who Mac Ritchie, Massey and Squire describe as dark, short, non-Aryan aborigines]; the Silures of South Wales [who both Squire, and Beddoe in *The Races of Britain* also label as dark, curly-haired non-Aryans]; Claudian's "nimble Blackamoors," routed by the legions of Roman General Theodosius; the "Ethiopian" indigenes of Britain, so-named in the second century by the Roman historian Pliny; the countless gypsy Moors of Scotland who gave allegiance to the Earls of Little Egypt; and numerous, swarthy sturdy beggars encountered in the Borderlands between England and Scotland in the medieval and Renaissance periods, indeed, all of these invisible Britons are added to the family tree by these so-called old cranks.

In *A Book of the Beginnings*, Massey, the mother of all cranks, attempts to uncover the origins of the Picts, arguing that they can be traced to the Gwyddyl or Gadhael race, and that the name Pict can ultimately be derived from the Egyptian goddess Pekht, whom, he claims, was the later name of the Goddess of the North who was earlier called Kheft. He further proposes that original race of Scotland, the Kymry, divided into the Picts and the Scots (1995, 464, 467, 471). He surmises that the Egyptian reckoning of directions is reflected in the geographical location in the British Isles of the Picts and Scots, the directions being known as Pekht for the northern area, a term which he derives from the Egyptian root *peh* for rump, and *sekhet* for the southern area (Massey 1995, 467). Interestingly enough, in Kent, he notes, a Gipsy or *Kheb-si* was in his day still known as a Pikey.

Arguing that these early Britons, like the Egyptians, were a solar cult, he traces the etymology of Pict, noting that Pascht and Sekhet were symbolic "of the twin lions of the equinox facing the north and the south. Our Pash or

Pasch of Easter is named after the goddess who presides at the place of the equinox, the Pekha, in her dual form. The Pekh or Bekh was the solar birthplace at the time of the vernal equinox" (Massey 1995, 468).

Massey goes on to argue that the goddess Pekh even "survives in the red lion of Scotland, red being the color of the northern, the lower crown [of Egypt], and of the female lion represented by Pekht. The wonderful temple at Bubastis [Egypt] was made of red granite. Bede wrote the name of the Picts as Pehtas, and in Egyptian Pekht became Peht" (Massey 1995, 468). Not yet finished with the lion imagery, Massey reasons that "in the arms of England the lion and the unicorn are united in a common support, and the unicorn is a type of Typhoon [the Egyptian Set] the one-horned, the Ramakh (hippopotamus or rhinoceros), called the mythical unicorn, the ancient Kheb or Kheft of Egypt and the Ked of Britain" (Massey 1995, 468). When the Picts vanished and the Scots prevailed, the Pekh became known as Pixy in Devonshire and Wales, argues Massey, as he goes on to observe that to his own day a drunk is said to be "Piksey-led" for "the goddess of drink thus protects her followers, or plays the devil with them, as the Puck or Pouke" (Massey 1995, 470).

The old cranks were clearly on to something. There seemed to have been a considerable, non-Aryan and, indeed, an African and Near Eastern presence in the British Isles in the Neolithic Age and beyond. But such theories were soon to be placed on the chopping block. For by the 1950s, these propositions appeared to have been rendered largely defunct by the carbon dating revolution.

One way to counter these theories which posited a diffusion of Afroasiatic languages and African and Near Eastern religions into Northern Europe and the British Isles in prehistory was to cite data from the Carbon-14 dating of the older megalithic tombs and monuments such as Carnac in Brittany and New Grange in Ireland. In *Before Civilization*, Colin Renfrew argues that since the advent of Carbon-14 dating in 1950, the chronology of several of the megalithic sites along the Northwestern European periphery should be revised back into the fifth or even the sixth millennium B.C.E. This redating process reveals that Carnac in Brittany and New Grange in Ireland, for example, are older by two or three millennia than the southern megalithic structures in Spain, Portugal, Crete, Malta, Greece, Egypt, and North Africa, which date to the third and second millennia B.C.E. Even in Spain sites such as Cuerva del Menga and Cuerva de Viera, much like other similar sites in France's Languedoc and Provence regions, appear to belong to the later group, given that copper spirals, flange-hilted daggers and bell beakers betray their Bronze Age identity. No such copper artifacts were excavated at the older northern sites except in those dating to the later passage grave period. This disturbing evidence, it was hoped, would place a chink in the armor of the diffusionists who proposed that a substantial African and Near Eastern population substratum moved in a south to north direction during the Neolithic Age. In light of C-14 dating, an opposite direction could be hypothesized. Advanced cultures could have sprung up in the far north and spread southwards!

Prior to C-14 dating, Childe and a score of like-minded anthropologists of the diffusionist and hyper-diffusionist schools argued that a megalithic race had slowly migrated from the Near East or Egypt, trekked across North Africa and fanned out into Spain, Brittany, the British Isles and Scandinavia, constructing their tombs as they went.   Renfrew cites Oscar Montelius' argument:

> One does not have to probe deeply into the study of the conditions . . . here in the north during the stone age . . . to see that the original homeland of the dolmens cannot be sought in Europe. They could not have spread from here to the southern shores of Mediterranean, to Palestine and to India. The entire discussion here shows that this would be absurd. So powerful a movement, able to influence the burial customs of so many and widely distributed peoples, simply cannot have originated here, thousands of years before our era. It is indeed remarkable that, originating in the Orient, it should have reached us here at such an early date. (1973, 32-33)

The origins of Stonehenge were also in question. In 1956, when radiocarbon dating was still in its infancy, R. J. C. Atkinson in *Stonehenge* goes further to argue that the stone-masonry skills needed to construct Stonehenge I could not have existed *in situ* and were likely imported by a Wessex chieftain in the form of a Mediterranean architect hailing either from either Minoan Crete or Mycenaean Greece.   Unfortunately for Atkinson, Stonehenge I was finally dated into the beginning of the third millennium B.C.E., well before the rise of the Mycenaeans and the Minoans.

Although more archeological data needs to surface before sound conclusions can be drawn about exactly who built many of these more ancient sixth and fifth century B.C.E. megalithic dolmens, "troy cities" of concentric rock circles, egg-shaped rings, chambered tombs, menhirs, standing stone avenues and the like, this study does not assume that because the Carnac and New Grange sites are older than later megalithic ruins, the movement of megalithic building necessarily spread from the north to the south rather from the south to north, or that it resulted from independent invention. Certainly radiocarbon data when properly correlated with bristlecone pine readings indicates that if these earliest sites were the result of diffusion rather than of independent invention, the movement of the so-called megalithic race in the sixth and fifth millennia could have still been from the south to the north, the direction that Montelius, Atkinson and host of others suggest, but not from where they suggest, as we shall see shortly.

Nonetheless, some historians proposed a possible avenue of culture emptying from Northern Europe into the Mediterranean basin, the exact opposite direction to that proposed by the diffusionists. Jurgen Spanuth's hypothesis presented in *Atlantis of the North* offers a case in point, albeit a late one. Hoping to account for the rapid rise of a Nordic population in the Eastern Mediterranean, an ingress which apparently joined forces with the Caucasoid, Libyan Tamahu and dark-skinned Tehennu indigenes of Libya to form the Peoples of the Sea before their defeat by Pharaoh Ramesses III, Spanuth presents evidence for a north to south migration. He notes that Jean R. Marechal, an authority on prehistoric metallurgy, concludes from artifact analysis that "one of the three great hordes that marched through Europe from the North at the end of the thirteenth century B.C., traveled along the great rivers of France-- the Seine, Rhone, Loire and Garonne-- to the French coast." Marechal goes on to place "the epicenter [of the great migration] in Southern Scandinavia and the Danish islands and the nearby sea," and speaks of "a far-flung Atlantic community, which spread from Scandinavia to the Iberian peninsula and even to the Mediterranean" (1959, 232ff.; Spanuth 1979, 128-29).

This evidence does not invalidate the original theory of the diffusion of higher forms of culture from south to north, however. For it will be argued in subsequent chapters that the Nordic types who joined forces with the other ethnic components of the Peoples of the Sea, may well have descended from ancestors who had trekked north from the Fertile Crescent, the Red Sea or the Mediterranean basin in more ancient times, and that these descendants appear to have simply retraced those earlier steps.

And in regard to attempts made to trace the ultimate origins of higher culture in the far north, common sense, if nothing else, should reveal that in the Boreal era, when glaciers were still in retreat and sea-levels were rising, a culture facing the vicissitudes of survival in the colder climes could hardly have developed into a society possessing the mathematical expertise required to construct a Carnac and a New Grange. In other words, there must have been two major waves of colonization from the much sunnier south, one likely from the Eastern Mediterranean or the Fertile Crescent in the Boreal period and a later wave, in the third and second millennia B.C.E., from the Mediterranean and Red Sea basins.

Ivimy also notes the diffusionist arguments which call for a south to north movement from the Mediterranean and Red Sea basins to Brittany and the British Isles, and the mistaken chronology supplied by the diffusionists for Carnac and New Grange, dates which they lodge in the third and second millennia B.C.E. rather than in the much earlier and much more accurate sixth or fifth millennium time-frame as the radiocarbon data indicates. In his attempt to propose a solution to the conundrum, Ivimy hypothesizes that primary migrations were indeed from south to north as Montelius, Childe, Atkinson and others argue. But he adds that there were two extensive waves from the south, each creating distinct megalithic industries-- an early, pre-Sumerian wave of colonists and mapmakers from the Euphrates valley, a wave which allegedly constructed Carnac and New Grange in the fifth millennium B.C.E., and a later African wave in the third and second millennia B.C.E. which built the newer stone circles and avenues of the Mediterranean basin, Portugal, Brittany and the British Isles (1974, 85).

The cornerstone of Ivimy's argument is a little known study of place-names entitled *The Key* by etymologist J. P. Cohane. Cohane bases his hyper-diffusionist hypotheses on his exhaustive survey of ancient place-names across the globe. This effort leads him to formulate two hypotheses. The first is that "certain key names and words were taken out in all directions from the Mediterranean, in some instances by water routes, and that these same names and words can still be found, in spite of corruptions, in the names of rivers, mountains, volcanoes, and waterfalls, lakes, islands, regions, towns and cities, scattered all across the face of the earth" (1969, 18). His second hypothesis is that these key place-names form two separate groups:

> The names in the first group, which appears to be older, are to be found in all parts of the world. Those in the second group are to be found in a more intensified level but in a limited portion of the world. This latter set of names permeates the Mediterranean basin, Europe, Africa, and parts of Asia, moves across the Atlantic into the West Indies, into Brazil, and are found along the gulf coast of Central America and up the East Coast of North America. (1969, 21)[3]

By separating prehistoric place-names from historical ones, Cohane identifies the recurrence of numerous prehistoric word roots in place-names around the so-called Old and New Worlds. A composite list of these place-name roots includes the following: Ber/Bar/Bor/Bur, Dan/Don, Elah/Ala, Hawwah/Avvah, Manna/Mana, Og/Oc/Aeg, and Tem/Tam (1969, 177, 216ff.).

Using this intriguing evidence, Ivimy argues, much as Jim Bailey in

Sailing to Paradise, that there were two ancient surveys of the globe, the first conducted by pre-Sumerians in the fifth millennium, and the second by Egyptians in the third and the second. As far as the western periphery of Europe is concerned, each produced a unique megalithic industry in its respective wake.

If this two wave theory has any merit, it is likely that sites such as Carnac and New Grange were perceived as ancient by the later waves of colonists who traveled north along the old Atlantic land and sea routes from the Mediterranean and Red Sea basins to the British Isles during this second industry. Indeed, Carnac's menhir of Er Grah, which was visible off shore for ten miles and which stood more sixty feet high and weighed approximately 340 tons, must have been an awesome and baffling sight. In any case, this proposed second Neolithic, African and Near Eastern wave may well have joined forces with the Wessex people to supervise the building of Stonehenge I and the stepped pyramid located nearby called Silbury Hill. For both of these structures, according to C-14 dating combined with bristlecone pine correlations, date to 2775 B.C.E. and 2745 B.C.E., respectively-- contemporaneous with the beginning of pyramid age in Egypt!

A possible link between the Egyptian stepped pyramids and Silbury Hill might be found at another unlikely site--Thebes, Greece. Excavated in 1971 by Greek archeologist Theodore Spyropoulas, the enigmatic tomb of Amphion and Zethos turned out not to be a mound as previously supposed, but a pyramid which was dated to the same time-frame of c. 2800 B.C.E. (Poe 1997, 321ff).

Silbury Hill, a lingering archeological enigma near the Neolithic camp of Windmill Hill in West Kennet, rises 130 feet above the plain with a base covering more than five acres. It is often described as the largest earthen mound in Europe, but, according to Ivimy, that description presents an inaccurate picture of what really amounts to a an Egyptian-style, stepped pyramid of chalk:

> That pyramid was not built the way one might expect Stone Age aboriginals to have built it, by simply digging a ditch and shoveling material from it into a heap in the middle, as children build sand-castles on the beach. Far from it. Silbury Hill was a complex piece of engineering involving advanced methods of construction similar to those used in the Egyptian pyramids. For the main part of the hill the material dug from the ditch was laid symmetrically in horizontal layers, the outer edges of which were riveted by means of sloping retaining walls made of large blocks of chalk. (1974, 84-85)

If this is an Ethiopian/Egyptian/Wessex construction, an Egyptian style sarcophagus lodged within the structure may still await discovery, Ivimy concludes (1974, 85).

But regardless of who built the megalithic monuments during the first industry of the fifth millennium B.C.E., enough evidence from other disciplines outside of archeology exists, as we shall see in a subsequent chapter of this study, to support a revision of the old diffusionist paradigm of Childe and others of his persuasion to reveal that two waves occurred, both originating from the south, and that secondary migrations also moved from north to south again when climatic conditions warranted.

For the rivers of Europe, and the Western Atlantic seaway stretching from the Straits of Gibraltar to Iceland, did not have one-way signs attached to them, and migrations doubtless moved in both directions depending on the time frame involved. Natural catastrophes that plagued Europe and the Mediterranean and Red Sea basins from the seventeenth to the twelfth centuries B.C.E. such as the Santorini [Thera] volcanic eruption/explosion, with the resultant ash clouds and tsunamis of c. 1628 B.C.E , could have forced a migration of Mediterranean survivors to the north with the British Isles being one of many eventual destinations. And at the opposite end of the Bronze Age, the Hekla III eruption in Iceland, which Bernal places at 1159 B.C.E., may have pumped enough ash into the atmosphere to force migrations back out of the chilly, drought-ridden, northern climes to the Eastern Mediterranean (1991, 275). He cites M. G. L. Baillie, who notes the impact of the Hekla III eruption on the Scottish Highland economy:

> The catastrophe was so sudden and severe that it appears to have forced hundreds of thousands of people to leave their upland homes to seek a new life in the already inhabited valleys and lowlands. Widespread warfare would have followed and in the later half of the twelfth century B.C., valley settlements start to be fortified. (Baillie 1989, 78ff.; Bernal 1991, 305)[4]

Then too, the numerous volcanoes and earthquakes that were ravaging the Mediterranean basin around 1220 B.C.E. may have served as trigger mechanisms for the Trojan War, which has been dated, interestingly enough, from 1220 to 1210 B.C.E. (Bernal 1991, 519). Earthquakes and catastrophic volcanism may have created more Mycenaean and North African argonauts than even Homer imagined. And many of these involuntary refugees were no doubt inclined to sail out of the Mediterranean for good as the Late Bronze Age collapsed around their heads. But earthquakes were not the only catastrophes to be endured, for as noted in the introduction to this study, a rogue comet or two appeared to be lurking overhead.

As Spanuth observes in *Atlantis of the North*, the second half of the thirteenth century B.C.E. did not spare Northern Europe. For this area suffered a period of catastrophic droughts leading to critical recessions of the water table, the temporary drying up the lakes and rivers, and raging forest and sphagnum bog fires. To back his claims about an environmental collapse in Northern Europe during the Late Bronze Age, Spanuth cites numerous studies, including one by W. Wilthum who locates a "burning horizon" in the sphagnum bogs of the Eastern Alps which pollen analysis placed at about 1000 B.C.E. (Wilthum 1953, 83; Spanuth 1979, 148). The wrath of meteor showers and the unbearable heat of fireballs aloft were apparently, then, experienced in Northern Europe as well, although Spanuth does not suggest this possibility.

A thirteenth century B.C.E. southern migration of Nordic stock most likely allied themselves not only with dark Libyan Tehennus but also with Caucasoid Libyan Tamahu whose ancestors appear to have migrated to North Africa from the Near East centuries earlier. This probable alliance appears to have created a formidable irritant to the Egyptians (Moller 1921, 428).⁵ It was, no doubt, the desperate combined forces of this racial potpourri that came to be called both the People of the Sea and Dene or Denyen, which invaded the western Delta of the Nile and infiltrated Memphis and Heliopolis during the reign of Merneptah. The Nordics are clearly depicted in the Medinet Habu reliefs with their horned helmets, rayed crowns of horsehair and flange-hilted swords. The final defeat of these forces during the reign of Ramesses III was carefully recorded on the walls and pillars of monuments at Medinet Habu. The stacks of severed hands and phalli of the captives point to a grim capitulation. And that defeat, along with the lingering North African drought, may well have encouraged some of these Nordic survivors and their defeated allies to trek westward across Europe to Iberia or to sail the Great Green, as the Mediterranean was called, and turn north to safer pastures as the climate of Northern Europe began to stabilize again.

Indeed, the descendants of some of these darker-skinned itinerants may well have been the elusive Tuatha de Danaan, an invader group which this study will examine in some detail, and still later in time, the "Ethiopians" and "blackamoors" described by the Romans during various campaigns though Southern Britain in the second century C.E. For as Don Luke observes, Pliny describes the complexion of several of the Britons encountered by the Roman forces as "Ethiopian," and Claudian describes the routing of a band of indigenous inhabitants by Theodosius, a Roman General, as "He subdued the nimble blackamoors" (Luke 1985, 225; Preston 1981, 67). The complete quote from Claudian that describes the victories of the Roman General Theodosius explains the reference, which in Latin reads: *"Ille leves Mauros, nec falso nomine Pictos Edomuit."* Translated it reads: "He subdued the nimble blackamoors, not wrongly named the painted people."

In a review of Don Luke's article, "African Presence in the Early History of the British Isles and Scandinavia," Paul Edwards questions whether or not the terms Ethiopians and blackamoors were used figuratively or literally by Roman observers such as Pliny and Claudian in their descriptions of some of the indigenous peoples of Britain: "Pliny describes how a dye is made from berries with which the Britons stain their skins and then *in sacris nudae incedunt Aethiopum colorem imitantes* (i. e. 'at some religious ceremonies parade naked, in a color resembling Ethiopians')" (Edwards 1987, 403).⁶ This caution seems warranted in some cases, but it also can be argued that these stained, indigenous people may have been donning the color of their darker Ethiopian or Ethiopian-Greek ancestors.

Despite counter theories regarding the migrations across Europe, the diffusionists were alive and kicking well into the era of carbon dating. The hypothesis that a potent African and Near Eastern presence existed in the ancient British Isles was far from dead and would continue to gain momentum, as we shall see.

Notes

1. Could certain members of the Basque population have been mixed with dark-skinned Africans, Rogers (1967, I, 151ff.) asks when he observes that: "Some Basques have a certain type of Negroid face, and it is not improbable that such are descendants of . . . Negro aborigines." By "Negro aborigines" Rogers is referring to early fossil remains unearthed in Mugem, Portugal. He refers to G. Young's conclusion: "It is easy to recognize not only the imported Negro type, but also a type generally confused with him: the aboriginal Negroid Iberian."

2. Also see G. Sergei (1914) *The Mediterranean Race*. Stoddard (1924, 31-32, 104-05) writes less euphemistically in his *Racial Realities of Europe*. Dividing the so-called races of Europe into Nordics, Alpines and Mediterraneans, he argues that racial blend in Britain offers "the key to English history and English character." He goes on to propose that: "Down to that time [the fall of Rome] the British Isles had been inhabited almost entirely by the slender, dark-complexioned race called Mediterranean, which still inhabits most of the lands about the Mediterranean Sea and which settled the British Isles long before the dawn of history." He further notes that "For a long while Britain was divided between two sharply contrasting races, the Nordics occupying most of the island, while the western fringes, especially Wales, Cornwall, and Scotch Highlands, were solidly Mediterranean." Unlike Sergei,

Stoddard admits that the dark complexion of the Mediterranean resulted from admixture with the Negro, although he greatly laments that state of affairs. He appears to solve the dilemma, however, by arguing that there were two strains of Mediterranean stock, thereby mirroring a racial bias of his day. "Any one who has traveled in Italy realizes the sudden change which takes place south of Rome. Rome is, indeed, the dividing line between two sharply contrasted regions. Northward are progress and prosperity; southward lie backwardness and poverty. This is precisely what the racial situation would lead us to expect. The two halves of Italy are inhabited by very different breeds of men.   The northern half contains the best of the old Mediterranean stock, plus a strong Alpine element and a considerable leavening of Nordic blood.   The southern half is inhabited by a racially impoverished Mediterranean stock, long since drained of its best strains and in places mongrelized by inferior Levantine and African elements." It appears that euphemism was required to deny an African admixture in the Caucasian, but when fantasies of creating a "superior race" were entertained, the African admixture in the "inferior" group was admitted and spurned.

    3. Brunson (1985, 38) notes that the Nea Nikomedea megalithic burial site, which has been dated to 6200 B.C.E. and which lies north of the Macedonian Haliacmon River, has yielded bushman-like skeletons, steatopygous female figurines, and libation vessels that appear to be linked to a ram cult. Citing Jennett (1970, 21), he further notes that local Irish traditions in the Connacht area indicate that the Nemedians and Fir Bolgs, groups that will be dealt with later in this study, migrated to Ireland from that Macedonian region. That certainly makes these matrifocal negritos possible candidates for the makers of the older megalithic structures such as Carnac and New Grange.

    4. Also see Keys (1988) and Baillie (1989, 78-81). For the controversy regarding the Thera dating and the shift from radiocarbon to dendrochronology [tree ring dating using Bristlecone pines] see Bernal (1991, 274-288).

    5. Citing Moller (1920\21, 428), Spanuth notes that the white, Nordic Tamahu, which he translates as 'north land' on p. 238, are first mentioned in Egypt in 2400 B.C.E., and they should not be confused with the Tehennu, who according to Holscher (1937, 16) were the black-haired, dark-skinned, original inhabitants of North Africa.

    6. Also see Graves (1966, p. 241, n. 1). He comments on woad dyeing as a mysterious rite of the female worshipers of the Triple Goddess.

Chapter 3

~~~~~~

Another Look at Cultural Diffusion Theories

Suspicions that a sizeable, non-Aryan population from the Near East, and the Mediterranean and Red Sea littorals roamed the British Isles in prehistoric and historic times were aroused again in another generation of commentators whom we label neo-diffusionists. Historians such as Winthrop Palmer Boswell, Bob Quinn, John Ivimy, Kevin Danaher, Jim Bailey, Edward Scobie, James Brunson, Dana Reynolds, Robert Graves, Ahmed and Ibrahim Ali and others writing in the mid and late-twentieth century, revisited both the diffusion theories of their predecessors and the testimony of folklore and classical accounts which spoke with one voice about the African and Near Eastern origins of numerous early inhabitants of Ireland and Wales in particular. In the process, hypotheses regarding the builders of Stonehenge, Silbury Hill and other ancient sites were posited.

Armed with new chronological data gleaned from the C-14 revolution of the 1950s and beyond, many of these neo-diffusionists reexamined documents such as *Lebor Gabala*, a product of Irish monks writing in the seventh century at Clonmacnoise Abbey, Geoffrey of Monmouth's *History of the Kings of Britain* and Raphael Holinshed's *Chronicles*. Aware that such documents had been dismissed by many in the Academy as so much pseudo-history, these neo-diffusionists, nevertheless, wished to reach their own conclusions regarding the veracity of such records.

A brief inventory of the various waves of "invaders" who reputedly arrived on Hibernian and Welsh and English shores during the Bronze and Iron Ages which are chronicled in the above-mentioned sources and in classical accounts by Pindar and Diodorus Sciculus is presented here to refresh the reader's memory. To the neo-diffusonists, accounts such as these provide several valuable leads, if not indisputable confirmation, of an extensive and enduring African and Near Eastern presence in the British Isles.

Long before the arrival of the Indo-European speaking Celts, an indeterminate lot who poured into the British Isles around 500 B.C.E., the earliest invaders were, according to the *Lebor Gabala*, led by "Seth" [also called Bith] and his consort Banba. In 3400 B.C.E. [2400 B.C.E. being an alternate date], they allegedly embarked on a journey from the Island of Meroe adjacent to the river Nile with fifty women of color, made sojourns along the shores of the Caspian Sea, arrived at an unnamed alpine region and wandered along the North African littoral of the Mediterranean, before arriving finally in Ireland centuries later (Boswell 1972a, 24a). Given that Seth was worshiped in Upper Egypt in the fourth millennium during the predynastic period of Egypt, the earlier date may be the correct one (Bailey 1994, 337).

Holinshed, writing in the sixteenth century, tells the story a bit differently. He proposes that the band of fifty women traveled under the leadership of Cesara, who, according Holinshed, was a niece of Noah (1965, I, 73) And who did these itinerants discover in Ireland? A population of black giants, descendants of Ham [Cham]:

> certain godless people of Nimrod's stock, worthily termed giants, as those that in bodily shape exceeded the common proportion of others, and used their strength to gain sovereignty, and to oppress the weak with rapine and violence. That lineage (Cham's brood) did grow in short while, always endeavored themselves wheresoever they came to bear rule over others. (Holinshed 1965, I, 74)

Since Nimrod was synonymous with Set or Seth, it may be the first of many ironies of Irish history that the dark Fomorians, likely the enemies of these colonists, worshiped at the same altar. Holinshed, goes on to mention three men, Bith, Finhain and Ladhra, included in the company of Cesara and her fifty female sojourners (1965, I, 74ff.). Given the emphasis placed upon Cesara's [or Banba's, in Keating's version] leadership, these invaders were doubtless a matrifocal group traveling with a harem of royal priestesses. After settling in Dun na Mbrac, which may have been in the area of county Cork, Cesara died, and, legend has it, she was laid to rest at Cuil Ceasair in the Connacht area. The citing of fifty women is reminiscent of two classical parallels: the voyage of the fifty Danides to Greece in Aeschylus' *The Suppliant Maidens,* and another more famous journey of fifty women to Carthage that occurred in 814 B.C.E. under the leadership of Princess Elissar, or Dido of the *Aeneid.*

Lebor Gabala relates that the second invasion was led by Partholon, who came to the island from Micil, Mygdonia and Sociana (Boswell 1972a, 24a). According to Boswell, Micil may indicate Sicily, or a strip of land on the opposite side of the Red Sea from today's former Abyssinian province of Eritrea (1972a, 24a). The other areas have not been identified. But *Lebor Gabala* does indicate that Partholon was the son of Baath or Sdairn and possibly either the brother or nephew of Starn, whom Boswell identifies with Seth/Saturn, placing the migration of Partholon at approximately 2000 B.C.E. (1972a, 24a). It seems likely then that this second wave of colonists may have been another remnant of Egyptian Seth-worshipers, possibly involved in the extensive incense and tin trade that will be examined in subsequent chapters. But that is not the entire story about the Partholonians.

The origins of this group is shrouded in mystery. Early Irish mythology attributes their origin to the Underworld, the land of the dead called Sera to the west (Fiore 1973, 42). According to *Lebor Gabala,* however, Partholon, known as the son of Sear, sailed the Mediterranean with his followers from some point in Greece to Sicily, then traveled around the Iberian peninsula and headed north to the west coast of Ireland. Dubbed the "Basclense" in Welsh folklore [recalling Basque], this band of seafarers allegedly originated from the Caucasus area and may have been related to the Colchians, a likely remnant of either Pharaoh Sesostris II's or Pharaoh Thutmoses III's army (Bernal 1991, 245). Herodotus' infamous Book II, reveals that the Colchians practiced circumcision as did the Egyptians, to whom they appeared to be related. And of equal interest is Herodotus' observation that like the Egyptians, the Colchians were also "black-skinned" and "woolly-haired" (Jairazbhoy 1985, 59).

Upon arriving in Ireland, the Partholonians' activities are equally obscure. Tradition has it that they lived in Ireland for ten years before engaging the Fomorians in a series of disastrous battles around 2000 B.C.E. Thirty years or so later Partholon died prior to the spread of a plague that ravaged the remaining Partholonians in what is today the Dublin area. According to Geoffrey of Monmouth, a small remnant fled to the Orkney Islands off the Scottish coast.

The Fomorians, often described as black, Hamitic pirates, allegedly made frequent voyages back to the Mediterranean area, and those who survived the plague appear to have thrived in Ireland for a time. The Fomorians were also called Fomoraig Afraic, or sons of *Dubh* [literally, the 'black'], who himself was the son of Fomore. Ham, the black son of Noah, was claimed as their ultimate ancestor, according to the *Annals of Clonmacnoise*. And the *Annals* go on to indicate that the Fomorians were descended from Phut, a son of Ham.

The Nemedians, the third wave of invaders to arrive in Ireland, are also assigned different origins depending on the source consulted. According to Boswell, Nemed, the son of Algenor of Tyre and grandson of Partholon, joined forces with his queen Macha to lead their band of colonists out of Scythia before arriving on Ireland's shores in 1921 B.C.E. (Boswell 1972a, 24a). Silvestro Fiore proposes that the Nemedians, like the Partholonians, journeyed to Ireland from the "Land of the Dead," which Nennius in his *Historia Britonum* rightly or wrongly equates with Spain (1973, 42). Although their name echoes 'Numidian,' the title of a North African Berber tribe, they set sail, according to the *Annals of Clonmacnoise*, from Greece. The Macedonian Neolithic site of Nea Nikomedia north of the Haliacmon River could have been one possible point of departure (Brunson 1985, 38). It is possible, then, that Greece was their point of embarkation, and that the Nemedians, like the Partholonians, may have been involved in the international Bronze Age trade network identified in Bailey's *Sailing to Paradise*.

For Bailey such trade was truly an intercontinental one and may have been conducted in areas as remote as Isle Royal in present day Lake Superior and in mineral-rich Bolivia, Peru and Brazil (1994, 20ff.). Bailey's controversial thesis which will be examined below appears to be supported by more western netherworld imagery found in the Welsh *Mabinogion* in which the hero Pryderi was the son of Pwyll, Prince of Annwyn, Annwyn being the Welsh name for the "Land of the Dead." Then too, in a tale entitled "Cuchulain's Sick Bed" in the *Book of the Dun Cow*, Cuchulain sailed to the Isle of the Blessed in a bronze boat. The traces of tobacco and cocaine that have been found in the tissues of the Munich sample of ancient Egyptian mummies may become less a mystery in light of these ancient chronicles (Balabonova, Parsche, and Pirsig 1992, 358).

The *Annals of Ireland* describe four major battles fought between the Nemedians and the Fomorians, with the Nemedians gaining costly victories in each. But when Faebar, the son of Nemedius, was killed at the present day site of Barrymore by the Fomorian general Conain, the Nemedians' fortunes went into a rapid decline. From their base at Tor Conain on Tory Island, two Fomorian princes, Conain and Moor, demanded tribute from the weakened

Nemedians. Unwilling to be subjected to Fomorian demands which included tributes of Nemedian children, butter, cattle, milk and wheat, the Nemedians formed an army under the command of Beothach, Fathach and Fergus who, with the help of a newly-arrived fleet of Greek allies, finally captured Tor Conain and killed Conain. But the tables turned when Moor, the other Fomorian prince who at the time had sailed his fleet into the Mediterranean on a mission to Africa, returned and defeated the Nemedian army and its Greek allies at Tory Island with the aid of a Fomorian druidess.[1]

Lebor Gabala describes how one band of the Nemedian remnant, under the leadership of Simeon Breac, escaped to Greece. There they were forced to work in unspecified mines for several generations. Boswell argues that their leader was Starn, another Set/Saturn avatar (Boswell 1972a, 24a). Generations later a new band of their descendants titled the Firbolgs, constituted the fourth wave of invaders. This group voyaged back to the British Isles, settling in Ireland, Wales and possibly Scotland. Two other Nemedian bands, however, went in different directions, according to Skene in *Celtic Scotland.* One band, led by Beothach, from whom the Tuatha de Danaan were allegedly descended, sailed to the north of Europe, while the other, under Briotan, sailed to the north of Britain (Skene 1886, I, 95). Boswell puts the possible dates for this activity at 1750 B.C.E. (1972a, 24a).

In *A Book of the Beginnings*, Massey, citing Wood's *Inquiry Respecting the Primitive Inhabitants of Ireland*, attempts a century earlier to derive the name 'Nemedian' from Egyptian origins:

> The Tuath-dadanan were reported to have descended from Nemethus, a native of Nem-thor, or Nemethi Turris; to have learned magic in Thebes, and waged war successfully against the Assyrians. They were led into Ireland by Nuadhah, the silver-handed. Now Ptah was the son of Nem, the god of Thebes. Nem-tes is Nem himself; the type of Nem; Nem-ter, the bourne or boundary of Nem, which was that of Thebes. Nnu is antennae, feelers, and may have been the hand, huta is silver, Nnu-huta, the silver-antennaed or handed. Thus the descent claimed for Nem himself by the Tuat-Dadanan is exactly that of Ptah-Tatanen in the divine dynasties of Egypt. (Massey 1995, 482)

The Firbolg occupied Irish lands in what is today Northern and Southern Munster, Ulster and Connacht. Their time in Ireland was to be short, however, because, as the Four Masters explain, more than 100,000 of the dark aborigines were killed by a new wave of invaders, the Tuatha De Danaan, at the battle of Magh Tuireadh Conga in Connacht, during which the Tuatha leader, Nuada of the silver hand, suffered the loss of his famous limb

(Grimal 1965, 352). According to Quinn, certain descriptions of that battle, embellished centuries later, appear to have been derived from an Arab epic. Quinn compares the Irish amputee to a pre-Islamic rain god named Hobbal. Like Nuada, Hobbal also lost an arm that was replaced with a golden one rather than with a limb of silver (1986, 128). In any case, escaping to several off-shore islands, the Firbolg remnant was finally driven to Leinster by the marauding Picts before settling finally in Connacht, where individuals claiming Firbolg descent live to this day.

The fifth wave of invaders, the Tuatha De Danaan, allegedly embarked from a homeland situated between Greece and the lands of the Philistines, according to *Lebor Gabala*. Boswell argues that they were an offshoot of the Nemedians, also known as the sons of Bith or Seth, and that their leaders were Dagan and Nuadu, wizards and Athenian poets who were driven out of Greece by the Philistines (1972a, 24a). But if Crete was that island, they may well have been the "negroized Libyans," or North African indigenes, the Tehennu, of whom Arthur Evans (1921) writes in the second volume of *The Palace of Minos* (Brunson 1985, 40). And one can only speculate on their reasons for heading to northern climes. Certainly there was no shortage of natural disasters in the Mediterranean basin during the Bronze Age, as noted in the introduction. And Boswell dates their movements to around 1730 B.C.E., which is a bit off the mark from Bernal's argument for a corrected date of 1628 B.C.E. for the Thera eruption, but not unreasonably so (Boswell 1972a, 24a).[2]

In his examination of the Dan/Don place-name complex that appears over much of Europe and the British Isles, Cohane speculates as to the etymology, deriving it from Danaus: "Danaus is first encountered sharing the throne of Egypt with his half-brother Aegyptus. Driven out of Egypt by Aegyptus, Danaus with his fifty daughters, the Danides, traveled via Rhodes to the Peloponnesus, where he ascended the throne of Argos" (1969, 45).

Interestingly enough, Aeschylus describes the Danides in *The Suppliant Maidens* as black and sun-smitten, the descendants of swarthy Epaphus, son of Zeus. And later they are described as most resembling Libya's daughters rather than the native women of Argos (Swanwick 1890, 273).

Cohane goes on to note that in Wales the mother of Arashod and father of the "children of Don," who comprise the royal house in the mythology of Wales, is none other than Don. And in Ireland, Cohane goes on, the "mother of all the gods" was called either Danaan, Danu or Diannan, and the early invaders of Ireland were known as the "children of Danaan" and "the Tuatha De Danaan," from which the "royal House of Munster" was derived (1969, 46).

In any case, disasters from the earth and sky were likely quite common during the period of the early migrations to Ireland. An inland lake called Lake Triton may have been ruptured by earthquakes, causing its contents to flow from what is today the northern Sahara into the Mediterranean during the Neolithic period. As Diodorus Siculus relates, Libya, formerly a lush grazing area, was devastated by earthquakes in the third millennium B.C.E. (Velikovsky 1977b, 178). And the Thera [Santorini] explosion must have been another horrific catastrophe to be endured centuries later. Possible pre-Theran meteor showers could have resulted in a brief colonization of Crete by Evans' so-called "negroized Libyans," and as Brunson notes, Libyan cultural elements such as "Libyan Bow" shield, and various fashion motifs surfaced in Crete:

> The ureaus or 'serpent lock', is often associated with Libya and it seems to have some connection with Crete. This protruding tuft of hair seems to have been associated with an initiatory rite dedicated to the Goddess Neith . . . . It is known that Neith, as Goddess of Sais, was synonymous with the 'Great Serpent' of cosmic, physical change and spiritual rebirth. (Brunson 1985, 40)

It is probable that the mother goddesses worshiped in the Mediterranean during the late Neolithic and early Bronze Ages were known by many names. Graves proposes in *The Greek Myths* that the Libyan Triple Mother Goddess later carried to Crete may have been named *Kar* or *Ker*, and that the bearers of her religion were called the Kuretes (1971, 33-34). Brunson notes that the Tuatha de Danaan worshiped the Triple Goddess under the names of Danu, Dana, Anu, Dinah and Diana, and that the ancient Libyans, from whom the Tuatha may have descended, were known as the Anu-Tehennu (1985, 45). The Tuatha also honored the goddess Neith [Net], who bore striking similarities to the Phoenician Tanit and the Greek Athena, names derived from Anat-ana or Athana (Brunson 1985, 45ff.). Going on to cite Irish legends, he argues for a Libyan origin of the Late Bronze Age Tuatha De Danaan who settled in Ireland. For proof, he points to the *Book of Ballymote*, an ancient Irish document, which lists an early Libyan script. Nearly a century earlier Massey argued much the same when he indicated that the Tuatha De Danaan called their goddess Anu, Danu-ana, or Neter-Kar, as Brunson notes (1985, 48). Interestingly enough, the *Annals of Ashurbanipal* describe an ancient Sabaean mother goddess trinity consisting of Al-Lat, Kore and Al-Uzza, a composite deity worshiped in Southern Arabia from time immemorial. Were the Tuatha De Danaan comprised, in part, of black Libyan colonists who migrated from the Sabaean Red Sea littoral?

The Tuatha were associated with magic, bronze weaponry, and horse-drawn chariots. The Greeks acknowledged their debt to the Libyans who taught them how to hitch horses to chariots (Brunson 1985, 49). Providing further insight, Reynolds, a Columbia University-trained specialist in North African anthropology, reveals that the Garamantes and the Tuareg of North Africa were charioteers as well (1993, 119). Since chariots are associated with the Libyans and the Hyksos during Bronze Age times, one more reason to assume that the Tuatha De Danaan may have been of Libyan origin emerges.

Added to this evidence are Egyptian blue faience beads [c. 1600 B.C.E.] that have turned up in the long barrows of Britain; the eight double spirals carved at the entranceway of New Grange that remind Graves of Mycenaean tomb drawings; parallel designs and riveting on a Bronze Age dagger excavated in Britain that compare with Mycenaean equivalents; fluted gold cups from Shaft Grave IV that are strikingly similar to designs on cups excavated in Cornwall; the purple dye industry found in Cornwall that is reminiscent of a similar industry of the Phoenicians; and the writing of the Tuatha which employed a mixture of Coptic, Middle Egyptian, and Nubian vocabulary (Brunson 1985, 49ff.).

Allied with the Greeks against the Philistines, the Tuatha De Danaan were reputed to have been driven out of the Mediterranean when the Philistines defeated their adversary. Sailing past the Iberian peninsula and heading north, they finally made landfall at Dobar in Northern Scotland prior to their invasion of Ireland, according to the *Lebor Gabala*. Taking exception, Keating in his *History of Ireland* proposes that they first settled in Denmark before sailing to Scotland and finally to Ireland, as Boswell notes (1972a, 24a). Their queens included Etan, Macha, Banba, and Brigit; their princes were Dengus and Lug; and their kings included Dagan and Midir (Grimal 1965, 352).

As previously stated, in the Irish battle of Magh Tuireadh Conga, Nuada of the silver hand is reputed to have defeated the Firbolgs. After a twenty year reign, however, Nuada was killed and his army defeated in the battle of Magh Tuirdeadh na bh-Fromorach in present day county Sligo by Fomorian forces under the command of Balor of the One Eye, a most cometary figure as we shall discover in a subsequent chapter (Clube and Napier 1982, 218).

Associated mainly with the New Grange megalithic site, the Tuatha De Danaan are said to have intermarried with their Fomorian adversaries when hostilities ceased and to have lingered there for several years. Given the fifth or sixth millennium B.C.E. dating of New Grange, the Tuatha could not possibly have been the builders of that site, but they may have later claimed it as their own.

The Tuatha were finally overthrown by the last wave of ancient invaders, the Milesians. Also known as Goidels, Gadelians and Scythians, the Milesians appear to have arrived from the Iberian peninsula after the biblical Exodus (Boswell 1972a, 24b). Incidentally Clube and Napier date the Exodus to 1369 B.C.E., the same date as the Zeus\Typhon cometary events (1982, 224). *Lebor Gabala* relates that at the time of the Exodus from Egypt, Gadelas was born on the island of Crete. His mother was called Scota, daughter of the Pharaoh, and his father was Niul, son of Fensa Farsa, the King of Scythia. Boswell suggests that the Milesians at first departed from Thebes, Egypt and settled in places as widespread as Crete, Ceylon and Scythia (1972a, 24b). Citing *Lebor Gabala*, she notes that the Scythian Greeks, namely the sons of Gaidel Glas who descend from Nel, his father Fenius and ultimately Cercrops, the Egyptian founder of Athens, trek to Carthage which was then controlled by the Philistines. Boswell goes on to cite that Agenor of Tyre, Tat [Set] and Erca [Hercules] are also ancestral to these wanderers. (1972, 24b). Boswell connects them with Horemheb, successor to Pharaoh Akhenaton, arguing that Nel is alleged to have married Scota, daughter of Pharaoh. Etan is one of the male Goidelic names found among these wanderers and Liben is one of the female names (1972, 24b).

Boswell appears to be onto something with her Horemheb reference, because if Clube and Napier are correct in their assigning the date of 1369 B.C.E. to the Exodus and the alleged meteor shower called the *barad*, and if the date of 1364 marks the last year of Akhenaton's troubled reign, then the Milesians could have been ousted from Egypt for their allegiance to Akhenaton's collapsing order which celebrated a benign god Aten instead of the roaring meteorites that were likely flashing overhead. Interestingly enough, the periodic Zeus/Typhon conflicts may have been the culprits as Clube and Napier argue, and in the aftermath, the Set or Seth comet fragment finally became associated with evil, Satanic forces (1982, 218ff.). Clearly, any Set follower would have been most unpopular in Horus-worshiping Egypt.

According to the *Annals of Ireland*, the Egyptians drove the Goidels out of Crete in retaliation for the Goidelian aid given to the Hebrews who were fleeing Egypt. This reference adds more detail to the events of the Exodus. And generations later, the *Annals* tell us, the Goidels landed on the Iberian peninsula, where Milesius finally became ruler before returning to Egypt. Back in Egypt, he married a second wife, also named Scota, who is not to be confused with the wife of Niul. Shortly thereafter, the Goidels arrived in Ulster under the leadership of Ith, son of Breoghan, who ruled from Muigh

Ith. Defeated by the Tuatha forces, however, the Goidels retreated to the Iberian peninsula, only to land again in Ireland on the coast of Leinster years later. There they disembarked, marched inland and defeated the Tuatha De Danaan in western Meath. But later, in an engagement with a Tuatha De Danaan remnant under the command of Eire, wife of a Tuatha ruler named Mac Greine, Scota, the Egyptian wife of Milesius, was killed in battle. The remaining sons of Milesius, Amergin, Heber and Heremon, defeated the remnant Tuatha forces and secured hegemony over the island that lasted for several centuries. Finally, according to Keating's *History of Ireland*, during Heremon's reign, the Picts, who initially served as the Goidel's ally against the Tuatha Fiodhga [an invading force of Britons], were driven out of Ireland as well (Grimal 1965, 352). Skene, citing the *Annals of Ireland*, argues that the Picts, also called the Cruithnigh and the race of Rughruidhe, were descended maternally from the Milesians through one of Milesius' sons, Ir of Ulster, whose followers were reputed to steal Milesian women (1886, I, 96).

Since an air-tight etymology for the term Goidel has yet to surface, it is useful to speculate that Goidel may have been derived from a tribe of black Libyans called the Fulanis of Takur, who according to Reynold's source, the *Annals of the Mauretanian Kings*, were called Beni Warith or Waritan of the Beni Goddala or Jedalla (Reynolds 1993, 120). Could these Libyans have joined the Milesians on their trek from Egypt? Were they also in flight? Interestingly enough, the Goddala may have originated from similar East African stock as the Tuareg, and a group of these Goddala, known as Gailtules, helped to found Numidia in Roman times, according to Reynolds. Today they are singular in North Africa in that they use their cows for milk and only infrequently use them for meat (Reynolds 1993, 120-21). One must wonder if the pastoral, pork-eating Tuatha/Milesian mixes were of a similar disposition in Ireland.

Centuries later, the Goddala may have accounted for another wave of settlers who allegedly settled in the British Isles during the Middle Ages. For the late Moorish dynasties were composed not only of Tuareg and Garamante descendants, but of Fulani descendants as well. Reynolds notes that both the Lamtuna Tuareg from Adrar in Mauretania and the Goddala spearheaded the Almoravid movement. She goes on to reveal that the Almoravid controlled Morocco, Western Algeria and Southern Spain by the eleventh century (1993, 142).

In *A Book of the Beginnings* Massey contends that the Milesians [Goidels] were a matriarchal tribe, and he attempts to derive the etymology of the term Goidel from tree worship, a theme that will be elaborated upon later in this study. He derives the Gadhael [Goidel] title from the mother goddess Ked. Her son is Har, Hel, or Ar. Ked is associated with the Tree of Life, the ash tree in northern climes, and her son, known as Pren in Welsh and Renpu in Egyptian, is likened to one of its branches. Massey goes on:

> The ash is one of the few trees on which the mistletoe branch can be found, but very rarely. The mistletoe was the Druidic Pren or branch, and Guidhel is one of the names of the mistletoe, which was especially venerated during the time of the winter solstice. Guidhel, the branch, is Hel or Har, the child of Ked whence Al, Welsh, for the race. Thus the Guidhel is the son or offspring of Ked. (1995, 479)

So how might the African and Near Eastern ancestors of many an ancient Briton have traveled to the British Isles, and for what reasons would they have come? Is *Lebor Gabala* the final word regarding the motivations of the invader groups, or was there additional traffic? That routine voyages between the Eastern Mediterranean and the British Isles, with stops in ports such as ancient Sarras and Spanish Galicia, were commonplace in Neolithic and Bronze Age time frames is proposed by E. G. Bowen in *Britain and the Western Seaways*. Arguing that ocean-going ships had been developed by the Minoans around 3000 B.C.E., Bowen states:

> in spite of the marked differences in physical geography, there was a close parallel between the maritime activity existing in prehistoric and historic times along the 2,500-mile axis of the Mediterranean from Gibraltar to Syria and that which took place along an axis from of almost equal length in Atlantic Europe from Gibraltar to Iceland during the same period. As in the Mediterranean, so on the Atlantic seaboard, there were times-- such as, for example, during the 'Megalithic Age,' or in the Early Christian period-- when the whole length of the coast lands of the Atlantic fringe were united in a common cultural inheritance dependent upon intensive maritime activity. (1972, 12-13)

Bowen argues that the final disappearance of the land bridges which connected the British Isles to the Continent in the Boreal period occurred about 5500 B.C.E. At that time, he argues, the sea lanes opened up and ancient traffic increased (1972, 16). Interestingly enough, 5500 B.C.E. is the approximate date of the building of Carnac in Brittany. But when he examines the activity along the Atlantic seaway c. 3000 B.C.E., Bowen makes an extraordinary statement:

> By this time, cultural influences from the great civilizations of the riverine

lands of the Middle East began to spread throughout the continent. The
valleys of the Nile, Tigris and Euphrates had already developed civilizations
and, in particular, had learned the arts of cultivation of the soil and the
domestication of animals. Very slowly, these new and vital skills began to
spread westward, and with them went other fundamental elements of
civilization such as the making of pottery and the manufacture of superior
tools, first of polished stone and later of metal. These new discoveries were
spread, partly by trade and partly by bands of settlers moving in search of
new homes. (1972, 22)

Citing   modern carbon dating breakthroughs, Bowen revises the
introduction of animal domestication and soil cultivation into the British Isles
to just before the third millennium B.C.E. During this period, he notes, three
sea routes were employed by immigrants to the British Isles: "across the
southern North Sea from the north European Plain; across the newly formed
Straits of Dover from northern France; and from Atlantic Europe by way of
the western sea-routes" (1972, 26). Bowen argues that the older diffusionist
model of southern to northern cultural influence needs to re-examined when
discussing the rise of the earliest megaliths and their possible diffusion up
the Atlantic seaway, given that megalithic passage graves ending in circular
chambers such as Carnac in Brittany pre-date by at least two millennia
similar sites in North Africa, the Iberian peninsula and Malta, to name a few
areas placed as origins by the old diffusionist camp (1972, 28ff.). He
concludes his discussion of the megalithic problem by restating Colin
Renfrew's independent invention argument: that the megaliths of Europe
[gallery graves and passage graves] in areas such as Malta, Portugal,
Brittany, the west of Britain, Ireland and Denmark did not share a "common
origin" located in either the Eastern and Mediterranean, Spanish Aegean
colonies or Portugal. Furthermore, he argues the megalithic tombs located
in Northwestern Europe did not spring from two colonizations from
Southern Europe, the first resulting in gallery graves and the second resulting
in passage graves (1972, 30ff.).
    As noted in the Introduction to this study, this anti-diffusionist position,
proposed by Bowen, Renfrew and others, may move the pendulum too far in
the opposite direction, for even though independent invention may have
occurred in some instances, the truth may be found in a modified diffusionist
hypothesis that allows for both the north-south and the south-north cultural
contacts along the Atlantic seaway. One should exercise caution when
examining the radical views of either extreme position.
    Bailey helps to explain the need for such caution in *Sailing to Paradise*.
He proposes that an Eastern Mediterranean-based network of bronze

markets were supplied by Near Eastern mariners who sailed world-wide to mine copper and tin, the components of bronze, and relay the refined ores back to Eastern Mediterranean markets. He cites R. J. Forbes' assertion to challenge historians: "Much of ancient history could be rewritten as a struggle for the domination of quarries and ore-deposits or metal supplies (Bailey 1994, 25; Forbes 1965, III, 212). According to Bailey, the first long-distance sailors were matrifocal thalassocrats, Near Eastern entrepreneurs, who from the sixth millennium B.C.E. or possibly earlier dominated the metals and incense trades, and, after patriarchal religion swept over the Near East, still managed to survive somewhat intact in the north. There they constructed Avebury, and Silbury Hill which has a circular base in homage to the Goddess (Bailey 1994, 157, 191). He further proposes that the appellation Sil, from which the name of Silbury Hill likely derived, was the title of the Great Goddess in Britain, and that the *Ave* root found in the title of the megalithic ruins at Avebury likely stems from the west Semitic designation for the Great Goddess, variously known as Eve, Hava or Hawa (1994, 191). This matrifocal, earth-worshiping order gave way further south to male-centered, sky-worshiping groups who began to revere a celestial male deity dubbed Ouranos by the Greeks, On by the Egyptians, and Anu by the Mesopotamians (Bailey 1994, 321). These sky-worshipers, were, for the purposes of this study, likely comet-worshipers in the early phase of this religion and only later sun-worshipers.

Once the sky-god religion insinuated itself into the Mediterranean and Red Sea basins, Bailey argues, Horus ruled ancient Egypt during this period, but the avatars of the god-king Seth ruled the rest of the world (1994, 147). For Bailey, the Seth-worshipers were the next wave of entrepreneurs to dominate the Atlantic seaway. Championing Hercules as one of their principal deities, and retaining vestiges of the old *mutterecht*, they were the miners, prospectors, smelterers, metal merchants, incense traders and incense manufacturers of the ancient world. For the purposes of this study, the earliest, pre-Christian invaders of Ireland, who will be examined closely in subsequent chapters, were likely splinter-members of this Seth-worshiping group, who over the centuries went into self-exile as this shift from matrifocal to patrifocal rule gained steam. Like their more mobile comrades, they were a mixed lot, for they too probably paid considerable homage to the cometary sky gods, one of which they deemed hermaphroditic, while retaining the kinship laws of royal incest in obeisance to ancient *mutterecht* and the Mother Goddess (Bailey 1994, 39).

Bailey goes on to propose that the various waves of Seth- worshipers were the builders of the later, Bronze Age megalithic calendar clocks on the

Mediterranean islands, in North Africa and along the western periphery of
Europe. They were also, he continues, the authors of the rock-carved
Oghams, or tally sticks distributed along the western Atlantic periphery
(1994, 234). The enigmatic Ogham script that has so puzzled the inventors
of the so-called Pictish problem can be derived from similar writing on
phallic standing stones or tally stones in North Africa which appear to have
recorded astronomical cycles, he explains, producing a photograph from
Algeria of a stone discovered in 1969 (1994, 236). He cites Swire's
contention, which Swire based upon local traditions, that the megalithic
stone circle at Callanish on the Isle of Lewis in the Hebrides was constructed
by priests and black men (1994, 156; Swire 1966, 45). Traditions can be
fanciful, of course, but coupled with this and other historical testimony,
Swire's observation may be correct regarding the Isle of Lewis site.
Stonehenge is the only larger circular megalith in Britain, and Geoffrey of
Monmouth attributed its construction to Africans as well. And Bailey cites
another tradition denoting a possible African presence in Ireland, namely that
black troops fought alongside the legendary Cuchulain (1994, 279).[3]

Language, for Bailey, is the key to much of this ancient unraveling. Noting
that the earliest name for 'copper' during the Copper Age, was *awa-ak*, he
defines *awa-ak* as the cave of the Mother Goddess, and argues that the
matrifocally supervised trade and mining network dug the copper mines of
the Atlantic periphery during the earliest period of copper smelting (1994,
24). Given that the oldest copper objects unearthed in Egypt date to 5000
B.C.E. and in Crete to 6000 B.C.E., and the earliest bronze objects at Ur date to
3500-3200 B.C.E., Bailey suggests that the megalithic site at Carnac, which
dates to c. 5445 B.C.E., may have been named [or renamed, perhaps] from the
Akkadian word for bronze or *anak* (1994, 27, 55). Noting the congruence
of ancient tin and copper mines with the megalithic sites of the western
periphery of the British Isles, he argues that these sites were better suited to
the needs of mariners than the needs of inland farmers, given that the
monuments were likely used as aids to cartography and navigation (Bailey
1994, 55). Then too, the ancient name for 'king' in Scots was Eocha, which,
Bailey argues, may be derived from the *awa-ak* root, given that the ancient
Eachan people of the Hebrides were matrifocal and inhabited the western
shores of the islands after the last Ice Age (1994, 30). He also cites another
of Swire's proposals based upon local traditions-- that the island of St. Kilda
was named after an Amazon queen called Kilder (Bailey 1994, 432; Swire
1966, 25).

Ancient female hegemony appears to be frozen in language as well.
Returning to the Late Bronze Age and beyond, he provides the name for

'mermaid' among the Bambara of Mali. They called her Faro, a title which is very close to the name of the Faroe Islands which lie to the immediate south and along which the North Atlantic current passes on its eastward course (Bailey 1994, 156). Interestingly enough, Norma Lee Goodrich notes in *Guinevere* that the Murray [or Moray] clan badge for Queen Guinevere was a mermaid holding a mirror and a comb (1992, 42). And Bailey cites another timeless mermaid who combs her hair, the *mami wata*, or siren of the West African coastal region (1994, 195).

Bailey poses another startling hypothesis based upon these and other apparent anomalies: Africa, especially West Africa, constituted an integral portion of a ancient global village that was collectively responsible for raising the Atlantic-based megalithic monuments from 5400-1200 B.C.E., the Mesopotamian temples and ziggurats from c. 4000-500 B.C.E. and the Egyptian pyramid and temple complexes of Egypt from 2800-500 B.C.E. (1994, 157).

To understand the identities of these Seth-worshiping, global villagers who likely trekked along the shores of the British Isles, it is necessary to refer to *Lebor Gabala*. The first Seth-worshipers, it argues, originated in the Isle of Meroe in the late fourth millennium B.C.E., and began a trek that allowed their descendants to eventually settle in Ireland. Two subsequent waves of Seth\Saturn-worshipers, the Partholonians from the Greek isles, and the Nemedians from Scythia, are alleged to have departed the Eastern Mediterranean for Ireland at the beginning of the second millennium. These first three groups likely opted for self-exile to escape the growing ostracization they may have experienced when they held fast to their matrifocal persuasion. And it is probable that the three later invader groups of Seth and Hercules-worshipers, the Fomorians, the Tuatha de Danaan and the Goidels [Milesians] that followed in the wake of the collapsing Late Bronze Age, were forcibly exiled to Tartaros [or the Coptic Amenti] by the followers of the sky god Zeus because of their matrifocal persuasion as well. And for our purposes, Tartaros was the extreme western periphery of Europe, or Ireland itself.

All of these Set-worshipers, who also revered the goddess of mariners, Isis and her various avatars, appear to have formed a dynastic succession of colonists. It is likely that they would have used the megalithic sites of earlier prospectors for their own channel markers, as much in awe of the ancient sites such as Carnac as we are today. For these Seth colonists appear to have been more concerned with prospecting for tin and gold and harvesting Scotch pine for resin than in building elaborate burial structures.

Bowen provides some evidence for this hypothesis. He notes that in lands bordering the sea-routes: "wealth was on the rise during megalithic times through the late Bronze Age and this prosperity involved the Bronze Age trade in gold, copper and tin" (1972, 43). Bowen indicates that Southeastern Ireland's Wicklow Hills held gold and copper deposits in their gravel; that Cork and Kerry, and Anglesey across the Irish Sea held deposits of copper; and tin abounded in Corwall, Brittany and Northwestern Spain (1972, 43). But who were these prospectors from Bowen's point of view? Certainly not the Stone Age, megalith tomb builders. Bowen explains:

> There can be little doubt that the megalithic folk, or those among them, who were prospectors, had already discovered the great mineralogical resources of the Atlantic margins before the end of the third millennium B.C. Yet . . . the builders of the great tombs were not the people who developed these resources, nor indeed were they the first to introduce metal implements into the western lands. It would appear that the use of metal reached the Irish Sea from the Near East by two channels. One was the invasion of the southeastern parts of our islands by the Beaker Folk who, about 1800 B.C., came to eastern Britain from the lower Rhineland. (1972, 43)

But there is a bit of a glitch here. Bowen notes that the Beaker Folk who entered Eastern Britain carried with them a small riveted dagger and flat axes of low quality continental bronze and copper (1972, 43). But higher grade, bronze reproductions of these daggers that appeared later and further to the west in Britain were sold to the Beaker Folk by Irish metal merchants (1972, 44). Bowen acknowledges the glitch, but fails to draw a coherent conclusion from it. He quotes Fox who argues that "the Bronze Age in Britain came not from the south or the east, but from the west" (Bowen 1972, 52). Bowen surmises from this odd state of affairs that the technology of metallurgy was diffused along the Atlantic seaway from Spain to Brittany and thence to Ireland, where metallurgy became firmly established. Given, he goes on, that bronze is found in Ireland, the "prime trade secret" of mixing small amounts of tin to copper must have been dispersed along the seaway since little tin has ever been mined in Ireland, but great quantities have been found in Cornwall, Brittany, and Galicia in Northwestern Spain (1972, 44).

If *Lebor Gabala* is to believed, it is more than likely that the secret of making bronze came from the Near East, where the process was first perfected, and later brought to Ireland not from Spain directly but from the Isle of Meroe. That tradition could have been continued by the additional waves of colonists cited in the *Lebor Gabala* and by the subsequent hordes of Phoenician merchants, metal workers and prospectors who flooded the western periphery of the British Isles in the centuries just prior to the collapse of the Late Bronze Age at the end of the second millennium B.C.E. For it was then, as noted earlier, that the so-called Typhonmachia occurred in Egypt circa 1182 B.C.E. and the Peoples of the Sea were defeated by Ramesses III (Bailey 1994, 357).

Bowen continues to ignore the obvious as he puzzles over the western origins of the bronze industry in Ireland. He argues that even though high grade bronze appears in Ireland during the Early Bronze Age, no workshops there were linked to Neolithic axe producing centers on the Continent. He goes on to propose that outside of the Eastern Mediterranean area, no tribe could support such an enterprise. As a result, he reasons, Irish bronze tools and weapons must have been made and distributed by itinerant smiths who worked the area (1972, 46, fn. 3). But he stumbles, for he realizes, based upon a map he displays, that Northeastern Ireland, lying beside the Atlantic sea route as it does, must have been well-positioned for bronze production (1972, 46).

Lebor Gabala appears to resolve this dilemma of advanced metallurgical techniques appearing in Ireland. Quite simply, there were people from the Eastern Mediterranean, where advanced techniques of metal working had been perfected, inhabiting Ireland. And these Seth-worshiping colonists may well have been established in Ireland when the more primitive Beaker People called upon their services (Bowen 1972 47, see fig. 19).

It is becoming clear then that two thriving industries, incense production and bronze and tin production, explain at least some of the African and Near Eastern migrations to the British Isles cited in *Lebor Gabala*. Regarding the incense industry, adjacent to the Axum area in Ethiopia were vast incense plantations complete with sacred groves, which as W. P. Boswell argues, later served as the prototype of the druidic groves of Italy, Provence, Greece, North Africa, and the British Isles. These plantations were the seat of an ancient industry, the distillation of myrrh, incense and other resins from the myrrh, frankincense, baobab, cedar and other sacred trees. The incense was used by the temple priests, priestesses and the cleansers of the altars. For the orgies of human and animal sacrifice in the Mediterranean and Red Sea basins produced much blood and entrail residue that had to be cleansed with the fatty acids of these trees. And incense also had to be burned to appease the cometary sky gods which, this study holds, periodically evoked general consternation. Additionally, the intricate process of embalming of the dead, once reserved for deceased royal families and their entourages, gradually was practiced on deceased commoners and their numerous pets. Soon nearly everyone of any caste at all, was being embalmed upon his or her demise. The result was an enormous industry that involved the processing of trees into the needed components. The second industry involved the mining of tin, the manufacturing of bronze, and the refining of gold and other precious metals. To make high grade bronze, tin was a scarce but necessary additive. As a result, the tin deposits of Cornwall, Galicia and other tin-rich areas along the Atlantic seaway were eagerly exploited, for bronze at times commanded a greater premium than gold.

It is more than likely that the balsam trade in Ireland also piggy-backed onto the tin trade, for the Red Sea and Tyrian supplies of fatty acids used in the making of incense and temple detergents must have fluctuated with climatic changes. An observation from a twelfth century B.C.E. monk, Giraldus Cambrensis, who wrote a description of Ireland centuries after the collapse of these twin industries, may harken back to them. In his *Topography of Ireland*, he states that "the forests of Ireland also abound with fir trees-- producing frankincense and incense" (Boswell 1972a, 89, fn. 267). What would make him use those archaic terms? What did he know? Boswell notes Lucas' and Harris' observation that Ireland's vast forests of Scotch pine and fir yielded resin and pitch that was and is quite similar in composition to the Syrian and Attican pines and firs that Egypt finally exploited in order to support its growing embalming industry (1972a, 90; Lucas and Harris 1926, 319ff.). Boswell cites another cryptic similarity between Egypt and Ireland when she reveals that the embalming caste of Egypt wore dog masks, the mask of Anubis, the jackal-headed son of Osiris, a dog that was also likened to a greyhound (1972a, 90; Budge 1962, cxvii). Is it a coincidence, Boswell asks, that St. Patrick's Druid-master was called the Greyhound (1972a, 90; 95ff. fn. 294)? As we shall see, Seth, like his 'son' Anubis, was also likened to a greyhound. And Seth was not only worshiped by the Irish prospectors and incense entrepreneurs, but he was also the great Lord of Meroe (Boswell 1972a, 90; Crowfoot 1911).

But Seth, the chief cometary deity of Ireland, as we shall see in subsequent chapters, became Luficer to the inhabitants of the Eastern Mediterranean basin as the Late Bronze Age likely collapsed under a hail of meteorites. The matrifocal Irish and the equally matrifocal Cathars of thirteenth century C.E. Languedoc in Southern France, however, refused to abandon the old God, and the *mutterecht* which the religion demanded. Hence, the matrifocal Irish Catholics became the exiles of Europe, a stigma from which they suffer even today, and most of the Cathars were brutally exterminated in the Albigensian Crusade.

Such is the testimony of folklore and extraneous sources regarding the various colonizers of the western periphery of the British Isles in the millennia prior to the arrival of the Saxons. But what else does folklore have to say about Geoffrey of Monmouth's theory of an African-built Stonehenge, which contemporary archeologists date to the third millennium B.C.E.? Was Geoffrey drawing from sources no longer extant? The neo-diffusionists began to take another look.

Regarding the who, what, where and why of Stonehenge, Monmouth's narrative and its mention of the original volcanic blue stones, which have been traced to the eastern end of the Prescelly range of Pembrokeshire in an area lying beneath Carn Meini and Foel Trigarn, may contain some elements of truth. In the following excerpt, Merlin of Camelot fame allegedly speaks: "These stones are connected with certain religious rites and they have various properties which are medicinally important. Many years ago the Giants transported them from the remotest confines of Africa and set them up in Ireland at a time when they inhabited that country" (Monmouth 1966, 196). Although Monmouth mistook Ireland for Wales, he knew that the stones had been moved. But could they have been moved by Africans? That is the question. Of the excerpt, R. J. C. Atkinson cites Stuart Piggott's theory that "we cannot rule out the possibility that Monmouth had access to written or oral tradition, now lost but then still current in Wales which embodied the carrying of the blue stones from Prescelly to Stonehenge" (Atkinson 1956, 184-85).

In the waning nineteenth century, Massey, who, as previously noted, identified Monmouth's Brutus myth as Egyptian debris in *A Book of the Beginnings*, proposed that the builders of Stonehenge were Egyptians who had migrated into the British Isles from the Nile Valley at a much earlier date than Geoffrey supposed (1995, 218). Massey's theory is echoed in the twentieth century by folklorist Kevin Danaher in *The Celtic Consciousness*. Danaher argues that the people who built Stonehenge were solar worshipers rather than lunar-worshiping Celts, and that they divided the year into four seasons (1982, 51ff.). John Ivimy joins the Massey camp as well in *The Sphinx and the Megaliths*, arguing that the first circle at Stonehenge could not have been built by Mycenaeans nor by the local residents, as some suggest, because at that time [c. 2750 B.C.E.] both the indigenous culture of Britain and the Aegean civilization were in their infancies. The nearest civilization that could have built Stonehenge I would have been the Solar-worshiping Egyptians, he argues, postulating that to better predict eclipses and thereby enhance the power of the Egyptian priesthood of Ra, the Hyperborean temple/computer [both before and after its removal from Pembrokeshire] was built contemporaneously with the great era of pyramid building in Old Kingdom Egypt (Ivimy 1974, 153ff.). Gerald Hawkins appears to corroborate Ivimy in *Beyond Stonehenge* when he proposes that

the same ancient quarrying techniques were used at Stonehenge and at
Aswan: "They used round, stone dolerite mauls (at Aswan) and the crude
bashing methods of the Stonehengers" (1973, 214).

Classical evidence for the rebuilding of Stonehenge I [c. 2750 B.C.E.] by
solar worshipers rather than by indigenous moon-worshipers comes from the
Greek poet Pindar and from Diodorus Siculus as well. Pindar, in a poem
written to praise the winners victors of Greek athletic contests, writes of the
"Hyperborean Apollo" from "the land of the Hyperboreans."[4] Siculus, who
lived during the time of Augustus, speaks of the fourth century B.C.E. in this
fragment from a lost work by Hecataeus of Abdera. Ivimy reproduces the
passage:

> Of those who have written about the ancient myths (relating to the
> Hyperboreans), Hecataeus and certain others say that in the regions beyond
> the land of the Celts there lies in the ocean an island no smaller than Sicily.
> This island, the account continues, is situated in the north and is inhabited by
> the Hyperboreans, who are called by that name because their home is beyond
> the point where the north wind (Boreas) blows; and the island is both fertile
> and productive of every crop, and since it has an unusually temperate climate
> it produces two harvests each year. Moreover, the following legend is told
> concerning it: Leto was born on this island, and for that reason Apollo is
> honored among them above all other gods; and the inhabitants are looked
> upon as priests of Apollo, after a manner, since daily they praise this god
> continuously in song and honor him exceedingly. And there is also on the
> island both a magnificent sacred precinct of Apollo and a notable temple
> which is adorned with many votive offerings and is spherical in shape.
> (Ivimy 1974, 94)[5]

Siculus goes on to convey that:

> The Hyperboreans also have a language, we are informed, which is peculiar
> to them, and are most friendly disposed toward the Greeks, and especially
> toward the Athenians and the Delians, who have inherited the good-will
> from most ancient times. The myth also relates that certain Greeks visited
> the Hyperboreans and left behind them their costly votive offerings bearing
> inscriptions in Greek letters. And in the same way, Abaris, a Hyperborean
> came to Greece in ancient times and renewed the good-will and kinship with
> the Delians. They say that the moon, as viewed from this island, appears a
> little distance from the earth and to have upon it prominences, like those of
> the earth which are visible to the eye . . . . (Ivimy 1974, 94-95)

Ivimy speculates that in later times Apollo, the Greek sun god, may well
have been substituted for Ra, given the Greek hegemony in the

Mediterranean, but, be that as it may, Siculus links the worship at the round temple [possibly Stonehenge] with solar worship. And citing the Neoplatonist philosopher Iamblichus' *Life of Pythagoras*, Ivimy argues that Abaris, reputed to have been an Egyptian priest at Stonehenge, actually met and formed a lasting relationship with Pythagoras. Ivimy then derives the name Abaris from an ancient city in the northern Nile Delta, also called Abaris, and further derives Avebury, Stonehenge's companion site, from Abaris as well (1974, 101-02, 170, 177).

Even the original egg shape of Stonehenge is traceable to Egypt, according to Ivimy. Proposing that the egg was an archetype in world religions for resurrection during the megalithic period, he cites the fact that Ra, the sun god, was said in ancient Egyptian myth to be reborn each morning from an egg (1974, 136).

In 1913, the Australian anthropologist Sir Grafton Elliot Smith also associates many of the megalithic tombs adjacent to Stonehenge and Avebury to megalithic tombs in Egypt, as Ivimy notes (1974, 136). And in a follow-up study, Sir Mortimer Wheeler (1935) argues "that the general analogy between *mastabas* and many types of chambered tombs is too close to be altogether accidental" (Ivimy 1974, 83).

Although Smith was pursuing a worthwhile hunch in regard to Stonehenge and Avebury, he, Wheeler and a host of diffusionists in their company were on shaky ground when it came to other megalithic sites such as Brittany's Carnac and Ireland's New Grange, both of which were later carbon-dated to at least the fifth millennium B.C.E., well before the rise of the pre-Pharaonic site of Ta-Seti.

Repeating the error, Quinn links the Irish site at New Grange to another site, M'Zora in Algeria, without revealing any data based upon C-14 testing. Citing Glyn Daniel's *Megalith Builders of Western Europe*, Quinn notes the structural similarities between the menhirs in Algeria, especially the tumulus of M'Zora, and standing stones on the Atlantic coasts (1986, 73). He proposes that an anti-African diffusion bias appears to be the reason why the M'zora site is mentioned so infrequently by archeologists (1986, 74-74).

Nonetheless, Quinn may be on the right track regarding an North African etiology for more recent standing stones found on the western periphery of Europe. Quinn also notes the existence of a snakelike undulating line, together with a grouping of concentric circles, which overlap one another on several North African stones, including the Stele Maaziz which is housed in the Moroccan Louis Chatelain Museum. The arrangement reminds him of the entrance stone to New Grange and various designs appearing on kerb-stones at the New Grange site, a design which he traces to ancient Egypt, a

Winter Solstice icon, he argues, which depicts a serpent guarding the entombed Sun God (Quinn 1986, 11). This is not surprising to him given that at New Grange the sun illuminates an inner chamber there on 21 December. Again, without the use of C-14 testing, his hypothesis is just that, a hypothesis, but it is possible that the New Grange spiral designs were added at a later date.

But closer to probability is Bernal's suggestion of an Egyptian connection with Silbury Hill. He is puzzled by the structural parallels that he observes between this flat-topped, stepped pyramid and the similarly shaped pyramid at Saqqara. In his discussion of the Egyptian style tombs of Amphion and Zethos found in Greece, which, he argues, were the products of early Egyptian colonization there, Bernal proposes more parallels between Egyptian-inspired megaliths in the Mediterranean basin and in Britain. He then notes that Silbury Hill appears to date between 2800 and 2700 B.C.E., and flatly states that its architects must have been familiar with contemporaneous pyramids in Egypt (1991, 131).

Cohane notes a curious pattern of prehistoric place-names which cluster just to the west of the Stonehenge site. These place-names contain either the Bar/Ber or Og roots discussed at length in *The Key*. Arguing that the pig, known as the *ber* or *bar*, was introduced into the British Isles around 2000 B.C.E., he speculates that both this sacred animal and barley, a crop then found in the Ethiopian uplands, were imported to the Salisbury Plain. A veritable "barley trail" that led from the Mediterranean and Red Sea littorals across Europe to Britain, Cohane argues, resulted in the place-names of ancient "barley villages" just to the west of Stonehenge. These include as Berwick Bassett, Berwick St. John, Berwick St. James and Berwick St. Leonard (Cohane, 1969, 70ff.). Cohane traces the *bar* element in Cochobar, King of Ulster, to another root, the Eber\Aber cluster. He notes that Eber was the great-grandson of Sem and an ancestor, five generations removed, of Abraham. Cohane argues that the title Hebrew can be derived from Eber as well (1969, 248; 218ff.).

In addition to these place-names, Cohane cites several villages in proximity to Stonehenge which bear the Og/Oc/Aeg root. Noting that Oc was not only a survivor of the Great Flood along with Noah and his passengers, but also the major deity of the ancient Irish and the inhabitants of Avebury and Stonehenge, Cohane links the Og/Oc/Aeg root to the Greek Achaeans, also called the Akhaioi or Akhaiwi, the "Sea People" who invaded the Mediterranean c. 1300 B.C.E. and created Mycenaean/Cretan culture; to the North African Acholi tribe; to Ogygios, the founder of ancient Thebes and the Achaean League of the Peloponnesus, and to the place-name Ogygios, the nomen of both Calypso's island in the *Odyssey* and of ancient Ireland; to the Irish word *Oc* meaning youth; to the word *egg*; to the word *hog*; to the Greek *aig* for goat, totem of the half-goat Pan; to Aegyptus, the co-ruler of Egypt with Danaus; to Aeetes, father of black Medea who sailed from Asia Minor to found Athens and to establish the Medes people there; to the royal Irish title Aengus or Aongus; to the sacred oak tree; and to Og, the half-brother of Eochaid Ollathair, or Dagda, brother of the goddess Brigid (Cohane 1969, 102ff.). This Irish Og fathers Ogma, the champion of the Tuatha De Danaan, through incest. And it is Ogma who reputedly handed down the written Ogham language (Cohane 1969, 81). Og may also be related to the cometary Gog and Magog of the books of Genesis, Ezekiel and Revelation. In Revelation 20, Gog, under the tutelage of Lucifer, is prophecized to appear just before the final world conflagration.

Towns bearing the Og/Oc/Aeg root in proximity to Stonehenge noted by Cohane include: Ogbourne, northeast of Stonehenge; Ogbourne St. Andrews and Ogbourne St. Georges (1969, p. 78). Cohane also notes that the Ock River, a tributary of the Thames, nearly intersects Stonehenge (Cohane 1969, 79).

Clustering around this root, are some oddities cited by Cohane. He notes that Varro argues that during the time of Ogygios, Venus changed color and shape, a phenomenon related to catastrophic floods (1969, 107). Cohane also mentions a conundrum from Irish mythology, namely that the world will not end until "Ogham and Achu mix together and the Sun and the Moon mix together" (1969, 85). Then too, the pre-Roman name for St. Michael's Mount on the Cornwall coast, was Ocrinum (Cohane 1969, 90).

One of the great disappointments for diffusionists and their intellectual progeny was the paucity of Egyptian hieroglyphic remains at the megalithic sites in Britain. Certainly the harsh winters, vandalism, the clearing of land and the like accounted for the general absence of hieroglyphic inscriptions, assuming that early dynastic or Coptic speaking Africans were involved in the construction and decoration of certain of the later megaliths.

Nonetheless, that problem is seemingly overcome by a select group of eighteenth and nineteenth century antiquarians who propose that several megalithic monuments in the British Isles are themselves hieroglyphs writ large. Eighteenth century antiquarian and Freemason Dr. William Stukeley notes several serpent and winged circle motifs in the ground plans of various megalithic sites, including Avebury itself. Although the giant serpent design at Avebury was destroyed in his own time by men such as a brawny farmer by the name of Stone-Killer Robinson, other examples, identifiable as druidic, of serpentine and winged disc shapes which may well have represented the Egyptian Cneph hieroglyph, are still extant, including one outline, still visible, at Navestock Common in Essex. Other sites where serpentine designs, albeit mangled, survive include Stanton Drew, Kanabre Hill in Cornwall, and the Tavistock site near Dartmoor.

But are there any examples of actual symbols engraved in the stonework of various ruins? In *The Serpent Symbol*, E. G. Squier notes that the Cneph serpent emblem was placed upon nearly all Egyptian temples and monuments as a consecration emblem and as an image of the supreme deity of the Egyptians (1851, 247ff.).⁵ And partially anticipating Bernal by two centuries, Squier notes Stukeley's observation regarding a possible ancient source for Britain's serpentine sites: "In the road between Thebes and Glisas [Greece], you may see a place encircled by select stones, which the Thebans call the Serpent's Head" (Squier 1851, 232). Using Ovid's *Metamorphoses* for his source, Squier argues that the Aeolian Python, which Medea observed during her flight from Attica to Colchis, was also a serpentine temple (1851, 233-34; Ovid, vii, 357). Could early Egyptian colonists, followers of Danaus, have built these serpentine monuments? It seems a reasonable question.

And there are still other markings inscribed on various ruins which point toward Egyptian origins. In *The Mediterranean Race*, G. Sergei notes that an ankh was clearly visible on a French dolmen (1914, 290). In the same work he notes the symbol of the feet of Osiris inscribed on various dolmens in Brittany. T. W. Rolleston explains the imagery:

> In Egypt the Feet of Osiris formed one of the portions into which his body was cut up, in the well-known myth. They were a symbol of possession or of visitation. 'I have come upon earth,' says the *Book of the Dead* (ch. xvii), 'and with my two feet have taken possession. I am Tmu.' (1995, 77)

Rolleston further notes that the two footed symbol also appears in India, Scandinavia, Ireland, and of all places in Mexico as well, where it may derive from the Aztec ceremony conducted during the Second Festival of the Sun God, Tezcatlipoca, in which the divine footprints were thought to appear in the maize flour strewn in his sanctuary by priests (1995, 77).

These ankh and feet symbols, combined with what appear to be Egyptian-style solar bark inscriptions that Rolleston notes were carved into megaliths at New Grange, Ireland, Hallande, Sweden and Locmariaker, Brittany, add more evidence for African and Near Eastern origins of the megalith builders and argue for the validity of the invader groups identified by *Lebor Gabala*, Holinshed and other sources (1995, 72ff.).

Compounded with other recent evidence that Jim Bailey identifies in *Sailing to Paradise*, a case may be made for an ancient global village that apparently coalesced around the world-wide tin and copper mining industries. Such New World trade appears to have been conducted at various times prior to and during the Bronze Age from bases in Egypt, the Indus Valley, Phoenicia, Minoan Crete and Mycenae. Various key sites in both North and South America would have been involved in this network (Bailey 1994, 74ff.).

Bailey notes that Brittany possesses deposits of tin and copper, both of which are used in the smelting of Bronze, and argues that various place-names such as Carnac in Brittany echo the Babylonian word *anak* for bronze (1994, 55). Referring to A. Thom, Bailey goes on to propose that megalithic sites such as Carnac, Stonehenge, Callanish on the Isle of Lewis in the Hebrides, and others were calendar clocks used not by farmers but by sailors to time their shipments of copper and tin to the Mediterranean during the Bronze Age (1994, 55). Furthermore, Bailey argues that symbols left by Mediterranean mariners can be found on various megalithic monuments. Notable among these are the New Grange labyrinthine patterns and other geometrical shapes, rock carvings which are strikingly similar to those found in ancient Iberian art. Bailey goes on to observe that megalithic monuments abound in areas where ancient Bronze Age gold and copper mines were worked such as Wicklow in Ireland, and Cornwall and other western British sites (1994, 55).[7]

The archeological record appeared, at the time, to offer potent evidence for the diffusionist cause advanced by several nineteenth century anthropologists. However, in light of modern C-14 dating, diffusionist origins for the earliest megalithic sites such as Carnac and New Grange are today viewed as rather specious. Nonetheless, a modified hypothesis arguing that an Egyptian/Mediterranean influence may have been exerted at sites contemporaneous with predynastic and dynastic Egypt such as Stonehenge and Silbury Hill, for example, still needs to be tested.

Folklore clearly provided a record that inspired the diffusionists. If the ethnicity of Gormund and his army raised questions, so too did the ethnicity of the builders of Stonehenge I, Silbury Hill and other megalithic sites. And what of the Phoenician presence in Bronze and Iron Age Cornwall? What did classical sources and the testimony of folklore tell the diffusionists and neo-diffusionists of these merchant sharks of the sea?

Phoenician contacts with Cornwall or the Cassiterides, as the Phoenicians called it, have been suggested by so many historians and anthropologists that Bronze Age, Phoenician tin and copper mining operations in the area are all but certain. According to the early nineteenth century ethnologist Godfrey Higgins, the place-name Cassiterides [countries of tin] can be derived as follows: "*Casse-tair* signifies the vulgar, or base sheet or bar, to distinguish it from silver, which is called *Airgad*-- i. e. 'the precious sheet or bar'" (1829, 90). Given the two destructions of the library at Alexandria, the first by Theodosius' Christian rabble in 389 c.e., and the second by the Arabs in 640 c.e., not much is known about this traffic. Added to these destructions is the fact that the Phoenicians, who provided the Mediterranean world with their alphabet, ironically enough, left little written record of their own exploits. This self-imposed obscurity largely resulted from their policy of not sharing trade secrets. Luckily, the ancient Greek geographer Strabo left a partial record of a Phoenician shipmaster who was sailing to the Cassiterides to collect a cargo of tin. When the Phoenician captain caught glimpse of a Roman vessel that was spying on his craft in what appears to have been the English Channel, he deliberately headed toward a shoal, wrecking his own ship and the Roman vessel that followed it (Irwin 1963, 198). Hailing from cities such as Tyre, Byblos, Sidon, Memphis and Carthage, the Phoenicians not only worshiped Baal and Ashtarte, but also absorbed several Egyptian gods into their pantheon such as Bast, the Egyptian cat goddess; Osiris; Ptah, the creator god of Memphis; and the Egyptian god of the Underworld, which they identified with Adonis.

And they were reputed to have set their course by the Little Bear constellation once they passed beyond the Pillars of Hercules. Certainly, by the twelfth century b.c.e. they were spreading their language and religion to outposts such as Gadid, the site of the present Cadiz, Spain, and from there to points north. Godfrey Higgins argues that Esmun [an avatar of Baal, the god of death] was the prototype of the Irish god Saman (1829, 30). And several Cornish, pre-Aryan place-names provide additional evidence for the extensive Phoenician mining operations conducted on the Cornish peninsula. These include Marazion (Jews Market), Para-Zabulon, Phillack, Menachin, Tamerton, Mullion, Preez, Ziklag, Zelah, Zepha, Parazeanbeeble, Zenor, and the Camel and Fal rivers (Ali and Ali, 1993, 153ff.).

More classical references to a Phoenician presence exist as well. Irwin notes Strabo's remarks about them: "The Phoenicians, I say, were the informants of Homer; and these people occupied the best of Iberia and Libya before the age of Homer" (1963, 206-207). Written in the fourth century c.e., the *Ora Maritima* by Avienus also describes a third century b.c.e. voyage of Hamilco to the Cassiterides.

In 1866 Palmer and Darling, following the lead of the much abused Col. Vallancey of the late eighteenth century, also extend the Phoenician territory to Ireland. Citing parallel traditions in the ancient Eastern Mediterranean and in Ireland, they note: "'The Patterns and Pilgrimages, Particular Holy Wells and Fountains, the celebration of La Beal-tinne, the Irish Ullagone, the lighting of fires on St. John's Eve, the Baalist names of bridges, towns, mountains, brooks, rivers & co.'" (Quinn 1986, 30).

Judging from the number of place-names with the prefix Bel, Bally, Bal etc. that are scattered across Ireland, the Phoenicians must have literally swarmed over the western periphery of the British Isles (Ali and Ali 1993, 153). Regarding their activity in the seventh century B.C.E., Quinn elaborates:

> There was good reason why the Carthaginians would want to venture on the Atlantic seaways. They had indeed blocked the Straits of Gibraltar in 600 B.C. to protect their valuable silver deposits at Tartessos on the Atlantic coast as well as to monopolize whatever rich mineral resources lay further north. The Mediterranean was, for centuries, divided between the two peoples: the Greeks controlled the eastern and northern shores, while the western and southern shores were dominated by the Carthaginians. But the Greeks had founded and controlled Massalia-- now Marseilles-- thus giving them an overland route to the Loire and thence to the tin deposits of the British Isles. The Carthaginians were, therefore, forced to seek a different route to this raw material, necessary for mixing with copper to make bronze weapons and implements. The uncolonized waters of the Atlantic seaways were theirs for the taking or, at least, the traversing and they made sure the Greeks had no access to this route. It would be centuries before a Greek from Massalia named Pytheas dared pass through the straits and enter the Atlantic and explore the sea route to the British Isles. (1986, 43)

According to Cornish legends, the original owners of the smelters (Jews' houses) and mines were alleged to be Semites who descended from the Phoenicians. Generations later, whatever remnant still clung to the mines in the eleventh century C.E. were banished in a pogrom conducted by Edward the Confessor.

Despite this evidence, Cohane disputes the Phoenician connection in Britain. Based upon C-14 dating, he argues that the Phoenicians and the Greeks received their alphabet from an earlier, more advanced Semitic people. Cohane asks: "If this is so, who were the pre-historic, seafaring ancestors of these Semitic owner-operators of the Cornish tin mines banished during the reign of Edward the Confessor?" These alleged precursors of the Phoenicians are identified with the "Sea People," or Akhaiwa, who long ago constructed the fifth century B.C.E. megalithic structures in sites such as Carnac, and whose descendants finally entered the

Mediterranean from the west around 1300 B.C.E. to raise considerable havoc in Egypt and the Mediterranean basin. Cohane argues that the "Sea People" were none other than the Philistines, descendants of an earlier wave of Semitic hegemony. That is why Exodus 23: 31 refers to the Mediterranean as "The Sea of the Philistines," Cohane reasons (1969, pp- 39-41).

In any case, the Semitic ancestors of these banished individuals may have been the same stock as a portion of the Milesians, who were allegedly blue-eyed and red-haired. Quinn notes that in 1833 Joachim de Villaneuve suggests in *Phoenician Ireland* that the Irish Druids were Phoenician snake-priests who worshiped Baal, from which the Irish god 'Balor of the Evil Eye' and Beltane, the name of the month of May meaning 'fire of Baal,' can be derived (1986, 123).[8]

The root *Bel* also appears frequently in regard to the North African and Abyssinian tribes which lived side by side with the Tuareg in Central and East Africa. In "The African Heritage and Ethnohistory of the Moors", Reynolds reveals: "The Beli of Chad and Sudan or Belin of Ethiopia/Eritrea were a people who were called the Bello of Adal [Adulis] in Abyssinian song." She goes on to explain that a tradition of the Beline of Ethiopia indicates that they descended from the House of Tarque, or the Pharaoh Taharqe, or Taharka, of the twenty-fifth Nubian Dynasty (1993, 138). This tribe is interesting for at least four reasons, according to Reynolds. First, evidence points to an eighth century B.C.E. invasion of Spain by Taharka prior to his becoming Pharaoh (van Sertima 1985, 134ff.). Hence, the Beli would have been quite mobile in ancient times. Second, the Beli were known to be miners and workers of Nilotic iron and may have been ancestral to the miners of Cornwall. Third, they revered their version of Hercules, who allegedly led a conquest of Libya. And fourth, they were known to call their ruler Kar, Ark, Ari or Areg in their Afroasiatic dialects, roots that may well have been modified into various place-names in the British Isles (Reynolds 1993, 138). Given the possibility that the ithyphallic, club-wielding Cerne Abbas Giant carved into a chalk hillside in Dorset, England may be a first century C.E. rendition of Hercules, the Beli/Belin reverence for their Hercules may afford a possible link between the North African Hercules and the Dorset figure. Then too, a few centuries before Christ, the sun gods Med and Mash, according to Reynolds, appear to have been deities associated with the Sun, fire altars and the hearth, and may have been members of the pantheon of the twenty-fifth Libyan dynasty (1993, 134). Given that Medr was the Underworld god of ancient Ethiopia, and given that Midir was an Irish Underworld deity, both of which were associated with celestial fire, it is well worth asking: Could these Beli-Tuareg or their later descendants have been ancestral to the fire-worshiping Druids?

If early folklore and a variety of other sources make a case for an African and Near Eastern presence in Ireland during the fourth to the first millennium, they are equally boisterous about the existence of Africoid inhabitants in the Isles during the Middle Ages. The *Annals of Ireland* and the Welsh *Mabinogion*, like their sister medieval works *The Song of Roland* and *Morien*, includea fairly substantial cast of dark-skinned characters, many of whom are described in less than flattering language. Several of these characters will be examined in subsequent chapters, but a sample will serve us here. In the *Mabinogion*, the tale entitled "The Lady of the Fountain" introduces an ominous black man who guards a hilltop with his club; a curly-headed woman with a black face and black hands who rides a mule to visit King Arthur at his court in South Wales; and a so-called Black Oppressor who reveals his battle prowess during a conflict at Ysbidinongyl castle.

It is, of course, extremely difficult to verify many of these legends, and caution needs to taken, since as Skene notes a century earlier, many of the Cymric tales were doctored by overzealous Welsh antiquarians in the eighteenth century (1886, 100ff.). Nevertheless, Skene argues that the *Book of Taliesin* can be trusted to reveal accurate information about three so-called races, the Gwyddyl, the Brython and the Romani, all of which lived south of the Firth of Forth. Using Bede as his source, Skene identifies the Gwyddyl with the Gaidheal or Irish Gaels from whom various lines of Galloway Picts [Welsh, Gwyddyl Ffichti, or Scoti Picti] also descended; the Brython both with the Cymry and with Bede's Brettones who lived in ancient Cumbria in districts which extended from the Derwent to the Clyde; and the Romani [using Nennius' testimony] with descendants of Roman civil and military commanders (1886, 100ff.). Referring to "The Descent of the Men of the North" found in *The Four Ancient Books of Wales*, Skene reveals that the Cymry were said to descend from Coel Hen of Kyle and his son Ceneu. And those descended from the Romans could trace their pedigree from Dyfnwal Hen, the grandson of the Roman Emperor Maximus. These Romani, Skene argues, settled in the districts of Annandale, Clydesdale and Tweeddale, a supposition which will be dealt with in a subsequent chapter. And regarding the clans of transmarine Scotland, Skene locates additional verisimilitude in the legends. Many of the West Highland clans, including the Clan O'Duibhn, later called the Campbell clan, and the MacLeods, can trace their pedigrees to Briotan, the Nemedian, Skene argues (1886, 101 ff.).

Given that much Welsh folklore largely followed the Irish legends when depicting the various invasions just summarized, this study will move to

Geoffrey Monmouth's *The History of the Kings of Britain* for his narrative
concerning Stonehenge's origins, and the activities of the enigmatic African
King Gormund of the sixth century c.e., whose African army of mercenaries
was allegedly hired by the invading Saxons to subdue the Britons.

Concerning the sixth-century African figure Gormund, Monmouth may
also be reporting actual events. Ashe notes that because of Gormund's
African army, the Saxons were able to conquer most of the country, forcing
the fleeing Britons to retreat to Wales and Cornwall (1985, 13). Although
Monmouth's *History* attempted to cast earlier legends into a medieval frame
by injecting the conventions of chivalry and courtly love into them, there is,
nonetheless, much that can be verified historically after the collapse of
Roman hegemony in Britain. Geoffrey of Monmouth recounts that during the
reign of the English Constantine, a Saxon revolt was thwarted, but after the
next king, Keredic, came to power, the Saxons, a pagan Germanic tribe that
had for years been infiltrating Southern England, successfully staged a revolt
with the help of mercenaries commanded by the Irish King Gormund the
African. Geoffrey describes how Gormund marshaled an impressive fleet of
ships, each loaded with African troops (Ashe 1985, 31). That such an
invasion force was assembled may be confirmed by a passage from the
Annals of Ireland which speaks of "Blue Men" who arrived from Morocco
during the same time frame (Ashe 1985, 31). At first the Saxons and
Africans were adversaries, according to Monmouth, but finally, after the
signing of an armistice, the African mercenaries were unleashed against the
Britons, forcing King Keredic to flee to the city of Cirencester. Gormund
followed him, burned the city, and drove Keredic from Ireland to Wales.
Monmouth then relates how the Africans allowed their Saxon allies to settle
in Central England in Loegria, displacing numerous Britons who fled to
Brittany (Ashe 1985, 31). Whether this account is true or false is yet to be
proven, but it is also retold with some variations in the *Welsh Triads*.

These   and other   such questions fueled the inquiries of the neo-
diffusionists. Clearly, the early inhabitants of the British Isles were a racially
mixed lot, and the existence of a substantial African and Near Eastern
presence there could no longer be doubted. This chapter has only provided
a brief sketch of that presence. Subsequent chapters will reveal a richer
canvas. And at this juncture a closer look at one of the more visible African
and Near Eastern invader groups-- the Tuatha De Danaan-- needs to be
taken.

Notes

1. See Keating (1901, I).

2. On the Thera eruption, see Bernal (1991, 274ff.).

3. Cuchulain is also called Setanta, a Set name in Bailey (1994,. 72). Also see Quinn (1986, 91-92), where he notes that in the Ulster Cycle, battles occur between Queen Maeve of Connacht and Setanta or Cuchulainn of Ulster. Connacht represents the area of the southern Q-Celts, and Ulster to the North was the domain of the P-Celts who came from Iberia. Cuchulainn then is also called Setanta because he bore the Hamitic Set name from North Africa. Note also that Anta and the Islamic Antar titles give the derivations of Setanta away. Chandler (1996, 301) notes that Antar was not Arabian but Ethiopian instead, and that he describes himself as "Black and swarthy as an elephant."

4. Also see Mac Manus (1975, p. 91) where he notes Tacitus' observation that Phoenician slaves of various hues were involved in the trade between the Mediterranean and Ireland in the first century C.E.

5. Pindar, *Pythian Odes*, X, 50-55.

6. Squier (1851, 233, 237).

7. Michell (1983, 131) argues that the Jewish sacred rod occurs not only at Stonehenge but at the Temple of Jerusalem and at Mexico's Teotihuacan.

8. Spence (1974, 156-57) summarizes his views and other opinions on the origins of Druidism: "In the first place, we are now justified in classing Druidism as a religion of Iberian origin, having its European beginnings in Spain, on which was later superimposed a mass of Celtic belief. Siret, the distinguished Belgian archeologist, is of the opinion that it was brought to the shores of the Iberian peninsula by certain 'Easterners' from Egypt or Syria, who introduced among the nations the worship of Egyptian or Syrian deities and symbols, for example, the sacred palm tree, and worshiped a goddess resembling the Egyptian Hathor, a form of Nut, the sky-goddess. Expelled from Spain, these adventurers settled in Gaul, Italy and North Africa. The goddess Hathor or Nut was regarded as the cow of the heavenly regions, and was, therefore, associated with milk, and the milk-exuding fig or sycamore. This lacteal fig, having no parallel in North-Western Europe, was replaced there by the milk-bearing hazelnut and similar plants, which gave forth an elixir symbolizing the life principle. The mistletoe berry was also regarded as a bearer of this magical milk. M. Siret has found evidence, too, that this cult was associated with the megalithic monuments usually regarded as Druidic. In a word, he has succeeded in showing that there unquestionably was a very ancient correspondence of belief between Egypt and Western Europe."

Chapter 4

~~~~~~

The Elusive Tuatha De Danaan

The Tuatha De Danaan have left such an indelible imprint on the myths and folklore of Ireland that this chapter, which will attempt to further trace their origins, is devoted solely to this elusive band of wanderers. One lead to Tuatha etiology comes from folklore, namely the presence of myriad dark and light elves woven into the fabric of the myths and legends of the British Isles. In the nineteenth century, James Bonwick gazed due south to locate the origins of the 'wee people' of the these legends in *Irish Druids and Old Irish Religions*:

> Because many are represented as little men, writers have fancied the idea was but a tradition of pre-existing races, small in stature, who were improved by visitors or marauders of larger growth. Dwarfs or Duzes are thought in Brittany to haunt the Dolmens, or ancient graves, though in some manner they are known as the ghosts of Druids. Certainly Africa bears evidence of a widespread pigmy race. There are *Dokos* of South Abyssinia, *Obongo* of West Africa, *Akka* of Central Africa, *Batua* living in trees like monkeys, and others in the Congo, etc. (1986, 92)

Further on, he links these diminutive groups with the Tuatha De Danaan and the Druids, terms which he uses interchangeably, and indicates that after their conquest by the Milesians, the wee folk escaped to the hills where they survived as fairies (Bonwick 1986, 92ff.).

In a similar attempt to trace the origins of both the Scandinavian Light Elves, fabled to have peopled the mythical landscapes of either Alfheimr,

Asgard, or Nilfheim, and the Scandinavian Black Elves of Svartlheim, Luke notes that in the *Prose Edda* the Dark Elves are said to have dwelled underground and to have been "blacker than pitch," while the Light Elves were described as being "fairer than the sun" (1985, 229-230). Luke ponders the fact that since "fair" is an imprecise term, this latter group could have been partly comprised of mulattos (1985, 230). Luke quotes Mac Ritchie's *Testimony of Tradition* in which Mac Ritchie cites Massey's contention that the Chaldean magi, or Babylonian priests, who themselves originated in Egypt, may have initiated the ancestors of the dark elves of the British Isles and Scandinavia into the secrets of Chaldean magic:

> In one aspect, the dwarf races appear as possessed of higher culture than the race or races who were physically their superiors. They forge swords of 'magic' temper, and armor of proof; beautiful-wrought goblets of gold and silver, silver-mounted bridles, garments of silk, and personal ornaments of precious metals and precious stones, are all associated with them. They are deeply versed in 'magic' (a term generally held to denote the science of the Chaldean Magi), and this renders them the teachers of the taller races, in religion, and in many forms of knowledge. In short, it is only in physical stature that they are below the latter people; in everything else they are above them. (1985, 230; Mac Ritchie 1890, 156)

Less boldly, Charles Squire proposes that the tradition of the wee people of the British Isles stems from a vague pre-Aryan source. Speaking of Shakespeare's Puck, he asserts that this character "is merely the personification of his race, the *pwccas* of Wales, *pooka* of Ireland, *poakes* of Worcestershire, and *pixies* of the West of England" (1975, 393). Squire goes on to comment: "The Welsh bwbach, too, is described as brown and hairy, and the coblynau as black or copper-faced" (1975, 393). These he considers to be "the degraded gods of a pre-Aryan race" which he compares to the Irish leprechauns and pookas. He then makes a disclaimer, for these "degraded gods," he supposes, have "nothing in common with the still beautiful, still noble figures of the Tuatha De Danaan" (Squire 1975, 393).

But who exactly were the Tuatha De Danaan? Was the racial background of some of the Tuatha identical to that of the wee people? And what did Squire mean by "beautiful" and "noble"? Was he responding to the misconception that the Mycenaean Greeks, or Danaans, as Homer called them, were exclusively a race of white Aryans?

In close competition with the testimonies of folklore, etymology is another avenue that can lead to origins, and when etymology is combined with an examination of additional classical references, the dark countenances of the ancestors of many an early Briton begin to emerge from forgotten northern mists. The derivation of *Danaan* provided by Bernal in *Black Athena*, suggests an African and Near Eastern rather than an Indo-European origin. Hence, a fifteenth century B.C.E. figure, Danaos, who appears to have been either an Egyptian colonizer of Greece responsible for introducing irrigation technology, or a Hyksos leader in Lower Egypt, or both, appears to provide the root (1991, 502).[1] Citing the Parian Marble as his source, Bernal dates Danaos' arrival at the Greek Thebes at 1511 B.C.E. (1991, 500). Bernal later notes that according to Hekataios Miletus of the sixth century B.C.E., Danaos introduced the Phoenician alphabet to Greece in the fifteenth century. Later, the Mycenaean Danaans, who appeared to have been associated with him, also carried it to Numidia, Spain and Northern Europe [where it evolved into the runes] during the *Pax Aegyptiaca* that smoothed the waters of the Mediterranean during the reign of Thutmoses III (1991, 502). With his characteristic thoroughness, Bernal goes on to argue that the generic term *Danaans* signified the people of the colonizer Danaos, and that evidence supports the contention that the term *Dane* predated any Hyksos entry into the Aegean. He cites a geographical list dating to the middle of the third millennium and excavated at the Mesopotamian site of Abu Salabikh. From that list, Bernal extrapolates the name *DA-ne*[h], noting that it appears as *an-ni*[h] in the parallel list from Ebla (1991, 502). Citing G. Pettinato, Bernal links *an-ni*[h] with Amnissos, which was none other that the Cretan port of Knossos. Bernal proposes that the name *DA-ne*[h] was an ancient one as a result of its appearance in both Linear A and in hieroglyphic texts dating from the middle of the second millennium. He goes on to argue that *DA-ne*[h] may have signified the "far west," namely the island of Crete and the Aegean Sea (1991, 422; Pettinato 1978, 69, fn. 188).

Bernal concludes that the best working hypothesis regarding the word *Danaan* derives from its probable cognate *Dane*, a third millennium Cretan place-name and ethnic title. "After the Hyksos settlement in the Western Peloponnese in the second millennium, punning with the Egyptian words *dn'i* and *tn'i*, and possibly the Semitic *dyn*, led to the naming of an eponym Danaos," he argues, proposing that by the fifteenth century B.C.E. *Danaioi* was the title of the people later called Mycenaeans. Transmuting to *Dnnym* and *Dan*, the title resurfaced in Cilicia and Palestine just as the incursions of the Sea Peoples commenced (1991, 422).

Brunson is fast on Bernal's heels when he also attempts to derive the elusive title. In "The African Presence in the Ancient Mediterranean Isles and Mainland Greece," Brunson refers to Aeschylus's *Suppliant Maidens*, noting that the Danides of the Mycenaean heroic epoch were described as

"Black and smitten by the sun," and that Danaus, the king of the Argolid, was, according to Aeschylus, not an Egyptian but related to black Epaphos, son of Zeus and Io. (1985, 48). Apollodorus attempts to clarify Danaos' genealogy as follows:

> [Io] gave birth to a son Epaphus by the river Nile . . . and was married to Telgonus, who then reigned over the Egyptians . . . . Reigning over the Egyptians, Epaphus married Memphis, daughter of Nile, founded and named the city of Memphis after her, and begat a daughter Libya, after whom the region of Libya was called. Libya had by Poseidon two sons, Agenor and Belus. Agenor departed to Phoenicia and reigned there. But Belus remained in Egypt, reigned over the country, and married Anchinoe, daughter of the Nile, by whom he had Egyptus and Danaus. (2. 1, 3-4)

If Danaus was not an Egyptian, but kin to Epaphos, what are the origins of Epaphos? Frank Snowden provides an answer in *Before Color Prejudice* when he observes that Epaphus was derived from black Libyans and Ethiopians (1983, 46). Clearly, Apollodorus suggests that Io herself was an Egyptian transplant in Greece: "And she set up the image of Demeter, whom the Egyptians call Isis, and Io likewise they called by the name of Isis" (2 .1, 5; Snowden 1983, 94).

Manetho's version of the Danaos saga argues that Danaos [or Harmais, in Egyptian], the brother of Pharaoh Ramesses [or Sethos], attempted to seize the throne of Egypt while Ramesses was engaged in attacks on both Cyprus and Phoenicia. Upon his return, Ramesses drove Danaos into exile (Poe, 1997).

Other sources admitted Egyptian origins for at least some of the ancient Greeks. Plato, it seems, held a certain contempt for these probable early Egyptian colonizers: "For are we not like many others, descendants of Pelops or Kadmos or Aigytos or Danaos, who are by nature barbarians . . . but we are pure Hellenes, uncontaminated by any foreign element" (*Menexenos*, 245d, Jowett, trans.). Herodotus was less squeamish: "If . . . we trace the ancestry of the Danae, the daughter of Acrisios, we find that the Dorian chieftains are genuine Egyptians" (*Histories*, VI, 53, de Selincourt, trans.).

So Zeus, Io, Epaphos, Danaus and the fifty maidens [Danides] were apparently dark-skinned Libyans and Ethiopians. Certainly Danu, the mother goddess of African origins, who Brunson argues was worshiped by Aeschylus' Danides, recalls the name of the Negro Libyan indigenes, the *Anu-Tehennu*, whom the People of the Sea came to know (1985, 48). Indeed, the euphemistic term "pre-Aryan" is taking on some needed coloration. And the fifty maidens motif, interestingly enough, recalls the *Book of Ballymote*'s description of the fifty maidens who accompanied the fifth invader group cited in *Lebor Gabala*. The probable symbolism of the number fifty will be examined in a subsequent chapter.

Not prepared to leave it at that, Brunson goes on to review the vicissitudes faced by the Libyan Anu-Tehennu [later known as the Tuatha de Danaan] as they colonized Crete and parts of Greece in the Prehellenic era. He notes that around 3200 B.C.E. the Theban king Menes, hoping to unify the lower delta with his southern empire, invaded Lower Egypt and drove out the Libyan Tehennu, who appear to have fled to Crete and points beyond (Brunson 1985, 48).[2] This study has already proposed an origin for the Tehennu, and Brunson cites several theories that corroborate earlier observations. First, he mentions Alan Gardiner, who in *Egypt of the Pharaohs* cautions scholars not to confuse this early people with later immigrants to the coast of North Africa:

The name [Libyan] is, strictly speaking, both a misnomer and an anachronism . . . . In earlier times two peoples are distinguished, the Tehennu and the Temehu, of whom the former were perhaps originally identical both in race and culture with the Egyptians of the Western Delta. . . . They wore phallus sheaths, had a large curl hanging from one side of their head, and carried feathers in their hair. (Gardiner 1961, 35)

Brunson also refers to Arthur Evans, the early excavator of Minoan Crete, who unequivocally links Libya with Crete in *The Palace of Minos II*: "The question even arises whether some other, in this case partly negroized elements, with whom the proto-Libyan race stood in close relations in the Nile Valley, may not also have found their way to this Cretan district in their wake" (Evans 1921, II, 45ff.). And regarding Crete, Evans goes on to observe: "Whether they like it or not, classical students must consider origins. The Grecians who we discern in the new dawn were not the pale-skinned northerners, but essentially the dark-haired, brown complexioned race" (1985, 62; Evans 1921, II, 45ff.). R. W. Hutchinson's *Prehistoric Crete* is also cited by Brunson. Hutchinson argues that a dolichocephalic [long-headed] substratum existed in Crete well into the Neolithic Age:

Early Minoan I bones from a rock shelter at Hagios Nikolaos (24 women) [are] described as being of pygmy dimensions [Bushmen] . . . . An Early Neolithic series of sixteen skulls of adults from other Mesara tombs, probably not earlier than Early Minoan III, or Late Minoan II fall as low as 74.2 [quite dolichocephalic on the c. i. index]. (1985, 56; Hutchinson 1968, 60-61)

Of this dolichocephalic substratum, Brunson cites D. A. MacKenzie's observation in *Footprints of Early Man* that the remains were of a long-headed, dark type "of the same type as the predynastic Egyptians" and the skulls, as MacKenzie notes in *Myths of Crete and Prehellenic Europe*, "resembled [those of] the people of Somaliland" (1985, 56; MacKenzie 1927, 58). And Brunson also cites Sean Jennet's observation in *Connacht* that a branch of this matriarchal people, known in Greece as the Nemid or Nemedians, journeyed to Ireland, where they suffered from a plague and retreated back to the Greek isles. The remnant which lingered in Ireland were known as the Firbolg, worshipers of Bolg, or the Goddess of Lightning (1985, 38; Jennet 1970, 21).

Weighing the growing evidence, Brunson insists that these migrating Libyans were African in origin:

> Among the eccentricities of wardrobe and attire associated with these people were double plumes in the hair, tails attached to short skirts, and most important, the 'Libyan Bow' shield, and a strange 'little tuft of hair standing upright above their foreheads which reminds one irresistibly of the uraeus on the Pharaoh's brow. The Libyan bow, which became the hieroglyphic symbol for Nubia or Ta-Seti, was a religious emblem known as 'Zeti.' (1985, 39-40)

Noting that the Anu-Tehennu worshiped an avatar of Danu, the goddess Neith, who reveals many parallels both in name and characteristics to the Phoenician Tanit and the Greek Athena [legend has it, she was born in Africa on the shores of the extinct Lake Triton], Brunson examines their connection to Ireland in the Late Bronze Age. Alluding to Barry Fell's *America B. C.*, Brunson cites the *Book of Ballymote* which contains a listing of ancient Libyan script (1985, 48; Fell 1976, 175ff.). Brunson then cites Gerald Massey, who in *Ancient Egypt: The Light of the World* proposes that the Tuatha De Danaan referred to their goddess as Anu, Danu-ana and Neter-Kar, and that the derivation of the title Tuatha De Danaan stems from Egyptian underworld imagery, "those in land beneath the waters" (1985, 48; Massey 1992, II, 635-36). And, although Brunson does not include it in his study, Massey offers an intriguing hint about the possible itinerary of the Tuatha:

> the Tuatha or tribes who brought the ancient wisdom out of Lower Egypt or the Tuat may have been genuine Egyptians after all, as the much derided traditions of the Keltae and Kymry yet allege and strenuously maintain. 'The

oasis of Tuat' is another bit of ancient Egypt still surviving in the country of Morocco, where it testifies, like some strange boulder on the surface, to the buried past. (1992, II, 636)

This migration could have resulted when and if the Tuatha De Danaan were pushed out of Greece by the proto-Achaeans.

The serpent designs at New Grange, the Irish megalithic complex which was certainly occupied, although not constructed by the Tuatha given its dating to at least the fifth millennium B.C.E., may have denoted the Tuatha's worship of the Triple Goddess. Her moon and serpent associations appear to have been African imports. Clearly, Triple Goddesses worshiped along the North African coast, i. e. the Phoenician Tanit, the Libyan Neith and Danu, had similar associations.

Brunson notes other connections: Long Barrow skulls, many of which may be the remains of the Tuatha, are uniformly dolichocephalic [long-headed] much like predynastic, Nilotic Egyptian skulls, and some are even prognathic [jaws projecting beyond the upper face], Brunson reveals (1985, 52). He cites T. Rice Holmes' theory proposed in *Ancient Britain and the Invasions of Julius Caesar* that these bones may be the remains of the "ancestors of the dark-skinned Silures, or 'Black Celts'" (Brunson 1985, 52; Holmes 1936, 79).[3]

But it is the overwhelming archeological evidence that links Libya and Mycenae to Ireland. Brunson summarizes the high points, noting that tradition reveals that the lands of the Firbolg were eventually occupied by Tuatha De Danaan, and that at New Grange, the entrance to a Firbolg shrine is carved with eight double spirals, attributed by Graves to the Tuatha De Danaan (1985, 49). Also discovered in these long barrows, were segmented blue beads of faience, Brunson notes, adding that these beads, which have also been unearthed in Mycenaean tombs, were crafted in Egypt around 1600 B.C.E. He also points to the resemblance between a Bronze Age dagger blade discovered in the Sixth Shaft Grave at Mycenae, and another excavated in Ireland from the same period: "Both of these bronze halberds are adorned at the hilt with five rivets, plated with gold conical caps, with straight back, and curvilinear outline, and a well-marked medium rib," he reveals (Brunson 1985, 49).[4] And even more convincing evidence is cited by Brunson, namely Eliott-Smith's observation that the purple dye industry of the Phoenicians originated in Minoan Crete. The Phoenicians marketed the product, and perhaps with their input a modified purple dye industry blossomed in Cornwall, where the product was known as "black purple" (Brunson 1985, 49). Recalling that purple was regarded as a sacred color by the Egyptians, Phoenicians and Nubians, Brunson notes one of the main uses of the purple dye as described by Graves in *The White Goddess*: "As late as the time of Pliny, girls and matrons stained themselves with this dye for 'certain rites,' until they were as swarthy as Ethiopians, then went about naked. Only women were allowed to indulge in this rite that sanctified them to the Goddess Anu" (1985, 52; Graves 1982, 76).

If this were not enough to link the Africoid Tuatha wanderers with pre-Celtic Britons, Brunson cites Holmes' observation that the vocabulary and even the script of the Tuatha De Danaan seems to have been derived from Coptic, Middle Egyptian and Nubian languages, arguing a point this study will deal with in a subsequent chapter, namely the existence of identical syntactical anomalies identifiable in both Insular Celtic and in certain Afroasiatic dialects. Brunson concludes that the linguistic evidence points toward African origins of the Long Barrow race (1985, 53; Holmes 1936, 67).

For Brunson, then, Crete was at first a refuge of Libyan Tehennu, who were known to be ardent worshipers of the Triple Goddess. Agreeing with that hypothesis, this study contends that as time passed the matriarchal elements of the religion at Crete were supplanted rather abruptly by a sinister patriarchal set of rituals. As a result, Evans' view of the persistence of a jubilant, liberated Cretan society of Tehennu inspiration, which he pictured in *The Palace of Minos*, is largely a naive and sentimental vision. For, unknown to Evans, more sinister forces appear to have come into play at Knossos as the centuries passed.

In *The Secret of Crete*, Hans Wunderlich (1974) argues that Evans grossly misinterpreted the *zeitgeist* of Cretan society and the function of the Palace of Knossos. Far from being an ebullient, life-centered society as Evans supposes, the Cretans appear by the eighteenth century B.C.E. to have been very much obsessed with a bizarre death cult that this study contends may have resurfaced in the British Isles. Certainly, Wunderlich observes, if the palace had been lived in by the royalty and their entourage, how could one explain the lack of a defensive wall around the palace, the fragile egg shell ceramic objects, the thin, militarily useless shields that lined the walls of various rooms, the gypsum stairways that could not withstand the normal wear of palace inhabitants, the odd-shaped "bathtubs," and other chair-like objects that Evans claimed were the prototypes of modern toilets. And why the lack of armament rooms and stables, the lack of a dining room, hearths and kitchen facilities, the orientation of the palace not to an easterly exposure but to westerly one, and the dreary, windowless rooms in the lower labyrinth? he asks. And why had Dedalus, the fabled architect of the labyrinth whom tradition says Princess Ariadne commissioned, constructed the palace on a barren plateau from which no springs flowed?

Thomas Munster, a visitor to the palace ruins, also found the site to be most peculiar. Wunderlich notes his reaction:

> What about the palace's access to light, air and sun? Where, for example, are the big windows without which we can scarcely imagine elegant living? When you look closer you see, to be sure, that the royal palace has open loggias, colonnaded halls, roofed over courts, but that there are scarcely any windows. A good many rooms are so completely boxed in within the complex structure that they don't not even border on an outside wall. There is something very odd about the idea of constructing a luxurious building in whose interior people would necessarily feel as if they were inside a cave. Yet they had all the means to build in totally modern windows, perhaps even glazed windows. (1974, 85)

For Wunderlich, the answer to these questions is obvious. Like similar Egyptian "palaces" such as the one constructed at Medinet el Fayum during the reign of the Seventh Dynasty Pharaoh Ammenemes, a site which may have served as the model for Dedalus's labyrinth, or the later Hawara and Mendinet Habu sites in Egypt, the Palace of Knossos was not a domicile for the living but a luxurious crypt for the dead. Although their labyrinths are not as convoluted as those of their counterpart at Knossos, all of these Egyptian funerary palaces, honeycombed as they are with underground rooms and hallways, become for Wunderlich, palpable symbols of the Egyptian Underworld and the shared religion of Egypt and Crete. For it was into that Underworld which Ra descended each evening in his sun barge in hopes that his passenger Horus would, just before the coming dawn, slay the Apap monster that guarded the eastern horizon. Then, much as the soul of man which was called the Osiris in the *Book of the Dead*, Ra could once again be resurrected at the sunrise.

The assertion that Egypt and Crete adhered to the same cultic rituals at least by the eighteenth century B.C.E. is linguistically justified for Wunderlich. For proof he traces the name of Minos, the daughter of Europa and the first king of Minoan Crete, to King Menes, the founder of a united Upper and Lower Egypt at the beginning of Egypt's dynastic era in the early third millennium B.C.E. (1974, 85ff.). And although Evans denied it, Wunderlich maintains that the word 'labyrinth' could be derived from the Egyptian *loperohunt* or "palace (or temple) by the lake" [Lake Moeris] (1974, 85ff.).

I. E. S. Edwards in *The Pyramids of Egypt* describes the Fayum and Hawara sites which were constructed during the reign of Ammenemes III:

Ammenemes III had been immortalized by the classical historians as the constructor of Lake Moeris in the Fayum and as the builder of a labyrinth in the neighborhood of a lake, which was considered to bear comparison with the labyrinth at Knossos in Crete . . . Ammenemes III's connection with the labyrinth has been proved . . . as Petrie was able to show when he excavated the king's second pyramid at Hawara and discovered that its mortuary temple was, in fact, designed as a kind of labyrinth. (1947, 174)

And the immense mortuary palace of Medinet Habu, constructed for Ramesses III [1181-1150 B.C.E.] in Thebes West, Wunderlich notes, was itself only inhabited by ten people who were assigned to perform various duties for the dead (1974, 248). That was certainly an eerie and frightening job description, for as Wunderlich explains, the labyrinth in Thebes West is neither a necropolis nor a mortuary temple, but a mortuary palace in which sacrifices, conjurations, ritual feedings, embalming and a host of other ceremonies were conducted for the edification of the dead which languished there (1974, 196).

The god who presided over these grim festivities in the Ta-Meran [Egyptian] Underworld was none other than Ptah, "'the mighty one, south of his wall, lord of Anch-tawi, Ta-tenen, father of the gods, tall in feathers, pointed in horns, beautiful in face, dwelling in the great place," the supreme deity of Lower Egypt whose sacred animal was the Bull (Wunderlich 1974, 54). As the centuries passed, however, Ptah was likely replaced by Zeti or Set. And if the reader hears the name Tuatha De Danaan echoing in his inner ear, Gerald Massey also heard it when he examined the reemergence of the cult of dead in the British Isles.

But from where did this cult of the dead arise? And why did the Egyptians of the second millennium believe that the dead were somehow living?

Wunderlich attempts to provide some answers. He argues that concept of the "living dead," so integral to the Egyptian and Cretan cult of the deceased, can be traced to black Africa. Citing John Mbiti's 1969 study entitled *African Religions and Philosophy*, he notes that in contemporary West Africa when the living move from the present world called *sasa* to the realm of the dead called *zamani*, their relatives consider that the dead are still alive and supply them with water, cola nuts and intimate conversation on a daily basis (1974, 250). Wunderlich also recalls that in twentieth century Burundi, when a king who had been expelled by his subjects finally died, the population was anxious to recover the body. If not, the spirit of the king might wreak vengeance on the living and take them along with him (1974,

251).

And although Wunderlich does not suggest it, this attitude toward the dead that existed in the patriarchal era of solar worship may have evolved from the moon-worshiping era of the Mother Goddess. Noting the existence of beehive shaped tombs that resulted from the initial Tehennu colonization of Crete, and, citing William L. Hansberry (1981), Brunson links them to similar pre-dynastic tombs excavated in the Sudan, Ethiopia, Egypt and the Western Sahara. He argues that these tombs derived from the African ghost house, where the ancestor's spirit allegedly resided, and that those tholos tombs were linked to the spiral or serpent image (1985, 62). Given that during the era of matriarchy the serpent was a sometimes benign symbol both of the Goddess herself and of the rebirth or reincarnation of the soul [i. e. the serpent sheds its skin and is reborn], the rites surrounding this early cult of the dead may have been initiatory in nature. Perhaps they involved the cutting of the male's valued lock of hair as a sacrifice to the goddess, and not the act of human sacrifice.

But, as noted in the introduction to this study, catastrophes occurred in the Mediterranean basin that may well have influenced how the mother goddess and her snake iconography came to be perceived. In *The Cosmic Serpent*, Clube and Napier provide considerable evidence for the proposition that either comet Encke, a short period comet with an average earth orbit of 3.3 years, or perhaps the long period comet Halley, began to break up as it passed the earth during the period of the Egyptian Old Kingdom. This disintegration may have led to catastrophic results for the Mediterranean basin in the form of forest fires, the desertification of North Africa, and other horrors noted in the introduction. According to Clube and Napier, the comet, whether comet Encke or Halley, was likened to Ptah during the Old Kingdom and seemed, from earth's perspective, to resemble a demonic celestial serpent (1982, 220). Clube and Napier summarize the profound influence of the comet on the religious pantheon of Egypt, noting that the primal Ptah, likely the symbol of either the comet-generating planet Jupiter, or a super comet breaking into two fragments, is linked with the Flood. Then, the cosmic serpent Nunet replaces Ptah and likely produces Osiris. That genealogy is logical, Clube and Napier argue:

> if the events describe the successive phases in the life of a huge comet in periodic Earth-crossing orbit, but after further break-up and decay, the main component ceases to be visible and presumably becomes an Apollo asteroid. Although not part of the principal family of gods, Apepi [Apap] may have been another mighty comet periodically dominating the sky: we can only speculate here but it is not impossible that Halley's comet may have been

recognized. (1982, 180-81)

Clube and Napier note that Hesiod's *Theogony* presents what may have been the Greek version of the Egyptian horror when it describes the birth of Typhoeus, conceived after the intercourse of Earth and Tartarus, and after Zeus [the Greek Ptah] had driven the Titans from the sky:

> But he thundered harshly and strongly, and all around the earth, the broad heaven above, the sea, Ocean's streams and the lowest part of the Earth resounded terribly . . . . Through two of them, heat seized the purple sea, from the thunder and lightning, the fire from the monster, the hurricane winds and the blazing thunderbolts. The whole earth, sky, and sea seethed; and moreover long waves raged around about the shores. . . . So when Zeus had raised up his strength he chose his weapons, thunder, lightning and the smoky thunderbolt. He leapt from Olympus and struck him and burned about the awful heads of the terrible monster. But when he had tamed him and lashed him with blows, he was thrown down lame and the large earth groaned. The flame from the thunderstruck lord shot out in the unseen rocky glens of the mountains, when he was struck. Much of the vast earth caught fire as a result of the awful blast, and melted just as tin melts . . . . Grieving at heart, he cast him down into broad Tartarus. (1982, 184-85)

Although speculative pending further digs at Knossos, the impact of this cometary activity may have had profound repercussions on the shared religion of Egyptian Thebes and Knossos, perhaps leading in both locations to a macabre cult of the dead dedicated to the bull god Ptah. That is the same Ptah who later became the gristly Phoenician Baal to whom thousands were sacrificed. And Ptah likely devolved into the British Beli in whose honor the Druids routinely set aflame giant wicker men packed with victims. It is also tempting to speculate that Zeus's son the Minotaur, that half bull, half man which languished in the Cretan labyrinth, might have been for a time at least deified as a comet roaming the Underworld. But it could just as well have stood for the earthquakes which rumbled beneath the islands. Until the spade uncovers any hard evidence, the identity of the Minotaur will remain enigmatic. In any case, the serpent image, venerated during the matriarchate, must have taken on mixed and even negative connotations at Knossos, given the less than flattering associations taken on by the serpent in the Greek myth of Apollo's slaying of Python at Delphi.

For Evans, however, the existence of any cult of the dead was out of the question at his idyllic Palace of Minos. In fact, he appears to have had several double-headed axes to grind, an intellectual exercise that biased many of the reconstructions of the frescoes his artist Edouard Gillerion completed under Evan's direction. C. W. Ceram (1972) was one of the first to protest, balking at the Art Nouveau style that seemed all too obvious in Gillerion's work, a style which often turned ancient temple prostitutes into blushing 1890's nouveau damsels. And Ceram went on to question the palace reconstruction as well, complaining of the free range of Evan's interpretation of its structure, and arguing, as Wunderlich notes, that "in his reconstructions he [Evans] put together elements of ancient buildings that were completely unknown to the Cretans. Many archeologists nowadays say that he erected a concrete Crete" (Wunderlich 1974, 80).

For Wunderlich as well, Evans failed to understand the pastness of the past in his reconstructions of Late Bronze Age Crete. Instead, Evans viewed the site through the subjective lens of a proper Victorian gentleman, placing King Minos and his spouse in the large palace and the crown prince in the adjacent little palace and so on down to the smaller estates of the princes and nobility. Wunderlich comments: "Thus even the social order of the Victorian era could be found anticipated and corroborated in Knossos (1974, 83). Wunderlich berates Evans further:

> Evans should properly have compared the Minoan world not with the British monarchy at the turn of the century, with its palaces and country houses, but with the practices and thought of Africa, where attitudes toward death are age-old and bear a strong relationship to those of ancient Egypt. (1974, 251)

Wunderlich goes on to answer various complaints lodged by his own critics regarding an Egyptian-Cretan connection. He cites the relaxed, naturalistic style used in Crete to represent the human form that seems most un-Egyptian, the absence of hieroglyphs on the walls of the Cretan labyrinth, and the apparent lack of mummies at the Knossos palace. Despite the fact that the frescoes of Knossos appear so drenched in the life-force, Wunderlich rebuts, the processions they depict were hardly celebrations designed to entertain and amuse the local populace. Instead, like similar, albeit stiffer, Egyptian processions of the Eighteenth Dynasty illustrated at Thebes, which should not to be mistaken for tribute marches of Cretan's in the act of obeisance, these Cretan marches were designed to appease the dead by offering up sacrifices of the vegetable, mineral, animal and human variety. And the flesh tones, Wunderlich recounts, are Egyptian, usually reddish-brown for the men and white for the women, with a large number of black-skinned subjects as well. And since a primitive form of Greek called Linear B was used to prepare the inventories of grave good listings, the hieroglyphic language of the Egyptian priesthood was not needed. The Cretans already had a written language which they used for the express purpose of maintaining their lucrative cult of the dead.

Examining the imagery depicted in the Cretan processions on the restored frescoes and the numerous shields and ceramic jars that Evans unearthed at Knossos, Wunderlich provides copious evidence to prove just how macabre these processions became. The bare-breasted maidens holding snakes in their outstretched arms, who so impressed Evans with their alleged liberality, are really mourning the dead, with the raised snakes serving as emblems of the soul's hoped-for resurrection. Given that bare-breasted, mourning women are depicted numerous times in the writings of Herodotus and Homer, Wunderlich regards the motif as a mourning convention. And the frolicking dolphins, fish and birds that fill the frescoes with their apparent life-force, are really funerary zootypes, transporters of the soul to the hereafter, he argues. And even the intense blues, which form the background of so many of the frescoes, symbolize nothing more than the color of mourning, he proposes, noting that Hecate, the goddess of the underworld centuries later, was often depicted with a dolphin on her belly, and that well into Roman times dolphins were painted on blue cinerary urns. And buxom maidens, who for Evans appear to be joyously leaping over the horns of bulls, creatures which Wunderlich derives from Ptah's bull zootype, are hardly emblematic of Evan's perception of Minoan *elan*:

> The girl at the raging beast's horn is not swinging over the horns, but dangling helplessly from them-- one of the sharp horns, which she clasps convulsively, has already passed through her chest instead of going by it on her side. The Spanish bullfighters were perfectly right when they told Evans that such a perilous leap over a bull was impossible. (1974, 277)

For the Minoans, Wunderlich argues, the dead continued to live on in their graves. Hence, they required feeding from the ceremonial bowls found *in situ*. But as cremation replaced burial, the concept of the Underworld changed from a substantial place to a realm of shades (1974, 237). And cremation became necessary, according to Wunderlich, to halt the epidemic of grave robberies that occurred at the Palace of Knossos and other such palaces and burial sites throughout the Mediterranean basin. For these grave robbers, the ill-favored poor, were not numbered among the potential living dead. Hence, they had nothing to lose as a result of their activities.

Finding no mummified human remains in the excavation proper, Evans became convinced that the Palace of Knossos was not a burial site. But he was puzzled by the debris piles of human bones that littered the surrounding area. In his attempt to create an Art Nouveau theme park in Crete, he apparently did not factor in grave robbers as the source of that debris, nor the insatiable demand in Europe right up until the last century for mummified flesh, both human and animal, which was used to prepare bogus potions and medicines. Crete was not Egypt. There were cultural differences. But for Wunderlich, the cult of the dead was a shared phenomenon.

Interestingly enough, the builders of certain megalithic sites of roughly the same period that are found in Brittany and Cornwall may have derived much of their ritual from the Egyptian/Mycenaean/Cretan ceremonies. Certainly, the archeological record shows that cremation abruptly replaced burials in these northerly sites much as it did in the Mediterranean basin. That shift in the rites of the dead in the British Isles is usually accounted for by an Aryan invasion, but cremation rites may have also been introduced in the north by non-Aryan Mediterranean colonists as well.

And that leads to a tie-in. For similar Egyptian faience beads and other funerary objects found in Knossos reappear in megalithic sites along the western periphery of Europe. Although this modified diffusionist argument, along with a closer examination of the rituals that occurred in Egypt, Knossos and most likely in Cornwall and Ireland, will be detailed in a subsequent chapter, Cretan diffusion to the western periphery shortly after the Thera explosion and the other alleged disasters that apparently plagued the basin should not be ruled out. For the Tuatha De Danaan may well have been Cretan Ptah-worshipers who brought the rituals of the Egyptian *Book of the Dead* with them to Ireland, along with the concept of Ptah's land of the living dead, which appears to have devolved into an orgy of human sacrifice by fire. And this macabre religion of sacrifice may have proliferated in the British Isles when Ptah was renamed Apollo, Zeit (or Set) and Baal by Phoenician sailors, before Ptah's avatars were finally transmuted into the British Beli.

Clube and Napier propose that both the linear array of stones and the later stone circles, constructed at sites such as Carnac in Brittany, Stonehenge and at Brodgar at Orkney, may not have always been designed to symbolize the stars, the sun or the moon, but the ever more impressive cosmic serpents (1982, 263-64). They note that many of the stone circles, which slowly evolved into elliptical, egg-shaped configurations, appear to have been added on at these sites from 2400 B.C.E. to the tumultuous 1300 B.C.E. when circle building reached a climax (1982, 264). They also discuss the many Neolithic "cup and ring" markings. For such shapes are common in numerous rock formations in the British Isles and appear to record the coma and tail of a comet. Putting two and two together, they come up with the startling hypothesis that Stonehenge's more obscure alignments and monuments "represent an attempt to track one particular comet" in all of its orbital changes over a specific time-frame (1982, 263).

And then, citing Lockeyer, they draw a telling analogy that may speak volumes about the proposed migrations of Africans into the early British Isles. For this comet may also have been tracked simultaneously in Egypt, a process which may explain "the adjustment to the alignments of Egyptian temples" which cannot be explained by "the luni-solar precession" (1982, 262-64).

Noting the observation that at least forty tons of meteoric material enter the earth's atmosphere each day, Robert Stephanos goes further still, when he proposes that the linear northeast-southwest standing stone and temple configurations found in the megalithic monuments of Britain and in the alignment of the West Bank Nile Temple complex may demarcate the regular pathways of meteorites aloft (1983, 44ff.). Typically called Ley lines and dragon paths in various cultures, these linear patterns resulting from similar northeast-southwest alignments of monuments worldwide, likely served as earthly representations of the cosmic serpents' heavenly and not so heavenly itineraries.

In any case, turning to the Greeks who appear to have intermingled with the Ptah-worshiping Tuatha De Danaan, Clube and Napier recall that the fourth century Greek Hecateus was convinced that a race called the Hyperboreans inhabited Britain. They cite Diodorus Siculus' recording of Hecateus' observations, previously mentioned in this study, which delineate how the worshipers at the round temple celebrated Apollo's deeds.

What deeds might they have been celebrating? In fact, who or what exactly was Apollo? Bernal derives Apollo's name and part of his nature from the Egyptian *Hprr*, the god of the dawn, which does not really settle the matter (1991, 587, fn. 93). For Clube and Napier, Apollo was emblematic of a comet, and by the fifth century B.C.E. Apollo would be linked by the Greeks with Horus, the killer of Set and avenger of the dead Osiris. And Clube and Napier also regard Set as the Egyptian version of the Typhon comet discussed in the introduction. So how could Greek and Egyptian gods be emblematic of comets?

For Clube and Napier, the two major combat myths that emerged in ancient Greece were those of Apollo vs. Python and Typhon vs. Zeus. And for these two astrophysicists, such myths were not idle tales but quite accurate accounts of the breakup of a comet that they believe shattered over the Mediterranean basin. The first myth, which concerns this study, comes from the Homeric *Hymn to Apollo* that dates back to at least 1200 B.C.E. Clube and Napier paraphrase the hymn, noting that shortly after his cometary nativity, Apollo travels across the sea and appears in Greece, seeking a temple site. A mountain called Parnassus is chosen by the god, and after he lays the foundations of his shrine at Delphi, he battles a she-dragon, which he dispatches with an arrow (1982, 192).

Suggesting that this myth was derived from an actual event, Clube and Napier argue that Apollo was clearly the survivor of some encounter. But what kind of encounter? Of what event was the Apollo v. Python combat an allegory? To answer these questions, they propose that "he was the surviving fragment of a disintegrating comet" which traversed the Greek skies, and in the process dropped a betel stone, later used as the cornerstone of the temple at Delphi. They go on to propose that his bow may have symbolized "the crescent head of a huge comet," hence the association of the Delphic temple with dangerous vapors (1982, 193). And later, they theorize that the exploits of both Python and Zeus' adversary Typhon were likely allegories of the gradual breakup of the Zeus comet, admitting the possibility, however, that if there had been one catastrophic meteor shower that emanated from the comet, Python and Typhon might have been two names for the same fragment (Clube and Napier, 1982, 197-98).

How Egyptian or Greek the British Apollo may have been will be examined in subsequent chapters. But speaking from the worm's eye view again, Wunderlich notes still more curious parallels between Crete and certain Celtic burial sites of the early Iron Age:

> It is amazing . . . that Etruscan and Celtic funerary architecture at this period developed forms quite similar to the tombs of the Middle Bronze Age. Along with simple inhumation we find rock tombs, large barrows, stone chamber tombs and even labyrinthine structures. Originally these were closely associated with the cult of the dead, but later became castles of refuge (oppida), to which the populace inhabiting the plains fled from attackers. (1974, 194)

That observation certainly raises questions about the ethnic origins of several tribes of the so-called Celts.

And he also notes Homer's description of what Wunderlich deemed to be a funeral dance performed both at Knossos and at Cornwall in which garlanded maidens strut with young men bearing golden knives (Wunderlich 1974, 324; Lattimore 1970, 391).

Although those golden knives may have raised some ancient eyebrows, the purpose of the dance may never be known. And Wunderlich, citing Pliny, holds that mazes similar to that at Knossos which may have been used for versions of that same dance have been found not only in Cornwall but in Scandinavia and Northern Russia as well (1974, 289). Were the Tuatha De

Danaan and their progeny numbered among these dancers in the British Isles?

As we have seen, folklore and classical testimonies whetted the appetites of scholars with a diffusionist persuasion. Aroused by that record, they would seek additional avenues to confirm their hypothesis of an African and Near Eastern presence in the early prehistory and history of the British Isles.

One avenue was littered both with unexplained phonetic, semantic and syntactical commonalities between English and Afroasiatic words and sentences. Another was replete with various place-names which dotted the British Isles, appellations that were neither Celtic, Roman, Saxon nor Norman. It is to phonetics, syntax and these fossilized place-names that this study now turns.

Notes

1. For his derivation of Danaos from a possible pun with the Egyptian *dn'i* for 'allocate' and 'irrigate,' see Bernal (1991, 47).

2. Also see Graves (1966, 238ff). He argues much the same, noting that the Goddess-worshiping Pelasgians of Greece who refused to worship Zeus were extruded from the coastal regions in successive Greek invasions and then driven from the Nile Delta as well.

3. Also see Holmes (1936, 79).

4. Also see Graves (1966, 104), and Evans (1921, II, 170-73).

Chapter 5

~~~~~~

Phonetics and Place-names

If likenesses between a select number of megalithic ruins scattered across Britain and those further south could provide a means to test the hypothesis of African and Near Eastern diffusion from southern climes to northern ones, so too could a study of comparative phonetics. Gerald Massey, more so than any other nineteenth century philologist, attempts to prove that Neolithic and Bronze Age migrations from Egypt and the Eastern Mediterranean to the British Isles occurred by arguing that many of the Egyptian word roots these colonists brought with them became imbedded in the earliest languages spoken in the Isles. And even more eccentric is Massey's notion that Egyptian roots preceded and informed elements of Sanskrit as well. He describes his method with no apologies: "The founders of philological science have worked without the most fundamental material of all, the Egyptian; this they neglected early and avoided late" (1995, 137). He goes on to argue that Egypt, not India, was the earliest source of the language first spoken in the British Isles, and derides his fellow philologists: "their theory of the Indo-European origin of languages and races is . . . the most spurious product of the century" (Massey 1995, 137).

Using phonetic likenesses as his method and largely avoiding the search for syntactical parallels, Massey deliberately violates Grimm's Law, the philologist's benchmark, which holds that the comparison of words from different languages based upon their agreement in sound is, independent of considerations of grammatical structure, specious.

It would be easy to relegate Massey, the self-schooled son of a poor

Hertfordshire boatman, to crank status were it not for Martin Bernal's new wave of philological research which appears to corroborate much of Massey's earlier word-spinning. Beginning in the late 1980s with the *Black Athena* series and numerous articles, Bernal conducts a similar survey of Afroasiatic-derived, Greek loan words, some of which filtered into the Romance languages, and challenges the much belabored theory of an invasion of pre-Hellenic Greece from the north by Indo-Europeans. Equipped with a more refined philological acumen which often outshines Massey's more frenetic and sometimes facile etymologies, Bernal argues that pre-Hellenic, Greek language was replete with Egyptian and Phoenician cognates. Many of these cognates, he goes on, cannot be derived from Sanskrit. In an article entitled "Black Athena: the African and Levantine Roots of Greece," he notes that nearly every word referring to weaponry or military organizations in early Greek is non-Indo-European in origin. How could that be the case if Greece endured an invasion by northern Aryans? he asks (1985, 75). His analysis is crucial for the purposes of this study, for to reiterate, these pre-Hellenic, Afroasiatic-speaking colonists who hugged the southern littoral of Greece were likely the ancestors of many an early Briton, assuming that the invasion scenarios of *Lebor Gabala* are credible,

Despite Bernal's more refined methodology, he often identifies, much as Massey did one-hundred years earlier in his comparisons between Egyptian and English roots, a simple concurrence of phonetic and semantic goodness of fit between early Greek words and their alleged Afroasiatic cognates. Like Massey before him, Bernal argues that one language system, the Afroasiatic [inclusive of Berber, Chad, Cushitic and Semitic tongues] co-existed with a later influx of the Indo-European language. For ammunition Bernal alludes to Herodotus' *Histories* VI, 55, Aeschylus' *The Suppliants* and Euripides' *The Phoenician Women* to argue that in pre-Hellenic times Greece was inhabited by primitive tribes such as the Pelasgians which absorbed waves of Egyptian and Phoenician settlers. Additionally, Bernal argues, it was these later colonists who not only constructed the cities and irrigation projects which studded the Greek Peloponnese, but also introduced the alphabet and a dusky pantheon of deities. For Bernal, this early diffusion of technology, language and religion partially explains the legends citing the Egyptians and Phoenicians as the founders the earliest royal dynasties of pre-Hellenic Greece (1985, 67). Although Greek is, in the main, an Indo-European language given that "its morphology, case, and personal endings, and . . . core vocabulary-- pronouns, prepositions, numbers and verbs and nouns of agricultural life," Bernal reasons, nonetheless, "over 50% of its lexicon, especially in the semantic areas of luxuries, political--not family--

relationships, law, religion and abstraction are non-Indo-European" (1985, 75).

He cites scores of surviving Afroasiatic toponyms and mythological names, and traces their derivation not from Indo-European roots, but from Egyptian and Phoenician ones. The following is a sample of non-Indo-European Greek words that he examines: 'ebony' from the Egyptian *hbny*; 'kudos' [divine glory] from the Egyptian *KDS* [divine glory or vileness]; 'markarios' (blessed) from the Egyptian *m3'hrw*; 'sophia' [wisdom] from the Egyptian *sb3* [teaching]; 'xiphos' [sword] from the Egyptian *sft*; the Greek river name 'Anigros' from the Egyptian *(N)GR* [spring forth, flow]; 'Samothrace' from the Semitic *sam* [high or sky]; 'Mount Ida' from the Semitic *YD* (hand); 'Thebes' from the Canaanite *tebah* [ark, chest] and the Egyptian *db3* [chest] and the Egyptian *db3t* [palace]; 'Sparta' from the Egyptian *Sp3t* [Jackal god Anubis epithet]; the Hyksos Greek capital 'Avaris' from the Egyptian *Db3*; 'Athens' and 'Athena' from the prothetic A and the Egyptian *Neit*; 'pontos' [distant ocean and land beyond] from the Egyptian *Pwnt* [distant land reached by sea]; and 'Hekate' from the Egyptian *Hkt* [old frog woman] and the Egyptian *h3k* [magic] (1987, 80).

To further support his hypothesis of a potent Afroasiatic sub-strata in an otherwise Indo-European, Greek tongue, Bernal echoes classical authors, reiterating that the majority of the Greek gods were of Egyptian origin. As partial evidence, he cites Book II of Herodotus' *Histories*, which, he notes, is the only Herodotus selection that is not required reading at England's Oxford University (Bernal 1985, 80).

In "African Women in Early Europe," Edward Scobie compliments Bernal's argument by providing more Egyptian-Greek influences regarding the gods of Greece. Scobie recalls that the progenitor of the gods, Zeus, who fathered black Epaphus, was of Ethiopian ancestry. He quotes the Greek poet Aeschylus, who wrote of Zeus: "And thou shalt bring forth Black Epaphus, thus named from the manner of Zeus' engendering" and goes on to note that Zeus was also called Ethiop (1985, 213-14). Scobie further reveals that the name of Artemis, the Greek Goddess of Chastity, was derived from a black Egyptian deity, and that the derivation of Minerva, the Goddess of Wisdom of Rome, leads to an African princess of the same name (1985, 214).

For Massey the great wash of Egyptian and Phoenician language, culture and technology which bathed Prehellenic, Greek shores also washed onto the litorals of the British Isles. A century before the insights of Bernal and others, Massey argues the case for the transmission of Egyptian loan words to the British Isles, and for an Egyptian and Phoenician presence in the

British Isles as well.

Using his complicated and sometimes rather contrived linguistic juggling, Massey concludes that there were at least three great migrations to the British Isles. The first wave was one of Egyptian pygmies, the Karfuti, or Kamruti, later called the Kymry, which translates, he argues, into the race [from Eg. *rekh*, pl. *ry*] of Kam, Kym, Kvm or Khebma (1995, 501).

The second wave, he continues, was that of the Ketti. This wave included the followers of the mother goddess Kheft [Ked], whose zootypes were the hippopotamus and the ape. Claiming that the ape zootype was transformed into various monsters still extant on ancient Scottish stones, he reasons that the Ketti were short, black itinerants who hailed both from the African interior and from Kush to the south of Upper Egypt. He goes on to argue that the complexion of the Ketti was retained in the names of their Irish descendants, the Corca Duibne and Corca Oidiche, and in the title of their Welsh descendants, the Kymry (1995, 501).

The third migration originated from Lower Egypt. This group, he argues, was known as the Ruti, or the men of monuments (Massey 1995, 502).

For Massey, the Kymry were the earliest dark-skinned immigrants. He proposes that they came by sea from the land of Hav, noting that in old Welsh and in Irish, Hav is equivalent to Ham or Kam (1995, 456).

He goes on to observe that a modified form of Kam was Kheb, the name given during the Twelfth Dynasty to a land in Egypt that lay below the second cataract, the land of Hab. He calls upon the following Su-Hathor allusion from a Twelfth Dynasty text to document the linkage: "I entered the land of Heb, visited its water places and opened its harbors" (1995, 456-57).

He also proposes that *Hav* is the root of the word Gypsy, deriving it from the Egyptian *Kheb* [Lower Egypt] and *Khept* ['to squat, to lie prostrate on the ground']. Aware that not all Gypsies who entered the British Isles came from Egypt, he realizes, nonetheless, that some may well have traced their genealogies to that locale (1995, 457). He explains that the word *gypsy* need not be viewed as a corruption of 'Egypt,' but may have been derived from *Kheb* with *si* being the added suffix for child (1995, 457).

He further notes that in Scotland the name Gypsy mutated from *Hfa* to *Faa* and concludes the etymology by arguing that *gipsy* can be derived as both 'the child of Kheb' and 'the child of Ked,' two names for the British mother goddess whose title was derived from Ketti (1995, 457).

In his introduction to the *History of the Gipsies*, Walter Simson, although unable to resolve the matter, also attempts to trace the ultimate origins of various gypsy bands to Egypt. In a footnote, he cites Ezekiel 29: 12-14, and 30: 10, 23 and 26, which all contain allusions to the scattering of the

Egyptians (1878, 40). Recalling that Nebuchadnezzar conquered Egypt and dispersed thousands of prisoners throughout his empire, Simson argues that the ancestors of many British Gypsies might have been partially comprised of that remnant which did not return to Egypt (1878, 40). That British Gypsies did not speak a Coptic tongue, but a form of Hindustan does not phase Simson, who goes on to argue that over time the generations would have learned and unlearned numerous tongues (1878, 41).

Brian Vesey-Fitzgerald notes in *Gypsies of Britain* that Irish Gypsies called Tinkers speak a different language than the Anglo-Romani or their English counterparts. The Tinkers' language is Shetla, and he reveals that Shetla is a secret tongue, not simply a jargon. Like the other secret languages of Ireland, Ogham, Hisperic Latin, Duil Laithne, Berlae na Filed, and Bearlagain na Saer, Shetla will require more study by scholars, he concludes (1973, 33ff.).

Massey attempts to construct a dictionary of Egyptian loan words spoken in ancient Egypt, cognates, he argues, which were retained in the English language after the Afroasiatic language systems had been absorbed by the later waves of invaders who spoke Indo-European tongues. Using a less scientific method than that employed by Bernal and later philologists, Massey, nonetheless, tries to prove that several ancient place-names extant the British Isles contain Egyptian loan words which stem from the pre-Aryan speech and writing of early Britons. Since Massey's etymologies can become quite labored at times, a sampling of his analysis of key place-names will be examined at this point.

As in Greece, pre-Aryan river names persist in Britain, albeit sometimes in modified forms, or so Massey argues in *A Book of the Beginnings*. The Thames and Tamar rivers are two examples. *Tem*, he argues, means 'totality, the perfect whole' in Egyptian, whereas Tam means 'to renew.' *Temi* [Eg.], he goes on, signifies the Inundation of the Nile. From this Egyptian root, then, he derives the titles of England's Thames, a tidal river, and the river Tamar in Devon (1995, 183).

As convincing as his etymology may be, he fails to note another possibility. *Tamar* in Hebrew also refers to a 'beautiful object' or literally 'date palm,' and may be derived from the Ethiopic *Tamr*.

Interestingly enough, Cohane also traces the etymologies of these river names to an Afroasiatic root: "At the time when Caesar invaded England in 51 B.C., the Thames was called the *Tamesis*, and was so recorded by Caesar. It has been variously spelled since then-- the *Tamesa, Tamensis, Tamisa, Temis*, and *Temes*" (1969, 47). Cohane derives the Thames place-name from a northeastern district of the Arabian peninsula called Tema. This district, which faced the western district of Dedan, was inhabited by thirteen tribes allegedly descended from Ishmael, who, banished into outer darkness by his father Abraham, fled there with his Egyptian mother Hagar. Cohane goes on to reveal that from the fourteenth to the seventh centuries B.C.E.: "Tema was in the finest strategic position in the world. Today a barren desert, seven thousand years ago it was a flowering paradise, watered by rivers as the Thamar and the Al Thamalai, the Thamri, Thumrayt, and Thumayl watercourses . . . " (1969, 198). Going further down the etymological trail, he links Tema to the primal Egyptian deity Tem, also known as Tum and Ptah, who populated the earth and skies through masturbation (Cohane 1969, 206). Not content to leave it at that, Cohane then links Tema to Themis, the first wife of Zeus and the mother goddess who gave birth not only to Prometheus but also to the Fates, the Horae, and the Hesperides, also known as the "Daughters of Night" (1969, 206). Although Themis was one of the original twelve Titans who lived with the next wave of deities which populated Mt. Olympus, Themis and her sister Dione, were exiled by Zeus much as Ishmael and Hagar were cast into outer darkness, Cohane notes. He goes on to make an interesting comparison linking the titles of two goddesses Themis and Dione with the two northern Arabian districts of Tema and Dedan (1969, 206). Cohane, then, like Bernal, follows in the footsteps of Massey.

Continuing his examination of river place-names, Massey provides an etymology for the river Shannon. Arguing that the Egyptian root *nen* is another name for the Inundation, he cites the Shannon as Ireland's version of the Nile. Noting the transit of alluvial soils by both the Nile and the Shannon, he goes to argue that *shen-nen* [Eg.] implies periodic renewal. The *nen* [*han*] suffix, he goes on, also means 'the bringer' (1995, 186).

The possible etymology of the river Usk in southeast Wales is equally intriguing to him. Citing Renouf's translation of the *Papyrus of Ani*, Massey indicates that *An* is the place of rebirth both for the soul and the sun. In this sacred place, he goes on, is found the mythic Hall of Two Truths called Uskh, the place where the soul is cleansed of its sins. Uskh, he argues, translates to 'the limit' or 'the division,' and an icon of that hall is three feathers from which he derives the three feathers of Wales, and the ancient name of the burgh of Caerlion, previously called *Caer-usk* (1995, 437-38).

Massey later proposes that the *uskh* name may have been transmitted from the Euskarians, a black-haired, pre-Celtic people who once populated the Basque region of Spain, Wales and Ireland, but the water name can, nonetheless, ultimately be traced to an Egyptian source (1995, 448).

Other place-names for rivers in the British Isles for which he does not trace etymologies, and which appear to be derived from Afroasiatic loan words are the rivers Fal and Camel in Cornwall; the rivers Tawy and Taff in Wales; the rivers Affric, Farra, Liver and Nevis in Scotland; the rivers Hafren, Ouse, Tama and Teviot in England; and the river Tawy in Devon, to name more notable examples (Ali and Ali 1993, 143ff.).

Several English, Scottish, Welsh and Irish cities still retain their pre-Aryan roots as well, Massey argues. Regarding Dover, he argues that the name can be derived from *ter-ru* [Eg.] meaning 'gate' or 'port.' Watling Street, a former Roman road which begins at Dover and runs north, is derived from *uat*, the Egyptian for 'north,' and *uati*, the Egyptian title for the goddess of the north (1995, 371). Given that Roman roads were often built over the mostly straight roads constructed by the earlier inhabitants of Britain, Massey may be correct in so deriving Watling Street.

The roots for Tenby, a town on the Welsh coast, are also traced by Massey to Afroasiatic cognates deriving both from Sabaean [Arabian] star cults and solar cults. Attributing Sabaean origins to Tenby may not be as far-fetched as it seems given Reynold's observation that a proto-language of the ancient Berber tongues was Sabaean, and that Abyssinian, Sabaean and Himyaritic colonists from Ethiopia and Somalia from at least the second millennium B.C.E. were the originators of modern Ethio-Semitic dialects (1993, 101). Massey attempts to derive the Tenby place-name from *ten* [Eg.] for 'the mount,' 'the throne,' and 'the birthplace of the Equinox,' or *bekh*. For evidence, he recalls that the name Tenby was originally known as Tenbick or Den-bigh, which he translates as 'the solar place of birth' (1995, 384).

Banff, along with its accompanying Gamrie Bay on the northeast coast of Scotland, is given a similar scrutiny by Massey. He derives the place-name from the Egyptian *ban* or *ben*, which he translates as 'to cap,' or 'tip.' Noting that *ben* also meant pyramidion, he muses over the many other *ben* place-names throughout the British Isles which designate mountains, for *ben* converts to mountain in Britain. Gamrie Bay is then derived from the Egyptian *ka* for 'headland,' or 'high place,' and the Egyptian *meri*, which he translates to 'the limit of land and sea' (1995, 372).

Not only do Egyptian cognates inform the names of towns and cities in the British Isles, Massey insists, but various British cities and towns were also named according to a sacred system first employed in Egypt which involved the dividing of the land into what in England were later called shires or counties. Noting that several towns in the British Isles contain the *car* root, Massey attempts to sort out the influence. Citing Nennius, Massey reveals that before the shires were designated, the land divisions were called

Caers. Massey goes on to derive *car* from the Egyptian *Kart* which he translates to 'dwelling in,' or 'dwellings of the damned in Hades.' Massey then reveals that in ancient Egypt the Kars were equivalent to the lower places or land divisions, and the concept was transmuted into the names of the lower counties in Wales when the ancient land surveys were done there (1995, 434).

The designation of Kent in Southeast England follows a similar pattern, Massey argues, assuming that it was named for the Egyptian cognate *Khent* [south]. The appellation also allowed, he proposes, a means of reckoning the year through the motion of the Great Bear constellation, and the rising of the Dog Star Sothis [Sirius] which announced the Inundation of the Nile (1995, 132).

Continuing with his train of thought, he cites a Basque proverb: ". . . in flying from the wolf [or dog] he met the bear" (1995, 133). That leads Massey to observe that the Great Bear constellation was associated with the north, and the Dog star Sothis [Sirius] with the south (1995, 133). Later in the tome, he continues to construe the Egyptian cognate *Khent*, arguing that as in Egypt where Khent was the title for the unexplored wastes of Upper Egypt, the British Kent also stood for south, citing also that Horus was designated Lord of the South, or Lord of Khent (1995, 406). He further notes that Ramesses III, in an address to Ammon, says, 'I made thee a grand house in the Land of Khent.' This is mentioned as one of the four quarters along with the north, east, and west" (1995, 406).

The Egyptian system was also used in naming counties designated with the *set* suffix, , Massey argues, noting the archaic titles that still obtain [i. e. Defenset, Dorset, Somerset, and Wilset, or today's Wiltshire]. These counties, he goes on, were previously mapped by Egyptians, arguing that *set* also means 'a portion of the land measured off, divided, and named' (1995, 435).

Then he proposes that several Egyptian roots are nested in the county names: Defenset from the ancient name for Wales, *Dyved*, with the set suffix added; Dorset from the Eg. *Tur-set*, 'the extreme limit of the land'; Somerset from the Egyptian *mer* for 'sea'; and Wilset from the Egyptian *hir* for 'uppermost boundary' (1995, 435).

Massey offers another observation regarding the naming of English counties bearing the *sex* suffix. Regarding Essex, Sussex, Middlesex, and Wessex, he derives the *sex* suffix from the Egyptian *sekh* [Eng. *soke*], which he translates as 'a division mapped out,' 'to cut out,' 'to rule,' etc. (1995, 432).

And if this were not complicated enough, Massey concludes:

Applied to territorial division on the large scale, the Sekh gives us the plural of Sex, our four counties. In Essex, Sussex, Middlesex, and Wessex, we have a complete system of the territorial sokes, arranged according to the four cardinal points, and named in Egyptian. Uas is in the west, a name of Western Thebes. Wes-sex [today it is called Hampshire] is Uas-sokes, the west divisions. . . . Both Sut and Su signify the south, and in Sussex, Wessex, and Essex the English follows the parent language in dropping terminal T. Sussex is the south sokes, and on the same principle Essex is the east sokes. (1995, 432)

According to Massey, Welsh counties which include *car* in their names [Cardigan, Carnavon and Carmarthen] also derive from the Egyptian cognate *kar*. For he argues that the Egyptians believed the upper and lower hemispheres of the night sky mirrored the topography of the land of Egypt that lay below. The upper [because of the mountainous terrain], southern hemisphere was broken down into the Sets, while the lower [because of the Delta's low elevation], northern hemisphere was divided into Kars. The two celestial hemispheres, he goes on, were divided by the imaginary equinoctial line which ran from east to west (1995, 436). Anticipating by decades the celestial mythology described in *Hamlet's Mill*, Massey reveals that the topographies of the Earth in both Egypt and early Britain were rendered as reflections of the heavens above.

Continuing his examination of the alleged, ancient divisions of Britain, Massey attempts to plumb the mystery of the counties ending in the *ster* suffix, as will be noted in the discussion on Stonehenge that follows.

The names of ancient megalithic sites in both Brittany and the British Isles present Massey with more opportunities to demonstrate his etymological gymnastics. The analyses Massey provides of Carnac and Avebury render a sampling. Brittany's Carnac is derived, he argues, from the Egyptian Karnak [Eg. *Kar-en-akh*, or 'the circle of the dead'] located at Thebes. He notes alternative spellings of the cognate in the British Isles which include *Cairn* in English, *Crwn* in Welsh, *Cruinn* in Gaelic, *Cern* in Cornish, and *Cren* in Armoric [in Brittany]. In each case, he argues, the cognate denotes a Cairn-Circle, and the *kar* root is translated to several derivatives which include: the 'Underworld,' and 'sarcophagus.' The variant *karas*, he argues, translates to 'a place of embalmment,' or 'a chamber for the mummy' (1995, 398). Unbeknownst to Massey, of course, the name Carnac may have been bestowed on these ruins at least two millennia after the megalith had been constructed in what is today's Brittany, given that Carnac is at least that much older than the Theban Karnak. Nonetheless, Avebury's [originally *Kaf-bury*, he argues] cognates are equally obvious to Massey, who derives the place-name from *Af* [Eg. 'born of'], another title for the mother goddess Ked, and *burui*, the Egyptian for 'roof,' 'supreme height,' etc. Hence, it meant a high, undampened place of the soul's resurrection, he argues, proposing that the inhabitants interred their dead much like the Egyptian dung beetle buried her eggs on high ground in hopes of a hatching [i.e. resurrection] of the offspring during the next flooding of the Nile. The tomb at Carnac is also linked by Massey to another term for a place of burial, the Egyptian *meskhen* (1995, 421).

Incidentally, Massey's *meskhen* reference echoes the name Meshken, a Libou king of the thirteenth century B.C.E. who Reynolds cites (1993, 114). And referring to Oric Bates' *The Eastern Libyans*, Reynolds reveals that a later Numidian king of the third century B.C.E. called Misagenes by the Romans, was a son of a ruler named Massinissa, which means 'son of heaven' (1993, 114-16). Once again, it appears, Massey was ahead of his time.

To strengthen his argument regarding Carnac's derivation, Massey notes that the remains of beetles have been found in several megalithic sites in the British Isles. Such sacramental insects, he reasons, point again toward the possibility that many of the megalithic architects were either Egyptians or individuals heavily influenced by Egyptian burial rites. Massey argues that the beetle (*khepr*) was sacred in Egypt and analogous to the druidic egg, and mistletoe branch in Britain. He recounts the Nile beetle's yearly habit of laying its eggs just prior to the Inundation, and then concealing them inside of doughy ball of earth before rolling the ball backward to the high water mark. Arriving at the sandy periphery, it buries the egg ball and itself and waits for the chrysalis' transformation.

Of the Stonehenge site, Massey proposes that in Welsh *Cor-Cyfoeth* was the early name of the temple. In Welsh, he argues the word *cyfawd* translates 'to rise up,' and *cyfodi* means 'resurrection' (1995, 421). Regarding the *henge* in Stonehenge, Massey reasons that it derives from the Egyptian ankh symbol (1995, 407). For the Egyptians, he argues, the stone ankh symbolizes eternal life, for the term meant 'the living,' but it was also used to denote the living dead (1995, 407).

In attempting to unravel the loan word for the *ystre*, or the name of the course into which one avenue at Stonehenge leads, Massey argues that it can be derived from the Egyptian *ster* or 'couch of the dead' (1995, 408). From this *ster* cognate, he proposes, rather than from the Norse *saeter* ['farm' or 'homestead'], three provinces of Ireland [and other cities ending *ster*] partially derive their names-- Ulster, Munster and Leinster (1995, 409). Arguing further that the word *minister* once applied to the *ster*, or 'layer out of the dead,' he derives the name of the English city of Manchester from the Egyptian *mena* [the dead] and *ster* (1995, 409). The word *menhir* also relates to this *mena* cognate complex, according to Massey, who wrests the word from the Egyptian *men* [Eg. 'heaven'] and *her* [the Eg. verb 'to ascend' and the noun 'the road'] and *mena* [Eg. 'the dead'] (1995, 400).

The etymology of the England title is also attempted, an effort that for Massey only reinforces evidence for the funereal uses made of the British Isles during the Bronze Age. Noting that the *Welsh Triads* refer to England as *Glas Merddyn* ['a green spot defended by water'], he notes the Egyptian roots *mer* or *meru* ['isle'] and *ten* [Eg. 'to cut off'] in the title (1995, 440). He also argues that the island was called the Island of Beli, after the Mediterranean god Baal (1995, 450). But he spends more space in breaking down the later name *England* into its possible Egyptian roots, denying that *England* is only to be derived from the *Angles* root. Rather, he traces the name from the Egyptian *ankhiu*, meaning 'the dead,' 'the departed.' This cognate explains why the people of Brittany once called England *Ancou*-land, 'the land of souls, to which the dead crossed over by night,' he insists, or why *ankow* means 'death' in Cornish (1995, 441).

Proposing that these early names ultimately derive from the Egyptian root *ankh*, he deduces that Ankh-land was, mythologically speaking, the land of the soul's rebirth, or the land of life transplanted from Egypt, as it were. He goes on to argue that "for the people on the mainland the white island beyond the waters was blended with the Ankhland that lay on the other side of the waters crossed by souls in death" (1995, 442). Citing further evidence for the etymology, he recalls that when Homer's Odysseus consults the dead in the far north, the hero enters the land of the Kimmeroi--which Massey wrests from *khema* [Eg. 'the dead'] and *rui* [Eg. 'the isles'] (1995, 441). Massey goes on to decipher the etymology of England, arguing that *Ankh-land* derives from the Egyptian *Ankh-ta*, a name for one of the quarters in ancient Memphis, and *Ankh-taui*, meaning 'the land of death and new life' which lay on the opposite bank of the Nile. Equating Brittany to *Ankh-ta* and England to *Ankh-taui*, he argues that the English Channel functioned much as the Nile in funerary rituals. Over both bodies of water, the dead were carried to their final resting places (1995, 441).

Island names such as the Isles of Sark, Orkney and Arran are also grist for Massey's etymological mill. Regarding the Isle of Sark, he argues that in Egyptian *sarkh* or *serkh* means 'temple,' 'place,' or 'shrine,' and *Serkh* was an Egyptian avatar of the goddess Isis, hence the name, the Isle of Sark (1995, 373). Massey then derives Orkney from *orch*, an old Kymric word that means 'border' or 'limit,' which, he argues, renders *ark*, the Egyptian for 'an

end,' 'limit,' 'to cease,' 'be perfected.' In Egyptian these denote the extremity
or end of the islands (1995, 392). Introducing another possible etymology,
he explains that the Egyptian for water is *nnui*, and the Egyptian word *ark-
nnui* denotes both the limits of land and water (1995, 392). Citing the
influence of the Egyptian root on Gaelic and Icelandic, he goes on to point
out that *arach* in Gaelic means 'a bier,' and the Icelandic *ork*, means
'sarcophagus' and 'womb' in Irish (1995, 392). As noted later in this study,
W. P. Boswell suggests a different etymology for the Orkney islands.

Scottish Arran is a bit more complicated for Massey's unravellings. The
name, he argues, should be derived from the Egyptian *aren*, the ancient title
of an ark or a floating island (1995, 415). The ancient symbolism to which
he refers involves Herodotus' transcription of the Egyptian legend of the Isle
of Chemmis, or 'floating island,' situated in a lake near Buto. Massey cites
the passage:

> The Egyptians, when they affirm that it floats, add the following story. They
> say that in this island, which before did not float, Latona, who was one of the
> eight primary deities dwelling in Buto, where this oracle of hers now is,
> received Apollo as a deposit from the hands of Isis, and saved him, by
> concealing him in this which is now called the floating island, when Typhon
> arrived, searching everywhere, and hoping to find the son of Osiris. For they
> say that Apollo and Diana are the offsprings of Bacchus and Isis, and that
> Latona is called Orus; Keres, Isis; and Diana, Bubastis. (1995, 414)

Missing the possible cometary level to all of this, Massey reasons that
Herodotus' account can be compared to a much later one by Diodorus
Siculus. Siculus' account noted a similar island opposite the coast of Keltica
in the lands of the Hyperboreans which the Hyperboreans did not inhabit.
On this island, Siculus states, Latona was born, and a round temple of Apollo
was built. And from this island, a priest named Abaris traveled to the Island
of Delos off the southern coast of Greece (1995, 414). Although many
historians assume that the Hyperborean island referred to is today's England,
Massey argues that this cannot been so, since the island in question "is self-
identified by name and the mythological scheme as Bute, one of the seven
isles of Buteshire, the namesake of Buto, both being sacred to Latona and
Apollo" (1995, 415). He goes on to indicate: "Bute [the companion island
of Arran] lies off the Keltic coast of Scotland . . . . Moreover, it has in Arran
the twin island, which was called Chemmis in Egypt and was known as the
floating island" (1995, 415).[1]

As ingenious as Massey's derivation of Arran may seem, there is another
possibility as well which may not be mutually exclusive. According to E. J.

Brill's (1982) *First Encyclopedia of Islam*, the Arabs captured what is today called the Eastern European country of Albania from 644-656 c.e. and named it *Arran* or *Al Ran*. Given the ragged, mountainous terrain of today's Albania, the possibility should not be ruled out that in later times Moors could have penetrated the two equally mountainous islands of that name, one off the coast of Galway and the other off the western coast of Scotland, and named them both after their previous conquest.

Although Massey does not attempt to derive the name of the Isle of Skye from Egyptian, he is quite emphatic about the complexion of its early inhabitants. He cites Martin's *Journey Through the Western Islands of Scotland*, noting the following description: "the inhabitants of the island of Skye were at that time for the most part black," and reasons: "Doubtless that is over-colored, but all who have traveled in the isles and in the remotest parts of Wales and Ireland have met with the old dark type, which has been greatly modified by admixture, but is not yet extinct" (1995, 454; Martin 1981, 174).

And regarding another more recently-named island, the Scottish Isle of Lewis, Massey reacts to the local tradition that the underground beehive structures found there were built by ancient black Africans known as the Kymry. He notes parallels between the Isle of Lewis ruins and similar underground structures discovered by Stanley in Southern Unyoro in the African interior, and argues that beehive structures in Hottentot villages are all but identical to similar beehive houses identified at Lewis (1995, 447). He goes on to type the early inhabitants of the Isle of Lewis, calling them *karti*, dark-skinned Egyptian pygmies not unlike the African Akka and Bushmen. He proposes that the *karti* were dwellers in huts and holes, describing them as spinners, potters, weavers and corn-men, judging from the spindle whorls and pottery shards found at the site (1995, 447, 449).

The name of Scotland itself is also traced back to its alleged source by Massey. Arguing that 'Scot' may have been derived from *sekh* or *uskh*, the Egyptian for 'water,' he also consults *Cormac's Glossary* and discovers that the oldest form of the name 'Scot' is *Scuit*, or 'wandering' (1995, 449). From that point he reasons that the place-name can be derived from the Egyptian *khet* ['to navigate'] with the S added later to create the word *skhet*, or 'vessel,' 'ark,' or 'boat.' He goes on to note that *Skute* is English for 'wherry,' and that Scot may also be derived from the Egyptian *uskht*, meaning 'wanderer of the waters' (1995, 449).

Assuming that Ireland was at first called Scotia, Massey provides what could be a much later origin of the word Scot from Scota, a daughter of Pharaoh [unnamed], who married a Celtic prince (1995, 465). He goes on to propose the following etymological unraveling when he recalls that Hesychius wrote that in Egypt, Venus was also called Scotia, a deity he likens to Sekhet [or Bast], the goddess of drink and pleasure (1995, 465-66). He also proposes, much as W. P. Boswell does nearly a century later, that the goddess Bridget, another representative of the mother goddess, may have been linked to Bast-Venus-Scotia (Massey 1995, 466).

Scholars may haggle over the veracity of the Massey's myriad etymologies. Some, like the derivation of England perhaps, may be spurious, but others ring true. For there appear to be too many phonetic parallels to entertain the notion that such copious goodness of fit is merely coincidental. And it is hard to dispute the contention that numerous non-Aryan loan words influenced the languages of the British Isles. Nearly a hundred years later, W. P. Boswell, in complete ignorance of Massey's works, comes to similar conclusions regarding the large number of apparent Afroasiatic loan words and place-names extant in the languages and landscapes of the British Isles.

But this study must now turn to quantitative matters. Given that the application of various qualitative approaches to African and Near Eastern cultural diffusion allowed scholars to uncover numerous ethnological leads, what about the scientific community? What conclusions did numerous blood specialists, craniologists and linguists draw regarding the alleged migration of Africans and Semites into the ancient British Isles? The next chapters will examine their evidence, hard data which appears to validate the diffusion hypotheses of the so-called old cranks.

Notes

1. In 1642 in the shire of Bute [originally Buto], there were a series of witch trials involving six defendants who all bore the Moore surname or a variant. Most notable of the defendants was Jonet Morisone, accused of consorting with a black man in the evenings and concocting herbal brews. See MacPhail (1916, III, 3-28).

Chapter 6

~~~~~~

Quantitative Methods: The Mediterranean basin and the western periphery of the British Isles, ABO blood analysis and correlations

Much early debate over the so-called ethnic purity of numerous inhabitants of the British Isles may finally be put to rest by examining several obscure yet extremely important scientific surveys of the distribution of ABO blood type variations along the western periphery of Ireland, Scotland and Wales. When medical technicians correlated this data with blood group data largely derived from the Eastern Mediterranean region, startling matches were discovered. Ali and Ali summarize a portion of this data in their pioneering work *The Black Celts* (1993, 111-125). This chapter takes its lead from that study and attempts to expand upon it.

For those unfamiliar with the ABO system, it is not complicated to understand. All human beings belong to one of the following blood type classifications: A; B; AB; or O. Ascertaining an individual's blood type is necessary to ensure that successful transfusions and organ transplant operations are performed. What is interesting about the system to the anthropologist is that certain blood types can remain intact for centuries in a given population, and this continuity of blood typology can often provide a biological trail, tracing the paths of human migrations over millennia.

A summary of data produced in the 1950s by A. E. Mourant and I. Morgan Watkin in an article entitled "Blood Groups, Anthropology and

Language in Wales and the Western Countries" offers a case in point. Using a sample of approximately 20,000 residents in Wales and along the western periphery of Scotland, Mourant and Watkin discover that many of these inhabitants carried roughly the same percentages of the O antigen in their blood as did populations of Sardinia and Crete and certain Berber groups of North Africa. Their data on the frequency of the O gene, clearly a marker variable in the study, indicates that the highest concentrations could be found in Northwestern Scotland and Northwestern Wales (Mourant and Watkin 1952, 19, 25).

Discounting the possibility that similar distributions of the O antigen in North Africa, Sardinia, Crete, and the western periphery of the British Isles could be accounted for by similar patterns of intermarriage and isolation in these geographically disparate areas, Mourant and Watkin argue that those whose blood revealed high O counts in the above-mentioned areas of the Mediterranean islands and North African littoral share a common ancestry with numerous inhabitants of the western Celtic periphery whose blood also contained like proportions of O counts (1952, 14ff.).

A similar conclusion regarding the origins of many of the early Welsh had been arrived at in another survey conducted by Watkin years earlier entitled "ABO Blood Groups and Racial Characteristics in Rural Wales." In that study Watkin makes some telling observations that are reproduced at length:

> Archeology offers support for the theory of human migration from the Eastern Mediterranean to Britain in Neolithic times. It is also known that the fundamental physical type in Wales is the long-headed [dolichocephalic] brunet, universally recognized as belonging to the Mediterranean race of Giuseppe Sergi. It has been noted that the children of certain Berber tribes, if attired in European dress, would be indistinguishable in a class of Welsh school children. There is evidence that the language spoken in Wales prior to the advent of the Celtic belonged to the Hamitic family. One wonders, therefore, whether the peoples having the North Welsh type of ABO frequencies, who are scattered from the Atlantic seaboard to the Eastern Mediterranean and the Caucasus, are the remnants of related human stock. If so, the distribution of these frequencies would seem to offer a clue to the route taken by some of the earliest colonists of Wales. (1956, 170-71)

Scientific as Watkin's observations are, he trusts what his eyes can see regarding the contemporary Berber racial mix and does not appear to inquire about what the racial composition of the North African might have been millennia earlier when Neolithic and Bronze Age migrations to the British

Isles may have occurred.

At this point, it is useful to understand how the term *Berber*, native to North Africa, is used today. Ivan van Sertima notes that the term does not refer to a race, but to a linguistic grouping of dialects. He goes on to argue that white Berbers and black Berbers inhabit North Africa, and that numerous metal workers, most of whom are blacksmiths by trade, are black (1985, 141). To further clarify the term, he cites C. A. Diop, who argues in *The African Origin of Civilization* that "similarities have been noted between Berber, Gaelic, Celtic and Cymric. But the Berbers [also] use as many Egyptian as African words and, depending on one's point of view, the basis of their language becomes Indo-European, Asian, or African" (van Sertima 1985, 141; Diop 1974, 68-69). Diop's facetiousness in the last part of this quote is understandable given the white-wash that has been applied to North Africa. Certainly, there was a greater diversity of African racial stock than most anthropologists care to admit. Van Sertima mentions one major archeological study conducted by S. Gsell at the site of ancient Carthage to the east of Berber territory that bears this out at least from the perspective of the waning third century B.C.E. In the same essay, van Sertima recalls that Gsell, after examining skeletons exhumed from graves located at the site dated roughly at the time of Hannibal, concludes that his skeletal sample proves that the bulk of Punic population remains in Carthage indicate African and Negro ancestry (van Sertima 1985, 137-38). Van Sertima further notes that in *Blacks in Antiquity*, Frank Snowden (1970) reproduces images of coins minted in Carthage during the era of Hannibal that show countenances which are clearly Africoid (van Sertima 1985, 138). Whether these faces are those of Indian elephant drivers called *mahouts* or leading Carthaginians has been the subject of a debate.

Van Sertima proposes that since these coins were minted at the time of Hannibal, the very time frame of Gsell's sample, they must have depicted Negroes of prominence. He takes issue with Snowden's rather illogical interpretation that these coins represent faces of several of Hannibal's lowly *mahouts* [elephant riders], noting that Carthaginians primarily used coins, statues and stelae to depict Carthaginian gods and aristocrats (van Sertima 1985, 139). And van Sertima further proposes that it is irrelevant whether or not Hannibal was a dark-skinned African. What is relevant to van Sertima is that Carthage was, in the main, a black African enclave prior to the Roman conquest (1985, 139). He goes on to question Alfred Church's and Arthur Gilmen's assertion proposed in *The Story of Carthage* that the population of pre-Roman Carthage, although a racially mixed one resulting from the intermarriage of Phoenicians and native Africans, was, nonetheless, predominantly Caucasian:

> How can a handful of people (the Phoenicians) of Princess Elissar, drowned
> in the genes of African races, using an African-based type of warfare to crush
> their greatest enemy, experimenting with types of political structure that vary
> significantly from that of Tyre, the Phoenician capital, mixing both their
> spirit and their blood so heavily with Africans to the point where the skeletal
> evidence almost wipes out their original physical identity, be credited with a
> civilization that is totally theirs, that owes nothing to the African? How can
> they be credited with the greatest victory of ancient times over any European
> power in which the African stands out so clearly, as the coins celebrating this
> victory show, in the van of the invading army? We shall have to look again
> and again at Carthage, for part of it rightfully belongs to the African heritage.
> (van Sertima 1985, 139-40)

Although ancient Carthage is distant in time and place from the Berber
territories, the white-washing of Carthage casts serious doubts on the "White
Berber" theory when examining many of the pre-Islamic populations in the
region.

But to return to the evidence of blood specialists, W. E. R. Hackett et al.,
in another important study, "The Pattern of the ABO Blood Group
Frequencies in Ireland," conducted with a sample of 21,894 donors, note that
one of the purposes of their study is "to consider the frequencies of the ABO
blood group genes in peoples in different parts of Ireland and to correlate
these frequencies with what is known about the history of the population
(1956, 69). Regarding the frequencies of A and O, they discover that the
highest concentrations of the A gene are found in Southeast Ireland and the
lowest in Western Ireland. The O gene, however, has the highest incidence
in Western Ireland, stopping abruptly in the Connacht area (1956, 75-76,
Figs. 1-3).

Their conclusions, then, are quite similar to those in Morant's earlier
study regarding the distribution of the O gene in particular, but their
comments on all the blood types need to examined so that the correlations
between the blood types of many of the inhabitants of Europe's western
periphery with the blood types of the North African, Mediterranean and
western Caucasian samples can be better understood. Noting that in
Western Europe on the whole there is a high frequency of A, and a rather
low incidence of group B, which is generally found among the Slavs and
other inhabitants of Eastern Europe, they go on to explain that the highest
incidence of the O group lies along the northwestern peripheries of Iceland,
Scotland, Ireland and Wales (1956, 78). The only other parts of the world

where such high O frequencies exist, they explain, are Sardinia, Crete, the Western Caucasus and the Berber areas of North Africa (1956, 79). In this particular study, Hackett and his associates correlate their new data with data from earlier studies conducted by Hooper (1947) and by Morant and Watkin (1952) especially in regard to the incidence of the O group:

> In the three southern provinces of Ireland the most striking feature of the country pattern of the ABO blood groups is the highly significant difference in the O and A gene frequencies between the western and the eastern counties . . . . The O gene occurs with the highest frequency (0.76 to 0.81) and the A gene with the lowest (0.13 to 0.16) in the western counties of Mayo, Galway, Clare, Kerry and Cork. (1956, 79)

Hackett and his associates note other correlations as well:

> In the three southern provinces the regions with the highest A gene frequency correspond to those regions which received the most settlers from England-- Anglo-Norman and Cromwellian settlements being the most important. In Ulster the high A gene frequency is primarily attributed to the English who entered the area under the scheme of plantations of James I. (1956, 82)

This data strongly suggests that during the Neolithic Age various migrations occurred from the Caucasus to North Africa and thence to the British Isles and Iceland probably via Spain and Brittany. It also suggests that groups fanned out in two directions from the Nile Valley, with one pathway leading east to the Caucasus and the other west across North Africa and thence into Spain, Brittany and the western periphery of the British Isles via the Atlantic sea route.

In another survey of the Welsh population entitled "Human Genetics in Worcestershire and Shakespeare County," I. Morgan Watkin speculates on the Atlantic sea route:

> The European and Mediterranean distribution of high O points to movement along the western Atlantic seaboard. If Wales is taken as an analogy the high O people of central or lowland Worcestershire were formerly hill folk and it is on the limestones of the Cotswolds, the White Horse Hills, and the chalk downs of Salisbury Plain that their kinsmen are most likely to be encountered. (1967, 354)

In the same article, Watkin suggests a link between these "ancient mariners," as he terms them, and the builders of Stonehenge, noting that "if the connection of the blue stones of Stonehenge with the Prescelly mountains, Pembrokeshire points to a relationship between the people of the two localities, high O frequency is a mutual characteristic" (1967, 354). For Watkin, these "ancient mariners" and/or nomads must have carried in their blood similar high percentages of the allelic O gene, and low levels of allelic A and B genes, resulting in present day populations in both areas maintaining similar ABO gene frequencies with the O gene exceeding 70%; the A gene varying from 15% to 20%; and the B gene varying from 4% to 7% in both populations (1967, 356). And Watkin makes another interesting observation regarding the high frequency of the B gene in part of the sample:

> In Wales a raised B gene frequency, regardless of variations of O and A, is characteristic of all the moorlands where Fleure and James (1916) discovered vestiges of very ancient human stocks (Watkin, 1956). Similarly in Ireland, Dawson (1964) observed that the highest B gene frequency occurred in county Roscommon, in the heart of the central boglands. Brown (1965) noted an association in Scotland between high B frequency areas and the presence of megalithic chambered tombs. It seems on the serological evidence, therefore, that the descendants of some of Britain's earlier inhabitants have survived at Stratford-on-Avon and neighborhood-- a conclusion which Beddoe drew on anthropological grounds over eighty years ago. (1967, 356)

Angus Fraser reveals in *The Gypsies* that much of the gypsy population of Europe has a high B gene frequency that is well above European levels, but similar to levels found on the Indian subcontinent (1995, 24). What Fraser fails to note, although he does refer to A. E. Mourant's *Blood Relations: Blood Groups and Anthropology*, is that equally high levels of B gene frequency (about 20-22%) are also found in-- of all places-- Egypt (1983, 51-52)! In comparing the similar ABO frequencies of contemporary Egyptian Copts and Muslims, Mourant reveals:

> The profession of Coptic Christianity has sometimes been regarded as a mark of ancient Egyptian descent, but Copts and Muslims do not differ significantly in their ABO frequencies. The remarkable feature of these frequencies is the consistently high level of B, in marked contrast to the low values found not only in the Arabs of the Arabian Peninsula but in all the neighboring populations as well. (1983, 51-52)

This concurrence may vindicate the claim made by many European Gypsies that ultimately their ancestry can be traced to Egypt. Upon leaving Egypt their ancestors may well have strayed into Northern India, with subsequent migrations from India to Europe. In the process, they may have forgotten their original language as they adopted those of their host countries.

But returning to the correlation of the high incidence of O along the western Celtic fringe with high O along Eastern Mediterranean islands, North Africa and the Caucasus [inclusive the northwestern shores of the Black Sea], Mourant and Watkin are careful to qualify it:

> That there should exist in most of North Wales, in Ireland, in Scotland and, to a certain extent, even south of Hadrian's Wall, people whose ABO group frequencies are almost identical with those of certain tribes belonging to the North African White race may . . . seem rather strange. Nevertheless, there is much evidence-- anthropological, archeological and linguistic-- to suggest that such a finding is more than an accidental coincidence. (1952, 23)

This North African data, of course, begs the question. Were there, as far as Mourant and Watkin are concerned, no dark-skinned individuals involved in the proposed migrations from the North African Mediterranean littoral to the periphery of the British Isles and even points north? The specious attempt to neatly classify North Africa as "white" and sub-Saharan Africa as "black" may have been at work in the Mourant and Watkin findings, and the possibility of an earlier, darker-skinned, aboriginal population, namely the Tehennu, bearing a high frequency of O, is not discussed. Clearly, the Sahara is a major barrier between the dark, sub-Saharan population and the generally lighter-skinned, white North African peoples, but if migrations moved both from the Eastern Mediterranean and up the Nile Valley from Ethiopia, dark-skinned and racially-mixed individuals would, doubtless, have made up a substantial component and, at times, if Irish folklore is to be given any credence, the majority of the itinerants. Otherwise, the Berber languages would not have been so strongly influenced by Hamitic [Afroasiatic] dialects, as will be demonstrated shortly. Nonetheless, Mourant's and Watkin's data was unexpected, and, with certain racial readjustments, it proves to be extremely useful in tracing the early migrations to the British Isles. But there are still more discoveries which result from their research.

Mourant and Watkin explain that Europe can largely be segmented into three unique areas based upon ABO blood groupings. A high frequency of group A is typical of most Western Europeans "with medium O and rather low B, the percentage gene frequencies being of the order: A=30; B=5; O=65." Moving to the East of the Baltic and Adriatic seas and along "a line running through Central Germany there is a rise of B, mainly at the expense of O, and this rise apparently continues steadily to give very high B levels in Central Asia and India." But, they go on to reveal:

> West of the main area of high A, and a number of other places on the periphery of Europe, we find very high O levels with B somewhat higher than in the high A area. These remarks apply to Iceland, Scotland and Ireland, and to much of Wales and, to a less marked degree, to Northern England. (1952, 12-13)

In short, on the western periphery of the British Isles as in North Africa, Crete, Sardinia and the Caucasus/Black Sea areas noted, genes A and B are relatively low and gene O incidence is high.

Is it any wonder that these studies have been gathering dust in the world's libraries? Conducted by the some of the top blood experts of the period, this research should have caused a radical revision of the history of the early British Isles. But our racially torn world was not going to lose any sleep over such pronouncements-- as long as they remained in intellectual cold storage.

In any case, what needs to be probed next, among other variables, is the existence of any possible correlations between populations sharing high incidences of O and the existence of pre-Aryan speech patterns. The next chapter will explore that syntactical possibility.

Chapter 7

~~~~~~

Syntactical anomalies in Welsh and Irish

Mourant's and Watkin's logical conclusion that Hamitic-speaking North Africans comprised a sizeable component of the colonizers who settled along the western periphery of the British Isles runs against the grain of the much-touted theory arguing for Indo-European as the singular ingredient of the languages spoken in the ancient British Isles. Given the impressive size of their samples, these blood specialists provide convincing evidence to substantiate their claim that high O blood antigen levels existed along the western periphery of the Isles and along much of the Mediterranean littoral, its island groups, and the Caucasus region as well. That data led them to reexamine the diffusion theories of Childe, Rhys, Morris Jones and Julius Pokorny among others, who noted other unexpected matches. These include the similar architectural styles of the later megalithic burial chambers which dot Crete, North Africa, Spain, France and the western peripheries of the British Isles, the existence of domesticated animals in the British Isles which are clearly of African derivation or admixture, and perhaps most important of all, the shared syntax [the order of words in sentences] of Berber and Insular Celtic, along with the phonetic similarities of various place-names in these two disparate areas.

Mourant and Watkin were intrigued by the archeological record that linked Western Britain and Ireland with the Mediterranean basin. This linkage applies especially in the Neolithic period when many of the megalithic monuments and burial chambers were constructed. They consult an article entitled "The Megalithic Monuments of Wales" by W. F. Grimes, and note Grimes' conclusion that of North and South Wales, North Wales received the strongest influx of megalithic culture. Was it a coincidence then that the living population of this northern portion of Wales contains the highest percentage of the O gene (Mourant and Watkin 1952, 23ff.)?

Turning their attention to an examination of research already completed by Morris Jones and others on various phonetic similarities of place-names in these designated locales, and syntactical anomalies noted in both Berber and Insular Celtic, they cite numerous parallels between Afroasiatic language systems, which include Semitic, Berber, ancient Egyptian, Cushitic and Chad, and the pre-Aryan language system that appeared to have existed along the western littoral of the British Isles prior to the arrival of the Celts.

In their search for phonetic parallels between various place-names of the Mediterranean and Red Sea basins and the British Isles, Mourant and Watkin, like Massey and W. P. Boswell, propose that although many river, mountain and valley titles in the British Isles are Celtic, a substantial number also appear to be pre-Celtic and non-Indo-European. *Cader Idris* [Idris' Chair], the chair-shaped Welsh mountain, for example, seems to echo the North African title *idris* which designates the royal line of Berber kings (Mourant and Watkin 1952, 27). They surmise from this and other apparent phonetic matches that prior to the invasions of the Celtic speaking tribes, large portions of Europe [mainly the western periphery] and of North Africa were "inhabited by a people speaking a common non-Indo-European tongue" (1952, 27).

Continuing with their inventory of linguistic parallels, they note additional matches in the areas of syntax, idiom, intonation and accent which had been documented earlier by various diffusionists. Citing John Davies, reviser of the 1588 Welsh Bible in 1621, and later students of Welsh such as John Rhys, Morris Jones, Heinrich Wagner and Julius Pokorny, Mourant and Watkin indicate that these scholars all discovered substantial evidence which points to a lingering pre-Aryan syntax in Welsh sentence structure. In the appendix to their article entitled "Blood Groups, Anthropology and Language in Wales and the Western Countries," Mourant and Watkin state:

> It is contended by Morris Jones and Pokorny that if the pre-Celtic inhabitants of Britain are related to the Berbers of North Africa it is not unnatural to expect that their language should also have belonged to the Hamitic family, a family which includes the Berber languages and ancient Egyptian. (1952, 32)

Paraphrasing Morris Jones, Mourant and Watkin go on to make another telling generalization that may unwittingly point to the ancestry of the so-called White Mediterranean peoples of North Africa:

> It is known that Egyptian preserves a form of Hamitic speech and there is
> reason to believe that it approaches the ancient type of Hamitic language
> much more closely than any of the modern Berber dialects. Consequently
> it is the Egyptian that one expects to bear the greater resemblance to the pre-
> Celtic speech of our islands. (1952, 32)

The underlying question begs to be answered: Why were so-called White
Mediterraneans speaking a modified Afroasiatic language in the ancient
world? The question is largely dodged.

In an important article by Wagner entitled "Near Eastern and African
Connections with the Celtic World," he argues that Basque, as spoken in the
Pyrenees, was a survivor of the pre-Indo-European languages of Western
Europe. The Pictish language of Northern Scotland, spoken as late as the
early Middle Ages, was another pre-Indo-European remnant (1982, 51).
Wagner goes on to propose that diminutive bands of Celts from the
Continent who spoke Indo-European tongues were likely influenced by the
speech of the more populous non-Celtic peoples inhabiting the British Isles
(1982, 51). Wagner relies heavily on Morris Jones' 1899 appendix to Rhys'
The Welsh People entitled "Pre-Aryan Syntax in Insular Celtic," as do
Mourant and Watkin, to establish the influence of what was then called the
Hamitic-Semitic language family [renamed Afroasiatic] on Celtic languages
which were largely Indo-European. Morris Jones earlier notes:

> When one language is supplanted by another [in this case a Hamito-Semitic
> by an Indo-European language] the speakers find it comparatively easy to
> adopt the new vocabulary, but not so easy to abandon the old modes of
> expression; and thus, whilst the old language dies, its idiom survives into the
> new. The neo-Celtic languages, then, which are Aryan in vocabulary, and
> largely non-Aryan in idiom, appear to be the acquired Aryan speech of a
> population originally speaking a non-Aryan language. (1899, 617; brackets
> mine)

Although Wagner does not quote Morris Jones' theory on the mechanism of
language transfer from the pre-Aryan, indigenous population of Ireland and
Wales to the waves of Celts who later descended upon them, Wagner does
speculate that the invading Celts must have annihilated the bulk of the
indigenous male population, while claiming the women as their own. Hence,
a hybrid race must have emerged whose children learned non-Aryan speech
from their non-Aryan mothers, as Morris Jones suggests (1899, 617-18).

An admonition from Carleton Coon's *The Races of Europe*, ironically enough, is relevant at this point in the discussion lest the importance of the non-Aryan influence is devalued. Coon writes that "in antiquity, while civilization of the first order was in the hands of the Hamites, Semites and Sumerians, all Indo-European and probably most Ural-Altaic speakers, if they existed as such, were illiterate barbarians" (1939, 178). He goes on to observe that even as late as the Middle Ages the cultures of Indo-European speakers lagged far behind the cultures of the Semites, Turks, and Chinese (1939, 178). If the Andalusian Moors were added to his list, the admonition would be even more pertinent.

So what are these syntactical anomalies that so fascinate Mourant and Watkin? They cite 1.) a lack of sentence connections; 2.) a unique word order; 3.) inflected prepositions; and 4.) periphrastic conjugations (1952, 32ff.). These anomalies need to be examined one at a time.

In regard to the lack of sentence connections, Mourant and Watkin note that in neo-Celtic languages there is "the tendency to break speech into a series of direct clause statements" (1952, 32). By this they mean that subordinate clauses and connectives are eschewed in written and spoken Irish and Welsh in favor of the asyndeton, a figure of speech common in Egyptian and Berber that omits connectives. In English an asyndeton can be expressed as 'I came, I saw, I conquered.'

Citing the agglutinative character of pre-Aryan languages and its partial survival in neo-Celtic languages, they further note the lack of certain personal pronouns in neo-Celtic. For example, the English 'I gave it to the man whose house lies at the top of the hill' could not be rendered into early and even later forms of Irish or Welsh. Instead, in Irish or Welsh one would say 'I gave it to the man. The man's house lies at the top of the hill' (Mourant and Watkin 1952, 33).

Other traces of the non-Aryan language system can be found in the rather unique syntax of Irish and Welsh sentences, according to Mourant and Watkin. Despite the fact that Indo-European languages are inflected so that the subject comes first, followed by the verb (the S.V.O. word order), Irish and Welsh retain the pre-Aryan syntax of the verb coming first in the sentence followed by the subject and object (the V.S.O. word order): "In Irish and Welsh," they reveal, "the verb normally comes first: thus in Welsh, *Codadd Arthur y garreg*, [but in English:] 'Arthur picked up the stone'; in medieval Irish, *Aliss Particc Dubthach*, [but in English]: 'Patrick requested Dubthach'" (Mourant and Watkin 1952, 33, brackets mine). Citing O'Donovan's *Irish Grammar*, they explain that the verb precedes the nominative and its trailing dependents in an Irish sentence (Mourant and Watkin 1952, 33). They go on to cite Renouf's *Egyptian Grammar*, noting that the verb comes before the subject in ancient Egyptian sentences (Mourant and Watkin 1952, 33). To further illustrate this pre-Aryan syntactical anomaly, they provide the following example: "There is a special form of sentence in Welsh in which a noun as subject comes first. This order is used to lay particular stress upon the subject; thus *Du a farn* . . .; for *(Ys) Duw a farn* . . .; '(it is) God who judges . . . '" (Mourant and Watkin 1952, 33). Mourant and Watkin trace this form of syntax to the Egyptian: "In Egyptian, according to Renouf, a noun at the beginning of a sentence implies the ellipsis of the verb 'to be'" (1952, 33).

Mourant and Watkin also note the lingering, pre-Aryan anomaly in Welsh and Irish of placing the adjective after the noun which it modifies, arguing that the Welsh *gwr mawr* and the Irish *fear mor* translated into English mean 'a great man' (1952, 33). Oddly enough, they recall, that identical syntax can be found in ancient Egyptian. It should be noted, however, that although this syntactical arrangement is rare in Indo-European languages, it is common in Latin and the Romance languages. But that fact only strengthens their argument, for these languages also harbor pre-Aryan structural anomalies. They conclude, then, that in terms of syntax, Irish and Welsh sentences often retain a Hamitic word order, a "divergence from the primitive Aryan order in the sentence and its replacement by the same order as found in Hamitic, a divergence which is also noticeable in some of the Romance languages which . . . display in the syntactical field certain pre-Aryan traits" (Mourant and Watkin 1952, 33).

The third syntactical anomaly Mourant and Watkin discuss in their appendix falls under the category of inflected prepositions:

> In the neo-Celtic languages when the object of a preposition happens to be a personal pronoun, it becomes attached to the preposition in a manner identical with an inflection. The fusion is complete for the appendage is not even hyphenated; thus in Welsh 'us' is *ni*, but 'for us' is not *er ni*, but *erom*. In the Egyptian the endings forming personal verbs are also affixed to prepositions. (1952, 33)

They note that the Celtic preposition *yn,* which has no adequate English equivalent, is amazingly similar to the Egyptian *em* in its syntactical positioning given that the Celtic *yn* like Egyptian *em* "is used after the verb 'to be' to introduce not only an attributive substantive but also an attributive adjective" (1952, 34). Morris Jones' example, which they cite, illustrates this characteristic:

Egyptian: *au-k   am-a*;   or   *au-a   am-ek*

Welsh:	*wyt ynn.of,*	or	*wy.f ynn.ot*
English:	art thou in me;	or	am I in thee,

which is to say in proper English syntax-- 'thou art in me; I am in thee' (Morris Jones 1899, 627).

The fourth syntactical anomaly they discuss falls under the category of periphrastic conjugations [a conjugation formed by the combination of a simple verb and an auxiliary, as distinct from a simple formation from the verb stem]. In English, this construction, the origin of which is unknown, occurs when an individual says 'he is a-coming,' for example. In Egyptian, they note, common examples of the periphrastic conjugation are the verb 'to be' followed by a noun or having a personal suffix joined to it; a preposition; and a verbal noun. They continue:

> Although Irish and Welsh retain many Indo-European tenses, the type of conjugation mentioned above is, nevertheless, extremely common. In Egyptian, the prepositions *em*, 'in,' *er*, 'to' or 'for,' her, 'above' or 'upon' are used to indicate the present, future and perfect tenses respectively. In Welsh, the corresponding prepositions are *yn* 'in,' *wedi* 'after,' while *am* 'for,' presumably an old future, is now only used optatively [in the expression of a wish]. (Mourant and Watkin 1952, 34)

Although they do not cite them, Morris Jones' examples illustrate the complexity:

Present tense:
Egyptian:	*au-k em meh*
Welsh:	*wy.t yn llanw*
English:	art thou in filling (i. e. thou art filling)

Future tense:
Egyptian:	*au-a er sem er ta ant*
Welsh:	*wy.f am fynd I 'r mynyd*
English:	am I for to the mountain (i. e. I shall go)

Perfect tense:
Egyptian:	*au-f her kem taif hemet*
Welsh:	*mae-ef wedi cael ei wraig*
English:	is he after (upon) finding his wife (i. e. he has found).

(1899, 625)

Mourant and Watkin provide the following example using *wedi*: "*Maent wedi cael bwyd* (literally) 'They are after having food'" (1952, 34). "This does not mean," they argue, "that 'they are in quest of food,' but the exact opposite 'they have had food'" (1952, 34).

Wagner's discussion of periphrastic verbs in old Gaelic and Basque sheds more light on Morant's and Watkin's summary of Morris Jones' "Pre-Aryan Syntax in Insular Celtic," from which they draw most of their observations. Noting the importance of social history in language development, a phenomenon which schools such as Neo-grammarianism that ignored Morris Jones' and Pokorny's similar findings missed, Wagner relates an experience he had when studying the remnants of Manx on the Isle of Man. Around 1950, when he was collecting material for his *Linguistic Atlas and Survey of Irish Dialects*, he and colleague Myles Dillon learned that there were still some very old speakers on the island of what was thought to be a defunct ancient Gaelic dialect. During their investigation of that speech, Wagner made a startling discovery about the construction of verbs in the Gaelic idiom:

> Practically every tense-form of every verb was expressed by a periphrastic construction which had become standardized. Examples: *nyim bu:la su* 'I shall strike you', lit. 'I shall do striking you'; . . . *ha ridhn mi gi:k sone* 'I did not pay for it', lit. 'I did not do paying for it'; . . . *dyin gol ta:i* 'go home!,' lit. 'do going home.' (1982, 53)

He further notes that Dillon, his colleague, attributed the verbal anomalies to "the moribund and degenerate status in which the language appeared in its last stage of development" (Wagner 1982, 53). But Wagner was not convinced. Years later, when he studied the Basque language under the brilliant Ernst Lewy, Wagner realized that although Basque is not considered to be a precursor of Celtic, many of its verbal constructions are similar to those of Manx (1982, 53).

Reinforcing Mourant's and Watkin's observations, Wagner notes that as a result of his studies of Gaelic, we find that the development of the Manx and the Scottish Gaelic verb often mimicked the evolution of Brythonic Celtic [the dialect once spoken in Cornwall]. He argues:

> In all three languages, but significantly not in Irish or Breton, the form of the Indo-European present tense had become, at an early stage, a future tense, while the original present tense was replaced generally by the periphrastic construction 'to be,' of the type W. *ydwyfl yn myned*, Sc. G. *tha mi do* or *tha mi ri dhol*. (1982, 53)

And to drive home the nail that Morris Jones set in place, Wagner observes that the evolution of verb constructions in Gaelic can be compared to a similar development of Egyptian verbs from roughly 3000 B.C.E. to the era of the Christian Copts, whose language still exists in its spoken form.

And then he concludes:

> The fact, however, that in Coptic the majority of the older synthetic constructions have been replaced by periphrastic constructions based upon the Old Egyptian verbal noun or verbal adjective conjugated by means of auxiliaries, recalls very much the situation found in Manx, late Cornish and Basque. (1982, 53)

As noted above, Mourant and Watkin present a formidable case for the proposition that the western periphery of the British Isles was inhabited in the Neolithic Age by highly advanced colonists from the Mediterranean, specifically from 'Berber' North Africa. But unwittingly they suggest the ultimate ancestry of these ancient wanderers, the Nile Valley itself, leading an objective researcher to wonder if a substantial component of these wanderers was not originally the black-skinned, Hamitic-speaking dwellers of that Valley. Why so? Later in the article they puzzle over the many Ogham inscriptions found throughout Cornwall, Wales, Ireland, and in Scotland as far north as the Shetlands, inscriptions that cannot be translated by scholars conversant in Celtic languages. They go on to make an interesting observation: "They [the Ogham inscriptions] appear to be written in a language termed by Rhys 'Pictish'-- a non-Indo-European tongue spoken in the British Isles before the advent of Celtic-speaking people" (1952, 27).

In "The Pictish Language," K. H. Jackson, attempting to resolve the so-called problem, has no doubt that Pictish, a lost tongue, is pre-Aryan. He cites the biographer Adomnan, who mentioned that on two separate occasions in the *Life of St. Columba,* written between 692 and 697 C.E., Columba required the use of interpreters when conversing with the Picts. The first incident occurred in a conversation with Brude, King of the Picts, whose fortification lay close to the mouth of the river Ness, and the other at Skye when two sons brought their father to him to be baptized. Jackson also cites Bede's *Ecclesiastical History,* completed in 731 C.E. when Pictish was still a spoken language. In that work Bede classified Pictish as a fourth language, distinct from Gaelic, Brythonic and English (1970, 133). Then too, Jackson cites Cormac, King and Bishop of Cashel, who noted in his *Glossary* the Pictish for 'thorn' or 'pin,' *catait* or *cartait*, which Cormac labeled as a Pictish expression, or a *berla Cruithnech* (1970, 134). Jackson goes on to reveal the deliberate avoidance by discrete scholars of mentioning pre-Aryan elements in Pictish inscriptions written in the Ogham alphabet (1970, 136). Citing the St. Vigeans stone, with its *ett*, and *ipe* prefixed to *Uoret*, which Jackson speculates can imply the Latin *et* or 'and,' and 'son of' or 'nephew of,' respectively, he concludes that the inscriptions do not appear to be either Celtic or Indo-European (1970, 140). Then, he mentions the Lunnasting inscription which reads *ettochuhetts ahehhttannn hccvvevo nehhtons*, arguing that it too belonged to a language other than Indo-European or Celtic 1970, 141). *The Pictish Chronicle*, or king-list, which was written in Latin probably near the end of the tenth century c.e. after the ascension of Kenneth Mac Alpin and the Gaelicization of the Church in Pictland, also does not provide any evidence that Pictish was in the Goedelic language family since the names were often "hideously Anglo-Gaelicized," according to Jackson (1970, 144--45).

Place-name elements are not of much help in reconstructing the language either, since most in Scotland have been replaced by Gaelic, Norse and English titles, except possibly place-names that began with *pit*, 323 in all, according to W. J. Watson, which cluster around Northeastern Scotland (Jackson 1970, 147).

Jackson further notes that place-name elements such as the *pett* or *peth*, which cannot be related to P-Celtic or Q-Celtic, appear to be remnants of the Pictish language. They are not to be found south of the Antonine Wall in Roman areas except four times (1970, 148). Much the same applies to other place-name elements appearing in Scotland such as *carden, lanerc, pert, pevr* and *aber*, which appear also in Northeastern Scotland in the same locale at the *pit* place-names (Jackson 1970, 150).

Concluding his discussion of the so-called Pictish problem, Jackson mentions Stuart Piggott's observation that since primitive Bronze Age populations inhabited the entirety of Northern Scotland during the first quarter of the second millennium b.c.e., it would have been highly unlikely that they could have spoken an Indo-European language (1970, 155). Jackson builds upon Piggott's observation:

> There were at least two languages current in northern Scotland before the coming of the Irish Gaels in the fifth century. One of them was a Gallo-Brittonic [Brythonic] dialect not identical with the British spoken south of the Antonine Wall, though related to it. The other was not Gaelic at all, nor apparently even Indo-European, but was presumably the speech of some very early set of inhabitants of Scotland. The people of Scotland before the coming of the Celts must, after all, have spoken some language, and that language must almost certainly have been a non Indo-European one. (1970, 152)

Given Tacitus' description of the Picts as being swarthy and curly-haired, Jackson's observations are particularly telling. Then too, Mourant and Watkin mention that the marriage customs of the aborigines differed radically from those practiced by the Romans in that descent was matrilineal as opposed to patrilineal. The practice of matrilineal descent is also characteristic of the Berbers, and of peoples living further east of the Berber lands, they note (1952, 30).

It is useful to recall that in *A Book of the Beginnings*, Massey deals with this deep matriarchal current in the British Isles. Examining Ogham inscriptions in Wales such as *Macc-Decceti*, *Macu-Treni* and *Maqvi-Treni*, he proposes that the Irish and Gaelic *Mac*, to which these earlier forms evolved, now stands for 'the son of,' 'or the child of'(1995, 476). But he traces the etymology of *Mac* backward again, citing the Cornish *maga* meaning 'feed,' and 'nourish,' the Welsh *mag* for 'nurture,' and the English *maeg* for 'blood relation.' He goes on to cite the Irish *Book of Armagh* in which *maccu*, *mocu*, and *corca* evoke the concept of clan, and then traces the titles back to the Egyptian *mahaut* and *makhaut* for mother clan (1995, 477).

A similar observation is made regarding the *O* prefix, which Massey argues was the earlier symbol of the mother circle. He traces the prefix to the Egyptian *aukhu* for 'diadem' and *khekh* for 'collar' and links it to circle called *Og* in Irish, meaning the primal virginal mother. The *O*, like the *Mac* symbol, he argues points to matrilineal descent during a time when lineage was not reckoned from the father (1995, 478-79).

Mourant's examination of the importation of domestic animals indigenous to the African continent reveals still more evidence that these Neolithic migrations occurred. Citing a 1920 study by L. Adametz entitled *Herkunft und Wanderungen der Hamiten*, Mourant argues that North African long-horn cattle and the greyhound, both native to the northern Hamitic lands of the African continent, were imported into Spain and as far north as Britain, where they evolved into the Black Cattle of Wales and the Reds of Devon (1952, 31). Mourant also proposes that Scottish deerhounds and Irish wolfhounds were the result of breeding the Hamitic greyhound with Scottish and Irish wolves, suggesting that tests should be made on these animals to determine their blood groups (1952, 31).

It may be helpful to recall another admonition from Carelton Coon on this subject, for he observes in *The Races of Europe* that Indo-European speech and civilization is a relatively recent occurrence, and that "linguists tell us that the Indo-European speakers did not initially domesticate one useful animal, or one cultivated plant" (1939, 178).

Yet another linguistic correlation between Wales and North Africa discussed by Mourant and Watkin is the use of chanting in Welsh oratory, what is called the *hwyl*, that sometimes occurs in Welsh sermons. The *hwyl* occurs when the preacher stops speaking and begins a sing-song wail. Regarding the musical score that many preachers use in this Welsh chanting, Mourant argues that it is uncannily similar to the chant of the African Muezzin, and he cites a BBC program produced on the subject in which the two forms are virtually indistinguishable (1952, 28).

Although they do not explore another area of commonality between Welsh, Irish and Afroasiatic languages, a cursory examination shall be made of it here-- i. e. the Welsh and Irish habit of counting in groups of five. The first mention of this anomaly appears in John Rhys' *Celtic Folklore*. Noting that the Irish and Welsh count by fives, he makes reference to a tale in which a lake fairy reckoned the livestock in her dowry by fives (1941, 664). From this and other early evidence, Rhys observes:

> Now the students of ethnology . . . tell us that we have among us, notably in Wales and Ireland, living representatives of a dark-haired, long-skulled race of the same description as one of the types which occur, as they allege, among the Basque populations of the Pyrenees. We turn accordingly to the Basque, and what do we find? Why, that the first five numerals in that language are *bat, bi, iru, lau, bost*, all of which appear to be native; but when we come to the sixth numeral we find *sei*, which looks like an Aryan word borrowed from Latin, Gaulish, or some related tongue. (1941, 664-65)

The same applies to *zazpi*, the Basque seven as well as *zortzi* and *bederatzi* (eight and nine, respectively) that also terminate in 'I' as does *sei*. Rhys concludes:

> we have evidence of the former existence of a people in the West of Europe who at one time only counted as far as five. Some of the early peoples of the British Isles may have been on the same level, so that our notions about the fairies have probably been derived, to a greater or lesser extent, from ideas formed by the Celts concerning those non-Celtic, non-Aryan natives of whose country they took possession. (1941, 665)

Hence, in Welsh sixteen becomes *un abbymptheq* (1 on [ar] 15) and so on from eleven [*un arddeg*] up to nineteen [*pedwar ar*]. And for numbers greater than twenty, the Irish and Welsh reckon in multiples of twenty. For example, in Welsh thirty becomes *deg ar ugain* (Ali and Ali 1993, 156ff.).

It should be recalled that the Indo-European method of counting was by tens as was the case with Latin.

Attempting to clarify once and for all the proposition of language diffusion from North Africa to the British Isles, Wagner agrees with Pokorny's earlier assumption that about 2000 years ago peoples in North Africa and the western littoral of Europe spoke African languages which could have been derived from invasions or migrations commencing in the Arabian and Syrian deserts (1982, 59). For Wagner, the fact that centuries later during the Middle Ages, Islamic expansion spread Arabic across North Africa and into Spain and Southern France was a case of history repeating itself with a new language and a new cast of characters. Reflecting on the pre-Islamic wave, Wagner argues that the verb constructions in Berber indicate that it is the "most archaic Hamito-Semitic language" (1982, 59). He goes on to propose that in early historical times the ancient Libyans spread a dialect of Berber or Libyan over the entirety of North Africa all the way to the Canary Islands and to the Mediterranean coast of Iberia. And when he speculates on the origin of that dialect, he rules out ancient Ugaritic or ancient Akkadian in Mesopotamia in favor of Cushite, which is in the Afroasiatic family (Wagner 1982, 59).

So what was the origin of the Berber dialects? According to Wagner, the key to understanding Northern African linguistics is discovered in various proto-Hamitic languages which include the Nubian employed in areas south of Aswan and on the frontier of Egypt and Abyssinia:

> Complicated as a detailed analysis of the verb of these languages might be, its conjunction seems to be based on similar principles to that of the Cushitic languages, namely upon inflection by means of suffixed auxiliaries. North-Eastern Africa, including Ethiopia, the Sudan and Somalia, presents itself as a linguistic field where the principles of area linguistics can be studied almost to perfection.   In this area, certain grammatical features such as the periphrastic verbal forms found their way into wave after wave of languages presumably imported from the East, the latest one-- if we exclude Northern Arabic-- being represented by Ethiopian Semitic. The southern varieties of Ethiopian in particular, including Amharic, the official language of the Abyssinian empire, exhibit strong Cushitic features such as inflection by means of auxiliaries. (1982, 59-60)

Morris Jones was adamant in his belief that present day Berber formed an evolutionary link between Hamitic and the pre-Aryan languages spoken in Iberia and ultimately in parts of the British Isles.   The two Berber dialects that he studied were Kabyle and Tamashek, the latter being the spoken dialect the Tuareg. In "Pre-Aryan Syntax in Insular Celtic" Morris Jones demonstrates how much Hamitic-based idiomatic syntax survives in Berber dialects, heavily influenced by Semitic as they are. He proposes that

> Egyptian preserves a very ancient form of Hamitic speech; and we can assume with confidence that it approaches much nearer to the primitive Hamitic type of language than the Berber tongues which we are acquainted with only in their modern form. Egyptian may therefore be expected to agree more closely in general structure with our hypothetical pre-Celtic dialect . . . . (1899, 618)

A summary of his detailed comparison will be examined at this point.

The syntax of the Berber sentence, its arrangement of words, agrees remarkably with the syntax of Egyptian, and with syntactical anomalies in Welsh, especially when the verb appears first. Citing several examples, Morris Jones notes that when a noun does appear first in Berber dialects, it serves as ". . . a complement of an implied verb 'to be'" which he renders as follows:

Tamashek:	*midden a nemous ourger' tidhidhin.*
Welsh:	*gwyr a ym nid gwraged.*
English:	(it is) men that we are no women.

Tamashek:	*s tamachek' as isioul ourger' s tarabt.*
Welsh:	*yn Tamashek' y sieryd nid yn Arabeg.*
English:	(it is) in Tamashek' that he speaks not in Arabic. (1899,
631).	

And in Berber, Welsh and Irish the verb 'to have' is expressed by the verb 'to be' plus the required suffix, as Morris Jones demonstrates:

Tamashek:	*illa r'our-ek*
Welsh:	*mae genn.yt*
Irish:	*ta le.at*
English:	'is with thee,' (i.e., 'thou hast'). (1899, 633)

Another area of syntactical agreement among Berber, Welsh and Irish lies in the area of suffixed pronouns. Morris Jones notes:

> The pronominal suffixes in Berber are added to the verb to denote the object direct or indirect: thus, Kabyle [a Berber dialect] *izera- thent*, Welsh, *gwelod-hwynt*, 'he saw them'; Tamashek' [another Berber dialect] *ekfet-I-tet*,

Welsh, *rhowch-imi-hi*, 'give (pl.) to me her,' give her me. (1899, 634)

As should be expected, the periphrastic conjugation of verbs is also as common in Berber dialects as it is in Egyptian and Welsh and Irish. In Berber dialects there is a deficiency of verb tenses; hence particles must be used, Morris Jones observes, noting that in the Kabyl dialect they are *ad'* and *r'a* to indicate the future, and *ai* to indicate the past (1899, 636). Morris Jones reveals that Berber tense particles attract objective pronominal suffixes which appear between the particle and the verb, just as in Irish and Welsh (1899, 636). He goes on to explain that the persistence of tense particles is clearly an anachronism in Irish and Welsh, given that both languages have no need for tense particles. Nonetheless, they cling to Irish as *no*, a particle indicating incomplete action used in front of present and future tenses, and *ro* and *do*, indicating completed action which appear with the past tense verb; and the medieval Welsh *dy* and *ry* (1899, 636). He illustrates these anachronisms: "Thus Tamashek *ad-I-inhi*, 'he will see me,' *ad-AS-enner*, 'I shall tell him.' Compare Irish, *No-T-alim*, 'I beseech thee,' *ro-M-gab*, 'he seized me'; *Welsh ry-TH-welas*, 'saw thee'" (Morris Jones 1899, 636).

Based upon these and other comparisons, Morris Jones asserts quite bluntly and unequivocally that "The whole structure of the neo-Celtic sentence and nearly all of its distinctly non-Aryan features are embraced in the principles discussed above, and have been shown to have parallels in Hamitic" (1899, 637). And quite unlike his contemporary, Massey, Morris Jones eschews making phonetic comparisons between the languages, with one exception, the lack of the Aryan *p* in Irish and Welsh, which he finds to be nearly non-existent in Berber as well (1899, 637ff.).

The persistence of pre-Aryan syntax and place-names, along with other matches generated from livestock diffusion and a shared numbering system, are all tools that can be used to trace the origins of the languages of the Berber as well as the tongues of numerous ancient inhabitants of the western periphery of the British Isles. That the earliest ancestors of the Berbers were to one degree or another dark-skinned Ethiopians, prior to their racial admixture with various white invaders, is an issue the linguists, as well as the blood specialists, who corroborate their own data with the data of the linguists, largely choose to ignore. But these are not the only tools that can be utilized to discover the ultimate origins of the Neolithic inhabitants of the western littorals of the British Isles. For the science of craniology also offers more grist for the diffusionst's mill with some equally startling results.

Chapter 8

~~~~~~

The Evidence of Craniology

Diffusion theories were strengthened by the testimony of craniologists who compared samples of Neolithic and Bronze Age skulls exhumed along the western periphery of the British Isles with earlier skulls excavated along the Mediterranean and Red Sea littorals and the Nile Valley. As a result of those comparisons, more empirical evidence for the alleged migrations of Africans and Eastern Mediterranean Semites into the British Isles during prehistoric and early historic times was brought to light. Ali and Ali (1993, 87-109) summarize a number of these comparisons in *The Black Celts*. This chapter builds upon their pioneering work.

By 1899, Morris Jones in "Pre-Aryan Syntax in Insular Celtic" could agree with I. Taylor's assertion: "The skulls of the pure Iberian race, such as those found in the long barrows of Britain of the Caverne de l'Homme Mort, are the same type as those of the Berbers and the Guanaches, and bear a considerable resemblance to the skulls of the ancient Egyptians" (1899, 618). It appeared early on that a connection was established between early peoples of the Nile Valley, the Mediterranean and Red Sea basins, and the British Isles.

Nonetheless, such a conclusion led to problems. Morris Jones had already argued the case that the Africans in question were "White" Africans. And the whole subject of craniology was a tortuous one that hinged upon dubious racial distinctions. Should the Negroid category, for example, sometimes include individual crania that contained narrow and medium nasal widths as well as broad ones? Should the entire range of the measurement of cranial width from narrow-skulled to broad-skulled called the cephalic index [defined below] sometimes apply to dark-skinned people then and now? Could craniologists reasonably infer the probable skin pigmentation of an ancient, borderline specimen from cranial and other skeletal characteristics? And where did one draw the line between the Negroid and Caucasoid? If a skull showed a slight "Negroid tendency" in its various structures, was it to be called Caucasoid? And how slight was slight?

The controversy surrounding the specious race classification system currently involves a raging debate over the persistence of African mitochondrial DNA in all the so-called races. Suffice it to say that for now racial characteristics will be referred to merely as imperfect indicators that may suggest tendencies toward one morphology or another. For racial characteristics can never provide infallible classification guides given that all *Homo Sapiens* belong to one species, and, in all probability, are all ultimately descended from primordial, dark-skinned Africans. For the purposes of this study, suffice it say that groups with Mediterranean and Red Sea and Caucasus origins of various hues entered the British Isles in the Neolithic and Bronze Age time frames. The first wave was, more than likely, a dark-skinned, long-skulled [dolichocephalic] Nilotic grouping that constructed the round barrows and other ceremonial megalithic monuments. Later, medium-skulled [mesocephalic] Goidels, and short-skulled [brachycephalic] Silures from ranges as diverse as sub-Saharan West and Northwest Africa and Central Europe also appear to have entered the British Isles during the Bronze Age. Since the later waves would likely have been of various hues from dark-skinned, dark-haired to near albino, it is rather pointless to draw a pigmentation line in the sand. Doubtless, as Coon argues, East Africa's Nile Valley, and Ethiopia especially contained individuals who today, using our current racial classification system, would be labeled both Negroid and Caucasoid. The same can be said for North Africa all the way to the Canary Islands. Caucasoid and Negroid racial types, as the world reckons them today, populated these regions, with the Negroid type likely being numerically dominant in prehistory. And more important than the pigmentation variable, this diverse population, according to *Lebor Gabala*, included the so-called invader groups who migrated to the British Isles. These individuals largely spoke and sometimes wrote in Afroasiatic languages derived from various populations which profoundly influenced the culture of the early British Isles.

Before proceeding, some terms need to be more carefully examined. Dolichocephaly forms a band which, according to Coon in *The Races of Europe*, "extends south of the Mediterranean from the Atlantic coast of Morocco across North Africa, Egypt, Arabia, and Persia into Afghani; to continue, off the map, over the Khyber Pass and into the Indus Valley" (1939, 256). Dolichocephalic skulls are long and narrow compared to mesocephalic [medium-headed] and brachycephalic [short-headed, broad-faced] specimens.

The measurement of skull breadth is called the cephalic index (ci), and is equal to skull breadth multiplied by 100 divided by skull length. On the cephalic index scale, dolichocephalic skulls measure 75 centimeters and less in width; mesocephalic skulls measure 76-80.9 centimeters; and brachycephalic skulls measure 81-85.4 centimeters. According to Coon, dolichocephalic skull distribution is rare in modern Europe with the exception of Portugal, given that most modern Europeans are mesocephalic and brachycephalic (1939, 257). Then too, head size is unrelated to head form, according to Coon, who notes: "Some of the largest heads are found among both dolichocephals and brachycephals, and the same is true of the smallest heads" (1939, 264).

Based upon the evidence presented in previous chapters, it is becoming evident that during the Neolithic and Bronze Ages migrations of the invader groups across North Africa usually moved from east to west, given that eastern Neolithic culture was older than western and extreme northwestern North African culture. *Lebor Gabala* indicates that some migrations originated from Egypt by way of Greece and Crete, but evidence will be presented that suggests sub-Saharan and Black Sea origins as well. And regardless of which itinerary, a sea route along the Mediterranean or a land route traversing the North African land mass and then across the Straits of Gibraltar, most of these migratory waves likely made stop-overs, perhaps lasting hundreds of years in some cases, in Northwest Africa and on the Iberian peninsula before heading to points north.

Whatever the route and regardless of the duration or any particular migration, it now appears, based upon the many studies of crania found in the megalithic sites of Spain, Brittany and the British Isles, that several rather distinct African types are represented. Appearing first are long-headed dolichocephals whose ancestors either embarked directly from the Nile Valley or from Crete, given that similar skull shapes have been exhumed in both regions. Later, in the waning Neolithic and Bronze Age periods, mesocephals and brachycephals who may have been directly or distantly related to mesocephals and brachycephals of the Ethiopian Highlands, become prominent, along with predominantly long-headed dolichocephals whose crania bear uncanny resemblances to those of many modern North-central and Northwest African Tuareg and other Berber tribal entities.

Regarding the eastern Nilotic and Ethiopian populations, Coon proposes in *The Races of Europe* that although there was and still is a high incidence of dolichocephalism in Egypt, further south in Ethiopia, individuals living in the Abyssinian plateau, regardless of ethnicity or language, reveal dolichocephalic and mesocephalic skull structures and morphologies that are comparable with those found among both North African Berbers and European Nordics (1939, 450).

Dolichocephalic skulls prevail in the numerous nineteenth and twentieth century archeological digs of Early Neolithic sites throughout the British Isles. And Coon reveals that the earliest Neolithic economy appears to be that of the Windmill Hill group (1939, 370). Ancestors of this group likely migrated from North Africa across the Straits of Gibraltar and thence across the Continent to Southern England, for Coon goes on to classify the racial morphology of the Windmill Hill group as a small Mediterranean type. Yet he notes that there is a paucity of evidence in England to confirm that conclusion (1939, 370). Nonetheless, for Coon the bulk of the Neolithic migration from the Eastern Mediterranean into Great Britain and Ireland was by sea with Spain used as a stopping point on the way. These Megalithic invaders, he argues, crossed the Irish Channel and fanned out into to Western and Northern Scotland and thence to Denmark and Sweden (Coon 1939, 370-71).[1] He describes the racial stock of these Megalithic people as tall, mostly brunette, extremely long-headed Mediterranean types (1939, 371). He goes on to note, tellingly, that: "This racial group furnished both Great Britain and Ireland, which consisted, before their arrival, of nearly empty land, with a numerous and civilized population which has left many descendants today" (1939, 371).

In an important article by Beatrix Hooke and G. M. Morant entitled "British Craniology in Late Prehistoric and Historic Times," the authors propose a similar hypothesis:

> In late Neolithic times, and probably in early Neolithic times also, the population of England and Scotland was racially homogenous and a type which is clearly distinguished from that of the races which predominated in later times. Its salient characters are a most extreme skull length and a low cephalic index. (1925, 99-101)

These early skulls compare remarkably well with predynastic Nile Valley skulls which Brenda S. Stoessiger examined in 1924 in a sample exhumed by the British School of Archeology in Egypt at Badari, thirty miles south of Asyut. In "A Study of the Badarian Crania," Stoessiger describes these skulls, which Coon dates at circa 4000 B.C.E., as being "markedly dolichocephalic, smooth, fragile and very feminine in type" (1927, 110).

T. L. Woo in "Seventy-one Ninth Dynasty Skulls from Sedment" notes striking similarities between the skulls in his Ninth Dynasty Egyptian sample and modern skulls observed on the island of Crete (1931, 76). Interestingly enough, ancient skulls unearthed in Crete were classified as belonging to C-Group Nubians who flourished for about 600 years after the close of the Old Kingdom in Egypt. This C-Group population becomes a prime candidate for some of the early Neolithic settlers who migrated to the British Isles. The evidence of bee-hive stone structures that are quite similar to C-Group Nubian graves along the Upper Nile Valley, indicate a considerable C-Group Nubian activity on the south coast of Crete, where similar bee-hive structures exist. Regarding the origin and probable use of these bee-hive structures, James Brunson proposes that not only did Libyans build them, but, citing William L. Hansberry's *Africa and the Africans*, they are also found in the Western Sahara, Egypt, the Sudan and Ethiopia (Brunson 1985, 62). Brunson goes on to paraphrase Albert Churchward's observation made in *Signs and Symbols of Primordial Man* that these tombs originated from the African concept of the ghost house in which the ancestor's spirit resided (1985, 62). Brunson concludes that such *tholos* tombs were connected to the spiral or serpent image, and recalls that Churchward believed the serpent was symbolic of the Egyptian imagery of the child, *Tmu*, and the initiated man, *Tem* (1985, 62). Brunson includes in his discussion Churchward's claim that rites conducted in these structures rejuvenated the serpent that was sacred to the mother goddess (1985, 62). That the serpent in question could have been both cosmic and phallic is a proposition which will be explored in subsequent chapters.

Regarding predynastic and dynastic Egyptian crania examined by the British School of Archeology, Morant lists two distinct racial types, which he labels "the Upper and Lower Egyptian types" (Stoessiger 1927, 116). Morant is careful to distinguish between those skulls which reveal a "Negro admixture" and those that do not, and Stoessiger proposes that the Badarian sample is closer in morphology to these Negro types than to the dynastic series of skulls examined (1927, 125). Stoessiger also cites the observation of French anthropologist, Pruner Bey, who, in an article entitled "Sur l'origine de l'ancienne Race Egyptienne," argues that the predynastic Egyptian skulls show a marked resemblance to the skulls of the modern Berber (Stoessiger 1927, 125).

For the purposes of this study, two basic types of dolichocephalism found in Africa need to be examined in some detail: the long, "feminine," smooth skulls of the Nile Valley, and the Berber long-headed types of the so-called white and racially-mixed Berber tribes whose skulls are often less narrow and more rugged. Coon notes that the Afalou influence, which he derives in part from a Cro-Magnon residue, was strong in North Africa, and he attempts to summarize the racial admixture that occurred in North Africa which led to the creation of the so-called White North African. He argues that many North African peoples, with the exception of Jews, Negroes and colonists from Europe, reveal an admixture of the ancient Afalou race, Mediterraneans from the Mesolithic and Neolithic periods, Hamitic speaking nomads from Asia, and two incursions of Arabs (1939, 467). The racial composition of the Hamitic-speaking tribesman is, of course, conspicuous by its absence in Coon's description. And he contradicts himself about the allegedly missing Negroid admixture of the Afalou component in *The Living Races of Man* when he argues:

> The many skeletons found in the caves of Afalou Bou Rhummel, Algeria, and Taforalt, Morocco, and individual ones from other sites, indicate the presence of a tall, heavy-boned people with massive skulls, wide faces, craggy jaws, and wide nasal openings. Although essentially Caucasoid, they clearly show the absorption of an indigenous element, which can only have come from the previous inhabitants, the Aterians. The Aterian people derived from the local Ternefine-Tangier line and . . . were ancestral bushmen. Traces of this indigenous element may still be seen in living populations of North Africa. (1965, 93-94)

Regarding the cephalic index of the skulls in the Afalou Bou Rhummel series, Coon reveals that they vary from the predominant dolichocephalic sizes to rounder-headed brachycephalic dimensions (1939, 42).

Drawing from this and other evidence, he makes two observations in *The Living Races of Europe*. First, despite the fact that North Africa was initially inhabited by non-Caucasoids, and despite the fact that the earliest waves of Caucasoids mixed their genes with these non-Caucasoid aborigines, later waves of Caucasoids finally drove the aborigines south of the Sahara, thus allowing the lightening of the population over a period of time. And second, this "massive penetration of Negro Africa by Caucasoid genes" occurred "in the last fourteen thousand years" (Coon 1965, 95). Now that is a safe conclusion, if ever there was one. And Coon can rest easy in the hopes that North Africa was Caucasoid in the Neolithic Age and earlier, even though the evidence for the fourteen thousand year figure is a bit thin. And having established that time frame in his mind, it is quite safe to argue the case for a North African migration to the British Isles.

But the cephalic index problem still loomed. The studies of T. H. Huxley, G. M. Morant, A. C. Haddon and others indicate that the Neolithic inhabitants of the British Isles were uniformly dolichocephalic. Huxley's 1862 study of the River Bed type found the cephalic index of his specimens to average around 70. According to Haddon and Huxley, the people who constructed the ancient stone monuments were descended from the older River Bed type which they trace to Northwest Africa. In Ireland, cephalic index measurements made on the Neolithic Whitepark Bay skull found in county Antrim in Northern Ireland indicate long-headedness with facial features reminiscent of the North African Afalou. Other Neolithic Irish skulls are also long-headed. These include the Ringbella, the Balbriggan, and the Kilgreany B skulls. The dolichocephalic Ringbella skull excavated in county Cork, and the Balbriggan skull uncovered in county Dublin were described as being similar to some predynastic Nile Valley types (Ali and Ali 1993, 87ff.).

Of the 296 predynastic and dynastic, Nile Valley skulls that J. M. Crichton compared by computer, Coon notes in *The Living Races of Man*:

> the predynastic Egyptians were more like the Negroes than the dynastic Egyptians were, and that the dynastic Egyptians were more Caucasoid than their predecessors. Differences between the two sets of Egyptian skulls were more marked in the face than in the vault. The predynastic skulls have broader, flatter nasal bones and more alveolar prognathism than the dynastic skulls. The predynastic skulls have relatively flat cranial base, as shown by the difference between the auricular and badion-bregma heights. In this case, the predynastic skulls were more like those of Negroes. (1965, 94)

The Kilgreany B cave skull from county Waterford was compared by Mollesun to the East African Elementeita type, a parallel which provides more evidence for a darker ancestry (Ali and Ali 1993, 91). And Fleure concludes that the average cephalic index of the Early Neolithic skulls discovered in Ireland was 75 (1922, 83).

The whole issue of the racial composition of the many North African Berber tribes, which in the Neolithic Age and Early Bronze Age may well have been partly responsible for the peopling of the British Isles, is an area of great controversy. Coon is less cautious than usual when he argues that north of the Sahara "non-Caucasoids" were once dominant. These "non-Caucasoids," he argues, originally mixed with other native Caucasoid populations and drove many tribes to the south. But then new waves of Caucasoids entered the picture, whitening the population until the Slave trade "reversed the trend" (1965, 95). According to Coon, this admixture explains: "the similarity between Caucasoids and Negroes in many genetic traits that are not closely related to environmental adaptation such as some of the blood groups . . . ." (1965, 95).

The confusion surrounding the racial classification of the Tuareg, a very ancient and still extant Berber tribe whose ancestors may have helped to people the British Isles in Neolithic times, offers a case in point. Coon, writing in *The Races of Europe*, is rather vague on the subject, arguing:

> The Tuareg probably represent in a general way the ancestral physical type of the bringers of Hamitic speech to North Africa, but their adherence to this type must be a matter of recombination and selection. They are by no means typical, but may be taken as an end type in the Berber racial complex. (1939, 374)

Again, the adjective Negroid is conspicuous by its absence.

In "The Origin of the Tuareg," which appeared in *The Geographical Journal* of the Royal Geographical Society, Francis Rodd reveals the complexity of the racial classification problem and helps to muddle it even further. Writing in 1926, Rodd notes that living among the Libyans is the nomadic tribe, the Tuareg, one of the oldest groups in North Africa that still ranges freely from the Fezzan to the Niger River. Rodd carefully distinguishes the Tuareg both from the Muslim Arabs who arrived much later and from the Negro groups who inhabit the expansive territory of the Tuareg. He argues that the Tuareg settled no further south than the Niger bend which is predominantly black (1926, 27ff.).[2] Nonetheless, Rodd notes matrifocal elements in Tuareg socialization, which, although he does not argue the case, may link the Tuareg to predynastic Nilotic origins:

> The most striking outward peculiarity of the Tuareg, which distinguishes them from all other races in the world, is that the men go about veiled, in such a manner that nothing is visible of their faces but the eyes, which peer through a narrow slit between the upper and lower folds of the long bandage-like veil. Their women never veil themselves at all. If they draw a fold of stuff half over their faces it is out of coquetry or a token of respect, but not to conceal their charms. The veil, or 'tagilmus,' of the men is worn by noble and servile tribes alike. In certain districts the latter wear a white veil and the former a dark indigo or black one, a practice which has given rise to the terms Black and White Tuareg; it is however not a universal habit and never refers to the complexion. (1926, 31)[3]

Rodd explains that contemporary Tuareg women are freer than English women, and that they choose their own husbands, teach their children how to read, serve as historians, and own and control property after marriage (1926, 32-33).[4] Such customs, of course, are anachronisms in Moslem countries, but the Tuareg are described by Rodd as being quite independent of Moslem customs. For although Moslem law allows Tuareg men to marry up to four wives, the Tuareg remain monogamous (1926, 32). Another peculiarity of the Tuareg is noted by Rodd. Even though they speak an Afroasiatic language, Berber, they write in a script that exists nowhere else in the world. The script is called *T'ifinagh* which means "signs," Rodd explains, revealing that several of its characters were derived from Punic origins (1926, 33). Rodd goes on to indicate that the mysterious Tuareg were at one time much more civilized than they appear during his own time, and that some but not all of their traditions can be traced to Egypt (1926, 33). Rodd further speculates that unraveling the enigma of Tuareg origins might cast light on the origins of the Garamantes (1926, 33).

The plot thickens as Rodd attempts to classify the Tuareg racially. He rejects the classification system of Sergi, who opts for a coloration synthesis by 'bleaching' the black into a brown Mediterranean man. Agreeing, however, with Sergi's argument that the Tuareg remained unmixed in more recent history, despite the incursions of the Phoenicians, Romans, Greeks, Vandals, Byzantines, Franks, Persians, Jews and Turks, and that the Tuareg only reaped certain cultural influences from them, Rodd attacks Sergi's classification of the Tuareg into the "Eurafrican race," or what Sergi also calls the "brown Mediterranean race":

> He [Sergi] has proposed that his Eurafrican race (using the word in the widest sense) had its cradle in Africa itself, either in the region of the Great Lakes or else in the Sahara when the deserts of today were lands flowing with milk and honey. Sergi has divided the this Eurafrican sub-species of man into two families of peoples, the Eastern and the Western or Northern Hamites. In the former category are included the Ancient and Modern Egyptians, Nubians, Bejas, Abyssinians (excluding Himyarites), Gallas (including Somals), Masai and Wahuma; in the latter are the Mediterranean Berbers, the Saharan Berbers (that is, the Tuareg and the Tebu), the Atlantic Berbers, the Fulani, and the Guanchos. The first difficulty encountered is that these categories include people with dissimilar characteristics as the fuzzy-haired Nilotic Hamites and the fair wavy Atlas Berbers. If this is so, racial distinctions as we know them must break down. (1926, 35)[5]

Admitting earlier that the Tuareg are prone to dolichocephalism and some brachycephalism, Rodd goes on to express his amazement at Sergi's classification system: "When tall men and small men, dolichocephals and brachycephals, woolly-haired and straight-haired, nomads and sedentaries, and black and tan all belong to a common stock, the implication is inevitable that the definitions hereto accepted by other anthropologists are worthless" (1926, 35). But that is not all. According to Rodd:

He [Sergi] explains the incidence of blonds in the Atlas by their geographical surroundings though he forgets that there are no indigenous blonds in the far higher mountains near the Great Lakes of Africa, nor indeed, elsewhere in the world, except where Nordic blonds are indigenous, namely in North-Eastern Europe. (1926, 35)

Even more incomprehensible to Rodd, is Sergi's proposal that the Ancient Egyptians and the Libyans [including the Tuareg] are ultimately descended from the same stock. For evidence, Rodd indicates that the elements of Tuareg and Egyptian painting and writing are radically different (1926, 35). Rodd waffles on, arguing: "These blonds are probably late Nordic immigrants, and they have little to do with the far more tenuous stratum of Nordic humanity which is spread much further afield, all over North Africa" (1926, 35).

Van Sertima reveals how the 'bleaching' or albinization process leading from black to white, so cleverly obfuscated by Rodd and to some degree by Sergi as well, is muddled further in the 1960s when Falkenburger attempts to prove that two-thirds of the ancient Egyptian crania he examines are Euro-African [a euphemistic spin-off of Sergi's "brown Mediterranean race"] and only one third Negroid (1989, 4). Van Sertima further notes that a comparative study conducted by B. K. Chatterjee and G. D. Kumar of a large sample of predynastic crania excavated at Naqada II, Badari, and Nubian Ariba and another Twelfth and Thirteenth Dynasty Old Kingdom sample from Saqqara indicates that all the skulls that are long-headed and broad-faced with "a low orbit and broad nasal aperture have the same characteristics features of the Negroid type" (van Sertima 1989, 4; Chatterjee and Kumar 1965, 17).

And of the hot-button adjective Nordic, Diop, citing Marcellin Boule and Henri-Victor Vallois, notes their insistence on the proposition that *homo nordicus* is a recent derivation resulting from interbreeding which transpired to the south of Denmark during the Neolithic Age of indigenous descendants of Upper Paleolithic Man and a band of interlopers from the south. The mixture resulted in "a diverse dolichocephaly with . . . slight Neolithic brachycephalic traits" (Diop 1991, 21; Boule and Vallois 1957, 238). As to whether or not these invaders could have been derived from Nilotic dolichocephals, Diop does not speculate.

Discounting another theory of Berber and Tuareg origins proposed by Ibn Khaldun, who traces them back to Ham, Rodd states his own theory, later restated by Jurgen Spanuth, which Rodd derives from Egyptian records. These records trace Tuareg origins to a rival nationality the Egyptians called Tamahu, literally, 'white people' or 'people of the north,' who inhabited

Eastern Libya, and who may have formed a series of military alliances with the People of the Sea in both the Nineteenth and Twentieth Egyptian Dynasties (Rodd 1926, 41ff.). During earlier dynasties, the Tamahu were constant irritants to the Egyptians, Rodd argues, citing accounts of military action in the Third and Fifth Dynasties. And in the Sixth Dynasty, he notes the conflicts occurring in the Upper Nile Negroes and the Tamahu and Rebu. He cites Diodorus Siculus's reference to the conquest of Libyan territory by Sesostris in the Eighteenth Dynasty. He also recalls the defeat of the Imukekek by Amenhotep I in the north, the push against the Ekbet by Thutmoses I, and the subjugation of the Libyan Tamahus by Thutomoses III, Hatshepsut and Amenhotep III. As late as the Nineteenth Dynasty a new influx of westerners into the Nile Delta area continued to command Egypt's attention, Rodd notes (1926, 42). Rodd cites Egyptian invasions mounted by the People of the Sea in the Nineteenth and Twentieth Dynasties, roughly between 1350 and 1200 B.C.E., and from 1200 to 1090 B.C.E., respectively. For an alliance against Egypt was made by various parties: the Sea Peoples, the largely Syrian-derived westerners, and the Semitic Lebu (Rodd 1926, 43-44).

Rodd concludes that Tuareg ancestors entered Africa either after the emergence of the Alpine race and the Bronze Age, or during later migrations, but he leaves the question open, suggesting that he is only positing a hypothesis as to Tuareg origins (1926, 46).

But Rodd appears to have gotten Tuareg racial etiology quite wrong, and it seems that Sergei was closer to the mark regarding the often racially-mixed modern Tuareg. Reynolds proposes that the Tuareg were originally dark-skinned inhabitants native to East Africa. Speaking of the term Berber, which may derive in part from the Afroasiatic root *bar, ber* or *bur* for 'phallus' or 'warrior,' and which, she surmises, was used to indicate Red Sea as well as North African peoples, she goes on to assert that "the peoples whom the classical Greek and Roman historians called *Berber* were 'black' and affiliated with the then contemporary peoples of the East African area" (1993, 93).

She further proposes that the derivation of *Berber* can also be traced to the word for wells and water sources which are so important in the lives of pastoralists (Reynolds 1993, 96). This proposed etymology is very interesting given, as will be noted in detail in a subsequent chapter, that the root of *Moor* in the British Isles is derived by some from the Anglo-Saxon *mor* for 'watery waste.' In any case, like Rodd, Reynolds notes that the infusion of whites into North Africa came from the waves of the People of the Sea, the Romans, Greeks, Turks, Iranians, Iraqis, and, in later times, from the importation of vast numbers of slaves of European and Slavic descent by Muslim slavers. But unlike Rodd, she does not believe that the white element was numerically significant in the North African population until the rise of the Moorish dynasties in Spain (Reynolds 1993, 96). She goes on to propose that the term Moor was used even during the Moorish domination of Spain to denote individuals called Moors who were ancestral to numerous current inhabitants of North Africa. These include the "dark brown and brown black" dwellers of today's Sahara and Sahel areas and the Fulani, Tuareg, and Southern Morocco's Zenagha. They also include the Kunta and Tebu dwellers of the Sahel region, she goes on, as well as additional dark-skinned Arabs who hail from Mauritania and the Sahel. The Senegalese and Mauritanian Trarza are also included on the list as well as the Mogharba, numerous Arab tribes of the Sudan, and the Alegerian Chaamba (Reynolds 1993, 96).

   And, interestingly enough, she does not attribute the narrow noses and fragile limbs of certain desert populations to Caucasian admixture, arguing instead that desert conditions caused Africoid desert dwellers to undergo a "specialized physical development" (Reynolds 1993, 104). Citing Hiernaux's *Peoples of Africa*, Reynolds proposes a more diverse morphology:

> Narrow noses and little or no prognathism are typical and associated with the modified aspect of their facial and cranial morphology. These characteristics, once presumed to be a legacy of a non-Negroid or Caucasoid intermixture, are now attributed, by some population biologists and geneticists, to the ancient adaptation of Africoids to certain specific. ecological factors including the change to a Neolithic diet in combination with dwelling in exceedingly hot, dry habitats. (1993, 104)

One tribe that she cites as an example of this peculiar Africoid morphology is the Sabaai, the Sabaeans of Southern Arabia and Macae, who may have been the ancestors of the Mesopotamian Saracens cited centuries later by the Romans (Reynolds 1993, 105). Regarding the Sabaai and similar dwellers on the Arabian peninsula in ancient times, Reynolds proposes, much as Druscilla Houston does decades earlier, that they were obviously Africoid, for "it is clear from ancient writings of the 'Arabs' that the peoples of the Arabian peninsula and the non-immigrant, indigenous nomads of the Horn were considered ethnically one and the same and thought to have originated in areas near the cataracts of the Nile. Troglodytes (Bedja) were said to have lived on both sides of the Red Sea" (1993, 105-06). Pursuing the matter, she lampoons euphemistic terms such as "hamite" and "brown" or "graceful

Mediterranean," which have been used by misinformed anthropologists to define indigenous Ethiopian people and racially mixed populations of modern day North Africa. These anthropologists, in her view, obfuscate the true ethnic complexity of Berber speakers of a much earlier era. By concentrating on the modern Berber rather than the ancient one, they attempt to belie "the fact that the original Berber and Arab populations of North Africa were biologically and ethnically affiliated with modern day peoples to the south of Egypt, especially those who now speak languages of Ethiopic and Cushitic groupings" (1993, 107).

Reynolds also cites numerous examples of classical references to Berbers and Moors to advance her hypothesis. Notably, in the fourth century c.e., the Roman Claudian complained about the "hideous Ethiopian hybrids" who were being produced during the reign of the Algerian Gildo from the union of Roman matrons of Sidon and their male Berber consorts (Reynolds 1993, 107). And regarding the Libyans, she notes that Roman sources described all of the prominent Libyan tribes as dark-skinned. These sources include Martial, Corripus, Procopius, Juvenal and Silius Italicus, all of whom described the Maures as black-skinned people. She notes further that Polemon in his *Physiognomical Scriptures* and Admantius both equated Libyans and Ethiopians as a result of the black skin of the two peoples. Then too, she notes, these groups were also described by chroniclers as being "light of build" and "woolly-haired" (Reynolds 1993, 114).

Another of Reynolds' observations casts more light on the elusive Tuareg when she notes that in ancient East Africa and in ancient Nubia, Egypt and Arabia, the predominant physique consisted of a light build, characterized by a lankiness that is typical also of the pastoralists of Abyssinia and Erythraea. That same body type can be found in Northern Kenya and in portions of modern Arabia, she continues, revealing that a similar morphology was typical of North African nomadic tribes speaking Cushitic and Nilo-Saharan dialects well into early medieval times, and is still typical of pastoral Fulani and other Sahelian pastoral nomads today (Reynolds 1993, 114).

Reynolds presents other evidence, indicating that the so-called Caucasoid Tamahu or Libou [Libyans], the name of which appears in the Nineteenth Dynasty [thirteenth century b.c.e.] during the reign of Ramesses II, were originally an Africoid group allied with the more obviously Caucasoid People of the Sea (1993, 114). She further reveals that during the Roman era, Procopius and other commentators of the period indicated that the Libou bore an "ethnic affinity" with Ethiopian and Sudanic hamites speaking Cushitic (1993, 116).

Shedding even more light on Tuareg ethnic origins, she indicates that Libyans invading Tunisia during the time of Diodorus Siculus, were known by the Romans as Afri or Afer, Afaricani or Frexus and also as Maures or Maurusioi (Reynolds 1993, 116-17). Reynolds goes on to cite additional classical sources, drawing from accounts written by Pliny, Josephus, Cleodemus and later Arab traditions, all of which indicated that these groups traversed the Red Sea area and the then Berber Abyssinia and Eritrea with Hercules, and that they traded in incense and inhabited both shores of the Red Sea (1993, 117). Then she reasons that the contemporary area of Afar in Djibouti and Ethiopia was once inhabited by Tuareg ancestors, given that an enclave of Tuareg tribes along the Niger assert that their ancestors were called *Argulen* (1993, 117).

In light of the river Affric place-name in Scotland, this Afer reference to Tuareg ancestry is particularly illuminating. And Reynolds recalls that the Afer were components of the Carthaginian army that invaded Europe under the command of Hannibal the Afar. To this day, dark-skinned Tuareg tribes of Irforas or Kel Faruwan near Ghat in Libya and Asben on the Niger are identical, Reynolds adds, to the Beni Ifren of Algeria [described by Pliny as the Ifuraces or Frexus], the Tunisian Aferi, and Pharusii, inhabitants of Morocco's Atlas Mountains from the time of the ancient Greeks and Romans (1993, 117).

Her assertion that the early Libyans were originally dark Africoids is shared by several scholars and clearly reveals the limitation of cranial studies that are not backed up with hard historical data. Although she does not cite him, Alan Gardiner in *Egypt of the Pharaohs* arrives at a similar conclusion about the Libyans of the early Neolithic Age:

> The name (Libyan) is, strictly speaking, both a misnomer and an anachronism . . . . In earlier times two peoples are distinguished, the Tehennu and the Temehu, of whom the former were perhaps originally identical both in race and culture with the Egyptians of the Western Delta . . . . They wore phallus sheaths, had a large curl hanging from one side of their head, and carried feathers in their hair. (1961, 35)

Brunson recalls that Diop in *The African Origin of Civilization* also notes that the early Libyans derived from a clan name of the Mande, *Anu-Tehennu*, and that the Anu-Tehennu herded cattle and built walled stone cities (1985, 37). Then too, Brunson cites linguist C. A. Winters' (1981) assertion that the Garamantes were descendants of the dark-skinned Mande as well (Brunson 1985, 37).

Additional observations by Reynolds shed even more light on the darker strains of the contemporary Tuareg, whose ancestors appear to have penetrated ancient Europe at least as far the British Isles.   Noting the existence in the Tripoli area of a fourth century c.e. tribe called the Mauri Mezikes, who were often confused with Ethiopians, Reynolds proposes that this same tribe, also dubbed Libyan, frequently attacked oases near Egypt and the Fezzan area of Libya (1993, 118). She cites the Roman Evagrius who writes that they were allied with the Blemmyes of Nubia (1993, 118). Reynolds then deduces that the Mezikes were related to the Blemmyes in Ethiopia, whose rulers were named Ilam Meshi. The nobles of the Tuareg to this day are called Imoshagh or Amazighen (Mazikes), which in the Tamashek language of certain Tuareg indicates kinship with the Mashek or Mezikes, she notes further on (1993, 118).   She describes them rather differently than Rodd, using adjectives such as dark brown, tall, long-faced, narrow-nosed, and long-headed, noting that these features suggest East African origins to Coon (Reynolds 1993, 118).

Citing their possible link to the C-group Libyans mentioned earlier, Reynolds makes an observation that is critical to this study. Citing Oric Bates' *The Eastern Libyans*, she mulls over his observation that the pre-Islamic "stone tumulus graves of Nubia typical of C-group and Pan- Grave culture closely resemble the type found in the Western Sahara called by the Tuareg *regem* or *argem*" (1993, 123). The description of these tombs, noted above, is uncannily similar to tumuli excavated in the British Isles, where bodies were also found buried in a contracted position. Citing Camps' *Aux Origines de la Berberie*, she notes that these North African tombs comprised the most commonly found burial monuments in North Africa in which the body was interred in a retracted position, and that they ranged from above the Atlas, across the Sahara south to the river Niger and west from the Nile to the Canary Islands.   Still alluding to Camps, Reynolds reveals that they also can be found in Rio d'Oro, Fezzan, Cyrenaica and Abyssinia, and that Camps believes the structures could have originated as early as the Memphite period in Egypt (1993, 124).

And Reynolds, consulting Camps again, includes another pertinent observation for this study. Interestingly enough, early Saharan rock paintings of military scenes replete with camels, warriors in triangular configurations, and various inscriptions written in Tifinagh, a Tuareg form of writing, are nearly identical to inscriptions found in pre-Christian Nubia (1993, 125).

And what do Arab sources indicate about the origins of the Tuareg? Reynolds reveals that certain Tuareg males, who wear the veil to prevent them from exhaling on the sacred fire of their Nubian sun god [called *Mesh* or *Mash*], are said by Ibn Khadun to have descended from similar veiled

Berbers who lived in the Abyssinian rift area. She then cites Mohammed Bello, who proposes in the *Infaq al-Mausri* that the Tuareg or Beri-beri are the remnant of the Berbers who inhabited the territory between Zinj and Habash or the Afar area (1993, 134). As noted later in this study, Mesh, or Mash, may represent the Ethiopian Underworld deity Midir, who in pre-Christian times was likely transmuted into an Irish god of the Underworld. Given that the meteoric betel stone has been regarded as a sacred object by most of these North African peoples into modern times, the fire worshiped may originally have been a cometary one as we shall see.

Drawing upon still more historical data, Reynolds surmises that the matrilineal Tuareg ancestors who herded camels, cattle and sheep, and drank milk mixed with blood, were related to a tribe of Ethiopian troglodytes called Blemmyes, Bedja and Madjayu or Medid and Afar, many of whom migrated westward across the Sahara in ancient times, (1993, 125).

Interestingly enough, during the Moorish rule in Spain, various descendants of these Tuareg, along with their fellow, black Garamante desert dwellers, would seize the extreme western portion of Southern France and assorted valleys of the Pyrenees as well, according to Reynolds. And roughly seven years after the fall of Gibraltar [Gebel el Tarik] in the early 800s, they mounted a successful invasion of Southern France capturing several cities including Marseilles and Arles before moving into Sicily in 837 c.e. and into Rome itself by 846 c.e. (Reynolds 1993, 125). Certain Tuareg and Garamante descendants, then, according to Reynolds, constituted a portion of the population of La Petite Afrique, or Little Africa, which stubbornly resisted expulsion from the French Riviera town of Camarque for centuries. And their descendants may have even served in the "blacker than ink" army of Moors depicted in the eleventh century *Song of Roland* as well. Then too, in the eleventh century the Ummayad Dynasty of Spain and North Africa was overtaken by a Tuareg-based dynasty called Al Murabatin or Almoravids, according to Reynolds (1993, 125).

Certainly Reynolds' insights take us far afield from Rodd's simplistic argument that the Tuareg were mainly a Caucasian cluster of tribes in ancient times. Apparently Rodd was drawing his ethnic conclusions largely from his inventory of the modern day Tuareg, who, in most cases, could easily be classified as Caucasian by a Eurocentric ethnologist. But he was not looking at the entire time frame and thus failed to see the bigger picture. And again, pairing off Rodd and Reynolds reveals how easily early crania can be classified as Caucasian if no one is watching the hen house but the fox.

Drawing upon *Crania Britannica* and other sources, John Beddoe in *The Races of Britain* also attempts to link the dolichocephalic Tamahu [who appear to Beddoe to be a component in the ancestry of the Tuareg] with certain Neolithic Britons, noting that "at the age when the dolmens and chambered tumuli began to be built, there is reason to think that extreme dolichocephaly was the prevailing type throughout most of the west and northwest of Europe, from the Baltic to the Straits of Gibraltar" (1885, 14). Beddoe goes on to suggest that descendants of the long-headed Tamahu may have been part of the traffic:

> French anthropologists think there were two Paleolithic races of long-heads in their country, those of Canstadt and of Cro-Magnon, before the Neolithic long-heads, the first constructors of the dolmens, came in from the northeast. If so, it is likely enough that the third race was a blond one, identical with the Tamahu, who are supposed to have imported dolmen-building and the fair complexion into North Africa, and who are portrayed with blue eyes and light hair upon the Egyptian monuments of 1500 B.C. (1885, 14)

He further speculates, not unlike Rodd and Spanuth, that these Tamahu may have at one time been northern Europeans who migrated into what is today called Libya and then returned to Europe again (1885, 15). Coon notes in *The Races of Europe* that a Berber sub-tribe of Riffians, many sporting red hair as do a small percentage of modern day Irish, appear to be directly related to the Libyan Tamahu, although some are descended from Arab missionaries (1939, 464, 480-81). They live in the Garet Desert, and he argues that they are the blondest and the most Nordic of all the Berbers. Additionally, they are all dolichocephalic with narrow, leptorrhine noses, and largely white-skinned like most northern Europeans (Coon 1939, 480ff.). The problem here is obvious, for extreme dolichocephally and leptorrhine noses can be found in both dark and white-skinned populations, a coincidence which can pose problems when one tries to determine the ethnicity of the dead. That there were people, who under our current classification system would be labeled Caucasians, dwelling along the North African littoral during the Neolithic period must be admitted but not overestimated.

In the same vein as Rodd, Coon notes further on that many of the ancestors of extreme dolichocephalic remnants who appear to have "concentrated in Hoggar and parts of the Algerian plateau, are the Tuareg and the purer families of ancestral nomadic Berbers, preserving the head form which they brought from East Africa, their Hamitic homeland" (1939, 257). Regarding the Tuareg desert nomads who still police the areas between the Libyan Desert and Rio de Oro and between the Algerian oases and the Niger, Coon adds:

Despite the close association between the Tuareg and the Negroes, who preceded them in the Sahara and with whom they are in close contact in Nigeria, the noble class has to a large extent preserved its freedom from Negroid admixture, although there are many individual exceptions to the rule. (1939, 471)

Yet Coon argues further on that the heads of the Tuareg are mainly dolichocephalic, and that the purest Tuareg belong to a specialized Mediterranean sub-type (1939, 472). Finally he notes that even though the Tuareg carried Hamitic tongues to North Africa, there must have been some intermingling of blood lines to accomplish this transfer (Coon 1939, 474).

This kind of description typifies Coon's [and, as noted earlier, Rodd's] avoidance of the mixed-race issue throughout his otherwise erudite *The Races of Europe*, the urge to coin euphemisms when dealing with the Negroid component, no matter how small it might be, in the modern North African. Coon continues his observations of the Tuareg in a similar vein, noting:

They resemble the East African Hamites very closely, and especially the whiter element among the Somali, but in their extreme stature and great head size they seem closer to most living Mediterraneans than to the pre-Neolithic East Africa men. Tuareg history does not support the view that they represent a survival in isolation of a pure East African strain from a remote period. (1939, 473)

And in describing the cephalic indices of the Tuareg, Coon throws a couple of pails of gasoline on the fire when he argues that the Tuareg are dolichocephalic with cephalic indexes varying from 72 to 75 and averaging out at 73. He goes on to observe that among the white nobles, brachycephals are not identified (Coon 1939, 472).

Coon does about as well as any European-schooled anthropologist of his day can in muddling through, given the racial classification system under which he labors. But much of his analysis, along with aspects of Rodd's, seems to blend an amount of racial wish-fulfillment with the hard data, leading perhaps to more questions than answers regarding the racial composition of North Africans then and now.

Regarding the Long Barrow group in the Neolithic British Isles, Coon notes in *The Races of Europe*: "In one particular feature, the nasal index, the Long Barrow people resemble the Egyptians more than most of the more northerly Mediterraneans, for the Long Barrow crania are leptorrhine [narrow-nosed]" (1939, 111). Earlier Coon applies his North African observations to the northern and southern peripheries of Europe in *The Races of Europe*, noting that there are two belts in Europe that possibly contain dolichochephals who are descendants of Neolithic African wanderers and seafarers. The first belt includes parts of the British Isles, Holland, Belgium, Scandinavia, the Frankish Palatinate, Finland, Estonia and Latvia. The other belt, Coon argues, lies in Iberia, the Dordogne Valley of France, the islands of Sardinia, Corsica, Crete and the Balearics, the southern tip of Italy, the Black and Aegean Sea littorals, and likely in the British Isles as well. (1939, 257)

Given that many Scandinavians emigrated to the British Isles, the skeletal remains of Scandinavia are relevant here, and it is interesting to note that when examining many Iron Age samples a reversal occurs-- long-headed individuals become fair-skinned and round-headed individuals are generally darker-complexioned. Gwyn Jones cites data that leads him to a more radical conclusion than that of Coon's, when Jones reveals:

> The Viking peoples who lived between the neck of Jutland, Lofotens, Sogn and Uppsala, were not all alike, and emphatically not of one 'pure' Nordic race. But two main types of Scandinavian have always been recognizable: the one tall of stature, fair or ruddy complexioned, light-haired, blue-eyed, long of face and skull; the other shorter, dark-complexioned, brown-or dark-haired, brown-eyed, broad-faced and round of skull. (1984, 67)

Jones cites evidence for this darker population. Of Norway's first royal dynasty, he reveals: "Harald Fairhair was the first king of all Norway; his father was Halfdan the Black (svarti), and two of his sons were likewise called Halfdan, one nicknamed the White (hyviti), the other, reminiscently, the Black" (1984, 68). Jones goes on to present more swarthy characters from *Egils Saga*, noting that:

> of the two famous sons of Kveldulf, Thorolf was tall and handsome like his mother's people, but Grim took after his father and was black and ugly. Grim's sons, Thorolf and Egil, born out of Iceland, repeated the pattern: Thorolf was the image of his uncle, tall, handsome, and sunny-natured; Egil was black, even uglier than his father, tortuous and incalculable. He became the greatest poet of his age, and many a hard-hewn line of verse testifies to the pride in his craggy head, broad nose, heavy jaw and swart visage. (1984, 68)[6]

In regard to possible itinerants to Britain from the Black Sea area, Coon glosses over the Africoid population found even today along its eastern shores. Bernal is not so avoidant when he cites the skeletal remains of dolichocephalic Africans who inhabited the Black Sea town of Colchis of Jason, Medea and Golden Fleece fame. Colchis may have been an Egyptian colony, Bernal argues, established by a remnant of Pharaoh Sesostris II's army (1991, 245ff.). Speaking of contemporary Georgia, Bernal notes that in contrast to Ibero-Georgian inhabitants of the mountainous regions who are short-skulled Caucasians, many dwellers of the coastline area of Colchis have long skulls characteristic of some Africans (1991, 249).

Bernal goes on to reveal that the Abkhaz linguist and ethnographer Dmitri Gulia, posits Abyssino-Egyptian origins for the Colchians, and cites an Egyptian influence in Abkhaz place-names, divine terms and surnames (1991, 249). Bernal also cites Herodotus' loomings about the Colchis area:

> My own idea on the subject was based first on the fact that they [the Colchians] have black skins and woolly hair (not that that amounts to much, as other nations have the same), and secondly, and more especially, on the fact that the Colchians, the Egyptians, and the Ethiopians are the only races which from ancient times have practiced circumcision. The Phoenicians and the Syrians of Palestine themselves admit that they adopted the practice from Egypt, and the Syrians who live near the rivers Thermodon and Parthenius, as well as their neighbors the Macronians say they learnt it only a short while ago from the Colchians . . . . And now I think of it, there is a further point of resemblance between the Colchians and Egyptians: They share a method of weaving linen different from that of any other people; and there is also a similarity between them in language and way of living. The linen made in Greece is known as Sardonian linen; that which comes from Egypt is called Egyptian. (1991, 248-49; Herodotus II 1954, 104-05)

Citing parallels between the Colchian ram/fleece and the Egyptian ram cults of Amon, R. A. Jairazbhoy also points out a major parallel between Colchis and Egypt in a short but important article entitled "Egyptian Civilization in Colchis on the Black Sea." Noting a passage in the *Argonautika* in which the fleece is shown with its serpent guard, Jairazbhoy links this iconography to the royal ram's head of Amon topped with a uraeus serpent and the solar disk (1985, 58ff.). Jairazbhoy also notes that the title of Aeetes, the King of Colchis and the father of black Medea, was referred to as "the son of the sun," the title held by the Pharaohs of Egypt (1985, 58ff.). Another observation by Herodotus, which Bernal cites, seems to close the book on the debate regarding Egyptian influences in the Colchis area:

> On his way back Sesostris came to the River Phasis, and it is quite possible

that he detached a body of troops from his army and left them behind to settle-- or, on the other hand, it may be that some of his men were sick of their travels and deserted. I cannot say with certainty which supposition is the right one, but it is undoubtedly a fact that the Colchians are of Egyptian descent. I noticed myself before I had heard anyone else mention it, and when it occurred to me I asked some questions both in Colchis and in Egypt, and found that the Colchians remembered the Egyptians more distinctly than the Egyptians remembered them. The Egyptians did, however, say that the original Colchians were men from Sesostris' army. (Bernal 1991, 246; Herodotus II, 105)

As previously noted, Irish folklore makes reference to possible migrations from the Black Sea area, and the ancestors of some present day dolichocephals may well have made the journey..

Given that many of the crania exhumed along the littorals of the Mediterranean, Red Sea, Black Sea and Northwestern Atlantic match so neatly during the Neolithic period, and that *Lebor Gabala* and Keating speak of Egyptian, North African and Black Sea points of embarkation for certain invader groups, there is good reason to assume that North Africa, the Nile Valley and Crete, and the Black Sea areas are likely prospects for the origins of many an early Briton. And based on the speculations of Reynolds and Bernal and their sources, whose arguments seem more plausible than Coon's and Rodd's regarding Neolithic racial characteristics, some of these early dolichocephals were likely dark, although Caucasian itinerants [many of whom may have been dubbed People of the Sea] would most likely have been well represented in later Bronze Age waves. But one thing seems certain, whether, Caucasoid, Negroid or Semite, as the world uses these terms, many were Africans, or at least the racially-mixed descendants of Africans.

The long-headed, Long Barrow people who streamed into the British Isles prior to the arrival of other long-headed types that followed over the ensuing centuries of the Neolithic and Early Bronze Ages were both finally replaced by a new wave of brachycephals, according to Morant's "A First Study of the Craniology of England and Scotland." For Morant, Bronze Age invaders were members of a distinctly brachycephalic type as indicated by the exhumed English and Scottish skulls of that period which contrast significantly with the earlier, long-headed crania (1925, 27). Although some skulls of the prior Neolithic type have been found in juxtaposition with various artifacts of the Bronze Age period indicating some admixture of the two races, he argues, the invading party won the day, doubtless driving the descendants of the Neolithic wave of invaders into extinction during the sunset of the Bronze Age (1925, 57).

Regarding the race of the brachycephalic wave, Beddoe makes mention of the darker African elements [dark referring both to skin and hair color] found in the British Isles on the eve of the Roman conquest of Britain. These elements include the swarthy Picts of Scotland, he argues, citing Tacitus' observations on the curly-haired, dark Silures whom the Roman historian believed to have come from the Iberian peninsula (1885, 3). Even today an observant traveler in the southern Welsh valleys of Rhonda, Bargoed and Caerphilly can locate numerous olive-skinned, brachycephalic inhabitants who are more likely than not the descendants of the Silures. Their presumed Silurian ancestors, associated as they are with the round barrows, may have come from West Africa via Spain during the Bronze Age.

Of these Silurian descendants Beddoe argues that "a physiogamy strikingly Iberian (or Basque-like, at least) is commoner in South Wales than in any other part of Great Britain. Many photographs of Basques," he continues, are "in no respect different from some of the ordinary types of features in South Wales" (1885, 26). Then too, Beddoe comments on the dark to black hair of present day inhabitants in parts of Scotland and Northern England where Cymric blood remains, areas such as Upper Galloway, Strathhaven, and Annandale (1885, 26).

Not everyone would agree with Beddoe on the origins or racial derivation of the Round Barrow people. Fleure in *The Peoples of Europe* labels this new brachycephalic type "Prospectors," arguing that they may have been a cross between Anatolians and Mediterraneans (1922, 57). Coon notes in *The Races of Europe* that the Bronze Age skeletal record is spotty resulting from the practice of cremation, and the paucity of bones that escaped the flames indicates to him that the cremation rites derived from a small migration from the Swiss Alpine area (1939, 371). Noting that the dolichocephalic types associated with passage graves and long barrows appear in the British Isles first, Fleure argues that around 2500 B.C.E.: "The distribution of this brachycephalic type around the coasts of South-west Europe is curiously like that of the ancient mines for gold, copper and tin, and these again are largely coincident with that of some types of Megalithic monuments" (1922, 57).

Examining later waves of mesocephals and brachycephals, the Goidels of Ireland and the Cymric A and B invaders of England, who displaced the earlier brachycephals in the Iron Age, Coon notes that the victorious Goidels after leaving a "distant homeland" trekked through Spain according to mythological accounts. Once in Ireland, they incorporated the aborigines into their clans which were ruled by Tara's line of high kings (1939, 372).

Although Coon rightly distinguishes the Goidels from the previous inhabitants, who, according to Irish traditions, disappeared underground to haunt the Megalithic monuments, he assumes, or appears to assume, that the Goidel and the Kymric A and B invaders were Nordic types belonging "to the Celtic Iron Age branch of the Nordic race; a type characterized by a medium-sized mesocephalic skull, with a low vault, a sloping forehead, a cylindrical lateral vault profile, a long, prominent nose, and a relatively small lower facial segment" (1939, 371). Nevertheless, Coon admits that the Celts, who arrived in the British Isles during the La Tene Iron Age era [c. 500 B.C.E. to the time of Christ], were culturally and racially mixed. This mix included elements of central European, Nordic long heads derived from Mediterranean sub-groups and brachycephals from Southwestern Germany who in the Early Bronze Age derived from an earlier mix of Mesolithic round heads and Dinarics. (1939, 293.)

His definition of Dinaric begs the racial question again: "*Dinarics*: A tall brachycephalic type of intermediate pigmentation, usually panoccipital, and showing facial and nasal prominence of Near Eastern peoples." He goes on to note that they form: "The basic population of the whole Dinaric-Alpine highlands from Switzerland to the Epirus, also in the Carpathians and Caucasus, as well as Syria and Asia Minor" (1939, 293). So far, so good, if one wishes to argue they were Nordic, but then the definition expands to include: "a brachycephalized blend in which Atlanto-Mediterranean and Cappadocian [Asia Minor] strains are important, with Alpine acting as the brachycephalizing agent in mixture. . ." (Coon 1939, 293). This sounds like a mixed group that could include so-called Negroid elements given the Atlanto-Mediterranean ingredient, but Coon does not speculate on that touchy issue.

Regarding the Goidel, an early people over whom Coon waxes so euphemistic, the appellation may bear a relationship to a Tuareg tribe called the Godala, members of which later joined the ranks of the Amoravid and Almohade Moorish dynasties of Spain. Reynolds explains that by tradition the Berbers are divided into two lineages, the Zenata and the Sanhaja (1993, 139). She goes on to indicate that the geographical origins of the Zenata tribe have been traced to Nubia, and that during the medieval period the Sanhaja tribe included the Tuareg, Lamta, Lamtuna, Kunta, Gomara and Masmuda groups, all of which lived in the Abyssinian riff. Their descendants include the Goddala and various other groups, she concludes (1993, 139).

If history repeated itself, it seems possible that the ancestors of these Moorish Goidels may have been the Goddala of North Africa, a proposition that warrants further investigation.

Nonetheless, Coon finds evidence of brachycephalism in Afalou and Tuareg Negro crania, and given that an incidence of brachycephalism has been found in Northwest Africa and in the Canary Islands, both likely points of embarkation to Spain and points north, it seems just as likely to conclude that brachycephals came not only from Central Europe but also from Northwest Africa and the Canaries, with the first wave probably departing from the African sources. The Bronze Age brachycephals, then, could have been fairly direct descendants of northwest Africans and African Canarians. Coon seems to stumble over this proposition when he compares the hair and features of Riffian Berbers with certain contemporary Irishmen, but, characteristically, he does not dwell on the similarities. Then too, the later La Tene Iron Age invaders could have been Europeans mixed with Negroid elements from the Atlanto-Mediterranean component.

To complicate matters, Gwyn Jones, as noted earlier, reveals that in Scandinavian populations, it was the dolichocephalic individuals who bore the Nordic characteristics and the brachycephalic individuals who tended to be dark-skinned. We need to re-examine his observation noted earlier where he argues that Viking populations revealed two types: "the one tall of stature, fair or ruddy complexioned, light-haired, blue-eyed, long of face and skull; the other shorter, dark-complexioned, brown-or dark-haired, brown-eyed, broad-faced and round of skull" (1984, 67). Given that the Viking's occupied nearly all of the British Isles during some point in the early Middle Ages, Viking racial stock is clearly relevant here, and adds further complexity to the whole issue of race and craniology.

In conclusion, there is good reason to believe that Africans and Semites with all three cephalic indices, the dolichocephalic, mesocephalic and brachycephalic, formed sizable components of the various invader groups which migrated to the British Isles in the Neolithic, Bronze and Iron Ages. How many of these invaders would have had dark skin is, of course, difficult to say based on many of the crania that have been exhumed, but it is likely that many were dark, just as many would have been light to medium-hued. In all fairness, Rodd is on the verge of reaching that conclusion in "The Origin of the Tuareg" when he broods over the racial composition of the Tuareg then and now. For he admits that a Negroid substratum existed in North Africa prior to the rise of the Libyans, and he draws upon classical sources which indicate that this substratum could be found much further to the north than the current Negroid populations (Rodd 1926, 44).

That lead, along with Sergi's suggestion [muddled as it is] that the Tuareg were not as they appeared, however, is not followed up by Rodd and anthropologists of similar persuasion. As a result, a clear picture of the racial dynamics operative along the western periphery of the British Isles in Neolithic, Bronze and Iron Age times also gets muddled, to say the least. An observation by Reynolds, cited by van Sertima, regarding the so-called "brown Mediterranean" of Sergi may help to reduce the confusion. Denying the proposition that his so-called brown Mediterranean type reveals a "perceived lack of 'Negroid' attributes," she proposes that the early Mediterraneans who first farmed in Europe and in the Middle East were descendants of Mechta-man, a Nilotic hunter who lived during the Upper Paleolithic period. In turn, she argues, these early Mediterraneans were also the early ancestors of persons maintaining traditions associated with the Khartoum, Saharan and Sudanese areas from the ninth to the fourth millennium B.C.E. (van Sertima 1989, 5).

So the old cranks may have been right after all. Their hunches, gleaned from a rapacious study of folklore, etymology and a sound diet of the classics, led to their often unequivocal conclusion that Africans and Semites once roamed the British Isles. These conclusions, as bizarre as they still may seem to many, are corroborated by the disciplines of blood analysis, linguistics and craniology. And although the more systematic, quantitative approaches used by science cannot always allow researchers to project the racial composition of whole populations from samples when dealing with the remote past, the studies of the blood specialists and the craniologists are still quite compelling and thorough enough to warrant some degree of external validity to earlier observations from diffusion camps, then and now.

Having established that Africans, Semites and their descendants comprised a portion of the prehistoric population of the ancient British Isles, this study now moves from pre-historic to historic times to assess the African and Near Eastern influences on pre-Christian and Christian Irish religion. This study maintains that the essence of Irish religious and kingship rituals were carried to the region by yet another wave of African and Near Eastern colonists.

Notes

1. Lewis Spence (1974, 74) quotes Elliot Smith's observation: "So striking is the family likeness between the early Neolithic peoples of the British Isles and the Mediterranean and the bulk of the population, both ancient and modern, of Egypt and East Africa, that a description of the bones of an early Briton of that remote epoch might apply in all essential details to an inhabitant of Somaliland."
2. In *The Golden Trade of the Moors*, E. M. Bovill (1958, 49) tells a different story

regarding the pre-Islamic ethnicities of North Africans: "Before the Arab invasions of the seventh and eleventh centuries the interior of northern Africa was peopled by two distinct types of man, Negroid and non-Negroid. The later, who were the northern Hamites, were called Libyans by the Romans and, subsequently, Berbers by the Arabs, the last name being derived from the Latin *barbari*. The Negroid peoples, infused with varying degrees of Hamitic blood, also inhabited the Sahara, but south of the desert Negro blood became increasingly predominant as the tropical rain forest of the Guinea coast was approached. These southerly regions beyond the Sahara were known to the Arabs as the Beled es-Sudan, the land of the Blacks. The name Sudan, therefore, originally applied to all the countries south of the Sahara but now connotes only the great corridor of savannah and orchard bush separating the desert from the forests and stretching from the Nile to the Atlantic." Nonetheless, like Rodd, Bovill argues that the Tuareg (sing. Targui), who the Arabs called Muleththemin or 'veiled people', "are a tall, slender, long-faced, fair-skinned people whose children often have fair wavy hair which afterwards turns black.". He goes on (1958, 52) to note that *The Chronicle of Biclarum* indicates that both the Garamantes and the Nubian Maccuritae, who lived near by became Christian converts in the sixth century. He argues further that some Tuareg may also have been converted. This conversion may have resulted during the Roman period when these Africans likely interfaced with religious refugees who fled to the Sahara from North Africa.

3. Bovill (1958, 51-53) further notes that the decorations on many Tuareg shields consisted of the cross let of heraldry rising from sea, which harmonized with the cross-hilted swords and cross-shaped pommels of their camel saddles. He assumes that they came from the Eastern Mediterranean and Southern Arabian regions, and argues that their chief contribution to history was that, through their camel caravans, they allowed the Negroid races south of the Sahara to remain in contact with Mediterranean influences

4. Bovill (1958, 34) deals with the rapprochement that existed between the Romans and the Garamantes in Chapter 3 of *The Golden Trade of the Moors*. Of the ethnicity of the Garamantes, Bovill argues: "Ethnologically the Garamantes are not easy to place, but we may presume them to have been Negroid."

5. Regarding this "Mediterranean Race" Sergei (1901, 39) argues: "But the original stock could not have its cradle in the basin of the Mediterranean, a basin more fitted for the confluence of peoples and for their active development; the cradle whence they dispersed in many directions was more probably in Africa. The study of fauna and flora of the Mediterranean exhibits the same phenomenon and becomes another argument in favor of the African origins of the Mediterranean peoples."

6. Could the darker strain in the Norwegian have stemmed from the early invader groups or from the later Phoenician prospectors? These kinds of questions are often taboo. Nonetheless, they must be asked if the diverse racial make-up of many northern Europeans is to be understood. Shore (1971, 112-13) adds these observations: "There is another odd word used by the Anglo-Saxons to denote black or brown-black-- the word *sweart*. The personal names Suart and Sueart may have been derived from this word, and may have originally denoted people of a dark-brown

or a black complexion. Some names of this kind are mentioned in the Domesday record of Buckinghamshire and Lincolnshire. These may be of Scandinavian origin, for the ekename or nickname Svarti is found in the Northern Sagas. Halfdan the Black was the name of a king of Norway who died in 863. The so-called black men of the Anglo-Saxon period probably included some of the darker Wendish people among them, immigrants or descendants of people of the same race as the ancestors of the Sorbs of Lausatia on the borders of Saxony and Prussia of present day."

Chapter 9

~~~~~~

Heading North to the Isle of Saints and Sages

The most cursory view of Irish history reveals that for centuries Irish Catholics have been regarded as aliens and outcasts by many of their British cousins. The standard explanations for this long-standing feud-- Ireland's dogged Catholic creed, its attempt to preserve the Gaelic tongue, and the 'odd' temperament of its people, betray deeper divisions that are, nonetheless, determined by religion and ethnicity. Much of the British rancor against the Irish can be explained by examining the early Irish Insular Church which was linked to pre-existent druidic rituals by more than a slender thread. For during the early centuries of the first millennium, the evolution of Irish religion from Druidism to Catholicism was a radically different process than England's religious engendering which occurred when England fell under the yoke of the Roman legions, and eventually under the aegis of the Church of Rome. Largely unfettered by Roman influence, early Irish Christians went their own way, a fact which caused the English to regard their creed as an embarrassing anomaly. Linked to Jerusalem, Byzantium, Egypt, Ethiopia, North Africa, Provence and Spain by the North Atlantic seaway, Irish ports such as Cork, Dublin, Galway and Limerick were bastions of the imported, heretical theology of the early Christian Church. These heresies included Pelagianism, Arianism and Gnosticism, theological counter-currents that were refined in the desert monasteries of Coptic Egypt, Carthage and Utica, and which were quickly exported north (Aberg 1943, 6). Many of these largely North African paradigms would be deemed heretical as Rome consolidated its power and spread the Pauline version of Christianity throughout the European countries into which its hegemony extended.

E. G. Bowen provides insight into the transmission of both the intellectual and material freight which moved back and forth along the Atlantic seaway beginning with the eclipse of Roman rule in Britain. He notes that Britain's lowland zone entered a chaotic period which opened the door to the invading Anglo-Saxons. The collapse of Roman hegemony in Europe reactivated the western sea routes, and during the Middle Ages, which might better be named the Age of Saints, Europe's entire western littoral was united under the tenets of Celtic Christianity (Bowen 1972, 71). Bowen notes that it was along these sea routes that pre-Patrician Christianity was likely carried to Gaul, Ireland and Scotland by the Desert Fathers of Egypt and the hermits of Cyrenaica prior to the end of the fourth century c.e. (1972, 71). Bowen goes on to propose that when the barbarian invasions commenced, numerous Gallo-Roman Christians traveled the western sea routes to the north. Citing an anonymous author, Bowen reveals that in the fifth century a group of refugees, armed with classical learning from Bordeaux and nearby towns, sailed to Southern Ireland (1972, 71-72). For Bowen "a great Celtic thalassocracy reaching from Iceland to Spain" began to develop as a result of the extensive activity along the Atlantic seaway (1972, 91). Rogers notes that members of that thalassocracy included African clerics, citing one North African cleric, St. Dimian the black, who prior to his death in Ulster in 658 c.e. performed numerous clerical duties in seventh century Ireland (1952, 71).[1] And there were others, as will noted shortly.

In *Visigothic Spain, Byzantium and the Irish*, J. N. Hillgarth appears to confirm Bowen's observations. He cites pottery shards of Eastern Mediterranean origin, dating to the fifth and sixth centuries c.e., that were discovered in Cornwall. He then proposes that since no such shards have been found along the land route from Marseilles to Bordeaux, the sea route was likely taken by these travelers (1985, 178). He goes on to observe that ships from the Mediterranean were routinely entering Irish ports in the seventh century c.e. He bases this observation on the testimonies of the contemporary Greek life of St. John the Almoner of Alexandria who died in 616, on the harrowing experiences of Arculf who was shipwrecked in Britain in the 680s, and on the Egyptian glass specimens cited by D. B. Harden (1956) that have been found in various English and Scottish sites (Hillgarth 1985, 176ff).[2] Hillgarth presents more evidence for a movement of North African and Spanish Christian monks to Ireland in the seventh century by citing the existence of an Irish copy of Donatus' grammatical teachings, and Irish copies of *Etymologies*, Book I, and the *Synonyma* by Isidore, Bishop of Seville, a prolific Visigothic writer (1985, 15-16). Hillgarth goes on to note that Isidore exerted a profound influence on Irish monastic writers. For proof, Hillgarth cites ten other treatises penned by Isidore that were alluded to by the Irish in the seventh century, including the *De natura rerum*, *Differentiae*, *Chronica* and *De officiis* (1985, 8). Hillgarth also mentions C. H. Beeson's *Isidor-Studien* which provides a very exact description of the Irish role in the transmission of Isidore's works. In fact, Beeson identifies thirty-nine manuscripts of Isidore's which were either corrected or copied by Insular scribes during the seventh century (1985, 449 and fn. 6).

Hillgarth   paints a vivid picture of the traffic, and the resulting diffusion of Egyptian monasticism, which flooded Spain and Ireland during the seventh century:

> From Carthage ships coming from Alexandria or Constantinople could gain the South of Spain, sail up the Guadalquivir to Seville or up the Guadiana to Merida or continue round into the Atlantic to reach Braga and the North. These ships brought with them travelers and artists from the East, with, in their luggage, books, Greek authors-- mostly, though not always, in Latin translations; Eastern silks and jewels such as adorn the treasures of Visigothic kings. In Spanish art of the sixth and seventh centuries historians now decry the successive waves of Eastern influence, coming either directly from Constantinople, Syria or Egypt. Over Spanish monasticism Egypt exercised the same predominant influence as over the religious life of Ireland. (1985, 445, fns. 1-4)

The anti-realist style of Spanish and Irish illuminated manuscripts also appears to have resulted from the Egyptian Coptic and Byzantine influence in both European centers, an influence which Hillgarth traces indirectly to Spain and not so extensively to France or Italy as Nils Aberg, mentioned below, argues (1985, 442-43).   Hillgarth cites land routes as well which linked Brittany and Ireland, branching out to St. Gall and Bobbio; and a Spanish route to Britonia, a Celtic See in North Galicia. These routes spread Eastern influences via an inland itinerary from Braga in the late sixth century, he proposes (Hillgarth 1985, 179).

According to Aziz S. Atiya, a student of the Coptic Church, it was not only missionary zeal that goaded various Copts to set sail for the British Isles. For they were also escaping the persecutions of their orders, a rancor that began in the early centuries of the first millennium. The rancor resulted largely from theological controversies which broke out between Arius and Athanasius at the time of the Edict of Milan in 312 c.e. The dispute centered around two contradictory assertions, namely that of Arius who adhered to the doctrine of "Homoiousion," the belief that although Christ was divine he was not as divine as God but only of 'like' essence to God; and that of Athanasius, who subscribed to the doctrine of "Homoousion," the belief that both God and Christ were of the same essence. These and other heresies such as Nestorianism, centering around the divinity or non-divinity of Christ, raged during the Council of Nicaea [325 c.e.] and during both Ephesus I [431 c.e.] and Ephesus II [449 c.e.]. The upshot of these councils was to set up a rivalry between the bishoprics of Constantinople and Alexandria. Atiya explains the impasse:

> Feeling was running high in Rome and in Constantinople, and the change of Emperors brought about changes in imperial policies. Theodosius II was succeeded by Marcian and his wife Puylcheria, a former nun, who deplored the Alexandrian supremacy in ecclesiastical matters. The two capitals were drawn nearer by the high-handed actions of Dioscorus, and Coptic patriarchs were described as the 'Pharaohs of the Church,' which was unpalatable to the authority of Byzantium. Thus Marcian summoned Dioscorus to answer for his actions at Ephesus II and to discuss his views of Christology at Chacedon in 451 c.e. The Romans quickly mustered a massive army of bishops from the West to join the East European prelates at Chacedon in Asia Minor, while Dioscorus was detained by the imperial guard under a kind of house arrest, and the Council summarily condemned and exiled him to the island of Gangra in Paphlagonia near the eastern shores of the Black Sea, where he died a few years later. (1996, 4-5)

As a result of the power struggle, the Byzantines assumed much of the influence once exercised by the Copts, inheriting the so-called legitimate line of succession, while the Copts experienced excruciating persecutions which lasted until the Arab conquest.

Graves notes C. S. Boswell's observations in Boswell's edition of the tenth-century Irish "The Vision of St. Adomnan" in which he cites the Egypto-Syrian-Irish connection, indicating that the important monastery of Lerins, reputedly where St. Patrick studied, was founded and operated by the Egyptian Church for several centuries. Other monasteries at Marseilles, Lyons and a number in Southern Gaul were also in constant communication with their brethren in Egypt and Syria. Because of Ireland's close contacts with these Gaulish monasteries, a relationship which lasted until the end of the eighth century, Oriental ideas were liberally imported to Ireland (Graves 1966, 147). Furthermore, Boswell reveals, the system of anchoretic and coenobitic life in Ireland derived from monastic communities in Egypt and Syria, and even the beehive cells found at Irish monasteries were copied from Syrian counterparts (Graves 1966, 147).

One likely cause of late seventh century and early eighth century land and sea-based migrations of Coptic monks to Ireland via Spain and Italy could have been the fall of Egypt, North Africa and eventually parts of Spain to the forces of Islam. Hillgarth tends to confirm this hypothesis in regard to a Spanish exodus. Citing Lowe's *Codices Latini Antiquiores*, he notes the vast number of manuscripts, housed now at sites such as Verona, Vercelli and Lucca, that were carried out of Spain by refugees escaping to Italy after the Arab invasion (Hillgarth 1985, 179-80).

Returning to the early years of the seventh century, Hillgarth notes C. W. Jones' observation that African tracts establishing the date of Easter passed from Spain to Ireland in the 630s (1985, 194; Jones 1943, 75ff., 97, 105, 122ff.). Hillgarth also cites the importance of Galicia in Northern Spain [also noted in *Lebor Gabala* as the last stopover of the Milesians] as a port of departure of Spanish manuscripts and tracts to Irish monasteries. Noting that Galicia remained independent in the seventh century, Hillgarth argues: "Perhaps we shall end by believing that after all the *Lebor Gabala* was not without some foundation in ascribing a Spanish origin to the Goidels and to Mil-- Miles Hispaniae" (1985, 194).

Atiya provides more evidence for the essentially African and Near Eastern-based substructure of Irish monasticism. He reveals that a fourth century Coptic monk named Pachomius was largely responsible for developing the blueprint which prescribed the rigid daily routine of monks in a tract entitled *Paradise of the Fathers*, which was distributed throughout the Mediterranean world. As a result, Atiya proposes, monks from Greece, Rome, Capadocia, Nubia and Ethiopia came to live with the desert fathers, and Pachomius set up a ward system for each national group inhabiting the monasteries under his purview (1996, 6). Although Atiya argues that the original Copts were neither Semitic nor Hamitic, he indicates that many of their converts were of both ethnic derivations (1996, 1). As a result of Pachomius' efforts, the monastic system, which began in Pachomian sites such as the Thebaid and the convents of Kellia, Scetis, and Nitrea in the western desert of Egypt, spread throughout North Africa and Europe. Although later discarded by the Benedictines who sought to derive their sustenance from the labor of the area farmers, the self-sufficient Pachomian system was revived again in the tenth century by the Cluniac reform (Atiya 1996, 7). But several centuries before that reform, Coptic missionaries appear to have penetrated the British Isles, according to Atiya, who argues that Christianity was introduced into Britain much earlier than the 597 date which marked the arrival of St. Augustine of Canterbury (1996, 10). He quotes Stanley Lane-Poole:

We do not know how much we in the British Isles owe to these remote hermits. It is more than probable that we are indebted for the first preaching of the Gospel in England, where, till the coming of Augustine, the Egyptian monastic rule prevailed. But more important is the belief that Irish Christianity, the great civilizing force of the early Middle Ages among the northern nations, was the child of the Egyptian Church. Seven Egyptian monks are buried at Desert Uldith, and there is much in the ceremonies and architecture of Ireland in the earliest time that reminds one of still earlier Christian remains in Egypt. Everyone knows that the handicraft of the Irish monks in the ninth and tenth centuries far excelled anything that could be found elsewhere in Europe; and if the Byzantine-looking decoration of their splendid gold and silver work, and their unrivaled illuminations, can be traced to the influence of Egyptian missionaries, we have more to thank the Copt for than had been imagined. (Atiya, 1996, 10)[3]

Quinn also reasons that the theological ties between Ireland and North African Berbers and Copts antedated the arrival of the Moors in Egypt, North Africa and Spain. For centuries before the Moorish hegemony in Southern Spain, the writings of the Algerians St. Augustine and Tertullian, two North Africans who believed that mankind should acknowledge "no border but the universe" and "no country but the world," may have been absorbed by many an early Irish scholar during the nascent years of the Irish church (1986, 76). Quinn further proposes that several Berber leaders such as Massinissa, Jugurtha and Juba allied themselves with the invaders while retaining intellectual independence in North Africa. For example, when paganism was rampant in Rome, Christianity and Judaism were practiced by the Berbers; and when the Pauline strain of Christianity swept over Rome, the Berbers accepted the Arian heresy. Later, when conquered by the Byzantines, the Berbers embraced Islam, but liberalized its theology to drive out the more oppressive doctrines. Finally, when decadence set in among their Muslim rulers, the Berbers rebelled and set up "a puritan regime" (Quinn, 1986, 76).

For Quinn, this maverick Berber spirit, combined with non-conformist Coptic ideas, must have added more peat to Irish intellectual fires. Quinn also cites the seven Egyptian monks who were martyred in Ireland. In the *Martyrology of Tallaght* these monks are said to have been buried in 'Diseart Ulidh,' the Desert of Ulster, in the extinct town of Ballymena in Ulster (1986, 140). Noting that Coptic, Syrian and Carthaginian Christian refugees fled religious persecution from Egypt and North Africa during the formative years of Christian dogma, Quinn argues that some of these refugees relocated from the middle eastern deserts to equally bleak Irish seascapes beyond the pale of the ecclesiastical control of Rome. In these new surroundings, Quinn argues, the practices of this transplanted faith in Ireland were all but identical to those of the solitary desert anchorites to the south (1986, 142). He also recalls that the first mention of the existence of the practice of Christianity on these isles came in the third century c.e. from Tertullian and Origen, who were both North Africans (1986, 141).

Quinn's discussion begs the question of the identity of the Tuareg, the North African amalgamation of Berber tribes discussed earlier in this study. Reynolds reveals that certain dark-skinned, Tuareg Berbers embraced Christianity when it was first implanted in East Africa. The Blemmyes, a group she links to the Tuareg, had been Jacobite Christians from the period the Copts introduced Christianity into Nubia, and the early Makhorritae or Makhorra of the Makkhorian kingdom migrated to Algeria and converted to Christianity in the 6th century (1993, 134). A migration of Blemmyes from Algeria to Ireland should not be ruled out given the persecution and instability of North Africa during this period.   The Nubian Blemmyes wielded considerable power, according to documents cited by Reynolds dating from the third and fourth centuries, but they were often at odds with Berber indigenes in Libya's Fezzan region (1993, 134).

Evidence that North African Christians flocked to the Isle of Saints and Sages during the spread of early Roman Christianity can also be located in various design motifs of Irish illuminated manuscripts such as the *Book of Kells*, according to Quinn. Coptic stylistic motifs including the naturalistic depictions of Isis and Horus [transformed into Mary and Jesus]; the Pharaonic symbol of the ankh, the prototype of the Coptic Cross; and the portrayal of human bodies with animal heads-- motifs that early Irish scribes appear to have copied from Egyptian tomb drawings and which informed the style of a stone cross in Monasterboice, Ireland-- reveal to Quinn that Coptic monks must have fled to Ireland in large numbers in order to escape the persecutions of the Orthodox Church which had denounced them for at least two hundred years prior to the Islamic conquest of Egypt (1986, 139, 154ff.).[4]

For Quinn, such a migration of rogue priests in the early Christian era explains the existence of several archeological anomalies in Ireland-- Alexandrian pottery shards found in Garranes, county Cork, hordes of Baghdad-minted coins, along with a cache of fourth century Egyptian pearls found in a grave in Plouhinec, Brittany, and the notoriety only in Ireland of the *Book of Adam and Eve* [the *Saltair na Rann*] that was composed in fifth-century Egypt (1986, 146-47). Then too, Quinn reveals that the Arabic for Jesus was *Issa*, while in Gaelic it was *Iosa*, both omitting the 'J'; and that the word shamrock seems to derive from the Arabic *shamrukh* which denotes any trefoil plant (1986, 27, 137).

And what should be made of the stylistic parallels David James cites in *Celtic and Islamic Art* between the *Book of Kells*, the *Book of Durrow* and an illuminated Koran reproduced in Baghdad during the tenth century? On selected pages of each document, James notes identical geometric designs which include the interlace and tree of life motifs. Intrigued by these parallels, Quinn cites James' conclusion that Christian Ireland and Islam "expressed spiritual and metaphysical ideas by means of an art that which was either wholly non-representational, abstract, or in which the human element was subordinated to anti-naturalistic concepts" (Quinn 1986, 31).

In concluding his discussion on the migrations from North Africa to the remote islands of Ireland and its periphery, Quinn reasons that itinerants fleeing the persecutions of the Arians, the Donatists, Montanists, Manicheans, Nestorians and Pelagians in North Africa must have regarded Ireland as a safe haven rather than as a place of exile (1986, 151).

C. Knight and R. Lomas note in *The Hiram Key* that St. Patrick subscribed to the Arian heresy which asserted that Christ was not immortal, and that the Virgin birth was bogus (1996, 258). They further note that like the theological stance of Christ's brother James, the Celtic Church denied the Virgin birth, the divinity of Christ, the prominence of the New Testament over the Old Testament, and the inevitability of Original Sin (1996, 259). More Jewish-based than Christian, the Celtic Church maintained the druidic tonsure [shaving the front of the head], and the Easter date honored there derived from the Jewish Calendar (Knight and Lomas 1996, 259).

In short, because of its access to the western seaway, Ireland went its own way in the early centuries of the first millennium, despite St. Patrick's symbolic act of driving the druidic serpent religion from the resistant pockets of pagan belief. Insular Christianity became somewhat Africanized and Jewish-based as it developed a belief system that endured for centuries in a time warp that was not unlike the suspension of time experienced by the Ethiopian and Egyptian Coptic Churches. For both of these African Churches were effectively sealed off from Rome first by geography and later by the Islamic sweep across Arabia, Egypt and North Africa beginning in the late seventh century.

Art historian Nils Aberg proposes that the flowering of seventh-century, Insular manuscript art was largely made possible both in Irish monasteries and in Scottish monasteries controlled by Irish monks, not by the importation of the Merovingian style from Germany, nor by the reworking of the La Tene style from Britain and the Continent, both of which are only rarely noticeable. Instead, the illuminated manuscript style was overtly Coptic and originated in various monastic centers in Egypt and in Carthage and Utica. To prove his hypothesis, Aberg identifies several Coptic stylistic motifs and their appearance in Insular manuscripts such as the *Book of Durrow* and the *Book of Lindnisfarne*. These motifs include the following: the use of dot-contoured initials and interlace with breaks; the doubling of animals such as doves, hippos, and elephants; the use of flatnosed animal designs; and other ornamental animal motifs such as the nose roll-up, and the roll up of jaws into spirals (1943, 31ff.).

In the *Book of Durrow* and the *Book of Lindnisfarne* and in the Irish and Pictish stone crosses such as the Fahan Mura example and others found as far south as Kent, England, the Coptic illuminated manuscript and grave stone carving style is dominant, according to Aberg (1943, 37ff., 41, 70, 93). Regarding Fahan Mura cross in Donegal, Hillgarth notes that its seventh century Greek inscription represents a doxology that dates to the Fourth Council of Toledo held in 634 (1985, 455, fn. 4). Based upon this evidence of Spanish contact, Hillgarth concludes:

> The presence in this remote cemetery in the extreme North of Ireland of a Spanish formula only promulgated half a century before is striking visual evidence of the influence of seventh century Spain on Ireland and it is none the less significant in that the cross should be covered by decoration of markedly Eastern origin. (1985, 455)

Based upon Aberg's thorough survey of these numerous Coptic stylistic motifs and their overwhelming presence in Insular art, direct and extensive communication between Ireland and its Dal Riada colony in Scotland with monasteries in Carthage, Utica, Egypt and Ethiopia is a certainty.

The Egyptian and Ethiopian monasteries mirror the Irish Church in another way as well for, like the druidic priesthood of their Irish sibling, the African desert and Ethiopian highland doctors were converted to Christianity at the same time, in the fourth century. Direct communication between the African monasteries and the converted Irish Druid colleges would have been made possible not only by the land route to Sarras [today's Marseilles, which was also a major sea terminus in the Phoenician tin trade with Cornwall], but also by the considerable traffic noted earlier along the Atlantic seaway during the era of Saints and Sages. Because of these two routes, one overland and one by sea, Irish monks had access to Egyptian Coptic monasteries such as Bawit, where many of these design motifs were created (Aberg 1943, 34ff.). The traffic of monks to and from Ireland, then, must have been extensive for such an elaborate style to be transmitted. Corroborating Quinn, P. W. Joyce in *A Social History of Ancient Ireland* also reveals that at least three Irish monks lived in Carthage for a time, and one produced a manuscript in 655 (1903, 345, 466). Coptic influence was also felt in Kent, England, where a number of Coptic ceramic vessels mixed with Byzantine bronzes have been unearthed (Aberg 1943, 45).

In his examination of the North African and Moorish influence on medieval Ireland, Quinn offers a plausible explanation for why Ireland flourished intellectually during that era while Europe, with the exception of Moorish Spain and Southern France, languished. Between the seventh and tenth centuries and again between the twelfth and fourteenth centuries, Quinn notes, Muslim Spain became the intellectual center of Northern Europe. Clearly, without the translations and refinements of Egyptian, Greek and Roman literary classics and scientific works that were being reproduced in the Muslim world during these eras, there might never have been a Renaissance in Europe. Quinn indicates that between the seventh and the tenth centuries the only two countries which experienced a golden age in learning were Muslim Spain, and, oddly enough, Ireland. That observation raises several questions which Quinn attempts to answer: How could such an isolated island on the periphery of Europe reach such heights when, logically speaking, quite the opposite should have happened? How could there have been such an explosion of leaning in the classical languages, geometry, mathematics, astronomy and the like at monasteries such as those located at Bangor, Lismore, Clonfert and Armagh? Why were scholars from throughout Europe braving the seas, drawn to Ireland as if by a magnet? Could it have been the native genius of the Celts? If so, from where did they procure the classics? From Byzantium, perhaps? But how, given that the Arabs controlled the Straits of Gibraltar? Could the Vikings have transported the classics from the Black Sea along the Dneiper River to the Baltic and points west? Would that be feasible, given that the Vikings seemed more interested in shipping booty?

The only logical place from which this material could have come would have been Muslim Spain, Quinn proposes, from Baghdad to Cordoba, Toledo and Seville and on up the Atlantic seaway. And other ideas, he surmises, such as the religious heresies, could have been imported from North Africa and Spain as well, given that Spain, especially, was on the Islamic periphery, a geographical fact that enabled less orthodox ideas to flourish there. Quinn argues further that in the thirteenth century it is indeed an irony that European Christendom was embroiled in a theological debate between the followers of two Muslim philosophers, Averrose and Avicenna. Unknown to many in the West, these names were, in fact, Latin translations of the Islamic philosophers Ibn Rushd and Ibn Sina (Quinn 1986, 113).

Quinn continues to question the historical status quo which too often denies Islamic connections with Ireland. Could Irish scholars have traveled to Moorish Spain and returned with outlawed doctrines that challenged Rome's dogma of Original Sin, or that argued that even pagans could gain salvation if they lived by right reason, or that promoted the idea that men could pray directly to God without the intervention of priests? Given that these heresies and others were rampant both in North Africa and in Moorish and Berber Spain, could there have been a mutual exchange of scholars between North Africa, Spain and Ireland? And why did the Celtic Church celebrate Easter on the very date it was celebrated at Alexandria? And why did Irish priests develop their own form of tonsure? he asks.

Contemplating these questions, Quinn concludes that the clerical free spirits of Ireland who chaffed against the grain of orthodox Christianity received much of their anti-doctrinal *elan* from the intellectual ferment of Moorish Spain and North Africa right up to the twelfth century when the Anglo-Normans, wielding their Papal authority, finally established hegemony (1986, 115ff.).

Noting also that the European word *troubadour* derives from an Arabic phrase *tarab dour* or 'House of Delight,' Quinn reveals that in Conamera, Ireland a humorous, improvised duet between two singers is called Luibini, whereas in Brittany it is known as Kan ha Diskan. This musical form, along with romantic chivalry, originated with the Arabs, who unwittingly bequeathed to Europe the equestrian aplomb of desert Bedouins and the Bedouin code of honor (Quinn 1986, 115ff.). Then too, Quinn notes, the pentatonic scale of *sean-nos* singing in Conamera has been compared to Bedouin singing by Irish composer Sean O'Riada, who argues that it probably came to Ireland from North Africa through Spain as did instruments such as the guitar and violin (1986, 16-17). Regarding the *sean-nos* form, Quinn cites an excerpt from an article written by Charles Acton in the *Irish Times*:

> If one has listened for hours in the desert of an evening of Bedouin Arabs singing narrative epics with as many stanzas as a long 'aisling' (vision poem, in Gaelic) and then returned to Ireland and heard a fine *sean-nos* singer using the same melismata and rhythm, one finds the resemblance uncanny. (1986, 19)

That the Moorish scientific Renaissance of the twelfth century made dramatic inroads into the curricula of medieval universities in the British Isles far removed from the western periphery is also not widely known. Referring to the origins of Oxford University, Jose V. Pimienta-Bey explains:

> Like Montpelier [and Chartres] and Bologna in Italy, Oxford did not
> originate as a Cathedral school under the regimented supervision of Vatican-
> sanctioned clerics. Consequently, such European academic institutions were
> able to adopt much Moorish learning without the Church's typically
> debilitating restrictions. (1992, 230)

He goes on to note that one of the earliest Oxford professors was a man
named Adam de Marisco, that is, Adam of the Moors or Adam of Moorish
blood (1992, 230). Clearly, Spain was a major distribution center for North
African, Egyptian and Byzantine intellectual and artistic motifs, a fact that
Aberg, despite his excellent analysis of Coptic influences, largely ignores.
    Leaping back to the sixth century again, it is intriguing to speculate that
Lebor Gabala, and the *Kebra Negast,* the history of the early Ethiopian
Church, both of which were codified concurrently into oral tradition in the
sixth century C.E. and transferred to written text in the thirteenth century, may
have been composed in an attempt to initiate a complete history of the
Ethiopian Coptic Church. The pairing of these documents then would have
resulted in a joint chronicle that included events occurring in the Irish branch
of that Church. This sounds absurd on the surface of it until the text of *Lebor
Gabala* is examined a bit more closely. For, as we shall see, *Lebor Gabala*
clearly states that the earliest Irish colonists departed from the Isle of Meroe
in the fourth millennium B.C.E. Today, the sacred Ethiopian city of Axum,
which did not exist in the fourth millennium, maintains, nonetheless, the
traditions and the ancient historical records of Cush, of which the Isle of
Meroe was a part. It is more than likely that *Lebor Gabala* was written
either by Coptic priests originating from Ethiopia and/or Egypt or by Irish
priests who were indoctrinated into the Coptic traditions by African priests,
or perhaps by both parties working in concert. It may even be true that
Emperor Yekuno Amlak's thirteenth century request that the *Kebra Negast*
be transcribed into print in Ethiopia was echoed in Ireland. If this hypothesis
is correct, relations between the two renegade churches of Christendom, that
of Ethiopia and Ireland, may have been more than casual even then. By
committing both the *Kebra Negast* and *Lebor Gabala* to text, the entire
history of the Ethiopian Coptic Church and its Irish-Pictish branch could
have been assembled, as previously stated.
    And if there is any question that the mysterious Picts, who used the
Ogham style of writing, were not of North African origin, one need only
consult Aberg on the matter. Norma Lee Goodrich in *Guinevere* makes a
weak, albeit meticulous, case that the non-Aryan Picts were Asians who

entered Scotland through Finland (1991-92, 175ff.). More convincingly, however, Aberg traces the origins of their artistic style to the Mediterranean basin (1943, 42-43). He concludes the matter with the following summary statement:

> During the period of the flowering of Irish art, the Irish development was very closely connected with the Pictish, which is evident, not only from the scroll, but also from a number of other motifs common to both areas, and further, from the Ogham writing. The majority of these motifs are not, however, of ancient Celtic origin but come direct from the Mediterranean world. Their domicile is not within the circles round the Roman mission in England, nor have they been passed by any Germanic art. Consequently, either Ireland or the land of the Picts must have been in direct connection with the Mediterranean world, and as such an assumption must be considered out of the question with respect to the distant land of the Picts, isolated by mountains, while on the other hand Irish connections with the Mediterranean are well documented, it would thus appear that the Mediterranean motifs came to the Picts by way of Ireland. (1943, 125-26)[5]

Given the overwhelming evidence of a pervasive Coptic influence on the Insular style of various seventh century Irish, Scottish and even some Kentish art works, the communication between the monks of Egypt and Carthage with Ireland and Britain is indisputable, although it appears to have been most pervasive in Ireland.

And now this study turns to a closer look at some of the more bizarre aspects of this imported Insular Christian religion in Ireland and Pictish Scotland, theological atavisms that so contrasted with the Pauline version rubber-stamped by Rome.

Notes

1. African connections with the Iberian peninsula existed long before Batrikus [his Latinized name] led his idol-worshiping followers across what are today called the Straits of Gibraltar to the site of today's Cadiz. He hoped to escape a catastrophic African drought, according to a manuscript located by Ivan van Sertima by Ibn-l-Khattib Al-Makkary entitled *History of the Mohammedan Dynasties in Spain*, and another entitled *Libro de las Grandezas de Espana*, published in Seville in 1549. These colonists, however, did not venture very far from the Seville area, for tradition has it that they were slaughtered 157 years after their arrival in Iberia by barbarians from the boot of Italy. Van Sertima (1985, 134), notes that the first manuscript also indicates "that Spain was in continuous contact, through trade, with Egypt all during the time of the Libyan kings, the Shishonqs to the Osorkons, a dynasty that was eventually overthrown by the Nubians." Nearly four-hundred years later during the twenty-fifth Egyptian Dynasty, Taharka [also called Taharco, Tarraco], a young,

black Ethiopian general who would later depose his uncle Shabataka and become Pharaoh of Egypt, invaded Southern Spain, and, according to van Sertima, left cartouches of contemporary Upper Egyptian and Libyan kings including Shisnonq throughout much of Southern Spain. Evidence for another migration is cited by Reynolds (1993, 110-11) who refers to accounts by the 6th century c.e. Latin poet Corippus and Byzantine historian Procopius. Corippus reveals that the Ethiopian Lagwathes included a blood-thirsty tribe called variously the Ausuriani, the Astures and the Astacures. The Mazikes, he notes, were a sub-grouping of the Luwata. Reynolds goes on to cite Procopius who reveals that the Luwata were related to the Maurusioi of Tripoli, Tunis, Byzacium and Numidia. Procopius further indicates that over one thousand years earlier, these groups migrated into the Iberian peninsula.

2. Also see D. B. Harden (1956) "Glass Vessels in Britain and Ireland, a.d. 400-1000," and C. A. Ralegh Radford, "Imported Pottery Found in Tintangel Cornwall," 59ff. Both in Harden (1956).

3. Atiya's statement regarding the racial identity of the Copts should be compared with that of a Muslim commentator, Al-Jahiz, written in 860 c.e. and quoted in Chandler (1995, 271): "The Copts are a race of Blacks. Khalil Ar-Rahman asked for a son from them, so there was born to him a great prophet from them, who was Ishmai'l, the Father of the Arabs. The Prophet Mohammed . . . also asked for a son, and Ibrahim was born to him, and [the angel] Gabriel made it his surname." Chandler goes on to propose that the Ethiopians were the original Arabs in Southern Arabia and that the title "Himyar" identified them. Hence, the term Himyaric language resulted, and that language, Chandler argues, is identical with Abyssinian, an African-based tongue.

4. Bovill (1958, 56) describes the religious ferment of North Africa prior to the arrival of Islam, citing the fourth century rebellion of the Donatists against both the Church and Rome; their alliances with the Circumcelliones, a fanatical sect; Count Boniface's attempts to restore order and his subsequent alliance with the Vandals in a rebellion against Rome; Genseric's invasion of Africa from Spain of 428 and the turmoil that ensued when the Donatists allied themselves with the invaders because of a mutual hatred of the Roman church; Genseric's conquest of Carthage, and his alliance with Attila; the subsequent flight of the Christians into the desert; the death of Genseric in 477 and the additional instability that caused many desert refugees to migrate to Spain and even further north; and the numerous Berber rebellions of the sixth century.

5. For a similar view on the origins of Ogham writing, see Bowen (1972, 72-74).

Chapter 10

~~~~~~

Merlin's Secret

In two obscure titles, *The Snake in the Grove* and *Irish Wizards in the Woods of Ethiopia* , W. P. Boswell advances several daring hypotheses that will be examined and employed to develop this study's contention that the religions worshiped during the Bronze and Iron Ages in the Mediterranean and Red Sea basins and in druidic Ireland were based upon the cyclical reappearance of menacing comet fragments. In *The Snake in the Grove*, Boswell argues that in pre-Patrician Ireland religious rituals to determine the succession of kings involved periodic and deadly conflicts between aging priest-kings and their younger supplanters, or tanists. These struggles were based upon matrifocal kinship rules derived from royal incest, and the resultant battle royal was designed not only to satisfy the queen's desire to co-rule with a virile consort, but also to magically control the rogue comets aloft. This Irish conflict, Boswell proposes, can be traced back to similar battles royal that originated in Ethiopian sacred groves during Egypt's early dynastic period. For millennia, in the highlands of Ethiopia each new set of snake priests engaged in a struggle for hegemony in accordance with the same matrifocal system.

For Boswell, these Ethiopian battles royal, much like their later Irish counterparts, were waged in commemoration of a strange conflict recorded in the First Dynasty of Egypt involving three principal deities of the twin sea basins. In Egypt these deities became known as Isis, Osiris, her brother and consort, and Set, also her brother. In that conflict, which occurred in several stages, Osiris was gradually driven from the heavens by his brother Set. Eventually Osiris became the judge of the dead in the land of Amenta, the Egyptian Otherworld.

In *Irish Wizards in the Woods of Ethiopia*, Boswell refines her earlier observations, and based on a series of field trips to the Abyssinian sacred city of Axum, she further proposes that the ancient names of Ethiopia's sacred incense trees, the frankincense, the myrrh, the baobab, the fig, the ebony and others, contain word roots also found not only in the pre-Christian clan names of the Irish druidic priesthood, but also embedded in the sacred titles of Ireland's kings and queens. And if this were not enough, she argues that the rituals of Ethiopian kingship were eventually transplanted into Upper Egypt in the second millennium B.C.E., where they heavily influenced Pharaonic succession. From there, she proposes, the modified Abyssinian ritual eventually filtered into the entire Mediterranean basin at Egyptian and Phoenician-founded coastal shrines in Greece, Italy and North Africa before finally being imported to Celtic Ireland. Influencing not only the Druids, this paradigm of kingship also aided in creating the peculiar brand of Christianity practiced in pre-Patrician Ireland. In fact, she argues, the lingering Ethiopian mythic debris was the main reason why St. Patrick was credited with driving the snakes [literally druidic snake priests] out of Ireland.

The next two chapters will examine Boswell's evidence. In the process this study will add another missing piece to the puzzle of that bizarre system of kingship by exploring the etiology of the conflicting dragon pair in Ireland. It will be suggested that this dyad was also derived from the celestial battle of Osiris and Set, a conflict which was, as it were, a cometary, euhemeristic combat myth. To accomplish this task, the unsettling hypotheses of two modern astrophysicists need to be examined.

Clube and Napier present disturbing evidence from our ancient past. For they argue that beginning in the Egyptian predynastic era the gods of the Eastern Mediterranean and Red Sea basins and their violent, celestial activities were modeled directly upon the appearance of and devastation wrought by a disintegrating, earth-grazing comet. In *The Cosmic Winter*, they propose:

> One of the most remarkable and widespread beliefs held in early civilizations was that of a god in the sky. Even in the Nile Valley, where the sun was eventually a principal object of worship, there was an earlier celestial religion, older even than the dynasties of the pharaohs. In the *Pyramid Texts* this early god is shown as the giver of life, of rain, and of 'celestial fire.' Worship of a sky-god has been the dominant religious feature of the Indo-European and Semitic peoples from the earliest times. (1990, 169)

In their earlier work, *The Cosmic Serpent*, Clube and Napier attempt to unravel the mystery of the god in the sky, arguing that many of the myths of the ancient world were based on empirical events centering around the disintegration of a comet or group of comets locked in short period orbits around the Earth. Speaking of the Zeus v. Typhon and Python v. Apollo combat myths of ancient Greece, events that will be referred to often in this study, they propose that such myths likely signify the various stages in the break-up of a super comet (1982, 197). Additionally, they argue, those comet fragments which stayed aloft over the planet were often likened to guardian angels of the Lord or benign saviors, whereas the fragments that crashed into the planet or threatened it were deemed sky dragons or devils (1982, 185). There may have been exceptions to this rule, however, especially if falling meteorites killed one's enemies.

The concept of a protector or guardian angel is a very important one for the purposes of this study. For Hebrew, druidic and early Christian beliefs mirrored the primal Ethiopian/Egyptian sky-battles of the dragon pair Set and Osiris, given that such beliefs were largely derived from the ancient ones. For the Hebrews the dragon pair was dubbed Behemoth and Leviathan, and later, in the second millennium, Yahweh and Satan. For the druids, Heracles and the bull god Tauriscus [also called Gargantua, an avatar of the Egyptian Ptah and the Greek Zeus] were the rivals (1990, 191). And for the Christians, Michael and Lucifer were the contenders as the skies once again rained death in the fifth and sixth centuries c.e. Shared religious beliefs clustered around the pyrotechnics of these dragon pairs: the doctrine of the elect and the damned; the transmigration and/or the resurrection of souls; the deity's descent into purgatory (which recapitulated Osiris' descent into the Underworld in *The Papyrus of Ani*); the messianic visitation of a celestial deity on Earth and that deity's return to a Father in heaven; and the possibility of an apocalypse by fire descending from on high (Clube and Napier 1990, 191).[1]

The Hebrew concept of election, of being a chosen people, first arose, according to Clube and Napier, during the flight from Egypt, when the departing Jews were spared the wrath of Yahweh, who was known as Set in Egypt (1982, 218ff.). In fact, Josephus relates that Moses, or Osarsiph, was a Set-worshiper (Whiston 1981, 607ff.). Velikovsky corroborates that observation and notes that the Exodus story and the Archangel Michael are also closely connected, for it was Michael who served as "a wall of fire" which separated the Egyptians and the Israelites, according to the *Midrash* (1977b, 297).[2] To better determine the identity of Michael's earthly counterpart, who reputedly lived during the time of the Exodus, Velikovsky quotes the *Haggadah*: "Michael was appointed High Priest of the celestial sanctuary at the same time that Aaron was made High Priest of Israel" (1977b, 279). Mistaking Michael for the planet Venus, Velikovsky goes on to reveal more about Michael:

> The celestial struggle at the Sea of Passage is depicted in the familiar image
> of the Archangel Michael slaying the dragon. Michael produces fire by
> touching the earth, and it was the emanation of this archangel that was seen
> in the burning bush. He has his abode in heaven and is the forerunner of
> Shehina or God's presence, but as Lucifer, Michael falls from heaven and his
> hands are bound by God. (1977b, 297)[3]

This equation of Michael and Lucifer would later puzzle certain Church
Fathers of North Africa, as will be discussed shortly. In any case, it was
Michael, according to Exodus 14:10, who separated the Red Sea, a tidal
aberration likely caused for Clube and Napier from a meteoric impact that
allowed the Israelites to escape and led to the drowning of Pharaoh's army.
That experience of election must have been reinvigorated again when,
hundreds of years later, the angel Gabriel intervened in the conflict between
Judah and Ethiopian General Taharka and their Assyrian enemies. The
intervention took the form of a blast from heaven, an *arad gibil*, or an *ignis
e coelo*, that miraculously slew and all but annihilated "a hundred fourscore
and five thousand" Assyrian troops who were encamped near the besieged
city of Jerusalem under the leadership of Sennacherib (Velikovsky 1977b,
38; Kings 19:17; Isaiah 37:7). The *Talmud* reveals that after a deafening
noise from heaven, the Assyrian army was nearly decimated: "Their souls
were burnt, though their garments remained intact" (Velikovsky 1977b, 123,
237).[4] This blast, then, may have been an enormous electrical discharge, not
unlike lightning but far wider and more potent, that emanated from the
friction of an earth grazing comet fragment aloft with the Earth's surface.
Regarding these fortuitous and cometary events, Velikovsky notes that
because of their interventions, Michael and Gabriel were considered to be
guardian angels by the Israelites (1977b, 298).

In any case, it was this concept of election that initially deviated from
other religious theology in the Eastern Mediterranean, and which fashioned
the Hebrews into a distinct entity, according to Clube and Napier (1990,
101). And what accounted for this devotion between Yahweh and his
followers? For Clube and Napier, as for Velikovsky, it resulted when
"cosmic forces were said to have wreaked destruction on their captors.
Henceforth the Jews regarded Yahweh as their particular protector and
themselves as His chosen people" (1990, 101). The retreating Jews were
apparently encamped outside the debris path of an earth-grazing comet
fragment. In Exodus 13:17-18 we learn:

> When Pharaoh had let the people go, God did not let them take the road to
> the land of the Philistines, although that was the nearest way. God thought

that the prospect of fighting would make the people lose heart and turn back to Egypt. Instead, God led the people by the roundabout way to the wilderness to the sea of reeds.

And what form did Yahweh take as he led them? The answer to that question is found in Exodus 13:21-22:

> Yahweh went before them, by day in the form of a pillar of cloud to show them the way, and by night in the form of a pillar of fire to give them light: thus they could continue their march by day and by night. The pillar of cloud never failed to go before the people during the day, nor the pillar of fire during the night.

Of this pillar, Clube and Napier argue: "A truly exceptional comet . . . visible by day, would appear in the pre-dawn sky as a red band of light, its nucleus below the horizon" (1982, 221). Assuming that this celestial body was comet Encke [a short period comet with an approximate earth orbit of 3.3 years] which still exists despite numerous disintegrations, they go on to observe:

> Should the comet lie anywhere near the ecliptic plane as does Encke, then with the anti-solar streaming and the latitude concerned, the tail would appear to rise vertically up; the people would be moving towards the pillar of fire during the night. After sunrise, the white inner tail would dominate and there would be a pillar of cloud. (1982, 221)

The Egyptians were not as lucky as the Hebrews according to the Old Testament description of the *barad*, or the stony 'hail' from heaven known as the eighth plague (Exodus 9:18). According to Exodus 9:24, this "very grievous hail, such has not been seen in Egypt since its foundation" appears to have been a mixture of meteorites, large chunks of ice, complex sun-spawned carbohydrates and ferric dust, for the meteoric debris of a comet can include all of these components. The above selection indicates that a rain of hail may have occurred in Egypt's predynastic period as well. And in *The Wisdom of Solomon*, it is stated that water, cometary ice perhaps, did not quench the hail when the Egyptians were "pursued with strange rains and hails and showers inexorable, and utterly consumed with fire: for most marvelous of all, in the water which quencheth all things the fire wrought yet more mightily" (Velikovsky 1977b, 71; Holmes 1913). In Daniel 1:10 the cause of the eighth plague is referred to as "a river of fire" or a "fiery stream."

And an apparent carbohydrate cluster embedded in the meteor shower, described as "naphtha," was also a deadly component of the *barad*, according to the *Papyrus Ipuwer*: "The Egyptians refused to let the Israelites go, and He poured out naphtha over them [the Egyptians] burning blains [blisters]." This substance fell in "a stream of hot naphtha" (Velikovsky 1977b, 71).⁵

For those who would argue that airborne cinders from the Santorini eruption were the agents here, an examination of time frames of that eruption and the *barad* do not match or even come close, as previously noted. The probable origin of the hail of stones and rain of blood cited in Exodus was a comet variously named Phaeton, Sekhmet, Anat and Typhon, likely ancient names for comet Encke, that either brushed the earth's atmosphere or collided with it during the fifth year of the reign of Pharaoh Merneptah (c. 1232-1222 B.C.E.). As noted in the Introduction, in the texts of Sethos II (c. 1215 B.C.E.) the threatening Sekmet comet is described prior to its descent: "Sekmet was a circling star, which spread out its flame in fire, a flame of fire in her tempest" (Velikovsky 1977b, 174; Breasted 1903, III, 117). Confirmation of the devastation possibly caused by impact also comes from Ras Shamra prior to that city's collapse near the end of the thirteenth century B.C.E.: "The star Anat has fallen from heaven; he slew the people of the Syrian land, and confused the two twilights and the seats of the constellations" (Bellamy 1949, 69; Velikovsky 1977b, 183ff.). And in the Carnac inscription it is written that in that fatal fifth year of Pharaoh Merneptah's reign, "Libya has become a barren desert; the Libyans come to Egypt to seek sustenance for their bodies" (Spanuth 1979, 193; Holscher 1937, 61ff.). And in the Medinet Habu texts, Ramesses III laments: "Libya has become a desert; a terrible torch hurled flame from heaven to destroy their souls and lay waste their land . . . their bones burn and roast within their limbs" (Spanuth 1979, 147). Centuries later, Pliny reflects on the event in his *Natural History*:

> A terrible comet was seen by the people of Ethiopia and Egypt, to which Typhon, the king of that period [of Ethiopia] gave his name; it had a fiery appearance and was twisted like a coil, and it was very grim to behold: it was really not a star so much as what might be called a ball of fire. (1962, 223)

As will be discussed shortly, a variant of the worship of Set, the protector of the Jews and the scourge of the Egyptians, relocated itself in the British Isles. However, in Lower Egypt and finally in Upper Egypt, Horus, the falcon god, who was the son of Isis and Osiris, the adversary of Set, and the prototype of Jesus, became the people's protector. According to Clube and Napier, Horus was "essentially a benevolent figure, he provided security and continuity going back to the very foundation of the new Egyptian state" (1990, 38). But in Ethiopia, Upper Egypt, and in much of the Eastern Mediterranean, for a time at least, Set still reigned, and he would later be called Typhon by the Greeks (Bailey 1994, 146ff.). When the Late Bronze Age ground to its screeching halt, however, Set fell from grace in the Eastern Mediterranean basin.

Bailey cites three great battles between the Peoples of the Sea, who hoped to conquer Egypt and the Egyptians. Although he does not argue that these land battles were spurred on by cometary pyrotechnics, this study proposes that the terrestrial conflicts may have mirrored the celestial conflicts, the land battles being encouraged by the chaos in the skies above. The first, the Titanmachia as the Greeks called it, was fought between the Zeus and Titans (c. 1575 B.C.E.). In its aftermath, the Set or Sutekh-worshiping Hyksos were expelled from Egypt, and their allies, the Chronos-worshiping Titans, were exiled to Tartarus by an angry Zeus (1994, 146ff.). The second battle, the Typhonmachia, was waged between Typhon, and Zeus and Athena about 1219 B.C.E. As a result, the Peoples of the Sea, known then as Peleset or Typhon followers in the Mediterranean, were driven back by the Egyptians and their allies (Bailey 1994, 354). The final battle, which likely ended the Bronze Age, was fought c. 1182 B.C.E. between Ramesses III and the Egyptians' old rivals, the Peoples of the Sea. About forty years earlier, a skirmish between the Peoples of the Sea and Pharaoh Merneptah had nearly broken the invader's back. But their culminating battle with Egyptians and their subsequent defeat by Ramesses III's forces in 1182 B.C.E. terminated their control of the Mediterranean sea routes and the bronze trade once and for all (Bailey 1994, 355). And as they licked their wounds, an economic disaster further weakened the rag-tag remnant, for iron became the metal of choice, and bronze prices crashed (Bailey 1994, 355ff.).

Suddenly, the deity Set was transformed into Lucifer the Devil, and the Semites adopted their prohibition against eating pork, given that the boar was one of Set's totems. But the Irish continued to eat pork with abandon far to the north, for many, in all probability, were descended from transplanted Ethiopian-Greeks, Libyan-Greeks, and Phoenicians, all of whom were likely Set-worshipers who fanned out across the Mediterranean basin and arrived in several invader waves prior to Set's transformation from a god to a devil.

Nonetheless, in Egypt a love-hate relationship developed between the Horus followers and the Set monster even after Set fell from grace in the night sky. Clube and Napier note Plutarch's description of this ambivalence:

as for the dimmed and shattered power of Typhon, though it is at its last gasp and in its final death-throes, the Egyptians still appease and soothe it with certain feasts and offerings. Yet again, every now and then, at certain festivals, they humiliate it dreadfully and treat it most disrespectfully-- even to rolling red-skinned men in the mud and driving an ass over a precipice (as the Koptos folk)-- because Typhon was born with his skin red and ass-like. (1990, 41)

The idea of the savior god resurfaced in Christianity, of course, but it is only in the very cometary Revelation to John, which appears to depict the celestial happenings during the final land battle between the Peoples of the Sea and the Egyptians, that the sky drama is nearly unmasked. For in Revelation 11 and 12, in the midst of a barely disguised meteor shower:

A great sign appeared in heaven: a woman, adorned with the sun, standing on the moon, and with twelve stars on her head for a crown. She was pregnant, and in labor, crying aloud in the pangs of childbirth. Then a second sign occurred in the sky, a huge red dragon which had seven heads and ten horns, and each of the seven heads crowned with a coronet. Its tail dragged a third of the stars from the sky and dropped them to the earth, and the dragon stopped in front of the woman as she was having the child, so that he could eat it as soon as it was born from its mother. The woman brought a male child into the world who was to rule all the nations with an iron scepter, and the child was taken straight up to God and to his throne, while the woman escaped into the desert where God had made a place of safety ready, for her to be looked after in the twelve hundred and sixty days.

And now war broke out in heaven when Michael with his angels attacked the dragon. The dragon fought back with his angels, but they were defeated and driven out of heaven. The great dragon, the primeval serpent, known as the Devil or Satan, who had deceived the whole world, was hurled down to earth and his angels were hurled down with him. (Revelation 11: 15-19)

Noting the frequent mention of the 'dragon pair' in world mythology which includes Osiris and Set in the Egyptian scenario, Clube and Napier cite the pair's permutations in the Africanized coastal areas of Greece:

A detailed study suggests that the duality has its origins in the fragmentation of a primary body which produces a meteor stream and a huge comet, the latter circulating around the former. These elements are treated as male and female respectively. But in due course, the great comet breaks up further: one of its components, Marduk of Babylonian mythology or Zeus of Greek mythology, engages in battle with its principal progenitors and emerges the dominant figure. (1982, 199)

In Egyptian Old Kingdom myth, the etiology of these world-wide dragon pairs is best seen. Clube and Napier note the primal myth of the heavens, recalling that Ptah produced two deities from his mouth, Shu and Tefnet, or Nun and Nunet, or Nut and Geb, depending on the version consulted. They go on to cite the births of Osiris, Isis, Seth and Nephthys from Nut, recalling that Osiris became the chief sky-deity during the Old and Middle Kingdoms. The accounts of Osiris, they go on, parallel accounts of Zeus and Jupiter in Greek and Roman mythological accounts. Hence, Horus, the son of Isis, the wife and sister of Osiris, can be matched with Apollo, they continue, noting that Horus became the dominant sky-god once Osiris entered the Underworld to assume his role as judge of the dead (1982, 180).

For the Egyptians, human ethics and morality were practiced not as ends in themselves, but to preserve the order of the heavens. Clube and Napier explain that the ethical concept of *ma'at* and the rituals called *hike* were utilized by the Egyptians to prevent the sky-deity from raining down on their heads. For twice, they note, Set killed Osiris in aerial battles. After the first slaying, Osiris was miraculously restored to the living by his sister and wife, Isis. But in the final conflict with Set, Osiris fragmented into pieces which rained down on Egypt. When Isis restored the corpse of Osiris, he entered the Underworld. Finally, Horus, the avenger, defeated Seth in another display of celestial pyrotechnics (1982, 180).

By this time Set/Seth was likened to Satan, and his defeat by Horus did not finish him off, but demoted him instead to the prow of Ra's solar barge, where he kept watch for Ra's cometary enemy Apepi. Clube and Napier transpose the Osiris myth into cometary form as follows:

> First of all there is Ptah, perhaps either the planet Jupiter spewing forth comets as a result of a close encounter, or simply a large comet splitting it two; then there is the universal flood followed by a period dominated by the sky-god Nunet; this god either produces or is identical to the god Osiris. The genealogy makes reasonable sense if the events describe successive phases in the life of a huge comet in periodic Earth-crossing orbit, but after further break-up and decay, the main component ceases to be visible and presumably becomes an Apollo asteroid. Although not part of the principal family of gods, Apepi may have been another comet periodically dominating the sky: we can only speculate here but it is not impossible that Halley's comet may have been recognized. (1982, 203)

Critical to this study is the notion, already touched upon, that Set was not always viewed as evil in his role of cosmic dragon or serpent. Depending on the part he played in the periodic sky battles overhead, he was either deemed beneficent or otherwise. Noting Set's opposition to the Apepi monster, which was probably Halley's comet threatening to eclipse the sun god Ra under the shroud of a cosmic winter, Clube and Napier note that in the later versions of the Egyptian myth which saturated the Mediterranean and Red Sea basins, the mysterious Set was the protector of Ra, for Set decimated Apepi. But later, Set was demoted to an evil deity (1982, 203).

Although W. P. Boswell does not examine the alleged cometary aspects of the dragon pair, the ancient battles of which were commemorated at Axum when the sky-drama resurfaced centuries later in Axum's sacred grove, she does reveal that just as the dragon Set/Seth was deified there and throughout the Africanized Mediterranean and Red Sea basins, so was he deified not only by the druidic priests of Ireland, but by the early Irish Church, which understood more about these celestial serpents than has been told. Indeed, even in the early Christian era, Ireland experienced an undercurrent of Lucifer worship, for Lucifer was a distant avatar of Seth himself. But before we can understand the reasons for Lucifer/Set worship in the pre-Christian and early Christian milieus, more foundation stones must be laid.

What Boswell and other students of cultural diffusion have not adequately explained is the true etiology of the cometary god-kings worshiped in the Mediterranean and Red Sea basins, in the druidic British Isles and in the early Irish Church [hereafter called the Insular Church]. Clube and Napier note in *The Cosmic Winter* the various dyads of benevolent and malevolent gods worshiped in these diverse regions. Those relevant to this study are listed below:

Egypt	Osiris and Set; Horus and Set [Seth]
Greece	Zeus and Typhon
Hebrew	Yahweh and Satan
Syria	Baal and Yam
Medieval	Michael and the Devil
Medieval	St. George and the Dragon (1982, 40).

These dyads did not evolve solely through cultural diffusion in the twin basins. Rather the meteor showers and close encounters were apparently regional and even world-wide phenomena, resulting in the mythology of cometary gods not only in the Eastern Hemisphere but in the Americas as well. Clube and Napier argue that the periodic return of these meteor showers and the "intense fear of the sky" that these events fostered, account for many of the so-called patterns of history which include key climate shifts, the various ensuing dark ages, mass migrations, mass exterminations such as the Crusades and other wars in which men imitated the fury of their cometary gods, and gradual shifts in religious paradigms. In *The Cosmic Winter* Clube and Napier correlate some of these patterns of history with periods of increased cometary activity over the planet. They note that peak cometary periods include: c. 3100 B.C.E. [leading, perhaps, to the Mesopotamian Dark Age]; c. 1100 B.C.E. [corresponding with the Mediterranean Dark Age and the collapse of the Bronze Age]; c. 450 C.E. [leading, perhaps, to the European Dark Age and the eclipse of King Arthur's Camelot]; and c. 1100 C.E. [leading, perhaps, to the First Crusade] (1990, 42).

Some interesting parallels emerge if we attempt to correlate this chart with the dates of the various migrations from the Eastern Mediterranean basin to Ireland as alleged in *Lebor Gabala*. The dates are the alternate ones which Boswell cites: 1.) 3400 B.C.E. to 2400 B.C.E.: The journey of Banba and Seth commences from the Isle of Meroe; 2.) 2000 B.C.E.: Partholon's emigres begin their journey from Micil [possibly Sicily or Cilicia, an area due north of Cyprus lying between the Mediterranean and the Taurus Mountains]; 3.) 1921 B.C.E.: Nemed and his queen Macha journey from Scythia. 4.) 1293 B.C.E.: The Firbolg journey to Ireland. The point of departure is Greece; 5.) 1213 B.C.E.: The Tuatha de Danaan under Dagan and Nuadur journey to Ireland. They depart from Greece; and 6.) 1016 B.C.E.: The Milesians, sons of Nel and Scota, journey to Ireland. Their final departure is from Thebes, Greece, long after the Exodus out of Egypt (1972a, 24a-24b).[6]

The dates of these migrations correlate fairly well with the pattern of increased cometary activity over the Eastern Mediterranean basin cited by Clube and Napier. The first migration could have occurred in the wake of the Osiris/Set combat that has been dated at approximately 3100 B.C.E. just prior to the time of the first Egyptian dynasty and the Mesopotamian Dark Age. The 2000 B.C.E. date for the departure of Partholon corresponds to increased cometary activity over the basin and the collapse of the Egyptian Old Kingdom which led to the First Intermediary Period. The Nemedian migration likewise falls in that unsettled period. And the migrations of the Firbolg and the Tuatha De Danaan occur around the time of the Exodus from Egypt, possibly during the period of the Ten Plagues when the not-so enigmatic pillar of fire likely convinced the Jews of their election by God. Since Clube and Napier date the Exodus at roughly 1369 B.C.E., the final migration date for the Milesian dispersal could be in error, for it falls much later than the Exodus date, but much closer to another heightened period of comet activity which culminated in the defeat of the Peoples of the Sea by

Ramesses III in 1182 B.C.E. and in the final crash of Late Bronze Age industry (1982, 224ff.). Given that for Boswell's sources the last migration is associated with the collapse of Akhenaton's rule at approximately 1364 B.C.E., it would appear that a monk added or subtracted incorrectly, and that the Milesian date should be set at that earlier date.

Or there may be another explanation. In *Centuries of Darkness*, Peter James argues that historians have made a "gigantic academic blunder" in their adherence to the Sothic dating system, based on Manetho's calculations, for determining the Pharaonic chronology of the Egyptian New Kingdom. Denying that an extensive Dark Age occurred in all of the Eastern Mediterranean basin after Ramesses III's victory over the People of the Sea [he admits it did occur in the Mycenaean areas] , James argues that the revised date for the collapse of Mycenaean civilization should be adjusted to the mid-tenth century, very close to the 1016 B.C.E. date given by some historians for the Milesian migration to Ireland (1991, 311ff.). What appears to have happened is that *Lebor Gabala* may be correct in associating the Milesians with the Exodus and Akhenaton's decline. But the migration to Ireland probably occurred later, and the colonists were likely members of the Greek Orphic cult. This cult traced its roots back to the priests of Akhenaton, who fled to Greece and adjusted their benign theology to an apocalyptic one (Clube and Napier 1990, 64). But whichever date is used, it appears that *Lebor Gabala's* accounts are not challenged.

For Clube and Napier, the *real presence* of the deity or deities made itself felt during times of heightened cometary activity, but during slack periods, more rational, abstract concepts of the god or gods predominated. They propose that in the third millennium B.C.E. a disintegrating comet was the cause of numerous cataclysms in Mesopotamia and Egypt. In the second millennium B.C.E., they go on, similar comet-inspired destruction occurred in the Minoan and Mycenaean centers. The "dread of the sky" that resulted in the ancient world, they reason, is difficult for modern people to understand (1990, 97).

But as the cometary display and disruption diminished around the time of Socrates, they argue, comets were regarded as somewhat benign (1990, 97). As a result, the frenzied, cometary religions of a Set or a Pan or a Dionysius or an Orpheus must have slowly gone out of fashion, as it were. Mankind entered into a "collective amnesia," forgot its dread of the sky, and replaced the earlier, irrational gods with an abstract, Aristotelian Unmoved Mover, a concept which, to say the least, created a false sense of security. At the same time, the concept of evil, they propose, also underwent a radical change. For during the first millennium B.C.E. it was yanked from the sky and humanized. Hence, they propose, an abstract, invisible, beneficent deity was fashioned, the skies ceased to be perceived as an evil domain, and the concept of evil was transferred to Earth, where it resided in the hearts of the worshipers of the monotheistic religions (1990, 67-68).

In the case of Akhenaton and his ill-fated priesthood, this process must have played itself out in reverse. For Akhenaton's worship of the monotheistic Atum, the beneficent energy fueling the solar disc, and the gentle religion that revolved around that worship, could not have arisen at a worse time. The Ten Plagues that marked the Exodus, the demise of Akhenaton and the dispersal of his priesthood revealed the Pharaoh's fatal underestimation of the havoc that cosmic serpents could wreak over Egypt. As a result, Clube and Napier reveal: "Tutankhamun restored the succession under Amon-Re after the death of Akhenaton and he was said to have 'driven out the disorder from the Two Lands, so that order was again established in its place, as at the creation'" (1990, 61). They go on to note that Akhenaton's priesthood was blamed for the chaos, and the priestly survivors made a bee-line for the Northern Aegean. Later, their benign theology formed the basis of the Orphic doctrine that evolved in Greece (1990, 64).

Interestingly enough, *Lebor Gabala* may again be vindicated, for Orphic doctrines greatly influenced the Druids, especially their belief in a magic egg. This egg, their mythology asserts, was produced by a serpent that was responsible for the creation of the earth as we know it, and the Herculean task of keeping constant tabs on the serpentine spawn of that egg (Clube and Napier 1982, 260). Clube and Napier discuss the Egyptian-Orphic connection, noting that the concepts of the dualism of soul and body, and the soul's immortality found in the Orphic cult were likely carried to Greece by Akhenaton's renegade priesthood (1990, 57).

And did the dispersed priests of Akhenaton learn their lesson when they resurfaced in Greece? Apparently they did because the cometary deity Heracles and the equally cometary Phaeton myth are closely linked with the new Orphic synthesis. Clube and Napier explain that in the Orphic tradition Phaeton is reputed to have fallen from his celestial course and lit the Earth on fire. They note that Homer not only links Phaeton and a particular labor of Heracles, but also associates Phaeton with the strange events leading to the collapse of Mycenae. Then too, they add, Phaeton means 'blazing star' and the title was a possible nickname for Zeus (1990, 57-58). That the Phaeton story is a cometary drama seems quite obvious when the account of the Roman poet Ovid is examined. Phaeton's inability to control the horses of the sun chariot causes pandemonium as Ovid explains in *The Metamorphoses*:

> The earth bursts into flame, the highest parts first, and splits into deep
> cracks, and its moisture is all dried up. The meadows are burned to white
> ashes; the trees are consumed, green leaves and all, and the ripe grain
> furnishes fuel for its own destruction . . . . Great cities perish with their walls,
> and the vast conflagration reduces whole nations to ashes.
>   The woods are ablaze with the mountains . . . . Aetna is blazing boundlessly
> . . . and twin-peaked Parnassus . . . . Nor does its chilling clime save Scythia;
> Caucasus burns . . . and the heaven-piercing Alps and cloud-capped
> Apennines." (Velikovsky 1977b, 154; *Metamorphoses*, Miller trans., bk. II)

Clearly this is not volcanism alone that is being described by Ovid, for the
havoc occurred in both volcanic and non-volcanic mountain chains.

The collapse of the nations of the Eastern Mediterranean, a catastrophe
which occurred in the later centuries of the second millennium B.C.E.
beginning in the time of the Exodus and culminating with Ramesses III's
defeat of the People of Sea, appears to be exactly coincidental with the havoc
wrought by Phaeton. And the Orphic hero Heracles, who was also identified
with the Egyptian Ptah and the Greek father-god Chronos, looms large in the
process. It should be recalled that one of the gods of the Irish Milesians, a
cult that likely began its wanderings from Egypt and Greece shortly after the
fall of Akhenaton, was, according to *Lebor Gabala*, along with *Tat* or Set,
none other than *Erca* or Heracles.

To understand the implications of this linkage and the importation of this
cometary religion of the Eastern Mediterranean to the British Isles, it is
necessary to understand with what celestial beings Heracles and his
'children,' the Heraclids, were associated during the collapse of the Late
Bronze Age. Despite his skepticism about the assertions that a major
cataclysm occurred in the Eastern Mediterranean basin at the close of the
Late Bronze Age, James admits:

> There can be no doubt that in many parts of the Old World there was a
> dramatic collapse of civilization at the end of the Late Bronze Age. The
> centralized economies controlled from the palaces disintegrated, the old
> trading markets broke up, diplomatic contacts were lost, and major
> settlements were abandoned. However, the cause or causes behind these
> momentous changes are unclear. (1991, 311)

James goes on to cite a host of reasons presented by scholars for this more
limited collapse, especially that of Mycenae, an area which figures as a point
of departure for the later migrations to Ireland. These reasons include:
"cultural decadence," "invasions by outside barbarians," "technological
change" associated with shift to more easily obtainable iron, "internal

conflicts" in Egypt, "food shortages," "prolonged drought," earthquakes, catastrophic volcanic eruptions, and the like (James 1991, 311ff.). Clube and Napier offer a more controversial explanation in the form of violence raining down from the heavens from a meteor shower linked with the enigmatic "Heraclids," or sons of Heracles. Discounting the effects of the Thera eruption, which, like Bernal, they date at mid-millennium, they identify the culprit as a comet, as we shall see (1990, 48).

But before the activities of the likely culprit are examined, a better feel for that chaotic period needs to be had. Clube and Napier explain that considerable destruction of forest, vegetation and topsoil occurred in the once heavily-wooded northern Mediterranean littoral. Much of the erosion and deforestation that characterizes this area today, may well have occurred during the Late Bronze Age when the civilization collapsed because of meteor showers, they go on. This catastrophe forced migrations from the area before the eventual resettlement of the area around 1100 B.C.E. by a much reduced human population, they conclude (1990, 48-49).

Interestingly enough, they note that the ancient project of building megarons, underground structures not unlike today's fallout shelters, within Mycenaean palaces was revived for the apparent purpose of defending against the enigmatic invaders called the Heraclids (1990, 51). These are enigmatic because, as Clube and Napier note, history shows no record of any invading land forces that fit such a description, unless, of course, these Heraclids were celestial in nature (1990, 52). Sir James Frazer links them to a Lydian dynasty of kings who regarded a death by fire as their inevitable end (1961, I, 182). Citing Herodotus I, 7, Frazer reveals that "the ancient dynasty of the Heraclids which preceded the house of Croesus on the throne traced their descent from . . . Heracles, and this Lydian Heracles appears to have been identical in name and in substance with the Cilician Heracles, . ." (1961, I, 182). Frazer goes on to observe that the double-headed ax was associated with the Cilician Heracles:

> For the double-headed ax was carried as part of the sacred regalia by Lydian kings from the time of the legendary queen Omphale down to the reign of Candaules, the last of the Heraclid kings. It is said to have been given to Omphale by Heracles himself, and was apparently regarded as a palladium of the Heraclid sovereignty; for after the dotard Candaules ceased to carry the ax itself, and had handed it over to the keeping of a courtier, a rebellion broke out, and the ancient dynasty of the Heraclids came to an end. (1961, I, 182)

Staying with the cometary scheme of things, however, the double-headed ax is an apt symbol for a comet, given that like Venus a comet appears brightest at dusk and dawn. And given that Heracles, during his journey to Libya, was said by the Greeks to have been attacked by none other than Typhon, Heracles appears to be yet another name for a comet and the cometary line of kings at Lydia (1961, I, 111). Clube and Napier may be correct when they propose that the enigmatic Heraclids were phantom plunderers which never actually inhabited the lands they allegedly conquered (1990, 52). A chronicle from the period, which they quote, may shed more light on the Heraclids:

> All at once the lands were on the move, scattered in war. No country could stand before their arms. Hatti, Kode, Kizzuwaka, Carchemish, Arzawa and Alishahya. They were cut off. . . . They desolated its people and its land was like that which never came into being. They were advancing on Egypt *while the flame was spread before them.* (1990, 53, italics mine)

For the Orphic cult which so influenced the Druids of the British Isles, Heracles was the son of Zeus. When Heracles was traversing the sky, according to Lucian's *Dialogi Deorum*, he refused to allow space for Aesculapius and started a brawl with him. To settle the argument, Zeus decided that the space should be awarded to Aesculapius "since he died before Heracles, and was therefore entitled to rank as senior god" (Frazer 1961, I, 210). For the Orphics, Heracles was a very ancient god who miraculously reappeared in a later age. And it was the Heraclids with whom Homer associated the downfall of Mycenaean Greece (Clube and Napier 1990, 66-67).

Bailey attempts to explain just how ancient their earliest worshipers may have been when he links the Heracles people to the Eastern Mediterranean Pelasgians. He cites traditions which indicate that the Pelasgians overran both the west and the north of Europe, and that Heracles was a Celtic deity in Gaul (1994, 39). He proposes that the Heracles people, who, he argues, originated in the Black Sea area, were metal prospectors on a world-wide scale; that the apples of the Isle of Avalon may be a reference to the copper ingots the Heracles people used in commerce; that the ancient name for copper, *akawa*, was associated with them; and that they had broken away from matrifocal copper prospectors in the early Copper Age, or about 7000 B.C.E. (1994, 343, 404). This breakaway explains, for Bailey, why Hera sent twin serpents to kill the infant Heracles. Nevertheless, these serpents are not seen as cometary by Bailey, but as symbols of the earth goddess (1994, 343). Given the possible antiquity of the Heracles people cited by Bailey, they could not be candidates for the Heraclids either, nor could the Lydians, cited by Herodotus, have been likely candidates, for no account of a war between the Lydians and the Mycenaeans exists in Homer. If the Heracles people were later reconstituted in the Eastern Mediterranean during the waning years of the Late Bronze Age, their alleged invasions in the region could have been linked to their cometary representatives in the heavens, but it seems most unlikely, given the time frame Bailey provides.

Curiously enough, the Pythagoreans, who profoundly influenced the Orphic cult, often wrote of a strange formation in the heavens associated with "hoops of fire" which emanated from a central fire, the Citadel of Zeus, around which the planet Earth revolved (Clube and Napier 1990, 78). For Clube and Napier, this so-called Citadel of Zeus, a phenomenon barely present in our night sky, was brilliantly present in the ancient heavens. They characterize it as follows, noting the Pythagoreans did not associate the central fire with the Sun. Instead, they argue, the priests of this cult must have been referring to the zodiacal cloud. This cloud, they note, barely visible today and unknown to many astronomers, is comprised of comet dust that has settled into "a discus-shaped swathe" through which the planets travel. They go on to propose that the cloud was probably much brighter in ancient times and likely populated with disintegrating comets, creating the impression of awesome 'hoops of fire' from the Earth's perspective (1990, 79).

Louis Winkler, a Pennsylvania State University astrophysicist, also proposes that several comets, or at least much of their trailing meteoric material including micro meteoroids, were captured by the earth's gravitational field in ancient times:

> The available evidence . . . that suggests that there may have been many near misses over perhaps the last ten thousand years, consists of all the annual or periodic meteor showers. These showers are produced by matter in the comet's orbit, whether the comet nucleus is present or not. If the comet is missing it was either evaporated by the sun or it was used up as a canopy. If a comet has an orbit that intersects Earth's orbit, and it can last long enough, there will eventually be a near miss. (1985a, 38)

Winkler goes on to cite meteor showers which could be considered likely candidates for the formation of a cloud canopy enveloping the Earth. These include the Virginids of March 20; the Arietids of June 7; the daytime Zeta Perseids of June 9; the daytime Beta Taurids of June 29; the Opiuchids of June 20; the Capricornids of July 25; the Pisces Australids of July 30; and the Phoenicids of December 5 (1985a, 39).

The classical Greeks write concretely about the likely orbits of comets, these "hoops of fire" that could have created the cloud canopy. Appealing to an earlier tradition, Anaxagoras (c. 500-428), cited by Clube and Napier, argues that "the Sun and Moon and all the stars are fiery stones carried round by the rotation of the ether. Below the stars are the Sun and Moon and also certain bodies which revolve around them but are invisible to us. . . . The Moon is eclipsed by the Earth screening the Sun's light from it and sometimes, too, *by the [other, invisible] bodies below the Moon coming in front of it*" (1990, 81, italics mine). Based upon this ancient lore and other accounts as well, Clube and Napier draw an inevitable conclusion:

> Jets issuing from rotating wheels of fire; bodies coming between Moon and Earth; temporary 'worlds' forming about the plane of the zodiac: its seems reasonable to conclude that the earliest philosophers were describing . . . as essentially correct association between cometary disintegration products and the formation of a luminous dust cloud in the plane of the ecliptic, albeit one which was also supposed to come between us and the Moon. We are beginning to see, perhaps, hints of a night sky which was not the one we see now; and perhaps even clues to the nature of the Heraclids. (1990, 81-82)

Was such cosmological baggage carried to Ireland? This study will present evidence that the ancients' dread of the sky was not only imported to Ireland but reinforced by cometary, close encounters over the British Isles during the middle of the first millennium C.E. For once again the night sky lit up like a torch parade and impinged upon the earth.

As noted above, cometary activity increased again around 450 C.E. as the early Insular Church was evolving out of Druidism, leading to some little-known Luciferian confessions by the priests of Ireland and England and some bizarre behavior on the part of the reigning *merlin* of King Arthur's Camelot. The activity heated up again before the Crusades, and appears to have had a direct influence on the rising popularity of the Grail legends. For as will be demonstrated in the next chapter, the Grail was likened not only to the Ark of the Covenant but to a meteorite as well, with some very interesting results.

When *The Anglo-Saxon Chronicles*, the writings of Geoffrey of Monmouth and treatises written by various Irish priests are examined for references to cometary activity over the British Isles during the fourth to the twelfth centuries C.E., some startling parallels emerge.

The Anglo-Saxon Chronicles contain several references of comet sightings and the resulting social pandemonium. In 678: "There appeared the star called a comet, in August; and it shone for three months each morning like the beam of the sun. Bishop Wilfred was driven from his bishopric by king Ecgferth . . . " (Savage 1983, 245). And prior to the sacking of the monastery at Lindisfarne in 793, the *Chronicles* state:

> In this year fierce, foreboding omens came over the land of Northumbria, and wretchedly terrified the people. There were excessive whirlwinds, lightning storms, and fiery dragons were seen flying in the sky. These signs were followed by a great famine, and shortly after in the same year, on January 8th, the ravaging of heathen men destroyed God's church as Lindisfarne through brutal robbery and slaughter . . . . (Savage 1983, 247)

Regarding this event, Clube and Napier note that archeologists have uncovered a curved stone, not unlike the shape of a comet's coma, at the Lindisfarne site on which is found cosmic imagery which includes the Cross, the Sun and the Moon, God's hands on one side, and on the flip side, Vikings brandishing swords (1990, 110).   And, according to *The Anglo-Saxon Chronicles*, in 891, both during and after several battles between Saxon and Breton forces, a star appeared after Easter "which men call in Latin *cometa*; some men say in English that it is a hairy star, because long beams stand out, sometimes on one side, sometimes on every side" (Savage 1983, 99). Oddly enough, there are no major references in the *Chronicles* to Halley's comet, so clearly outlined on the Bayeux tapestry, a comet which appeared in the spring of 1066 prior to William the Conqueror's invasion of England. This omission leads one to assume other omissions may also exist.

Nonetheless, the birth of the Crusades is also linked by Clube and Napier to cometary activity, for in November 1095, immediately after a fierce meteor shower, Pope Urban II initiated the First Crusade at the Council of Cleremont (1990, 112). In *Recueil des historiens des Croisades*, which Clube and Napier cite, the apocalyptic atmosphere of the era is spelled out:

> In the time of the emperor Henry IV . . . according to the prophecies in the Gospels, everywhere nation arose against nation and kingdom against kingdom; and there were great earthquakes in divers places, and pestilences and famines and *terrors from heaven* and great signs.   And because already in all nations the evangelical trumpet was sounding the coming of the Last Judge, the universal Church beheld throughout the whole world the portents in prophetic signs . . . . [Thus] when it was God's will and pleasure to free the Holy Sepulcher [at Jerusalem], in which his son had lain for the sins of men, from the power of the pagans and to open the way for Christians desiring to travel there for the redemption of their souls, he showed many signs, powers, prodigies and portents to sharpen the minds of Christians so that they would want to hurry there. *For the stars in the sky were seen throughout the whole world to fall towards the earth, crowded together and dense, like hail, or*

snowflakes. A short while later a fiery way appeared in the heavens; and then after another short period half the sky turned the color of blood. (1990, 112, italics mine)

According to *The Anglo-Saxon Chronicles*, heavenly activity peaked again in 1106, 1107, 1110 and 1111, which likely increased the Crusaders' zeal. The entry for 1106 reads:

In the first week of Lent, on Friday, February 16th, there appeared in the evening an unusual star, and for a long time thereafter it was seen each evening, shining for a while. This star appeared in the southwest; it seemed little and dark, but the light which stood out from it was very bright, and a beam so immense that it seemed to be shining in the northeast; and one evening it was seen that the beam was streaming towards the star in the opposite direction. Some said that they had seen more unknown stars in these times, but we did not write about it freely because we did not see them ourselves. On the night of the morning of which was Cena Domini, that is the Thursday before Easter, two moons were seen in the heavens before day, one in the east and the other in the west, both full . . . . (Savage 1983, 245)

In 1107, Mauricius, the bishop of London passed away, and the entry seems to indicate that some celestial body was interfering with the transmission of moonlight to the earth: "Many said that they saw in the Moon this year various signs, and against nature its light waxing and waning" (Savage 1983, 246). The year 1110 was not propitious either, for "in the month of June appeared a star in the northeast, and the light stood out before it to the southwest; thus it was seen for many nights. Further on in the night, when it rose higher, it was going back to the northwest." The entry for that year goes on to record the following: "This was a very grievous year in the land," for all the crops were destroyed through "bad weather" (Savage 1983, 247). And in 1111 there was an exceptionally long winter with the worst die-off of livestock "that anyone could remember" (Savage 1983, 247).

The sightings continued in 1114 when "toward the end of May was seen a rare star with a long beam of light shining for many nights. Also in this year was so great an ebb-tide everywhere that no one remembered the like of it before. . . " (Savage 1983, 247). And in 1122, an earthquake struck on July 25th. Later that year sailors reported fire in the northeast quadrant of the sky, "and it waxed in height up to the sky; the sky undid unto four parts and fought there against it, as if to quench it, and the fire waxed no more up to the heavens. They saw that fire in the dawn and it lasted until it was light overall; that was on December 7th" (Savage 1983, 251). And finally in 1127, a reference to mysterious black hunters, observed from Lent to Easter, appears:

> The hunters were black, and great and loathly, and their hounds all black, and wide-eyed and loathly, and they rode on black horses and he-goats. This was seen in the very deer park in the town of Peterborough, and in all the woods from that same town to Stamford; and the monks heard the horns blowing that they blew at night. (Savage 1983, 261)

Were these hunters real men or celestial ghost-riders? The entry does not clear up the matter, but they seem quite similar to a cometary image pattern clustering around Merlin and the Italian Grove of Nemi, a motif examined shortly.

These sightings seem ominous in themselves, but when coupled with a rather obscure tract written by the British priest Gildas, entitled "De Excidio et Conquestu Britanniae," which details events leading to the so-called "ruin of Britain," they appear even more unsettling. Written approximately 130 years after the withdrawal of the Romans from Britain, the tract chronicles both a terrible slaughter that occurred during the reign of King Vortigern and a period of near complete devastation in England. Strangely, neither of these events were caused by the Anglo-Saxons, the Picts or the Scots. Clube and Napier note that Gildas attributes the destruction to a mysterious "feathered flight":

> the fire of righteous vengeance, kindled by the sins of the past, [which] blazed from sea to sea, its fuel prepared by the arms of the impious from the east. Once lit it did not die down. When it had wasted town and country in that area, it burnt up almost the whole surface of the island, until its red and savage tongue had licked the western ocean . . . . All the greater towns fell to the enemy's battering rams; all their inhabitants, bishops, priests and people, were mowed down together, while swords flashed and flames crackled. Horrible it was to see the foundation stones of towers and high walls thrown down bottom upwards in the squares, mixing with the holy altars and fragments of human bodies . . . . there was no burial save in the ruins of the houses, or in the bellies of the beasts and the birds. (Clube and Napier 1990, 108; Winterbottom 1978, 41)[7]

Citing soil evidence indicating that radical deforestation occurred from the Midlands to East Anglia, and presenting evidence for an ensuing mass migration from England to Brittany during this time, Clube and Napier argue that Gildas' account is not exaggerated (1990, 108). And if no major military incursion either from the Picts, Scots, Huns, Visigoths or Anglo-Saxons can account for this destruction, could these "impious from the east" have been meteorites? History tells us that the Anglo-Saxon invasions came a century later. But during this period the Anglo-Saxons were King Vortigern's uneasy allies. So is this scenario reminiscent of the mysterious invasion of Mycenae by the unearthly Heraclids?

Noting evidence for a one-hundred mile recession of the treelines that occurred in Canada and Scandinavia during this period, Clube and Napier reveal that the *Annales Cambriae* record several days that were as dark as night either in 444 c.e. or 447 c.e. (1990, 108).[8] Then too, they indicate that Nennius, reflecting back on that period of history, writes of "*a fire sent from heaven*" that annihilated Vortigern's fortress and Vortigern and his entourage along with it (1990, 109, italics mine).[9] Ironically, Vortigern had consulted his magi and moved his fortress prior to the catastrophe, but the magi, a title suggesting a druidic cult with Eastern Mediterranean roots, made a bad call.

Clube and Napier draw the following conclusions from the incidents described:

> Such hints as there may be in this course of events of a heaven-sent force which effectively ruined Britain, argue in favor of a celestial rather than an Anglo-Saxon agency for 'the fire of righteous vengeance' cited by Gildas. Indeed, the 'battering rams' which he also cited, in their Latin equivalent, are 'aries,' a term relating to stars as much as sheep . . . . (1990, 109)

Gildas, writing of events in the mid-fifth century, mentions that the inhabitants of Britain turned "to darkness instead of the sun, to receiving Satan as the Angel of Light" (Tolstoy 1985, 107). He also estimates that the quantity of Britain's pagan idols nearly surpassed "Egypt's in number" (Tolstoy 1985, 119; see 285 fn. 37). Were these 'aries' really meteors from the largest meteor shower in the current night sky, the Taurids, which Clube and Napier associate with comet Encke (Clube and Napier 1982, 148)? Was there any connection between the increased cometary activity of this period, and the eleventh and twelfth century obsession with Merlin, who was depicted in various Grail legends as the leading celestial figure of the Arthurian Age?

The death of Vortigern is described in Geoffrey of Monmouth's *History of the Kings of Britain*. In that work Vortigern's coronation; his hiring of Hengist and the Saxon mercenaries; his squabbles with Germanus, the Romano-Gaulish monitor of Britain's heresies; and his downfall are delineated. They are also chronicled in greater detail in *Liber Beati Germani*, the *Book of the Blessed Germanus*, one of Monmouth's sources for Merlin's prophecy which shall be examined shortly. In *Liber Beati*

Germani, Vortigern's incest with his daughter is decried, and his flight with his magi to a supernatural stronghold in Snowdonia in north Wales to escape the plotting of the Saxons and the "barbarian nations" is detailed (Tolstoy 1985, 103). But strange events occur. When Vortigern's druids attempt to build the fortress, the timber and stones vanish each night. To halt the disappearance, his druids advise him to find a fatherless child, kill him and sprinkle his blood on the foundation of the fortress. Vortigern's messengers find such a boy named Ambrosius [or Embreis Guletic as he later explains, son of a Roman consul!] who is playing ball with another youth on the "campus Elleti" (Tolstoy 1985, 104).[10] Gaining confirmation from the boy's mother that he is indeed fatherless, a situation which implies perhaps that he is the son of the mother through royal incest, and a likely tanist, the messengers bring him to Vortigern and his magi. But the boy demands that the druids dig a hole in the ground before them. They begin to dig and discover an underground pool containing two vases placed end to end and a folded tent. The following is a portion of Tolstoy's paraphrase of events that follow:

> 'What is in the tent?' demanded the boy. Again the druids were silent, and when the tent was unfolded two snakes (vermes) were found sleeping within. One was red and one white, and they began to fight within (or upon) the tent. At first the red snake was beaten almost to the tent's margin, but after a stiff struggle it recovered and drove its white opponent out of the tent. There was a pursuit across the pool, and the tent vanished.
>
> 'Now,' declared the boy triumphantly to the wondering druids, 'what does all this mean?' And on their confessing their bafflement, he explained. The tent represented Vortigern's kingdom, and the snakes two dragons. The red dragon (still, of course, the emblem of Wales) stood for the Britons, and the white for the Saxons. So far the latter had been victorious, and would conquer the land almost from sea to sea. But eventually the Britons would reassert themselves and repel the invader back to his homeland. (1985, 103-104)

As the story unfolds, the boy is put in charge of the uncompleted fortress, while Vortigern, accompanied by his druids, heads north. An interlude ensues in which the Saxons are driven from the island at Kent by Vortigern's son. Then Vortigern agrees to negotiate with Hengist, whose men carry knives hidden in their boots. When they draw their knives, the frightened Vortigern cedes Essex and Sussex to them. Then, almost as an afterthought, Germanus arrives and calls fire down from heaven, which incinerates Vortigern and his entourage once and for all (Tolstoy 1985, 104).

What concerns this study is not only the apparent subliminal, cometary imagery, but also the source of that imagery. For the symbolism clearly harkens back to the mythology of the Eastern Mediterranean, especially to the tanistry conflict waged between the snake and the pig-priests of Axum, Ethiopia, a struggle that will be examined in a subsequent chapter. Another version of the fighting dragons motif, the Welsh story of *The Contention of Lludd and Llevelys* found in *The White Book of Rhydderch* and *The Red Book of Hergest*, drives this point home. Again, Tolstoy's paraphrase is useful:

> Lludd, King of Britain, finds his country plagued by mysterious oppressions. Upon inquiry he is told that one of them is caused by the hidden contest of two dragons. One of them is 'your dragon' (i. e. representative of the Isle of Britain), who is fighting with a foreign dragon seeking to overthrow him, this is causing him to utter a horrible scream every May-day eve, heard the length and breadth of the Island. Lludd is told how to discover the dragons: he must cause the Island to be measured in length and breadth so as to discover its precise center. At that point he must dig a trench, place a vatful of mead in it, and cover the vat with a piece of brocaded silk. Then, if he watches, he will witness the dragons' fight. First they appear as horrible animals, then they grapple in the air as dragons, and finally they fall back exhausted in the shape of pigs. Sinking down into the vat, they drink the mead and fall asleep. Immediately [when] that happens, Lludd is to bundle up the creatures into the silk cover and bury them in a store chest in the strongest place in his kingdom. 'And as long as they remain in that safe place, no foreign oppression shall visit the Isle of Britain.' (1985, 105)

Lludd follows the advice, buries them in Snowdonia and rules in peace.

Tolstoy does not put the parts of this puzzle together, however. But he does ask the deeper question when he concludes: "Clearly a common source must lie behind the kernel of both versions of the Fighting Dragons story, and it seems possible that it rests ultimately on a grain of historical fact" (1985, 105).

It certainly may, for now the possible origins of these fighting dragons can be proposed. Doubtless, the totemism of the King of the sacred grove, who was both a serpent or dragon and a Set-pig, is unmistakable. The sacred grove imagery, of course, mirrors the archetypal Osiris serpent and its adversary, Set, the wild boar who tears up the cypress swamps of Lower Egypt. The silk imagery is also significant. On one level silk is the strongest of fabrics, but it also made by the silk worm, a safer, lesser worm, a creature that was revered at Sarras where the silk industry was not only lucrative but also symbolic of this lesser worm. The Egyptian concept of *ma'at*, the attempt by mortals to halt the ravages of these cosmic worms, is also apparent here as well. The tent and pool imagery are also obvious.

Without understanding the possible cometary etiology of the symbolism, Tolstoy correctly interprets the meaning. He notes that Siberian shamans liken the sky to a cosmic tent. Hence, he goes on, the dragon's activities beneath the tent would symbolize their gyrations in the night sky. Then too, the pool symbolizes the 'world lake' above which the battle between God and the devil occurred (1985, 113).

The sacred center imagery is also significant, for Delphi, site of a meteoric impact on Mt. Parnassus, was also a sacred omphalos designed to contain the cosmic serpents through the sympathetic magic of priestly ritual. Lucian, a Greek sophist, went so far as to propose that the ritual of the Otherworld journey at Delphi was first practiced by the Hyperboreans (Tolstoy 1985, 285 fn. 7). In any case, Tolstoy is on the mark when he cites the pool imagery in ancient Greece. He reveals that a serpent was housed in the Athenian Erechtheum. Also found in the Erechtheum was a vat of water, 'the sea of Erechtheus' which symbolized the ocean (1985, 113).

There is evidence that homage to celestial serpents occurred on May Day eve when Beltane fires may well have been lit to commemorate and, in fact, imitate a catastrophic meteor shower, for the fires were dedicated to Aries the Ram (Goodrich 1992, 241-42). And in the month of May, as any English snake fancier knows, the male adders do their odd head-bobbing dance as they contend for the choice female serpents. Clube and Napier also explain that such a festival was originally celebrated in Egypt on the first day of the month of Pachons which was coincident in Amenhotep I's time with May Day (1982, 241). They go on to reveal that in ancient Egypt the festival commemorated Horus' voyage to Dendera although in the ancient world the festival evolved into a celebration of fertility and the rebirth of the land, perhaps a rebirth after a cataclysm (1982, 241-42). Other such festivals with more likely cometary origins will also be noted when the celestial nature of Merlin, or the succession of *merlin* priests, is explored. And it is to the true meaning of Merlin, his prophecy, and the Grail legends that this study now turns.

When dealing with the problem of Merlin, this study must ask: "Which Merlin"? For *merlin* was not a family name but a title that was spoken in deference to the taboo against naming noted by Frazer in *The Golden Bough*. A *merlin*, according to Goodrich, also referred to Heracles' club, a weapon that this study deems cometary, given that Heracles himself had such associations (1987, 23). Then too, she reveals, the weapon that Cain used to dispatch Abel was also called a *merlin* (1987, 23). When Geoffrey of Monmouth proposes that Merlin, most likely an avatar of a figure whom

Monmouth called Morien, supervised the building of Stonehenge, he may be correct about the personage but definitely wrong about the fifth century C.E. date. This Merlin-Morien figure could have been a merlin priest descended from the first invader group which arrived in Ireland well before the approximate date of 2800 B.C.E. for the construction of Stonehenge I. Interestingly enough, the Arthurian knight who represented the ideal of chivalry during the rebirth of Arthurian legend was a black knight called Morien, whose story Jesse Weston (1901) translated.

All of this begs the question: Was Arthur's Merlin, later called the old Moore, dark-skinned? Was he also an avatar of the Ethiopian god-king Set, who was himself described in cometary language as grotesquely red-haired with brilliant, cometary, perhaps, white skin?

The legends of Merlin's birth are peculiar, to say the least. Goodrich notes that the Latin name used by Monmouth for Merlin is Merlinus. She goes on to parse the title:

merul + inus> merula = blackbird
meruleus = colored like a blackbird,
mru; a solivaga = a wandering bird, solitary, not gregarious. (1987, 22)

The bird reference has been derived from Shamanism by Tolstoy, but this study offers an alternative suggestion. Like Kukulcan of Mexico, Merlin was described as a feathered serpent. If Merlin was the earthly, human representative of a comet, this metaphor would make perfect sense. The description of the druidic dress of Mog Ruith, casts some light on the bird imagery: "Mog Ruith's skin of the hornless, dun-colored bull was brought to him then and his speckled bird-dress, with its winged flying, and his druidic gear besides. And he rose up, in company with the fire, into the air and the heavens" (Tostoy 1985, 145). This penchant for flight, as Tolstoy argues, may be shamanic in origin, but if Merlin was a cometary surrogate, the fiery flight also implies the imitation of the cometary deity as well, a deity characterized by at least two colors- black and white, black when invisible and white when viewed overhead. But there is another hint as to Merlin's color. Since, as Goodrich points out, Merlin's Welsh name was *Annbab y llaiann*, or 'Son-of-the-Mother,' it is possible that we are dealing here with an Africoid Pict, or a half-breed Pict, given that the Picts were matrifocal (1987, 30). Guinevere was also part Pict, as were several other Arthurian characters. Goodrich also proposes that Merlin, who was often likened to a mythical 'brownie,' was surely a prophet in the Judaic tradition (1987, 30-31). She goes on to depict him as type of Father Time, and a healer like Aesculapius (1987, 38). And she reveals another aspect of Merlin's extraordinary birth as described in Robert de Boron's late twelfth and early thirteenth century *The Story of the Grail*. Boron's version of Merlin's virgin birth reveals that his mother was raped not by a mortal, but by a demon, and that baby Merlin, named after his maternal grandfather, emerged from the womb *with swarthy skin and thick black hair* (Goodrich 1987, 45-46, italics mine). This incubus-father imparted the power of prophecy to Merlin, according to Boron's version. Tolstoy notes that Geoffrey of Monmouth provides additional details about Merlin's demon-father, for he was alleged to inhabit "*the aery space between moon and earth*" (1985, 2, italics mine). Is this not the same celestial landscape through which a short period comet may pass? Was Arthur's Merlin, and indeed were all *merlins*, earthly symbols of cosmic serpents? If so, there should be a sufficient number of extraterrestrial associations with Merlin that would shed light on that incubus father of his. There are.

The madness of Merlin [or Myrddin in Welsh] occurs, according to one version of the old Welsh *Annals*, after he gazes at what appears to have been a meteor shower. For after the battle of Arderydd, Merlin, hearing a voice from heaven, stares at the night sky and sees "numberless warlike battalions in the heavens like flashing lightning, holding in their hands fiery lances and glittering spears which they brandished furiously at me" (Tolstoy 1985, 57). And in the Irish tale of *Buile Suibhne*, based upon a character who ascends the Cosmic Tree, Merlin [Suibhne] views a similar celestial display which leads to an appropriate response reproduced by Tolstoy: "His fingers were palsied, his feet trembled, his heart beat quick, his senses were overcome, his sight was distorted, his weapons fell naked from his hands, so that . . . he went, like any bird of the air, in madness and imbecility" (1985, 56 ff.).[11] Graves, who does not probe the cometary nature of this madness, attributes it to Suibne's torrid love affair with the Triple Goddess. Citing D. Justin Schove, Tolstoy, however, reveals that the passing of a brilliant comet in 574 C.E. may account for Merlin's madness (1985, 57 ff.; Schove 1950, xiii, 42).[12] And there are other such associations as well. In the *Romance of Owain*, the knight encounters an ugly, one-eyed, black *merlin* holding an iron club, who is surrounded by a thousand wild animals.

Owain finds the Black Man, and asks him what power he holds over these animals. The Black Man then swings his club at a stag, which bellows and calls forth herds of wild animals which compare in number to the stars of the heavens.

The iron club recalls the *merlin* of Heracles, and it is commonly known that meteorites are composed largely of iron. The massing animals, and the bellowing stag, with its horns shaped like a comet's coma, also appear to be symbolic of meteor showers which accompany cometary pyrotechnics. Despite the obvious echoes of one-eyed Polyphemus, Goliath, Balor, and Odin, who was present when the sky fell during Ragnarok, Tolstoy identifies the Black Man only with Merlin (1985, 79). This study agrees with that observation.

And more cometary associations with Merlin can be found related to Merlin's role as leader of ghostly hunters. Near the end of *The Anglo-Saxon Chronicles*, as noted above, a reference for the year 1127 c.e. indicates that a terrifying ghostly hunt was witnessed near [or above?] the town of Peterborough after the arrival of Henry, an unpopular abbot from Poitou.

Was a band of blackamoors hunting in the vicinity of Peterborough? Or were these creatures *celestial* black riders, symbols of a meteor shower lasting until Easter? Or are both options possible? Anglo-Saxon superstition held that these huntsmen were symbolic of unbaptized, pagan souls doomed to chase the hart across forest and sky for all eternity (Tolstoy 1985, 79).

In any case, Tolstoy convincingly links the leader of the Wild Hunt not only to the horned god Cernunnos, whose image adorns many antique cauldrons, but to one-eyed Odin and to Merlin lore (1985, 79 ff.). And Goodrich indicates that Merlin, as the wild man of the woods, was depicted as mounting a stag during the Whitsuntide Mummer's play (1987, 97). She also reveals that the wild man of the woods "is a medieval descendant of the pagan Italian priest of Nemi in Diana's sacred Italian Grove, [who] is chased by the younger king, or younger 'stag' who will supplant him" (1987, 97).

We have moved through time. The cosmic serpent pair transmute into a stag pair, but they are still Osiris and Set underneath.   Because it is the same old Egyptian practice of *ma'at*, the attempt to prevent the feared arrival of more cosmic rocks, to ensure that the bloodline of the protector god-king is preserved through time. Merlin's association with beasts noted above, or his alternate title as King of the Beasts, may derive from predynastic Egypt. Bailey reproduces a sketch of a predynastic stela that pictures a male figure standing between two raised lions and above a menagerie of other beasts. Bailey likens the male figure to "the Master of the Animals" (1994, 172). What is astonishing here is that the lions are positioned almost exactly as the griffons and other beasts, depicted on Pictish standing stones, which likewise stare into one another's eyes!

To further understand the imagery surrounding Merlin, another account of his birth needs to be examined. Goodrich refers to an article by Moses Gaster (1928) entitled "The Legend of Merlin" in which Gaster traces Merlin's birth story to an Eastern Mediterranean source-- the birth of

Merlin's demonic prototype Asmodeus and a twin from an avatar of the Queen of Sheba (1987, 53).[13] Gaster reveals that the Asmodeus tale can be found in several versions of the Solomon cycle in which the mother, usually the Queen of Sheba [or her avatar, perhaps?], is either depicted as the daughter of the prophet Jeremiah or of King David" (Goodrich 1987, 79). What is so revealing about the Gaster thesis is his linking of Merlin's birth to an excerpt from a Rumanian manuscript which states:

> The Archangel Gabriel was dispatched to take away the soul of a widow, but when he found her suckling twins, he left her soul alone. God punished Gabriel for disobedience, by sending him for a stone at the bottom of the sea. But when the archangel cut it in half, he found two 'worms' (dragons) inside.
>
> 'If I feed worms,' said the Lord, 'do you think I would let twins starve?' God punished the erring angel for thirty years, and took the woman's soul. (Goodrich 1987, 71, 79)

Gaster traces the twin underwater dragons to a dream of Mordecai in the Book of Esther 6:3-5 in which cosmic serpent imagery is most pronounced:

> Beloved, there was a great noise and tumult and the voice of terrible uproar upon the whole land and terror and fear seized all the inhabitants of the earth: and behold there appeared two mighty dragons and they came one against the other to fight and all the nations of the earth trembled at the noise of their fury. And there was a small nation between these two dragons, and all the nations of the earth rose up against it to swallow it up. And there were clouds and darkness and obscurity upon the face of the earth . . . and the dragons fought one another with cruel fury and frenzy, and no one separated them. And Mordecai beheld and lo! a fountain of the living water sprang and flowed between the two fighting dragons and stopped their fight. And the small fountain swelled into a mighty river and overflowed like a mighty sea and swept everything off the face of the earth. And the sun rose up and the rays lighted the whole earth.

Is this passage not the archetype of Merlin's prophecy of future battles between the red dragon (the British) and the white dragon (the Anglo-Saxons)?

As noted earlier, Clube and Napier propose that such dragon pairs are cometary in nature, the duality arising from a fragmenting comet which spawns comet fragments (1982, 199).

Recalling that Merlin's father passed somewhere between the earth and the moon, Merlin is quite probably symbolic of a celestial dragon of the dragon pair, a dyad first discovered in the mythology of Ethiopia and Upper Egypt. The Near Eastern origins of Merlin's birth story help to explain why the Pentangle symbol, the Seal of Solomon, was the logo of Arthur's court (Lasater 1972, 184). They may also explain why Merlin's birth occurred, according to the *Prose Lancelot*, in the Scottish Rhinn of Galloway on Hart Fell mountain next to the Fountain of Bredigan near the river Dyfrig (Goodrich 1987, 309). If *Dyfrig* can be derived from David, another apparent cometary god-king whose celestial double killed the one-eyed giant/comet Goliath, one more dragon pair can be mixed into this Irish stew. For this single-eye imagery may stem from the cometary eye imagery of Egypt. African and Near Eastern origins also help to explain why Merlin's alias was Saint Dubricus [*dubh* meaning 'black' in Gaelic], who was, among other things, an accomplished astronomer and equal to the Pope at Dubricus' Church of Saint David in Wales (Goodrich 1987, 241). African and Near Eastern etiology also clarifies Merlin's association with Lug, the pig-god of the Underworld, himself likely derived from the raging boar Set who dug up the cypress swamp in the legend of Isis and Osiris. And the etiology also explains Merlin's association with the prophet and doctor Aesculapius, son of the cometary Apollo, and favorite of Black Athena, whose avatars are, according to Goodrich, Queen Morgan and the Lady of the Lake (Goodrich 1987, 228). Despite his mythological pedigree, Arthur's Merlin did not ascend to the throne likely because of the complexities of matrifocal genealogy. Hence, he became an initiator of prospective Grail king candidates.

As an initiator, Merlin must have known the periodic orbits of the short period comets that were careening over the British Isles. Perhaps he utilized the celestial computer at Stonehenge, or deciphered the cup and ring markings etched on sacred stones found throughout the British Isles, markings which Clube and Napier associate with comet tally records (1982, 79 ff., 263). Tolstoy indicates that the presence of Lug assured High Kingship in Ireland. Merlin also assumed some of Lug's powers, for Merlin could foretell who would rule in the future, even from the grave or Otherworld [symbolized by the woods to the north of Hadrian's Wall] (1985, 89, 278 fn. 3).

And who was Lug? He was born in Avalon, the Otherworld Isle of Apples which Cohane derives from a Near Eastern Ava/Haue/Hawa/Eva complex of roots, referring, he argues, to a lost mother goddess religion, and from *aballon*, the Welsh for apple (Cohane 1969, 96). Lug's name seems to derive from the Latin *lux* for 'light" and the Latin *lucus* for 'grove' [an ingenious linkage if there ever was one]. He is the Otherworld god who presides over the Festival of Lughnasa, an event associated with a dying serpent, sacred wells, lakes, mountain tops and standing stones, and celebrated in early spring during a meteor shower; he is the protector of mankind; he can transform himself into a pig-god; he leads an Otherworld Host; and the brilliance of his face rivals that of the sun. But as Tolstoy reiterates: he cannot be solar god for his glory is reflected by the sun (1985, 89). Given that description, he appears to be the protective comet in the dragon-pair that Clube and Napier have delineated. Graves tells us that Lug or Lugh was a celestial Heracles who rose appropriately enough from the west on horseback, brandishing a spear with which he defeated the African army of Balor of the One Eye during the battle of Moytura (1966, 302). Lug, who died on the first of August, was a progenitor of Cuchulain, having flown in the form of a May-fly into the mouth of Cuchulain's mother (Graves 1966, 301).[14] And he may well have appeared before Arthur completed his coronation rites by drawing the fiery Excalibur from a stone anvil, for this apparent cometary sword also recalls the magical spears possessed by both Lug and his cousin Odin.

But to truly understand the *real presence* of Lug in early Ireland, we must understand the descriptions of his father Balor and his son Cuchulain.

Regarding the enigmatic Cuchulain in "The Cattle-raid of Cooley," the final chapter of *Tain Bo Cuailnge*, Dorothea Kenny argues that his exploits are allegorical of cometary activity. "The Begetting of the Two Swineherds," the first chapter, sets up the action when it depicts the battles of the swineherds as they try to destroy one another. Their reincarnations as ravens, sea monsters, warriors, demons, dragon-like worms, and finally as bulls, which comprise their shapes in *Tain Bo Cuailnge*, are reminiscent of a pair of earth grazing comets locked in a periodic orbit around the planet (Kenny 1987, 15). Donn Cuailnge, "the brown (bull) of Cooley," which Queen Medb wishes to steal, is described as a gargantuan beast able to support the weight of fifty young men. As the story proceeds, Cuchulain, aged five, travels across the mountains in search of the king's foster children. When he finds them, they attempt to harm him on a playing field, but Cuchulain overpowers them, scattering some on the ground and driving others to the edge of the field.

Any doubts that an allegory of a meteor shower is being presented may be dispelled as the imagery surrounding Cuchulain builds. For when Medb mobilizes her army to capture the Donn, Cuchulain's actions, Kenny argues, mimic "the conditions and events often marked as accompanying comets or large meteors: terrifying noises, mass deaths, severe weather, unwonted darkness, and burning heat" (1987, 16). As Medb's army continues to engage Cuchulain, the gargantuan figure radiates intense heat. Kenny notes his description in a related tale, "The Pursuit of Gruaidh Ghriansholus," in which he

> began to drink the water [of the river] into his mouth and pulses and joints, so that the sand and the bottom gravel were visible and he did not allow any length of the river past him, up or down, which he did not drink or suck up by reason of the greatness of his heat and fierceness, so that the fierceness and the frenzy which possessed him were quenched and submerged . . . . (1987, 16)

Further on in the same tale, she argues, more cometary imagery attaches to Cuchulain:

> every stream of fiery flakes which came into his mouth from his throat was as large as the skin of a the three-year old sheep. The loud beating of his heart . . . was heard like the baying of a bloodhound . . . . The torches of the war-goddess, the virulent rain-clouds, the sparks of blazing fire were seen in the clouds and in the air above his head. (1987, 18)

When Kenny mentions that Balor of the Evil Eye was not only the grandfather of Cuchulain, but the leader of the Fomorians, a people that this study holds were Africoid wanderers, the importation of cometary religion to Ireland from Africa becomes clearer. One description of Balor is particularly telling: "An evil eye had Balor. That eye was never opened save only on a battlefield. Four men used to lift up the lid of that eye with a polished handle which passed through its lid. If an army looked at that eye, though they were many thousands in number, they could not resist a few warriors" (1987, 19). Another oral source cited by Kenny appears to clinch her argument that Cuchulain's grandfather was a parent comet:

> Balor . . . had a single eye in his forehead: it was a venomous, fiery eye. There were always seven coverings over his eye, and the coverings kept the eye cold, and everything else cold as well. One by one, Balor removed the coverings from his eye. With the first covering the bracken began to wither; with the second the grass began to grow copper-colored; with the third the woods and all wooden things began to grow hot; with the fourth heat and smoke came from the trees and all wooden things; with the fifth everything began to grow red; . . . with the seventh they were all set on fire, and the whole country was ablaze . . . . And that now is the reason why black deal [fir and pine] and black oak are to be found in every bog throughout the country. (1987, 19)

Are these tales part of a tradition inherited from African and Near Eastern sources? we must ask. Or did those traditions come alive when the British Isles experienced cometary horrors similar to those recorded along the Mediterranean and Red Sea littorals?

Lug, Cuchulain's father, inherits the imagery as he fatally pierces his father Balor in the eye with a magic spear. And other battlefield characteristics of Balor's grandson recall cometary coma imagery, according to Kenny, who cites the *Tain* and its description of an aerial battle between Cuchulain and Ferdia:

> Cuchulain rose up quick as the wind, swift as a swallow, in a storm of strength and dragonish fury, and landed on the knob of Ferdia's shield and tried to strike down at him over the shield-rim. But that battle-warrior gave a shake of his shield that sent Cuchulain off, as though he had never landed on it, into the middle of the ford. Cuchulain warped in his fury-spasm; he blew up and swelled like a bladder full of breath and bent himself in a fearful hideous arch, mottled and terrifying, and the huge high hero loomed straight up over Fredia, vast as a Fomorian giant or a man from the sea-kingdom. (1987, 19-20)

Kenny mentions additional cometary imagery that surrounds Cuchulain's description and his exploits on the field of battle. This imagery includes his description of a terrifying chariot with iron wheels that lays waste the land; the fall of blood from his wounded body that stains the earth; his ability to hurl great stones on the camps of Fergus and Ailill; and Cuchulain's cometary hair:

> You would think he had three distinct heads of hair-- brown at the base, blood red in the middle, and a crown of golden yellow. This hair was settled strikingly into three coils on the cleft of the back of his head. Each long loose-flowing strand hung down in shining splendor over his shoulders, deep-gold and beautiful and fine as a thread of gold. A hundred neat red-gold curls shone darkly on his neck, and his head was covered with a hundred crimson threads matted with gems. (Kenny 1987, 21)

These sudden color changes remind Kenny of the breakup of a comet into meteors. She concludes her discussion of *Tain Bo Cuailnge* and its hero Cuchulain, proposing: "a comet, Balor of the Evil Eye, broke apart, perhaps in two pieces, Lug and Balor, and . . . its last cometary or meteoric appearance, with loud noises, fireballs, atmospheric dust, and falls of rock and fiery stuff" comprises the real meaning of this epic (1987, 23).

In *The Book of Taliesin* is found a poem called *Cad Goddeu* or *The*

Battle of the Trees. It is a title that makes perfect sense given that meteors and comets were often likened to trees in the ancient world, and warring ones at that. In its descriptions of three catastrophes, the Flood, the Crucifixion of Christ, and Doomsday, the poem contains several references to Merlin's prophecies. Tolstoy indicates that it was recited at Lughnasa, and that it describes a massive scaly animal which the speaker claims to have wounded. Virtually the entire gamut of meteoric mythology is then recited: Yahweh's defeat on the cosmic serpent Rahab, Thor's attack on the serpent Midgard, and on and on (1985, 153). And then, just before Taliesin's admission that he transformed himself into an enchanted, hilltop serpent and a viper swimming in a lake, the cryptic lines of the shape-changer Taliesin appear:

> I was with my Lord in the heavens
> When Lucifer fell into the depths of Hell; . . .(Tolstoy 1985, 134, 138 ff.)[15]

Taliesin may well have been a god-king who represented the protector comet, given that a "radiant forehead" was his trademark. Using D. W. Nash's mid-Victorian rendition, Graves cites the line "I have been an evil star formerly," and Tolstoy compares the Lughnasa rituals to three precursors which also reenacted the slaying of a cosmic serpent and celebrated the emergence of a new era of history that followed. These include the Babylonian New Year's festival in which Marduk's slaying of Tiamat and the creation of a new earth was commemorated; rites conducted at Heliopolis during which Nun emerged from the primeval hill; and the Hebrew New Year's festival honoring Yahweh's triumph over his dragon adversary, Rahab (1985, 153).[16] Like these ceremonies, Lughnasa celebrated not only the renewal of the year, but the birth of the age that commenced after the slaying as well. And if the rituals of Lughnasa were not conducted, it was feared that the natural world and society would disintegrate into chaos. For all of the dragon pairs, Marduk and Tiamat, Yahweh and Rahab and the like, have been identified by Clube and Napier as different names for the same fragments of a disintegrating comet (1982, 210 ff.). What the Egyptians called *ma'at*, which, for the purposes of this study, consisted of orderly living and ritual incantations designed to preserve the protector comet, the Greeks called *Themis*, and the pagans of the British Isles called *fir flatha*, for as Tolstoy notes, God ascended the primordial hill during Creation and ordered the world with his laws, rules that should not be transgressed (1985, 232).

The Battle of the Trees addresses the chaos that can result when order gives way by personifying two combative groves of trees. Like soldiers, or trailing hordes of meteorites, perhaps, they war against one another, vast forests of them. Tolstoy notes Ford's observation that the tree animation must emanate from rituals related to sacred trees and sacred groves (1985, 159). Certainly, the sacred groves at Axum, Delphi, Nemi and a host of others are likely candidates for one of those traditions.

The Irish *Baile in Scail* or *The Phantom's Frenzy* provides more insight into Lug, his avatar Arthur's Merlin, and the cometary nature of Irish, pre-Christian gods in general. The essence of the drama that occurred at Tailtiu or Teltown in Cornwall, where the Festival of Lughnasa was held, goes like this. Conn rises at dawn, calls forth three druids and three poets, and goes to the hill of Tara to ward off the demons of the Underworld who would do harm to Ireland. During that journey, Conn steps on the sacred Fal stone which issues deafening screams. At the same time a mist surrounds Conn and his companions, and the ghostly thunder of horses' hooves is heard. Suddenly the rider throws three spears at Conn, but then ceases his attack without identifying himself. Then the rider trots over to Conn and leads him to a house with a golden tree emblazoned on the front door. Entering the house, Conn discovers a crowned maiden standing before a tub filled with a crimson beverage beside which rests a can and goblet of gold. Looking now to a throne, which lies next to tub, Conn sees that the phantom rider, whose features are more comely than any man's, is seated there. Subsequently, his druids explain that the number of screams made by that stone presage the number of the future kings of Tara. The stone is then moved to Tailtiu, where it will be consulted at the annual games. This is done to preserve Ireland's sovereignty.

This study proposes that the talking Fal stone and the "golden tree" represent a meteorite that separated from a parent comet once deemed protective of mankind. Additionally, that comet likely maintained a measurable orbit. Hence, the Fal stone would be a fallen meteorite not unlike the betel stones or arks housed at Axum, Delphi, Mecca and other sacred sites. The tree operates on another level as well. Tolstoy cites the Pole Star as the omphalos of the heavens. The Cosmic Tree, he goes on, is rooted in the Underworld and it joins the omphali of Earth and sky. This sacred tree, represents the bounty enjoyed by men (1985, 122-23).

In "Lleu of the Sure Hand," however, Lug's Welsh counterpart does not find the tree so bountiful, for he, not unlike other cometary heroes such as Christ and Odin, hangs on the sacred oak tree for nine days, is pierced by a spear, and finally gains both the knowledge of the eagle which has flown to the soul's haven at the Pole Star, and the knowledge of the cosmic serpents that roam the Underworld. The spear image is an important one as well. In

John 19:31-35, the book so dear to the Cathars, when Christ's side is pierced by the centurion's spear, both blood and water pour from the wound. If Christ is also a cometary deity as this study holds, the flowing water is emblematic of the floods that have resulted when cometary fragments slammed into the open seas or deposited a gargantuan vapor cloud into the Earth's atmosphere. The Welsh *Math vob Mathonwy*, reveals another consequence of the spear-piercing, for after receiving his wound, Lleu discarded his rotting flesh for the waiting swine at the base of the tree, and promptly ascended to the heavens on eagle's wings. And then his wizard uncle Gwydion [on his mother's side of the family, perhaps] used his magic to restore Lleu's body to life in a garbled version of the legend of Isis and Osiris in which Osiris is dismembered by the wild boar Set and reconstituted, *sans* penis, by his sister-wife Isis. Clearly, the World Pillar or Cosmic Tree is a two way street. Ascending it, the hero reaches the sanctuary of his immortal soul, the Pole Star, but descending to its roots, the hero becomes wise when he encounters the *real presence* of the cometary deities.

Tolstoy does not provide insight into the cometary nature of the omphalos and its pillar or tree. Nonetheless, the omphalos was often located at the strike zone of a meteorite. This was likely true for Tara, and for Delphi as well, given that on Mount Parnassus the remains of the she-dragon Python, slain by Apollo, were said to have fallen (Clube and Napier 1982, 192ff.). This rationale for the location of the omphalos may also explain why Stonehenge was moved.

In any case, what is to be made of the other symbols in the passage quoted above from *Baile in Scail*? The mist is likely indicative of the memory of a cosmic winter and of the smoke from burning vegetation that must have hung over crash sites when the Otherworld beings descended during meteor showers. The horsemen are reminiscent of Merlin's black ghost riders examined above, and they desist from throwing their spears [meteorites?] at Lug for he, like Osiris, is already dead. The "golden goblet" offered by the matriarch, which contains the red [ferrous?] drink conferring Sovereignty, is part of the image pattern that makes up the composite Grail symbolism, complete with Grail maiden. Tolstoy explains that the Phantom declared he was the god Lug who had come to recite the names of the future High Kings of Tara, and that Lug performed the marriage ceremony of the King and the goddess who symbolized Ireland's Sovereignty. Lug, therefore was the divine representation of earthly kingship, and the king was Lug's "earthly incarnation" (1985, 97). Apparently Lug was also emblematic of a comet.

Goodrich mentions that the appearance of comets often determined the fate of Irish kings: "Those gods who ruled on earth as kings were often replaced at certain fixed intervals, either by custom or because their strength magical-religious potency had diminished. Some ruled for five years, others for twelve. Some were warned by comets or meteors that their tenures had elapsed" (1992, 318). Tolstoy observes that the stories of the demise of Lug or Odin may have symbolized "real events" which required the sacrifice of "a divinity cast in human form" (1985, 183). For the purposes of this study, that precedent was the tanistry commemorated in the sacred groves along the Mediterranean and Red Sea littorals

Echoes, albeit garbled, of the rituals of tanistry practiced at various sites in the twin sea littorals and at the Festival of Lughnasa as well, reverberate in the apparent description of Lughnasa found in *The Life of Samson*, composed c. 610-615 C.E. from older material. In that tale, which Tolstoy cites, Samson makes an interesting discovery as he passes a temple where a group of men are encountered who are worshiping much as the Bacchantes of Greece were known to do. Angered, Samson steps down from his chariot and climbs a nearby hill, where discovers a terrifying idol that is being adored there. As Samson admonishes the worshipers for their pagan ways, a boy involved in a horse race gallops up the hill and is thrown off his mount. St. Samson miraculously restores the boy and destroys the idol. And what that idol may have represented is unclear from the text, but Jocelin of Furnes' description of another such druid idol, cited by W. P. Boswell, may prove useful in understanding this one:

> Even to this day, I am credibly informed, a brazen Serpent (like that which was lifted up in the wilderness) has been preserved in the northern part of Ireland and handed down in one family through a series of ages. Their tradition records it as one of the original objects of the idolatrous worship in this Island; it is curiously inscribed with Hieroglyphics, now unintelligible . . . . (1972a, 18)

In any case, Saint Samson's miracles are not over. For when Guedianus, one of the worshipers, asks St. Samson to help them kill a giant serpent that is destroying the countryside, Samson agrees. Upon crossing a river and entering a cave, Samson uses his girdle to lasso the serpentine troglodyte that is holed up within its depths. Subduing the creature, he summarily *strangles* the beast. By this time St. Samson has developed a powerful thirst, so he causes a shower of water to emanate from a spring located atop the cave's ceiling. As the water pours over him, Samson [his name recalls the biblical figure whose phenomenal strength only diminishes when his hair is cut] quenches his thirst.

Although this story likely serves as an attack on the practice of tanistry in a still pagan Ireland, Tolstoy does not identify any cometary elements in the narrative, while this study finds them everywhere. The standing stone or Tree of Life that [metaphorically] extends to the Pole Star and supports the sky is emblematic of the protector comet; the Bacchantes, or frenzied followers of Dionysius/Osiris in the Greek mystery cult tradition, symbolize the meteor showers which fell in the wake of the celestial battle of the dragon pair; the strangulation of the serpent can be likened to the strangulation of old snake-king Awri Nahir at Axum [noted later]; the hill, which Tolstoy does indicate is analogous to the primordial Benben sandhill of Egypt out of which the sun god Atum-Re-Kepri emerged from the waters, is emblematic of none other than the mountain-top encampments where stranded survivors likely waited out floods and the ensuing cosmic winters; the shower of water is reminiscent of the meteor shower that occurred during the Festival of Lughnasa on August 1; and the non-descript, abominable idol on the top of the hill, which by juxtaposition with the dragon imagery and the shower, appears to be emblematic of a cosmic serpent. And Samson may not be such a high-brow prelate after all, for this water-sucker recalls another, Set. Bailey reveals that Set, or Seth, means 'one who drinks water,' the fluid which Bailey rightly equates with wisdom (1994, 233).[17] Samson, then, is equated with Set-Lucifer, the fallen angel of the Underworld, as pagan lore leaks into Christian didacticism.

The Celtic rituals of kingly succession, like those of the Mediterranean and Red Sea basins, were, then, likely conjoined with the cycles of comets. According to Goodrich, Merlin prophecized King Vortigern's death to his face (1987, 319). Since Arthur's Merlin lived about a century later than Vortigern, the *merlin* referred to must have been one of the hereditary line of *merlins*. And Vortigern's demise was likely a death by fireball, as previously noted. So this *merlin* must have known when the celestial serpent was going to pay another visit. And the later Merlin, as Dubricus, presided over Arthur's coronation, rejected the candidacy of Gawain and Lancelot for kingship of the Grail Castle, and predicted his own death during a solar eclipse (Goodrich 1987, 319). One must also wonder if he conspired with Queen Morgue, the sister of Arthur and the wife of King Urian of Murray [which sounds like Awri of Axum fame] in the poisoning of Uther Pendragon, Arthur's dragon-father, to maintain the ideal of tanistry, namely that the old king must die to propitiate the mother goddess.

When it is recalled that Morgue, according to the Welsh *Triads*, utilized a chariot not unlike black Medea's escape vehicle, more African-based cometary imagery obtains, for Medea was the daughter of Aeetes, a Colchian king whose title was identical with Pharaoh's, "the son of the sun." And in Euripides' version, a whitened Medea finally ascends from Colchis on a celestial chariot, after providing Jason's bride with a fiery dress and, in the Greek version only, killing her children. When it is recalled that Morgue also sends Arthur a fiery garment in hopes of killing him, and that Medea was, as Graves notes in *The White Goddess*, called a Hyperborean by the ancient Greeks, heads have to be scratched. Herodotus emphatically states that the Colchians were as black-skinned and woolly-haired as the Egyptians; that, like the Egyptians, they practiced the rare custom of circumcision; and that they were descended from an abandoned garrison dating to the Asian exploits of Pharaoh Sesostris III (Herodotus, II, 105, 136).

Noting that Sesostris III can be dated to the pre-Hebraic, nineteenth century B.C.E., R. A. Jairazbhoy follows the lead of Herodotus by proposing that the Colchians could have been descended not from Sesostris III's garrison, but from an abandoned garrison of the Twelfth Egyptian Dynasty of Ramesses III, given that archeological evidence points to the activity of that dynasty in the Black Sea area. Citing archeological and historical evidence, Jairazbhoy argues that the story of Jason's pursuit of the golden fleece reveals numerous Egyptian echoes. A representative sample of his argument is quoted here:

> The fleece had been spread on an oak in front of Aeetes' city at the mouth of the Phasis [river]. The fleece is described as being 'watched over by a serpent.' Such a golden ram's head overlooked by a serpent occurs nowhere else than on the prow of a ship of Ramesses III (and of one of his predecessors). The ship was named Userhet, it was 130 cubits long (about 200 feet), and had golden rams on both prow and stern, each with a uraeus serpent overtopping it surmounted with the sun's disk. Below is a grand collar that could have been mistaken for its fleece. (1985, 60)

Could that be why the Greeks equated the Colchians with the Hyperboreans, the inhabitants of the British Isles?

Indeed, Merlin's prophecies in Monmouth's *History of the Kings of Britain* are replete with myriad references to a similar cosmic bestiary and various combats waged by those beasts, namely a "flying serpent"; a "horned dragon"; a "war-like boar" that will "lay waste provinces" before hiding its "head in the deeps of Solway Firth"; "a ram with golden horns" which emits a fog from its nostrils [signifying the meteor shower in Aries, perhaps]; "seven lions crowned with the heads of goats"; a celestial "bull" [reminiscent of the Apis bull, sacred to Osiris, perhaps]; a celestial "adder"; a "fire-breathing worm"; and other such "overgrown animals" (Goodrich 1987,

136ff.). The very essence of his great secret, his final prophecy of the occurrence of a meteor shower and an ensuing cosmic winter found in the *Bern* manuscript and quoted by Goodrich, must be examined at length:

> The stars shall turn their faces away from them & shall quit their usual tracks across the sky. In the wrath of the stars crops shall wither & the rain from the vault of heaven will be withheld. Roots and branches shall exchange places & the novelty of this shall seem a miracle.
>
> The shining sun shall dim under the amber of Mercury & this shall be visible to those who see it. The planet Mercury from Arcadia shall change its shield and the helmet of Mars shall call to Venus. The helmet of Mars shall cast its shadow; the fury of Mercury shall pass the bounds. Iron Orion shall draw his naked sword. Oceanic Apollo shall whip up the clouds. Jupiter shall emerge from his established bounds & Venus shall abandon her statutory tracks. *The star of Saturn shall rush forth in lead-colored [rain?] & a crooked sickle shall kill mortals. The twice six houses of the stars shall weep that their hosts jump their tracks. The twins shall depart from their usual embrace & shall call the bowl to the water-bearer. The scales of Libra shall swing free until Aries shall place his crooked horns under the balance. The tail of Scorpio shall ferment lightning & Cancer shall contend with the sun.* Virgo shall rise on the back of Sagittarius & shall forget her virginal flowers.
>
> *The chariot of the moon shall disturb the zodiac & the Pleiades shall burst into tears. None shall return to their appointed course*, but Adriana behind a closed door shall seek refuge in her causeways. At a stroke of the wand the winds shall rush forth & the dust of our forefathers shall blow on us again.
>
> The winds shall collide with a dire thunderclap & their blast shall echo among the stars (1987, 156-57, italics mine).

Around 50 B.C.E., Siculus made an observation about the Hyperboreans of Britain that is most relevant to Merlin's prophecy. Goodrich reproduces this passage, noted earlier in this study, regarding the nineteen year Saros cycle:

> The Moon as viewed from this island (Britain) appears to be but a little distance from the Earth and to have on it prominences like those of the Earth, which are visible to the eye. The account is also given that the god visits the island every nineteen years, the period in which the return of the stars to the same place in heaven is accomplished . . . . There is also on the island both a magnificent sacred precinct of Apollo and a notable temple . . . . and the supervisors are called Boreadae, and succession to these positions is always kept in their family. (Goodrich 1987, 320)

The god to which Diodorus refers may have been associated with eclipses that occurred from time to time at the end of the 18.61 year metonic moon cycle which Gerard Hawkins describes in *Stonehenge Decoded* (1979, 182ff.).[18] An eclipse of the sun likely symbolized a half-remembered cometary winter.

If Merlin prophecized as from the grave, as Tolstoy indicates, that grave, or the Otherworld itself, may at times have been the inner sanctum of a Grail castle, preferably the castle on the Isle of Man off the coast of the Rhinn of Galloway. It is to the cometary imagery of the Grail castles and to the many versions of the Grail legend which echo that imagery that this study now turns its attention.

What really transpired during the initiation rituals conducted in the bowels of the Grail castles which extended from Provence to Northern Europe? We may never completely answer that question, just as we may never uncover the intricacies of the female rites conducted during the Eleusinian Mysteries of ancient Greece. But we can take some educated guesses, nonetheless. If the Grail castle represented the Otherworld, that Otherworld may have been the mythical place where the comets set, a nether realm beneath the horizon where the Lord of the Underworld, a royal hermaphrodite, himself/herself a comet, wandered in its elliptical orbit that would bring it back for another close encounter with Earth. Arthur's Avalon to the west, [which, incidentally, Bailey equates with the Americas] was associated with eternal youth. Given that the Cosmic Tree was a two-way street with its roots in the Otherworld and its zenith pointing to the Pole Star, the hero had to go down before he could go up, as it were. For the upward journey of the hero, which could only be made after his descent, led to the Pole Star and its seven rotating companions-- the stars of Ursa Minor, the abode of the elect, the one fixed, unfrenzied portion of the sky. For as Gerald Massey explains, the stars of this constellation never set (1992, I, 322).

Massey proposes that Arthur, descendant of his Sabaean/Egyptian counterpart Horus, the avenger of his father, was derived, however, from the Ursa Major constellation which the Sabaean desert wanderers, the apparent ancestors of certain Celtic Irish, called Art, a constellation whose stars appeared from an earthly perspective to revolve around the Pole star. Seneca argued in his drama *Thyestes* that Ursa Major, also known as the Wain, in very ancient times "plunged below the all-engulfing waves" of the horizon because of Typhon (Velikovsky 1977b, 224ff.). Prior to that time, it contained the pole star, and the entire constellation never set. For Velikovsky, this indicates that a polar shift occurred during a Typhon encounter with the earth and as a result: "The polar axis now is turned toward one of the stars, the North Star, of the Little Bear" (1977b, 225). Arthur, first associated with Ursa Major, was later associated with Ursa Minor, which became the new symbol of order and kingship par excellence (Massey 1992, I, 310).   And we must not forget Arthur's dog, Garad. Massey explains that in ancient Wales as in ancient Egypt, there were eight gods of which Arthur was the eighth. Massey goes on to mention that pesky dog, which he identifies with Anup, the golden dog or jackal that inhabits the pole. After Shu raised a new heaven [after a cosmic winter caused by meteor shower dissipated, perhaps], Anup was equated with Set, or Sut, as god of the north celestial pole (1992, I, 322). And in ancient Egypt the jackal-headed Anup was the judge of the dead, superseded finally by Atum and Osiris (Massey 1992, I, 323). Massey reveals that in most ancient times, Anup serving as the ultimate power of the northern pole, positioned the stars in a reconstituted heaven of eight potent gods, of which Anup was the eighth (1992, I, 323).

But Anup was demoted, presumably, for our purposes, after another bone and teeth-rattling, close encounter. In the judgment hall, the *Ritual* depicts him as an inspector of weights and measures under the gaze of Osiris, now Amenta's judge (Massey 1992, I, 323). For Massey, ancient Ireland initially embraced the older Sabaean version of star mythology that existed prior to Set's demotion.   For Set-Sut-Anup [for our purposes, his cometary son Anubis] was first perceived as a savior before he was likened to a devil. Somehow, Set-worship [which was perceived as devil-worship by many a Christian missionary of the Roman persuasion] remained frozen in time in Ireland, and it probably arrived etched in the hearts of the first invader group which originally hailed, according to *Lebor Gabala*, from the Isle of Meroe in Ethiopia. No doubt, the modified view of Set was imported in subsequent migrations, but the older beliefs must have exhibited a certain resiliency.

Another   phenomenon also appears to have transpired in early Britain. The cometary myths probably became nested with earlier, Sabaean stellar mythology and with later solar mythology as well. For if the west was the direction of the Otherworld, the comets were likened to the Sun or later confused with it, humans being understandably forgetful of the legends passed down to them of traumatic visitations from the heavens. Clearly, all earth-grazing comets, asteroids and meteorites did not 'set' beneath the western horizon as they arched over the planet. But if the cometary and solar myths became confused and intertwined, the west, the direction of the setting sun, would have prevailed as the entrance to the Otherworld. To be sure, neither Massey nor W. P. Boswell make cometary associations with these gods. That is a hypothesis of this study which may be proven by a unique examination of Grail mythology.

In the Grail castle, the battle of the celestial dragon pair was likely re-enacted between the god-kings of tanistry. A beheading probably occurred, unlike the death by strangulation that was employed at Axum. This beheading was not so comical as the one that occurs in *Sir Gawain and the Green Knight*.[19] For in the Grail castle the young tanist or candidate for kingship likely decapitated the old king. In committing that act, the young king played the Set role when the later Egyptian mythology filtered into the Isles. In the act of dying, the old king played the role of Osiris, rudely nudged from the night sky by Set. But the young king could not feel too triumphant, for, in the glint of the ax, he had become a maturing Osiris awaiting his own execution by the next Set contender. *Thus each king was both Set and Osiris.*

Since Arthur's Merlin never became king, he must have been the officiator of tanistry along with Queen Morgue, united in a pact with her for as long as possible to preserve the protector comet, symbolized by Osiris-Horus-Arthur. Otherwise, if the spell failed, the sky would fall, that is, a deadly meteor shower would occur. Such is the logic of Merlin's over-determined prophecy. And as sideline coaches for the young Grail kings, all the *merlins*, like the young kings whom they initiated, played the role of Set-Baal-Lucifer-Lug-Orcus-Midir and all the other Set avatars that reigned in Ireland throughout the pre- Christian era. For the *merlins* were paradoxical figures. As agents of death, they, like Judas, were necessary agents-- not to be deemed evil in the modern sense, but behovely instead. Without a Set figure, the system of tanistry would degenerate like the night sky itself. Graves does not fathom the cometary nature of the White Goddess, whom in his Postscript he likens to the Moon-goddess Ngame worshiped along the Niger River banks in sub-Saharan Africa. Nonetheless, he almost sees the light, as it were, when he proposes that the goddess initially reigned unchallenged in ancient Europe when she cohabited with two lovers, the Serpent of Wisdom, and the Star of life, who was her son. He goes on to describe her two consorts:

> The Son was incarnate in the male demons of the various totem societies ruled by her, who assisted in the erotic dances held in her honor. The Serpent, incarnate in the sacred serpents which were the ghosts of the dead, sent the winds. The Son, who was also called Lucifer or Phosphorous ('bringer of light') because as the evening-star he led in the light of the Moon, was reborn every year, grew up as the year advanced, destroyed the Serpent, and won the Goddess's love. Her love destroyed him, but from his ashes was

born another Serpent which, at Easter, laid the *glain* or red egg which she
ate; so that the son was reborn to her as a child once more. Osiris was a Star-
son, and though after his death he looped himself around the world like a
serpent, yet when his fifty-yard long phallus was carried in procession it was
topped with a golden star; this stood for himself renewed as the Child Horus,
son of Isis, who had been his bride and his layer-out and was now his mother
once again. (1966, 387-88)[20]

Graves further notes that Pythagoras, a proponent of the Transmigration
of Souls whose rites recurred in Britain, was a Pelasgian from Samos.
During his initiation at Crete, the priests "ritually purified him with a
thunderbolt, that is to say they made a pretense of killing him with either a
meteoric stone or a Neolithic ax popularly mistaken for a thunderbolt . . . "
(1966, 283).

Clearly, Merlin's prophecy derived in part from a terrible memory that had
been transported to the British Isles. *In situ*, this memory was revived by
local cometary pyrotechnics. The memory of past and present impacts, then,
triggered the grim mechanisms of tanistry which spread from the
Mediterranean and Red Sea littorals to points north. These mechanisms
operated in the depths of the Grail castle, which came in the British Isles as
in Southern France to emblemize the Otherworld. But before this study turns
its attention to the landscape of that Otherworld and the lessons that its
landscape conveyed to the initiands who entered the Grail Castle's terrifying
depths, the complex African and Near Eastern-based totemism that
determined the family titles of the sacred priests, priestesses, kings and
queens of ancient Ireland needs to be examined.

Notes

1. See Graves (1966, 179). He mentions the "Gwyn, 'the White One', son of Llyr
or Lludd was buried in a boat-shaped coffin in his father's honor: he was a sort of
Osiris (his rival 'Victor son of Scorcher' being a sort of Set) and came to be identified
with King Arthur." This suggests that Guinevere was a cometary demon like Arthur.
Gwyn was probably a feminized title. And Arthur, whose title may be derived from
Artemis, was likely a masculinized one. Massey (1995, 128, 291-92) attempts to
explain Guinevere's function, using the imagery of the solar barge. Given that *nefer*
in Egyptian means 'good,' ' beautiful,' or 'perfect,' all of this suggests to Massey
that Guinevere is "derived from Khen-nefer, the beautiful Khen, queen, accompanier,
or mate. Khen (Eg.) is the boat, the ark, the feminine abode of the waters, and
Guinevere is the lady of the summit of the water in the triad of Arthur's wives."
The derivation of the word Camelot is also attempted by Massey (1995, 401-02).

Regarding the etymology, Massey argues in *A Book of the Beginnings* that the title evolves from two Egyptian cognates. The first is *kham*, meaning 'a shrine for the dead,' and *ret* [lot], meaning 'to retain the form,' 'steps,' and 'ascent.' Camelot, goes on, was the burial vault of the dead, the shrine to which the deceased was carried to be laid out. From Massey's perspective, Camelot becomes a miniature version of the Egyptian Masteba, of which the Great Pyramid is the grandest example, a place of duality, of burial and of birth-- specifically the birthplace of the divine child Arthur from the Great Mother's womb.

2. See Vilna (1887, *Midrash Shemot Raba*, 18:5); Ginzberg (1925, II, 307ff.); Exodus 14: 19; Velikovsky notes that Michael dwelt in heaven and was the precursor of "Shehina or God's presence, but as Lucifer, Michael falls from heaven and his hands are bound by God."

3. See Ginzburg's *Legends*, Index Volume under "Michael." Using C. Doumas (1982) as his source, Pellegrino (1991) suggests that it was the Sea of Reeds (*jam suf* in Hebrew) that Moses and his refugees crossed. It was this more northern body that may have experienced a retreat of waters just prior to the arrival of a Theran tsunami, and not the Red Sea proper.

4. See *Tractate Shabbat*, p. 113b; Sanhedrin, p. 941.

5. See Papyrus Ipuwer (2: 10; 7: 1; 1: 11;11: 11; 12: 6). Also see Velikovsky (1977, 71).

6. Cilicia lay northeast of the ancient city of Tarsus. Also see Sandars (1978, 158).

7. Winterbottom (1978, 41) provides the following translation: "'Howl! The day of the Lord is near . . . for destruction is on its way from the Lord. Because of this every hand shall lose its grip, every man's heart shall melt and be crushed; tortures and torments shall take hold, and they shall have pain like a woman in labor. Each man shall be astonished as he looks at his neighbor, their faces aflame. Behold the day of the Lord shall come, cruel and full of wrath and anger and indignation, to make a wilderness of the land, to wipe its sinners of its face; the brilliant stars in the sky shall cease to spread their light, and the sun shall be shadowed at its rising, and the moon shall not be bright at its due time. I shall punish the evils of this world, visit their wickedness on the wicked; I shall silence the pride of the rebellious, and lay low the arrogant and the strong.' And again: 'Behold, the Lord will scatter the land, and lay it bare, scar its face, disperse its inhabitants.'" No great leap of the imagination is required to infer that a cometary winter is being described by Gildas. References to a cometary "flying sickle twenty cubits long" from Zechariah, to the destruction of Sodom and Gomorrah, and to Elijah, who hears the voice of the Lord issuing from the fire, add to the cometary image pattern that emerges from *The Ruin of Britain*. Also see Winterbottom (1978, 47, 38-39).

8. In an important article in the British journal *Nature* entitled "Irish Tree Rings, Santorini and Volcanic Dust Veils," M. G. L. Baillie and M. A. R. Munro test the hypothesis that in 4735, 3195, 1626, and 1150 B.C.E. world-wide atmospheric dust veils shrouded the earth as a result of volcanism at eruption sites such as Santorini in the Mediterranean and Hekla in Iceland. Correlating tree ring data from several bog oak samples in Northern Ireland with bristlecone pine tree ring data obtained in the western US and with high acidic readings [resulting from acid rain] in core samples

from the southern Greenland icepack, they discover that all three sources provide the above-mentioned dates for world-wide climate recessions, along with one more date-- 550 C.E. plus or minus 50 years. Clube and Napier also lean toward the revised Santorini date of 1626 B.C.E., but they go on to note that in the case of the 550 C.E. date, there is no recorded evidence of volcanism. This lack of proof leads them to propose that the severe climate recession and the world-wide dust veil of that date that caused high acid readings in the corresponding ice sample and narrow tree ring formation in the U.S. and Irish samples, were caused not by volcanism but by a Tunguska-like aerial explosion of a comet fragment over Britain. They also point to the likelihood of an accompanying meteor shower and numerous fire-ball induced forest fires that could have caused the catastrophe which Gildas labeled "the ruin of Britain." For evidence, Clube and Napier (1990, 285, fn. 62) cite two obscure passages from Klinkerfues' *Gottinger Nachrichten*. The first reads: "In this year [524 C.E.], though, there occurred also much running of the stars from evening quite to daybreak, so that everybody was frightened, and we know of no such event beside." And the second: "For twenty days there appeared a comet, and after some time there occurred a running of the stars from evening till early [morning], so that the people said all the stars were falling." Aware that no impact is described in these passages, Clube and Napier reproduce a telling quote from an 1834 edition of the London *Penny Magazine*: "in the process of draining the Isle of Axholme in Lincolnshire, evidence has everywhere been found not only of previous vegetation but that this spot must have been suddenly overwhelmed by some violent convulsion of nature. Great numbers of oak, fir and other trees were lying 5 feet underground." The article goes on to reveal the north-west/south-east configuration of the trees which had not been "dissevered by the axe but had been burnt assunder near the ground, the ends still presenting a charred surface." (Clube and Napier (1990 , 284-85, fn. 61). Although the above-mentioned comet sightings and theTunguska-like configurations of the downed trees at Axholme are not absolute proof of a circa 540 C.E. meteoric impact in the British Isles, all of this information, coupled with Merlin's prophecy, calls for further study of the hypothesis that Camelot was eclipsed by an impact-induced, cosmic winter that heralded the beginning a climate recession history books call the Dark Ages.

    9. The death of another king, Aurelius Ambrosius, was attributed to the passing of a comet by Merlin in Monmouth's *History of the Kings of Britain*, 8.14-15.

    10. Tolstoy (1985, 115) derives the name Ambrosius, whom Geoffrey of Monmouth argues was the builder of Stonehenge [also referred to as Morien], from the Welsh for 'immortal', and in a footnote he indicates that Ambrosius might have meant 'lords of Britain.' These may be correct definitions, but there could have been an earlier source, namely Abyssinia's term for the serpent king of the sacred grove, the possible cognate *Awri*, for 'beast' (Boswell 1972b, 3ff.). Then too, during the wandering of the Jews during the Exodus, ambrosia, or "manna from heaven," was consumed by the Israelites. Exodus 16:14-34. Associated with the notorious "pillar of fire" and "pillar of smoke," this mysterious "bread of heaven" was known as the food of the gods in the Greek tradition, and it has been identified with complex carbohydrates by Velikovsky (1977, 145ff) who argues that it could have been

introduced into Earth's atmosphere by meteorites. Hence, ambrosia and Ambrosius may have much in common, and the hallucinogenic mushroom which induces trances should not be ruled out either.

11. This cometary madness is echoed in the twelfth century grove in the forest of Broceliande, where a monk named Eon de l'Etoile resided. Much as Robin Hood, Eon advocated the fleecing of the rich. Markale (1995, 126-28) notes that "his activities took place in about 1148. In that same year a comet appeared that terrified his contemporaries, and Eon was given the name 'de l'Etoile ['of the Star'], adding a fantastic aura to his image." Eon is likened to Merlin by Markale because, like his Scottish forerunner, Eon was deemed to be mad. Later, he was jailed on charges of heresy and died shortly thereafter. Interestingly enough, his haunt was a sacred grove or nemeton at Barenton complete with a Cosmic Tree and spring, where heaven and earth were thought to meet. What could more cometary? And Eon was not the only Frenchman of the era associated with a comet. Provencal rulers of the early thirteenth century, the lords of Les Baux, were a bloodthirsty lot. According to Payne (1963, 107) they dubbed themselves the "comet" race, and legend has it that Bergere des Baux cut out the heart of the famous troubadour poet Guillen de Cabestanh, and offered the organ to his wife who ate it with relish. An immense, sixteen-rayed, star of silver was reputed to have hovered over the head of Alix de Baux, the last of the so-called comet race, when she expired in 1426. This death star tradition was not uncommon in France and appears to result from the association of dying saints and ignominious sinners with the passing of a comet. Van Dam (1988, 103-04) in his translation of Gregory of Tours' *Glory of the Confession*, notes the following legend of the death of Pelagia of Limoge in 586 c.e.: "Before she was buried on the fourth day such a sweet fragrance flowed from her body that everyone was surprised. During the night a huge ball of fire appeared that rose in the east, moved across the circuit of the sky, and stopped over the church in which the body of the dead woman was lying. The sudden brightness of the ball of fire so filled the entire church that people thought they saw the middle of the day." Cometary imagery was ubiquitous in the Middle Ages. The imagery often appears in the descriptions of the lives of saints and sinners alike. Another likely cometary saint of the fourth century was Catherine of Alexandria. On St. Catherine's day, celebrated appropriately enough during the November meteor shower, wagon wheels alight with candles, called Catherine Wheels, were whirled in honor of her death.

12. See Tolstoy (1985, 55; 269, fn. 2) on sky warriors as emblematic of the Aurora Borealis. Also see Graves (1966, 451ff.).

13. See Gaster (1924-1928). According to Freeman (1992, 499), Asmodeus was an evil demon who killed Sarah's first seven husbands. According to the *Book of Tobit*, 3:8, each died on his wedding night. Her next husband Tobias tricked the demon by setting a trap. After placing the heart and the liver of a fish on burning incense following the advice of the angel Raphael, he captured Asmodeus. Also see Graves (1966, 130-31), who cites the *Book of Tobit*. Graves argues that "Asmodeus is the Persian counterpart of Set, the yearly murderer of Osiris, but he is charmed away with the fish of immortality and flees to his southern deserts. Tobit's dog is a helpful clue; he always accompanied Hercules Melkarth, or his Persian counterpart

Sarosha, or the Greek Aesculapius, wherever he went." In Ireland, Graves goes on, Hercules becomes in the eleventh-century *Book of Leinster* Cenn Cruaich, or "the Lord of the Mound," a deity which Graves estimates was introduced into Ireland around 1267 c.e. by the Milesian Heremon, the nineteenth king of Ireland whose ancestors likely migrated from Caria, Crete, and whose descendants founded a city by the same name in Ireland.

14 . Graves (1966, 332) also notes that a related deity, leonine Llew, did not die for his Achille's heel did not touch the ground, given that his hair held him aloft. Many of the protector comets were lame such as Dionysius and, with a stretch of the imagination, the Essenic Yeshua, or Jesus. The Essenes believed that Yeshua would judge the world by fire. Llew, Graves tells us on p. 321, floated in a coffer like Osiris. Cuchulain is also called Setanta, a Set name in Bailey (1994, 72). Also see Quinn (1986, 91-92), where he notes that in the Ulster Cycle, battles occur between Queen Maeve of Connacht and Setanta or Cuchulain of Ulster. Connacht represents the area of the southern Q-Celts and Ulster was the domain of the P-Celts who came from Iberia. Cuchulain then is also called Setanta because he bore the Hamitic Set name from North Africa, as noted earlier.

15. Graves (1966, 171) notes that Phaeton's sisters turned into a poplar grove. He also notes that the alder tree is the tree of resurrection in *Cad Goddeu*.

16. O'Keefe ed. (1913, 62-68). See Graves (1966, 35). Also on p. 138 Graves interprets the mill stone image as the actions of the double-headed "White Goddess in her complementary moods of creation and destruction." On p. 179 Graves recalls that Artemis Calliste, or Callisto, was another name for the Goddess of the Mill. Her totem was the she-bear, and a girl would often dress the part of the Little Bear in festivals at Athens. He concludes: "The Great She-bear and the Little She-bear are still the names of the two constellations that turn the mill around." Although Graves does not consider this possibility, could Artemis be the root of Arthur, masculinized by the firth century, who returns again and again as the earth's surface was periodically ground up as in a mill by falling meteorites?

Massey (1995, 503, 314-15) also tries to unravel the root of the Arthur title. He argues that the first wave of myth diffusion in Britain was Sabaean, and its principal gods were the Great Mother and her son Sut. During that era, which Massey does not date, Britain was allegedly called the Island of Beli, the Star-God of fire, a deity which Massey argues, represented the seven stars of the Great Bear constellation. Regarding the Great Mother of the Sabaean system, a paradigm that Druscilla Houston links to Ethiopian origins, Massey proposes that the most ancient version of the deity, symbolized by the Great Bear constellation, was born in the minds of desert star-gazers of Arabia. In Egypt, Massey goes on, she was known by such names as Taurt, Khephsh, Kheft, Aft, Apt, Khebt, Kheb, Kep, Ap, and her full title was identical with the name of Egypt itself. *Af*, he argues, means 'born of'; *ap* means 'the first,' and *aft* signified 'the abode of,' 'the four corners,' and 'the north.' As noted previously, her zootype was the hippopotamus. And she was also identified with the cow, or 'horse of the waters.' Then too, *Khebt* means 'the birthplace in the north.' Massey further proposes that *Kheft* evolved into *Hat*, leading eventually to Hathor and finally to Ked, goddess of the British Druids. He insists that Kheft or Aft was worshiped as the Ked avatar by the Druids at Stonehenge. For Massey (1995, 359) Sothis, the dog-star Sirius, was a potent deity that later evolved into both the solar version of the Egyptian Horus and his northern counterpart, the British Arthur. And when Sabaean star-worship arrived in the British Isles, Massey proposes, the primal Arthur, which appears to have been a title rather than a name, took his totemic name from the Great Bear constellation previously known to the Egyptians as Ta-Urt, the Great Mother, who gave birth to Sothis on the 25th of July just as the Nile inundation commenced to make the land of Egypt fertile again. Massey explains that Arthur was an avatar of the Sabaean Mercury, son of the Great Bear mother goddess. He was also an avatar of Sydik and Sutekh, and the later Egyptian god Sut-Har, who was associated with the sun and Sirius-cycle. Massey argues that a prototype of Arthur was also the Negro called Sut Nahsi and Sut Nubti, who was a combination of a Sabaean star god and an Egyptian solar deity.

Massey (1995, 316) goes on to fine-tune his Sabaean-derived version of Arthur, arguing that in the first phase of the Round Table, Ked reigned as the Great Bear, with her harp symbolized by the constellation Lyra. The name Arth [Arthur], then, was derived from the Egyptian name of the Great Bear, Ta Urt, because in the matriarchal scheme of things, men took their names from the mother and not from the father. To illustrate the derivation, Massey (1995, 358-359) attempts to clarify the alleged word roots deriving the Welsh *Arthen* from 'the bear's cub,' and 'utterance of the Bear.' As expected, he traces the name to the Egyptian root *ar*, har and khar, meaning 'speech.' Continuing with Sabaean Arthur's celestial genealogy, Massey (1995, 359) proposes that Arthur's parents were the Great Dragon, the female Typhon, and Eigyr. And the British Arthur is, for Massey, associated with the seven stars of the Great Bear constellation, the 'Seven in the Ark,' which being circumpolar in nature, escaped the so-called Deluge, or the gradual sinking of the lower stars below the horizon during the Precession of the Equinoxes. Massey (1992, I, 305) clarifies the imagery, noting that the Great Bear constellation served as a stellar clock, as it were. In Egypt, he goes on, when the tail of the constellation pointed south, the inundation of the Nile began. For Massey, then, the tail star pointed to the south of Egypt to the source of the inundation, the southern lakes or birthplace of the waters. It was at this time, in the later solar version, that Horus, adrift in his ark or sun boat, confronted the dragon of drought and saved Egypt by delivering it once again.

Interestingly enough, Graves notes on p. 136 of *The White Goddess* that the Welsh for Taliesin is 'radiant brow,' a nomenclature that likens Taliesin with Apollo. Graves further argues that the syllable 'Tal' can be found in the earliest names of Hercules, namely one Talus, the bronze man, who was killed by Medea in Crete. Graves goes on to note that the Irish Tailltean Games were played in honor of an agrarian Hercules, whose name also bore the Tal syllable. Furthermore, he was called Telmen in Syria, Atlas Telamon, in Greece. He traces the cognate to *Tla* or *Tal*, to "'take upon oneself', 'dare', and 'suffer'." If Taliesin was a barley god as well, that grain identification could link him with the corn god Osiris, and grain may symbolize more than it seems, for it could emblemize meteoric dust.

17. Hancock and Bauval (1996, 204ff.) note that the capstone of an Egyptian

pyramid was called a Benben. The Benben was likened to the Bennu Bird which was a symbol of rebirth and immortality. The Benben was symbolic of a cone-shaped, oriented meteorite which was reputed to have fallen from the sky, they argue. Bauval and Gilbert (1994, 203-04) note in *The Orion Mystery* that Wallis Budge was the first to suggest that the Benben stone was styled after a meteorite, not unlike the Black Stone of Ka-aba. They propose the following: "It is thus quite likely that a large oriented meteorite fell near Memphis at some time in the third millennium B.C., perhaps during the Second or Third Dynasty. From depictions of the Benben stone, it would seem that the frightful spectacle of its fiery fall would have been very impressive. The fall would have been presaged by loud detonations caused by the shock waves and even in daylight a fireball with a long, pluming tail would have been visible from considerable distances. This fire-bird would have evoked the notion of a returning phoenix crashing in from the east . . . . Rushing to the spot where it landed, the people would have seen that the fire-bird had disappeared, leaving only a black, pyramid-shaped *bja* object or cosmic egg [the oriented iron meteorite]."

18. Hawkins (1979, 182ff.) likens the 19 year Saros cycle to the moon's metonic cycle of 18.61 years, the time it takes the moon to complete one full movement cycle. Three times 18.61, then, is roughly 56 years, a figure equal to the number of the 56 Aubrey holes associated with Stonehenge I. These holes were used to predict eclipses of the sun, events that likely recalled memories of cometary winters, for our purposes. He argues: "When the full moon rises opposite the setting sun, an eclipse of the moon is possible. An eclipse of the sun may occur 15 days later, when the moon has moved around in its orbit to line up with the sun. The periods in which eclipses are possible are known as 'eclipse seasons.' Their occurrence in the calendar is controlled by the 18.61-year cyclic precession of the seasons. After 56 years the sequence of the eclipse returns within 3 or 4 days of the starting point in the Gregorian calendar." Regarding the uses of Stonehenge II, Hawkins is unable to say. "What about Stonehenge II, the abortive double circle of bluestones? Here, unfortunately, there is too little evidence for solid theorizing. Until archeology determines the exact number of spokes the builders intended to put in that wheel, one can only guess what its purpose might have been."

19. *Sir Gawain and the Green Knight* is filled with hints about Merlin's function as an initiator of potential young Grail kings. That Merlin should be equated with the Green Knight Bercilak has been so well delineated by Zimmer (1968), who provides thirteen reasons for the association, we need not labor the point. See Goodrich (1987, 320). In an important and often overlooked study of the Islamic influence on medieval English literature by Alice E. Lasater (1972, 172-73, fn. 54) entitled *Spain to England*, Lasater traces the figure of Bercilak-Merlin to pre-Islamic mythology. Denying that *Sir Gawain and the Green Knight* depicts a fertility ritual given that "there is no restoration of a wasteland to greenness at his beheading as would be expected in a ritual enactment of the death-and- rebirth cycle," Lasater proposes that the poem is focused on testing Gawain for characteristics such as "bravery and the ability to keep one's word even if it means death," "chastity" and "patience." Lasater (1972, 175) goes on to argue that the poem is designed to test Gawain, who unfortunately does not live up to the ideals established for the perfect Christian

Knight. For even though Gawain resists the seductions of Bercilak's lady, who appears to be not only the virgin aspect of the Triple Goddess, Morgan le Fey, but later the Loathly Lady hag as well, Gawain deceives Bercilak by concealing the girdle which the Lady has given him as a love token. Lasater provides a reason for Gawain's resistance to seduction, citing yet another, later Near Eastern influence: "The tradition within which the Lady is operating, in addition to a pre-courtly love Celtic tradition, is that of Ibn-Quzman, of troubadours and romance writers, in which the lady is married and of higher station than her suitor." See Loomis (1956, 89). Lasater (1972, 180) goes on to note that along with the concept of Christian chastity, Gawain "appears to be acting in accordance with an earlier courtly-love tradition, that found in Ibn-Hazm and in Jean de Meun, in which the lady must not be married." For the purposes of this study, *Sir Gawain and the Green Knight* is clearly a poem about tanistry, the beheading of the old king by the new one, but a comic approach is being used, given that the pagan ritual has become obsolete and that Gawain is unfit to play the Set role. Bercilak-Merlin corresponds to the initiator of the tanist, the prospective king, and Morgan la Fey, who recalls Aso, the co-conspirator with Set in the death of Osiris, according to one version of the legend, is the Mother Goddess who demands a worthy and potent consort to replace the old king.

This all comes out in the wash when another Eastern influence, this one pre-Islamic, is proposed by Lasater. For Bercilak is not only reminiscent of Cuchulain of the Middle-Irish narrative *Fled Bricrend* (*Feast of Bririu*), who, like Bercilak, is willing to submit to an ax blow, but Bercilak also echoes the pre-Islamic, Arabic figure al-Khadir, another Green Man, and yet another African and Near Eastern influence.

To prove her point, she traces more Oriental and French influences in the poem. Agreeing that two of the three plot components are Celtic in origin, the challenge to behead and the test of chastity, Lasater (1972, 181) argues that third plot component, the exchange of winnings "derives from an Oriental *fabliau* written in Latin, found in France in the twelfth century and in the *Arabian Knights*, suggesting that it may have reached Europe through Spain." Other Oriental and French influences are also identified by Lasater: The pentangle that Gawain sports upon his shield is associated with Solomon; the prosody of *Sir Gawain* is similar to the *chante-fable* form which was practiced in Arab and Persian courts [one excellent example is the Old French tale *Aucassin et Nicolette*], and the fiery red eyes of Bercilak are reminiscent of the blackamoors and Saracens depicted in the *chanson de geste* tradition.

Since Bercilak does not appear to be a fertility figure like the English Green Man, and since no European green figure has been discovered who resembles the Green Knight, Lasater (1972, 187) traces Bercilak's provenance to the pre-Islamic al-Khadir, noting in the legends surrounding him that "He appeared to be a contemporary of Alexander the Great . . . Adam, Noah and Moses; and he was later confused with such figures as Elijah and St. George." She cites Baring-Gould who referred to England's patron Saint George the dragon-slayer "as a 'Christianized, Semitic god,' who is none other than a manifestation of the older Khadir." Even more interesting for our purposes is Lasater's (1972, 189) observation, following Baring-Gould's lead, that al-Khadir was viewed as an avatar of the Phoenician god Baal and Egypt's Osiris.

Where there is an Osiris, there must always be a Set. When Bercilak allows Gawain to decapitate him, he is jokingly playing the role of Osiris, but in the pagan tanistry of pre-Christian, druidic Europe, the beheading was no joke. So as the initiator of the tanist working in concert and in collusion with the Queen, Merlin, Bercilak's other precursor, was performing his Set role. As James Joyce puts it, past times become pastimes. Goodrich (1987, 233) understands the nuts and bolts of the ritual of tanistry when she argues that the sacred chapel corresponds to Delphi, and notes that Bercilak: "the high priest of the chapel does not behead Gawain. At this ritual initiation, or final examination, the priest gives him only three dolorous strokes upon the bare neck with his ceremonial ax, and recall that a 'merlin' is a ceremonial Celtic ax." She goes on to propose (1987, 233): "Perhaps Gawain as the lascivious Aries was supplanted by a greater springtime hero" Saint George as pagan memories subsided. Dragon pairs all.

Sir Gawain and the Green Knight has many of the elements of the tree worship and tanistry rites practiced in the Mediterranean and Red Sea basins: The contest between the old and new king, the conspiratorial matriarch for whom the contest was waged, the linden tree sacred to the Mother Goddess, the sacred oak grove, the holly branch which Merlin carries, the location of the Green Chapel on St. Patrick's Isle [which recalls Axum's location in the Isle of Meroe], and the association of Gawain with Aries the Ram [and likely its meteor shower at Beltane]. It is a comic view of the past, spun for Yuletide revelers in Christian Britain, but underlying the comedy, the cosmic serpents and the pathetic attempt to control their movements, loom.

20. Spence (1974, 161-62) notes similarities to the druidic and Osirian cults in regard to their use of the bull totem: "In Egypt the bull was worshiped under the form of Apis. Apis was merely a form of Osiris, the calf of the sky-goddess Nut, and to the bull which represented him other cattle were sacrificed. The cult of Serapis (Osiris-Apis) was of widespread distribution, and brought by the Romans to Britain, where it flourished, chiefly at York. The bull was also sacred to the Druids, and was sacrificed at the ancient rite of Beltane (Bile's Fire), when the cattle were driven into the flames."

Chapter 11

~~~~~~

Comets and Trees

One of the puzzling aspects of the English attitude toward Africa from the High Middle Ages to the Renaissance involves the contradictory ways in which many of England's writers described the Ethiopian. In *Anti-Blackness in English Religion, 1500-1800*, Joseph R. Washington reveals that numerous literati mirrored national sentiments about blackness in the early sixteenth century. On the one hand, they largely accepted the Old Testament view alleging that Ham was doubly cursed not only because of his blackness but also because of the invective regarding his and his descendants' slavery. Despite this sentiment, the attitude often swung like a pendulum in the opposite direction, toward an articulation of human equality between black and white people and even toward an over-idealization of the Ethiopian (1984, 1).

Swinging in the direction of over-idealization, many medieval and Renaissance English thinkers depicted the Ethiopian in a manner quite unlike portraits of Ham's descendants, from whom the Ethiopian was carefully distinguished. Rather, the Ethiopian was placed at the top of list of most-favored Africans. Why should this be so? To derive the answer, we need to go back in time to the era of the Crusades, for it was during that protracted ordeal that the English imaginatively rediscovered Ethiopia. In his analysis of the fourteenth century *Voiage and Travaile of Syr John Maundeville*, Washington explains the phenomenon:

> This sudden awakening to a world unknown for centuries in the West produced in its mixture of magic, reverence, and hope, the myth of paradise lost; the idea that Christian Ethiopians resided near the Garden of Eden and thereby naturally reflected its innocence and simplicity in their lives, and that through their priest-king (the legendary Prester John) Christian Ethiopians would become the other prong of a pincher movement against Islam. (1984,

41-42)

In his zeal, Maundeville even reshaped the image of Ham and attempted to rewrite Genesis, as Washington notes:

> ... ye knowe that all the worlde was destroied with Noes floud by Noe, his wife & children. Noe had three sons, Sem, Cham, and Japhet. Cham whan he saw his father's privities naked when he slept and scorned it, & therefore he was cursed, and Japeth covered it againe. These three bretherne hadde all the land. Cham took the best parte eastward that is called Asia. Sem took Afryke, and Japeth toke Europe. Cham was the mightiest and rychest of his bretherne and of him are come the Paynem folke, and divers maner of men of the yles, some headless, and other men disfigured, and for this Cham the Emperour ther called him Cham and lord of all. (1984, 42-43)[1]

Earlier, in the twelfth century, another tactic had been employed to elevate the status of the Ethiopian, namely the tracing of the Ethiopians' lineage not to Ham, but, as Washington notes, to Croesus, the ancestor of Nimrod (1984, 42). Although this myth of the beneficent Ethiopian ally was largely deflated by Shakespeare's day, Washington goes on to reveal: "The Crusades, which unleashed a holocaust against Jews and a vendetta against the Islamic faithful, established blacks as a holy, respected, and endeared people. They were the good black Christian Ethiopians and equals of the good white Christian Europeans" (1984, 42).

Even as late as the sixteenth century, Washington argues, some Englishmen still perpetuated the twelfth century view which exempted the Ethiopian from the curse of Ham. Johan Boemus in *The Fardle of Facions* could write that the Ethiopians were "never under the bondage of any: but ever a free nation" (1984, 45). Washington goes on to paraphrase more of Boemus' thoughts:

> Instead of declaring blacks heathens to be shunned, Ethiopians were honored as literate, virtuous, law-abiding, orderly Christians led by the honored 'man of such power,' the 'King of Ethiope,' 'Prestonnes and Presbiter John,' 'of him given a benefices, and spiritual promotions, which prerogative the Pope hath given, to the matresie of Kinges.' (1984, 45)

Boemus went so far as to consider, if not to completely accept, the ancient view that the Ethiopians were "the firste of all menne." In making this assertion, Boemus identified Adam and Eve as Ethiopians and placed the Garden of Eden in the vicinity of that African locale (Washington 1984, 45).[2] Unwittingly perhaps, a dialectic had been established, the biblical view of the cursed Ham and his unfortunate descendants versus the lingering medieval view of idealized Ethiopians deemed "the firste of all menne" (Washington 1984, 45).

This English ambivalence regarding the value of blackness is profusely illustrated by Washington, and we need not explore it further. For the Irish monks of Clonmacnoise Abbey in medieval Ireland, Ethiopians were also viewed with favor and cited as one component of the ancestry of the early invaders of Ireland. For these invaders were clearly linked to Ethiopia and Upper Egypt in *Lebor Gabala.*

Apparently this over-idealization of the Ethiopian continued in the popular imagination and may have informed some twentieth century anthropological thinking. For example, Charles B. Seligman in the *Races of Africa*, seemingly echoing Rodd, writes with confidence:

> The Hamites-- who are Caucasians, i.e. belong to the same great branch of mankind as almost all Europeans-- are commonly divided into two great branches, Eastern and Northern . . . . The Eastern Hamites comprise the ancient and modern Egyptians . . . the Beja, the . . . Nubians, the Galla, the Somali and the Danakil and . . . most Abyssinians [Ethiopians]. The Northern Hamites included the Berbers . . . the Tuareg and Tibu of the Sahara, the Fula of Nigeria and the extinct Guanache of the Canary Islands. (1930, 157-58)

Could such over-idealization of the Ethiopian, regardless as to whether the people were perceived as white or black, have derived from another motivation? Was an ancient kinship dimly intuited?

Lebor Gabala delineates six pre-Christian invasions, or migrations, which apparently originated from places quite remote from Ireland: The Isle of Meroe, North Africa, coastal Greece, the island of Crete, the Caucasus Mountains, and the Black Sea littoral. The time frame for the migrations also seems excessively remote, for it extends from the fourth through the second millennium B.C.E.. Given this odd distance in time and place, many scholars reject *Lebor Gabala* out of hand, assuming it to be the product of the overactive imaginations of anonymous sixth century monks of Clonmacnoise Abbey.

This study is not so hasty in its evaluation of that chronicle. Instead, arguments have and will be presented that appear to substantiate many of *Lebor Gabala's* claims. To begin that endeavor the bizarre hypothesis proposed by W. P. Boswell in *Irish Wizards in the Woods of Ethiopia* and in *The Snake in the Grove* that *Lebor Gabala* depicts the Sabaean-Egyptian, Greek and North African colonization of Ireland in pre-Christian times will be examined.

For Boswell, the title of *Lebor Gabala* is itself illuminating. Citing Jean Doresse's *Ethiopia*, Boswell states that an ancient Ethiopian tribe of royal status was called the *Gabala*, and that a royal Irish clan was named *Ui Gabhla* (Boswell 1972b, 12; Doresse 1959, 28, 32). Additionally, she notes that the word *gabala* may also mean 'tribe,' and the *ab* suffix could refer to the 'Abbots' or 'Abs,' who in both pre-Christian and Christian Ireland traced their descent from druid chiefs and practiced a violent kingship rituals (1972b, 12). Citing Geoffrey Keating's *History of Ireland*, she finds a place-name, an apparent cognate to *Gabala*, in the Gabhail Liuin parish which includes the towns of Clonkelly, Knockninney and Coole (Boswell 1972b, 12). She fails to mention another possible cognate, however, for as E. Renan (1895) explains in *Mission de Phenicie*, the name of the Phoenician city of Byblus or Byblos is a Greek corruption of the Semitic place-name for Byblos or *Gebal*. Nonetheless, Boswell argues that there were two tribal entities, the Angabo and the Gabala, which tended the vast incense groves of ancient Abyssinia and monopolized the incense production there. She goes on to note that members of these tribal entrepreneurs migrated into Ireland, setting up potent druidic and monastic branches (1972a, 1919; Keating 1908, IV, 311).

Regarding this incense industry, Alfred Lucas in *Ancient Egyptian Materials and Industries* explains that Egyptian unguents and perfumes were derived from frankincense, myrrh, and resin, and that the perfume was fixed by the gummy resin (Frazer 1961, I, 13). This was no small industry, for one of the by-products of the sacred trees was myrrh, a key component in the embalming process. Boswell explains: "God had to be propitiated and wooed in his temple, but the human body was also his temple and had to be preserved so that the Ka . . . could make the trip to the Otherworld where the great God welcomed his child" (1972a, 4-5).

Shifting to the Angabo tribe of Ethiopia, the companion tribe of the Gabala, Boswell reveals that according to the *Kebra Negast*, the dynastic history of Ethiopia, Solomon's wife, the Queen of Sheba, had a father named Anghabo (1972a, 93 fns. 269, 270). Boswell finds an Irish place-name for the father's name as well-- the Anghabo monastery in Kilkenny, founded by Saint Cainnech (1972b, 5). She goes on to reveal that in pagan Ireland Anghabe was Aengus, the Culdee's father, and that Aengus was the monk who wrote the *Martyrology of Oengus* (1972a, 15). Intrigued by the semantic goodness of fit, she notes further that Anghabe and his son Aengus belonged to a caste of Irish royal magicians. Indicating that Ingube was the sister of the Irish god ancestor Aengus, Boswell then surmises that in Ireland

Anghabe was both a tribal name and a variant of Aengus (1972a, 15).

Discovering what may be a key link in the alleged Ethiopian origins of the early Irish royal line of kings and priests, Boswell concludes that given the fact that Aengus and Ingube ruled at Tara, and given that Tara means 'incense' in Semitic languages, *Lebor Gabala* echoes the name of the Gabala tribe (1972a, 15). Could this be why incense cups have been found in ancient tombs of the Salisbury Plain and the Boyne River valley? she asks (Boswell 1972a, 16).

Cohane offers a different spin on the etymology of Tara. Noting that, exclusive of the capital, there are more than 300 Tareh-based place-names in Ireland, he traces the Tara complex to Tareh, the father of Abraham (Cohane 1969, 266ff.).

In any case, if the monastic records of Clonmacnoise are accurate, Boswell goes on, there is "a black man in the very woodpile that provided papyrus, balsa and cedar boats, paper, ropes, perfumes, coffins, shrines, temples, and every other kind of cultural contribution" (1972b, 3). And what is more: "The God of Genesis was the ancestral magus who owned that woodpile and ruled the Garden of Aden [Eden]. The Garden was a place where resin and gum trees grew--otherwise the South Arabian and Abyssinian Red Sea coast lands which adjoin the Plain of Sennaar in East Africa" (1972a, 3).

Interestingly enough, pagan Ireland and Ethiopia, Boswell explains, were both matrifocal societies, each ruled by a succession of High Priestess Queens (1972a, 3). And what is to be made of the assertion found in *The Irish Liber Hymnorum* that Ireland's line of High Priestesses descended from the Queen of Sheba? she asks (1972a, 41- 42, fn. 134).

Adding to these parallels, she notes other parallels in chronology. For one, the earliest redactions of both *Lebor Gabala*, and the *Kebra Negast*, Ethiopia's dynastic chronicles, were compiled in the sixth century C.E. As mentioned, a more comprehensive written version of the *Kebra Negast* was compiled in the thirteenth century C.E. to legitimize the Solomonid bid for the kingship of Ethiopia. And interesting too is the historical fact that Ireland and Ethiopia converted to Christianity at about the same time, in the fourth century. Could the monasteries of these two widely separated countries have been in communication with one another during those conversions? Could that communication have extended well into the sixth and seventh centuries as well? Were the two works written in synchronization with the goal of chronicling a double history, one of the mother church and the other of its sibling? Boswell notes that according to E. A. Wallis Budge in *The Queen of Sheba*, the *Kebra Negast* was written by a Coptic priest, and Eugene

O'Curry states in his *Lectures* that the earliest text of *Lebor Gabala* was composed at the monastery of Clonmacnoise during the sixth century (1972a, 20 fn. 58; Budge 1932, xiv; O'Curry 1861, IX, 171). Given the overwhelming Coptic influence on the design motifs of seventh century Irish illuminated manuscripts and the presence of foreign priests noted previously in this study, the argument for rather intimate communication between the two countries in the sixth century c.e. is warranted. But the contacts between Ethiopia and Ireland may be even more ancient, going back to the era of predynastic Egypt, if *Lebor Gabala* is to be believed. For the departure date of the first invader group is set at 3400 b.c.e. (Boswell 1972a, 24a).

Therefore, it may be no coincidence, as Boswell proposes, that the titles of Ireland's ancient druid gods, clans and rulers bear the names of Ethiopia's most important trees, the very trees involved in the extensive processing of frankincense, myrrh, and other key by-products for the embalming of the dead and the cleansing of the myriad sacrificial altars of the Red Sea and the Mediterranean littorals. For Ethiopia, with its vast highland, riverine and sea-side aromatic groves, held a virtual monopoly over the incense trade, and, as Boswell reveals: "The people who sacrificed and who embalmed were God's ministers, and incense was their monopoly product-- symbol of their investiture by God as his agents" (1972a, 5). Citing *The Passions and the Homilies from Leabhar Breac* as her source, Boswell further proposes that all of these semantic parallels might be deemed coincidental were it not for the fact that the Irish Druids dubbed themselves Magi and traced their druidic ancestry to the Magi who inhabited the Sabaean deserts (1972a, 14; Atkinson 1962, 472).

Fortuitously, Boswell's argument lends itself to one of this study's venues, the use of sacred trees in ancient times to symbolize cosmic serpents. And Boswell offers copious evidence to advance her hypothesis that druid gods, clans and rulers bore the names of Ethiopia's sacred trees. Two trips to Ethiopia and countless dialogues with living Ethiopian holy men called Dabtara whose traditions extend back to pre-Christian times, convinced Boswell that the pagan tree worship still practiced at the Abyssinian town of Axum, where the Ark of the Covenant is allegedly housed, closely resembles the tree worship practiced in ancient Abyssinia and in druidic Europe as well.

To depart from our examination of Boswell's hypothesis for a moment, the symbolic use of sacred trees in cometary religion needs to be clarified. Trees were often emblematic of the cometary deities, given that the branching tail of a comet was often likened to a comet or a meteor by the ancients (Clube and Napier 1982, 155). And ancient tree worship was a frightening and widespread religion throughout the Mediterranean and Red Sea littorals and in Celtic Europe, for it was in the more prominent sacred groves such as Delphi in Greece, Nemi in Italy, Sarras in Provence, Utica and Carthage in North Africa, and Tara in Ireland that various high kings were crowned after each old king was either strangled or decapitated. Throughout these sites such ritual murders were conducted with the mixed-blessings of the reigning matriarch for whom the ceremony was ultimately conducted.

These and other sacrifices, such as infanticide and the burning of scores of victims in giant wicker men, were likely enacted in the sacred groves, this study maintains, to propitiate the sometimes half-remembered cosmic serpents of the respective dragon-pairs. For the sacred grove with its central Cosmic Tree was likely symbolic of the protector comet and its meteoric train. The Cosmic Tree itself was often visualized as an imaginary pillar holding up the sky, with the Otherworld lurking beneath the roots of that tree. For it was in the Otherworld that the celestial serpents appeared to set, if they were gracious enough not to come crashing to Earth during close encounters. In Ireland, these groves were replete with taboos. Even a Druid dared not enter one at noon or from sunset to sunrise, for evil spirits lurked. And the high noon taboo appears to be a result of solar myth layering over cometary myth, for the sun is the most potent at noon.

The worship of the celestial tree was inextricably linked with the worship of its counterpart, the cometary, hermaphroditic god-king and his totems. These cosmic serpents, who the various kings symbolized, would later devolve into the half-understood sky deities after the folk memory of the horrendous meteor showers of the Late Bronze Age began to fade.

In his attempt to link the etiology of these gods with fertility rituals instead of falling meteors, Frazer was often baffled as to why animals such as pigs, dogs, bulls, birds etc. should be linked to tree deities instead of vegetation gods (1940, 455). Stressing the dismemberment of gods such as Osiris, Dionysius, Adonis etc., and the dispersal of their body parts over large portions of the planet, he convinced himself that these deities were somehow understood to symbolically fertilize the Earth and thus invigorate the vegetable and animal world (1940, 543). For the purposes of this study, however, these gods are deemed cometary in nature.

It would be up to later astrophysicists to propose a cometary pedigree for the various pantheons of the cults of the Mediterranean and Red Sea littorals and beyond once aerial photographs of the Earth's surface revealed numerous previously undiscovered impact craters around the globe. Events such as the Tunguska catastrophe of 1908 and the dramatic descent of the Sikhote-Alin meteorite of 1947 provided more insight into the horrors that must have been endured by our ancestors.

Still puzzled, Frazer states categorically that Osiris was regarded as a tree spirit, and that this arboreal identity may well have been his most primal one, given that tree worship predated grain worship (1940, 441). He goes on to describe a ceremony recorded by Firmicus Maternus, noting that the center of a cut pine was hollowed and the core wood was fashioned into an icon of Osiris. That icon was then placed in the hollowed pine, which served as a kind of coffin (1940, 441). Frazer then explains that in Denderah's famous Osirian hall can be found a coffin encased in a branching conifer tree. That coffin houses the hawk-headed mummy of Osiris (1966, III, 110).

Osiris is a very ancient and puzzling god, and his origins appear to be Ethiopian rather than Egyptian. Chandler notes that both Diodorus Siculus and Herodotus argue that Ethiopians, also called the Anu, first settled Egypt when portions of the Delta were still under water (1989, 122, 180 fn. 17). Druscilla Houston, he notes, summarizes their observations: "They even allege that this country [Egypt] was originally under water, but that Nile, dragging much mud as it flowed from Ethiopia, had finally filled it in and made it part of the continent" (1989, 121; Houston 1985, 67). Chandler cites Diodorus Siculus again:

> the Ethiopians say that the Egyptians are one of their colonies which was brought into Egypt by Osiris . . . They add that from them, as from their authors and ancestors, the Egyptians get most of their laws. It is from them that the Egyptians have learned to honor kings and gods and bury them with such pomp; sculpture and writing were invented by the Ethiopians. The Ethiopians cite evidence that they are more ancient than the Egyptians . . . . (1989, 122)

Chandler goes on to reproduce a proto-dynastic statue of Osiris from Abydos (1989, 128). Its features are clearly Negroid as are the features of an Old Kingdom rendition of a seated statue of Isis and Horus (c. 2635) which he also reproduces (1989, 129). If classical sources are correct, it would appear that the Ethiopians invented the rituals of the god-kings, observances that apparently spread from the Red Sea basin to Upper Egypt and finally throughout the Mediterranean littoral to points north.

Having argued the case for Abyssinian origins for the primal cometary tree-king, more tree-king imagery needs to be examined in order to understand its cometary associations. Frazer describes a strange, annual journey of the dead Osiris:

On the twenty-fourth of Khoiak, at the eighth hour, the images of Osiris, attended by thirty-four images of deities, performed a mysterious voyage in thirty-four tiny boats made of papyrus, which were illuminated by three hundred and sixty-five lights. On the twenty-fourth of Khoiak, after sunset, the effigy of Osiris in a coffin of mulberry wood was laid in the grave, and at the ninth hour of the night the effigy which had been made and deposited the year before was removed and placed upon the boughs of a sycamore. (1961, III, 88)

He goes on to note that on the thirteenth day of Khoiak the worshipers entered an underground holy chamber over which a cluster Persea-trees grew. After carrying the image of the deceased deity through the western doorway, they placed the casketed icon on the sandy floor of the chamber and departed from the eastern door (1961, III, 88).

The ritual was likely designed to ensure that Osiris did not lose his potency, and that the King or Pharaoh did not lose his either. The older, eight year fixed reign of the king was apparently superimposed on the yearly ritual of fertility, for in these rites the yearly death and resurrection of Osiris as a fertility deity is layered with the eight year tenure of the king, a virtual death sentence, the duration of which, this study contends, was likely equivalent to the orbit of an earth-grazing comet. Hence the older cometary mythology was telescoped with the later fertility rituals which so fascinated Frazer. For the Pharaoh was the living embodiment of Osiris as was each Pharaoh after him. The sycamore tree, then, had to stand tall and strong as emblematic of the protector comet, but the Pharaohs were expendable in the process of maintaining the integrity of the that all-important tree.

In Plutarch's account of the legend of Isis and Osiris, more tree imagery is encountered. The coffer containing the dead Osiris, whom Set in the form of a celestial boar thrust out of the sky, floats to Byblus where it somehow becomes entombed in an erica-tree which springs up and surrounds it. Admiring the tree, the King of Byblus cuts it down and places its pillar-like trunk inside his palace. Overcome with grief, Isis eventually visits that palace, discovers the pillar and flies around it in the form of a mourning sparrow. When she finally releases the coffer from the pillar, the children of the King die from fright. Undaunted, Isis wraps the tree trunk in linen, covers it with ointment and gives it to the King. Then she departs for Egypt with the body of Osiris which Set later discovers and scatters over the papyrus swamp of Lower Egypt (Frazer 1940, 423).

But this study has only scratched the surface of this imagery. For the worship of dismembered gods began to proliferate. Why was this so? Bailey dates one of the Set v. Horus combat myths to the time of Ramesses

III's engagement of the Peoples of the Sea. Concurrent with this conflict, he argues: "It was the attack by Typhon [or Set] that finally persuaded the Egyptians to convert Set, the god, into Satan, the devil" (1994, 357). The year was c. 1182 B.C.E. But there is more to the story. From at least the seventh century B.C.E., Frazer explains, Tammuz, equated to a shining cedar, was likewise killed in the Adonis version of the myth by Ares who takes the shape of a boar and scatters Adonis' remains. Adonis' death is mourned by his lover Ishtar, and by her priestesses who anoint his body with oils and cover it with a red robe (1961, I, 8ff, fn. 1).

In the Adonis version of the myth, Adonis is born from a myrrh tree [the tree from which embalming unguents are derived] appearing from an gash scraped by the horns of a bull (Frazer 1961, I, 228 fn. 2). Marked by the rise of Venus, which likely symbolized an ancient, disintegrating comet most visible at first, like Venus, at sunrise and sunset, the rites of Attis enacted another dismemberment story. In this version, Attis castrated himself under a pine tree and bled to death, staining, for our purposes, the lands and waters of the Eastern Mediterranean blood-red with his ferrous debris (Frazer 1961, I, 264ff.). Then too, Frazer explains, in the Boetian rites Dionysius was titled Dionysius in the tree. The deity's presence was often marked by an armless post topped by a bearded mask, surrounded by a cape and leafed branches (Frazer 1940, 387). Like the bull Osiris, with whom he is often compared, horned Dionysius, also equated to a bull, was dismembered and his parts scattered over the earth. It may be recalled that Dionysius was conceived when Zeus visited Persephone. Frazer explains the aftermath, noting that just after his birth, Dionysius climbed to Zeus' throne and mocked god by casting lightning from his tiny hand. This brief hegemony ended, however, when the chalk-faced Titans swung their knives at the infant as the child gazed at its image in a mirror. To evade the Titans, the infant Dionysius became a shape-changer, not unlike the Celtic Taliesin, turning into Zeus, then into Chronos, then into a youth, a lion, a horse, a snake, and finally into a bull which the Titans slashed to pieces (1940, 388).

The myth presents a veritable cometary bestiary as the Dionysius fragment likely disintegrates, followed by his own spawn of meteorites, perhaps, that are likened to the Titans' knives. The chalk-faced Titans are likely white-hot, much as Set is described as being white when he displays his own pyrotechnics. In both cases, then, whiteness may have nothing to do with the pigmentation of the god's followers or enemies.

Trees and comets were not only linked to male deities, but to the even more potent female goddesses, or sacred Amazons, the true sovereigns of the holy groves. For it was these Amazons who served as prototypes for

Europe's Christianized black Madonnas. Diana's title also derives from her cometary appearance, it seems, for *Di* derives from the Aryan root *Di* for 'bright,' according to Frazer, and it may be possible to derive the *ana* suffix from the Ethiopian Anu people, making her the 'bright one of the Anu' (Frazer 1961, I, 191). When it is recalled that at Ephesus a many-breasted, black Diana was worshiped, Ethiopian origins for Nemi's Diana cannot be ruled out (Rogers 1967, I, 135). At Nemi's sacred grove Diana was an oak goddess, Frazer explains, going on to reveal that she "presided over a perpetual fire, which . . . was fed with oak wood. But a goddess of fire not far removed from a goddess of the fuel which burns up in the fire; primitive thought perhaps drew no sharp distinction between the blaze and the wood that blazes" (1940, 164).

In his discussion of Diana, and her Greek counterpart Artemis, who bears associations with the Delphic oracle, Bernal cites Victor Bernard's discussion of a Semitic cult called the Dilbat. For it was the Dilbat who paid obeisance to the morning star which bore the titles Thelpousa/Telphousa/Delphousia, all, Bernal explains, likely roots for Delphi (1991, 92, fn. 82; Berard 1894, 136-37). Bernal goes on to write of Melaina, the mother of the god Delphos, deriving the name Melaina/Melantho from the Greek root *melan* for 'black.' Citing ancient coins from Delphi and Athens which show Delphos rendered with unmistakable African features, Bernal concludes that both Melaina and her son were African imports. (1991, 92; Snowden 1970, 307-08 fn. 6). So what is the relationship between Melaina and Diana or Artemis? Deriving *Melaina* from the Egyptian name *M3nw*, which translates 'to the Mountain in the West where the sun goes down,' Bernal argues that Melaina/Melantho may indicate not only 'black' but the blackness of the West and of dusk (1991, 93). For Bernal, this dusk association equates Melaina/Melantho with "one of two Egypto-Greek goddesses-- Hrt Tmt/Artemis, the ferocious lion goddess of the evening sun, or Nephthys/Persephone, the divinity of the margin between life and death and day and night" (1991, 93). Not yet finished with the derivation, Bernal notes Plutarch's allegorical interpretation of the illicit sex practiced between Osiris and Nephthys in *De Iside et Osiride*:

> The outmost parts of the land beside the mountains bordering on the sea the Egyptians call Nephthys. This is why they give to Nephthys the name of 'Finality' [*teleute*] and say that she is the wife of Typhon. Whenever, then, the Nile overflows and with abounding waters spreads far away to those who dwell in the outermost regions, they call this the union of Osiris with Nephthys, which is proved by the up springing of plants. (1991, 93;

Plutarch, Babbit, trans., 93)

Hence, Nephthys, who this study regards as a cometary deity along with her husband/brother Set and her other siblings, Isis and Osiris, is equated with the benign Nile flood. But the flood depicted in the Greek version of the mythology in question is hardly benign. Bernal explains that Hades seized Persephone, and that Erinys, equated with Melaina/Melantha, was sexually assaulted at Thelpousa/Telphousa by Poseidon (1991, 93). Bernal ends his discussion by equating Poseidon with Set, and Persephone with Nephthys.

The cometary level of this allegory is not advanced by Bernal. Nonetheless, the curious association of early Delphi with a Venus cult that likely used the planet to symbolize a comet appearing brightest at dusk and dawn, and the associations with Set/Typhon and a violent flood, leave little room for doubt that Delphi was initially a temple designed to track and predict the motions of a cometary deity or a series of such cosmic serpents.

In referring to ritual events that occurred within the sacred groves, Frazer indicates that the queen of the sacred grove often died in a ritual manner (1961, I, 114). In Greece, he continues, Artemis may have been hanged in effigy in her sacred grove on an annual basis, for she was called the Hanged One (1961, I, 291). It is speculative at this point, but the battle between the old and new king may have been preceded by a ritual battle fought between two female Amazons in more ancient times during a period of stricter matrifocal rule in Ethiopia. Nonetheless, Diana's perpetual fire of oak timbers likely symbolized the protector comet much as did the sacred tree. And in Ireland, Brigit's perpetual fire is probably a derivative. In pre-Christian times it probably served the same purpose.

Hippolytus, Diana's consort at Nemi, also went by the name Viribus, the appellation of his tanist son. Hippolytus' duty was to tend to one of the sacred grove's trees which, if nurtured, would allow the grove itself to escape some vague attack, Frazer explains (1940, 10). But Hippolytus met with a bad end. Enraged that he gave all of his love to Diana, Aphrodite arranged for his demise. Frazer describes the fall of Hippolytus, noting that as Hippolytus drove his chariot on a coastal route, Poseidon directed a bull to arise from the waves, terrify the horses, and cause Hippolytus to slide off the chariot and expire after being dragged to death by his own steeds. But Diana, Hippolytus's lover, bade Aesculapius to bring the dead man back to life. Enraged by such interference by a mortal, Jupiter tried to cast Hippolytus into Hades. But Diana outsmarted him by shrouding her lover in a cloud, changing him to an old man, and then carrying Hippolytus off to the sacred grove at Nemi. There the nymph Egeria cared for him, and his name was changed to Viribus. Later, Viribus had a son, also named Viribus. (1940, 4-5). As a result of Hippolytus' fall, no horses were allowed in the sacred grove of Nemi (Frazer 1940, 552ff.).

It seems that the Greeks manufactured an endless array of myths with countless variations to describe the periodic disintegrations of comets aloft. The names of the gods changed, but the events remained horribly simple.

In Scandinavia, Balder was likened to a deciduous oak tree. He met his demise when Hodur, the tanist, impaled him with the sacred, celestially-conceived mistletoe which Hodur carefully cut with a golden knife from the metaphorical tree (Frazer 1940, 708, 823). For mistletoe was the only weapon that could kill him. Otherwise, he would have remained immortal (Frazer 1940, 772). Frazer notes that the immortal, evergreen mistletoe was deemed the very essence of the oak's life, and as long as the mistletoe thrived, the oak was invincible (1940, 772). Speaking of the mistletoe bough, the Roman historian Pliny reveals the druidic belief "that whatever grows on these trees was sent from heaven, and is a sign that the tree has been chosen by the god himself" (Frazer 1940, 763-64). Frazer goes on to explain that in the sacred groves a white-robed druid priest climbed the tree and using a golden sickle cut the mistletoe which fell onto a white cloth (1940, 764). Two druidic taboos were linked with this act, he explains. First, the mistletoe, which was associated as much with its healing powers as with its reputation as a weapon, must never touch the ground lest it lose its potency. Second, the knife must be made of gold, and never of iron (Frazer 1940, 686ff., 764).

For the purposes of this study, cometary imagery appears to abound in these taboos. Iron is a key ingredient of a comet. Hence, the introduction of iron into the ritual likely meant that the protector comet would be attacked by another comet fragment instead, of by the priest who was trying preserve cosmic equilibrium by ensuring the continuance of the protector king-comet-god. Given that the mistletoe was the agent of rebirth of the king, the very image of his reincarnating spirit, the old king would die, but the new king, now identified with the mistletoe, would be his incarnation (Frazer 1940, 689).

The taboo against using iron was widespread in the ancient world. The god-king's hair could only be cut with a golden knife and not with an iron one, according to Frazer (1940, 261). Since the Greeks called the *kometa* or comet a hairy star, the tabooed iron must have harkened back to the instability of the ferrous comet as it disintegrated above the Earth (Clube and Napier 1982, 162). To prevent that fate happening to the protector-comet, iron was not introduced, and hair-cutting remained a benign act. The taboo

of using iron also existed in Jerusalem. Solomon's Temple, which housed
the betel stone called the Ark of the Covenant, was not built with any iron
tools, Frazer explains, revealing a variation of the same taboo (1940, 266).
Iron could, however, serve as a talisman against the elves of Britain, who
were often associated with the Tuatha de Danaan and their descendants, the
Picts (Frazer 1940, 262). Since these inhabitants were associated with the
religion of the dragon pair, the Anglo-Saxon could, it seems, frighten them
with the metal.

   And   regarding   the taboo of not touching the ground, a cometary
explanation may also be appropriate, for if the mistletoe touched the earth,
willy-nilly, the protector comet might itself fall.   Frazer notes that in
Ethiopia, the king was sequestered, and if he left his palace he faced the
prospect of being stoned to death (1940, 263).   And in sixth century Britain,
Merlin was likewise sequestered by Vivian.

   The oak tree, upon which the mistletoe grew, was also sacred to Zeus,
for as Frazer notes, at Dodona, the most sacred of Zeus' shrines, Zeus was
worshiped in the oak, to which was attributed oracular qualities (1940, 184).
And in Boetia, Zeus and Hera, the oak god and oak goddess, respectively,
were joined in sacred marriage (Frazer 1940, 184). Zeus' and Hera's
cometary characteristics are delineated by Clube and Napier and have been
noted previously in this study.

   In the sacred, druid groves of Northern Europe, the Abyssinian trees
noted by Boswell were replaced with native species such as the live-oak, the
yew, the kingly alder tree, and the cypress. Nonetheless, these trees, as their
counterparts in Abyssinia, Greece, Italy, Provence and North Africa,
maintained their funereal associations with sacrifice and embalming, and,
more than likely, with the death and rebirth of the god-king as representative
of his respective celestial serpent.   In the *Pharsalia*, Lucan writes of a
superstition which held that snakes infested the sacred oaks, causing the trees
to ignite into a fire that did not consume them (Lucan III, 383ff.) Here is the
linkage of serpent, tree and, we argue, celestial fire, the earthly symbol of a
comet, meteor or asteroid. During the fire-festivals celebrated throughout
Europe and the Mediterranean and Red Sea littorals, the image of the fiery
tree was ubiquitous (Frazer 1940, 732).[3] Often a tree was cut from the
sacred grove and burned (Frazer 1940, 754). Since even for Frazer the
tree=king equation was absolute, the tree that was burned was the emblem
of the old king who was replaced by the new king either at the end of the
orbital cycle of a returning comet, or when the old king grew gray hairs and
could no longer endure the combat with his adversary (1940, 3, 346).

   For Frazer, who did not link the kingly tree image with the tail pattern of a comet or falling meteorite, the fixed term of kingship derived from the earliest tradition of tree worship (1940, 345-46). He notes that in Southern India the complete revolution of Jupiter around the Sun ended the king's reign, while in Greece the king's tenure lasted eight years, ending with the appearance of a falling star (1940, 280). Apparently, one of the short period comets had locked into an eight year orbit around the earth. Given that the Biela comet and its debris have an orbit of 6.6 years, that comet Encke returns every 3.3 years, that Hephaistos revisits every 3.1 years, and the daytime Taurids arrive every 3.26 years, it is understandable that the eight year orbit of a disintegrating comet, no longer known to science today, could have fixed the king's term (Clube and Napier 1982, 153ff.).

The spirit of the dead king was also likened to a serpent or a star, associations that for this study, evoke more cometary imagery. Citing Apollodorus' *Biblioteca*, Frazer reveals that in Greek myth Cadmus and his wife Harmonia were turned into serpents just as they died (1961, I, 86-87 fn. 1). And, according to Plutarch's *Cleomenes*, he notes, a giant snake coiled around the face of the slain Spartan king Cleomenes as he hung on his cross. Given that the snake drove away the vultures which were about to prey upon the king's body, the bystanders concluded that Cleomenes was a son of the gods (Frazer 1961, 1, 87). In the legend of Isis and Osiris, the souls of the dead brother and sister pair become stars. This metaphor could be glossed over were not for an odd coincidence. The annual flooding of the Nile was attributed to Isis. And Isis was likened to the star Sirius which rose from the horizon to herald the late July inundation of the Nile. The linkage of a star that disappears and reappears again with a benign flood seems to have, in part at least, commemorated the appearance of a comet, its fall, and the consequential, disastrous Flood recorded in world mythologies. Hence, the star was likely the *momento mori* of a cosmic serpent.

Proposing that the names of certain Abyssinian trees reappeared in the British Isles, Boswell explains that in Ireland, the sacred oak tree was called *Daro*, an old Gaelic word, which, she claims, is identical to the name given to the live-oak species of fig by the Ethiopians of Axum (1972a, 35, 105 fn. 37). In Axum, she continues, the fig tree is still called Pharaoh's tree and is alleged to contain a *ganen* or evil spirit, the name of which name is identical to two Irish Firbolg chiefs, Gann and Genan, according to Macalister (1972a, 35; Macalister 1931, 104, 116). Deriving the place-names Kildare, Durrow and Derry from the Ethiopian *Daru*, Boswell reveals that the *ganen* is reputed to own the fig tree, and to both speak to and light up the tree each night (1972a, 36). So potent was Eden's tree that two winged Cherubs were assigned to guard it, much as two Cherubim seemingly hovered over the Ark of the Covenant on either side of the tree-shaped candelabra that rested above the sacred chest in the Temple of Jerusalem.

This tree imagery remains quite obscure unless it is understood that it likely symbolized a brilliant object in the night sky, also described as the wise, talking serpent in Eden. The superstition surrounding the Ethiopian fig tree, had variants in Ireland, Boswell notes, citing the folklore of tree demons in that country. For druid healers cleansed victims of tree demons with water or by incense fumigation (1972a, 36; Rodinson 1967, 39, 59, 60, 97). And the Ethiopian version of these healers, still women at contemporary Axum, are called Balatta, Boswell reveals, noting that Bellat, an ancestress of the Gaidel tribe, was the name of Fenius Farsaid's wife of the sixth invasion group cited in *Lebor Gabala* (1972a, 36).

Another Abyssinian-Irish parallel is drawn by Boswell, for in today's Ethiopian monastic churches, exorcists, cantors and musicians are called *Dabtara*. Similarly in St. Patrick's era, the head of the Irish bardic caste was called *Dubthach* (1972a, 36). The *dub* prefix which is Gaelic for 'black' should not go unnoticed either.

The derivation of Banba (also called Cesair in *Lebor Gabala*), a title additionally applied to the fifty women of color who accompanied Banba during the first migration to Ireland from the Isle of Meroe, can also be traced to Ethiopian origins, she argues. For Boswell reveals that *banba* is precisely the Abyssinian name of the baobob tree which has the widest girth of any tree known (1972a, 39, 97, 119 fn. 43). Banba, like her avatar Brigit, was a tree goddess who tended the sacred oak groves.

Interesting enough, Banba, according to *Lebor Gabala*, arrived in Ireland before the Flood, a catastrophe which Clube and Napier argue may well have been triggered by an earth-striking meteorite and its trailing debris. They date the Flood to the mid fourth millennium B.C.E., right in line with *Lebor Gabala's* first migration, placed by de Jubainville at 3451 B.C.E.. Furthermore, they trace the Flood's origins to the Earth's close encounter with a comet fragment that not only would have terrified the populace, but also would have generated the Flood. For they go on to propose that "there do exist astronomical mechanisms, e. g. sea impact, whereby massive floods might be generated, especially in the Near East where almost closed seas do not allow dissipation of wave energy into the open seas" (1982, 211). Breasted in *The Development of Thought and Religion in Ancient Egypt* also places the beginning of the Pharaonic period at 3400 B.C.E. (1912, 5).

Winkler describes another Flood scenario. Like Clube and Napier, he believes that either a close encounter with a comet or a cometary capture caused the Flood, but the capture incident is pushed back centuries before the actual Flood itself. How could this be so? Arguing that the large quantities of ice, a major component of the comet mix, could be dispersed into Earth's atmosphere during a capture event, Winkler proposes that a cloud canopy composed largely of water vapor which could have encircled the Earth might have been the result. Centuries after such a capture, he explains:

> Melted water ice from the canopy itself would be a supply of water for the Flood. Removal of the canopy would also allow the greenhouse heat to escape and cool the atmosphere so as to precipitate the water vapor and further feed the Flood. If the canopy extended near or into the Arctic regions, the melting canopy would also release the embedded micro meteorites which in turn would cause water droplets to crystallize and form snow. This of course would explain the deluge of snow that entombed many animals in the Arctic in the remote past. (1985b, 6)

Winkler goes on to propose that the comet responsible for this canopy was likely captured thousands of years before the flood, and its resultant canopy melted because of "a cyclical perturbation in the earth's revolution" (1985b, 6).

In any case, why was Banba and her male consort accompanied by fifty women? The female entourage was doubtless part of the king's royal harem. But why fifty? Again, cometary imagery may provide the answer. For each woman may have stood for one year of the fifty-year orbit of a contemporaneous comet. In ancient Mexico, the number fifty was also regarded with dread. Fifty-two years comprised the Aztec century, and according to Fernando de Alva Ixtlilxochitl's *Obras Historica*, world catastrophes, heralded by the appearance of Venus, were predicted based on the multiple of 52 years (Tompkins 1976, 289).[4] The same tradition existed with the Etruscans as well, according to Censorinus' *Liber de Die Natali*, in which twice 52 or 104 was the time that elapsed between two world catastrophes that were announced by heavenly signs (Velikovsky 1977b, 163 fn. 1). Fifty year cycles also marked the Jubilee year for the Israelites. Velikovsky explains:

> The fiftieth year was a jubilee year, when the land not only had to be left fallow, but had to be returned to its original proprietors. According to the law, one could not convey his land forever; the deed of sale was but a lease for whatever number of years remained until the jubilee year. The year was proclaimed by the blowing of horns on the Day of Atonement. 'In the Day of Atonement shall ye make the trumpet sound throughout all of your land. And ye shall hallow the fiftieth year, and proclaim liberty throughout all the

land unto all the inhabitants thereof: it shall be a jubilee unto you, and ye
shall return every man unto his possession, and ye shall return every man
[slave] unto his family' (1977b, 164-65; Leviticus 25: 9ff.).

The jubilee was celebrated in order to forestall the Day of Judgment,
according to Velikovsky, and that Day of Judgment was predicated upon a
close encounter with a comet having a fifty year orbit (1977b, 165). The
discrepancy between fifty-two and fifty years is also explained by
Velikovsky: "Comets do not return at exact periods because of the
perturbations caused by the [gravitational fields] of the larger planets"
(1977b, 165). For proof, he cites the irregular orbit of Halley's comet which
varies from 74 ½ to 79 ½ years (1977b, 165). He goes on to reveal that
when the Day of Atonement arrived, a scapegoat was chosen by the Israelites
and sent to a desert location called Azazel [a.k.a., Azzael, Azza or Uzza,
which means 'a fallen star of Lucifer']. This scapegoat, he argues, parallels
Satan, and in the Egyptian version the scapegoat figure was linked to Seth-
Typhon. And then Velikovsky hits pay dirt: "According to rabbinical
legend, Uzza was the star of Egypt: it was thrown into the Red [Reed?] Sea
when the Israelites made their passage" (1977, 166-67).[5]
   In any case, for Boswell, ancient Banba, like first millennium Sheba,
belonged to a line of sacred priestesses who initially owned the immense spice
and aromatic groves in the Saba-Sheba area (1972a, 41). She goes on to
suggest that Banba, who journeyed from the Isle of Meroe to Greece and then
across North Africa to arrive finally in Ireland, may have been one of
thousands of early Greeks who were described as Ethiopian colonists by
Strabo, Diodorus Siculus and Herodotus (1972a, 41).[6] And the by-products
of the baobab tree, after which the Irish Banba was apparently named, had
several uses-- in embalming the dead, in treating snake and insect bites,
malaria, small pox and dysentery, and in the construction of boat hulls
(Boswell 1972a, 42). Then too, in the Sudan the dead were sometimes
interred in the hollowed trunk of the baobab, making it a truly funereal tree
(Boswell 1972a, 42).
   But what of Banba's consort, who is called Seth in Keating's *History of
Ireland* (1908, I, 161)? Was his name derived from a sacred Abyssinian tree?
Boswell asks. Before this study can reveal her answer to that question, it is
necessary to refine the comet-tree image pattern, for Set, according to Clube
and Napier, was the earthly name for a comet or comet fragment that drove its
'brother' Osiris into the Otherworld after scattering Osiris' body parts over
Lower Egypt (1982, 202ff.). This catastrophe likely occurred in stages, some
of which transpired during the middle to the end of the third millennium, very

close to the alleged migration period of Banba and Seth. It is logical, then, that Seth would have been likened to a tree. And sure enough, Boswell explains, the Abyssinian name for another aromatic tree, the cedar, which in the Tigrinya dialect, a vestige of the ancient royal language of Ethiopia, is called *Zeddi* or *Seddi* (1972a, 47). She also reveals that *Seddi* is a cognate for *Seth*, the deity of the later Phoenician sailors who would corner the market in the incense trade (1972a, 47). He also went by the title of the Phoenician Baal (Boswell 1972a, 47, 52 fn. 155; Te Velde 1967, 1-3).

The Irish stew thicks when Boswell explains that the Sabaean/Phoenician incense growers, processors, traders and temple priests consorted with priestesses who owned the plantations of the tree called the Cedar of Lebanon. This is the wood that was used by Solomon to construct the Temple of Jerusalem which housed the Ark of the Covenant (1972a, 47). Hiram of Tyre provided Solomon with that wood, and, so it turns out, Hiram was the cousin of the Queen of Sheba, that same woman who would later become Solomon's consort and wife. And cedar was also used to construct the coffin of Osiris which somehow drifted to Byblos in Plutarch's account. Cedar, then, had a relationship with the sacred betel stones or meteorites, for this study holds that the Ark was such, as were the fallen fragments of Osiris. Cedar like the baobab, then, also appears to have been a most funereal tree.

The Seth nomenclature has other spin-offs in Ireland, for as Boswell notes, in Egypt and Phoenicia as in Ireland, the avatars of Seth were god priest-kings called *Baraks*, or *Barcas*, all associated with lightning (1972a, 48). As we might expect, there is an Ethiopian cognate here too, for *Barak* means 'forest' or 'lightning' in Abyssinian dialects (Boswell 1972a, 48, 52 fn. 159; Shearman 1882, 204, 208ff.). This royal title had a certain longevity as it spread across North Africa, for much later in history, Hannibal's full name was Hannibal Barka (Boswell 1972a, 63, 67 fn. 205).[7] And this brings us again to the fifty women of color who accompanied Seth and Banba as described in the *Lebor Gabala*. For Boswell, they were probably Seth's sisters and consorts, virgin priestesses or sacred prostitutes, whose descendants inhabited the sacred groves and temples of druidic Ireland (1972a, 48).

Given that the Phoenicians wrote down their consonants from right to left and eschewed vowels, a simple consonant reversal unlocks another mystery for Boswell. *Barak* or *Barca* yields the *C-R-B* or *K-R-B* consonant string which stands for the most ancient title for South Arabian and Abyssinian regents (Boswell 1972a, 63; Contenau 1949, 93). She derives the *K-R-B* consonant string from the chief priest of the *Egyptian Book of the Dead, Kher-Heb*, as well (1972a, 93; Budge 1962, 265ff.).

Unknowingly, Boswell appears to have unearthed yet another layer of the cometary lore which informs the imagery of the sacred, Edenic grove. For the *Karib,* or *Mukarib,* were associated with the cherubim, guardians of the gates of Eden and the agents of both a god and a goddess (1972a, 63; Doresse 1959, 22-23, 49; Pankhurst 1965, 1965, 4). During the period 1550-1000 B.C.E., roughly the era of Saul, David and Solomon, meteor shower activity likely became more intense on the planet, and, as noted earlier, celestial angel references in the Old Testament started coming out of the woodwork (Clube and Napier 1982, 243).

These Sabaean Mukaribs were the entrepreneurs who harvested and processed the incense and myrrh groves, tended the vineyards and wheat fields and worked the gold mines. And in Ireland farming and gold mining were also joint concerns, especially among the O'Neill clan, a name that echoes Niul or Nel, an apparent avatar of Seth, of the sixth invader group, from whom the Irish Saint Columba was descended. In the Red Sea basin, the Mukaribs lived a highly regulated monastic life because of their need to maintain the irrigation dikes, channels and dams, Boswell explains, noting that in Ireland a similar monastic form of government was put in place long before the Christian era (1972a, 64). To prove her assertion, Boswell cites Alexander de Bertrand, who demonstrates that the early Christian monasteries in Ireland were originally druid colleges (1972a, 64, 68 fn. 214).

And whether pagan or Christian, these monastic estates fell under the authority of holy men called *Korbes.* Boswell reveals that each new Korb represented a previous saint of Korb or Barce nomenclature (1972a, 64, 68 fn. 215; Todd 1864, 155ff.). Hence, Boswell continues, the *K-R-B* consonant groupings found in Ireland, which represented the name of a sacred clan leader and entrepreneur in the incense industry, stemmed from a clan name in Saba (1972a, 64). And, she adds, that same cluster of consonants reversed in Semitic style to *B-R-K* appears as a clan name once associated with an African king. The same nomenclature also applied in Phoenicia and its colony at Carthage (1972a, 64). Both Hamilcar I, who was a fifth century B.C.E. general routed finally by Sicilian Greeks under Gelon at the sea battle of Himera, and Hamilcar II, the third century B.C.E. Carthaginian commander and father of Hannibal, were of the Barca [or Baraq, 'lightning'] clan.

Hannibal's defeat in Italy was, by the way, attributed to a small black stone, likely a meteoric betel, that symbolized the Phrygian Mother Goddess, Cybele, according to Pliny, Herodian, Livy, Arnobius and Ovid (Frazer 1961, I, 265 fns. 4 and 5). Prophecies current in Rome had indicated that Cybele would protect the Romans if this Goddess were adored in the Temple of Victory on the Palatine Hill (Frazer 1961, I, 265). The stone was eagerly placed there, and a year later Hannibal retreated to Africa.

Recalling that the fig tree at Axum was called *Warka* and *Daro*, and citing Edward Ullendorf's *Semitic Languages in Ethiopia*, Boswell suggests more phonetic parallels between Ethiopia and Ireland. For the Warka/Daro tree was replaced in Ireland by the oak or Daro, and *Warka* becomes *Barak* or *Barca*, since there is an interchange between B and W in Semitic languages with B becoming M and finally W over time (1972a, 69 fn. 220; Ullendorf 1955, 90ff., 104ff.).

Boswell continues her examination of the Seth figure and his avatars, arguing that in Ireland, a Seth avatar was probably the father or brother of Banba, wedded to her in royal incest, like Isis and Osiris (1972a, 48). *Lebor Gabala* II, 264-65 reveals that, seeking the kingdom, Seth murdered his brother, [recalling Set's 'murder' of Osiris], and Partholon of the second invasion was an avatar of Seth or Bith, who was Banba's consort and father as well (Boswell 1972a, 48; Keating 1908, I, 233). And Niul of the Milesian invader group is described in *Lebor Gabala* as another Seth avatar, who, for services rendered, received Pharaoh's cedar wood fleet from Moses during the Exodus. For Niul [also called Nel] was reputed to have donated wine and wheat from his estate in Southern in Egypt and to have received the fleet as Pharaoh's gift prior to the Red [Reed?] Sea crossing which Nel and his party allegedly observed, as noted in *Lebor Gabala* (II, 49).

What is the derivation of Nel? Boswell asks. She proposes that it comes from an Ethiopian Tigrinya cognate for the cedar tree-- pronounced *Niul-ret* and written as *Nerret*. Since Keating calls Nel, Niul, a good case for the derivation emerges, she argues (1972a, 49).

And why is Nel important? *Lebor Gabala*, II, 49 proposes that he was married to Pharaoh's daughter Scota from whom the name for Scotland appears to have been derived, and for Boswell, Nel and Scota, are both descendants and avatars of the original, sacred god-hermaphrodite, Seth\ Banba (Boswell 1972a, 49). An alternate date of 1016 B.C.E. provided by Boswell for their migration is close to the 1182 B.C.E. date advanced by Bailey for the final repulsion of the Peoples of the Sea, or Seth-worshiping Titans, from Egypt (1992, 357). This event may have corresponded to the heightened activity of the Typhon comet, as noted earlier. Assuming a protracted migration period for the sixth invader group, these itinerants may have been members of that defeated group as well, mixed, perhaps, with the descendants of an earlier wave of emigrants from Egypt, namely the Priests of Akhenaton who fled Egypt during the Exodus and greatly influenced the Orphic traditions in Greece.

Regarding the matrifocal, marital customs of these invader groups, Boswell concludes that undergirding such legendary relations could be found an incestuous royal marriage that all early divine kings practiced, which, if properly consummated, could result in the birth of a Son of God (1972a, 49). This same royal incest was imported to Ireland, according to Boswell, by both the Druids and the priests of Christ, for many fourth and fifth century C.E. priests were married to their sisters, mothers or daughters, a practice that was later denounced by numerous horrified clerics adhering to the Romano-Gaulish brand of Christianity after they visited Scotland and Ireland (1972a, 50, 53-54 fn. 175).

This Son of God motif, indeed the whole impetus of royal incest, this study argues, has an apparent cometary base to it. In order to preserve the earthly equivalent of the protector-comet, the god-king, great pains were taken to ensure that a god-king would always be in place, and that the royal blood line, carried by his queen, would never be sullied. And this is where the Ark of the Covenant comes in. For the Banba\Queen of the Sheba line of priestesses were, for Boswell,who did not see the cometary base of all this, "the royal proprietors of the groves of aromatic gum called incense from which civilization as we know it flowered. If the Tree of Life was the Sabaean tree of perfume and preservation, it also bears a name in Ethiopic which becomes dynastic in Irish" (1972a, 50). The Tree of Life symbol, carefully examined later in this study, was the emblem of the protector-comet. It was also the symbol of the comet's earthly hermaphroditic god-king. As a result, the *titular* king must never die, even though his representatives did. So long as the *titular* king drew breath, the Tree of Life would not die. But if the worst happened, the tree would buckle and the sky would once again degenerate, or so the logic of sympathetic magic goes. Therefore, the queen of the grove arranged the old king's eventual replacement with a virile male born of a royal matriarch. This young tanist would accept the challenge and collude with her in the process when the king's old age approached. For royal blood was preserved in the veins of the female queen and her priestesses. In effect, the marriage of the new king and the queen of the grove involved the union of a brother and a sister, or a father and a daughter in the event that the queen had aged, or a mother with her son, for all female children of the queen's bloodline shared in that royal bloodline. Hence, Boswell demonstrates, Isis married Osiris or Set. Banba married Seth. Baobab married cedar, and, mixed together, these gums made up the embalming fluid which preserved the body and therefore the soul. It was all a pathetic denial of death and doomsday.

Frazer speculates on some of the mechanisms of royal incest, noting that in some countries women were the bearers of the royal bloodline, and that male kingship rested solely on marriage to "a hereditary princess," the princess royal, who was the real sovereign and often the king's sister (1961, I, 44). He goes on to examine the father-daughter union, arguing that the need to preserve the royal bloodline sometimes required father/daughter incest. For if the king's wife died, how better to maintain the bloodline than to marry his own daughter (1961, I, 44)?

Frazer concludes his discussion of royal incest by noting its presence in mythology. He cites the tales of Cronus and Rhea, of Zeus and Hera, of Isis and Osiris, all of which depict kings wedded to their sisters. For the royal blood was assumed to flow not in men but in women (1961, II, 316).

But we are only part way through this saga of cometary trees. Other invader groups bore Ethiopian tree names as well, according to Boswell. A type of frankincense tree that grows today along the Mareb and Takezze rivers is called *Etan* or *Liban* in the Tigrinya dialect. Its other names are *Angua*, *Makker* and *Magher* (Boswell 1972a, 55). Boswell notes that variants of these names also appear in *Lebor Gabala* as the titles of major druidic divinities. They include Etan of the fifth group of invaders, a goddess of poetic inspiration who was loved by the death god Midir [Angus], himself associated with the necropolis at Tara. She argues that these names were allegorical, for Tara, Midir and Etan stood for incense and its ritual use in mortuary ceremonies. She derives the Irish Midir from Medr, the underworld god of Axum. Medr transmutes, she argues, to Aden in Plutarch's *De Iside*, and to Adin in Ireland, another version of Etan's name. Midir [Angus], Etan's lover, has a father named in Irish Anghave or Aengoba, which she derives from Anghaba, who fathered the Queen of Sheba and killed Axum's snake king in the Axumite legend. She concludes from this phonetic parallelism that the records of ancient Ireland depict divine people with names derived from the titles of kings and queens who ruled at the Island of Meroe (1972a, 55-56, 59-60, fns. 187-189).[8]

It appears that various members of the so-called invasion groups knew exactly where they were going when they either trekked overland or set sail for Ireland along the Atlantic seaway. They did not just drift in. Apparently they were members of successive dynasties who not only worshiped the same cometary god, Set-Typhon, but also shared a common purpose in tending the sacred groves of Ireland-- to keep the sky from falling on their heads. Boswell continues to unravel the complexities of the royal incest without discovering its deeper purpose:

> Since Dagan or Dagda is a rotating title, passed on to males of succeeding generations, Aengus, brother of Etan or Liban, is also the father Dagda. Similarly, Seth was the brother and father and husband of Banba and Isis in Ireland's and Egypt's first dynasties. The sacrifice of sacred kings in a matrilineal society ensured the immortality of names or titles. (1972a, 56-57)

It also ensured the immortality of the protector comet, which was its *raison de' etre*. In a footnote, Boswell cites Macalister's observation in *Tara* of the equivalency of Dagda with Set, the heavenly twin of Osiris. This celestial twin theme runs rampant throughout *Lebor Gabala*. In this instance, Dagda is described as the Red One of Great Knowledge. Macalister, she goes on, notes that Set was red-haired, and that he represented the priestly ranks from which the Pharaohs were selected. He goes on to note that upon his death the Pharaoh was called Osiris (Macalister 1931, 115ff.).

Boswell proposes that the same royal incest theme was operative with the invaders bearing the Ethiopic M-names. Makker or Magher, she notes, can be derived from the Ethiopian word *angua* which stands for the frankincense tree. The Makker/Magher title, she goes on, can be found in *Lebor Gabala's* descriptions of the second, third and fifth invader groups, where she appears as the Irish queen Macha, associated with Cuchulain and the Red Branch knights. Then too, Boswell notes that Armagh was founded by St. Patrick to honor Macha, who may well have been named for Mackeda, the Queen of Sheba (1972a, 57).

The Ethiopian tradition of royal incest lived on for generations both in Ethiopia and in Ireland, it would seem, and, for our purposes, the cometary iconography of these far distant religions remained current as the priests of the Abyssinian and the Irish cults scanned the night sky from their mountaintop and hilltop monasteries, fearing the worst.

The Irish title *Eochu* also appears to have a pedigree. Yet another Irish title for the divine male ruler, *Eochu* or *Eochaid*, which in Irish is pronounced *Yohy*, is also an Ethiopian derivative, according to Boswell (1972a, 70). Bailey surmises that it might derive from the Scottish word for 'copper', or *eachan*, which makes sense given the value placed on copper in the making of tin, and given that the incense industry was also tied in with mining both along the Mediterranean and Red Sea littorals and on the western periphery of Europe (1994, 147). Variations or cognates of the *eachan* copper term have been located in all the areas in which Phoenicians traded, in Africa, Asia, Europe, the Mediterranean and Red Sea littorals and possibly even in the New World, Bailey argues, suggesting that Carnac, the megalithic site in Brittany dated to 5445 B.C.E., may have been named [or renamed?] after the Babylonian term for bronze, or *anak* (1994, 147, 55). Boswell takes a different tack in deriving *Eochu*, arguing that Seth corresponds to the Greek Zeus and the Roman Jove, a course which for our purposes fits well with the cometary etiology of kingship in Ireland and along Mediterranean and Red Sea shores. In Ireland, Boswell explains, the Set name was frequently Yohe, and the ebony tree is called *Ahieh* or *Aiyeh* in Tigrinya (1972a, 70, 71). Both Bailey and Boswell may be correct. For the *Eochu*, or divine rulers, would have likely been active in trade negotiations conducted by various Eastern Mediterranean 'corporations' involving the movement of goods back and forth along the Atlantic seaway, perhaps for several millennia.

The next word associations Boswell examines reveal the complex totemism existing in the Mediterranean and Red Sea basins during the first millennium B.C.E. She notes the Geez title *ahiya* for donkey which leads her to believe that since the Queen of Sheba walked on a donkey's foot, her father Anghabo may have been associated with both a dog and a donkey totem. She goes on to cite the Greek word for 'holy,' *aghia*, which has an identical pronunciation as the Ethiopic term for 'ass.' Then too, Apollo was revered at the Ionian city of Miletus as a donkey, and Pindar's *Pythian Ode* 10 describes the sacrifice of asses on Apollo's Hyperborean island (1972a, 71) Additionally, the ass, along with the boar, was one of Set's zoomorphs.

So why is the Queen of Sheba associated with a donkey's foot? According to Budge in *The Queen of Sheba*, Sheba and her allies attacked and killed a dragon, but unhappily, some of the blood spurted onto her foot during the skirmish, turning her heel into that of a donkey (1932, lxvii). This makes no sense at all unless we understand that the donkey Set was also the celestial serpent who was switch-hitting in Sheba's time, sometimes protecting and sometimes threatening various portions of the Mediterranean of Red Sea basins.

And why was Apollo wintering in Britain? Perhaps because his partner at Delphi, Osiris-Dionysius, who, for our purposes, may have represented the spasmodic fall of the defeated, celestial serpent Osiris, an event which led to a cosmic winter, was consulted by the pythoness only during the winter months. Apollo, on the other hand, who was reputedly born under the sacred palm tree of Delos, received his queries during the warmer months, given that he appears to have represented the benign Horus, the protective incarnation of the dead Osiris (Clube and Napier 1982, 192ff.).

Citing an Etruscan statue of a black Apollo housed in the Villa Julia museum in Rome, Boswell reasons that Eochaid, also known as Dagda in Ireland, was a black deity as well. In fact, she argues, he secretly went by the name Zeus Ethiops (1972a, 71).[9] Apollo may have been depicted as black to indicate his invisibility during the unseen portion of his orbit after he had set on the horizon, in contradistinction to Set, who may have been depicted as white, or white hot, as he sputtered above the Earth in a close encounter.

Boswell continues her examination of the Eochaid associations, arguing that Eochaid was split into a divine trinity in Ireland: Yohy Airem, son of Finn the White; Yohy Fedlech, the brother of Yohy Airem and the father of Maeve, a derivative of the Medusa; and Yohy Salbuide, Conchobar's father and grandfather as a result of his incest with his daughter Nessa (1972a, 71, 79 fn. 234).

Do we not have the makings of a cometary trinity here, Set, Isis [Aso] and Osiris? And when it is recalled that Perseus watched ass sacrifices in the land of the Hyperboreans, it should also be recalled that he slew the snake-headed, cometary Medusa, the daughter of the second figure in the Yohy trinity. Lactantius argues that Isis was really Set's mother (Frazer 1951, 434). Since cometary Isis is later associated with Set, she is represented in her more threatening form. For, as the original matriarch of the grove, Isis-Aso, who assisted Set in the demise of Osiris, had a threatening aspect to her, and, given the conventions of royal incest and tanistry, the new king could be the queen's own father, brother or son. Boswell notes that the king symbolized the Abyssinian cedar, fig, frankincense and ebony trees (1972a, 72). As the new king then, Set would change to Osiris again, a black Osiris, probably because he was no longer deemed threatening, no longer visible in the night sky.

Fortuitously again, Boswell's derivations lead us to more cometary imagery. Now the sacred Irish mound called *Tara* which Boswell derives from *Temair* [Ethiopian for date palm] or *Temrach* [the Abyssinian for incense], was the site of the oracular, 'talking' Fal Stone and of the inauguration of the High Kings of Ireland, who were periodically supplanted through the vicissitudes of matrifocal tanistry (1972a, 80). Interestingly enough, the cometary Phoenix bird [which like a comet, leaves and then returns in an awesome show of pyrotechnics] was associated with the date palm by the Greeks, and the date palm was also called *Hosanna* in Ethiopic, Hosanna being the familiar cry made during Jesus' entry into Jerusalem on an ass (Boswell 1972a, 71, 84 fn. 246). But even more interesting is the earliest tradition associated with the Fal Stone. Pat Gerber notes the following in *The Search for the Stone of Destiny*: "Every legend about the Stone begins by saying that it was the pillow on which Jacob had his dream" (1992, 26). But just exactly what did that dream denote? Genesis 28 provides the answer. For one evening as Jacob was making his way from Beer-sheba to Haran, he

> took of the stones of that place, and put them for his pillows, and lay down
> in that place to sleep. And he dreamed, and behold a ladder set up on the

earth, and the top of it reached to heaven: and behold the angels of God ascending and descending on it. And, behold, the Lord stood above it, and said, 'I am the Lord God of Abraham thy father, and the God of Isaac: the land whereon thou liest, to thee will I give it, and to thy seed; And thy seed shall be as the dust of the earth, and thou shalt spread abroad to the west, and the to the east, and to the north, and to the south . . . and Jacob awaked out of his sleep, and he said, Surely the Lord is in this place; and I knew it not . . . this is none other but the house of God, and this is the gate of heaven.

And Jacob rose up early in the morning, and took the stone that he had put for his pillow, and set it up for a pillar, and poured oil upon the top of it. And he called the name of that place Beth-el . . . . And Jacob vowed a vow, saying . . . this stone, which I have set for a pillar, shall be God's house.'

Given that the time frame for this dream is roughly 1700 B.C.E., and the fact that Jacob anoints the pillow/pillar with oil, the cometary origins of anointing kings from David and Solomon to the High Kings of Ireland and the Kings and Queens of England seems to have been identified by Gerber. For as she notes, twenty-two years later God beseeches Jacob, whom He names Israel, to return to Beth-el. As Jacob proceeds, God tells him that "a company of nations shall be of thee, and kings shall come out of thy loins; And the land which I gave Abraham and Isaac, to thee I will give it, and thy seed after thee." After hearing these words, Jacob sets up a stone pillar and makes an animal sacrifice.   Since Jacob's twelve sons sire the twelve tribes of Israel; and since one those sons is Dan of whom the prophetess Deborah says in Judges 5: "Why did Dan remain in ships?"; and since the tribe of Dan may be the origin of the Tuatha de Danaan, it certainly raises a question. Was "The Stone of Israel," which Gerber admits appears to be meteoric, the prototype of the Fal Stone at Tara and the Coronation Stone or the Stone of Scone? For just as Zadok anointed Solomon before a sacred throne when David neared death, so at Westminster, the choir bellows out "Zadok the priest" as the Archbishop of Canterbury anoints the next King's or Queen's head, breast and hands with oil that dribbles from the a golden eagle's beak. Given that the Coronation Stone which rests beneath the seat of Coronation is made of sandstone and therefore not meteoric, Gerber indicates that the Stone of Scone is likely a copy of an earlier meteorite that was transported to Dal Riada in Argyll well before the defeat of the Picts by Kenneth Mac Alpin. And from Mac Alpin it apparently passed to MacBeth's castle and thence to MacAlpin's descendant, Robert Bruce, along the female line. The real stone may even have even been carried in an Ark-like container by the Templars during the Battle of Bannockburn. Gerber notes that on 1 January 1819, the London *Times* ran an article entitled "Macbeth's Castle-- A

Curious Discovery" in which the following translation of writing on a bronze tablet lying next to a "meteoric or semi-meteoric" stone unearthed on the grounds read: "The sconce [or shadow] of kingdom come, until sylphs in air carry me again to Bethel" (1992, 105).

It is not improbable that the excavated stone or its prototype came from Ireland after a circuitous voyage along the Atlantic seaway from the land of the Phoenicians. For the Tuatha de Danaan are reputed to have brought four sacred objects with them on their journey north: the Sword of Nuada, Lugh's blood-dripping spear, the Cauldron of Dagda, and the Stone of Destiny, the Lia Faill.

The Black Stone of the University of Glasgow, an apparent cousin of the original coronation rock, is actually mounted on the seat of a throne. A leafed tree branch encircling an hour glass appears to be growing from the back of the chair and looms above it. No great leap of the imagination is required to make the equations: meteor=tree=throne=king, when that relic is observed in Glasgow. Also, no great leap of the imagination is required to link the cometary "King of Kings" with the tanistry practiced in Upper Egypt, the Near East and Ireland-- for Jesus was a Horus-Set figure (Bailey 1994, 117; Jackson 1993, 111ff.). In one version of the myth of Isis and Osiris, Isis resides with her son Horus. This Isis consort for a cometary Christ becomes Mary Magdalen. Interestingly enough, the Pseudo-Tertullian, author of the *Gospel of the Egyptians*, equates Christ with Seth, and one of Seth's totems, like Christ's, was a fish (Bailey 1994, 239). When it is understood that Saint Columba, whose birth, much like Christ's, was associated not with a star but with "a great flame," and heralded by an angel who presented Eithne, Columba's mother, with a glowing cloak, and that Columba's body was interred under a pillow stone upon which he allegedly laid his head each night, the meteor=tree=kingship equations become even more likely.

In any case, Boswell concludes her ground-breaking study, *Irish Wizards in the Woods of Ethiopia*, by arguing that all the trees noted in her study were instrumental in Egyptian death rites. For coffins, she notes, fig, oak, cedar and juniper wood were used, and to ensure proper embalming frankincense was mixed with juniper oil. She goes on to explain that substances then called cedar oil, cedar juice, and cedar pitch, were employed in the Egyptian perfume industry and also used for the eviscerating and the anointing of corpses (1972a, 88). In Egypt, Boswell explains, embalmers were members of the priesthood of Anubis who ritually wore the mask of the jackal or greyhound deity. Hence, the druid master of St. Patrick was known as the "Greyhound," and Irish monks, according to ancient records, were described as "sharp-nosed dogs" and "dog-headed" (1972a, 90, 95-96 fn. 290).

According to Boswell, Seth or Osiris, depending on the version of the myth, fathered Anubis, and the Ethiopian goddess Anu was ultimately the mother of all the gods of the Egyptians (1972a, 95 fn. 291). Boswell further observes that the Greyhound was the symbol of Seth, and that this animal was lord of Meroe and Axum (1972a, 96 fn. 292). Recalling that Greek writers attributed the original rule of the Red Sea coast to dog-headed kings, she argues that the tribes which followed these kings were nomadic shepherds who were also labeled Troglodytes and Bolg or Volgios, the same titles used for the tribal names, Bolg or Volg, by which early Irish tribes were known (1972a, 96 fn. 294; 90, 96 fn. 295).[10] She goes on to reveal that one of the other agents used in the embalming process was olive oil, and that the olive tree to this day is called *Zeit* in the Ethiopian town of Lalibela. *Zeit* then becomes another cognate for Set (1972a, 91).

Boswell's analysis of the etiology of Irish titles for gods, priests, priestesses and hermaphroditic dyads called god-kings, takes us a long way in confirming the twin hypotheses that Irish druidic religion was derived from the Mediterranean and Red Sea littorals, and that it was cometary in nature. What came out of Ethiopia and Africanized Mediterranean shores was an eerie cult of the dead, so great was the terror evoked by these celestial serpents. The immortality of the soul, which could only be ensured through mummification, became an obsession in Egypt. For life was cheap when the serpent reappeared, and death must have been wholesale.

In 1991 an asteroid ten miles wide passed between the Earth and the Moon. Had it crossed Earth's path, there would have been no one left to explore these or any other hypotheses. Civilization and its half-understood rituals would have gone the way of the dinosaurs. Little has changed, then, from those ancient evenings. Potentially, civilization is still under the cometary gun.

For Boswell as for Gerald Massey before her, the British Isles reverberated with funereal, non-Aryan traditions in pre-Christian times. And both Boswell and Massey are in agreement with the testimony of the monks of Clonmacnoise-- that Ireland was the Saba of the North. Homer's puzzling quote in Book I of the *Odyssey* regarding the itinerary of the Otherworld god Poseidon may now be decrypted:

> But now that god
> had gone far off among the sunburnt races,
> most remote of men, at earth's two verges,
> in sunset lands and lands of the rising sun,

to be regaled by smoke and thighbones burning,
haunches of rams and bulls, a hundred fold (Mack, et al. 1985, 173).

This study maintains that one of those "sunset lands" was Ireland, and that
Ethiopia was one of the "lands of the rising sun." If Delphi was indeed
founded by the Hyperboreans, as the ancients indicate, it seems clear that
Saba, and Ireland, the Saba of the North, were the twin Edens where
cherubim priests and priestesses and royal hermaphrodites pathetically
attempted to cast spells upon the celestial serpents, and where the god-kings
periodically slaughtered one another for succession in the futile attempt to
ward off Doomsday.

Notes

1. Washington (1984) also refers to the nineteenth century editor, James Simson,
who in his preface to Walter Simson's *A History of the Gipsies*, also wobbles at the
same end of the pendulum. In effect, Simson attempts to remove the curse of Ham
from England's black gypsy population: "The peculiar feeling that is entertained for
what is popularly understood to be a Gipsy, differs from that which is displayed
toward the Negro, in that it attaches to his traditional character and mode of life alone.
The general prejudice against the Negro is, to a certain extent, natural, and what
anyone can realize."
2. Washington (1984, 20) also refers to the loomings of Bishop Hall, a seventeenth
century cleric who did a bit of soul-searching after he eyed a 'Blackamoor' who was
ambling along the streets of London. Observing in his *Occasional Meditations* that
all races are the "children of one father," Hall decided that beauty in regard to skin
color was not an absolute, but relative to the observer. "That which is beauty to one
is deformity to another; we should be looked upon in this man's country with no less
wonder and strange eyeness that he is here; our whiteness could pass there for an
unpleasing disposition of term. Outward beauty is more in the eye of the beholder
than in the face that is seen. In every color that is fair which pleaseth: the very
spouse of Christ can say, I am black, but comely. . . . The true Moses marries a
blackamoor, Christ his Church. It is not for us to regard the skin, but the soul."
3. The origin of this fiery tree appears to be the Egyptian/Abyssinian image of the
cometary Phoenix bird, symbol of immortality. According to Hancock and Bauval
(1996, 204), "the Bennu bird, the legendary Phoenix, which at certain widely
separated intervals fashioned a nest of aromatic boughs and spices, set it on fire and
was consumed in its flames. From the pyre miraculously sprang a new Phoenix,
which after embalming its feather's ashes, flew with the ashes to Heliopolis where it
deposited them on the altar of the sun-god Re."
4. For the 105 year figure see Velikovsky (1977, 163, fn. 1).
5. Also see Graves (1966, 129). He links the tales of the demon Asmodeus to the

murders of the husbands of the fifty Danides: "The Argive myth of the fifty Danides who were married to the fifty sons of Aegyptus and killed all but one on their common wedding night, and Perso-Egypto-Greek myth of Tobit and Raguel's daughter whose seven previous husbands had all been killed by the demon Asmodeus-- in Persian, Aeshma Daeva-- on their wedding night, are originally identical." Graves goes on to note that "Every four years at the fiftieth lunar month a contest was held as to who should become the Hercules, or Zeus, of the next four years and the lover of the fifty priestesses."

6. Also see the following: Strabo (I, 1, 2, 26). Apollodorus (II, 1, 4). Homer (I, 22). Siculus (I, 10, 28). Herodotus (I, 1-3).

7. Also see Walsh and Bradley (1991, 75, 82). They note that Columba's feast day is held on the 9th of June and in Derry oak leaves are worn in lapels in his honor.

8. See especially O'Rahilly (1967, 293) for the equation of Midir and Oengus. Boswell (1972b, 22) sheds some additional light on the Art title, linking it ultimately to the Otherworld God of ancient Ethiopia. In *The Snake in the Grove* she proposes that versions of the Anghabo title for the Ethiopian king who saved the Sheba avatar from the old python king in the Axumite version "turn up in Ireland and are all connected with the God of the Otherworld, Aengus or Midir . . . . " As we might expect, Midir was also called Art, a title which Boswell argues was "a name for a god in Irish and for a cobra in Egyptian." Boswell goes on to argue that in Ethiopian tanistry, the cobra equates to the new king, Neos Awri [or Set, in the Egyptian version], and the python symbolizes the old king Abi Awri [or Osiris in the Egyptian]. This linkage of Arthur with Horus implies an equation with Osiris as well, since Horus was Osiris's avatar and avenger in Egypt. And the Ethiopian Midir undergoes another transformation in North African Tuareg mythology, as Reynolds (1993, 122) explains. She cites the ancient title Meshi which becomes in today's Tuareg speech Imoshagh or Mashek [i. e. 'nobles]. She traces the title to an ancient Nubian solar deity called Mesh or Mash, a name which she associates with the Abyssinian Medir, also called Med, Mad and Midir. She then cites an ancient inscription for the Nubian Mad which indicates that 'he that is great among the deserts come from Puani (Punt).' She goes on to reveal that Medir was worshiped at the Nubian Talmis during the earlier centuries c.e. The godly titles Mit (Mid, Mad) and Mash have also been found in ancient Karanog inscriptions, she continues, noting that Med and Mash were likely solar and fire deities. Given that Reynolds speculates on a non-solar layer to the lore of this deity, it may well have been a cometary layer given the fact that desert nomads routinely carried betel stones in caravans to ensure safe passage. Nevertheless, based upon this obvious diffusion of the Ethiopian Otherworld God Midir to North Africa, the deity was likely transmitted to Ireland as well by the various invader groups which sojourned across North Africa.

9. Vallancey also notes that Aethiops was a title for Zeus. It did not necessarily refer to complexion.

10. See Crowfoot (1911, I.). See Lynch (1848, I, p. 214, fn. c) for a derivation of the 'Volg' and 'Bolg' titles.

Chapter 12

Comets and Kings

The processes of tanistry were not pretty. Only by the ritual slaying of the old king and the immediate installation of the tanist could order on Earth and in heaven be maintained, according to the understandably paranoid logic of our ancestors. In order to be viable, the god-king, as the earthly emblem of a benign protector comet, had to cast a magical spell to ensure that each periodic return of the cosmic serpent in question would be a non-event. As long as the king was virile, it was hoped, the stars would not fall from the sky. But when gray hairs began to fleck his head, it was time to call in the tanist.

The sovereignty or well-being of the mother goddess on earth was symbolized by the goddess-concubine of the king who could be his mother, sister or daughter. This incestuous bonding may well have mirrored the lascivious movements of the cometary gods and goddesses aloft. Hence Osiris, who Diodorus Siculus argued was reared Nysa in Arabia Felix and who was identical to the later Greek Dionysius, became the husband of Isis, but, depending on the version of the myth, sometimes the son or the brother of Isis as well. If a line of descent could be maintained through royal incest, if the earthly representative of the protector comet, the royal hermaphrodite composed of the king and his consort, could be reconstituted in perpetuity through tanistry, as it were, Doomsday could be averted. Such was the illogic of our traumatized ancestors.

Although the first father-son, or brother-brother dragon-pair of tanistry was traced to the cometary Osiris/Set dyad in the middle of the third millennium B.C.E., more than two millennia later, David, who founded his dynasty during an especially virulent period of cometary activity, was for a time substituted by the Israelites for Set of the first god-king dragon pair. This substitution was an easy one to make, given that Set's cometary slaying of Osiris paralleled David's pact with Joab to place Uriah in the front line of a military engagement against the Ammonites. For that position would ensure Uriah's demise. And why was Uriah important to David? Uriah was in possession of the Ark of the Covenant, and he was also Bathsheba's first husband. Uriah appears to be the Osiris figure, according to W. P. Boswell, given that Uriah's name is apparently derived from the Egyptian for 'cobra,' or *ouro*, a title for Osiris as well (1972b, 43-44). If Bathsheba cooperated in the killing of Uriah, tanistry may have been involved, for in a matriarchal society wealth is inherited by the female heir. Bathsheba does not appear to have offered any resistance to David's advances in 2 Samuel 11: 2-5:

> It happened towards evening when David had got up from resting and was strolling on the palace roof, that from the roof he saw a woman bathing; the woman was very beautiful. David made inquiries about this woman and was told, 'Why, that is Bathsheba's daughter of Eliam and wife of Uriah the Hittite.' David then sent messengers to fetch her. She came to him and he lay with her, just after she had purified herself from her period. She then went home again. The woman conceived and sent word to David, 'I am pregnant.'

Bathsheba, who may well have been a sacred concubine and thus a receptacle of what would later be called the *sang real*, the royal female blood line, could have played the role of Aso in the version of the Osiris myth in which Isis-Aso colluded with the supplanter Set. When David summons Uriah to Jerusalem, Uriah nervously replies in 2 Samuel 11: 11 that "'The ark, Israel and Judah are lodged in my huts.'" The Ark of the Covenant was apparently as great a trophy as Bathsheba, and David, no doubt, wished to possess it in order to play the god-king role. In any case, the murder of Uriah united David's empire with the territories once ruled by dead king Uriah, for Bathsheba was the heir of Uriah's holdings. The two peoples joined by David's chicanery became known as the Habashats, a title that will resurface later in this chapter.

The upshot of David's intrigue was the angering of Yahweh, who sent the prophet Nathan to inform David that his "household will never be free of the sword," and that Bathsheba's first child will die, but the next child, Solomon, will be spared Yahweh's anger. The reason for Yahweh's condemnation of David is unclear, but it results, according to 2 Samuel 24: 10-17, in an epidemic, administered by an angel, which killed seventy-thousand of David's subjects. Saddened by the devastation, Yahweh finally restrained the angel: "when it stretched his hand toward Jerusalem to destroy it." Was the angel a metaphor for a comet?

This study argues that tanistry, as in the example involving David, Uriah and Bathsheba, involved the use of sympathetic magic that was employed to thwart a feared doomsday encounter with a comet or asteroid and any attendant meteor shower. The reigning snake-king and his female consort formed a divine hermaphrodite. And what exactly is the upshot of the hermaphrodite image? Its import, like the image itself, appears to be dual. First, the hermaphrodite seems to harken back to a golden age when Isis and Osiris, two closely joined fragments of the same comet perhaps, reappeared at their regular orbital interval to put on the most awesome and benign light show ever witnessed by mankind. Second, bolstered by sacred incest, the hermaphrodite represents the unity of opposites, of male and female, of good and evil, the condition of that pre-sexual innocence that allegedly existed in the unfallen world, the ideal and perfect order which prevailed when the child was suckled at its mother's breast, and, by extension, before the sky 'fell' and the respective cosmic serpent became demonized (Markale 1995, 130-31).[1] Sometimes in the ancient skies the protective snake-king was Set, but later, as the process of cometary disintegration continued, the king was likened to both Set and Horus: Set for the Israelites and other tribes of the Mediterranean and Red Sea basins until the collapse of the Late Bronze Age, and Horus for the Egyptians. The honor apparently depended on the strike zones of the meteorites which distended from the fragmenting comet overhead. The earthly agent of the protector comet had to be both moral and virile enough to continue the spell and thus prevent the sky from falling in a hail of meteorites. This concept of kingly morality, called *ma'at* in Egypt, is apparently what David violated when he engineered the death of Uriah. For David was ruled by passion instead of by a concern for the welfare of his people. In any case, when the reigning king finally became the old king, the new king, or tanist, was installed.

The process was more complicated, however, for the king had a dual identity. He began his career by strangling the snake king, for the tanist was the Set avatar who forced the cobra-like Osiris avatar from the heavens. But when age and infirmity caught up with him, he terminated his contract as king in the guise of the defeated ouros-Osiris. The cryptic death of Absalom, David's rebellious son, reveals that Absalom, playing the role of tanist, sought his father's demise too early in his father's career. As a result, Absalom, associated with a mule, a Set totem, paid the price in 2 Samuel 18:9: "Absalom was riding his mule and the mule passed under the thick branches of a great oak. Absalom's head got caught in the oak and he was hanging between heaven and earth, while the mule he was riding went on."

All of this Old Testament background is quite relevant to the tanistry practiced in the druidic British Isles. Solomon, the second of the kingly line of David to which Christ's genealogy and that of the kings of Ireland and Britain were traced, had a wife called the Queen of Sheba. Not surprisingly, then, in the Grail legends, Mackeda, as she was called, was considered to be Guinevere's ancestor, just as Solomon was deemed to be Arthur's. These claims to kinship may at first appear fanciful until the ritual beheading that occurred periodically at the Grail castle is understood and derived from the more ancient version of the primal murder preserved at Axum in Ethiopia, an alleged resting place of the Ark of the Covenant.

Around the year 1000 B.C.E., Menelik, the dark-skinned son of Solomon and Sheba, preserved the dynasty of David when he fled from Jerusalem with the Ark of the Covenant. Centuries after the hiatus of the Ark at Elephantine, Menelik's avatar, who bore the same title, arrived at Axum, bringing with him the matrifocal system of tanistry. According to Boswell, the priests of the Tigray tribe of the Axum area relate that either Mackeda/Sheba's avatar or her father, Anghabo's avatar, destroyed a giant snake at Axum. That snake is identified as a high priest by the faithful of Eritrea and Tigray (1972a, 14). Jean Doresse in *Ethiopia* explains that for millennia Abyssinian natives have deified a huge snake named *Awre Midre* or *Awri Medr* (1959, 15). A mural at Axum provides another version of the serpent worship. Boswell interprets the mural, noting the cobra worship of the Ethiopians around 3000 B.C.E. which required that first born infants be routinely sacrificed to the reptile. This cycle was allegedly broken when Anghabo, the father of the Queen of Sheba, decided that the people kill the cobra. Shortly thereafter, Anghabo became the emperor (1972b, 21).

In still another version of the myth from Tigray province, Anghabo is distressed by the sacrifice of the tribe's daughters to the cobra. To break the cycle of female sacrifice, he saves his own daughter Sheba from the jaws of the serpent, marries her, and rules the groves of Tigray province himself (Boswell 1972b, 23ff.). The sparing of Sheba, or of Sheba's avatar, would appear to involve the restoration of matriarchal *mutterrecht* in Ethiopia, a right which may have been threatened because of a lethal display by a 'female' cometary fragment. Her rescue is also a Christlike act, in that the sacrifice of the snake-king whom Anghabo dispatched, ended the sacrifice of young children to the serpent, a gesture that was certainly not honored at Carthage, itself an early Ethiopian colony, according to Strabo (II, 26-27).

This version of the Axum-Tembien drama [Tembien being another sacred grove near Axum in Tigray province which is now a part of the nation of Eritrea] may, for the purposes of this study, translate into the following: To restore the order of the unfallen world through sacred marriage, to protect Mother Earth, symbolized by the Sheba avatar, from potential destruction by the potentially lethal, serpentine comet aloft, a virile, potent god-king, emblematic of the protector comet, must take the place of the older representative of the cosmic serpent on earth. The Sheba-avatar would then marry her father under the terms of royal incest and remain married to him until such time as his failing powers required his substitution by a younger king whom the queen or her avatar might also marry. This younger supplanter-king could, in fact, be her brother or son. For such were the tenets of royal incest. And after the older king's execution by strangulation, the Anghabo title of her father would then be taken on by the new virile king, the new husband of the Sheba-avatar.

Boswell, who does not link any of this drama to comets *per se*, argues that the old king at Axum, where the ritual was preserved intact until the arrival of Christianity, was called by the Geez name for 'Huge Beast' or *Abi Awri*. Another name for Abi Awri is *Gebel*, which in contemporary Tigrinya means 'snake,' and in Phoenician meant both 'mountain' and the city of Byblos, the very place to which Osiris's coffin floated, Boswell continues (1972a, 16). Given the cometary nature of Osiris, that destination was no accident. And the young, tanist-supplanter king is titled the "Small Beast" or *Neos Awri* in the contemporary Geez dialect even today, for the Dabtara or pagan priests of Tigray province still invoke pre-Christian traditions, she notes (1972b, 15, 3-4). The Awri title will reappear shortly in conjunction with numerous pre-Christian Irish deities, priests and kings.

The various titles and roles of the participants in tanistry need further amplification. If Neos Awri is called Anghabo, then the Sheba avatar has married her father in order to restore the unfallen world of matriarchy and to ensure the survival of the protector comet by associating her royal bloodline with his kingship. Additionally, when age afflicted Sheba, her Sheba-avatar would inherit the sacred grove. Since Boswell indicates that an alternate name for Neos Awri in Tigrinya is *Temen* for 'snake,' and in Amharic *Tenishe* for 'small beast,' the etymology of tanistry may be traced to East Africa, and, with a simple reversal from Phoenician right-left to Greek left-right, *Temen* becomes *Nemet* or *Nemed*, which is nearly identical to the name of the famous Italian sacred grove highlighted in Frazer's *The Golden Bough* (1972b, 18). For at Nemi and other sacred sites dotting the Mediterranean and Red Sea basins the tradition of tanistry persisted. Incidentally, *temen* also means darkness in Old Irish, according to Cohane. (1969, p. 246).

Applying this terminology to pre-Christian Ireland and ancient Greece, Boswell proposes that Nemed was titular of various priest-kings who were in line to inhabit the sacred grove. This Nemed was also an avatar of the various divine Irish priest-kings from Seth, who originated in Abyssinia, to Mil, who originated in Spain. Nemed's consort was none other than a sacred virginal Amazon who could be his mother, sister or daughter. Nemed and his consort, then, comprised an hermaphroditic "holy reptile" (197b, 6).

Boswell also reveals that in Ireland, the new king was called either *Tanaise* or *Tanaise Ri*, which means second in command (1972b, 5). She cites E. O'Curry's *Manners and Customs of the Ancient Irish*, who writes of the Tanaise Ri or tanist of a king, the second in command to the king, as it were, who was elected as the king's successor by the vote of the people (O'Curry 1873, 468 fn. 461). And there is one more spin-off from the Temen synonym, for as Boswell notes the title *Temenites* was an alternate name for Apollo, who was both the deity of doctors and the father of Aesculapius (1972b, 18).

But Boswell's Aso-Sheba figure is more complex. In some versions of the snake killing myth which may derive from an earlier era of unchallenged matriarchy, Sheba was the murderer. And her description was not that of a helpless victim of the snake's [old king's] appetite, but that of a lethal Amazon, a warrior queen (1972b, 25ff.). In another Ethiopian version of the ritual of tanistry called the Hirut myth, the Sheba avatar is likened to a weeping frankincense tree, according to Boswell's Dabtara source. Boswell notes that at Abi Sahafti outside of Axum there is a mountain called Pentelion that was, according to the myth, inhabited by a serpent king. When thirsty, the serpent would slither down to the Mareb River to drink. Once a year, sacrifices of a first born daughter, medicinal leaves, milk and other items were presented to the serpent-king. The daughter's title was Hirut or Sheba. At the chosen time, Sheba climbed the sacred oak [Daro] to await her demise, weeping so intensely that her tears landed on an angel which took pity on her and killed the serpent by cutting it into two pieces. Debra Damo monastery, Boswell goes on, was founded on that site (1972, 27-28).

Interestingly enough, the Sheba figure is in the tree, weeping meteorites perhaps, much as the frankincense or Etan tree 'weeps' moisture as it matures, for, although Boswell does not identify any cometary imagery, Sheba appears, for the purposes of this study, to be emblematic of a comet fragment. Sheba's tears may well be the prototype of those of the Virgin Mary's, Boswell notes, and the appellation *Hirut* for the Goddess appears to be echoed centuries later as the *hiruphin,* or angels referred to in *The Irish Liber Hymnorum*: "He came to Axala, great crowds, archangels, i. e. he came to the place where is the angel, Axal, . . . i. e. he came to the land in which conversation is made . . . ." In the original Latin, a portion of this passage reads: "*quia dicunt hiruphin et zaraphin, sanctus, sanctus dominus deus sabaoth dicentes*" (1972b, 39, fn. 41).² Is this Axala reference made not only to commemorate the French monastery at Auxerre southeast of Paris, but, ultimately, the mountain near Axum where a meteorite descended, and the monastery that was built in obeisance to this sacred stone from heaven? And the Abi Awri snake as river sucker and doctor who collects medicinal leaves, is echoed later perhaps in the Saint Samson's escapades at the Lughnasa celebration cited earlier in this study, where the Saint, another Set-Wainaba river sucker to be sure, swallows the water that gushes from the 'shower' welling up from the underground cave after slaying the cometary dragon. These are likely possibilities given that in another Ethiopian version of this myth, a more benign serpent transforms itself into a rock at Debra Damo mountain (1972b, 30). Could this imagery point to a comet fragment's or meteorite's abilities not only to dry up the land as it passes overhead and/or impacts and thus create drought, but also to deposit water vapor in an immense cloud canopy that might form overhead from melting cometary ice?

In the Abi Sahafti Abyssinian version noted above, the cometary angel, for our purposes, pities the Sheba avatar, and cuts in twain the threatening celestial serpent that hopes to devour her as the comet fragment disintegrates further. Unaware of the possible cometary nature of this myth, Boswell correctly identifies the killer angel with Set or Seth, who is alternately known as the Egyptian Angel of Death and the cutter (1972b, 28). During the early stages of the embalming of the deceased in Egypt, a Set/Anubis *Cherheb* priest, adorned in his jackal-headed mask, would make a small incision on the body with an Ethiopian stone knife so that the liver could later be removed from the belly cavity (Budge 1967, 265-66). Just after he cut the incision, the ritual required that the *Cherheb* priest be driven away by the other embalmers. Only then could the deceased's organs be removed and the myrrh placed into the hollowed cavity. Clearly, Set was an anathema to the resultant mummy who represented Osiris in the *Book of the Dead,* and who would make Osiris' journey into the Underworld where the celestial demons threatened. Interestingly enough, as Boswell notes, I. J. Gelb reveals that the verbs 'to cut' and 'to write' may have been synonymous in Semitic writing, both coming from the *STR* root, which, she argues, may have initially meant 'to cut,' given that the Arabic *satur* means a large 'knife,' and *satir* means a 'butcher' (1972b, 38 fn. 29; Gelb 1952, 7). Boswell concludes the following from this etymology: "The association between cutting and writing explains the ritual tattooing of letters on the skins of the Celtic chiefs which were memorials to the sacred letters first cut out by Neos Awri when he killed Abi Awri" (1972b, 28).

Do we have a clue to the tattooing noted on the bodies of numerous Britons by the Roman invaders? Pliny observes that the Druids performed snake sacrifices, and in his day, these Druids were the priests of the Phoenicians, themselves engaged in both mining and incense production in Ireland and Cornwall. Pliny makes another relevant observation. The tattoo marks borne by the Druids, which *Lebor Gabala* calls "snake bites," were of Ethiopian origin (Boswell 1972b, 39 fn. 38; Siculus, IV, 41, 4-6). Boswell notes that *Lebor Gabala* also relates an incident in which the Goidel chief in Egypt was cured of such a snake bite by Moses' serpent wand when it was placed on the chief's wound (1972a, 14; *Lebor Gabala*, II, 35, 61, 134). Velikovsky elaborates on this cure. He cites Numbers 21:9: "And Moses made a serpent of brass, and put it upon a pole." Pondering this image, Velikovsky suggests:

> The brazen serpent was most probably the image of the pillar of cloud and fire which appeared as a moving serpent to all peoples of the world. St. Jerome apparently had this image in view when he interpreted the star mentioned in Amos as Lucifer. Or was it the 'star of David,' the six-pointed star? (1977b, 185)

But we are not finished with the language theme yet. Boswell reveals that in Ireland as in Ethiopia, learning and language started with the worship of the trees of the sacred groves. This phenomena, she argues, is demonstrated in the Celtic tree alphabet which Graves attempted to decipher in *The White Goddess* (Boswell 1972b, 5; Graves 1966, 165ff.).

Why trees? And why were standing stones always found in the sacred groves? What is the connection between the tree and the stone? And why was the primal Word of God or Logos linked with trees? In *The Cosmic Serpent*, Clube and Napier demonstrate that nearly every culture has likened comet shapes with tree shapes. One visual from China, dated 168 B.C.E., which they display, is particularly telling. It depicts a series of diagrams of comets with various tree branch and swastika-like appendages (1982, 155, 193). As noted earlier, the benign comet, or protector comet, was likened to the World Tree which extended metaphorically from the Otherworld into which its roots were anchored to the Tree's zenith which pointed toward the

Pole Star. This Tree was thought to hold up the sky and prevent it from falling. At times the Tree was likened to a pillar of smoke, or to Atlas or Hercules who held up the sky. For a falling sky was likely a euphemism for a meteor shower.

But why was a comet or meteor as tree associated with a talking serpent [as is the case with the Genesis account of the Fall of Man] and with speech and writing? And why did early cultures produce sacred sound-image patterns involving snakes, speech and written language, rocks or sacred stones, and trees?

The loudest sound that an inhabitant of Earth could experience would likely emanate from the entry of a large meteor or a comet into Earth's atmosphere. The pealing of thunder or the quaking of a volcano win second place, as the Tunguska event of 1908 clearly demonstrates (Clube and Napier 1982, 140). If the comet and its careening meteorites were viewed as gods, the deafening roar of a meteorite's entry into Earth's atmosphere must have been likened to the voice of a god or a goddess, the Logos, or sacred speech uttered at the beginning of time. Graves is on the verge of discovering this phenomenon when he writes of the Gorgon's head, which he derives from the Greek Lamia and her progenitor the Triple Goddess Neith of Libya, of whom Black Athena, the Goddess of Wisdom, is also an avatar. Graves describes the effects of the Gorgon's head contained in Perseus' bag, lopped off he believes by the sickle-shaped moon rather than by a meteoric, coma-shaped sickle:

> Peeping from his bag there is now a Gorgon's head, which is merely an ugly mask assumed by priestesses on ceremonial occasions to frighten away trespassers; at the same time they made hissing noises, which account for Medusa's snake locks . . . . The ugly face at the mouth of the bag, symbolizes that the secrets of the alphabet, which are the real contents, are not to be divulged or misused. (1966, 231)

Interestingly enough, Graves reveals that Perseus' crane skin bag, which is derived from the bag Mercury used when he carried the Pelasgian language from Egypt to Greece, is also found in the parallel myth of Manannan, son of Lyr, whom Graves identifies as a Goidelic Sun-hero and precursor of Fionn and Cuchulain. For Manannan carried sea treasures, which Graves equates with the Peoples of the Sea's alphabet, in a sack of crane skin. Graves goes on to note that Mider, the god of the Goildelic Underworld, parallels the British Arawn, King of Annwyn and keeper of the castle on Manannan's sacred Isle of Man. The island's castle gates, he goes on, were guarded by three intimidating cranes which warded off potential visitors (Graves 1966, 233)³

Referring to the *Book of the Dead*, but missing the full import of its message, Graves equates Cuchulain with Osiris, Ixion and the Orphic Ophion-serpent, who travels through the twelve signs of the zodiac:

> Osiris [is] captured by his rival Set and tied, like Ixion and Cuchulain, in that five-fold bond that joined wrists, neck and ankles together. 'Osiris whose circuit is the Otherworld' is also the economical way of identifying the god with the snake Ophion, coiled around the . . . earth, a symbol of universal fertility out of death. (1966, 279)⁴

A more graphic picture of the immense tail of an earth-grazing comet seems to present itself here rather than "a symbol of universal fertility out of death."

Given that a meteorite is a metallic stone and that the comet from which it may become detached often takes the shape of a branching tree, the association of speech, tree, stone and serpent makes perfect sense. That rich intertwining may explain why the Ten Commandments were reputed to have been inscribed on stones, likely meteoric in origin, that were placed in the Ark of the Covenant. For can it be disputed that the Ark of the Covenant was linked to a meteor shower in Revelation 11? "Then the sanctuary of God in heaven opened, and the ark of the covenant could be seen inside it." This association of speech and rock also explains the talking Fal stone of Tara, the seat of Irish kings, noted later in this study.

The tree-serpent association may account for the fact that the sacred sycamore, or fig tree at Axum, was likened to both a snake and a god. Citing to Ira J. Condit's study entitled *Ficus, The Exotic Species*, Boswell notes that the Ethiopian strangler fig is also referred to by botanists as the "Scotchman." Boswell speculates that the ancients viewed the fig as a sacred tree, for much as the divine serpent reproduces itself, so the fig is capable of reproducing itself through its root system (1972a, 92; Condit 1969, 21).

Linking the vocabulary of Ethiopian tanistry to the invaders of Ireland, Boswell argues that the sacred tanist, whose prototype was Nemed, leader of the third invasion group, looms large in each of *Lebor Gabala's* invasion accounts (1972b, 6). She explores some of the facets of Nemed, revealing that the title was synonymous with 'the Beast' and the verb 'to be,' or the great 'I AM,' the God of the Oath (1972b, 6). The Oath was the doctor's oath, or the Hippocratic Oath as it came to be known at the Greek shrine of Delphi. In swearing it the priest vowed to assist the sick and insulate them from the ravages of disease. For both in Ethiopia and in the Ethiopian colonies that stretched along coastal Greece, the priest-king and his priests and/or priestesses, were 'doctors' who distilled medicines from the trees of the sacred incense groves. Given that Rendell Harris in *Origin of the Cult of Aphrodite* proposes that a black Goddess named Melaina, or the Black Lady, was credited with being the mother of Delphos, founder of the oracle at Delphi, and given that coins of Delphos picture Delphos as a Negro, the argument for an Ethiopian colonization of coastal Greece gains strength (Harris 1916, 16-17; Rogers 1967, I, 136, 80-81).

In Greece, the earth-bound representatives of the dragon pair, consisting of the old king and his would-be tanist-supplanter, were symbolized by the caduceus, replete with its intertwined serpent pair, Apollo and Dionysius. And this caduceus became the symbol of Apollo's son, Aesculapius, who appears to have been killed by one of Zeus' cometary thunderbolts. The doctor-protector, then, was a spin-off of the protector comet figure itself, which makes perfect sense given that the younger members of the priesthood were potential tanists. Interestingly enough, Boswell, citing Frazer's *The Golden Bough*, indicates that "the Ethiopian Emperor, Haile Selassie, like Queen Elizabeth of England, represents the persistence of a tradition which began with the inauguration of magicians under an East African tree of sacrifice" (1972b, 7; Frazer 1951, 703ff.).

Boswell traces the movement of the god-kings from the Island of Meroe to Greece, Crete, North Africa, and Ireland, for in each of these areas the invader groups' footprints can be identified. She does this by identifying Ethiopic/Upper Egyptian animal totems associated with the god-kings of Carthage and Utica, Greece and Ireland, and the persistence of Ethiopian tanistry practiced in these places as well. She argues that the Dog Priest King was the grandson of the Snake Priest King in early Ethiopia, while their avatars, the priests or 'dogs' of God in Phoenicia, were involved in preparing sacrifices and garnering tribute in recognition of their ancestor (1972b, 27). To trace the diffusion, she provides the following king list from Axum produced by Budge in *The Queen of Sheba*. The following kings or dynasties, perhaps, were reputed to have ruled before Mackeda: Arawi, Anghabo, Gieder, Siebadom and Kawnasy, she notes, revealing that the alternate Ethiopic spelling for *Gieder* is *Gadar*, which is an Irish word for 'dog' (1972b, 24-25; Budge 1932, p. xliii). Additionally, it is the name of King Arthur's dog, Gadar.

She then cites the Wainaba myth, another current Ethiopian version of the ascent of the Queen of Sheba, Mackeda, to the rule of the sacred grove, which today stands in the vicinity of contemporary Axum. Boswell notes the Dabtara myth which posits King Malakya, reputed to be Noah's African great grandson, and his six sons as the founders of Axum. After the founding, the Axumites made yearly offerings of a maiden, livestock, milk and beer to a dragon named Wainaba. This obeisance came to an abrupt end, however, when the maiden Mackeda was about to be offered. To prevent her demise, Anghabo, possibly with the assistance of Mackeda, killed Wainaba, and Mackeda ascended to the throne as the Queen of Sheba (1972b, 24).

Malakya, the reputed founder of the incense grove in the vicinity of Axum, appears to be a cognate for another Irish word for 'dog' known as *Milco*, Boswell argues, noting that *Milco* or *Milcu* in Irish means 'Dog King,' and that the Druid Chief of Ulster, Saint Patrick's foster-father and master, was a Milco (1972b, 25). Wainaba, for Boswell, becomes the *ouros* cobra king Osiris/Dionysius (1972b, 25; Siculus I, 15). These totemic associations are important, for the Egyptian Set was equated with the cometary pig or boar that ravaged the cypress swamp of Lower Egypt, and his son Anubis [or Osiris' son by Set's wife and sister Nephthys in one version of the myth of Osiris] was a jackal-headed [dog-headed] priest of embalmers.

This pig-dog and serpent imagery for kings and priests was ubiquitous along the alleged trail of the invaders leading from Egypt to Ireland. In fact, Boswell notes that in much Insular Irish art, snakes and dogs are merged (1972b, 27). Dog and snake kings ruled Punt, based upon the snake imagery and the genealogy Boswell cites. Set, she adds, appears to become the Malakya dog figure in Ethiopia, and linguistic evidence exists indicating that in pre-Christian and early Christian times at Carthage, snakes and dogs were alternate titles for the same ruling family (1972b, 27).

The Island of Meroe was once a vast oasis of incense and myrrh groves, a lush garden contained by an ocean of sand. The desert oases of Carthage and Utica, on a much smaller scale, were sacred cypress and fig groves as well, and these groves were replete with springs and additional water-drinking pythons. Curiously enough, both the pig and pythonic snake totemism found at the monastic sites of these smaller oases, along with the imagery of the Ethiopian tree doctors, who in Greece clustered at Delphi in homage to Apollo's son Aesculapius, are also prominent. At Utica, Boswell identifies a giant fig, and, at the adjacent museum, both a statue of Apollo's son Aesculapius, the Greek god of medicine, and images of Apollo's Muses. One of the legends at Utica which she cites is that of a thirsty python still reputed to sleep on a hilltop tree, a wily serpent which comes down the hill daily to drink from Poseidon's pool that bubbles out of the desert. And this spring is not unlike the sacred springs so common in Irish folklore (1972b, 75). Apparently the Greek version of the tree doctors, whose totems were both snakes and pigs, blended with the earlier Ethiopian tradition, recalling two of the various conquests of the area, one by the Ethiopians and the other by the Greeks. It should also be mentioned that at Delphi, a python was known to eat humans and livestock.

Carthage presents an even more dramatic picture for Boswell. For it was the home of prominent royal families such as the Magonis clan of Himilco Magonis, who before 484 B.C.E. sailed from Gades to Brittany and possibly to Britain as well. It was also the home of the Barcas of whom Hamilcar I and II and Hannibal Barca are the most famous representatives.

Ancient testimonies provide more clues. Strabo indicates that Libya, by which he means all of North Africa, was colonized by the Phoenicians and Ethiopians in ancient times (1972b, 81; Strabo I, ii, 26ff.; Autran 1920, 39). And Diodorus Siculus noted that Amazons, dressed in protective snake skins, roamed the oases. Were these Amazons related to a Sheba cult? Boswell asks. For she recalls that in Irish myth, Maeve is a multiple avatar of a queen of Ethiopia and an Amazon queen descended from an Egyptian Pharaoh (1972b, 81 fn. 119; Siculus III, 543; Herodotus IV, 9, 1991). Then too, she reveals that the Libyan Medusa figure was called "the Daughter of the Oath," an oath which the doctors swore in order to preserve human life with their knowledge of tree medicines (1972b, 61, 81 fn. 120). In both Greece and North Africa, Medusa and her gorgons were associated with the other serpent twin of Apollo at Delphi, namely the sometimes irrational, sometimes intuitive Dionysius. Clearly then, Apollo was deified in North Africa, for his son's statue is prominent in the Utica museum. As mentioned earlier, the British Isles were reputed to be the winter home of Apollo, a Set avatar, when Dionysius took over the Pythian Shrine at Delphi.

More parallels begin to accrete for Boswell: Axum's sacred precinct is called *Doctor*, and its pagan priests are called *Dabtara* to this day; the early Christian priests of Carthage, including Augustine, were called doctors of the Church; the sacred seat of high kingship in Ireland was called Tara; Carthage, in the early centuries of Christianity, had virtually hummed with pagan, druidic-style magician-doctors-astrologers, as Augustine reveals in his *Confessions*. And there are more. The older walls of the monasteries at Carthage and Utica are lined with cauldrons shaped like the three-pointed crowns atop ancient Phoenician gravestones. In fact, these cauldrons look identical to Dagda's cauldron or three pointed crown that Arthur hoped to fetch from Dagda's Otherworld with the help of the Irish Amazon Maeve in *The Cattle Raid of Coole*. Additionally, numerous shapes of incense and medicine phials, some resembling stelae tops at Axum, can also be found atop Phoenician graves, recalling the incense jars found in ancient barrows beneath the Salisbury Plain and the incense monopoly of the Ethiopians and later of the Phoenicians (Boswell 1972b, 61ff.; 121 fn. 121).[5] Boswell quotes the *Treasures of the Bardo Museum* to call up more associations:

> The oldest stelae and ex-votos were shaped like miniature chapels of Egyptizing or Hellenizing style, or thrones, the whole being of porous sandstone. They were adorned with roughly made anthropomorphic statues and betels. Some ex-votos bear consecrations to Baal-Hammon . . . . The most commonly represented picture is that of the symbol of Tanit. One also sees a symbol in the shape of a bottle, lunar crescents (emblem of Tanit) associated with solar disks (emblem of Baal Hammon), doves, palm trees, ivy (Bacchic), hands, caducei, oars, rose-windows, dolphins. On one of the stelae, one picture represents a priest in transparent linen dress, just like the Pharaonic priests, carrying a child he was undoubtedly about to offer to Tanit in sacrifice. (1972b, 67; Driss 1966, 12-13)

For the purposes of this study, the antique cauldrons that are so ubiquitous both in North African monastic architecture and in Irish folklore, may not be volcanic memorials, as Boswell suggests, but symbolic of the impact craters of meteorites (1972b, 65). Such craters may also have been commemorated by the megalithic stone circles scattered across the British Isles. These crater shapes may also be the origin of the crowns of kings and queens, headpieces which are often associated with cauldrons in Irish folklore.

And the orgy of child sacrifice documented at Carthage may point to a frenetic zeal to propitiate cometary Baal and his Medusa-like consort Tanit, for their respective lunar and solar connotations may not have always obtained, especially during the collapse of the Late Bronze Age and its prior disasters. In the British Isles, the Beltane fires celebrated on May Day, bear testimony to the cometary nature of Bel or Baal, to whom they were dedicated (Clube and Napier 1982, 242).

Seeking more Ethiopian genealogical debris in North Africa, Boswell further notes that the leading Christian figure at Carthage was Aurelius, also known as Augustine, Bishop of Hippo. Could that name be derived from the ruler at Axum, namely Awri, the python king? she wonders (1972b, 77). And could the name of the first king of the British Isles in the English tradition, one Lucius Aurelius, who was also called *Luciferus* in British accounts and *Lugh* in Irish accounts, be similarly derived? she wonders (1972b, 77). Ultimately, the name Lugh, she argues, may be traced to the Ethiopian Galla title *Lugo* (1972b, 38). And what of the Irish equation of Lucius, or Lugh Aurelius, with Cormac mac Art, the King of Tara? Boswell asks (1972b 77, 85).[6]

Other nomenclature in ancient Carthage appears to be cognate with titles both in Ethiopia and in Ireland for Boswell. Malchus, she notes, a sixth century Carthaginian general, is the first recorded historical personage of Carthage (1972b, 78). She cites B. H. Warmington, who argues that the Semitic title *Melek* for 'king' forms the root of both the Malchus title and the title of the founder of Axum or Malakya (1972b, 77; Warmington 1960, 52ff.). And Malchus was succeeded at Carthage by Magon, the ancestor of Himilco Barca who possibly explored the British Isles in the fifth century B.C.E. Interestingly enough, Magonis was the family name of Ireland's Saint Patrick, son of a Romano-British tax collector called a *decurion* (1972b, 78 fn. 158). And Columba was related to Patrick Magonus, Boswell reveals, for Columba was a Barcid on his mother's side of the family, and an Ui Neill on his father's side, a clan name that Boswell derives from Pharaoh Neil of Egypt, a Set avatar (1972b, 80, 29 fn. 35; Strabo, 5,1 14, 16). Columba's mother was an Irish princess named Eithne, and Columba was baptized by Cruithnecan, his foster-father, with the sobriquet *Criomhthann*, meaning 'fox,' a totemic dog title (Walsh and Bradley 1991, 75-76).

Is it any wonder that Columba is described as black in the account presented of him further on in this study. Kathleen Hughes cites two later members of the Ui Neill clan who, for the purposes of this study, have *dun* and *muir* roots in their names. Referring to the battles against the Vikings in the tenth century, she notes that Donnchad of the southern Ui Neill and Muircrtach, son of Niall of the of the northern Ui Neill, warred against Viking marauders (1987, 28-29). Although Columba is not described as swarthy in Adomnan's biography, it is possible that previous intermarriages of his ancestors may have lightened the clan. As a result, he may have been perceived to be black-hearted, at any rate, by English Christians because of his probable North African roots, his Africanized Christian practices and his Luciferian genealogy. And it is to an understanding of that Luciferian genealogy that this study now turns.

For Boswell, the Goidels of Ireland carried on the tradition of serpent and pig-dog totemism. So is this the meaning of St. Patrick's act of driving the serpents from Ireland in 431 C.E.? Edmund Swift argues that Jocelin of Furnes' *Life of Saint Patrick* depicts snakes, emblematic of serpent worship, that fled before Patrick's preaching (1972a, 29 fn. 61).[7] If so, Boswell observes that the task of converting the druid priests, who maintained an Old Testament mythology, could not have been very difficult. Conversion problems would have been expedited, given that Christianity posited the worship of a divine mother and her crucified son, both of whom were deemed kin to Ethiopia's Prester Johns, the succession of Emperors praised

in the *Kebra Negast* (1972a, 17). For according to the *Kebra Negast*, Christ
is kin to Menelik, the son of Solomon and the Queen of Sheba, and swarthy
Menelik founded the sacred line of *Negush*, or god-kings of Ethiopia. It was
from this line of descent that Columba as a Barcid and a Ui Neill appears to
have emerged, a genealogy which put him squarely in the camp of the
Hamitic Seth. But to understand what being in the camp of the Hamitic Seth
means requires some more digging.

The Tree of Life in Genesis is often thought to be an apple tree, given that
Eve accepts the apple from the talking serpent. It is also linked to the fig
tree, for Adam and Eve hide their shame with fig leaves. Boswell notes that
Lebor Gabala calls the snake-devil in the Tree of Knowledge, *Iofer Niger*,
or the Black Man: "Thereafter Lucifer had envy against Adam, for he was
assured that this would be given him (Adam), the filling of Heaven in his
(Lucifer's) room. Wherefore, he (*Iofer Niger*) came in the form of the
serpent . . . "(1972a, 22, 28 fn. 59; *Lebor Gabala*, I, 19). Citing Petrides,
Boswell explains that the Negus or King of Ethiopia was also linked to
Lucifer, as the bearer of light and the ruler of the abyss (1972a, 21 fn. 57;
Petrides 1966, 13). Interestingly enough, then, *Lebor Gabala* begins with
the creation story and likens Ireland to Eden, the abode of the serpent-devil.

The ambivalence that revolves around the figure of Lucifer can be
resolved. The reptile was well chosen to be the bearer of wisdom and
sadness, if he represented the celestial reptile called Set. Set or Seth is
regarded as the ancestor of all people in Genesis. And in Ireland, Boswell
notes, Seth and his variant titles, Saturn, Starn and Sdairn, and Banba, his
queen, were not individual names but royal titles used to denote each
successive king and queen (1972a, 26). These Irish rulers were literally gods
on earth, emblems of the sacred hermaphrodite, for God was fashioned to
encompass the male and female genders, as noted earlier.

The ritual slayings enacted in the sacred groves of the Mediterranean and
Red Sea basins, were, for Boswell, duplicated in Ireland, for the invader
groups carried the matriarchal system of tanistry with them.

The earliest invasion groups under Queen Banba were Hamite pirates
called by two names, the Fomorions and the Bolg. According to *Lebor
Gabala*, the Fomorions came from Africa to Ireland to escape the Semites,
or the sons of Shem. Keating translates the reference this way: "Neimheadh
won three battles on the Fomorions, namely navigators of the race of Cham,
who fared from Africa; they came fleeing to the island of the west of Europe
. . . and . . . fleeing the race of Sem . . . " (1908, I, 179). Citing Diodorus
Siculus, Boswell links this Fomorion or Bolg tribe to the Bolg clan of ancient
Abyssinia (1972a, 25; *Lebor Gabala*, I, 7ff, 27). Since Pliny observes in

his *Natural History* that the Celts adorned themselves with blue-black tattoos in honor of the Ethiopians, a fairly air-tight case for origins is suggested (xxii, 1).

Boswell explains that the Irish queens of prehistory were called Banba, Macha, Etan or Ethne, and Brigit. Given that the early inhabitants of Ireland were matrifocal, what role did these queens play in the rituals of kingly succession? She notes that Banba was the queen's title in the first and fifth invasion groups, and that Keating observes Ireland was first called Banbha (1972a, 25; Keating 1908, II, 109, 199). The queens of the second, third, and fifth invasion groups from Scythia were called Macha, from which Boswell derives the place-name for the See of Armagh in Ulster (1972a, 25; *Lebor Gabala*, IV, 149). Etan or Ethne was the title of the queens of the second invader group, and of the fifth invader group from Athens (Boswell 1972a, 25). Brigit is a generic title, Boswell agues, which can be substituted for all Irish queens of the invader groups (1972a, 25). Brigit's alternate name was Baalba which means 'flame' in Ethiopian (Boswell 1972a, 25, 31 fn. 80; *Lebor Gabala*, III, 24; IV, 117, 123, 131). Brigit was the daughter of the God of the Dead who was also called Dagda (*Lebor Gabala*, IV, 139). Boswell goes on to reveal that the Brigit title, which this study argues referred to a cometary deity, was passed on to each subsequent High Priestess, both pagan and Christian. Each of her avatars followed in her footsteps at Kildare monastery by maintaining the sacred oak and the perpetual fire (Boswell 1972a, 26, 32 fn. 85; Kenney 1929, 356-58). And not surprisingly, *The Irish Liber Hymnorum* equates Brigit with the Queen of Sheba (Boswell 1972a, 26, 32 fn. 86; Bernard and Atkinson 1898, I, 161).

Of what was the perpetual fire symbolic? History is mute on that point. Based on the cometary image patterns this study has proposed, it may well have represented both the protector-comet and the Sun, in that order. Given that the king/queen dyad was the protector of the Earth, the returning comet's benign light would have been held dear. And if the memory of a cosmic winter was still taught in the druid colleges, the Sun is a good candidate as well. Brigit's other duties were to serve as the consort of the god-king, and to ensure that a priestess from the royal blood line would produce suitable offspring. And one, if proven worthy, might then play the role of the tanist.

Boswell proposes that the titles of all the kings of the invasion groups are variations of Ireland's first king, Seth, and that his subsequent avatars in the five invader groups or dynasties prior to the Goidels were named Seithurn, Sethor, Setgh, Soethecht, Starn and Sdarin (1972a, 26 fn, 88; *Lebor Gabala*, IV, 307). Citing Macalister, she derives Seithurn from Saturnus, thus linking the Greco-Roman Saturn with the god of the Hebrews and Egyptians, namely the red-haired, white-skinned Set/Seth (1972a, 26 fn. 89). The color white, for the purposes of this study, would appear to denote the glow of a comet rather than the epidermal coloration of his followers, as noted earlier.

Boswell cites another title that will reappear later in this study, Oengus or Angus, which *Lebor Gabala* links to the fourth invasion group, the Fir Bolg (1972a, 26: *Lebor Gabala*, IV, 11, 25, 79). The Angus, she notes, is an alias for Midir of the Tuatha de Danaan (1972a, 26, 33 fn. 91). O'Rahilly in *Early Irish History and Mythology* reveals that Midir is an alias for Dagda, the father of Angus, and that all three names, Angus, Dagda and Midir, denote the god of the Underworld.[8] What is going on here? Why are all of these gods ruling the Underworld? It all relates to the ritual of tanistry, as this study will demonstrate.

Arriving with the sixth invader group, the Goidels, whose ancestors had once been priests in Thebes, Greece, is a leader called Soethecht, a Set avatar (1972a, 27; *Lebor Gabala*, II, 25, 79). They traced their descent from Cecrops, the Egyptian Pharaoh reputed to have established kingship in Athens. Now Soethecht's genealogy is interesting, for, as Boswell notes, in *Lebor Gabala* he is described as descending from Tat or Thoth, the Egyptian dog-god who was the son of Set (*Lebor Gabala*, II, 129). According to Macalister's *Tara*, Boswell continues, Thoth was regarded in Ireland as the druidic deity of learning (1972a, 34; Macalister 1931, 91ff.). The sixth invader group is linked ultimately to Ethiopia, however, for earlier in their wanderings across the Plain of Sennaar, or the Island of Meroe, their leader had been Fenius Farsaid, according to *Lebor Gabala* (II, 9ff.).[9]

Now, after a long detour, we return to Saint Columba, dweller in the Hyperborean lands of Set-Apollo, and by extension, of the Picts, over whom he ruled in Scotland like a Pharaoh. We need to recall Boswell's line of thought, that the first two Abyssinian snake kings, or Awris, were supplanted by the dog-king Gadar; that Shem, and Ham, his brother, were the ancestors of the Ethiopians, according to Auxumite priests; and that the founder of Axum was reputed to be the dog-king Malaky. Traditions at Utica and Carthage point to a similar totemism regarding kingship. These snake and dog totems allegedly refer to the zoomorphs of the cometary pair Osiris and Set, respectively, and they served as the totems, then, for both the Ethiopians and the Hamitic rulers of the North African Phoenicians (Boswell 1972b, 88). These totems, snake and dog, were also affixed to the Habashat people, joined as one by the marriage of David and Bathsheba, the same Habashat people who eventually ruled Ethiopia and Southern Arabia during the period of Ethiopian Christianization in the fourth century c.e. And just as Kings

Kaleb and Gebel, of the dog and python clans, respectively, ruled during the Christian conversion of Ethiopia, so Patrick, the foster son of Milco [or dog] and the son of Aurelius [or Awri-lius, the python, as Boswell insists] established Christianity in Ireland at roughly the same time (1972b, 89, 106 fn. 173). But now the totem enters the picture, representative of Set and of the Habashat rulers of the emerging Christian era.

The totemism surrounding Columba's genealogy is revealing. Being an Ui Bairrche, or a Barcid on his mother's side [the name of the Carthaginian dog-king clan], he was called *Milcolumb* by the Scots, a title which means greyhound (Boswell 1972b, 88-89, 106 fns. 173 and 176). And Milcolumb also recalls the non-descript "Milcom, the Ammonite abomination," described in I Kings 11: 6-8, which the aging Solomon worshiped in place of Yahweh. Interestingly enough, Columba's Pictish patron was Brude mac Maelcon, which translates to 'Brother-Son of the Greyhound' (Boswell 1972b, 90, 100, 106 fns. 179 and 180). Boswell notes this title indicates that under the matrifocal kinship system of the Picts, the king, who ruled at the pleasure of the queen, was the queen's brother (1972b, 91). Citing J. H. Todd's extensive study entitled *The Irish Version of the Historium Britonum*, Boswell argues that the Picts' totems were the serpent, dog and pig; that they were matrifocal, with wives sometimes claiming as many as a dozen husbands; that they were the first inhabitants of Ireland; and that their chiefs, who tattooed themselves in homage to their Ethiopian ancestors, likely constructed the Tara site (1972b, 91). Todd reveals that the Picts "must have been incapable of transmitting paternal inheritances and must have lived under pure tanistry" (1864, xlv-lvii).

Until Boswell's study, no one could adequately demonstrate why Brude mac Maelcon awarded Columba the Island of Iona, that is, why it was handed to Insular and not to Romano-Gaulish Christians. For with that gift [or inheritance, given, as Boswell insists, that Columba maintained his mother as his consort under the terms of royal incest in order to govern *her* inheritance] came the supremacy over the Druids of Scotland, who were in a converted or half-converted stage (1972b, 92ff.). Clearly, this honor was kept within the family, as it were. And Boswell explains how. For Brude mac Maelcon, whose last name means dog, was branded "the island dragon" by an angry Gildas who denounced Brude and Columba and their associates in his *De Excidio Britanniae* as Lucifers of the Atlantic Eden, Lucifers who were backsliding to their pagan roots much as Lucifer had fallen out of heaven (1972b, 91, 106 fn. 183; Gildas 1899, 69). In a futile effort to repair the damage and deflect the prying eyes of the English to someone else, Boswell argues, Brude, whose totems were the snake and the dog, awarded the monastery of Iona to Columba at the approximate time that the Debra Damo monastery in Ethiopia was awarded to the Christian Aregawi by Kings Kaleb [the dog] and Gebel [the python] (1972b, 92, 96).

There seem to be too many coincidences here, and again, Boswell presents circumstantial evidence for direct communication between the twin Edens, Ireland and Ethiopia, during the early days of the conversions, along with more evidence, hardly circumstantial, for the Columba-Lucifer connection.

Iona, Boswell proposes, was deviously kept within the family. To better understand that succession, the pig totemism described by Boswell needs to be better comprehended. Given that the Pictish kings claimed the Orcades or Orkney Islands as their seat of power, she inquires into the meaning of Orcades and discovers that the place-name means the 'Pig Islands' (Boswell 1972b, 92, 107 fn. 186). These Pig Islands, it turns out, were alternately ruled by kings of the dog and dragon [snake] clan of the Maelcons, and by kings called Forcus, the Pig, who also went by the eponyms of Fergus and Fergus Orc (1972b, 107 fns. 187 and 188). She cites Nicholson's *Keltic Researches*: "Forcus may have been a Scot. Pictish has Uurgust as late as the ninth century, whereas Forcus is given by Adomnan (*Vit. Col.* I,7) as the name of an Irish Prince of the sixth century, called Fergus" (1972b, 92, 107 fn. 191). Cutting through the totemism, Boswell argues that Saint Columba's grandfather was Fergus of the Ui Neill. This connects Fergus, the Picts and Brude mac Maelcon's clan (1972b, 93). So that is why Columba was awarded Iona. He was, Boswell argues, a typical Phoenician priest-king (1972b, 90, 106 fn. 176). When it is recalled that Graves in *The White Goddess* indicates that the pig was sacred to the Mother Goddess, and that Lucifer-Set was her lover, this matrifocal pig worship begins to make even more sense. Boswell goes on to reveal that Brude's title, Brother-Son of the Greyhound, may also indicate that Columba, called the Greyhound, and Brude were 'brothers,' the father being Columba, the Greyhound, the son being Brude, and the mother being Columba's *mother* in accordance with the royal incest practiced among the pharaohs of Egypt (1972b, 100).

As suggested earlier, incest was likely practiced to restore the pre-fallen world and to keep the protector king/comet intact. And the king was dual, serving initially as the Set-tanist and finally as the murdered Osiris, strangled by the next Set. "The king is dead. Long live the king!" was the logic. In any case, the tanistry and kinship patterns of Ethiopia and North Africa were apparently mirrored in the Irish Eden. Thus it appears that the Ethiopians, North Africans, and the Irish and Scots, many of whom were originally Irish Picts, formed a separate Church. And this Church was often at odds with its Romano-Gaulish rival, for its reverence for Lucifer lingered until the rise of

Islam, which finally cut Ethiopia off from access to the Atlantic seaway.

Druid priests, secretive though they were, wrote of the Ethiopian origins of the Irish royalty and of the genealogy of both Saints Patrick and Columba in *The Amra of Saint Columba*, Boswell reveals. For as it celebrates Patrick's successor Columba, referred to as the 'Lord of Iona,' it describes a portion of Columba's family tree, namely a Scythian king who betrothed not his mother but his own daughter in accordance with royal incest, and an Ethiopian queen, whom Boswell identifies with the Anghabo and Sheba pair. She draws that conclusion based upon an apparent reference to Axum which is spelled Axala, or 'the city of auxilium,' *auxilium* being the Latin for 'place of rescue' and 'medical help' (1972b, 93, 107 fn. 199). A key passage from *The Irish Liber Hymnorum* speaks volumes about Columba's Africanized ancestors on the Greek side of the Mediterranean: "Three daughters of Orcus who were called by different names in heaven, on earth and in hell; in heaven they were known as Stenna and Euriale and Medusa; on earth Clotho, Lachesis, Atropos; in hell Electo, Megeara, Tisiphone" (Boswell 1972b, 93, 107 fn. 200; Graves 1966, 229-230).

Although some of the names have evolved in transit, the nine daughters of Orcus echo the nine daughters of Apollo, who were called the Muses. They went by many names which included: Calliope of the heroic epic, Clio of history, Euterpe of flutes, Terpsichore of lyric poetry, Erato of hymns, Melpomene of tragedy, Thalia of comedy, Polyhymnia of the mimic art, and Urania of astronomy (Hammond and Scullard 1970, 704).

So why is Medusa entered as one the Muses of Orcus? And why does she reside in heaven? According to Clube and Napier, at Delphi, the Muses were originally the Gorgons of Apollo's cometary serpent brother Dionysius [also called Osiris by Diodorus Siculus], and they were led by none other than Medusa (1982, 192ff.). Boswell derives Medusa from Med-Aso, given that the Medusa of Greece was derived from Aso [and her avatar Sheba] of Egypt and Ethiopia, who was herself the co-conspirator in Osiris' death in the Ethiopian version, the daughter of the Otherworld Ethiopic god called Medr, alias Anghabo (1972b, 94, 102, 109 fn. 233). Medusa, according to *The Oxford Classical Dictionary*, was "the daughter of the marine deities Phorcys and Ceto. She had a round, ugly face, snakes instead of hair, a belt of the teeth of a boar, sometimes a beard, huge wings, and eyes that could transform people into stone" (Hammond and Scullard 1970, 472). For the purposes of this study, even though the less pugnacious version of comet-Apollo domesticated Medusa and these Gorgons into the more serene Muses, they were, nonetheless, capable of backsliding themselves. For according to *The Oxford Classical Dictionary*, these Muses took off the gloves when they drove the Sirens into the sea: "The Sirens tried once to compete with the Muses; defeated, they lost their wings and jumped into the sea" (Hammond and Scullard 1970, 704). They went at it bare-knuckled again when they blinded the Thracian poet Thamyris and deprived him of his ability to sing, for he had made the mistake of competing against them (Hammond and Scullard 1970, 704).

Boswell mixes the pieces of the Irish edition of Columba's genealogical puzzle with the Greek and Egyptian/Ethiopian pieces when she explains that, according to historians such as Diodorus, Dionysius was an avatar of Osiris, just as Apollo was an avatar of Set. She then reasons that Abi Awri equates to Dionysius-Osiris, and Neos Awri to Apollo-Set. Together Abi Awri and Neos Awri comprise the Ethiopian double serpent icon, she recalls, adding that the Celtic pig god Orcus-Phorcys could be an avatar of that icon. If this is true, she goes on, St. Columba's mythic ancestors were Apollo and Dionysius (1972b, 94).

Then Boswell goes on to locate the etiology of the North African pieces of this puzzle. Consulting the much-lauded eleventh edition of the *Britannica,* she discovers that the Orcus deity was the god of the Oath, and that he paired with another deity called Dis, who like *Dis Pater* of the Romans, was a father god of the Celts: "Orcus (Horkos), meaning 'Oath' in Greek mythology, an infernal deity who punishes perjury. In Roman religion, Orcus is apparently a synonym of Dis . . . God of the Underworld" (1972b, 95, 108 fn. 207). Could this Oath equate to what would later be called the Hippocratic Oath that likely originated with the doctors of Ethiopian sacred groves and was later transported to the Greek Delphi and to the sacred groves of Phoenician North Africa? Boswell wonders. Although she misses the following reference, *The Oxford Classical Dictionary* provides the answer, for at Delphi, which was likely founded by Ethiopians, Apollo's son Aesculapius used the blood of the fallen Medusa to revive the dead (Hammond and Scullard 1970, 472).

The *Britannica* article also states that Orcus and Dis were gods who went by the same title. Dis was a god of plenty who ruled the dead in the Otherworld, whereas Orcus was known as the 'Angel of Death' and 'the actual slayer' (1972b, 95, 108 fn. 208). Given this information, Boswell proposes that the Ethiopian Awris resembled Orcus. She goes on to observe the parallels between the Ethiopian and the Irish-Scottish divine pairs, noting that the Irish angel of death Orcus may derive from the Ethiopian Anghabo, who served as Neos Awri, the killer of the old king of the grove, Abi Awri. The fact that Anghabo willed his kingdom to the Queen of Sheba falls in place with the particulars of Pictish succession, Boswell argues, for the

Pictish king was killed when he was too old to mate with his queen much as Abi Awri met his demise from a plot hatched by an Amazon queen and her father (1972b, 96).

So Columba was both Osiris and Set, or in the Christian version, Michael and Lucifer. Clearly, this old time religion, as it were, had to clash with the Romano-Gaulish version of the Gospel that was being touted in England and on the Continent. For Columba's Insular interpretation of Christianity, with its roots in the so-called heresies of many of the North African and Coptic Christian doctors, was deemed blasphemous by the Continental bishops. The Muses of Ireland and their leader Set-Apollo had to go. Three observations made earlier in this chapter should be recalled 1] that *Lebor Gabala* calls the snake-devil in the Tree of Knowledge, *Iofer Niger*, or the Black Man: "Thereafter Lucifer had envy against Adam, for he was assured that this would be given him (Adam), the filling of Heaven in his (Lucifer's) room. Wherefore, he (Iofer Niger) came in the form of the serpent . . . ."; 2] that the Negus or King of Ethiopia was also linked to Lucifer, as the bearer of light and the ruler of the abyss; and 3] that *Lebor Gabala* begins with the creation story and likens Ireland to Eden, the abode of the serpent-devil (*Lebor Gabala*, I, 2, 19).

St. Columba was born into the royal O'Neill family about 521 C.E. at Galtan in Donegal. In a twelfth century Welsh poem attributed to Merlin which Markale reproduces, Columba, here called *Yscolan*, or *Scot*, which appropriately enough translates to 'wise,' is pictured after the clan rivalry he incited between the northern and southern branches of the O'Neills. As a result, he was forced into exile:

> Black is your horse, black is your cloak,
> black your face, black yourself,
> yes, quite black! Is it you Yscolan?
>   I am Yscolan the wiseman [or the Scot],
> giddy is my cloud-covered mind.
> Is there no redeeming an injury to the Master?
> I have burnt a church, killed the cows of a school,
>   I have thrown the Book on the waves,
> I am heavily punished.
> Creator of the created, you, of all my protectors
> the greatest, forgive me my sin,
> he who betrayed you, deceived me (Markale 1978, 144).

Markale reveals that royal Columkill, then abbot of Kerry, was exiled 563 C.E. as a result of the clan war waged between the northern O'Neills and the southern O'Neills (1978, 143). His expulsion occurred shortly after the death of Arthur of Camelot fame, and upon founding the monastery at Iona, Columba ministered to the pagan Picts and Britons, maintained the Irish date of Easter, and insisted on retaining the Irish style of tonsure. Before his death in 597, Columba returned to Ireland, founding the monasteries at Kells and Glencolumkill. According to Markale, who refers to Adomnan's biography, Columba had copied a psaltar on the sly, an unethical act which kindled the feud (1978, 144). But leaping out of the passage is the assertion that Columba was black. Clearly he was black in sense of having committed an evil act. And Adomnan never describes him as black-skinned in Columba's biography. So the reference could refer to his genealogy, given that he was a Barcid on his mother's side and an O'Neill on his father's, and, were it not for the in-flow of Christianity, a potential Pharaoh of Ireland, descended from the Seth avatar, Anghabo, and the Sheba avatar. Boswell unwittingly sheds some light on this passage as well, for she argues that the Seth avatars of the invader groups described in *Lebor Gabala* were ultimately Hamitic in origin. She then explains the Hamitic puzzle, noting that the Fomoire sea pirate Seth, whom *Lebor Gabala* likens to Noah's son Ham, and the pig/fig goddess Banba were the first recorded takers of Ireland during the era of King Solomon. Calling upon Irish records, she goes on to argue that those accompanying Seth and Banba were people titled *Cu Corb* (Dog Angel) and *Mu Corb* (Pig Angel). Later, she goes on, these Celts were ruled by the Celtic King Cormac at Tara (1972b, 54, 60, fns. 108, 109). It should also be kept in mind that the pig and dog were the Set-Lucifer totems. It appears, then, that comets and kings was the name of the game.

Boswell derives this new wave of invaders from the South Arabian Habashat incense growers and entrepreneurs, who, before allegedly settling in Ireland, arrived in Ethiopia around 1000 B.C.E. Their god-king, as mentioned earlier, was Uriah the Hittite, a title which to Boswell sounds like Awri. Mackeda's mother, Bathsheba, married Uriah, and in the tradition of Egyptian tanistry, the murder of Osiris by Set in concert with Aso, Boswell argues, David, father of Solomon, killed Uriah and united his lands with the those of his deceased rival. It was this combined empire that Solomon and Sheba would eventually rule. Given that right into the early Christian era, the Celtic royal Corb, Mugh Corb, and Cormac titles at Tara match the Hamitic Habashat Mukarib or Karib titles, and since the Tara place-name appears to be derived in part from the date palm of Ethiopia, the *Temrach*, these Celts must have been part of the later Ethiopian and Phoenician invader groups, or black Celts, as it were (Boswell 1972b, 44).

Boswell reveals that the great and mysterious god of the Habashats during this 1000 B.C.E. time-frame was *Al-Mukah*, a name which for Boswell becomes Michoe or Michael in Europe and in Ireland, the pig-angel in Ireland and the adversary of Lucifer in the Christian Revelation. And Michoe, Boswell notes, was also the name of the father of the Troglodytes of the caves located in the Isle of Meroe, a name intimately connected with the South Arabian deity, Al-Mukah (1973b, 45).[10]

In Gaelic, 'pig' is called *Mucc* or *El Mucc*, adding the Spanish 'the' (Boswell 1972b, 45). And this is where Columba's name enters the picture. For Boswell indicates that Irish records reveal that the names for king among the Hamitic Irish Fir Bolg at Tara were: Aengus Oll-Muchach, Great Hog or Great Quencher; Aengus Olmccaidh; Aengus Ollum; and Aengus Cinn Nathrach, of the Serpent's Head (1972b, 46 fns. 70-72).

Ollum, the title embedded in C*olum*ba's name, meant 'chief druid' or 'bard,' Boswell notes (1972b, 46). And referring to O'Rahilly and de Jubainville, Boswell reveals that the King of the Bolg was the King of the Dead or Underworld, who was called Aengus-Midir or Dagda (1972b, 46 fn. 73). By this time in Egyptian history, Set, or for the purposes of this study, the Set comet, had lost its potency and was depicted as defending the Barge of Ra in the Otherworld from the threats of a new celestial serpent, Apepi, which Clube and Napier identify with comet Halley (1982, 203). Set or Seth, the pig-dog, had, like the Christian Lucifer, finally set, having likely wreaked its havoc at the close of the Late Bronze Age as Seth-Typhon.

With that in mind, this same King Cormac was also called Cormac mac Art, High King of Tara, and his title, Boswell argues, is indicative of a composite derived from numerous kings (1972b, 54). Deriving *Cormac* from the Habashat Ethiopian royal title of the *Mukarib* by reversing the consonant string, Boswell quotes Keating to tie the knot: "As to Conchobar, he had twenty-one sons; and in a fit of drunkenness, he committed incest with his own mother, and she bore him Cormac Conluigeas. Now Cormac is the same as Corbmac, an incestuous son; for it was through *corbadh* or incest that Cormac was the offspring of Conchobar by his own mother whose name was Neasa" (1972b, 55, 60 fn. 110). Then Boswell proposes that incestuous Cormac in his role as the Mukarib of Ireland was the 'dual' king of tanistry, who, carrying a pig on his back, killed the old king of the grove, and was later killed by his successor (1972b, 55, 60 fn. 112).

Reinforcement for Boswell's Ethiopian etiology can be found in Paul Edwards *Essays on the History of Blacks in Britain*. Edwards cites a ninth century medieval Irish tale, *Mesca Ulad* or *The Intoxication of the Ulstermen*, the setting of which was the first century C.E. Roimid, King Conchobar's jestor, is described as having "'an Ethiop face, shiny blue-black'

(Old Irish, *ethiopacda slemangorm*) and 'short sharp-edged (bristly) black hair' (*suasmael dubrintach*)" (1987, 11). The passage has been translated as follows:

> 'Lo, to the east of these, outside,' said Crom Deroil, 'I have seen here a band of their rabble host. One man is among them, with a close-shorn, black bristly poll; great eyes in his head, all white and bulging; he has a smooth blue Ethiopian face. A cloak of striped cloth is gathered about him; a hook of brass is in his cloak above his front; a long crook of bronze is in his hand. He has with him a sweet-sounding little bell, and flourishes his rod above the host, so that he affords mirth and merriment to the high king and to all the host.'
>
> 'Laughable and entertaining is the description,' said Medb.
>
> 'Laughable is the one whose description it is,' said Cu Rui.
>
> 'Who is there?' said Ailill.
>
> 'Not hard to answer,' said Cu Rui: 'that is Roimid the royal fool,' said he, 'Conchobar's fool.
>
> Never was there upon one of the men of Ulster as much of want or of grief as he would heed, if only he should see Roimid, the royal fool.' (Edwards 1987, 12)

An observation Boswell cites from O'Rahilly also drives the Columba-Set-Hamitic linkage home. For O'Rahilly notes that the name Cormac was awarded to the god-kings who played the role of Lucifer, or the Irish Lug at Tara (1972b, 60 fn. 113). Added to that, Boswell reveals that *Conluingeas*, the sobriquet for Cormac, means 'Head of the Exiled Bands' (1972b, 55, 60 fn. 114). Like the black tanist devil, Neos Awri, Boswell argues, who was exiled to a mountain monastery in Ethiopia lest he kill the old king before the old king's time, Cormac was both the king's brother and son as a result of an incestuous relationship with the reigning mother goddess. Then too, she notes, in Egypt Seth was also Osiris's brother and son. Likewise, Lucifer, leader of his band of fallen angels, was a pig/dog angel who fell from the sky, which she likens to the sacred Incense Grove. Lucifer's crime, she goes on, was his threat to God and Adam (Boswell 1972b, 55-56, 60 fns. 115 and 116). The above is a paraphrase of Columba's own hymn, the "Altus Prosator," which Boswell quotes:

> The Dragon, great, most foul, terrible and old which was the slimy serpent, more subtle than all the beasts and fiercer than all living things on earth, drew with him the third part of the stars into the abyss of the infernal regions and of divers prisons, apostate from the True Light, headlong cast by the parasite. (1972b, 60 fn. 117)

But how did Columba, himself exiled like his Set-Lucifer ancestor, regard the devil? Rather warmly, it turns out. For the Korbs, of which Columba was one, ruled the monasteries during their druidic and early Christian phases. Like the Karibs of the Habashat in Ethiopia, the Korbs were likened to the protective Cherubim of the Garden of Eden, the angels of the Lord. And in Irish monasteries as in Ethiopian ones, their totems were the snake, dog and pig, which comprised the monastic dragon (Boswell 1972b, 46). Like the Karibs of Punt, Boswell notes, the Korbs referred to themselves as slaves and/or dogs of God (1972b, 47). Therefore, Boswell reasons, Ham, who was a slave of slaves, became a kind of role model for monastic discipline and self-sacrifice (1972b, 48).

A problem arises, however, for in Hamitic Ethiopia and in Israel, pork was finally regarded as unclean. Why then did pork become the food of choice both at the Irish monasteries and in secular Ireland itself? It would seem that if the distant descendants of Ethiopian Hamites eventually landed in Ireland, they would have upheld the prohibition. Boswell attempts to solve this puzzle by reasoning that Seth and Banba of the first invader group entered Ireland after their ancestors fled from their Semite relatives. In the process, this fleeing group abandoned their patriarchal religion long before their descendants entered Ireland (1972b, 48-49). The Habashats, Boswell argues, were a matrifocal collection of tribes which arrived as newcomers to Ethiopia. Under their rule, Al-Mucah became the major deity of the Island of Meroe, and upon the arrival of their descendants in Ireland, the old Mukarib kings and priestly retinue titles became Cormacs (Boswell 1972b, 50). But something strange had happened, Boswell goes on, for in Ethiopia Serpent Kings, Dogs, and Mukaribs ruled in that order (1972b, 50). Citing the snake titles, *Negush* and *Nahash* titles for Haile Selassie, Boswell proposes that the emperors of Ethiopia finally represented Abi Awri, the old king, and the Habashat, who ultimately lost their hegemony in Ethiopia, became associated with Neos Awri, the young tanist king and his matrifocal queen (1972b, 50). This process appears to have occurred with each invader group, she argues, for each Banba would have asked her people to reject the God of Noah, and place their allegiance in her. Totemism also evolved in North Africa, for there the Dog priest prevailed, while in Ethiopia, the Snake Priest King was still regarded as the grandfather of the Dog Priest King (Boswell 1972b, 27). Boswell attempts to explain the evolution of the totemism involved, arguing that snake and dog regents, whose sons were likened to sacrificial pigs, ruled in ancient Ethiopia. Seth, Ham, Aengus or Anghabo was the title for the tanist son who challenged his father to a battle royal in order to win the kingship of the grove and to possess the sacred woman (1972b, 53).

The cometary thesis that this study is advancing gets to the root of the prohibition against eating pork a bit more efficiently. As noted earlier, the boar-like comet fragment Set-Typhon was worshiped outside of Egypt, while Horus was worshiped inside Egypt. The Israelites may well have derived their odd belief of being a chosen people because the Set-Typhon comet likely spared them twice, first during the Red Sea crossing, and, centuries later, when Set-Typhon annihilated Sennacherib's Assyrian forces with a 'bolt' from heaven. Set was not so considerate of the Egyptians and the Ethiopians. As the comet made its successive orbital rounds, it probably became less a protector and more of a heavenly pariah. As a result, pork was finally tabooed in those areas where Set-Typhon was likely casting his meteorites. And when Set-Typhon finally turned, as it were, on the Israelites near the end of the Late Bronze Age, new deities had to be smelted. The invader groups, however, had arrived in Ireland prior to Set-Typhon's conversion into a devil by the Israelites and their neighbors. Hence, Set remained in favor in the lands of the Celts, and pork was consumed with abandon as a food of the god. But in lands to the south, the battered Set-Typhon comet was equated with the Devil, who, along with Lucifer's angels, had made the symbolic plunge into the Otherworld, the scrap-heap of the gods. The resulting truisms are often spoken but seldom understood, snakes cannot live in Ireland, and pigs cannot live in Ethiopia. Hence, the Hamitic Seth-worshipers, the ancestors of Columba, had already migrated to the Otherworld of the West, that pig-shaped island of Ireland which Gildas depicted as an island of Lucifers. There they awaited the next Flood on the omphalos of Iona, hoping to postpone the catastrophe for as long as possible by preserving the *sang real* of Sheba which flowed, they believed, in the veins of their Queen-mothers at Tara (Keating 1908, II, 4-5).

It strains credulity to accept the argument that Irish monks could have invented all of this genealogy and totemism in their spare time. As we shall see later in this study, Gerald Massey argues that the British Isles served as an equivalent to the Egyptian Otherworld of the West which was called Amenta by the Copts. Boswell agrees. For the Ethiopian god of the Otherworld was called Medr. And this very Medr eventually became the Irish god Midir, synonymous also with Angus and Art. Angus, Boswell goes on, can ultimately be derived from Sheba's father Anghabo, in his dual roles as supplanter and supplanted, both cobra and python, who became Lancelot and Arthur in King Arthur's Court. For, as Boswell reminds us, the Irish Angus, Dagda and Midir, were not names but titles of the old king and his tanist-supplanter, the Angus (1972a, 26, 33 fn. 91; O'Rahilly 1967, 516).

The Christian conversion of Ethiopia and Ireland finally ended the ritual of tanistry. But tanistry survived imaginatively in the British Isles and in France during the High Middle Ages. It simply took on a new form: the Grail legends.

Notes

1. Markale equates the Holy Grail with the spring of the sacred grove and indicates that the womb-like water restores the drinker to a pre-fallen, maternal paradise.

2. See *The Irish Liber Hymnorum* (II, 65).

3. Graves (1966) notes that cranes migrate from Africa to the arctic. Could these invader groups followed the routes of their sacred cranes who were linked with the ibis-headed Thoth?. Also see Graves (1966, 235-36). There he discusses the possible Cretan and Egyptian hieroglyphic origins of the Phoenician language. Graves notes on p. 272 that the Pelasgians spoke a Greek language of Cretan extraction that was ultimately Hamitic. On p. 281 Graves proposes that the language of trees was used by the Bronze Age Pelasgians and the Britons.

4. Twentieth century Egyptian scholar and oceanographer A. A. Aleem also notes interesting parallels between the fifth century voyage described in the ninth century text [pre-Crusades] of *Navigatio Sancti Brendani Abbatas* and Sinbad's voyages in the *Tales of the Arabian Nights*. Citing Aleem, Bob Quinn discusses numerous likeness between the two works: "Both Sinbad and Brendan discover island paradises, see monstrous fish, find underground palaces and meet strange people. The similarity between the two voyages is particularly noteworthy because they are attributed to the same period (the ninth century) and happened to be representatives of cultures apparently separated by geography and religion-- Ireland and the Middle East." (1986, 52). Then too, E. L. Ranelagh (1972, 153) identifies some striking parallels between the two leading heroes of Ireland and Arabia-- pre-Christian Cuchulain and the early seventh century figure Antar-- especially in *The Cattle Raid of Cooley* [*Tain Bo Cuailgne*]. Noting that both the Antar and Cuchulain sagas were set in a cattle economies, Quinn (1986, 127-28) summarizes the major likenesses, noting that both Antar and Cuchulain kill small dogs when boys [leading to Cuchulain's name change from Seandanda to 'Hound of Culain']; both were reared by single women; both receive arms from male relatives; both have a horrific eye which frightens their adversaries [one-eyed Cuchulain's terrible eye protrudes like a cauldron]; both, although mortally wounded, deceive their enemies; and both have horses which attack their enemies. For Ranelagh, stories such as the exploits of Antar are especially important because they do not appear to have traveled through the continent to Ireland. Interestingly enough Antar was an Ethiopian character spawned from the imagination of the dark Yemenite Abbasids who delivered the golden age of Islam to Spain after the overthrow of the lighter-skinned Umayyads of northern Arabia in the eighth century C.E., according to Chandler (1996, 300ff.).

5. See *The Irish Liber Hymnorum* (I, 164; II, 56, 64, 79, 223-35). See O'Rahilly (1967, 68-69) where he equates Arthur with Cuchulain.

6. See O'Rahilly (1967, 283-84). John Michell (1983, 67) notes a legend of a giant serpent that at various times slithered down Serpent Lane in the town of Mordiford to drink at the river Lugg.

7. She notes that Edmund Swift writes: "St. Patrick expelled the Serpents and drove them into the sea. So says the Legend; which divested of its allegory and restored to its simple truth, tells us that-- St. Patrick's Conversion of Ireland and his Extirpation of the Serpents, are one and the same act; his introduction or rather confirmation of Christianity, and his expulsion from the Island of the Ophi-Sebia, or serpent worship, which fled before his preaching."

8. See O'Rahilly (1967, 516). He equates Dagda=Elcmar=Midir=Oengus.

9. For more insights on this figure, including his association with Dionysus, see Graves (1966, 237ff.).

10. Clube and Napier provide some cometary insight into the term 'troglodyte,' noting that the Feast of the Repelling of the Troglodytes was celebrated during the tenure of Amenhotep I on the 21rst Phamuti [which corresponds to the modern Easter during April]. The ceremony, they go on, was designed as an appeasement to underground meteorites associated with Typhon's [Set's] celestial thunderbolts (1982, 203).

Discussing the curious linear arrangement of churches, shrines and other religious and secular sites across Britain that crisscross the Isles, Michell (1996, 70ff.) notes that: "St. Michael rules over the rocky crags and pinnacles and St. George over the lower hills, like the white tiger and the blue dragon in the Chinese landscape. St. Michael's shrines are especially characteristic. All over Europe, particularly on the coasts of Brittany and Cornwall, his churches and chapels crown the summits and rocks and mountaintops . . . . It was on such an eminence that he was said to have killed the dragon, and he became a natural successor to the pre-Christian deity, the guardian of the dragon current, whom he supplanted. Like St. Patrick's in Ireland, the story of his victory over the dragon or serpent, originally illustrating his control over a natural, elemental force, was taken by early Christians to represent the defeat of the old religion by the new." Michell assumes that the straight line that can be traced on the map of Cornwall to Berkshire which connects St. Michael's Mount in Cornwall with the Hurlers stone circles and the Cheesewring; St. Michael's church in Brentor; Trull church; St. Michael's, the Mump in Burrowbridge; St. Michael's church in Othery; St. Michael's Tor in Glastonbury; the Avebury rings; Ogbourne St. George's church; and St. Michael's church in Clifton, Hampden can be likened to a Chinese ley line which indicates underground magnetic lines of force. These lines may have functioned as Michell suggests, but originally they may have marked the passage of fireballs and meteors aloft. Given that the underground water supplies that may fuel alleged magnetic Earth currents do not occur in straight lines, it appears that the debris of mythology may be layered. Mann (1996, 81) unwittingly provides more information that could support this cometary interpretation: "John Michell dubbed the alignment of the 'St. Michael Line' because of the number of hills with churches on their summit dedicated to the saint, if not exactly on the line, then not far from its route. Another name is the 'May Day Line' because of its astronomical orientation, of the 'Dragon Line' because wherever St. Michael goes, there goes a dragon." He continues to note on p. 82: "The sixty-three degree alignment of the St. Michael Line through Glastonbury Tor indicates sunrise at the beginning of May and August. These are the cross-quarter days of Beltane and Lughnasa, the calendar days mid-day between the solstice and the equinox. The alignment also indicates sunset on the remaining cross-quarter days of Samhain and Imbolc. This means . . . that from Burrowbridge Mump on the 1rst of May or August, the sun will set over the Mump. All these days were major fire festivals in the pagan Celtic world and are likely to be part of an older tradition." Indeed, the desired survival of the sun and the nerve-shattering appearance of meteor showers that could induce cometary winters are what that "older tradition" must have been all about, given that the Tor was associated with the dragon twins of the underworld and the "Day of Doom." As to the meaning of the "cross-quarter days," Mann (1996, 104) explains: "These lie between the solstices and the equinoxes, dividing the year cross-wise: northeast, northwest, southeast, southwest. They are important points on the agricultural calendar."

Mann goes on to depict an interesting scenario, proposing that a labyrinth may have existed at Glastonbury Tor: "they may have entered the labyrinth at Beltane and Lughnasa when the axis of the Tor pointed to where the sun rose on the eastern horizon. They lit a fire on the hilltop and saw that a line of fires extended along the pathway of the sun, through other sacred hills, and continued unerringly to the great ceremonial sanctuary at Avebury-- the 'mother circle' of ancient Britain."

On p. 87, Mann proposes that there are two sets of great circle alignments that can be discovered at Glastonbury. These great circles, he argues, pass through the following sacred centers, some associated with falling stars: Zagrost, Russia; Bandiagara, Mali; Chaco Canyon, USA; Tiahuanaco, Bolivia and Lake Titicaca, Peru/Bolivia; Lalibela, Ethiopia; Iguaza Falls, Argentina/Brazil; Ponape, Micronesia; Carnac, France; Callanish, Scotland; Mt. Kilimanjero, Tanzania; Mecca, Saudi Arabia; Persepolis, Iran; Bali, Indonesia; Fatima, Portugal; Table Mountain, South Africa; Filitosa, Corsica; Delphi, Greece; and Mt. Kailas, Tibet. Mann's following description of the ritual conflict between the Bright King of Summer and the Dark King of Winter (1996, 178-79) reveals how the original cometary imagery likely became nested into fertility imagery: "Although we must be careful not to read too much into the symbols, when so little actual evidence exists for pre-Christian beliefs, May Day in the Celtic tradition is the festival of Beltane that ushers in the light half of the year. Six months later, Samhain or Halloween ushers in the dark half of the year. Gwynn, or in the legend, Melwas, is the Dark King of Winter and Gwythyr, or Arthur, is the Bright King of Summer. They are the Lords of the Waxing and Waning Year." Closely associated with these two Lords, Mann goes on, are the exploits of the Ash God Gwydion and the Alder God Bran, King of the Underworld, in *Cad Goddeu*, who replace one another but do not destroy one another, for that would spell doom for the natural world rather than seasonal change.

Chapter 13

~~~~~~

The Grail: *per ignum missum de caelo*

The Cosmic Tree or Tree of Life was a ubiquitous symbol in the ancient world, given that the meteor showers discussed earlier likely covered large areas of the globe (Clube and Napier 1990, 48ff.). And that Tree was a two-way street. Properly initiated, the shaman could imaginatively ascend to its peak, the Pole Star, on eagle's wings, or enter the fearsome Otherworld that clung to its roots. And that Otherworld, or Underworld, was an emblem of the mysterious place beneath the horizon, the repository of the cometary demons which set either temporarily or permanently. The upward destination of the Cosmic Tree, the Pole Star, appeared from Earth's vantage point to be the only fixed spot in the heavens. As a result of that trickery of earthly perspective, it was deemed the location of paradise in the era of the earliest stellar mythology, according to Massey (1992, II, 599ff.). For ancient mythmakers world-wide it was a magical place, a refuge for the soul, a destination of perfect peace, a sanctuary where the soul's immortality seemed assured.

The Cosmic Tree grew out of the earthly omphalos, and each omphalos, whether in Ethiopia, Greece, Italy, North Africa or Celtic Europe, included the same sacred landscape: A magical spring often inhabited by a serpent or dragon; a chapel; and a sacred grove with the Cosmic Tree as its centerpiece. Iona, seat of Columba's power, was one such omphalos, a place to bide one's time until the next cataclysm. Because it was considered flood-proof, as it were, Iona became the sacred Necropolis of Scottish Kings and Queens who hoped to rise on the Day of Judgment and partake of their immortality.

Interestingly enough, the worship of trees, with the exception of the Tree

of Life, was abandoned by the Israelites upon their return from the
Babylonian exile (Tolstoy 1985, 179). The reason for the Tree's persistence
in informing both Hebrew and Christian iconography was that this sacred
icon was worshiped for a time at least as a symbol of the protector-comet,
which for the Hebrews was none other than Set. The concept of a chosen
people, noted earlier, appears to have initially arisen during the Exodus when
Earth's likely encounter with the Set comet failed to harm the fleeing
Israelites, but decimated the Egyptians instead. The cross upon which Jesus
hung continued the Tree of Life symbolism for Christians. For the cross, like
the Tree of Life, was perched upon a hill, the omphalos called Golgotha.[1]

Stonehenge and Delphi, both founded by the Hyperboreans according to
ancient sources, were also sacred centers (Tolstoy 1985, 124).[2] Regarding
the rituals of the former, Tolstoy proposes that the Dragon Conflict was set
at Stonehenge, or, in Geoffrey of Monmouth terms, Mons Ambrii, the hill of
Ambrius (1985, 112).

And it was during the final stage of initiation that the Grail heroes were
introduced to these twin dragon contenders, to a simulation of the *real
presence* of the cometary deities, presented with an immediacy that the
heroes, no doubt, would not soon forget. At both Stonehenge and Delphi
the dragon conflict occurred in the Otherworld, the lower terminus of the
two-way street that is the Cosmic Tree. For the Otherworld was the abode
of the celestial serpents, and a properly simulated journey to the Otherworld
would evoke in the priest or priestess, Grail king, or Grail king candidate,
the kind of raw terror and submission needed to produce a true believer.
This is the core meaning of the Grail legends, which often depict the
initiation of the Grail king candidate into a visceral knowledge of the terrors
of the Otherworld. For its was here that the dragon pair, having dropped
below the horizon at last, executed their head-bobbing adders' dance.

A disintegrating comet is an untrustworthy god. On one passage by the
Earth a comet or comet fragment may appear benign, but during a later
periodic encounter, the formerly benign fragment may turn into Set, "the
great deceiver," and pummel an unlucky area of the planet with fireballs.
Therefore, the cometary deity had a dual nature. Because of this apparent
fickleness, the god-king, who was the earthly representative of the protector-
comet, had to remain strong and under the strict control of his subjects at all
costs. If weakened by disease or impotency, or if disposed to immorality, the
protector comet, the king's counterpart in the heavens, might sprout horns
and spew debris during an inevitable return. Hence the constant supplanting
of the old king with the new one. For Osiris could become Set.

As a result, tanistry must have imitated this ambiguity, and to preserve the protector comet through sympathetic magic, the young contender apparently had to play the role of Set and kill the old king. Upon the contender's coronation, which included the placing of the cometary crown upon his head, however, he became Osiris, the original protector, until the next round of tanistry occurred when he, now approaching middle or old age, was strangled or beheaded and symbolically cast into the Otherworld. Hence the ambiguity of the World Tree as a charm and a place of crucifixion, for each new king was equated with that tree. And it was the tree that had to be preserved for as long as possible. Kings were expendable, and the seemingly benign tree was eventually their place agony.

In the numerous Grail legends that welled out of Europe during the Middle Ages, the initiand's symbolic journey to the Otherworld is officiated by the ranking *merlin*. And this ordeal, if survived, leads the hero to the knowledge of good and evil and an appreciation of their ambiguity-- the good being associated with the protector comet and the evil emanating from the Set figure of the dragon pair. The Welsh *Cad Goddeu* or *Battle of the Trees* must have imparted some of this wisdom to the initiands to whom it was chanted (Evans 1910). For its main themes are as follows: the creation of man by Gwydion, the Otherworld wizard after whom the Milky Way was named; an ancient combat that results in the injury of a primordial dragon; rumors of an eventual return of demons from *Annwfyn* or the Celtic Hades; and references to the Flood, the Crucifixion of Christ and to the inevitability of Doomsday (Clube and Napier 1990, 79ff.).[3]

During his symbolic journey to the Otherworld, the initiand sometimes discovers a benign sacred grove replete with the Cosmic Tree at the eastern door, and, at the western one, the ominous cometary steeds, variations of which also occur in Revelation 19: 11-21. And also found in the Otherworld is the "vat of merry mead," a drink of which allows the hero an hallucinogenic plunge into mankind's pre-fallen state.[4]

Upon entering the Otherworld, the Grail hero, Diarmait, discovers a similar pre-fallen landscape replete with a flowery plain, singing birds, humming bees, the soothing hiss of waterfalls and streams, and a sacred grove. Enchanted, Diarmait traverses the plain and approaches the grove. There he happens upon a giant, fruit-laden tree [the Cosmic Tree] that dwarfs those growing around it. The tree is ringed by standing stones, and the tallest stone stands next to the tree. And adjacent to the tree and stone lies a pool of crystal-clear water fed by a bubbling spring.

Beneath this halcyon description, the potential for chaos looms. The ominous steeds recall those celestial horses which trampled Nemi's Hippolytus, and which were therefore banned from Nemi. Also, the grove of sacred trees and the description of the Tree of Life surrounded by the pillar-stones offer a precise rendition of the landscape of Axum and other such sacred centers such as Delphi and Nemi. Then too, the tallest stone evokes the image of the protector comet and its trailing debris. And the seemingly benign pool of water may also symbolize a future flood.

Without suggesting its cometary possibilities, Tolstoy cites the sinister aspect of the tallest standing stone, noting its analogue at Stonehenge, the center Altar Stone upon which a fatherless child was ritually killed to safeguard World Tree and its pillar (1985, 132).

But Diarmait sees more. To quench his thirst he attempts drink from the well that rests beneath the tallest pillar, but he is interrupted by the din of approaching warriors whose armor clatters as if a heavenly host were approaching. Drinking finally from a golden drinking horn that lies atop the pillar, he sees an apparition-- an giant, careening out of the East, covered in armor and sporting a crown of gold. As the demon approaches, he berates Diarmait for encroaching on his land and drinking from his drinking horn. A fight commences between them, four fights, in fact, before the giant is carried beneath the earth by the enraged hero.

In accord with the ritual of tanistry, the young king encounters the old king. The otherworldly warriors loom, hoping to descend if the young king loses the match. The well and its Grail-like drinking horn contain the water that will give Dairmait the knowledge of the serpent battles and the potency to defeat the giant, the old king. For Dairmait, like comet Set, the water sucker who likely dried up considerable areas along the Mediterranean basin with its fireballs, is playing the role of the tanist. And these cometary giants abound in African and Near Eastern and Celtic myths, from one-eyed Cyclops to Goliath to Balor of the One Eye.

Still more trees and beasts populate the Arthurian version of the Otherworld called Avalon, or Arthur's Happy Isle. Two key examples are the apple tree and the fig.

It does not take a great leap of the imagination to understand why the sacred apple tree, known as the Celtic Tree of Life, substitutes for the hallowed fig of Abyssinia. Falling apples can be likened to falling stars. And anyone who has wandered the Irish countryside in early September has probably witnessed pigs eagerly devouring fallen apples to the point of incontinence. So who devours those cometary apples as they fall? Set, the raging boar of Lower Egypt's cypress swamp, the winner of celestial battle with Osiris, or his comet-successors, for as meteorites burn up in the atmosphere, it may appear from the worm's eye view that they are being eaten.

Clearly, this apple image has Mediterranean origins. Zeus is awarded the cometary Apples of the Hesperides after his marriage to Hera, and in the Otherworld, where they dangle ominously, a dragon with a hundred heads stands guard over them (Bailey 1994, 380).[5] Hercules, who Graves argues is a fusion of Apollo and Dionysius, is made immortal when he is given the golden apples by the Three Daughters of the West. Without sensing the likely cometary implications, Graves notes that five-pointed star in the apple core symbolized immortality, outlining, as it were, the five stages of the White Goddess' life from birth to death to reincarnation (1966, 257). He goes on to observe that the apple was sacred to Venus, and was worshiped as Hesper, the evening star, on half of the apple, and as Lucifer, on the other half (1966, 257). In other words, the apple likely symbolized the cometary dragon-pair, for Venus mimics the dawn and dusk appearance of comets, and comets symbolize immortal souls because of their periodic orbits. The apple of immortality has other associations with the Thracian Orphic cult; with Bran; with Apollo; and with Dionysius who was revered as a kid stuffed with apples; and with the Greek word for 'goat' [or scapegoat-king, perhaps], a zoomorph of both Osiris and Dionysius. And the Greek word for 'goat' is identical to the Greek title for 'apple' which is *melon* (Graves 1966, 257). And does not the apple, the emblem of the soul in the Cuchulain saga, a fruit carried in the belly of the salmon [a word that echoes Solomon] which returns every seven years in a magic spring, recall the fish that swallows the phallus of Osiris after he is dismembered by Set? Jonah asks the question, "Where shall wisdom be found?" The answer is under the apple tree. Is it the same wisdom that the Grail hero will discover in his initiation rite in the Grail castle? Diana, the title of whose grove at Nemi echoes the dreaded deity Nemesis, served cider in a sacred, crater-like bowl, which was embossed with the human figures of black Ethiopians, according to Frazer (1961, I, 316).

Frazer goes on, telling more than he knows: "Nemesis carries a wheel in her other hand to show that she is the goddess of the turning year, like Egyptian Isis and Latin Fortuna, but this is generally understood as meaning that the wheel will one day come full circle and vengeance be exacted on the sinner" (1961, I, 255). Generally understood by whom? we might ask. This wheel finds its way to Ireland, according to Frazer, who cites the *Coir Anmann* in which the wheel's use by the Irish Druid Mogh Ruith for divination purposes is described (1961, I, 255). Was Merlin also a wizard of the wheel? Did he use the wheel of Nemesis in his *nemeton* or sacred grove to predict the return of the cosmic serpents? Did he consult with Queen Guinevere on this matter? Was Guinevere an avatar of the bloodsucking, snake goddess Lamia, a remnant of the Libyan Set cult? Did Guinevere's nemeton mimic the dread rituals of those due south. Was Arthur her comet-king?

Much like W. P. Boswell, Tolstoy also probes the all-important pig totem of Ireland, noting that the major Celtic cult animal was the boar. For not only did the Celt gorge himself on the meat, but the Marnian tribe also placed choice cuts of pork in the graves of their dead kings to provide them with a proper send-off (1985, 72). He goes on to cite the magic pig that Diarmait slays, and the local Irish folklore about sacred pigs of gargantuan sizes being credited with making many of the ancient earthworks (1985, 73). Then he notes that the pig was identified as originating from the Otherworld, where it often served as a guide (1985, 73). Given the fact that druids frequently made prophecies when wrapped in the flayed skin of a pig or a wolf, the Egyptian Set=Boar equation appears to be the source of the pig imagery that is interlaced throughout Celtic folklore. Then too, Merlin often took the form of a wolf as well as a pig in the *Vita Merlini* (Monmouth 1973). Boswell's pig-dog totemism as it relates to kinship was ubiquitous in Ethiopia, North Africa, Greece and in Ireland, as noted earlier in this study. During the female-inspired Eleusinian rites, pig sacrifices also occurred, and the meat was ritually eaten. The purpose of this ritual meal may likewise have been the acquisition of the wisdom of the cometary boar Set, who finally suffered the fate of his 'brother' Osiris.

The Grail hero experiences a longing for immortality after he descends to this Celtic Otherworld and encounters his Set-devil, his *doppelganger*. This tradition can also be found in Christianity, for, like the Grail hero, Christ visits Hell after his crucifixion. There the Devil, the head *merlin*, as it were, is his broker of initiation. Again in the Christian tradition, Christ spends forty days in the desert, where he receives instruction from the Devil and the angels of Satan. Staring into the cometary jaws of death, Christ longs for immortality.

And if Christ is himself a cometary god-king as his antecedent Horus appears to have been, *The Gospel of the Egyptians* and the *Pseudo-Tertullian* are correct when they emphatically state that Set is the ancestor of Christ. Even Luke 3:38 traces Jesus' descent from Set-Seth. Following the Horus logic, Set was Horus-Christ's uncle.[6] And it was with these kinds of apocryphal, Coptic texts that the Irish priests of the early Insular Church were in tune. For Insular Christianity was likely little more than the old cometary wine in a new bottle. The proposition also occurs in the Orphic mystery rites, for at Delphi, Plutarch reveals, Orpheus, the counterpart of the Celtic Lug, was said to have entered the Underworld through "the great krater from which dreams draw their mixture of truth and falsehood" (Tolstoy 1985, 186, 298 fn. 1).[7] A meteor crater is not to be ruled out here, symbolically speaking, and in the Celtic tradition, which was heavily influenced by the Orphic, Arthur, with the help of the Medusa-like Maeve, searches for the crown of Dagda in the Otherworld in the *Spoils of the Abyss*. But that crown seems more like an impact crater, for it is blue-rimmed and pearl-ringed. And as might be expected, it contains Lucifer's cometary sword, the weapon of Lugh, as well.[8] In the *Murder of Curoi*, Cuchulain also enters the Otherworld and returns with a cauldron. But Bran is not so lucky in the Welsh tale *Branwen*. Rebuffed by her husband, who is the king of Ireland, Bran's sister, Branwen, sends a message to her brother Bran which goads him to enter the Otherworld of Ireland, avenge her, and locate the magic cauldron of rebirth. The quest fails when Bran, upon discovering the cauldron, realizes that it is broken.

In the thirteenth century romance entitled *Fergus*, the hero also enters the Otherworld, where he encounters a devil in the form of a black giant (Martin 1872). Ascending the Black Mountain, Fergus snatches a horn and a wimple from a lion's neck and kills the Black Knight, who appears to be another *merlin*. Having survived the Wild Hunt, Fergus returns to the Moat of Liddel. Here again, the young king supplants the old one and takes possession of the horn, or what in the Christianized versions of the Grail quest becomes one component of the Holy Grail image pattern.

Otherworld imagery is also found in the *Prose Lancelot*. In this narrative the Black Knight becomes a monstrous Ethiopian who occupies a castle named the Dolorous Gard. Lancelot must defeat him there and enter the copper chamber of the Otherworld, for copper was associated with the underground mines of Cornwall, the Hades of the West (Markale 1995, 13ff). The fact that the Knight is an Ethiopian tags the ritual of tanistry with Abyssinian origins. For another black figure, slain by Apollo, also guarded the Delphic Oracle, and Delphi was certainly within the Greek periphery that certain invader groups of *Lebor Gabala* inhabited on their long journeys to Ireland (Boswell 1972b, 78).

So exactly what is the Grail? Can it be equated to the Ark of the Covenant and the other arks carried by various religious sects throughout the Mediterranean and Red Sea littorals? Why was the Grail so terrifying and awe-inspiring? Why was it associated Christ's self-sacrifice? Why did the knight, the candidate for the kingship of the Grail Castle, have to view it in order to pass the initiation test? And why did the initiation rite occur on November 1rst, the night of the Celtic New Year and the Taurid meteor shower?

In the premiere Grail legend, *Parzifal* by Wolfram von Eschenbach, who was himself a member of the Templars, the Holy Grail is unambiguously described as a meteorite. Its place of origin, according to Eschenbach's contemporary Robert Boron, is Jerusalem (Goodrich 1992, 203). Graham Hancock notes in *The Sign and the Seal* medievalist Helen Adolf's argument that Wolfram was influenced not only by Chretien de Troyes' interpretation of the Grail legend, but by an Oriental version as well (1992, 61ff.; Adolf 1947, 306ff.). That source, Adolf argues, is the *Kebra Negast*, which chronicles the story of Menelik's removal of the Ark of the Covenant from the Temple of Solomon and its subsequent arrival in Axum centuries later. Hancock reasons that the Ark of the Covenant was a stone, written upon by the hand of God (1992, 65). Recalling the oracular uses made of the Grail in *Parzifal*, Hancock compares them to similar uses exacted from the Ark of the Covenant. He notes the following passage in the Book of Judges, "where the identity of God Himself was often completely fused with that of the Ark":

> And the children of Israel inquired of the Lord, (for the Ark of the Covenant of God was there in those days, and Phinehas, the son of Eleazar, the son of Aaron, stood before it in those days), saying 'Shall I yet go out to battle against the children of Benjamin my brother, or shall I cease?' And the Lord said, 'Go up: for tomorrow I will deliver them into thine hand.' (1992, 65-66; Judges 20: 27-28)

Continuing his investigation, Hancock discovers a passage in Chapter 9 of *Parzifal* which describes Flegetanis, a Moslem seer allegedly descended from Solomon. Flegetanis, Eschenbach tells us, understood the secrets of the Grail, the orbits of the various planets, and certain "hidden secrets in the constellations." Regarding the Grail, Flegetanis wrote: "A troop [of Angels] left it on the earth and then rose high above the stars, as if their innocence drew them back again" (von Eschenbach 1980, 232). Hancock does not comment on the line that follows, but we add it here. "Afterwards a Christian progeny bred to a pure life had the duty of keeping it. Those humans who are summoned to the Gral are ever worthy" (von Eshenbach 1980, 232).

Mulling over the significance of both the sacred Black Stone of Ka'aba, reputed to have fallen from heaven and given to Adam to absolve his sins after the expulsion from Eden, and over the meteoric betel stones carried by pre-Islamic desert nomads, Hancock discovers that a betel was known as *lapis betilis* in Europe, the name: "stemming from Semitic origins and taken over a late date by the Greeks and the Romans for sacred stones that were assumed to possess a divine life, stones with a soul [that were used] for divers superstitions, for magic and for fortune telling. They were meteoric stones fallen from the sky" (1992, 67-69; See Rosche 1884). Hancock then uncovers terms that Wolfram used to describe the Grail: *lapis ex caelis* ['stone from heaven'], *lapsit ex caelis* ['it fell from heaven'], and *lapsus ex caelis* ['stone fallen from heaven']. Following these leads, he learns that the Grail was associated with abundance both in *Parzifal* and in the Old Testament, noting: "When Solomon brought the Ark into the Temple, all the golden trees that were in the Temple were filled with moisture and produced abundant fruit, to the great profit and enjoyment of the priestly guild"; and that in both works the Grail was described as emitting a blinding light (1992, 462).

Hancock concludes that the Grail, then, was equated with both the Ark of the Covenant and a meteorite or sacred betel stone; that Wolfram must have used the *Kebra Negast* as a source for *Parzifal*; and that a splinter-group of Hebrews, originally under the leadership of Menelik, the son of Solomon and Sheba, centuries later carried the Ark from Elephantine in Egypt to Ethiopia (1992, 62ff.). Since the *Kebra Negast* insists that the Ark was brought to Axum by Menelik, the Abyssinian chronicle would appear to be in error, for if the Ark had been secreted out of Jerusalem around 1000 B.C.E. by Menelik, he would have been long deceased by then. Unless the *Kebra Negast* means a *menelik*, which, like the term *merlin*, would refer to a priestly title rather than to a personal name. In *The Golden Bough*, Frazer explains that the names of sacred individuals were often tabooed and only their titles employed because of the fear that sorcerers might cast spells upon these persons (1940, 302).

But who was Flegetanis? Interestingly enough, Flegetanis, the reputed author of the Grail papers which Wolfram claims to have used in writing *Parzifal*, is said by Wolfram to have descended from Solomon's royal line. Although many scholars regard the existence of Wolfram's Flegetanis with tongue in cheek, Lasater argues that the character was based on an historical figure, Alfraganus, one of the most widely known astronomers and astrologers in medieval Europe (1972, 164ff.). Dante even referred to him in the *Convivio*, she notes, and his Arab name was Abu-al'Abbas Ahmad Ibn-Muhammad Ibn-Kathir al-Farghani of Baghdad, mercifully shortened to Alfraganus. She goes on to reveal that his *De Scientia Astorum* was translated first into Latin by John of Seville in 1137 and later by Gerard of Cremona around 1172 (1972, 164ff.). So it appears that Wolfram was no hack, and that he may have been looking into exactly what this study is proposing, the verisimilitude of recurring comets in Earth-grazing, periodic orbits and the conversion of these cosmic serpents from naturalistic phenomena into religious symbols.

This study proposes that the initiation rites practiced in the Osirions of Egypt and at sacred sites marking meteoric impacts such as the vapor-filled Otherworld at Delphi were repeated in the Grail castles of Europe, and that the imagery associated with Grail castles and Grail processions is overtly cometary.

Several classical Greek accounts reflect events that occurred during the protracted decline and fall of the Late Bronze Age, an eclipse which transpired from roughly 1300 to 1000 B.C.E., and which serves as a backdrop to the Grail motif. Clube and Napier cite Pliny's *Natural History* in which Pliny, drawing from much earlier accounts, describes the Typhon comet that would certainly have been invoked in the underworld of Delphi (1982, 197). Lydus in *De Ostentis* described it as well, as Clube and Napier note:

> They say that the sixth comet is called 'Typhon' after the name of king Typhon, seeing that it was once seen in Egypt and which is said to be not of a fiery but a blood-red color. Its globe is said to be modest and swollen and it is said that its 'hair' appears with a thin light and is said to have been for some time in the north. The Ethiopians and Persians are said to have seen this and endured the necessities of all evils and famines. (1982, 197)

Speaking of a Typhon variety of comet, Lydus goes on to explain that:

> it is sickle-shaped, white, smoky, and sullen. Wherever it looks, there are general evils. Grave foreign and civil wars, public disturbances and lack of necessities. Glorious leaders will be taken away in wars and especially if it appears for three or four days. If it appears for more, it threatens the destruction and overthrow of everything and no end to evils anywhere. (Clube and Napier 1982, 197)

As they reflect on these and numerous other classical accounts, Clube and Napier propose, as noted earlier, that the Zeus vs Typhon and Python vs Apollo myths were originally based upon major celestial combats which occurred in the skies of ancient Greece. They go on to argue that these myths likely chronicled the ongoing disintegration of the Zeus comet. They point to the real possibility that Typhon's fragments struck Earth as this cosmic serpent and Zeus battled overhead, and that another disintegration also resulted from Apollo's challenge of Python (1982, 197-98).

During the Late Bronze Age and its aftermath, then, there were apparently two celestial, Greek combat myths which were reenacted in the

Otherworld during the Delphic initiation rites-- Typhon vs. Zeus and Apollo vs. Python. As noted earlier, Clube and Napier summarize the pertinent events of the Homeric *Hymn to Apollo*, which dates to 1200-850 B.C.E., near enough to the collapse of the Late Bronze Age. They note Apollo's arrival at Delphi, his creation of the temple [with a meteorite for a cornerstone], and his slaying of the she-dragon with an arrow from his cometary bow (1982, 192). And, interestingly enough, one of the admonitions of the Delphic oracle was: "Leave no stone unturned!"

The versions of the combat myths are many, and we need not review them all here, for each generally has the same cometary elements. In any case, the genealogy of the dragoness Python supplied by Homer indicates that Python had previously nursed Typhon, after Hera gave birth to it. Because Zeus had not involved Hera in the birth of Athena, whom he yanked from his own head, Hera exacted her revenge by birthing Python. In time, Apollo was alleged to have killed Python at Delphi, and in Simonides' version the female Python is deemed to be a male (Clube and Napier 1982, 193). It appears that Typhon disintegrated, producing a Python fragment, and Hesiod describes him as being Ge's and Tartarus' youngest son. Referring to Hesiod's *Theogony*, Clube and Napier note that his head "reached to the stars," and where his fingers should have been he sported "a hundred serpents' heads." They go on to cite his threats to Olympus when he flashed his fiery eyes and spewed fiery stones from his mouth, all of which caused the Egyptian gods to flee the country in animal disguises. Finally, they note, Zeus came to Earth and defeated the demon with his celestial thunderbolts (1982, 194).

All of this imagery and more persisted in the numerous Grail legends when comet activity began to peak just before the period of the Crusades, as noted earlier in this study. So how did this cometary imagery manifest itself in those legends?

In *The Holy Grail*, Goodrich mentions that the Grail castle itself was called the *Corbenie* in the *Grand-Saint-Graal* and *Queste del Saint Graal* versions of the Grail legend, both of which relate the alleged wanderings Joseph of Arimathea and his companions in Sarras [today's Marseilles] and in Glastonbury (1992, 79). The term *Corbenie* recalls Boswell's etymology of the term *Corb* or *Korb*, a title which Boswell derives from the Ethiopian priestly *Mukarib* title. *Corb* or *Korb*, she notes, signified both an Irish druid priest and a Christian one in later times (1972a, 63ff.). And for the Grail knight initiand, the Corbenie is a place of great ambiguity, dangerous to the point of death, but it is also the domain of epiphany and beatific vision. Fire-breathing dragons often surround it, and as Saint Theresa of Avila explains, it is a sacred region where the Grail hero and worshiper gain a triple knowledge: The knowledge of the Majesty of God; the knowledge of self, and of the soul which resembles the lush Tree of Life in springtime; and the knowledge of the valuelessness of earthly things (Goodrich 1992, 120). For the true jewels, Saint Theresa asserts, are to be found in the Seventh Heaven, or as Massey knew so well, the stars of the constellation Ursa Minor, the *Art*, from which the name Arthur may have been derived (1992, II, 599ff.). For these seven stars, which revolve around the Pole Star, mark the zenith of the Cosmic Tree. But added to that, they never fall below the ecliptic during the Precession of the Equinoxes (Massey 1992, II, 306, 376). Hence they are flood proof, as it were, much as Columba hoped his omphalos at Iona might be. For the earthly Flood was mirrored in the heavens, given that as the Earth wobbles on its axis during the 26,000 year Precession, those stars which slip below the ecliptic over the years are deemed to have 'drowned' in the celestial Flood (de Santilla and von Dechend 1977, 56ff.).[9]

Goodrich cites Saint Theresa's description of the cometary, beatific vision of a saint and a Grail hero, for as: "fire awakens the worshiper . . . it comes in the form of a comet, or as thunder and lightning from the zenith, or like the red phoenix bird that catches fire, is consumed, but arises young again, each time, from its black ashes" (1992, 121). No wonder the Templars were accused of devil worship, or the worship of the red haired Set. And no wonder, too, that after piebald Feirefiz experienced the Grail vision in *Parzifal*, Repanse de Schoye journeyed to India [a generic term for Ethiopia as numerous scholars have discovered] to give birth to Prester John, the next guardian of Axum's Ark of the Covenant (Hancock 1992, 81).

But what is contained in a Corbenie? Below is a list of some of the more conspicuous objects and characters drawn from numerous versions of the Grail legend which this study regards as cometary:

--A white dove;
--censors filled with crackling, red-burning balsam, the Irish equivalent to Abyssinian frankincense;
--glass vessels filled with burning incense [as found, perhaps, in the Phoenician necropoli of North Africa];
--candelabras;
--blinding mystical lights;
--Longinus's spear which pierced Christ's side, drawing both water and blood;
--a harlot Queen wearing a golden crown whose face glows like the sunrise, or the devil's concubine who must be freed by the Grail hero;
--a lance;

--a broken sword;
--a procession of female Grail bearers;
--a weeping maiden;
--a plate holding a decapitated head;
--the Grail itself, or Wolfram's *'lapsis ex coelus*,' 'the stone from the sky';
--Lucifer, Aurora's son, with an emerald on his forehead;
--a sacred cup;
--the impotent Fisher King; and
--four bronze or copper pillars, signifying the entrance to the Otherworld.

Little general comment need be made about these objects and characters, for they speak for themselves. The finer points may not be so obvious, however. The white dove of the Annunciation also appears to indicate the presence of the protector comet. The red-burning balsam links the comet and the sacred incense tree to Set, whose 'hair' was red. Longinus' spear or lance, which causes Christ to bleed water and blood, ties in not only with the various floods that, catastrophists argue, meteoric impacts especially when occurring on the open sea likely caused, but also with the sacred spring associated with the Grail castle and the sacred groves of Ethiopia, Greece, North Africa, and Celtic Europe. The broken sword easily translates into the truncated tail of a disintegrating comet. The emerald in Lucifer's forehead evokes the third eye of wisdom in Hindu texts and its likely precursor, the cometary eye of Horus. The Harlot Queen or Devil's Concubine is reminiscent of the sacred concubine who births the protector comet and flees to the desert in the Revelation to John. The weeping maiden recalls Boswell's description of the weeping frankincense tree at Axum and its association with the tears of Sheba, those of Mary, the mother of Christ, and those of the grief-stricken Mary Magdalen, his alleged consort (1972b, 29ff.). The weeping maiden, in the *Prose Lancelot* version of the Grail legend, especially, may be shedding tears of guilt, for there is the suggestion that as Sheba-Aso, Queen of the Sacred Grove, she assisted the tanist in the murder of the old king or even carried out the deed herself (Goodrich 1992, 144). The plate, which may or may not have a representation of John the Baptist's head on it, evokes the decapitation motif found in Eastern Mediterranean and Celtic tanistry. The sacred cup recalls the drinking horns and the crater-like cauldrons found in various Celtic tales of the Otherworld. It is also associated with Christ's chalice, a fact that has misled many explicators of the Grail legends, for the *sang real* or sacred female blood that extends to Sheba and beyond, blood which the Grail as chalice was alleged to have contained, is only one dimension of the complex Grail image pattern. And the female Grail bearers, who derive from Islamic Sufic traditions, likely evoke, as do the tears of the incense tree mentioned above, the trail of meteors that follow a disintegrating comet. The four pillars, which become standing stones in the sacred groves, likely represent the columns that were imagined to hold up the sky, and derive ultimately from Solomon's Temple. And it should be noted that the tree, especially the cypress, and the branching candelabra, have over the ages been commonly used to symbolize the shapes of various comets and fireballs (Clube and Napier 1982, 155). Finally, the impotent Fisher King ultimately points both to the old king in tanistry and to the devastated earth as well.

It was in the Grail castle that the initiate was introduced to the *real presence* of God or the gods through the use of such imagery as, step by step, the merlin figure removed the veils of repression. For as Velikovsky proposed for the wrong reasons, mankind may well have driven the horror of the comet deep into the unconscious, a process resulting in the acquisition of a "collective amnesia" (1977b, 302ff).

Goodrich notes that two Grail knights, Lancelot and Perceval, were considered by Grail authors to be direct descendants of David and Solomon, and that the Grail castle itself has been compared to Solomon's Temple, the one-time home of the Ark of the Covenant. Noting Josephus' description of the Temple, which from a distance appeared "like a mountain covered with snow," Goodrich goes on to mention that its main altar contained four horn-like raised corners, and that the Avalon Grail castle, which she locates on the Isle of Man, was situated in a horned-shaped bay and contained a similar horned altar (1992, 18). Therefore, based on these and other similarities, she proposes that Solomon's Temple, situated on a hill, must have served as the architectural prototype for the Grail castle, similarly perched atop a hill (1992, 18). She goes on to cite other features of Solomon's Temple that are similar to those described in the Grail legends: "an outer portico, lofty towers, bronze or copper columns, a Holy of Holies, golden candlesticks, a fire or fireplace for sacrifices, manna for the worshipers, angels ascending or descending like doves, and a sacred rock " (1992, 207-08). Solomon likely had the sword, which the Angel of the Plague spread over Jerusalem in David's time, in the front of his mind as the Temple was being constructed (2 Samuel 24; I Chronicles 21). Paranoia reached a crescendo, for to improve the harvest that year, David sacrificed seven of Saul's offspring (2 Samuel 21: 19).

Grail castles are also associated with sacred groves, whose origins Boswell traces to Ethiopia. Holy Trinity Abbey in Fecamp, Normandy, founded in 658 c.e., is a case in point. Goodrich notes that the title Fecamp "is a shortened, French form for the abbey's name Fig Tree Field, *Fici*

Campus" (1992, 136). Not surprisingly, its folklore associates the abbey with miraculous events such as the appearance of "brilliant lights" and roaring "choirs of heavenly angels" (1992, 137).

Boswell indicates that the Tree of Life, both at the sacred incense grove at Axum and in Genesis, is a fig tree, and this study equates that Tree both with the protector comet and with the trunk-like pillar extending to the North Star, a pillar that allegedly holds up the sky. Eating the fig, as eating the pig, appears to be equivalent to learning the mysteries of the Underworld, a process which involves the epiphanic vision of the *real presence* of the cometary deity or deities. Given the number of Grail castle sites in Europe, it is likely that each contained its own Grail or betel stone, and these taken together with others housed in scattered shrines throughout the Mediterranean region, formed part of the meaning of the complex Grail image. Velikovsky reveals that nearly every sacred shrine along the Mediterranean basin possessed a betel stone:

> The stone of Cronus at Delphi, the image of Diana at Ephesus, which, according to Acts (19:35), was the image that fell down from Jupiter, the stones of Amon and Seth at Thebes, were meteorites. Also the image of Venus on Cyprus was a stone that fell from the sky. The Palladium of Troy was a stone that fell on the earth from 'Pallas Athene' . . . . The sacred stone of Tyre, too, was a meteorite related to Astarte . . . 'Traveling around the world, she [Astarte] found a star falling from air, or sky, which she taking up, consecrated on the holy island [Tyre].' (1977b, 293)

Citing I Chronicles 21 and 2 Samuel 24, he goes on to corroborate the findings of Hancock: "The stone on which the Temple of Solomon was built-- Eben Shetiya, or fire stone-- is a bolide that fell in the beginning of the tenth century B.C.E., in the time of David, when a comet, which bore the appearance of a sword was seen in the sky" (Velikovsky 1977b, 293-94; fns. 3-11).

Goodrich summarizes some of the folklore that surrounds Fecamp, tales that appear to confirm many of this study's assertions:

> One story attributes the name to the Gospel of Luke where Jesus tells the parable of the barren fig tree that the Master wanted to cut down (Luke 13: 6-9). The gardener begged for another year's grace; there is, in other words, a final chance before the sentence of uselessness becomes irrevocable. Or, as Luke makes clear again (Luke 13: 18, 19), the tree is a cherished symbol of empire where nations and peoples seek and find refuge; it must be spared. Or Jesus reads a lesson in history (Luke 21: 25-37) that just as one sees in the fig tree the coming of the fall harvest, so similar indications point

certainly to the approaching Kingdom of God . . . . The monks at Fecamp
will connect the fig tree to the Holy Grail and to King Arthur alive in
Scotland not much more than a hundred years earlier than themselves.
(1992, 136-137)

Preserved in Fecamp's legends, the sacred Ethiopian fig of Anghabo and
Mackeda appears to survive intact. And this study proposes that the fig tree
is but one symbol of the cometary deity, the protector comet, associated with
the next 'coming' of that deity.

Another Grail castle, the Church of Les Saintes-Maries in Provence,
where the Grail procession is still held annually, bears several similarities
with the sacred landscape at Axum. Instead of Abyssinian incense trees, its
necropolis is situated in what once must have been a sacred grove which still
nourishes numerous alder trees, symbols of the Celtic kingship.

And Goodrich cites Alyscamps, another necropolis and grove that sits
next to the eleventh century Saint Tromphime cathedral, noting that in 314
c.e. resident men of the cloth were forbidden by a Council of the Roman
Church to join forces with Bishop Donat of North Africa and support his
claim that they were heirs of the Apostles of Jesus (1992, 50). Clearly, the
doctors and the matrifocal tanistry practiced in Ethiopia, Greece and North
Africa posed a direct threat to the concept of Apostolic Succession. For that
Roman, female-avoidant, ecclesiastical system was patriarchal to the core.

Montsegur, the Languedoc Grail castle in which the Cathars made their
last stand against the Albigensian crusaders, is also replete with cometary
imagery. The Cathar's apocalyptic theology, no doubt, accounts for these
associations. Goodrich cites Otto Rahn's conviction that the Cathars were
the last to own the Holy Grail, and that it perished with them when crusaders
assaulted Montsegur in the early 1300s (1992, 271). She goes on to cite his
account of the final, desperate hours of Montsegur, noting how "the troops
of Lucifer" besieged the fortress in hopes of recovering the Holy Grail that
adorned Lucifer's crown, symbolized here by a "lost emerald" that fell to
Earth when Lucifer was driven from the heavens (1992, 271).

And there is more cometary imagery associated with Montsegur. For this
mountaintop monastery/castle perched on a site above the clouds could
easily be confused with the equally heavenly site of the Coptic mountaintop
monastery of Bizen near Asmara in Eritrea. [An excellent photograph of the
Bizen site can be found on pp. 98-99 in the June 1996 *National
Geographic.*] According to legends, Montsegur even contained a dark
goddess in its subterranean depths with whom a knight such as Roland
allegedly cohabited (Goodrich 1992, 270). Is this dark woman a Sheba
avatar? Is Roland symbolic of the avatar of the Axumite Neos Awri, the

tanist?

The Cathars regarded the Gospel of John, which they called the Gospel of Light, and the Revelation to John, in which Lucifer's cometary fall and the birth of the protector comet are graphically chronicled in an undisguised meteor shower, as their principal guides to life. Indeed, the untold story of Catharism appears to be as follows: The Cathars embraced a life of poverty and simplicity because they were convinced that wealth could profit a man or woman nothing in a world at the mercy of cometary demons. The linkage of divinity with comets, an association that is validated by their Grail lore and their observatory-like monasteries, indicates that the Cathars, probably more than any Christian sect of their day, understood the *real presence* of their cometary Christ and the import of the more ancient dragon-pair. Like the Dabtara, the so-called pagan priests of Axum, they knew the dread secret and could bear up under it. For both the Cathars and the Dabtara, the Grail was the essence of God. Cometary theology, then, appears to have informed Catharist heresy, with, perhaps, a touch of collective amnesia thrown in for good measure. Doubtless, neither the Crusaders nor the Pope nor the King of France fully understood this heresy. They likely reacted to the outer symbolism of Catharism without understanding that symbolism's rocky core.

The Templars appear to have been cognizant of it, however, and that apparent understanding must have resulted from their veiled activities in Ethiopia, and their desire to make Languedoc an autonomous Templar nation. The Catharist cleric Nicetas from Constantinople seems to have understood it as well. Could that be why he argued in Toulouse in 1167 at a Catharist Council that the Revelation to John contained the truest expression of Catharist belief?[10] For in Languedoc, as in Ireland, the cometary interpretation of Christianity that this study is advancing seems to have prevailed. And it is likely that Catharism and its component rites in Ireland were transferred to Europe from Ethiopia and Delphi by the Doctors of Carthage, Utica and Origen of Alexandria as early as the second century C. E..

Notes

1. Clube and Napier (1990, 102-03) note that the Essenes studied ancient prophecies which spoke of the end of the world and the beginning of a new age. The Essenes, they go on, advanced the proposition that heavenly portents announced the birth and resurrection of Christ, but when the Kingdom of Heaven did not arrive on schedule, as it were, the Pauline view of Christ began to replace the Essenic viewpoint. That Pauline version stressed, they ague, a milder Aristotelian reading of

divinity. Hence, no flaming end-of-the-world scenario was stressed in the Pauline version. As a result, Paul transferred the earlier messianic material and wed it with Jesus' expected return. The upshot of Pauline Christianity was, for Clube and Napier, to elevate Jesus from an astrological prophet to a divine entity who would be associated with and thus legitimize the Apostolic Succession.

2. Tolstoy recounts the legend that Delphi was founded by the Hyperboreans from the Far North.

3. They argue that the Milky Way later came to symbolize the zodiacal cloud, a debris trail that partially extended between Earth and the Moon.

4. Horses are used in many cometary accounts, and clearly The Book of Revelation is well within that genre.

5. Hercules' eleventh labor is to steal the golden apples from the dragon with a thousand heads which guards them in the Hesperides.

6. Spence (1974, 158-59), like Massey before him, equates Arthur [a title which he derives from "Asar," another name for Osiris] with Osiris; Modred with Set; and Avalon with the Egyptian Aalu: "Slain in his last battle with his treacherous nephew, Modred, Arthur is carried off by his sisters in a barque to the mysterious Isle of Avalon, an overseas, or underworld locality, 'the place of Apples,' in the Western Sea. There he remains, neither dead nor alive, awaiting the fateful day when Britain shall require his aid once more. Slain by his treacherous brother Set, the body of Osiris . . . is ferried in the sacred barque across the Nile, accompanied by his wailing sisters Isis and Nephthys to the region of the Aalu, in the west, a place of plenteous fruits and grain. There Osiris rules as god of the not-dead-- that is-- the neither dead nor alive--awaiting a glorious resurrection.

The island paradise of Avalon to which Arthur was taken was undoubtedly associated with Druidism. We find it alluded to in such stories as that of Thomas the Rhymer, . . . and in several old Breton tales. It is the same as the Anwynn of the Welsh myths, the Tir-nan-ogue of Celtic tradition-- a place of rest and refreshment for the un-dead . . . . In some tales it is an island, in others a submarine locality. That it is one and the same as the Osirian Aalu can hardly be doubted."

7. See West (198311-13).Tolstoy (1985, 186) equates Merlin with Orpheus.

8. See Loomis (1959, 15-17).

9. For them, the precession equates with a celestial flood that ushers in each new age.

10. See Goodrich (1992, 288).

Chapter 14

~~~~~~

The Heresy of the Grail Legends

No examination of the African and Near Eastern presence in the British
Isles during the Middle Ages can be complete without an understanding of
the profound and divisive influence that esoteric ideas exerted on Ireland's
maverick Insular Church. Flowing from Moorish Spain and from cities such
as Carthage, Byzantium [Constantinople], Jerusalem and its sister city of
Sarras [Marseilles] in the earliest centuries of the Christian era, these
heresies shaped the theology of both the Insular Church and its apparent
theological double, the Cathars of the Languedoc region of Southern France.
The schisms included Arianism, which stressed that Christ, although more
spiritual than most men, was, nonetheless, a man; Pelagianism, which argued
that divine grace was not needed given that men had free will; and
Gnosticism, which attempted to solve the problem of evil by ascribing its
creation not to God, but to an emanation of God instead.[1]   In subsequent
centuries a continued influx of additional esoterica also moved overland from
Egypt, the Holy Land and Moorish Spain along the Crusaders' highways. It
came by sea from North Africa and Spain through bustling medieval ports
such as Limerick and Galway and, after the Flemish Renaissance, from
enlightened enclaves such as Flanders (Baigent and Leigh 1989, 70). That
converted Saracens accompanied returning Crusaders and assorted
Templars, all of whom could have carried this esoterica, adds still more
evidence for a significant African and Near Eastern presence both in the
Catharist, Languedoc region of Southern France and in the British Isles
during the Middle Ages.

To understand the divided mind of medieval Europe both during and after the era of the Crusades, it is necessary to review the impetus for the Albigensian Crusade [c. 1208-1278]. For many twelfth and thirteenth century Christians, Catholicism had come to resemble an open sewer clogged with Papal indulgences, clerical hypocrisy, church-sponsored genocide and dashed hopes for regaining the Holy Land. Unable to vanquish the Muslim heretics to the south, Rome hoped to eliminate another perceived threat to its continued existence, a schism concentrated in the Languedoc. The heresy was Catharism, as noted previously, and it ignited the best and the worst minds of Europe.

Catharism had been brewing in the Languedoc region from the earliest centuries of Christianity. Brought there by Bulgarian missionaries in the tenth century under the title of Bogomilism [Bogomil means the Beloved of God], it reached its defiant maturity in the Languedoc region during the mid-twelfth century. There it bore the imprint of early Christian and later Muslim ideas as well. Zoe Oldenbourg cites the arrival in Languedoc during the year 1167 c.e. of Nikta, a Bulgarian Bishop who traveled from Constantinople to consecrate churches in the region and to call a Council of Cathar bishops outside of Toulouse. She observes that this conclave alone indicates that, in defiance of the Church of Rome, the Cathar church was emerging as a universal, supra-national church in its own right (1961, 30-31).

Catharism took hold in the Languedoc region partly because of the area's strong Eastern European and Muslim ambience. Oldenbourg explains that routine contact existed in the region with the Muslim world, indicating that Arab physicians and merchants were frequently trekking across the Pyrenees to Languedoc. She goes on to reveal:

> The infidel could no longer be regarded as a natural enemy. The Jews, who formed a large and powerful community in every major business center, were not debarred from public life through any sort of religious prejudice. Their doctors and savants were held in high regard by the general populace throughout the cities of the area; they had their own schools, where they gave free courses of lectures, some of which were open to the public. . . . The influence of Jewish and Moslem apocryphal writings was widespread among the clergy, and even reached the common people. (1961, 24-25)[2]

The region's prohibition against killing Saracens, which it only compromised under extreme pressure from Rome, enraged the Catholic hierarchy which the Cathars openly flaunted. And the Catharist's tolerant stance resulted, if the countless Moors' heads that appear on local family crests are any indication, in countless interracial marriages that occurred both in the Eastern Pyrenees and to the west in Aragon (Oldenbourg 1961, 319).

When the Albigensian Crusade heated up, luckier victims of the Inquisition which marked that Crusade, countless thousands of penitents some of whom were of mixed blood, were spared the flames if they agreed to endure a pilgrimage to sacred sites such as Saint James of Compostella, or Rome, Jerusalem, or Canterbury in Southern England. How many penitents might have remained and/or cavorted in Britain during the early thirteenth century may never be determined (Oldenbourg 1961, 304ff.).

In any case, from a theological perspective, Catharism was not always a homogenous creed. Some strains portrayed a Gnostic Christ, who was viewed as divine, an impalpable, ethereal emanation of the Godhead rather a flesh and blood man. Malcolm Lambert explains this view:

> Cathars could not admit that Christ was God-- an angel, perhaps, or a son of God, but still not equal with the Father. Nor could they logically admit that he was a man, with a body like that of other men. So the hinge of traditional Christian belief, the Incarnation, was destroyed. Radical dualism went still further in its destruction of Christian belief, and can hardly be regarded even as extreme Christian heresy. With its belief in two gods and two creations, it might almost be described as another religion altogether. (1977, 126).

Two gods and two creations? In order to account for the problem of God's introduction of evil into his Creation, the Catharists, who felt that Bogomilism had not solved the problem of evil in its tracts on the fall of Satan, decided to take a new approach. Lambert explains:

> The dilemma remained: How was evil compatible with the creation of a good God? To satisfy themselves, they postulated two creations, distinct and equally eternal, and bravely followed out the consequences of their belief-- two heavens, two earths, for example or a life of Christ in another world, judgment already passed, hell identified *tout court* with this earth. (1977, 124-25)

Two gods, then, were proposed in the most radical Catharism-- one good and the other evil. And as we might expect, given the cometary nature of the creed, both were co-eternal. Lambert goes on to explain that:

> the fall and imprisonment of the angels in bodies was caused by an invasion of heaven, which captured the good angels and imprisoned them in bodies of the evil creation against their will. In this version the evil principle and his creation would never come to an end, although the good angels would be

released from their prison; in the older Bogomil version, as in orthodoxy,
Satan in the end was subject to the power of God; his evil creation would in
the Last Days be consumed. (1977, 122)

It was almost as if the Cathars sensed that Jesus and the Devil were
emblematic of naturalistic events. Satan was not to be despised, and his
angels were deemed innocent of all charges. The awareness of the cometary
nature of both the King of Kings and Lucifer, his tanist, was, if not on the
surface of consciousness, likely repressed.

Derived from raging schisms such as the Manichean and Arian heresies,
strains of Catharist heresy rubbed salt in several more theological wounds.
In its extreme doctrine, it held, as does the Nag Hammadi *Gospel of Philip*
(57.19-20), that the Crucifixion and Resurrection of Christ were not
historical events. Then too, it advocated the doctrine of reincarnation,
asserting that even animals had souls that could transmigrate into humans at
birth; it supported and encouraged abortion; it celebrated Mary Magdalene
as the most initiated disciple of Christ and sometimes preached that the two
were literally married; it worshiped the Black Madonna, linking the icon to
Mary Magdalene and peripherally to Mary, the mother of Christ; it held that
women should serve as priestesses on an equal basis with priests; it denied
the validity of the sacraments; it proscribed vegetarianism and forbade the
killing of animals for food; and like Protestantism of which it was a
precursor, it encouraged a direct, almost Gnostic relationship between the
individual and God, a union which devalued the role of clergy as
intermediaries in the experience (Baigent, Leigh and Lincoln 1981, 306-
307). Most curious perhaps was its hatred of other key Christian doctrine.
Oldenbourg explains: "The Cathars expressed especial hatred both for the
Cross, as the instrument of God's agony, and for the Mass, which was in their
eyes supremely sacrilegious, since it regarded as the true Body of God a
scrap of gross matter destined to decompose in the guts of the faithful"
(1961, 74). This notorious contempt for the cross would return to haunt the
Templars in the early thirteenth century.

Catharism evolved out of an esoteric tradition of *contemptus mundi*
which declared that the earth and all who dwelt on it had been created by the
Spirit of Evil. The cultivation of a life that would attune one to pure spirit
was the creed's goal. Therefore, the Church, graven images, the sacraments
and the family, all embodiments of earthly life, were eschewed with
considerable vigor. Clearly, the influence of the Hindu doctrine of
metempsychosis and karma, Islam's disdain for graven images, and
Gnosticism's and Manicheanism's articulation of two opposed principles of

Good and Evil were at work here. But something else was at work. It amounted to an almost pagan understanding of the cometary *real presence* of the deity and of the ancient queen's central role in the ritual of tanistry, all of which likely created in the minds of the Cathars an overpowering desire to restore the broken pieces of an earlier, matrifocal era of history.

The assertion that Mary Magdalene was the most initiated of Christ's disciples, put forward in *The Gospel of Philip*, 62:32-64, greatly influenced the Cathars:

> . . . the companion of the [Savior is] Mary Magdalene. [But Christ loved] her more than [all] the disciples and used to kiss her [often] on her [mouth]. The rest of [the disciples were offended by it . . .]. They said to him, 'Why do you love her more than all of us?' The Savior answered and said to them, 'Why do I not love you as [I love] her?'

Such matrifocal ideas created tensions with the Romish Church. Infused with early Christian sentiments, an attempt to include the active engagement of women in the Church had been championed by Clement of Alexandria (150-c.216 c.e.). Elaine Pagels notes that his cosmopolitan Alexandrian temperament, which largely resulted from his traffic with well-heeled, educated members of Egyptian society, was most offensive to Western Christian communities which adopted the misogyny of Clement's provincial contemporary, Tertullian, who wrote: 'It is not permitted for a woman to speak in the church, nor is it permitted for her to teach, nor to baptize, nor to offer [the Eucharist], nor to claim for herself any share in the masculine function-- least of all, in priestly office" (1981, 92-93). Godwin explains that a result of the devaluation of the female the Church fathers not only eviscerated Christianity but relegated the cult of the Virgin to underground status. Only later did the worship of Mary in the guise of the Black Virgin experience a revival when the Cathars' Church of Love, which the Templars and the Grail romancers supported, arose as a potent adversary to the patriarchal establishment (1994, 211).

The Church of Love was also supported by Eleanor of Aquitaine, who after wedding England's Henry II established several Courts of Love dedicated to Mary Magdalene, or, as the Gnostics held, the triple aspects of the mother goddess, Mary Lucifer the Light-Giver, Mary the Virgin and Mary the Harlot. Oddly enough, a source for much of the *fin amor* tradition of Eleanor's court, a tradition which placed the female object of devotion on a pedestal, was Muslim Spain. Roger Sherman Loomis explains that

> it is no accident that we find in the literature of Moslem Spain metrical forms

approximating those of the troubadours, and similar conventions such as
addressing the mistress as 'my lord', in Provencal 'midons'. Most significant
is the fact that a book called *The Dove's Neck Ring*, written by the
Andalusian, Ibn Hazm, about 1022, might almost serve as a textbook on *fin
amor*, so close are its idealistic doctrines on all points-- except one. The
object of one's adoration must not be married. (1970, 53-54)

Loomis concludes that southern French literature of the period, along with
the Italian works of Dante and Petrarch, was strongly influenced by the
music and love-tracts pouring out of the south of Spain (1970, 54). Norman
Daniel   reluctantly concurs with Loomis in regard to the etiology of
European courtly love tradition when he speculates: "If however, European
concepts of courtly love derive from the petty courts of the *taifas*, the whole
romantic tradition in European literature owes an almost disproportionate
debt to eleventh century Spain" (1975, 104).

In any case, the Moslem insistence on placing the female on a pedestal
was certainly amenable to those clinging to lingering Celtic traditions
regarding the woman's role in the sacred grove, and that compatibility
accounts for the goodness of fit between the two traditions, a gender ideal
that did not go unnoticed by Wolfram von Eschenbach when he composed
Parzifal.

Many of the less secular ideas current in Southern France also derived
from a virulent Manicheanism that had gained a foothold in Provence by the
fourth century C.E. Founded by Mani, who was born near Baghdad in 214
C.E., Manicheanism became a religion in its own right, and Mani, before his
decapitation in 276 C.E., was regarded by his followers as a latter-day Jesus,
much as Saint Columba [not to be confused with Colomban, who founded
the monasteries of Luxeuil and Bobbio] was so deemed in Ireland. Michael
Baigent and Richard Leigh explain the intricacies of Mani's thought:

> He regarded Zarathustra, Buddha, and Jesus as his forerunners and declared
> that he, like them, had received essentially the same enlightenment from the
> same source. His teachings consisted of a gnostic dualism wedded to an
> imposing and elaborate cosmological edifice. Pervading everything was the
> universal conflict of light and darkness; and the most important battlefield for
> these two opposed principles was the human soul. Like the later Cathars,
> Mani espoused the doctrine of reincarnation. Like the Cathars, too, he
> insisted on an intimate class, an 'illuminated elect'. . . . At the same time he
> declared Jesus to be mortal-- or, if divine at all, divine only in a symbolic or
> metaphorical sense, by virtue of enlightenment. And Mani . . . maintained
> that Jesus did not die on the cross but was replaced by a substitute. (1982,
> 386)

This assertion that a substitute died for Christ is also found in the Koran which states "they did not kill him, nor did they crucify him, but they thought they did." Later Muslim commentators also argue that Simon of Cyrene may have been the victim, and that Christ only looked on, a scenario also found in the Nag Hammadi scrolls (Baigent and Leigh 1982, 386ff.). And what was also operating in Mani's thought was the half-forgotten concept of tanistry, the succession of god-kings fueled by the periodic murder of the aging king by his tanist successor. For Mani likely felt, much like Frazer's king of the grove, that tanistry preserved a royal bloodline, and with it, the order of light over the darkness that would follow a vaguely understood chaos.

Other Cathar doctrine derived from the Arian heresy, an even more potent paradigm that nearly overwhelmed Christian theology during the early centuries of the Church, and that influenced certain devotees of Catharism who were less inclined to view Christ as a mystical entity. Begun by Arius, a presbyter of Alexandria (d. 355 c.e.), its assertion that Christ was mortal and capable of sin won the sympathies of Emperor Constantine and his successor Constantius, despite the fact that Arianism was officially condemned at the Council of Nicea in 325. And in the waning fourth century c.e. it became an especially potent force among entities such as the recently converted Goths, the Visigoths, the Burgundians, the Lombards, and especially the Merovingians, who claimed to be the direct blood-descendants of Christ. It was largely through the Visigothic influence that Arianism was sown in the Pyrenees region of Southern France and in the intellectual soil of Moorish Spain. Arianism, like Manicheanism, was very compatible with both Judaic and Islamic beliefs. Like the Jews, the Arians regarded Christ as a prophet of the female bloodline of Sheba of the House of David. Muslims were equally comfortable with Arian thought, for although Christ is mentioned thirty-five times in the Koran, he is deemed to be nothing more than a very human prophet, one of Mohammed's precursors. Arianism also fit in well with the Templars' efforts to fuse Christianity, Judaism and Islam into one religion. For the Templar Order had been founded in 1118 in Jerusalem, and, as Norman MacKenzie reveals: "its organization was based on that of the Saracen fraternity of the hashishim, 'hashhish-takers,' whom Christians called Assassins" (1967, 117).

Baigent, Leigh and Lincoln reveal the Arthur appears to have been an historical figure living in late fifth and early sixth centuries, a period which marked the apex of Merovingian hegemony in Gaul. They conclude: "If the term *Ursus*--'bear'-- was applied to the Merovingian royal line, the name 'Arthur,' which also means 'bear,' may have been an attempt to confer a comparable dignity on a British chieftain (1981, 306-307). This apparent coincidence may not be accidental at all, for if the Grail really symbolized, on one level at least, the *sang real* or the royal blood of the Merovingian bloodline, as several commentators have hypothesized, Arthur himself may have been in the line of descent from Mary Magdalene and Christ, and, ultimately, from Solomon and Sheba. Baigent, Leigh and Henry Lincoln, proposing that the bloodline might have been exiled from Provence to England in the ninth and tenth centuries C.E., speculate as much:

> Perhaps the Arthur in the Grail romances was really *Ursus*-- another name for 'bear.' Perhaps the legendary Arthur in the chronicles of Geoffrey of Monmouth had been appropriated by writers on the Grail and deliberately transformed into the vehicle for a quite different, and secret, tradition. If so, this would explain why the Templars-- established by the Priere de Sion as guardians of the Merovingian blood line-- were declared to be guardians of the Grail and the Grail family. If the Grail family and the Merovingian blood were one and the same, the Templars would indeed be guardians of the Grail-- at the time, more or less, that the Grail legends were composed. Their presence in the Grail romances would not, therefore, have been anachronistic" (1981, 308).

Interestingly enough, they note that in Robert de Boron's poem *Queste del Saint Graal*, Galahad is presumed to be the son of Joseph of Arimathea by an unknown mother, and that both Jesus and Galahad are regarded as descendants of the House of David. In fact, Galahad's name may derive from *Gilead*, a mystical title for Jesus (1981, 308-309).[3]

The Arian position of the Merovingians involved two main assertions. First, Christ was a human being who fathered children, most likely by Mary Magdalene. And second, the Merovingians claimed blood descent from both Solomon and Sheba and their avatars, Christ and Mary Magdalen. Had a Merovingian-Catharist-Templar alliance been forged in medieval Europe, this political union could have restored the rituals of tanistry once practiced in the sacred groves. Clearly then, the role of women in the Church would have become far more potent, leading, perhaps, to a redefinition of popery and the derailing of the Apostolic Succession that was maintained by appointment and not through a royal, *female* bloodline. If these counter currents seem exaggerated, it should be remembered that a holocaust involving untold thousands occurred in Languedoc during the Albigensian Crusade. Clearly the Papacy assumed that its back was against the wall. Given that the Templars, the most powerful extra-governmental force in Europe, were contemplating the establishment of an independent country in

Languedoc, the Avignon papacy could have been mortally wounded, and with it, the Pauline strain of patrifocal Christianity.

Because a less virulent interpretation of Catharism stressed the humanity of Christ while denying his equality with the Godhead, this earthier form bore the potential of becoming a kind of theological glue that could bind the seemingly disparate religions of Christianity, Judaism and Islam. The location of Languedoc with its port of Sarras, named for the Saracens who once populated it, played a vital role in the shaping of the region's radical theology. For since its founding in 49 B.C.E., Sarras had been a key port in Euro-African-Asian trade that moved vigorously across the Mediterranean. No European backwater, Sarras was from the outset an international city, and a multi-ethnic one at that.

And Catharism's value as a theological glue was strengthened by its tendency to value the female, a radical viewpoint that had been resurfacing in Judaism, Islam, and the Eastern Church through Sufism, Shiite theology and Gnosticism (Godwin 1994, 194ff.). Certain strains of Gnosticism, which emanated from such religious centers as the Hagia Sophia in Constantinople, argued that the Church of Rome [or Avignon, as the case may be] was a negative patriarchal force, more of an impediment than an impetus to spirituality. Godwin notes a tradition which argued that the female aspect of God's soul was personified as Sophia, who was said to have birthed Christ and his sister, Achamoth, prior to Jehovah's birth. It was Achamoth, the tradition goes on, who gave birth to Jehovah and to the Son of Darkness, as well. As the story continues, we find Jehovah barring humans from partaking of the fruit of the Tree of Knowledge, while Sophia, in the guise of the serpent Ophis, also known as Christ, pressures Adam and Eve to disobey Jehovah's injunction (1994, 203).

Some Cathars elevated a primary exponent of Gnosticism, Simon Magus, a disciple of John the Baptist, to cult status. In extolling the virtues of Sophia, Magus had argued that homage was not only due the Creator but the Creatrix as well. In fact, it was the Creatrix, Magus believed, who birthed the Creator. In other words, the female was the prime deity and the male was relegated to second place, a situation which recalls the very essence of tanistry. And in Languedoc, Simon's association with a sacred 'harlot' named Helen, who symbolized Sophia, the Gnostic Virgin of Light, was likened to Jesus' relationship with Mary Magdalene, who was also invested with Sophia-like qualities. If this were not enough to incite the Church Fathers, the Gnostic Gospels argued that it was Mary Magdalene and not Simon Peter who received the Keys to the Kingdom from Christ. Hence the rock of the church was founded upon the female and not upon a male priesthood, or the

Apostolic Succession.

The fair Shulamite of *The Song of Solomon*, an obvious avatar of the Egyptian Isis, was the prototype of Sophia and likely a female component of the protector comet as well. In *The Wisdom of Solomon*, vii, this blessed little sister [Isis was, we recall, was the sister of Osiris according to the tenets of royal incest] is described as

> the breath of the power of God, and a pure influence flowing from the glory of the Almighty: therefore can no defiled thing fall into her. For she is the brightness of the everlasting light, the unspotted mirror of the power of God, and the image of His goodness. And being but one, she can do all things: and remaining in herself, she maketh all things new: and in all ages entering into holy souls, she maketh them friends of God, and prophets. For God loveth none but him that dwelleth with wisdom. *For she is more beautiful than the sun, and above all the orders of the stars: being compared with the light, she is found before it.* [italics mine]

In *The Song of Solomon*, vi, 10, the perplexed author is not quite sure what to make of this female charmer: "Who is she that looketh forth as the morning, fair as the moon, clear as the sun, and terrible as any army with banners?" Clearly, the little sister is not only the Bride but also the double of the Bridegroom, for both are described with contradictory black and white imagery, both are associated with armies waving terrible banners, and both are associated with lilies, with the shepherding of a celestial flock, with a garden or sacred grove, and with celestial chariots. In short, the Bride and the Bridegroom comprise the divine, pre-sexual hermaphrodite of the pre-fallen, Edenic grove that W. P. Boswell identifies, and likely a composite image of the protector comet as well.

Harold Bayley links the dovish, little sister of *The Song of Solomon* to Sophia, and, unwittingly, describes a very cometary scenario:

> Among the Gnostics, Wisdom was known as Sophia, the Virgin of Light. This heavenly maiden was said to have been co-existent with God, and as His Master Workwoman to have descended to earth glorying in the work of creation. But by some dolorous mischance the maiden Sophia became entangled in the very matter she had helped to bring into being. Finding herself unable to regain her heavenly estate, and having no rest either above or below the earth, she cried out in lamentation to her Great Mother, who pitying her daughter's distress, invoked the aid of the Creator. Whereupon Eusoph, the Great Light, sent Christ, his Son, who 'emanated and descended to His own sister.' Here again, we meet with the conjunction of a brother and sister, which is one of the conspicuous elements of the Isis and Osiris

myth, and likewise of *The Song of Solomon.* (1988, 175)

Is the Gnostic account of Sophia's fall from grace symbolic of the descent of a female-designated comet or of its disappearance beneath the horizon? Is that why the Shulamite laments in *The Song of Solomon* I, 6: "Mine own vineyard have I not kept?"

Clearly the fair Shulamite is not a solar symbol, for as previously noted, she "is more beautiful than the sun." She is also not a lunar symbol, for she is described as being "fair as the moon," but not equated to it. What else could be more awesome than the sun and the moon but a comet?

In a Slav tale called *A Maid with Hair of Gold,* a variant of the Shulamite is identified by Bayley as the Cinderella-like princess of the tale:

> This princess is the daughter of a King whose crystal palace is built upon an island. She sits accompanied by twelve maidens at a round table-- a table which may be likened to the Round Table of King Arthur and his twelve knights. The golden light from the princess's hair is reflected on the sea and sky every morning as she combs it. The hero's name is George, and this George is evidently not unrelated to the St. George of Christianity. (1988, 184-85)[4]

And George's tasks, Bayley explains, are to find the scattered pearls of the princess' broken necklace, and to locate her fallen ring which lies at the bottom of the sea. Recalling that the Greeks described a comet as a hairy star and that part of Queen Guinevere's Moray clan badge was a comb, we need to examine Bayley's description of this dazzling princess. When George looks the princess in the face:

> she arose from her seat and loosening her headdress exposed to full view the splendor of her wonderful hair, which had the appearance of a waterfall of golden rays and covered her from head to foot. The glorious light that glittered from it dazzled the hero's eyes and he [like Solomon with the Shulamite, and Arthur with Guinevere, we may suppose] immediately fell in love with her. (1988, 185, brackets mine)

The upshot of this love affair results in George's immediate demise, but he is miraculously brought back to life again by the princess, not unlike Osiris who is revived by his sister Isis. This Slavic tale, like the variants of the Cinderella myth which spread across Europe, likely preserves the beatific vision of the *real presence* of the protector comet. It is not unlike Elisha's so-called *Vision of Adonai* in which the mountain of the Lord appears topped with celestial chariots pulled by flaming horses. In *The Song of Solomon* vi, 10, a similar vision is described by the poet: "I went down into the garden of nuts to see the fruits of the valley and to see whether the vine flourished and the pomegranates budded. Or ever I was aware my soul made me like the chariots of Amni-nadib." Later the poet cries: "Return, return, O Shulamite, return, return that we may look upon thee. What will ye see in the Shulamite?" And the answer is: "As it were the company of two armies"-- an image pattern which Bayley compares to the hosts of chariots observed by Elisha: "It came to pass as they still went on and talked that behold, there appeared a chariot of fire and horses of fire and parted them asunder, and Elijah went up by a whirlwind into Heaven" (Bayley 1988, 154ff.). Such was the tradition that informed Arthur and his consort Guinevere, who were viewed as the descendants of Solomon and Sheba.

In order to understand the theology of the renegade North African Church, and of the matrifocal Cathar and Irish Insular churches of the fourth century c.e. and beyond, we must understand the influence of Catharism in the British Isles. Their female-centered version of Christianity that was carried by missionaries from Sarras and from the fringes of North Africa and Egypt found a fertile soil in Ireland and Scotland. For Catharism was extremely palatable to the Celtic Church partly because the role of women in Celtic society had for centuries been a potent one. Extending to Arthur's day, the queen and her female priestesses remained the dominant force in tanistry as bearers of the royal blood line. For in the Insular Celtic Church female priests called *conhospitae*, distributed the communion wine, while their male counterparts administered the wafers. And that sacramental wine, dispensed only by women, would appear to be symbolic of the female bloodline, or *sang real*, the prerequisite for royal incest and tanisty.

Rightly or wrongly, Celtic clerics argued that Christianity was first introduced in Britain either by the Virgin Mary, or by Mary Magdalen, or by Joseph of Arimathea who had allegedly removed Christ from the cross.[5] As a result, the matrifocal Insular Church in Ireland and in its Scottish colony of Dal Riada antedated the patrifocal version brought by Augustine to Britain. An outraged Gildas would later lament that the Celtic Church in Britain was "opposed to all the world, hostile to Roman usages, not only in the Mass, but even in the tonsure, sheltering themselves under the shadow of the Jews"(Goodrich 1986, 123). For Gildas, as noted earlier in this study, Celtic Christianity with its lingering practices of tanistry and royal incest was nothing but old wine in a new bottle, an extension of the sexual practices of the 'backsliding' Hebrews, of David and Solomon, and of the half-Jewish Merovingians.

Early Christian doctrine in Ireland and Scotland clearly mirrored that of the Pyrenees and Northern Spain during the early years of the Celtic Church. Godwin explains that in areas such as Britain, the Pyrenees, and Northern Spain, early Christians were very cognizant of the Gospel of St. John and its key personages such as Nicodemus and Joseph of Arimathea. Godwin goes on to note that Merlin himself adopted the life-style of John the Baptist, and that the Gospel of St. John, likely written around 100 c.e. at Ephesus, was transported to the Pyrenees first by Polycarp, John's pupil, and later disseminated in the area by Bishop Iraneaus of Lyons. A French historian, Fernand Niel, argues that Montsegur in Provence was an early Grail Castle. Montsegur was a center of initiation not unlike Peel Castle on the Isle of Man, sacred ground that Goodrich identifies with the mysterious Avalon. Here the link between Languedoc and Scotland becomes stronger. Goodrich argues that the devotions at the chapel of the Virgin at Montsegur were practiced by King Arthur and the Templars as well (1992, 12). She goes on to explain that Niel was convinced that originally Montsegur was a solar temple built by Merlin and governed by Tinturel (1992, 286). Citing Stephen Runciman, an English authority on Catharism, Goodrich notes that these so-called heretics, who met secretly in Arthur's Broceliande forest, opposed baptism, the Eucharist, marriage, a male priesthood, a hierarchy, and the worship of the cross (1992, 287).

Apparently the twelfth and thirteenth century French interpreters of the Arthurian Grail legends who relocated Arthur and his court in Northwest France were aware of the earlier links between Sarras and England during the turbulent centuries of the first millennium c.e. Nonetheless, they could not resist the urge to devalue the characters of Guinevere and Lancelot, and the dark sister of Arthur, Morgan Le Fay, which they erroneously depicted as adulterous. This prurience resulted, in part, from the fascination with adultery at the court of Marie de Champagne, patroness of Chretien de Troyes, and from the perverse, clerical anti-feminism that shrouded France in a murky haze. Apparently, as Goodrich proposes in *King Arthur*, the Continental writers were unfamiliar with the privileges of the royal daughter, or heretrix chief, who was free to consort with various members of the warrior class (1986, 148-49).[6] Goodrich reasons: "Chretien's confusion and his accusation of adultery may have resulted from his failure to realize that Northern Britain, especially the Rhinn of Galloway but also the whole northern part of Scotland above the Forth-Clyde line, was once Pictish" (1986, 149). For the distorted Gaulish portrait of Arthur and the equally twisted French versions of Guinevere, Lancelot and company invented by Chretien de Troyes, were, nonetheless, based upon historical figures.

Baigent and Leigh explain that Chretien's hero, Perceval le Galois, originates not from Wales but from Galloway in Scotland (1989, 81).

The French and German twelfth and thirteenth century Grail legends written by authors such as the converted Jew Chretien de Troyes, author of *Conte del Graal*, and Templar Wolfram von Eschenbach, author of *Parzifal*, were attempting, albeit crudely, to make a philosophical-religious synthesis among the matrifocal, Cathar and Insular versions of Christianity and similar matrifocal esoterica that was surfacing in Islam and Judaism. After all, Wolfram believed that the story upon which he based his *Parzifal* originated among Sephardic Jews in the Visigothic capital of Toledo, Spain. And the ultimate Grail bearer in *Parzifal*, Repanse de Schoye, although virginal in Wolfram's version, presents in the Moorish version not the Grail but "a blood-filled vessel" signifying "the womb which represents rebirth and reincarnation" (Godwin 1994, 160). And the tale derives, according to Godwin, from an Islamic tradition in which Repanse de Schoye is labeled with the venerated title of Holy Whore (1994, 160). A remark by Godwin regarding *Parzifal* and its antecedents is particularly telling:

> In this account, the Knights Templar were named as the Grail guardians, who awaited the *Mahdi*, the desired knight, to reestablish paradise on earth, halting the spreading desert wasteland brought about by the loss of the Goddess. So once again we encounter the female aura permeating the deepest strata of the myth, radiant, yet partially hidden within the work. This time its origins lie in the hot and dry deserts of the mystical East rather than in the rain-swept lands of the Celtic North. This thirst for an essentially female principle within myth and romance became more exaggerated and urgent the more the Church, with its particular phobia against potent women, tried to repress her. The effect could be witnessed in the popularity of the cult of the Virgin Mary which was relentlessly repressed by the Church Fathers. It is small wonder that in the Middle Ages people often viewed God as their persecutor and Mary as their defender. (1994, 160-61)

The Templar concept of the Mahdi and his queen apparently harkened back to pagan king and queen of the sacred grove, the divine hermaphrodite of which W. P. Boswell writes, and the protector comet concept which this study is advancing.

Using southern traditions mixed with a dash of Welsh mythology derived from the *conteurs* or storytellers who had migrated from Southern Wales to Brittany, and material from Geoffrey of Monmouth's account of Arthur's court, these twelfth and thirteenth century Continental grail-spinners were attempting to replicate in a clumsy kind of way a similar matrifocal synthesis that had already occurred in the Irish and Scottish creeds. And it was that orientation that had partially survived the onslaught of the Roman occupation and Roman Christianity and flowered in the time of King Arthur.

Ironically enough, much as African and Near Eastern esoterica informed Wolfram in the late twelfth century, an earlier brand of that African and Near Eastern esoterica appears to have influenced the Insular Church of Arthur's time. It should not be overlooked that pre-Aryan, African and Near Eastern influences inherited from the martrifocally-oriented Picts may have greatly contributed to the racial and theological amalgamation that became the Celtic Church in the British Isles. For, according to Goodrich, Guinevere was a Pictish warrior queen (1991-92, 3). Then too, Arthur's Aryan pedigree has been questioned. Goodrich reveals that historian Edmond Faral theorizes [much as Gerald Massey argues before him] that *Arthur* is not an Indo-European name, given that no sound derivation from any Aryan roots has been forthcoming (1992, 230). For Goodrich, its origins might be found in the Pictish tongue, which, much as Hebrew and Aramaic, is neither an Indo-European nor a Celtic language (1992, 230). But she appears to arrive at a dead end when she traces the Pictish tongue to alleged oriental influences in Finland, as noted earlier in this study.

Around the time of the historical King Arthur (c. 475-542 c.e.), the Celtic Church was making plenty of waves in Rome. Goodrich notes that a heretical Briton named Morgan, who is today called Pelagius, was none too popular with the Roman ecclesiasts. She cites Bede's *Ecclesiastical History* (II,2), noting that the Pelagian heresy was commonplace in Britain by 429 and that Continental writers such as Orosius and Prosper of Aquitane vilified Pelagius and his Irish associate Celestius, calling the former "a low scribbler, a cunning snake, a sinuous viper, and a sea-green Briton" (1986, 204).

As a result of the perceived impudence of the Celtic Church, Germanus of Auxerre, and Lupus, his associate, were assigned to Britain in the mid fifth century to douse the heresies that were smouldering there. And earlier that century, Saint. Patrick had made his second trip to Ireland from 432-33. Particularly irksome to these itinerants was the fact that the Insular Church did not honor celibacy among its priests and priestesses. To their horror, many clerics, both male and female, had founded dynasties in accordance with the older concept of royal incest, a practice allowing the marriage of a priest with his mother, sister or daughter. This lingering kinship system remained virulent because under Pictish law property could only be transferred down the female line of descent.[7]

Certain influential Islamic esoterica also carried similar anti-patriarchal messages. Godwin notes that this female-centered thinking was shared not only by early Christians but also in the Near East for at least a millennium prior to the seventh-century arrival of Islam's patriarchs. In fact, Sheba was revered in the form of "a black aniconic stone" which today rests at the site of the old Temple of Women called Ka'aba. Additionally Sufi and Shiite mystical traditions credited the female sexual force with maintaining the equilibrium of the world (Godwin 1994, 203ff.).[8]

Catharism and the Insular Church absorbed so much of this matrifocal esoterica that both institutions were finally deemed noxious threats to the male-dominated Church. So great were the fears that this ecumenical heresy might depose the order of Rome that the Albigensian Crusade was conducted in Languedoc, resulting in a civilian genocide that rivals in intensity, if not in size, the atrocities of Nazi Germany. But what did the ferment in Languedoc have to do with the British Isles? A great deal, it turns out.

Precisely at the time of this Crusade, Europe experienced its second wave of Grail legends, and it was primarily in support of the martyrs of Catharism that this second wave came into being. The first wave of legends had described real and imagined events that had occurred mainly in Scotland in the sixth century and earlier. For as Goodrich observes, Arthur, Merlin, Guinevere and Lancelot were doubtless historical Scots, and their escapades took place not in Glastonbury, but in the southern Scottish Borders and further north near both Glasgow and Edinburgh (1992, 85). Spread orally by Welsh bards and Breton and Anglo-Norman *conteurs*, works such as the Irish *echtrai* or Grail adventures, with their mysterious cauldrons of rebirth, drinking horns of plenty, magic swords and spears, and Blessed Isles, and the Welsh *Mabinogion*, with its wasteland, wounded Fisher King, Knights of the Round Table and Grail knight Perceval, were being taken seriously not only in Christian Europe but in Moorish Spain as well where the tales were embellished with Eastern imagery from the Jewish Cabala and Sufism. And by the thirteenth century, Scottish, Irish and Welsh characters such as Arthur, Merlin, Perceval, Galahad and Lancelot were speaking in the dialects of Old French and Old High German, penned by writers such as Chretien de Troyes in *Le Conte del Graal* and Wolfram von Eschenbach in *Parzifal* as these characters experienced visions derived more from the Jewish and Islamic esoterica than from Celtic source material.

In the Celtic originals, the major crisis of the Grail legend was the attack upon female sovereignty, a concept which for the purposes of this study evolved from the dominant role of the queen of the sacred grove. This attack not only degraded the women involved, but for the Celtic imagination, threw out of synchronization the real world with the enchanted otherworldly state that existed parallel to it. Godwin explains that in the mythic arena, maidens inhabited sacred areas such as grottoes, wells and springs. And in the Celtic imagination, the mundane world and the Otherworld "were twin universes running parallel to each other." When arriving at a sacred place, the visitor was magically transported into the Otherworld (Godwin 1994, 20). The Celtic Logres that ultimately informed *Le Conte del Graal* and *Parzifal* had been a kind of heaven on earth, but that paradisal state was disrupted when King Amangons seduced one of the well maidens who guarded a sacred spring and stole her sacred bowl. Not to be outdone, King Amangons' retainers imitated the King's act with the remaining well maidens, and soon the grottoes, which quickly dried up, were abandoned. As a result, the once fertile ground withered into a wasteland, a sacred landscape that likely resulted from a meteor shower and a resultant cosmic winter. Godwin cites the prologue to *Le Conte del Graal* which reveals:

> since that time the court of the Rich Fisher, which made the land to shine with gold and silver, with furs and precious stuffs, with abundant foods of all kinds, with falcons, hawks and sparrow-hawks, could no longer be found. In those previous days, when the court could still be found, there were riches in abundance everywhere. But now all of these are lost to the Land of Logres. (1994, 20)

How could the land be restored? How could the magical fairyland once again merge with the natural world in mystical epiphanies? How could a communion between the female queen of the innerland occur with the king of the outer realm? How could the crime visited upon the well maidens be expiated? How, in short, could the ritual of tanistry and the periodic election of the divine hermaphrodite, the protector-comet, be maintained? Those burdens were placed upon the shoulders of the Grail hero. Only he could reestablish a proper kingship which would revere the female principle and restore the lost sovereignty of the female queen of the innerland. In order to accomplish his task, the hero had to undergo a radical transformation from a patrifocal set of values to a restorative, benign matrifocal set. Only then could he preside over the Golden Age that supposedly existed before the arrival of the devastating cosmic serpents.

This transformation is illustrated in miniature in "The Lady of the Fountain," a tale in the Welsh *Mabinogion*. When Owein arrives at the Countess' fountain which bubbles beneath an ancient tree, he finds a stone and a silver bowl beneath its branches. On cue, he fills the bowl and pours the water over the stone. This act results in a cometary hailstorm that not only injures him but rips the leaves from the tree. As a flock of birds begin to fill the denuded tree branches, a Black Knight appears before Owein and accuses him of authoring the destruction. Clearly, the Black Knight, who is associated with female sovereignty as are the three cup-bearing knights [two of whom are black] in the *Peredur* legend, has been the Countess's consort and champion. And his blackness also recalls W. P. Boswell's assertion that tanistry stemmed from Ethiopic roots. In the logic of this tanistry, mother nature now requires a younger, more virile champion to ensure her safety. Deeply infatuated with the Countess, Owein slays the rival, marries the woman and lives with her for three years. But as time passes Owein becomes restless and asks the Countess's leave so that he can find the court of King Arthur. Successful in that adventure, he forgets about the Countess until some time later when Luned, her messenger, berates Owein for his callousness. This admonishment causes a tremendous sadness to overwhelm Owein, and after several humiliations in his quest to find her, he, a changed man to be sure, is finally reunited with the Lady of the Fountain.

This theme of the restoration of female sovereignty became wedded in the European imagination with the ideal of the Service to Women, a concept based partly upon the Crusaders' exposure to Sufi mysticism and other Eastern marvels such as Islamic and Persian love poetry (Godwin 1994, 9). It is also likely that the Templars' travels in Ethiopia exposed them to Axumite tanistry. Additionally, the theme of female sovereignty was a not-so-veiled attack against a male Church.

If a defeated, Crusade-weary Europe had come to symbolize the castrated Fisher King, it was the patrifocal Catholic Church that had been the castrator, not the Saracen. And there were plenty of bones bleaching in the sun across the ravaged landscapes of Languedoc and the Holy Land to testify to the fate of female sovereignty. Barely hidden in the Grail quest was the Catharist belief that the rule of the mother goddess must be restored, that the Church must be feminized, that the European male must undergo a transvaluation of values, and that the Grail-bearers, the elders who officiated over that transformation, must be priestesses. And the reinstatement of ancient tanistry and royal incest, based upon Merovingian claims to descent from the bloodline of the Queen of Sheba, could not be far behind. Like the devotees of Sufism and Gnosticism to the south, Celts such Robert Bruce longed to restore the lost maternal paradise, the sanctities of royal incest and tanistry, all of which had become casualties of the invasions of Caesar and the emissaries of the Popes.

Monica Sjoo and Barbara Mor explain the Celtic matrifocal world view in more practical terms:

Celtic women owned their own property and were free to choose their mates, or 'husbands.' In marriage, women didn't enter legally into the man's family, but retained independent status and property. Desiring divorce, the woman simply took back her belongings and dowry. Marriage was not a religious ceremony, and there was no concept of adultery. There were even 'annual marriages,' entered into by both women and men, in which both parties agreed to be bonded for one year; at the end of each year the bond was mutually renewed, or abolished. Polyandry was practiced by some tribes; women belonged to the tuath. Legal contracts were made by the 'wife' independently of her mate, and women were often the economic 'heads' of families, with daughters inheriting equally with sons. Celtic heroes were named after their mothers-- and 'heroism' was not confined to men. (1987, 259)

To restore a matrifocal value system to Europe through the use of Celtic and African and Near Eastern mother goddess traditions, to end the Catholic wasteland caused in a later era by a debased patriarchy, and to bring the European male up to moral speed, these were the goals of Wolfram von Eschenbach's *Parzifal*. Reacting to the horrors of the Albigensian Crusade, von Eschenbach created both a playful and a daring scenario. The true culture bearers of a spiritually regenerated Europe would not only be the Nordic Parzifal, but also his half-black, pie-bald, half-brother Feirefiz.[9] That such a proposition could be made reflected the times. Goodrich notes "That hero's brother was half black and half white. No wonder. The Crusaders left children in Syria and brought others home. King Richard I struggled mightily to wed his royal sister to the Sultan Saladin. He failed and had to have her escorted back to southern France" (1992, 171). And if that pie-bald Knight were not insult enough to the Church, Feirefiz, son of Parzifal's father Gahmuret and the black queen Belacane, would be a none-too-subtle take-off on Menelik, the mixed son of Solomon and the black Queen of Sheba [known as Mackeda in the Jewish tradition and Belquis in the Muslim]. This same Menelik was reputed to have removed the Ark of the Covenant from the Temple of Solomon.

Menelik-Feirefiz is not the only person of color in Grail legends, to be sure, for dark-skinned, redemptive females such as Morgan le Fay, Kundrie, Esclarmonde and Repanse de Schoye, are ubiquitous in Grail lore. In the Welsh *Peredur*, Cundrie, the dark-skinned dwarf reputed to be the sister of the equally dwarfish Gawain, emerges as an archetype (Goodrich 1992, 66, 196). And in the Celtic imagination, black queens and priestesses and assorted black knights often stood not for evil, but both for the wisdom of an earlier, matrifocal race that swept across the British Isles, and for the dark men and women of the East such as Menelik and Sheba, potent figures that missionaries such as Saint Columba, one of the first to spread early Catharist doctrine from Ireland to Scotland in the sixth century, carried with them.

And what is the full upshot of the character Feirefiz? Clearly, he represented the hoped-for union of the Christian, the Moor and the Jew, in typical Languedoc style. This was bold, in-your-face kind of stuff. The very idea! A mulatto reaching the beatific vision in the Grail castle; a mulatto born of a black Queen who carried all the baggage of the half-repressed mother goddesses worshiped in the tanistry rituals of Europe, the Near East and Africa for millennia; a mulatto serving as a symbol for a new Europe rid of the religious intolerance and all the stupidity that had led to the Crusades? Yes, Wolfram nodded. A mulatto was the very symbol of an Islamic-Jewish-Cathar-Insular synthesis that would fulfill the wildest dreams of the displaced Templars. It was all too much then, and perhaps it is too much today, for a modern version of the Crusades may well be looming in Europe, with Bosnia or Iraq serving as the fuse on the powder-keg.

Notes

1. Also see Hughes (1966, 20). She notes that Pelagius was called an Irishman by Jerome who used the invective 'Scotorum pultibus praegravitus."

2. More Catharist thought may entered England in the thirteenth century. For from 1251-1253 Roncelin de Fos, who had been Master of Provence from 1248-1250, was elected Master of England. Baigent and Leigh (1989, 59) argue that more heretical Catharist thought was carried from Provence to England, based upon testimony before the Inquisition given by Geoffroy of Gonneville, Preceptor of Aquitaine and Poitou, who charged de Fos with "perverse rules and innovation."

3. Godwin (1994, 186) cites the Merovingian belief as stated in numerous Grail romances that Mary, the mother of Christ, carried the Nazarene bloodline which merged with the bloodline of the Franks, founders of the Merovingian dynasty. For Godwin, this explains several Merovingian traditions: Mary's landing at Marseilles; the supernatural birth of Merovee, the founder of the Frankish bloodline; his claim of having two fathers and his association with the fish symbol designating Christ; and the overall Merovingian claim of descent from Christ.

4. On p. 154 Bayley notes: "King Solomon was sometimes represented in the St. George-like attitude of a dragon-slayer, and the Arabians credit him with waging a perpetual warfare against wicked genii and giants."

5. Also see Hughes (1986, 21). She notes that Tertullian, writing c. 200 c.e. in "Britannorum inaccessa Romanis loca Christo vero subdita" believed Christianity had reached the British Isles prior to the second century.

6. Goodrich argues: "It seems among the Pictish peoples of ancient Scotland the crown passed to the royal daughter, who was called heretrix chief. She was free to

bestow it on the consort of her choice. Thus, the kings of the Picts were most frequently noble sons of non-Pictish origin."

7. See Hughes (1966, 42, 95). She notes that Gildas was protesting against the polygamous behavior of the British clerics. See notes 4 and 5. She also discusses the activity of Irish priests in Merovingian Gaul.

8. And so we come to the etiology of the cometary Black Madonna in Europe. Godwin (1994, 203) links the worship of the Black Madonna to the worship of Sheba in pre-Islamic times when at Mecca Sheba was venerated in the image of a black, meteoric stone now housed at Ka'aba, a shrine earlier known as the Temple of Women. J. A. Rogers (1980, 29) notes religious aspects of the Egyptian influence in the British Isles and the Continent. He observes that during the Roman era the worship of Black Isis and Horus was practiced "as far north as Britain" and that Henry II was a devotee of the Black Madonna of Valle Tenebreuse, evolved by then from the earlier Black Isis. The existence of the Black Madonna and Baby Horus prototype for Mary and Jesus, of course, can be found in churches and museums throughout Europe. See Redd (1985, 116ff.).

9. See Godwin (1994, 78) for the Menelik=Feirefiz equation.

Chapter 15

~~~~~~

Lucifer's Emerald Isle

That Saint Columba embraced heresies that would later resurface in Cathar theology is a certainty. In Frazer's discussion of the god-kings of the past, he notes that Columba's disciples regarded him as Christ's very embodiment, that is, as an actual god-king whom they equated with Christ (1940, 117).[1] This could mean that for Columba and his disciples, Christ was viewed as both a man [in harmony with the Arian heresy] and one of a long line of cometary kings of the sacred groves. Frazer goes on to reveal that judging from hundreds of records drawn from the fourteenth century Inquisition at Toulouse, the Albigenses, steeped in Arianism, also regarded one another as they regarded Christ himself (1940, 117).

It seems that when the *real presence* of the god was understood, the symbolic overlay was stripped away and deemed as so much mumbo-jumbo which masked the deity's true cometary nature. That explains why in *The Legend of Saint Columba*, Columba was reputed to speak of Doomsday and of the cryptic "lightning flash of the Western World" that he believed would signal that traumatic day (Colum 1967, 57ff.). This understanding accounts for his ambivalence toward Set-Lucifer, whom he likely knew to be the former *real presence*, symbolized by his god-king ancestor and replaced, finally, by the tanist Christ-Michael.

Origen, the North African Church Father, was also ambivalent. And so was Isaiah shortly after Set-Lucifer was finally driven from the sky in the Late Bronze Age: "How art thou fallen from heaven, O Lucifer, son of the morning! How art thou cut down to the ground, which didst weaken the nations! For thou hast said in thine heart, I will ascend into heaven, I will exalt my throne above the stars of God" (Isaiah 14: 12-13). Given that the Set-Lucifer comet was later associated with the benign planet Venus, and given that the comet had previously been adored by the Israelites as their protector but reviled by the Egyptians as their scourge, Origen was justifiably confused when he wrote in response to Isaiah's observation:

> Most evidently by these words he is shown to have fallen from heaven, who formerly was Lucifer, and who used to arise in the morning. For if, as some think, he was a nature of darkness, how is Lucifer said to have existed before? Or how could he arise in the morning, who had in himself nothing but the light? (Crombie 1869, 51)

Origen was probing the collective memory to ascertain the mystery of the god-comet linkage. Columba would probe even deeper into the heresy.

And the heresy lived in the Grail legends as well. What is probably the earliest version of the Perceval Grail legend in the British Isles can be found in the Welsh *Mabinogion*. In 1838 Lady Charlotte Guest translated a section of the folk anthology, and this section became the English text called *Peredur*.

The plot of *Peredur* unfolds like a dream, for as in the dream work, much is revealed but even more is hidden. The hero Peredur, a candidate for kingship, undergoes an initiation process involving lengthy and varied ritual ordeals. Buried in the particulars of these ordeals, cometary imagery and its component, tanistry, can be uncovered. For Peredur, like Lancelot and Arthur, traced his descent from a royal line extending back to David and Bath-Sheba of Israel (Goodrich 1992, 191). Goodrich notes that neither name, Peredur nor Arthur, is an Indo-European title (1992, 310ff.). Hence, the tale was likely transmitted to Wales from North Africa via Provence. Peredur's ritual of initiation into kingship can be traced to Egypt and Greece, and, ultimately, to Ethiopia, given W. P. Boswell's discovery of the oldest version of the ritual in the highlands. The fifteen episodes of *Peredur* propel the hero through this most ancient initiation process, and the highlights of that ordeal need to be summarized.

Peredur is King Arthur's last nephew to face the rigors of initiation that may lead to his crowning. Like comet Horus, perhaps, he is fated to avenge the death of his father Osiris. He must also avenge the demise of his mother and brothers.

Jolted out of his boyhood routine when the emissaries of Arthur, who Peredur associates with dazzling "angels," visit him, he suffers his first major loss, the death of his mother who succumbs to pure fright. As is made clear in the second section, she knew that Peredur would endure the rites of kingship which effectively would remove him from the realm of mere mortals and brand him a god-king. W. P. Boswell's *Awri* serpent title for the Ethiopian snake priest-king seems to be a cognate for one of those "angels," Urien of Moray, a title which recalls the generic one held both by the king of the sacred grove and by his priests in Abyssinia. And such priests were also likened at the twin Thebes [both in Egypt and in Greece] and at the Irish Tara to a dragon as well (Goodrich 1992, 317).

Having mauled sixteen knights in the forests surrounding his uncle's castle, Peredur enters the great hall where he is told by two dwarves, one male and the other female, that he will succeed in his quest. So mounting his piebald nag, he proceeds to the castle of the Fisher King, who is none other than his mother's aged, lame brother and Peredur's second maternal uncle. For, as expected, traces of the royal incest inherent in Ethiopian tanistry cling to this tale. At the castle of the Fisher King Peredur's education is continued, and, upon leaving that castle, he goes to a third castle where, wielding his sword, he slices an iron bar in half.

And then the dreamy symbolism appears, for two Grail processions occur at the Castle of Wonders. In the first, he witnesses two youths carrying a large spear that drips blood. And in the second, a pair of Grail maidens bear a salver upon which rests a bloodied, severed head. This head likely represents that of John the Baptist, the precursor of Christ. It is also symbolic of the tanistry underlying most Grail legends, the strangulation or beheading of the old king of the sacred grove by the new king.

In a later episode, Peredur is given still more instruction on the art of combat at the Witches' Court. Here he is attended by muscular female creatures, reminiscent of the Amazons reputed to have once roamed North Africa. And these witches may well harken back to a more ancient matrifocal period of history when the queen of the sacred grove and her priestesses were the dominant figures there, as Graves suggests in *The White Goddess* (1948, 109ff.).

Leaving his female teachers, Peredur journeys to a Hermit's cave where a strange event occurs. Startled by the sound of horse's hooves, a hawk that has just killed a duck, flies to safety. Then a raven swoops down to claim the carcass. This causes Peredur to fall into one of his many hallucinatory trances. When he awakes, he gazes at the blood-stained black raven that is perched on a field of white snow and thinks of his black haired, snow-white lady, Blanchefleur.

Encountering more challengers, including Sir Kay, Peredur unhorses them, and dropping from exhaustion and hallucinating again, Peredur is carried to his own tent by one of Arthur's men. Revived finally, he marries his lady at Arthur's castle, and promptly joins Arthur's dog in a stag hunt. Finally the dog, not Peredur, brings the stag down.

More ordeals face him. He defeats a giant Black Oppressor who guards a Neolithic black barrow, a reference likely to the dark-skinned inhabitants interred in those underworld crypts. Descending into the barrow, he kills a Black Worm that grasps a magical stone in its tail. Then, after choosing the correct path from three itineraries, Peredur enlists the aid of a magic stone given him by a voluptuous fairy and thereafter kills Addanc, a non-descript monster that has dammed up a black lake. Using a spear made not of wood but of stone, Addanc was reputed to kill passers-by at a stone pillar.

Having survived these ordeals, Peredur joins his new bride and begins his fourteen-year tenure as king. But he is afforded another honor as well, for when his term as king expires, he is inaugurated to a higher level of kingship at the Grail castle. As a result, he is forced to abandon his wife and to practice celibacy, for, it would appear, he is now a god-king who must be sequestered to preserve the sovereignty of Mother Earth.

Cometary imagery is intertwined throughout this tale with the masked presence of the tanistry practiced in the Mediterranean and Red Sea littorals. The cosmic serpent imagery seems obvious: The "angels" of Arthur who represent the Cherubim which guarded Eden, the first sacred grove; the hoofbeats of the celestial horsemen that are so often associated both with Merlin as the leader of the celestial hunt and with Diana's sacred grove of Nemi, also replete with cometary hunters; the fallen duck, and the cometary hawk's replacement by the cometary raven; the stag [a northern variant for the Bull of Osiris, perhaps], gored, by the symbolic dog, one of Set's zoomorphs; the image of the iron bar that Peredur cuts with his cometary sword; the stone talisman given to Peredur by the fairy; the cometary spear dripping blood which the maidens bear; the Black Oppressor who harkens back to the old python king of the Abyssinian sacred grove; and the equally cometary Black Worm and Addanc monsters, both associated with meteoric betel stones.

All of these images occur in a dream-like haze, for collective amnesia is likely alive and well in *Peredur*. The dream symbolism that flickers through that haze barely unmasks the true horror of the cosmic serpent and the beheading ritual of the old king by Peredur, who for the time being must play the role of the tanist Awri Neos. No wonder Peredur's mother dies on the spot.

In tanistry, this study argues, the two dragon kings reenact on Earth the celestial battle of the dragon pair, Osiris and Set But the plot line is different, *for time magically reverses, and Set transforms himself into Osiris in the attempt to deny that the catastrophe ever happened.* And just as Peredur, playing the Set role, will slay the old king, so will he be slain by the next supplanter. For the gory head that appears on the platter is the head of the old king and likely symbolic of a vanquished comet fragment. Thus Peredur's inauguration at the Grail castle is the beginning of his end. For Peredur's name means "Longspear," and he is just that, for as the earthy representation of the dragon-pair, he must first play the Set role and finally the Osiris part. When it is recalled that in some versions of the Grail legend Lancelot dies on the castle bridge, tanistry, no matter how disguised, raises its bloody head.

Still more cometary imagery lies submerged in the Peredur narrative. The fairy who provides Peredur with the talismanic stone, which Peredur uses to kill the monster Addanc, hints at the female's role in the ritual of tanistry. For the fairy is a vestige of Sheba, just as the witches who train Peredur in the art of combat recall the Sheba-like Amazons of the aromatic groves of North Africa. Then too, the death of Peredur's mother is not an unusual occurrence in Grail legends, for Merlin's and Guinevere's mothers also expire shortly after giving birth. For the purposes of this study, the death of the mother makes perfect cometary sense. Indeed, much of the mumbo-jumbo surrounding the virgin-births of mythological figures can be dispelled if it is realized that a disintegrating comet will appear to give birth from its head, as it were, autonomously (Clube and Napier 1982, 178ff.). The Pictish custom of embalming heads with cedar oil may have been associated with this cometary head imagery, but there is as yet no way to be certain.

The other nasty habit of drowning a royal twin at birth, an activity that runs rampant throughout Celtic folklore, probably derives from the fear evoked by the dragon-pair in the heavens. No unsequestered, earthly reminder of that celestial pair was to be tolerated, for when the time for the reinstatement of the god-king arrived, both of the 'official' twins, the old king and the tanist, were literally imprisoned in their respective Grail castles.

In his role of Grail king, Peredur becomes dual. First, he is the avatar of both Osiris and the Ethiopian Otherworld god, Medr. Secondly, he is also the tanist, a red-haired Lugh, himself an avatar of Set, who careened into Otherworld at the end of the Late Bronze Age. Given these allusions, is it far-fetched to suggest that the Arthurian Age ended and the Dark Ages began as a result of a cosmic winter? As the avatar of Lugh, Peredur's true cometary symbolism is pronounced. For Lugh's arms were bigger than the sun's rays as he rolled the solar wheel across the sky at high noon. That wheel was likely changed to a solar one when the sky waxed more cheerful. High noon, it may be recalled, was a dangerous time to enter the druids' sacred grove, for the tree serpent was particularly venomous then. This taboo appears to result from the layering of solar mythology onto cometary mythology, for the sun is at its peak at noon. And like Peredur's mother, Lugh's mother also died prematurely on November 1rst, the first day of the Celtic New Year, and the beginning of the Taurid meteor showers (Clube and Napier 1990, 191). Horse races were held in her honor, and the horse, with its flashing mane and rumbling hooves, serves as a cometary symbol in several cultures.

Loomis is correct when, for a number of reasons, he equates leonine Lancelot with red Lugh and further associates Lancelot with the kingly title of Angus (1970, 225ff.; Goodrich 1992, 154). Boswell goes even further, however, when she derives Lancelot from Angus and Angus from Sheba's father Anghabo, the Abyssinian version of red-haired Set (1972b, 21ff.). For red was Lancelot's color as well, and both he and Lugh were players in the rites of tanistry, despite the fact that Lancelot failed his final initiation.

For Loomis, the Grail hero was solar, and Guinevere, Arthur and the Knights of the Roundtable were deemed symbols of the zodiac through which the sun journeyed. These associations doubtless obtained during periods of cometary inactivity. But when the sky degenerated, as it periodically did, the Grail hero would have reverted back to his earlier identity, and the goals of tanistry would have been defogged, as it were.

Referring to the *Perlesvaus,* c. 1190, Goodrich sheds light on the survival of the imagery of tanistry when she argues that many of Lancelot's so-called adventures were really "beheading games" in disguise (1992, 155). Lancelot's ordeal in the Castle of Griffins [or Dragons] offers a case in point. Lining the doorway, the severed heads of fifteen champions stare back at him blankly as Lancelot draws a sword from a copper column. Clearly, Lancelot, like Lugh, is in the Otherworld, for, as was the case with Solomon's Temple, copper and bronze denoted the infernal regions. Sensing that the residing king wishes to behead him, Lancelot joins up with a maiden and enters the Otherworld, the entrance of which is guarded by a lion which he promptly dispatches. Two cometary griffins [Set monsters, it would seem] with birds' beaks, dogs' teeth, asses' ears, and serpents' tails also fall prey to his sword. And finally, like the lovely fairy in Peredur, the Lady [playing the Isis-Aso role] offers Lancelot a talisman. It is not a rock this time, but a puppy, which Lancelot accepts but refuses to carry. Once again, the puppy harkens back to the cometary Set-Anubis zoomorph, for Anubis was jackal-headed-- hence, Lancelot's fear of holding it. And this puppy, or incubating tanist-symbol, perhaps, charms the other griffins so that they allow Lancelot and the maiden to pass. Leaving the Otherworld, Lancelot and the maiden enter a sacred grove, an orchard it turns out, as the dream landscape created by repression barely masks the underlying ritual of tanistry.

The symbolism of African and Near Eastern tanistry and comet lore also informs the exploits of Gawain, as noted previously in a footnote which discusses the imagery of tanistry in *Sir Gawain and the Green Knight*. In that equally dreamlike work, Gawain plays the role of Set or Awri Neos, and Merlin, disguised as Bercilak, mimics the role of the old king. In Malory's accounts, Gawain's totemism links him to both members of the kingly dragon pair, for his red hair recalls the cometary locks of Set, but his association with Taurus the Bull likens him to the Apis Bull of Osiris (Goodrich 1992, 294). The king, or would-be king, then, is dual as this study argues. *Gwallt-advwyn*, or 'Bright-hair,' is the Welsh version of Gawain's name in the *Mabinogion* (Goodrich 1992, 292). And his birth date, May 1rst, links him to the Egyptian Feast of the Repelling of the Troglodytes, celebrated in Egypt in late April (Clube and Napier 1982, 241). His association with Ares, the Ram, completes the cometary imagery, for Gawain's true identity is entwined with the Taurid meteor shower which comes from the constellations Tauris and Ares (Clube and Napier 1990, 169). Loomis regards Gawain as an avatar of Cuchulain, for Cuchulain, after killing old man winter, departs with Blanchefleur (Goodrich 1992, 293). Nevertheless, it seems that the cometary ritual of tanistry forms the lowest mythic layers of the Grail legends, while the fertility myths depicting young summer killing old man winter to renew the land are likely superimposed later on. This phenomenon has gone largely unnoticed by students of Arthurian romance, and their own collective amnesia, perhaps, has led to other misreadings.

Tanistry was primarily a matrifocal institution which operated under the kinship rules of royal incest, as mentioned earlier. If Aso-Isis colluded with Set in the murder of Osiris so that Set could become the king of the cometary grove, does her counterpart do the same in the Grail legends?

In Wolfram von Eschenbach's *Parzifal*, Cundrie, who appears to act out a rather subdued version of the Isis-Aso role, knows her tree lore. Much as Sibyl advises Aeneas to search for the Golden Bough and use it as a ticket with which to exit the Otherworld, Cundrie implores Gawain to seek the branch of an indeterminate tree in order to make his own exit from the infernal regions. Steeped in the esoterica of the East, Wolfram's Cundrie has memorized the arboreal language. Indeed, she preserves a version of the sacred language of incense-bearing trees and the complicated numerical symbolism associated with those trees, both of which evolved in the sacred groves of Abyssinia. It is a language that was used by the Doctors of North Africa to induce cures for their patients under the aegis of the Doctor's oath of which W. P. Boswell writes. For the Celts as for the Ethiopians, cometary trees and the rituals of tanistry were linked. And after the oracular methodology diffused, each member of the royal caste in Scotland was associated with a tree, a linkage that was, no doubt, passed down to future offspring. Perceval was the birch; Morgan le Fay, the willow; Arthur, was Chronos, the kingly alder; Guinevere was the avatar of Banba, herself associated with the apple tree which replaces Axum's fig tree; Lancelot, the oak of Baal; Merlin, the ash of Aesculapius, patron of the Doctors; and Gawain, the holly tree of Ares (Goodrich 1992, 221). But even more importantly, Cundrie can plot the orbit of the planets. And sure enough, her planets have cometary characteristics, for planets are not her real interest.

Clube and Napier reveal that when cometary activity diminished, astronomers shifted their focus from comets to planets, which they had previously ignored, given that cometary horrors had commanded their predecessors' complete attention. (1990, 84). As a result of reduced meteoric activity, Clube and Napier argue, the rational Apollonian view of the cosmos as opposed to a frenetic, Dionysian one, took hold among intellectuals in Classical Greece. Hence, cometary gods devolved into quaint folk memories (1990, 85).[2] Comets lost caste, as it were, and cometary astrology degenerated into planetary astrology.

In Arab thinking about the heavens, however, there was less of an inclination to relegate comets to a lowly status. Possessed of a more ancient knowledge, perhaps, Arab astronomers compromised and projected cometary characteristics onto the planets. Hence, Jupiter grew a beard; Mars became a lamp; Mercury a spear; Venus a horseman, and Saturn a kettle (Clube and Napier 1990, 85).

When Wolfram's Cundrie presents her astronomy lesson and speaks of the orbits of the planets in *Parzifal*, she attributes similar arboreal, zodiacal, and ancient god-like characteristics to them, until we must wonder if Wolfram, a Templar, knows more than he tells. Hence Mars is associated with the Holly tree, the Ares constellation, Ares, and Marduk; Mercury with the Ash, Gemini and Aesculapius; Jupiter with the Oak, Leo the Lion and Baal; Venus with the apple tree, Virgo and Isis; Saturn with the kingly alder, Sagittarius and Chronos (Goodrich 1992, 221). Her likeness to Nemi's Aesculapius gives Cundrie's act away. Like the incense lords of Punt, Cundrie is a Doctor, sworn to the Oath of Aesculapius to protect mankind from illness. With its myriad associations to orbits, gods and zodiacs, her language of trees is an astrological code ultimately derived from Abyssinia, and not just so much narrative filler. It is an ancient oracular and astrological language designed to cast spells, to keep the protector comet appeased, to drive away the demons of the night. For meteor showers are named in accordance with the constellations from which they appear to emanate--the Taurids, the Leonids, the Andromedids, the Aquarids, the Lyrids, the Orionids, the Perseids and so on. Like dark Sheba, this dark woman understands the cometary language of the sacred grove. Richard Wagner almost understands when his Cundrie, like a female Dabtara of Ethiopia, provides Amfortas with healing balsam in *Parsifal.*

And Cundrie's astronomy lesson in Wolfram's version bears a striking resemblance to Merlin's attribution of cometary characteristics to planets during his prophecy. For Merlin, the planet Saturn is Chronos waving his crooked sickle; the Moon is a chariot that disturbs the constellations; Mercury glows with amber rage; etc. All of this proved confusing to Velikovsky, who came to the unfortunate conclusion that the planet Venus was once a comet (1977b, 171ff.).

Cundrie appears to be derived from the more ancient symbolism of the celestial serpent, recalling a time when the sacred groves were home not to the god but to the goddess. And that cometary goddess, a virgin, mother and hag, became a black dwarf, hag, gorgon or a Medusa with splayed nostrils, serpentine hair, grotesque eye-brows and boar's teeth when the sky degenerated.

In Wolfram's *Parzifal,* there are two Cundrie figures. One is the Otherworld sorceress who provides the astronomy lesson, and the other is Gawain's dwarfish sister. Wolfram is somewhat kinder in his rather sarcastic description of the dark sorceress, describing her boar-like bristled, black hair; her dog-like nose; her protruding tusks; her curving, elongated eyebrows, her bear-like ears; her ape-like skin; her leonine fingernails. Clearly, von Eschenbach goes on, lances were seldom broken for her (1989, 164).

The function of the Otherworld queen of the Grail castle and her role as the consort of the Grail king is shrouded in mystery. Did the Grail king conceive a child with her, or was she celibate? Did the king practice royal incest with her double-- his second sister or aunt perhaps? Goodrich argues that as Queen of the Dead, Guinevere did not cohabit either with Arthur or Lancelot as later traditions hold. In arguing this position she makes two very interesting observations. First, Guinevere, she proposes, like the winged, female angels who guarded and protected the initiands at the Delphic Oracle, was a guardian angel herself and was so regarded by Lancelot (Goodrich 1991-92, 156). Second, Goodrich categorically states that no sexual relations could have transpired between Guinevere and Lancelot. Consequently, she goes on to propose that "Guinevere was not merely a crowned queen, but higher than that, a virginal priestess" (1991-92, 157). Tradition argues that Guinevere was also the wife of Midir, a title of the Celtic Otherworld god that Boswell derives from Medr, the ancient, Abyssinian Underworld deity (1972b, 53). In the Irish story "The Wooing of Etain," the source of which can be traced at least as far back as pre-Classical Greece, Guinevere, as an avatar of Etain who was married to King Airem[a name suspiciously similar to Boswell's Awri title from Ethiopia], played the role of summer, and as the Greek Eurydice, was lured from the world of mortals and willingly taken into the Otherworld (1972b, 52).

If celibacy was a characteristic of this Otherworld Queen and of her ancient predecessors, why should this be so? The answers seem to go like this: As the daughter of the Lord of the Dead and as a variant of the Triple Goddess, who was virgin, mother and hag, it was likely feared that Guinevere, who was also called Stone Flower, could transmute herself from a guardian angel into a hag or Gorgon and turn on her worshipers (Goodrich 1991-92, 249). It is also likely that she, as part of the royal hermaphrodite along with Arthur, represented a pre-sexual innocence. For was she not a symbol of the pre-cometary, Golden Age that existed before the sky degenerated again in the middle of the sixth century C.E., well within the time-frame of Camelot's demise?

Goodrich clears up the problem of Guinevere's pre-sexual identity a bit when she observes: "Aspersions cast on Arthur and family prove their long and close association with a foreign, pre-Christian culture" (1991-92, 48). For royal incest, she goes on, may have been practiced at Camelot not between Arthur and Guinevere but between Arthur and his sister. For just as Gawain and Modred were Arthur's sons by his sister, Roland was also the son of Charlemagne and Charlemagne's sister (1991-92, 48). Hence, Guinevere would have remained unsullied. And if the name Arthur can also be derived, in part, from *athair* or 'father,' then Arthur would be the distant avatar of Osiris, and of his kingly cousin Uriah who was murdered by David. In any case, there is little doubt that such brother-sister betrothals were widespread. Hence Guinevere could have functioned as Queen of the Dead and thus have produced no heirs. Her value would have resided not in her powers of procreation, but in her ability to caste spells, perhaps, on the celestial serpents and keep them at bay, or to descend to the otherworldly Grail castle with Arthur and Merlin and officiate in the Grail hero's initiation rite, or, most importantly of all, to serve as a symbol of Mother Earth in the Golden Age, inviolate, and free of threatening rogue comets. As the female component of the hermaphroditic ruler of the sacred grove, her role, like the king's, would have been ceremonial. And adding to her symbolic complexity, she is likely a disembodied guardian angel, more benign comet-spirit than flesh, and the daughter of Orcus-Phorcys, the Roman and Pictish God of the Underworld and ogre, who, as Goodrich observes, "sometimes assumed the guise of a black snake (priest)" (1991-92, 193). Goodrich explains one of the cardinal tenets of royal incest, noting that the king had no specified wife, nor prospects of producing an heir, but, rather, he "borrowed" wives. Furthermore:

> The only king's son who could reign was the king's son by his sister. Ergo, Arthur was accused of incest by other Celts who mistook his choice of Modred [for the next king] as an admission of guilt. Thus Modred was intended to be king because he was the son of Arthur's eldest half-sister, and she belonged to the Pictish or 'female royal race.' (Goodrich,1991-92, 180-81)

Earlier in *Guinevere*, she observes that based upon the Celtic concept of primogeniture: "The chief named his heir, ergo, Modred, by law of tanistry. Being next highest in blood and name, and by Pictish law the rightful heir as his sister's son, Modred, and not Kay, was the 'tanist,' or 'second' person" (1991-92, 56).

This study disputes Goodrich's conclusion advanced in *Guinevere* that the Pictish female royal race was Finnish, however (Goodrich 1991-92, 53, 181). Guinevere's name may imply that she was a 'white phantom' I. e. *gwen*=white and *hwyfar*=ghost, or phantom (Goodrich 1992, 181ff.). But the whiteness in question most likely applies to her cometary appearance. Victorian painters may have been correct when they depicted the earthly Guinevere as dark-skinned and saturnine (Goodrich 1991-92, 177). Given that she was a member of the Moray or Murray clan which sports a badge depicting a mermaid holding both a comb and a divination mirror [a comb which West African mermaids also held] , and given also that her father was reputed to be Ogre Vran, a black raven, a figure not unlike the cometary raven in Peredur's vision, perhaps, a good case can be made that she was a tawny Pict (Bailey 1994, 156; Goodrich 1991-92, 44ff.). Similarly, Elaine, the Lady of the Lake, marries Pelles whose name likely derives from the Phoenician Baal, another god of the North African, Phoenician Otherworld. In the case of Guinevere, since there is no time machine to take us back the sixth century, we can only speculate about her melanin level. But that level is really not the point. The point is that her ancestors were likely African, even if she, through numerous intermarriages of her ancestors, may have been white.

In any case, it all appears to have vanished in a cosmic flash: Arthur, Guinevere, Lancelot, Galahad, Camelot. The sky likely degenerated once again, transforming Arthur's Golden Age to dreary cosmic winter. As a result of these heavenly pyrotechnics, the Dark Ages commenced.

Clearly, the existence of a potent African and Near Eastern presence in ancient Britain is an indisputable proposition. That collective amnesia has set in regarding the religion which was transplanted on British shores, is another hypothesis that this study puts forth.

In the next chapter, this study will leap-frog across time to examine the persistence of Britain's "old dark race," as Massey calls it, during the reign of the Tudors and of Charles II.

Notes

1. Graves (1960) explores that proposition, minus the cometary equation, in *King Jesus.*
2. Clube and Napier (1980, 84ff.) cite the calm period of the classical age when meteor showers diminished.

Chapter 16

~~~~~~

Charles II and the Cavalier lifestyle:
The persistence of the dark type in Britain

This study has identified a considerable African and Near Eastern presence that profoundly influenced the religion, governance and culture of pre-Roman, Roman and medieval Britain. As time passed, the descendants of these darker inhabitants gradually began to blend into the woodwork, as it were, and their cometary religion was eventually subsumed after the night sky grew benign again. But by the time of Charles I that presence took a strange turn, for what can be described as an ethnic political faction, which apparently drew some sustenance from both the indigenous, swarthy inhabitants and the additional infusions of Moorish, Cathar and Gypsy immigrants to England and Scotland during the thirteenth to the seventeenth centuries, gradually began to form a potent countercurrent in English political life. And this countercurrent reached its crescendo during the Restoration period when swarthy Charles II and his Cavalier faction assumed the reigns of power.

Indeed, the more we study the history of the British Isles with an open mind, the more we stumble over the paradox of ethnicity. The 'colorful' career of Charles II is a case in point. Imagine the surprise of his mother, Henrietta Maria, when she first noticed what poet Andrew Marvell would later call Charles' "sable hue." Luckily, the reaction of Henrietta Marie was recorded for posterity. Lady Antonia Fraser, one of Charles II's modern biographers, reveals: "His mother wrote jokingly to her sister-in-law that she had given birth to a black baby and to a friend in France that 'he was so dark that she was ashamed of him.' She would send his portrait 'as soon as he is a little fairer'" (1979, 9). But he never became fairer, Fraser notes, recalling also that the Black Boy became his nickname, a sobriquet that still is used to name certain British inns in his honor (1979, 9).

A black man as the King of England? Far-fetched? To be precise, he was not the color of ebony, but he was *swarthy, saturnine, grim, Italianate, sable*, or any other of the myriad adjectives that were used to describe him during his lifetime. Certainly, someone as dark who lived in the today's United Kingdom or United States would not be able to pass. So what exactly was the pedigree of Charles II?

Fraser reveals that Charles was one-quarter Scots, one-quarter French and one-quarter Italian:

> Further back, the marriage of the cousins Mary Queen of Scots and Darnley increased the proportion of Scottish noble blood; while Mary's Guise mother supplemented his French inheritance. For the thin but vital trickle of English-- Tudor-- which had ensured the family's succession to the English throne, it was necessary to go back five generations to his great-grandmother's grandmother, Margaret Tudor, daughter of Henry VII. And even that Tudor blood was basically Welsh. (1979, 9)

She further notes that an embarrassed King James took the politically correct approach of eschewing normal discussions of the newly crowned Charles' heredity, and attempted to link him somehow to vague, shadowy kings concocted by Geoffrey of Monmouth. Then too, Aurelian Cook's eulogy over the dead Charles II, which Fraser cites, proclaimed that the blood of Christians of all the world had flowed through the veins of Charles: British, Saxon, Danish, Norman and Scottish from his father's side, and Bourbon of France, Austrian of Spain, and de Medici of Florence from his mother's descent. But it was English blood that came up short in the mix, Fraser explains (1979, 9).

What could have been the origin of what Fraser labels his "abnormal darkness of complexion," his "truly saturnine tint"? His Italian ancestry is Fraser's explanation, resulting in "a strain of very dark, swarthy Italian blood in the French royal family, inherited through Marie de Medici, which might and did emerge from time to time" (1979, 9-10). She concludes the matter by comparing Charles to the other, fairer grandchildren of Marie de Medici: "Charles was the only one to look purely Italian; the rest being both frailer and paler. But his appearance was certainly a complete throwback to his Italian ancestors, the Medici Dukes of Tuscany" (1979, 10).

Fraser's genealogy is corroborated by Edward Scobie in "African Women in Early Europe." He cites one particular interracial marriage that occurred in the de Medici family. It involved the celebrated African beauty Anna, a respected member of Italian society who served Alfonsina Orsini, himself related to Cardinal de Medici, the future Pope Clement VII. Alessandro de Medici, the Duke of Florence, issued from this relationship in 1511, and Scobie reveals:

> All the writers of the period agree that Alessandro was of African origin and his portrait by Bronzino reflects this fact. Alessandro married Margaret, daughter of Charles V, Emperor of Germany, Spain and Austria in 1536. His mother, Anna, was so beautiful that she was called the Italian Cleopatra. (1985, 217)[1]

Scobie goes on to propose that marriages such as this one could hardly hold a candle to the countless discrete, interracial amours that occurred in Europe during the Renaissance, arguing that "traces of Africa have disappeared in . . . literally thousands of such families in Europe and also in Britain" (1985, 217).

Little Charles was not the only embarrassment to the royals, Fraser explains, for Anne of Austria, wife of Henrietta Maria's brother Louis XIII, also birthed "a baby having the 'color and visage of a blackamoor', which died a month after its birth" (1979, 10). And Fraser tells more. For in 1664 yet "another Queen of France, wife of Charles' first cousin Louis, was supposed to have given birth to a black child" (1979, 10).

Hoping to identify the origins of that alleged "black bastard" Charles, the rumor mongers had their day. For as Fraser explains, during the time of the Popish Plot in the waning 1670s, a rumor circulated that Charles was the end product of Henrietta Maria's cohabitation with a "black Scotsman." Fraser goes on to argue that the black adjective revealed "a neat combination of two prejudices of the time, against the Catholics and the Scots" (1979, 10).

Based upon the swarthy visages examined in the next chapter which appear on the family crests of several prominent British families, the black adjective employed by these rumor-mongers may not have been used metaphorically but quite literally when referring to certain Scots of that time. And Charles II's lineage becomes less bizarre when it is realized that Moors even figured into in the pedigree of Tudor royalty. J. A. Rogers notes the connection in *Nature Knows No Color Line*, revealing that Elizabeth, the daughter of Edward IV and the mother of Henry VIII, counted numerous Moors in her family tree. Two of note were Count More and Count Morienn, Rogers explains (1980, 87).

The adjectives of darkness clung to Charles II throughout his adult life.

Noting a contemporary stereotype warning that a dark character lurks beneath a dark complexion, Fraser reveals Lord Mulgrave's surprise that "Charles being swarthy and cheerful was an exception to the rule" (1979, 11). Years later, Fraser reveals, witnesses to Charles II's Restoration procession were surprised at his dark visage. One bemused witness called the King "black and very slender faced" (1979, 183 fn. 7). And at the same procession, another witness, 14-year-old James Boddington, ran back to his father after seeing the King and informed him that the monarch was "a black grim man" (1979, 183 fn. 11).

But the swarthy complexion had its advantages. Citing Charles' attractiveness to women, a trait which resulted in numerous affairs and the production of an unknown quantity of love-children, Sir John Reresby attributed the King's appeal to the regent's amorous complexion, an appeal, Defoe commented ironically after Charles' death which, in part, accounted for the fact that: "Six bastard Dukes survive his luscious Reign" (1979, 284, 414).

MacRitchie probes deeply into the ethnic origins of Charles II and many of Charles' subjects in his monumental and much ignored work *Ancient and Modern Britons*. His investigations lead to many genealogical discoveries that speak volumes about the mixed pedigrees of numerous Britons. MacRitchie asks the hard questions. Was swarthy Charles II an ethnic aberration, the end-product, as it were, of ancestral bedroom antics between the Italian royals and their black consorts? Was there a considerable number racially mixed English and Scots? In his attempt to answer these and other questions, MacRitchie explores an avenue that few others care to travel, a circuitous route, to be sure, that allows us to understand the Cavaliers' fascination with England's darker population.

MacRitchie begins his investigation of Charles' pedigree by dropping a bombshell: The Stewarts, who provided the surname of Charles II, were not originally Scots but Normans, for they arrived with William the Conqueror in 1066 (1991, II, 341). Were all the Normans fair? he asks. Were some racially mixed with transplanted Semites and Africans? In an attempt to answer that question, Mac Ritchie speculates on the origin of some of the swarthier Norman complexions and proposes that these darker Normans were "a cross between the white-skinned Northmen and the Moors of Picardy-- or some other dark-skinned race" (1991, II, 340-41).

Regarding the ethnicity of Charles II and the make-up of several of his Scoto-Norman ancestors, Mac Ritchie goes on to argue in a footnote that the dynasty's scion, James I, was of Norman extraction, and that for decades after the Norman Conquest, the successful race still remained on the surface, little affected by the strata underneath (although by the time of Charles II . . . they had reverted to a 'gypsy' type whether through his French mother, or by earlier alliances). (1991, II, 29)

And what kind of indigenous population did Norman families such as the Stewarts, the Bruces, and the Wallaces find in Scotland when they began to establish their plantations? Inhabitants, in many instances, of a still darker hue, Mac Ritchie proposes, as he traces the bitter racial wars in Scotland between certain indigenous "Moorish" clans and the attacking Scoto-Normans. Two passages in *Ancient and Modern Britons* which serve as paraphrases of various sources, including Mackenzie's *History of Galloway*, Skene's *Celtic Scotland* and Nicholson's *Historical and Traditional Tales*, describe a twelfth century battle waged by Robert Bruce against a field of dark-skinned *moss-troopers* otherwise known as *dubh-glasses*. The passages reveal that the swarthy warriors, or *dubh-glasses*, strutted about quite naked, decked in war paint and tattoos that dated back to the Roman occupation. Their hair was plaited into 'glibbes' to prevent sword strikes to the neck and the back of the head. As they approached on their saddleless mustangs, they sounded "the frightful war-hoops of their race" (1991, II, 176-77).

For Mac Ritchie, the conquest of Scotland and the displacement of the indigenous aristocracy by the Scoto-Norman conquerors is to be understood, especially in the Galloway area during the twelfth century, as a bizarre race war. On one side, according to Mac Ritchie, stood both fair-skinned Normans and assorted swarthy Norman half-breeds, and mixed with the other side, a number of the darker, indigenous inhabitants of Scotland. And Mac Ritchie notes that during the twelfth century, this dark population of Faws, or *dubh-glasses*, especially in Galloway, was angry and dissaffected (1991, II, 179). He goes on to comment on the fate of the Pictish tribes in Scotland: "It is generally believed that the conquering Scots nearly exterminated the native North-Britons-- those 'nimble blackamoors,' or 'painted men,' whom the Romans had previously encountered" (1991, II, 179).

As Mac Ritchie sees it, with the indigenous race conquered, Scoto-Norman families such as the Stewarts could begin their occupation. And Mac Ritchie describes the incompatibility of many of the natives and their conquerors. Citing the indigenous moss-troopers, or mossers, he notes their radical difference from the more gentile inhabitants of Scotland. Only through extermination or assimilation, could this population be neutralized, Mac Ritchie argues. (1991, I, 229).

Drawing a comparison with Indian reservations in America, Mac Ritchie further notes that the indigenous Moors, some likely of early Pictish or Danish extraction, were eventually overwhelmed. And when this task was completed, Mac Ritchie explains that in the early part of the eleventh century, Malcolm IV "removed them all from the land of their birth, and scattered them throughout the other districts of Scotland, both beyond the hills and on this side thereof, so that not even a native of that land abode there, and he installed therein his own peaceful people" (1991, I, 230).

Skene in *Celtic Scotland* characterizes the decline of Pictish hegemony after the transition. Speaking of Scotland in the early eleventh century c.e., he notes that the

> line of the kings of Scottish descent has now been for a century and a half in possession of the Pictish throne. During the first half-century, they had borne the title of kings of the Picts, but during the remainder of this period their title had passed over into that of kings of Alban, and what formerly had been known as Cruithintuath and Pictavia, or the territory of the Picts, and, from its capital, the kingdom of Scone, had now become Albania or the kingdom of Alban, extending from the Firth of Forth to the river Spey . . . . (1886, I, 384)[2]

By 1587, Mac Ritchie adds, the indigenous remnant of *dubh galls,* or "black foreigners" [as they were called by their conquerors] who had not been formed into regiments and shipped off to Continental battles or deported to Ireland, slowly transformed themselves into marauding bands of Gypsies. These Gypsies lived by stealth and cunning, often terrorizing their conquerors with guerrilla-like raids on outlying farms and hapless travelers.

In England, Henry VIII declared unconditional war against the Gypsies, a faction that would, ironically enough, become the vogue during Charles II's reign. Mac Ritchie explains that the sixteenth century campaigns against gypsyism were also directed against various priestly castes which, in the words of a letter he reproduces from a north Briton to Henry VIII: "derived themselves from a certain lady, named Scota," whom they traced to Egypt (1991, II, 371). Henry VIII's rage was triggered, Mac Ritchie explains, by reports that they used books of spells and magic, replete with hieroglyphs that appeared to link these individuals to Egypt (1991, I, 255). He further notes how infuriated Henry became when Henry discovered that the vagabonds practiced their own marriage, baptismal and inheritance rites, which were often at odds with Christian practices. MacRitchie summarizes the intent of the various Tudor laws enacted against the Gypsies. For they threatened to kill, enslave, burn as witches, or outlaw any who did not adapt the so-called civilized manners of the gentile English and Scots (1991, I, 256).

The numerous acts of the Privy Councils of England and Scotland in regard to gypsy matters are carefully reviewed by Skene in *Celtic Scotland* and more recently by Brian Vesey-Fitzgerald in *Gypsies of Britain* (1973, 13ff.). For the purposes of this study, some of the more relevant wording of pertinent acts, along with selected eye-witness accounts regarding the gypsy population, will be noted to document the persistence of the type in the British Isles.

According to Mac Ritchie, swarthy people of mixed ethnicity, whose descendants would later be branded with the generic name Gypsy, had been arriving to the shores of the British Isles throughout the Roman and medieval periods, but no formal mention of migrations of dark-skinned people to Britain had been recorded.

That situation would change. For in 1417 a band of roughly 200 Gypsies, many of whom would enter the British Isles years later, was nervously observed as it made its way across the Continent. And in 1438 another much larger band was also eyed suspiciously by observers on the Continent.

However, the first formal mention of the term 'Gypsy' to describe such swarthy itinerants did not occur in the British Isles, Vesey-Fitzgerald notes, until the name appeared in the Lord High Treasurer for Scotland's records dated 22 April 1505 (1973, 13ff.).

Simson in *History of the Scottish Gipsies* locates another reference to the term. It appears in a letter, dated 1506 from James IV of Scotland to the King of Denmark which includes a petition for one Anthonius Gawino, a self-styled Earl of Little Egypt (1878, 99). According to Simson, *Crawford's Peerage* indicates that in Bombie, Galloway a company that he presumed to be gypsy corsairs, although they were not so-named, were committing various crimes in Scotland prior to the death of James II in 1460 (1878, 98).

The following descriptions of the Gypsies, who presented forged documents announcing to one and all that they were conducting a religious pilgrimage sanctioned by the Pope himself, were recorded on the Continent during their fifteenth century sojourns which began there in 1417. Among other eyewitnesses, Vesey-Fitzgerald cites a Swiss chronicler, Justinger, who wrote after seeing them pass through Zurich, Basel, Berne and Soleure in Switzerland:

> they were from Egypt, pitiful, black, miserable, with women and children;
> and they camped before the town in the fields, until there came a prohibition
> because they had become unbearable to the inhabitants on account of their

thefts, for they stole all they could. They had among them dukes and earls, who were provided with good silver belts, and who rode on horseback; the others were poor and pitiful. (1973, 14)

In another chronicle they were described at Bologna:

Observe that they were the ugliest brood ever seen in this country. They were thin and black, and they ate like swine: their women went in smocks and wore a pilgrim's cloak across the shoulder, rings in their ears, and a long veil on their head. One of them gave birth to a child in the market place, and at the end of three days, she went to join her people. (Vesey-Fitzgerald 1973, 16)

And at La Chapelle in Paris, which was then held by the English, they were described most unflatteringly by a chronicler:

Item, The men were very black, their hair was fuzzled; the women were the ugliest that could be seen, and the blackest; all had their faces covered with wounds (tattoo marks?), their hair as black as a horse's tail, . . . In short, they were the poorest creatures ever seen in France in the memory of man. And, notwithstanding their poverty, there were witches in their company who looked into peoples' hands and told what had happened to them or would happen, and sowed discord in several marriages, for they said to the husband 'your wife has played you false,' or to the wife, 'your husband has played you false.' And, what was worse, whilst they were speaking to folks by magic or otherwise, or by the enemy in hell, or by dexterity and skill, it was said that they emptied peoples' purses and put into theirs. (Vesey Fitzgerald 1973, 30)

Simson reveals that the first recorded arrival of Gypsies in England appears to have taken place in 1512. He quotes from a history written by Hoyland a century later which mentions their activities:

this kind of people, about a hundred years ago, began to gather and head about the southern parts. And this, I am informed and can gather, was their beginning: Certain Egyptians, banished from their country, (belike not for their good condition), arrived here in England; who, for quaint tricks and devices not known here at that time among us, were esteemed, and held in great admiration; insomuch that many of our English loiterers joined with them, and in time learned their crafty cozening. . . . The speech which they used was the right Egyptian language, with whom our Englishmen conversing at last learned their language. These people, continuing about the country, and practicing their cozening art, purchased themselves great credit among the country people, and got much by palmistry and telling of fortunes; insomuch that they pitifully cozened poor country girls both of money, silver spoons, and the best of their apparel, or any goods they could make. (Simson 1878, 90)

Vesey-Fitzgerald notes another early reference to the gypsy presence in England which he locates in *A Dyalog of Syr Thomas More, Knyght*. That document concerns itself with an inquiry ordered by the King regarding the death of Richard Hunne in the Lollard's Tower. It turned out that an "Egyptian" woman, an alleged fortune teller who was lodging at Lambeth, was called as a witness (Vesey-Fitzgerald 1973, 28).

The British gypsy population reached the thousands and tens of thousands in subsequent decades, and as it swelled, a curious ambivalence developed among the Scottish royals and their subjects regarding the gypsy life-style. On the one hand the lure of the Gypsy, who was largely free of the legal and religious constraints that shackled non-gypsy Britons, loomed large. Yet at the same time the royals and their subjects also experienced a seething rage against the crimes and peccadillos committed by the so-called Egyptians, mixed, perhaps, with a certain jealousy of the freedom enjoyed by these foreigners. This ambivalence often manifested itself in the harsh gypsy and vagabond laws found in certain Acts of the Privy Council passed in England and especially in Scotland. Yearly, however, the courtly emulation of gypsy fashions was becoming more and more the vogue in both the Scottish and the English courts. Edward Hale attests to that vogue in his *Chronicles* when he describes two ladies at a 1517 Court Mummery donned in the gypsy headgear of the day (Vesey-Fitzgerald 1973, 28). Then too, countless Englishmen either entertained the fantasy or the reality of denouncing their country and joining the Barbary pirates of Muslim North Africa.

Focusing on Scottish royals, Vesey-Fitzgerald attempts to come to terms with the three James' troubling ambivalence directed toward the Gypsies, noting that although James II had nothing but contempt for the sorners and beggars who flooded the realm, James IV awarded the Egyptians financial support and even sang their praises to the ruler of the next country which they chose to visit. And in 1530 James V went a bit further when he invited them to perform the morris dance at his residence at Holyrood House, paying them for his pleasure (Vesey-Fitzgerald 1973, 21.[3]

But James V would become ambivalent. According to Simson, James V placed a naive trust in a certain gypsy leader named John Faw, Lord and Earl of little Egypt, and ten years later deferred to Faw's entreaty that Faw should not be deported, despite his crimes. Faw had argued that he would be needed in Scotland to suppress a rebellion that was about to occur among his people. As a result of James V's influence, the Scottish Privy Council passed an Act in 1540 that allowed the Gypsies the right to follow their own laws and customs in Scotland (Vesey-Fitzgerald 1973, 23-25). But the King underwent a radical turn-around after an incident that transpired in a cave near Wemyss in Fifeshire. In disguise, practicing as Simson puts it, "his low and vague amours," the regent caroused with a band of Faw's Gypsies who roughed him up for allegedly abusing a gypsy woman in their party (1878, 104). In a rage, the scuffed-up King forthwith had the Privy Council of Scotland pass a very harsh Act against Faw and his band of Gypsies. So on 6 June 1541, the 1540 Act was countermanded by the Scottish Privy Council. John Faw was cited along with his brother, and Sebastiane Lalow, all described as Egyptians, and they were ordered "to depart forth of this realm, with their wives and children and companies, within thirty days after they be charged thereto, under the pain of death . . . with certification that if they be found in this realm, the said thirty days being past, they shall be taken and put to death" (Vesey-Fitzgerald 1973, 27).

Simson notes, however, that despite the period of about one year in which James V's severe order was in force [it expired upon his death], the Gypsies experienced little molestation in Scotland for a 73 year period which lasted from 1506 until 1579. For 1579 was year in which James VI assumed the Scottish throne (1878, 104). And in a footnote, Simson observes that during that 73 year period the gypsy population in Scotland:

> must have multiplied prodigiously, and, in all probability, drawn much of the native blood into their body. Not being at the time, a prescribed race, but, on the contrary, honored by leagues and covenants with the king himself, the ignorant public generally would have few of those objections to intermarry with them, which they have had in subsequent times. (1878, 104)

During Queen Mary's reign, Simson further reveals, factional strife was so severe that the crimes of the Gypsies and the other bandit groups, were largely ignored (1878, 104).

In 1579, however, the pressure was reapplied through a Scottish Privy Council statute that named certain Gypsies and noted their practices. According to *Glenrock's Scots Acts*, the statute dictated that

> idle people calling themselves Egyptians . . . or any that fancy themselves to have the knowledge of prophecy, charming, or other abused sciences, whereby they persuade the people that they can tell their weirds, deaths, and fortunes . . . being apprehended, shall be put in the king's ward, or irons, so long as they have any goods of their own to live on, and they have not whereupon to live of their own, that their ears be nailed to the tron or other tree, and cut off, and (themselves) banished from the country; and if

thereafter they be found again, that they be hanged. (Oct. 20, 1579, 6th par., cap. 74)

And in 1587, as Mac Ritchie notes, more pressure was applied when another Scottish statute was passed "for the quieting and keeping in obedience of the disorderit subjectis inhabitants of the Borders, Highlands, and Isles" (1991, II, 328). The Scottish Privy Council was by then carefully keeping track of landowners, tenants and itinerants. And as expected, Skene uses the term "colored" to describe the area under surveillance: "It is unnecessary to enter into any detail as to the description given in this Act of the state of these parts of the country, which is sufficiently highly colored" (1886, III, 328).

Simson lists additional statutes emanating from the Scottish Privy Council in 1592, 1597 and 1600. The Act of 5 June 1592 clearly referred to Gypsies: "And for the better trial of common sorners (forcible obtruders), vagabonds, and masterful beggars, fancied fools, and counterfeit Egyptians, and to the effect that they may be still preserved till they be compelled to settle at some certain dwelling or be expelled forth from the country, &c." (Simson 1878, 110). The Act of 19 December 1597 titled, "Strong beggars, vagabonds, and Egyptians should be punished," reads:

> Our sovereign lord and estates of parliament ratify and approve the acts of parliament made before, against strong and idle beggars, vagabonds, and Egyptians . . . . That strong beggars and their children be employed in common works, and their service mentioned in the said act of parliament, in year of God, 1597, to be prorogate in during their lifetimes, &c. (Simson 1878, 111)

Simson further notes that the 1597 Act condoned the abduction of gypsy and non-gypsy beggars by coal and salt-masters into virtual slavery (1878, 111). And the servitude was a long and bitter one, for as Simson reveals, the descendants of these Gypsies in Lothian, called Colliers, were not emancipated until the early nineteenth century. And although the 15 November 1600 Act ratified the previous Act, Simson reveals that the Scottish Privy Council, despite these crimes of kidnaping, lamented that the Acts passed to restrain gypsy and non-gypsy beggars were not well enough enforced (1878, 111).

Quoting Simson's *History of the Gipsies*, Mac Ritchie recalls the extreme hatred that resurfaced in 1603 when the Scottish Privy Council ordered "the whole race to leave the kingdom by a certain day, and never to return under penalty of death" (1991, I, 252). Mac Ritchie argues that race was indeed the issue for the Privy Council for in that statute "the race of *Graemes*, or swarthy people" was included in the wording (1991, I, 252).

And Simson cites an even harsher Scottish Act passed in 1609, the only one to exclusively target Gypsies *per se*, which made it lawful to condemn and execute an "Egyptian" simply because the individual could be proven to be a Gypsy. It ordered that those "commonly called Egyptians, to pass forth of this kingdom, and remain perpetually forth thereof, and never to return with the same, under pain of death" (1878, 112).

Despite the severity of the Acts, many respectable and well-heeled Scots protected Gypsies on their property, Simson reveals, and as a result, the gypsy problem remained a concern the Scottish Privy Council could not legislate away despite numerous trials of individuals connected to the Faw [Faa], Baillie and Douglas gypsy clans in 1611, 1616, 1624 and 1636 (1878, 113-15).

Surveying the 'Egyptian' influx to England and Scotland, Simson reveals that during Elizabeth's reign there were roughly 36,000 Gypsies in Great Britain (1878, 92). And Fletcher of Saltoun, cited by Simson, states that in his time [the end of the seventeenth century], about one-fifth the population of Scotland, approximately 200,000 people, were beggars (1878, 111). How many of those were gypsy beggars we can only guess. And if Mac Ritchie is to be believed, several droves of what would have been called Gypsies or Moorish Picts arrived in waves either by sea from Moorish Spain through Ireland to transmarine Scotland or from the Continent beginning in the eighth century c.e. Many of these refugees were likely dark-skinned blackamoors and white and mixed Berbers who may have been driven to the less desirable, mountainous areas of Moorish Spain, perhaps only to flee during the Berber revolts that occurred often during the Moorish occupation of Spain from the eighth to the fifteenth centuries.

In their relentless pursuit of the gypsy 'look,' the seventeenth century Cavaliers would later embrace the mannerisms of this darker, allegedly freer strain of humanity that roamed the ragged landscapes of the Continent and the British Isles. But there appears to have been another ingress of dark people into Scotland going as far back as the thirteenth century c.e., for accompanying a vagabond group of Templars were, doubtless, scores of Saracens. These Saracens, many of whom could have been people of color, appear to have added another dimension to the ethnic countercurrent in Britain. But to understand that ingress, a little backtracking is required.

Graham Hancock in *The Sign and the Seal* makes an intriguing case for the proposition that a detachment of Templars traveled from Jerusalem to Ethiopia in 1185 with the exiled Prince Lalibela, a descendant of the non-

Solomonic Zagwe dynasty, and helped to install him on the Ethiopian throne (1992, 162). As we shall see, this intervention into the affairs of Ethiopia may well have had a ripple effect on the Continent and in Scotland as well.

Hancock argues that thereafter subsequent waves of Templars, recruited largely from the Holy Land, were tending the Ark of the Covenant and building churches and stelae at the Ethiopian sacred centers of Axum and Lalibela. The Templars allegedly remained in those centers until shortly after Yekuno Amlak, a monarch claiming Solomonic descent, requested that the oral history of Ethiopia be written down in the *Kebra Negast* (1992, 162). Yekuno's purpose in ordering the writing of that history was to validate his Solomonic genealogy and wrest Ethiopia from the rule of the Zagwe dynasty, which had considerably less interest in the Ark of the Covenant than did the Solomonids. Given that in 1270, Naakuto Labab, the reigning monarch of the Zagwe dynasty, was pressured to abdicate his throne, the *Kebra Negast* transcription was begun.

The political strategy worked, according to Hancock. Yekuno Amlak ascended to the throne, restoring the dynasty of Solomon, Sheba, and their son Menelik, who centuries before had smuggled the Ark of the Covenant out of Jerusalem. From Jerusalem, Hancock argues, the Ark began its centuries-long journey first to the island of Elephantine on the Egyptian Nile, then to the shores of Lake Tana in Ethiopia, and eventually to the church of St. Mary of Zion in Axum where it still rests to this day high in the Ethiopian mountains (1992, 422ff.). But what was good news for the Solomonids was bad news for the Templars, for the project of tending the Ark ensured that the Templar remnant would eventually be killed or expelled from Ethiopia during the reign of Yakuno Amlak's grandson, Wedem Ara'ad. Hancock reveals that Wedem Ara'ad sent a delegation of about thirty ambassadors to the headquarters of the Papacy at Avignon, France between 1305 and 1306 to discuss matters unknown to historians with Pope Clement V, recently crowned at Lyon, and with King Philip IV of France (1992, 153). Hancock speculates that the Ethiopian delegation warned the Pope and France's King that the Order was conspiring to remove the Ark from Ethiopia. This Templar strategy, Hancock argues, would have transformed the already powerful Templars, the money brokers and bankers of Europe, into an invincible political force that might well have attempted to replace Papal authority with the Templars' Catharist theology. If Hancock is correct, this delegation served as the trip-wire which led to the demise of the Templar Order. For in 1307, just one year after the visit of the Ethiopian delegation, mass arrests of Templars occurred in France, leading to the trial and execution of thousands of Templars, including their Grand Master, Jacques de Molay (1992, 164ff.).

The reasons for the Templar plight are varied and intriguing. The Templars were perceived, rightly or wrongly, as a threat both to European royalty and clerics. Sir Stephen Runciman compares the fate of the two military orders, the Templars and the Hospitallers, in his three volume *History of the Crusades*:

> The Temple was less enterprising and less fortunate. It had always aroused more enmity than the Hospital. It was wealthier. It had long been the chief banker and money-lender in the East, successful at a profession which does not inspire affection. Its policy had always been notoriously selfish and irresponsible. Gallantly though its knights had always fought in times of war, their financial activities had brought them into close contact with the Moslems. Many of them had Moslem friends and took an interest in Moslem religion and learning. There were rumors that behind its castle walls the Order studied a strange esoteric philosophy and indulged in ceremonies that were tainted with heresy. There were said to be initiation rites that were both blasphemous and indecent; and there were whispers of orgies for the practice of unnatural vices. It would be unwise to dismiss these rumors as the unfounded invention of enemies. There was probably just enough substance in them to suggest the line along which the Order could be most convincingly attacked. (1954, II, 317-18)

The Church over-reacted. It declared the Grail legends heretical, and sought to end the Templar Order whose theology was, in the popular imagination at least, so irrevocably fused with those legends. And the Church may have played the ace in its hand, an ace to be used in the event of general public outcry, the potential news that the Templars were about to seize the Ark of the Covenant from Ethiopian hands. According to Hancock, Clement V and Philip IV were justly alarmed by reports that a contingent of Templars had discovered the Ark of the Covenant in Ethiopia. Given the Old Testament mystique of the Ark [which was fused with the image of the Grail, as noted previously], of its alleged ability to lay waste entire armies, level whole mountains and numerous other horrors, Clement V and Philip IV may have been so unnerved by the reports of Templar activity in the Axum area that they requested that an Ethiopian delegation be sent to Avignon. It may be simple cause and effect then that led to the arrests of numerous Templars, the common enemy of Axum and Avignon, just one year later. Certainly, the tableau that appears on the north porch of Chartres Cathedral should raise some eyebrows. For it depicts the Queen of Sheba, and the Ark of the Covenant resting on an ox cart. Hancock speculates that the intent of the Ethiopian embassy at Avignon was to recommend the liquidation of the Templar Order (Hancock 1992, 164). Such an intent could have been caused, by the Ethiopian's fear that the Templars planned to transport the Ark to French soil (Hancock 1992, 164).

Suffice it to say that the risky venture of decimating the Templar Order may well have been partially motivated by the testimony provided at Avignon by the Ethiopian delegation, which itself would have wished the Templars out of Ethiopia altogether. Or perhaps all of this was so much potential public relations to be used by the Church in order to influence the masses in case the Templar liquidation backfired and an angry flock stampeded toward Avignon and Paris. Perhaps it was naked greed alone that motivated Philip IV and Clement V and their lackeys, an overwhelming desire to confiscate the lands and the fortunes which the Templars had amassed during the two centuries in which they had served as the international bank of Europe, as it were.

But again. What does all of this have to do with the British Isles and to Scotland in particular? A great deal, for the mythic tide that had poured from Scotland, Ireland and Wales to the shores of Brittany in the form of the Grail legends seemingly flowed back to its source again in the form of a retreat of the Templars from France via Ireland to lowland Scotland, the original stomping grounds of Arthur, Guinevere, Merlin and the Knights of the Roundtable.

It would have been interesting to have been a fly on the wall during the off-and-on trial of Jacques de Molay and his fellow Templars who were unlucky enough to have been trapped by the fingers of the iron fist that Philip IV and Clement V squeezed round them. The over-blown and often specious linkage of the Templars' philosophy with the playful mockery of the Church found in Wolfram von Eschenbach's *Parzifal* must have been too tempting for the Inquisitors to dismiss, however, as their attempt to impose fiction onto reality spun out of control. After all, the Inquisition argued, Wolfram von Eschenbach claimed to be a Templar; the Templars all but refused to march against the heretics of Languedoc during the Albigensian Crusade, that same Languedoc that they hoped someday to rule as autonomous country; and Lancelot and Galahad, who bore the Templar's cross, were reputed to be descendants of David. And did not the Templars have a special interest in Solomon's Temple, the foundations of which they had excavated for several years? And did not I Kings 11: 4-5 clearly state that when Solomon grew old he openly worshiped the Mother Goddess Astharte and the Ammonite abomination Milco, instead of the patriarchal Yahweh? And was not the initiand knight required to wear the Pentangle,

Solomon's and Astharte's notorious love knot, when he entered the Grail castle before his final initiation? And were not the grail bearers themselves, of all things, women, and women in the esoteric, Sufic tradition at that (Godwin 1994, 137).

Underlying the trial of the Templars was the suspicion, rightly or wrongly held, that the Templars were poised to institute a new order in Europe and to unleash a new supra-national religion complete with a matrifocal, Languedoc-style hierarchy issuing forth the proper measure of Arianism needed to allow for a synthesis of Islam, Judaism and Christianity. Rightly or wrongly, the Templars were partially judged by the fanciful Grail legends that had been associated with them. And when fiction failed to provide the 'evidence' needed, tall tales of secret rites replete with lascivious sex, the worship of the head of Baphomet, the deification of both Mary Magdalene and the Sheba-inspired Black Madonna, were called into play. Bernard Clairvaux, founder of the Cistercian Order which finally rose to even greater prominence than the Templars, had not only written the rules of the Templars, but a song, based upon the Song of Songs, in which he depicted the Virgin as the beloved Shulamite, wife to both Solomon and Christ. Godwin notes that Sheba's cry: "I am black, but I am beautiful, O ye daughters of Jerusalem" reverberates in the Black Virgin cult to which Bernard subscribed (Godwin 1994, 208).

Doubtless, from Avignon's point of view some of the charges directed against the Templar Order were well-founded. Otherwise, Raymond Lull, who also hoped for a marriage of Islam and Christianity, would not have testified against the Templars and their Grand Master Jacques de Molay. But most had been blown out of all proportion by a greedy and paranoid Philip IV and his puppet Pope, who were synchronously salivating over the Templar riches which they were already confiscating. The Templar Order was like any other military group. It had its visionary philosophers and its practical men. Clearly, the soldiers and master stone masons and their extensive entourages were, in the main, practical men, not flaming revolutionaries and zealots.

In any case, it was certainly not ironic that contemporaneously with the demise of Jacques de Molay, and Geoffroi de Charnay, preceptor of Normandy, who were both slow-roasted over charcoal on a Parisian isle in 1314, and the curse of Molay that was about to be visited upon Philip IV and the Pope [who both died mysteriously within the year], the Templar remnant had reestablished itself in the land of the Grail to fight the English beside Robert Bruce, who had himself been excommunicated in 1306 for the murder of John Commyn. As Baigent and Leigh note, the western sea route around Ireland was likely used by the Templars from 1307-1309 given that English fleets did not patrol these waters (1989, 72). And after this alleged Templar hiatus, Robert Bruce, James Douglas and the Earl of Moray, were fairing as poorly during the Avignon Captivity as the Templars had a few years earlier. For by 1318 these heady Scots were again excommunicated by the Pope for refusing to collude with Edward I of England in demoting a group of nationalistic Scottish Bishops.

Converted or not-so-converted Saracens of various hues must have become a common sight in Scotland during the thirteenth and fourteenth centuries. The mention of transplanted Saracens included in the entourage of the Templar knight Sir Brian de Bois-Guilbert in Walter Scott's *Ivanhoe* points to this avenue of Moorish emigration prior to and after the battle of Bannochburn. Although Scott promoted the myth of the unscrupulous Templar in his portraits of both Bois-Guilbert, and Lucas de Beaumanior, the Grandmaster who chastises the lecherous Bois-Guilbert, Scott researched his novels carefully, and it can be assumed that in reality as in fiction numerous Saracens entered the midlands of Scotland in the service of their aging and retreating Templars.

John J. Robinson notes a little-known policy of the Templars during the period of the Crusades regarding prisoners:

> Before being killed or sold to the slave merchants, the prisoners were interrogated as to their occupations. All craftsmen were held aside to become lifetime slaves of the Order. There was a constant need for carpenters and stonemasons to maintain the Templar fortifications and a constant need for war materiel and equipment. It was simply not practical to import everything from Europe. At every Templar commandery there were craft shops turning out saddles, bridles, chain mail, and weapons. Supply wagons had to be built, and there were tents to be cut and sewn, horses in need of shoes, bread to be baked. The Muslim craftsmen became a vital part of the Templar war machine . . . . (1991, 347-48)

After the fall of Acre in 1291, the Templars likely would have retained their Muslim entourages as they fled the Holy Land, given that the members fully intended to serve in subsequent Crusades. Many Muslim craftsmen, several of whom could well have been stonemasons at Chartres and other sites, would have entered France and Britain shortly thereafter.

And when Clement V and Philip IV were orchestrating the destruction of the Templar Order in France from 1307-1311, the band of French Templars [which numbered more than 1000] who fled the wrath of that Inquisition appear to have made a series of escapes from Rochelle to

Scotland in order to serve in the army of Robert Bruce (Robinson 1991, 459). That a remnant of Templars escaped from France to Scotland is documented by so many historians and evidenced by so many grave sites in Scotland, that their arrival in the north is a certainty (Baigent and Leigh 1989, 472). Baigent and Leigh record Addison's observations: "Many [Templars], however, were still at large, having successfully evaded capture by obliterating all marks of their previous profession, and some had escaped in disguise to the wild and mountainous parts of Wales, Scotland and Ireland" (Baigent and Leigh 1989, 213). Or as A. Bothwell-Gosse explains: "In 1309 when the persecutions began, an inquisition was held at Holyrood, only two knights appeared, the others were legitimately occupied in the fighting, having joined Bruce's army, which was marching against the English" (1912, 105). And as the Templars disembarked at either the Mull of Kintyre or the Mull of Oa in Western Scotland, their Muslim entourages must have accompanied them, for if Baigent and Leigh are correct, they were preparing for battle against the English (1989, 32-34, 74-75).

In the wilds of Scotland, the Templars would certainly have required the skills of the converted Muslim craftsman just as they had in the adverse conditions of the Holy Land. Then too, massive shipments of arms were no doubt being funneled under an air of strict secrecy to Templar holdings in Ireland through ports such as Limerick, Galway and Donegal and on to Bruce's Scotland, thanks to the marriage consummated between Bruce and Elizabeth de Burgh, daughter of the Earl of Ulster. Given that neither Ireland nor Scotland was at that time capable of any massive arms industry, the materiel, as Baigent and Leigh propose, must have come from the Continent, for royal authorities had raided supply depots in Ireland (1989, 34). These installations were scattered throughout Ireland, notably in Dublin, counties Waterford, Wexford and Louth and outside of the town of Sligo (Baigent and Leigh 1989, 46-47). Clearly, numerous entourages would have been necessary to handle the logistics of transport, inventory, unloading, and maintenance of this extensive cache of arms that was being shipped by the remnant of the powerful Templar merchant marine fleet.

The victory at Bannochburn, secured with Templar support on their most holy St. John's Day, 24 June 1314, allowed the Templars, along with the members of their foreign entourage, to implant themselves and their Near Eastern and African-based esoterica more deeply into Scottish soil and to irrevocably alter the history of Scotland and England as well. It also furthered Robert Bruce's dream of restoring ancient Celtic traditions to Scotland and Ulster, traditions that were extremely compatible with esoterica espoused by the Templars. Not only did the victory at Bannochburn assure that Scotland would remain sovereign for another 289 years, but as Baigent and Leigh note, Scottish Templar traditions survived for another four centuries (1989, 76).

The upshot of the presence of the Templars in Scotland has often been overlooked. Clearly, Scottish Protestantism was heavily influenced by Freemasonry, which was the major legacy of the Templars. And Freemasonry was the receptacle of ancient Egyptian mathematics and science which had filtered down over the ages to Pythagoras, to the Jewish Cabala and to Sufism and other Muslim esoterica. For the Templars had learned much during their long hiatus in the Near East. One of those lessons was the taboo against making graven images, a prohibition which Islam had inherited from Judaism. The taboo resulted from the belief that man's attempt to depict the human form as well as any other natural shape revealed an attack on the Master Architect, God. Representational art was considered to be an insult to God, an attempt by man to compete with the Creator and to usurp His role. And this shibboleth against representational art led to Protestant architectural austerity especially in Scotland.

The building of the fifteenth century, Gothic-style Rosslyn Chapel by Freemasons in the valley of the North Esk, symbolized this viewpoint in Scotland. Maintained primarily by the descendants of the Black Douglas clan [Sir James Douglas], and of the Sinclair clan, whose ancestors stood with Robert Bruce at Bannochburn, Rossyln Chapel was also sacred to area Gypsies who made pilgrimages to its grounds each May and June. In an atmosphere that harkened back to pre-Christian, matrifocal Celtic rituals, the Gypsies would perform Robin Hood and Little John dramas and dance the morris dance every spring (Baigent and Leigh 1989, 118ff.).[4] In fact, this tradition of gypsy visitations began after 1559, for it was during that year that Sir William Sinclair, who was then Queen Mary's Lord Justice General of Scotland, opposed the harsh laws that were being passed to punish and deport Gypsies and saved at least one Gypsy from the hangman's noose (Baigent and Leigh 1989, 118).[5] Even today, Gypsies make annual pilgrimages to Rosslyn Chapel in Scotland.

The arrival of the Templars in Scotland before and shortly after Bannochburn certainly amounted to a resurgence of Catharist and related esoteric thinking in Scotland. But it was not the only resurgence. The *Domesday Book*, commissioned by William the Conqueror in 1085-1086, which, ironically enough, used the *plateae* census techniques learned from the Moslems in Sicily, records several intriguing surnames. As even the most casual glance reveals, many Normans bore surnames with the ubiquitous *moor* or 'black' root in them (Lindsay 1974, 275). This peculiarity is not overlooked by Mark Anthony Lower in Vol. 1 of *English Surnames*. Speaking of prominent Norman families such as the Morrices, Fitz-Morrices and Mountmorrises, he notes the following:

> They are supposed to be of Moorish blood, their progenitors having come from Africa by way of Spain into various countries of Western Europe. It is a well known fact that the peculiar species of saltation called the morrice dance and several branches of magic lore, were introduced into these centuries ago by natives of Morocco. The professors of these arts, enriching themselves by their trade, seem in some instances to have embraced Christianity and to have become founders of eminent families. Certain it is that several magnates bearing the name of Morice, Fitzmorice and Mountmorris attended William the Conqueror in his descent upon England and acquiring lands settled in this country (1875, 54).

Some of these transplanted Moors who found their way to Britain may have also come to England by way Sicily, thus adding to the ethnic countercurrent that resurfaced later in the Cavalier lifestyle. It is not widely known that numerous descendants of the Vikings who had conquered Normandy took a rather long hiatus in Italy and Sicily in the eleventh and twelfth centuries. Regarded by Rome as Saracens when convenient to do so and as allies when it was not, many Norman kings of Sicily revealed a coziness with their Moslem subjects and mercenary troops, an arrangement that angered Rome on numerous occasions. Often more concerned with accumulating wealth than participating in the Crusades, many of these Norman occupiers of Italy and Sicily helped to nurture a similar pragmatic, political bonding of Europeans and certain Moslem favorites, a venue which numerous Templars also followed.

The occupation of Mediterranean territory conducted by the Normans was a profitable one. According to Jack Lindsay, during the Norman conquest of Sicily, which dragged on from 1068 to 1072, Roger de Hauteville and his brother Robert Guiscard made an alliance with the Moslems of Catania before taking over the port and staging their siege of Palermo, a city also replete with Moslem inhabitants (1974, 266). It should be recalled that Moslem forces had established hegemony in much of Southern Italy and in all of Sicily by the middle of the tenth century. But by 1072 the Normans had secured Palermo, and, as Lindsay reveals, unlike the Crusaders who often made a habit of slaughtering Moslem captives, Robert Guiscard spared the populace, demanded a yearly tribute and tolerated Moslem religious and legal practices (Lindsay 1974, 269-70). Moslem affiliations with Normans, then, were ubiquitous. Learning early on that it was better to pit Moslem factions against one another and to built strong alliances with Moslem allies, the Normans also employed willing Saracens as mercenary soldiers. Without them, it is doubtful whether Robert would have been as successful in attacking Rome, defeating Emperor Henry IV and sacking the city in March 1084 (Lindsay 1974, 272). So enamored did Roger, Robert Guiscard's brother, become with Moslem customs during his rule in Sicily and in much of Southern Italy before his death in 1101, that he maintained an extensive harem stocked both with Moslem women and captured nuns from Reggio, Italy (Lindsay 1974, 272). His son Roger II became even more acclimated to this Mediterranean life-style. Lindsay explains: "He kept a harem in Moslem style, exercised the authority of a papal legate, and thus had more complete control of his church that had any western ruler; he issued orders in Latin, Greek, and Arabic to officials variously called justiciars, constables, logothetes, catapans and emirs" (1974, 273). Combining Roman, Byzantine and Moslem law and feudal customs, he, according to Lindsay, occupied the major North African ports that lay to the south of Sicily and elevated Sicily to the most prominent sea power in the region (1974, 274).

Norman Daniel appears to devalue the intermingling when he notes:

> In the East, changes in doctrine among Sufi sects are commonly attributed to the influence of Christians absorbed into Islam, but there seems to have been no [sic!] influence exerted by captured Arabs in Europe. We must assume that their numbers were small and that their social standing remained depressed. (1975, 141)

Despite Daniel's apparent disregard for Moslem influence and his lack of documentation to back that assertion up, he further notes Ibn Jubayr's contradictory observations in Ibn Jabayr's chronicling of the rule of the Norman vizier William II in Sicily:

> All the palace concubines were Muslim, but they had converted many Frankish palace women secretly to Islam. All these crypto-Muslims were particularly pious and given to good works, including the ransom of prisoners. Ibn Jubayr states specifically that William (who lived in great luxury) acted altogether like a Muslim king, especially in his methods of government, and that he was the gentlest of Christian kings-- towards Muslims, is implied. (1975, 147)

The hundred year period of relative harmony between the Norman rulers and the favored Moslems ended with the reign of Frederick II, the last of the Norman rulers. Unlike his predecessors, Frederick II felt little empathy toward the Arab population of Sicily. For it was he who transferred the remaining Arab enclave to the Italian mainland. Daniel reveals the consequences:

> He wanted them extirpated from Sicily, but he still had a use for them which was quite in the tradition of his Norman ancestors. Perhaps no racial group has ever been more callously treated, because these were not only uprooted and re-established in an alien environment, but they were isolated at Lucera on the Italian mainland, where they must have been wholly dependent for their safety on the Emperor, who therefore used them, willing or unwilling, as mercenaries to be expended at his will; the more unpopular they became, the more they were dependent on him. (1975, 154)

Oddly enough, in the 1220s Frederick II used various Lucera Arabs as mercenary soldiers. This angered not only Christian Crusaders but Pope Gregory as well, who sent a group of Dominicans to convert them (Daniel 1975, 154). Daniel mentions that the *Annales Siculi* frequently cite the use of Saracen mercenaries in the Crusades, and these notations include invectives against those particular mercenaries who allegedly raped and debauched Christian women (1975, 155). In fact, Frederick II, who was excommunicated for not crusading and then for crusading in his most unorthodox way, was viewed by many Christians as a kind of thirteenth century beast of the apocalypse. Mathew Paris, a chronicler of the time, notes that Frederick II's enemies accused him of such crimes as visiting the bed chambers of his little Arab girls [*muliercularum sarracenarum*], of embracing Islam more than Christianity, and of conspiring against the Catholic hierarchy (Daniel 1975, 163).

Frederick II's alleged Mediterranean internationalism, which so infuriated the Catholic hierarchy, finally ended with his death and the subsequent demise of Norman control in Sicily, the rule of which was taken up by the House of France and Charles of Anjou.

Despite Daniel's devaluation of Arab influence during this period, it must be admitted that the Arab presence was more alluring to the West than most European chroniclers care to admit. And another wave of Arab influence would also occur in the late sixteenth and early seventeenth centuries. Baigent and Leigh set up the prologue to this next wave, noting that a

> corpus of 'esoteric' material from Constantinople had found its way initially to Italy and finally to Scotland. Of the corpus from Spain forty years later,

much also reached Italy from the Low Countries, the Spanish dominions of Flanders and the Netherlands, along with hundreds of thousands of Moriscos who managed to escape Spain with little but their lives. There, the influx of refugees and ideas generated the Flemish Renaissance which paralleled the Italian. And by the beginning of the sixteenth century, the strands originating in Italy and the Low Countries had converged under the patronage of the Houses of Guise and Lorraine Thus, for example, the first French edition of the seminal *Corpus Hermeticum*, published in 1549, was dedicated to Charles de Guise, Cardinal of Lorraine-- brother of Marie de Guise, who married James V of Scotland and bore Mary Queen of Scots. (1989, 138)

This newly unearthed esoterica [the translations of which had largely been funded by the de Medicis of Florence] was sent to Scotland via Flanders with the aid of families such as the Stewarts, Setons, Hamiltons, Montgomerys and Sinclairs, and the newly-formed Scots Guard. In this there is an irony, for by now Scotland was firmly Protestant, and yet the imported material was being sent by Catholics and being consumed largely by anti-Papists of Rosicrucian convictions in Scotland. It was no secret that the hyper-Catholic Guise and Lorraine coalition, through its nascent, anti-Protestant Holy League, had ambitions of first ruling France and then the whole of Europe including the Papacy itself. But with the execution of Mary Queen of Scots and Duc de Guise's assassination shortly thereafter, the Holy League was history, as it were, and the esoterica, which was simultaneously fueling an anti-Papist Rosicrucian movement on the Continent, was no longer associated with the Holy League's propaganda campaign against Rome. As the months passed it was even more avidly absorbed by the Rosicrucians of Scotland with the assistance of the moderate Catholic, Stewart King of the Guise-Lorraine bloodline, James VI of Scotland. In 1603 this same James VI became James I of England.

Given that James I was himself a Freemason, Scottish Masonry filtered south to London. The outbreak of the Thirty Years War in 1617, precipitated when the nobles of the King of Bohemia awarded Frederick [who by then had married Elizabeth Stewart, daughter of James I] with the Bohemian crown, resulted in the mass exodus of thousands of highly educated German Protestants, many schooled in Rosicrucian enlightenment. They poured into England from Flanders and the Netherlands, narrowly escaping the German Catholic forces. Many of these refugees would later join the English and Scottish Masonic Lodges, giving birth to modern Freemasonry, which became known as the "Invisible College" during the upheaval of the English Civil War and the inimical Protectorate of Oliver

Cromwell. When the Restoration of Charles II was proclaimed in 1660, these progressive thinkers, who included Robert Boyle and John Locke, resurfaced and many were inducted into the Stewart-sponsored Royal Society.

But we need to return to the big picture of foreign ingress into the British Isles during this time frame. Clearly, the more well-heeled Saracens who arrived in Britain with William the Conqueror, or with returning Crusaders from Sicily and adjacent lands, or through the back door with the Templars, founded hybrid families of their own when they intermarried with the members of established or not-so-established Scottish and English families.

Others may have not fared so well. Years later the descendants of some of the less successful transplants may have joined the roving bands of sturdy beggars and Gypsies which the Tudors tried their best to extirpate from the realm.

To better understand the complex ethnic constituency of the Cavaliers, other migrations of people of color need to be cited. Simson attempts to document a migration from Spain, noting that nearly all of the Scottish Gypsies claimed that their ancestors came into Scotland by way of Ireland (1878, 91). More waves may have followed as the Reconquista reached its grisly culmination. In a footnote to *A History of the Gipsies* regarding an "infestation" of Gypsies in the Bombie territory of Galloway, the following information is presented: "On the publication of the edict of Ferdinand of Spain in 1492, some of the Spanish Gipsies would likely pass over to the south of Ireland, and thence find their way into Scotland, before 1506. Anthonius Gawino [referred to above], would seem to be a Spanish name. We may, therefore, very safely assume that the Gipsies of Scotland are of Spanish Gipsy descent" (1878, 98-99). And with all of these various immigrants, no doubt, came the essential elements of the Cavalier 'look.'

In regard to these later refugees, it is clear that fifteenth and sixteenth century Spain had ceased to be a safe haven for Muslims as one Moorish stronghold after another fell to the Christians. As a result of the overwhelming Spanish victories during the sunset of the *Reconquista*, the tables had turned, resulting in the expulsion of countless Moors and Berbers into North Africa. A fact not widely known, however, is that hundreds of thousands of Moors [known as Moriscos] who had converted to Christianity also escaped into Europe either across the Pyrenees or from Andalusian ports. Free of the Spanish, many settled in countries such as France, Germany, Holland, Italy and Britain. Doubtless, a number of these Moors would have been the descendants of of mixed blood marriages, for as Robert

Briffault observes in *The Troubadours*, in twelfth century Moorish Spain prior to the *Reconquista*: "Mixed marriages were of regular occurrence in all classes, whether plebeian, noble or royal" (1965, 62).

Before continuing our discussion of Moorish arrivals to the British Isles, the problem of the pigmentation of the Moors and Berbers who occupied Spain from the eighth century to the end the Reconquista needs to be dealt with briefly. Clearly, the Moors and the Berbers were by the late Middle Ages both white and black and all shades in between, but dark-skinned populations appear to have comprised the vast majority of the inhabitants prior to that later period. Van Sertima argues that much nonsense has been written about the subject of Moorish ethnicity. Many commentators, he notes, have concluded that since the first army to invade Spain under the command of Tarif and Tarik was a Berber army, the Moors and Berbers were predominantly and even exclusively Caucasoid (van Sertima 1985, 140). He cites two historians in particular-- Lane Poole, author of *The History of the Berbers in Spain*, in which the term Moor is often deemed synonymous with the terms Berber and Arab, and Charlotte Yonge, who, in *The Story of the Christians and Moors of Spain*, asserts that the Berbers were exclusively unmixed, blond-haired, blue-eyed Caucasoids. Van Sertima satirizes them all: "The Berbers have been called Caucasoids, Asiatics, Libyans, Semites, Ethiopians, even racially indistinguishable from the Arab of the Arabian peninsula. Every European who has chosen to write history has been free to take his pick" (1985, 141) He notes that Yonge, especially, is extraordinarily careful to dissociate Moors from Africans when the Moors have the upper hand in Spain, but then on page 175 of her study *The Story of the Christians and Moors of Spain*, she slips up, as it were, and indicates that when the Muslims experienced military defeats at the hands of the Europeans, the Muslim armies are suddenly described as Negroes, and "there was a frightful slaughter of the Africans." Van Sertima muses: "One wonders how they could have been practically non-existent in life and have such great presence in death" (1985, 141). That glimpse into one of several cover-ups offers a clearer lens with which to view the ethnicity of countless Moors during the Middle Ages.

It should be noted that many of the trappings and conventions of European knight errantry and courtly love were Moorish inspired. So great was their influence that Dante could write:

> Throughout the Islamic world there were brotherhoods, that may be described as orders of knights, which were . . . enriched by mysticism, as in the case of the Christian orders of knights. Their motto was the Arabic

expression *futuwa* [meaning] magnanimity . . . the chivalrous virtues of
fearlessness, charity and generosity. *'L'amor e il cuor gentil sono una coas'*-
- 'love and a generous heart are one and the same thing' (Carew 1992, 273).

The largely Moorish origins of the conventions of European knighthood may
explain why the character Morien was regarded as the model knight in the
Romance of Morien.

Paul Edwards cites other influxes of Moors into the British Isles which did
not directly stem from the Crusades nor the flight from the Reconquista.
Referring to an account in the *Orkneyinga Saga*, written during the period
of the Crusades, in which the fleet of Earl Rognvald Kali captured and later
freed a blue man off the Mediterranean coast, Edwards speculates that the
Vikings were not conducting a systematic slave trade during the period of the
Crusades. He goes on to state that "although the 'blue men' make an
appearance from time to time in the sagas, they do so as berserk figures in
a legendary and fantastic context and it seems unlikely that very many
Africans reached Britain by way of Viking ships." Nonetheless, he attributes
the remains of an African girl dated at c. 1000 c.e. at North Elmham to
Viking capture, as Quinn notes (1986, 52).

All was not so rosy regarding this Moorish influence in the British Isles.
Brunson and Runoko Rashidi indicate that a Viking raid in 862 c.e. on both
Spain and North Africa is recorded in Irish records entitled "Three
Fragments Copied from Ancient Sources." Many of the black Moorish
captives called "blue men," or *fir gorma* in Gaelic, finally disembarked in
Dublin: "After that, the Scandinavians went through the country, and
ravaged it; and they burned the whole land; and they brought a great host of
[the Moors] in captivity with them to Ireland. These are the 'blue men' (*fir
gorma*); because the Moors are the same as Negroes; Mauretania is the same
as negro-land" (1993, 28).⁶ To be sure, the Icelandic poet Snorri Sturlusson
in his thirteenth century *Heimskringla: History of the Kings of Norway*
notes that further north in Scandinavia: "There are many tribes and many
tongues . . . . There are giants and dwarfs; there are black men and many
kinds of strange tribes" (1967, 6). Then too, Rogers recalls that after their
expulsion from Spain, bands of Moors routinely raided the shores of the
British Isles for slaves, selling them later in the white market at Sallee. He
also notes that in 1631: "they attacked Baltimore Castle, Ireland, and their
leader, 'black Ali Krussa,' carried off Mary, daughter of Sir Fineen
O'Driscoll" (1980, 62, 70). Of the 17 June 1631 Baltimore raid in West
Cork, Quinn reveals that, in fact, 163 persons, the entire population, were

carried off to North Africa (1986, 44-45). Rogers further notes that in 1150 the Trinitarians were founded in Britain with the purpose of freeing Britons taken into slavery by Moors through purchasing them back (1980, 70).

The number of white 'slaves' taken from various parts of Europe and sold in North African markets appears to have been greatly underestimated. Possibly numbering in the millions, this influx of Caucasians significantly lightened the complexions of new generations of North Africans. Noting that large numbers of blacks were also imported from the Sudan into North Africa by Arab slave traders, Reynolds cites James Wellard's observation in *Lost Worlds of Africa* that millions of white Europeans slaves also entered the mix after being imported by Muslim Africans over a period of centuries into the North African ports such as Sallee, Tangier, Algiers, Tunis, Tripoli, Fez and Marrakesh. She goes on to note that various Christian organizations freed millions from North Africa in later times (1993, 93-94).

All relations between Scandinavia and the Arabs, however, were not antagonistic, for Eric Oxenstierna notes a report written by Ibn Hauqual around 850 C.E. regarding the fur trade conducted between Baghdad and the Vikings [the Rus] who had established trading posts around Kiev:

> Beaver pelts are found only on the northern rivers, which lie in the vicinity of Bolgar and Rus in Kiev. And what is found in Spain in the way of beaver also comes from the rivers of the Slavonic lands. The greater part of these furs, or should I say all of them, are to be found in the land of the Rus. (1965, 120)

The Russian 'backdoor' route was preferred for several reasons. Oxenstierna explains:

> Since the Vikings already dominated the Russian rivers, had even reached the Black Sea and encountered Arabic traders from the Caliphate in the Ukraine . . . why not shorten the whole, laborious, immeasurably longer trade route through France and across the Mediterranean and sell one's furs directly to the Caliph in Baghdad, without any irritating middlemen at all? (1965, 94)

The numerous hordes of Arabic coins found throughout Scandinavia and Scotland speak to the extent of Arab trade (Oxenstierna 1965, 131). Then too, the arrival of Arab delegates in Denmark in 848 for the purposes of trade negotiation indicate how extensive the ties between north and south really were (Oxenstierna 1965, 76). Although he doubted that Mac Ritchie was a credible source, the late Paul Edwards in *Essays on the History of*

Blacks in Britain, describes a scenario with which Mac Ritchie would no doubt agree:

> There is a curious story about McLelland of Bombie in Galloway, which refers to a supposed North African raid on Scotland around 1460. It is said of McLelland, whose son had quarreled with the King, that his crest bore a Moor's head 'because his Son killed a More, who came with some Sarazins to infest Galloway; to the killer of whom, the King promised the forfeiture of Bombie; and thereupon he was restored to his father's land.' (1982, 16)

Edwards goes on to note that "there is unquestionable evidence that Africans were reaching and settling in Scotland by the end of the fifteenth century, as a result, quite possibly, of attacks being made by the Scottish privateers on Portuguese shipping, the Portuguese being involved at this time in the growing slave trade" (1982, 16). Edwards cites a letter of reprisal from *Extracts from the Records of the Burgh of Edinburgh* regarding the sons of a Scottish merchant turned privateer, one Andrew Barton, who after being captured and imprisoned by the Portuguese, died in captivity in 1507. After his death, his two sons,

> having procured from James [IV] a renewal of their letters of reprisal, fitted out a squadron, which intercepted and captured at various times many richly laden carracks returning from the Portuguese settlements in India and Africa; and the unwanted appearance of blackamoors at the Scottish court, and sable empresses presiding over the royal tournaments, is to be traced to the spirit and success of the Scottish privateers. (1982, 16)

The "sable empress," Edwards explains, using the poet William Dunbar's recollections, was the Black Queen of Beauty at the tournament of the black knight and the black lady, one Elen More. However, Edwards is skeptical of Dunbar's account and argues that Elen's title was given in mockery of her blackness. Still, Edwards reveals that many of the Africans at the Scottish court in the late medieval and early Renaissance periods were not viewed as or treated as slaves (1982, 17-18).

In light of Edward's research, Mac Ritchie's often ignored assertions of a Moorish presence in Scotland are more plausible. Suffice it say that between roughly 1492 and 1610, especially during the period when Phillip III issued the Moorish expulsion orders, approximately three and a half million Moriscos exited Spain, with at least a million settling in France, and thousands more migrating to Holland, Germany and the British Isles (Lea 1968, 340-41).[7] A case in point was Elen More, previously mentioned, who in 1507 played the role of the black lady with James IV assuming the role of the black knight at the Edinburgh court. Elen, in regal fashion, had brought with her a veritable entourage of Moorish ladies and male attendants from Spain who entered Scotland at the port of Leith, and who for a time became a diversion at the Scottish court. And by 1596, a frustrated Queen Elizabeth decided to remove the swelling numbers of Spanish Moors from the kingdom by informing the lord mayors of various cities that "there are of late divers blakamores brought into this realm, of which kinde of people there are already too many, considerying howe God hath blessed this land with great increase of people of our nation as anie countrie in the world." The solution to this Moorish problem, according to the Queen, was that such persons should be banished from England, a threat repeated once again a year later (Vesey-Fitzgerald 1973, 30ff.).

Despite such royal pronouncements, things Moorish, including Spanish Cavalier dress, became quite fashionable in the British Isles during the Tudor era and beyond. Suffice it to say that during the fifteen, sixteenth and seventeenth centuries, light and dark-skinned mummers were ubiquitous in the village squares and courtly halls of the British Isles. Quinn refers to the Wexford Mummers, who

> dress in a kind of bishop's garb and face each other in a line. They use shorter sticks than the Egyptians and produce a greater noise, accompanied by fiddles and flutes of traditional Irish music. It is also a ritual of battle-- the military ranks in contrast with the man-to-man combat suggested by the North Africans-- but has definite religious overtones. It so happens that the term 'mummer' comes from the term 'Mohammedan,' itself a pejorative description used by Westerners to describe the religion of Islam. 'Mummery' is consequently defined in Western dictionaries as 'an absurd, superstitious rite.' (1986, 163)

Noting the xenophobia, Quinn cites the resemblance between these mummeries and the stick dance of North Africa, arguing that mummery commemorated the battles between Christians and Muslims (1986, 164).

The weight of such evidence and more caused Mac Ritchie to do some considerable soul-searching. Speaking of the ethnicities of the gypsy tribes, many of which traced their descent to the Moorish influx just examined, Mac Ritchie speculates on the racial composition of many modern Britons, using T. H. Huxley's slippery term "darkened whites." For Mac Ritchie proposes that although the population of Britain contains numerous "dark whites," it is obvious that these individuals are far more white than black, given that no Briton of his day could deemed as dark as a Negro. Nonetheless, there has been considerable racial admixture in the past, he insists (1991, II, 245).

Darkened whites? we may ask. With the term ringing in his ears, Mac Ritchie digs deeper into the gypsiology of his day, noting that although some Gypsies are clearly white, the conventional Gypsy is dark-haired, dark-eyed and swarthy (1991, II, 101).

Then Mac Ritchie hits the nerve when he argues that the contemporary darkened white of Briton, whether descended from a dark-haired, or a dark-skinned ancestor, may be akin to the ninth or the nineteenth-century Gypsy (1991, II, 101).

But to continue with the gypsy ingress, it is clear that in England Gypsies received a chillier reception during the sixteenth and seventeenth centuries than they had experienced in Scotland. In 1530 the English Privy Council passed an Act that cited the problem and offered a remedy. The problem was stated as follows:

> Afore this tyme dyverse and many outlandyeshe People callynge themselfes Egyptians, usying no Crafte nore faicte of Merchaundyce had comen into this Realme and gone from Shire to Shire and Place to Place in greate Company, and used greate subtyll and crafty means to deceyve the People, berying them in Hande that they by Palmestre could tellem Menne and Womens Fortunes and som many tymes by crafte and subtyltie had deceyved the People of theyr Money and also had comytted many and haynous Felonyes and Robberies to the greate Hurte and Deceyte of the People that they had comyn amonge . . . . (Vesey-Fitzgerald 1973, 29-30)

And for a remedy, the Council decreed that "From hensforth no suche Persone be suffred to come within this the Kynge's Realme" (Vesey-Fitzgerald 1973, 30). The Act went on to warn that if they did enter the realm, their goods would be confiscated and they would be jailed, and any Sheriff etc. who seized these goods would be awarded half of them (Vesey-Fitzgerald 1973, 31). Then too, it made one other significant change in the law by countermanding a provision of an Act that had been passed years earlier during the reign of Henry VI. That earlier Act allowed a jury to be packed with up to fifty-percent of Gypsies. But the 1530 Act decreed that juries from then on would be composed only of English non-Gypsies. Although the enforcement of the English Act of 1530 was difficult, greater pressure was applied in 1544 when several Gypsies were deported from Huntingtonshire to Calais, and from Lincolnshire to Norway. During Cromwell's dictatorship Gypsies faired poorly again, and, as Vesey-Fitzgerald reveals, near the end of the Commonwealth period thirteen Gypsies were sentenced and hung at one Suffolk assize, based upon the language of the 1530 Act (1973, 31).

But gypsy persecution ended abruptly during the Restoration of Charles II with the exception of an Act beyond Charles' immediate purview that had been passed in Edinburgh in 1665. That Act ordered the deportation of certain Gypsies to Barbados and Jamaica. Simson explains in *A History of the Gipsies*:

> In carrying out the foregoing extraordinary enactments, the public was at the expense of exporting Gipsies to the continent; and it may reasonably be assumed that great numbers of these unhappy people were executed under these sanguinary laws. A few years later before the restoration of Charles II, thirteen Gipsies were executed 'at one Suffolk assize.' This appears to have been the last instance of inflicting the penalty of death on these unfortunate people in England, merely because they were Gipsies. (1878, 92)

And in a footnote, Simson reveals that the problem of social ostracization was partially solved by the intermarriage between Gypsies and English non-Gypsies that began during this period (1878, 92).

All of this ethnic mayhem brings us back to Charles II and a question: Why did the scourge of the Tudor countryside become the vogue during the Restoration? And why had the Gypsies been relatively unmolested in Scotland for the 73 year period mentioned earlier? Mac Ritchie sets up the dialectic, stating a popular opinion that "'during the reigns of James I and his immediate successors, [the English] presented two different forms of national life, character, and customs, as if they belonged to two entirely different and even hostile races'" (1991, II, 363). The parties which represented these "entirely different" societies were the Cavaliers and the Parliamentarians. And, according to Mac Ritchie, their chief social differences manifested themselves in the fact that the Cavaliers, or 'Riders,' were of the horsemen caste with marked gypsy mannerisms. This caste was marked by flamboyant dress of fine silks and velvets; long hair, a lock of which was fastened with a colored ribbon; feathered sombreros worn at jaunty angles; and rough manners punctuated with a fair amount of cursing. Their antithesis, the Roundheads, were characterized by closely-cropped hair; plain dress; hats centered upon their heads; and language devoid of cursing. These Parliamentarians [Roundheads] eschewed the activities of the Cavaliers--cock-fighting, gambling, bear-baiting, horse racing, minstrelsy and the like (1991, II, 363-64). Mac Ritchie concludes: The two societies were totally dissimilar; and there is much reason for believing that this difference was, to a great extent, a matter of race. (1991, II, 364)

And one prominent Cavalier of the time, Prince Rupert, upon being defeated by the Parliamentarian party, espoused the life of a buccaneer. Mac Ritchie notes that he was not not as swarthy as his sable cousin, Charles II, but possessed of a "sallow complexion," nonetheless. He wore his shoulder-length hair in long tresses, one of which was tied by a gaudy ribbon which made him resemble a gypsy prince (1991, II, 253-54).

The single 'tress' referred to was the notorious love-lock, which Mac Ritchie, using Dekker's *Gulls Hornbook*, likens to a similar lock worn by gypsy, Hebridean women of the swarthy variety (1991, II, 8).

And Prince Rupert was not the only of Charles II's rogue associates, for Charles also awarded the notorious, Welsh-born pirate Henry Morgan a full pardon before appointing that cold-blooded killer to the post of Governor of Jamaica. Unfortunately, no accurate likeness of Morgan exists.

A period description, biased as it may be, of the Cavalier life-style dating to the English Civil War, reveals some of the frictions of the times. Christopher Hibbert cites it:

> divers of the Cavaliers will not be content to feed upon good beef, but must have mutton and veal, and chickens, with wine and tobacco each meal, and much ado to please them at all; causing also, men, women, and children to lie upon boards, while these Cavaliers possess their beds, which they fill with vermin. Besides, they fill the ears of the inhabitants with their blasphemous, filthy, and wicked language, which no chaste ear, nor honest heart, can endure; yea so desperately wicked are they, that those that billet them dare not perform any act of religion, neither to give thanks at meals, nor yet to pray, read, or sing Psalms; but, instead thereof, they fill their houses with swearing and cursings, insomuch that they corrupt men's servants and children, that those who were formerly civil have now learned to curse and swear almost as bad as they. And on the Lord's day these beasts spend their time in dicing, drinking, and carding, and other such abominations. And, whereas the chaplains that go with them should teach them better, some of them swear as bad as any of the soldiers. As, namely, one of the prince's chaplains swore by the flesh of God . . . with many other horrible oaths. And in a tavern the Friday after they came into the city, a lord's chaplain wished the devil might roast his soul in hell, if he did not preach such a sermon next Sunday as was never preached at Bristol, some part of which sermon was railing at the doctrine of predestination, calling it damnable doctrine of the Roundheads, and his very sermon in the pulpit burst out into a fearful oath. (1993, 128-129)

So what motivated the Cavaliers of the Restoration period to adopt the mannerisms of what, for Mac Ritchie and his sources, amounted to a conquered race?

Mac Ritchie provides a partial answer, noted earlier in this chapter, when he notes that Charles II was part Scoto-Norman, and that the Bruces, the Wallaces, the Stewarts and numerous other families were Normans and Flemings and not Scots (1991, I, 203). Hence, they felt some affinity with the gypsy population they encountered, and, as a result, the gypsy life-style became the fashion during Charles II's reign (1991, II, 373).

For Mac Ritchie, this dialectical attitude toward that life-style resulted from see-saw movements of these two disparate and at times hostile races. But what had caused Charles II to swing toward his darker side? And what other ethnic extractions helped to make up his darker side?

Mac Ritchie probes deeper, suggesting that there were four major waves of swarthy settlement in the British Isles prior to the entry of the fifteenth century itinerants noted earlier: These were: 1] a group he characterizes as painted "Moors" [Silurians, Druids, Blueskins, and Green Men], who occupied Britain prior the Roman occupation; 2] the Scots of ancient Ireland and Scotland, a group he links with the Italian Romani of the fourth century; and 3] the ninth-century Cimbri [Dani, East Men], also known as the black Danars, or black heathen, a group which demanded for a time "the tribute of the black army" from the Britons (1991, II, 400-01).

Jones also mulls over the identity of these Danes: "The Irish annalists were a lesson to all of us with their division of Norse invaders into White Foreigners, Norwegians (*Finn-gall*), and Black Foreigners, Danes (*Dubh-gaill*), but it was a lesson no one heeded; nor do we know why they distinguished them by color" (1984, 77). In a footnote, Jones notes that for the Welsh chroniclers: "Danes coming in by way of England and the Norwegians by way of Ireland were pretty well all black: Black Gentiles (*y Kenedloed Duon*), Black Norsemen (*y Normanyeit Duon*), Black Host, Pagans, Devils, and the like" (1984, 77). But the unknown author of *Breuddwyt Rhonabwy*, Jones observes "makes a brilliant if fantastic play with the 'pure white troop' of Llychlyn (Locklan) and the 'pure black troop' of Denmark, but even so the generalization carries truth" (1994, 77). The adjective 'black' in this instance does not appear to stand for evil, but for complexion, or why would not both invaders be described as black?

In any case, did Charles II, because of both his Norman and Italian 'blood,' exhibit an affinity toward the Romani remnant in the British Isles? Did that remnant form a large portion of his political constituency? And was the racial composition of Charles II rather common for the period, rather than atypical? In an attempt to answer these questions, it is necessary to reexamine Mac Ritchie's observations about this 'Romani' segment of the population of the British Isles.

As suggested earlier in this study, Mac Ritchie speculates that the Norman side of Charles' family may have been dark. Comparing period descriptions of the Northmen [Vikings who settled in Northern France] and the Normans, Mac Ritchie proposes that various Normans who may have been the products of mixed marriages with groups such as the Picardy Moors of France, were, comparatively speaking, a swarthy bunch, or in Borrow's words in regard to the Lovels, Bosvilles, Rolands and more-- "dark but not disagreeably so" (1991, II, 241).

Rogers' reference to Lower's *English Surnames*, also quoted earlier, in which Lower argues that eminent British families such as the Morrices, Fitz-Morices, and Mountmorrices [all variations of 'Moor'], were of Moorish blood, their ancestors having migrated from Africa to Spain, France and thence to the British Isles with the army of William the Conqueror, should also be kept in mind (1980, 81-82). Rogers further notes that in the *Domesday Book*, the survey ordered by William the Conqueror in 1085-1086, surname derivatives of Moor such as Morinus, Moriton, Moretania etc. were common as well as a "number of Blac's (Black) as Blackeman . . . and Blackmer, another form of Blackmoor. This is quite independent of the fact that Anglo-Saxon for black and white sounded much the same. They were spelt the same, *blaec*, meaning absence of color. White, however, was accented. I am dealing with families named 'black' that had Negroes" (1980, 81-82).

And Charles' possible dark Norman strain was darkened still, as previously noted, by the de Medici infusion, a pedigree that could have derived in part from a Romani-gypsy and Latin mixture in earlier times. But, recalling that Charles' father was also described as being dark, and that coins of the period which feature his likeness reveal unmistakable Negroid features, could his Scottish ancestry also have accounted for his swarthiness? To answer this question and to further understand Charles II's proclivity toward the gypsy life-style that he and his fellow Cavaliers embraced, it is necessary to examine yet another page that has been deleted from many recent history books, the Romani exegesis in both ancient Italy and in the ante-Caesarian British Isles.

There were fair-skinned as well as dark-skinned Gypsies living in the British Isles during the Restoration period, according to Mac Ritchie. Drawing from various legends and studies of gypsyism [which include Borrow's *The Romany Rye* and *Lavengro*], he indicates that there were probably three predominant classes of Gypsies in the British Isles-- the Gwyddyl, Brython and Romani. He proposes that the Cavaliers appeared to feel a kinship with the Romani segment emblemized by John the Faw, who, in a ballad of the period, was described as "black, but very bonny" (1991, I, 541ff.; II, 346ff.). Mac Ritchie mulls over the Romani remnant which still inhabited Scottish Clydesdale, Tweeddale and Annandale during the eighteenth century, and proposes that they spoke the language of the Romani because of a Romani invasion of the area one thousand to fifteen hundred years earlier (1991, II, 348). Arguing that more distant countries such as Romania and India were not likely candidates for the origins of certain Scottish and Welsh Romani, he reasons, based upon the testimony of many a Scottish Gypsy, that a migration from Ethiopia and Nubia to Italy, a country much nearer at hand, should also be considered as a possible point of departure (1991, II, 345). He then attempts to weave the Romani strain into the genealogy of the black Scots who once ruled lower Scotland. These black clans of Southern Scotland include certain branches of the Kennedys, Marshalls and Black Douglases, whom, he argues, may well trace their descent from mixed Scots and Egyptians, and black strangers called *dubh galls* who were not associated with the Romani (1991, II, 349).

Referring to common surnames in Southern Scotland such as Romney, Romsey and Romford, and the term 'black speech' or *dubh chainnt*, which in James Boswell's and Samuel Johnson's vocabulary evolved into the term 'cant,' Mac Ritchie probes more deeply into the alleged Romani connection in Scotland, arguing that those who identify themselves as Romanes, and who call their speech Romanes, are members of the some of the darkest-skinned elements of the British Isles of his day (1991, II, 350). He goes on to propose that this group speaks a language called *Romani Fib* and *Kaulo Fib* [black speech, or *dubh chainnt*] and argues that the Romani invaders were black (1991, II, 350).

To distinguish the ancestors of the Romani remnant in the British Isles from the Latins, who ruled ancient Rome at the time that these Romani ancestors were still living in Italy, Mac Ritchie argues that as late as the twelfth century c.e. Latin and Roman were two distinct languages, and that the ancient Latins were not the Romans Proper, given the numerous ethnological differences between the two groups (1991, II, 350). The Latins, he reasons, had been white-skinned Northmen, who, upon conquest of the Roman peninsula, regarded the indigenous, dark-skinned population as being quite as amusing as the white gentry in Edinburgh later regarded their Moorish court minstrels. He reveals "that the Latin-speaking classes of the time of Agricola-- though calling themselves Roman-- amused themselves after dinner by 'bringing in the Moors,' much in the fashion of the Edinburgh citizens of three or four centuries ago" (1991, II, 359). He goes on to note that if it can be admitted "that a red-skinned Coptic people called themselves

Romi or *Romani*, then it is easy to see how-- if they emigrated from Egypt--
they would be called *Egyptians* (afterwards shortened to *Gypsies*) to other
people" (1991, II, 352). To verify his claim, Mac Ritchie once again refers
to Simson's *A History of the Gipsies*, where Simson notes that various
Scottish Gypsies referred to themselves as "Pharaoh's people" and
"Ethiopians" (1991, II, 352).

So   what exactly is going on here? Who were the Romani of ancient
Rome and ante-Caesarian Britain, if they were not Latins?

Although MacRitchie formed his hypothesis about the dark Romans and
the white Latins prior to the advent of modern archeology, later excavations
in Southern Italy, Sardinia and Sicily tend to support his view.   According
to B. H. Warmington (1960), in the eighth century B.C.E. Southern Italy was
a melting pot controlled by the Phoenicians, the Carthaginians and the
Greeks, with the Carthaginians being the major players (Sherrat 1980, 227).
Recalling Gsell's conclusion mentioned earlier in this study that skeletons
exhumed at Carthage revealed an overwhelming Negroid proportion, and the
proposition that some Phoenicians and pre-Hellenic Greeks were dark-
skinned, a considerable African presence must have existed in Southern Italy
well up to the vicinity of Rome itself.   Phoenician-Carthaginian hegemony
in Western Sicily at the port of Motya and in Sardinian cities such as
Tharros, Sulcis, Caralis, and Olbia was, of course, canceled out by the Latin
speaking Romans who temporarily subdued the Carthaginians during the
first Punic War.[8] That war ended in 146 B.C.E. with the Roman conquest of
Sicily, Tunisia and much of Spain, and the victory may have dispossessed
many of the darker survivors of Punic origin both in Southern Italy and in
Sicily.

Mac Ritchie attempts to backtrack to a Romani-gypsy migration from
Ethiopia and Egypt to Italy and eventually to parts north, a trek that may have
washed onto Italy's southern shores in the wake of the Phoenician-
Cathaginian hegemony that existed prior to the first Punic War. From there
some Ethiopian and Egyptian itinerants may well have migrated to Scotland,
he proposes (1991, II, 353). Arguing that Nubians and Ethiopians could
have arrived in the British Isles prior to the Christian era, Mac Ritchie cites
the observations of Pliny and Claudian who had observed that tribes of
Ethiopians and Moors inhabited Britain prior to Caesar's invasion (1991, II,
353).   Mac Ritchie stresses the point, recalling traditions noted earlier in
this study that in the pre-Caesarean era, Gadela, an Egyptian tribal chief, and
Scota, the alleged daughter of an unnamed Pharaoh, landed in Ireland, and
that the Emerald Isle harbored an Egyptian influence that lasted for centuries
(1991, II, 323).

And then Mac Ritchie speculates as to why Charles II found his royal self to be so at home with gypsyism. First, he proposes, the Scots of ancient Ireland, also known as Egyptians, may have been of the same racial stock as Italy's Romani. In the fourth century c. e., he goes on, these Egyptians "swarmed across St. George's Channel in Wales," bringing with them the harp and their oracular acumen. For evidence, he argues that in Ireland, the purest Romanes' tongue can still be heard, and, anticipating Morris Jones, he notes that Welsh contains a number of Romanes cognates. He goes on to reveal that the place-names Wales, Galloway, and Inchegall mean the country of "The Foreigners" (1991, II, 354).

He concludes the matter, arguing that Egyptians likely colonized Italy, Iberia, the Islands of the Oestryminides, and the British Islands, prior to the invasion of Julius Caesar. This group probably identified themselves by the Coptic word for 'man' in variants of *Rom, Romi*, or *Romani* (1991, II, 360).

Not finished, he adds a dash of spice to the stew. The Roman armies themselves could have brought still more Romanis to Britain during their invasion, for Caesar's soldiers did not find Druidism exotic, and, in anticipation of Birley's biography on Septimus Severus, Caesar may have included a number of Blueskins and Green Men in his own forces (1991, II, 360.

Citing Skene again, Mac Ritchie goes from there to indicate that a considerable number of the descendants of the Roman soldiers, allegedly comprising part of Caesar's armies, remained in areas such as York, Tweeddale and Clydesdale after the Roman Empire disintegrated (1991, II, 361). When we combine these dark Romanes into the mix, it is no wonder that a Cavalier movement arose centuries later.

The latest biography of the African Emperor of Rome Septimus Severus corroborates Mac Ritchie's observation. Anthony Birley relates an incident that occurred in 209 c.e. near the end of Septimus' life when he was hold up near Carpow in Northern England:

> After giving a Moor his discharge from the army, on the Wall . . . a certain 'Ethiopian' (black man) from the military numerus, with a wide reputation as a buffoon, and always noted for his jokes, met him with a garland made from cypress-boughs. When he ordered that the man should be removed from his presence, in a rage, being upset by the man's color and the ill-omened nature of his garland, the man is said to have called out, as a joke: 'You have overthrown all things, conquered all things, now be a conquering god!' When he [Septimus Severus] reached the town he wanted to make sacrifice, by a mistake on the part of the rustic soothsayer, in the first place he was taken to the Temple of Bellona, and then the sacrificial victims that were

provided were black. Then, when he had abandoned the sacrifice in disgust, and had withdrawn to the Palace, through the attendant's carelessness the black victims followed him right up to its doors.' (Birley 1972, 10-11)[9]

This is an ironic incident since the Numidian-born Septimus was himself rather swarthy as indicated by his portrait that Birley reproduces. And clearly Septimus' tantrum indicates that race prejudice must have existed at least from Roman times whether black on black or white on black.

In any case, Birley reveals that Moors in the Roman Legions were not uncommon in Britain, adding that "curiously enough, at the fort of Abavalla (Burgh-by-Sands), west of Luguvalium (Carlisle) on Hadrian's Wall, the garrison in the third century included a *numerus Maurorum*, an auxiliary unit of Moors" (1982, 10). Regarding this numerus, Edwards proposes that it was probably founded by the Emperor Marcus Aurelius (161-80 A.D.) and would therefore have served both on the Continent and in Britain (1982, 10). Edwards and Walvin also reveal that archeological evidence indicating the likely presence of an Africoid component of the Roman armies surfaced from digs at Roman-British cemeteries, where several skull measurements indicate the burials of Negroid Africans (1976, 172). These sites include York and Trentlholme. And they also mention the excavation of a skull that doubtless came from a "Negress or a woman with predominantly Negro genes in her chromosomes" (1976, 173). Edwards and Walvin also refer to a funerary inscription located on the Wall of South Shields recording the demise of 'Victor, aged 20, of the Moorish nation, freed by Numerianus,' and a recent dig at the Roman site at Southwark Bridge in London that produced a spoon of wood with an African head carved on it (1982, 10). Finally, Edwards and Walvin cite evidence of Anglo-Saxon trade beads discovered on the East African coast, beads that date prior to the sixteenth century C.E. They conclude that there must have been considerable trade between Africa and Europe in the late Middle Ages (1976, 173).

Moving to the thirteenth century C.E., Mac Ritchie again thickens the ethnic stew by referring to a Cornish chief, Richard, Earl of Cornwall and member of the Cheshire family, who styled himself as the "King of the Romans." This alleged Romani Earl, is credited with the founding of Burnham Abbey, an enclave of black priests, Mac Ritchie explains. Henry VIII broke up such Romani-founded establishments hundreds of years later, he goes on, forcing many a swarthy monk into a life of beggary (1991, II, 361-62).

Was Charles II privy to all of this? Probably not to all of it. But he likely knew enough about his mixed origins to figure out exactly where he stood after the raging battles of the Civil War that finally led to the beheading of his father Charles Stewart. Hibbert, biographer of the English Civil War, notes that Charles I was himself described as "a tall black man over two yards high" (1993, 290). And Charles II, along with his fellow caballeros, knew enough about his bizarre heritage to remain loyal to the mores of foreign Catholics and, perhaps, to those dark-skinned descendants of ancient Rome which the Tudors had attempted to drive out of England.

Were these dark-skinned, gypsy and Romani inhabitants of the British Isles numerous enough in times past to have altered the gene pool of nineteenth and twentieth century Britain? Mac Ritchie hazards a guess, noting the hybridization of the English population, whose diverse *histories* are quite brief (1991, II, 399). And he goes on to propose, as Daniel Defoe did before him in a satiric poem ironically entitled "The True-born Englishman," that most Britons cannot trace their genealogies to ancient times. As a result, he continues, "Unless the chain that appears to join him to the man of a thousand years ago is one unbroken series of links, the reputed pedigree is no pedigree at all" (1991, II, 399).

Notes

1. Also see Rogers (1972, II, 24ff.). He provides a profile of Alessandro de' Medici, who was nicknamed the Moor.
2. As a point of information, the origin of the name 'Alban' is still up for grabs. According to E. J. Brill's *First Encyclopedia of Islam* (1982), Arran or Al Ran was the ancient name of the mountainous, Eastern European country the Greeks would later call Albania or Ariania. The Muslims conquered Arran [today's Albania] during engagements lasting from 644-656 C.E. It is possible, then, that the Scottish nomenclature could be a corruption of Arran and Al Ra and that the two main islands, one off the coast of Galway and the other off the coast of Scottish Kyle, could be of the same Islamic derivation. Another possibility is that Alban is derived from a late first millennium B.C.E. and early first millennium C.E. kingdom of Albani located to the west of Colchis on the eastern shores of the Black Sea. Interestingly enough, sandwiched between Armenia, Colchis and Albani was another tiny kingdom called Iberia. See McEvedy (1982, 74-81).
3. J. Lawson (1955, 14-15) sheds more light on the origins of the Morris dance explaining that "when the Crusading armies met it among their allies, and their enemies, they might attach the name of 'Morris' and 'Morisco' to it. Probably, too, when attempting to dramatize current events, they would blacken their faces and pretend to be Moors. This may explain the curious Morris Dances of Bacchus in Lancashire and Provence, where the dancers wear half coconuts on their knees, waists, and hands, and clap out intricate rhythms as they dance energetically, in much

the way that young men in certain Turki tribal rituals slap themselves with their bare hands. The use of the coconut reinforces the suggestion that this dance was a copy of Moorish antics, for the coconut is of African origin, just as the floating ostrich plumes of the Basque Morris dancers also originated from Africa."

For Massey (1995, 306-307) the doubling of Horus was preserved intact in pre-Christian Britain and still exists in modern rituals that parallel the Christian mythology superimposed onto the Egyptian debris. The Christmas mummers offer a case in point, for, he argues, during the Christmas season, when the mummers performed at each house, the sun was in its darkest depths, a plight which was symbolized by the mummers in black face.

4. See Graves (1966, 396). He provides the matrifocal base of the Robin Hood myth . Rogers notes another Moorish presence in the British Isles. Evidence for the growing influence of Moors both in France and the British Isles could be derived from literary works such as *Chanson de Roland* (ca. 1100) which depicts events that occurred nearly three hundred years before the Norman Conquest. Rogers (1980, 56) explains that the work was originally composed in 718 C.E., shortly after the Moorish invasion of Spain and Southern France, noting that the Moorish forces were "50,000 strong and led by Marganice, Emperor of Ethiopia and Carthage. Their most valiant figure is Abisme" which may signify Abyssinia. The epic describes Abisme as follows: "At their head rides the Saracen Abisme: no worse criminal rides in that company, stained with the marks of his crimes and great treasons, lacking faith in God, Saint Mary's son. And he is black, as black as melted pitch . . ." See *The Song of Roland*, trans. F. Goldin (1978, 99). In the *Chanson*, the Moors are said to have come from: "Ethiope, a cursed land indeed;/ The blackamoors from there are in his keep,/Broad in the nose they are and flat in ear,/Fifty thousand and more in company." See *The Song of Roland*, (1938, 58). And later in the epic, the Moors are demonized further when Roland spots a race of infidels, "those hordes and hordes blacker than the blackest--/ no shred of white on them except their teeth." See *The Song of Roland*, trans. F. Goldin (1938, 107). Rogers (1980, 56) also cites the existence of black characters in the King Arthur legends: "in the *Romance of Morien* . . . Sir Morien (that is, Moor) is described as 'all black, his head, his body, and his hands were all black, saving his teeth . . . Moors are black as burnt brands. But in all that men would praise in a knight he was fair, after his kind. Though he were black what was the worse? In him was naught unsightly; he was taller by half a foot than any knight who stood beside him . . . Morien was blacker than any son of man whom Christian had ever beheld." Rogers (1980, p. 56) also mentions that another of King Arthur's knights was none other than the black knight Sir Palamedes. He goes on to reveal that Morien and Palamedes both converted to Christianity and fought against the forces of Islam.

5. Sinclair (1992, 123) notes that the Sinclair surname was originally Mor and Moray, but that it was changed in the tenth century in Normandy.

6. Jones (1984, 216) reveals more about this interesting ingress of Moors into Ireland, speaking of the African captives taken during Viking raids into Moorish Andalusia and into North Africa the ninth century: "We next hear of them at the Guadalquivir, where they seem not to have prospered. It is doubtful whether, as

some Moorish sources say, they preceded upriver as far as Seville. Soon they had
passed through the Straits of Gibraltar, put in at Algeciras, plundered it, then made
for the North African shore in the region of Cabo Tres Forcas. The local defense
force panicked, and the Vikings spent an unharassed week of rounding up prisoners
for ransom, though some, probably Negroes, they kept as *souvenirs de voyage*.
These poor wretches, *fir gorm*, blue men, *blamenn*, black men (or merely men with
dark skins), for the most part ended up in Ireland." In *Essays on the History of Blacks
in Britain*, Edwards (1982, 11), citing one of the fragments of the ancient Irish
Annals recopied by John O'Donavan, notes an 862 C.E. Viking raid in what is today
Morocco: "After this the Locklann (i. e. the Vikings) passed over the country (i. e.
Mauretania, mod. Morocco) and they plundered, and burned the whole country, and
carried off a great host of them [the Mauretani] as captives to Erin, and these are the
blue men [of Erin] (O. I. *fir gorma*), for they are the same as the black men (nigri);
Mauretania is the same as blackness (nigritudo). It is a marvel if every third man of
the Locklanns escaped between the numbers who were killed and those who were
drowned of them in the Gaditanean Straits [i.e. the Straits of Cadiz]. Long indeed
were these blue men in Erin. Mauretania is opposite the Balearic Islands.'" Edwards
further speculates that like the black African Roman soldiers, these 'blue men' must
have been assimilated into the local populations.

7. Lea (1968, 340-41) notes that in 1610, 20,000 to 25,000 Moriscos from Aragon
passed both through Navarre and over the Pyrenees to France. He goes on: "The
Spanish writers give a deplorable account of their sufferings on the road and state
that they were at first refused admittance, but were subsequently allowed to enter on
payment of a ducat a head; and they eagerly purchased licences to carry arms, and
then, after spending money on the weapons, they were deprived of them. In fact, this
was a very different outcome than the French had expected from their intrigues with
the Moriscos, and this dumping upon them without notice or agreement, of what was
regarded as an undesirable population, was not likely to be looked upon favorably.
In anticipation of it, Henry IV, in February, issued an ordinance permitting those who
would profess the Catholic faith to settle in the lands beyond the Garonne and the
Dordogne, while vessels should be provided to convey those who desired to go to
Barbary. Under this . . . nearly 17,000 from Castille had entered France up to May
1rst, soon after which the assassination of Henry threw everything into confusion."

8. See Sherrat (1980, p. 227) for a diagram of Phoenician, Carthaginian and Greek
influence in Italy during the eighth century B.C.E.

9. See Magie (1922, I, 434-37). Also see Edwards (1955, 14-15). He examines
race prejudice amongst the Romans when he questions Frank M. Snowden's
unwarranted assumption that racism as we know it today rarely existed in the Roman
and early Christian period in Europe. Noting the self-hate implicit in Severus's
reaction cited above, he discovers early Christian prejudices which exalted the
whiteness of the souls of virtuous blacks. Indeed, Edwards proposes, for the early
Christians blackness was synonymous with everything evil and threatening, as in
Snowden's quotation from Paulinus of Nola: 'Black people burnt not only by the sun
but black with vices and dark with sin.' Edwards also quotes a Greek epitaph:
'Among the living I was very black, darkened by the rays of the sun but my soul,

everblooming with white flowers, won my master's goodwill, for beauty is second to my noble soul, and it is this which covered well my black body.'" Edwards concludes from these and other early racial epitaphs that the color of the black African symbolized devilry and witchcraft to the late Roman and early medieval mind-sets and justified the Christian concepts of racism, for to many early Christians "black skin was God's punishment inflicted on certain descendants of Noah, the family of Noah's son Ham, or Cham, for disobeying a divine command requiring sexual continence in the floating ark."

Chapter17

~~~~~~

What's that Moor's head doing on my family crest? A purposive sample of Heraldry and surnames in the British Isles

It is safe to assume that not many people have seen Sir Thomas More's family crest. It is all but buried in an obscure document entitled the *Yorkshire Genealogist*, Volume 2, page 78. And what appears on page 78? The visage of a blackamoor with curly hair, thick lips and jet black skin. The figure is positioned above a field of bearded unicorns and exotic sea birds.[1]

Regarding More's more distant ancestry, little is yet known. However, Margaret Hastings (1961) traces his immediate precursors in *The Ancestry of Sir Thomas More*. Hastings notes that Thomas' father was named John More. John, a London lawyer, was born around 1450 and died at the extraordinary age of 79 in 1530. And Thomas' grandfather was William More, a London baker, who married Johanna, daughter of a London brewer named John Joye. Johanna's grandfather on her mother's side was John Leycester, a London Chancery clerk, who died in 1455. According to one of Sir Thomas More's biographers, E. E. Reynolds, Herald's records of Henry VIII's reign reveal that Thomas' father, John More, was awarded his grant of arms during Edward IV's reign, and that he inherited More Park, an estate in North Mimms, Hertfordshire from his mother's grandfather, John Leycester (1965, 19).

More's crest, according to Reynolds, consists of "a Moor's head (*affrontee sable*) with two gold earrings." Its other features, she notes, are described in heraldic language as "*Argent a chevron engrailed between three moorcocks sable crested gules*" (1965, 19 fn. 5). But why was such a crest selected?

Other biographers of More provide similar information. Richard Marius' chapter on More's genealogy in *Thomas More: A Biography* corroborates Hasting's and Reynold's findings. Marius reveals that "we lose track of More's family swiftly once we go back before his father," noting that the family tree abruptly ends with Thomas' grandfather William (1984, 5). Thomas More's earlier ancestry then appears to be lost. All that may be left to posterity beyond that genealogical dead end is the crest itself.

What   is to be made of similar heraldic images of Moors' heads that appear on the crests of several families which spell the surname More somewhat differently? J. A. Rogers indicates that blackamoors appear on the crests of other families with the More or Moore surname in "London, Berkshire, Kent, Canterbury, Wiltshire, Suffolk, Derbyshire, Ireland, and many others including some mentioned in *Burke's Peerage* as the Earls of Drogheda" (1980, 81).

So   how and why did the blackamoor image find its way to these and the Lord Chancellor's family crests? E. L. Ranelagh notes that the three components of European chivalry-- the conventions of knighthood, strong class distinctions, and respect for the female-- were in reality medieval exports from Moorish Spain to Christian Europe (1979, 151). Accompanying these came another Moorish export that was eagerly adopted by the English upper crust, namely the trappings of heraldry (Ranelagh 1979, 153). Might that explain the Moor's head on Sir Thomas' family crest? Was it simply the fashion to adapt Moorish heraldry to the English style without effacing or modifying the original crests?   Or was the surname More in all its various forms really a modification of the Anglo-Saxon *mor*, meaning 'damp wasteland,' rather than *Moor*? Would the phonetic similarity between *mor* and the surname More, then, have led to the use of a visual pun? Or did the Moor's head appear not to signify the likeness of a family progenitor, but to celebrate the victory of family heroes over the Saracens during the Crusades? Or did it merely extol the triumphs of English mercenaries who may have secretly fought with the Spanish against the al-Andalusian Moors and Berbers prior to the Moorish expulsions from France and Spain?

To answer the first question, the use of the Moor's head could have been a borrowing from Islamic crests. The Templars adopted a Triple Head of Wisdom for one of their insignias which likely honored the Saracen

Hashimiyyah fraternity after which the Templars modeled their controversial order. Given that the conventions of Islamic secular art allowed for human representation during the period of Third Crusade, when Fox-Davies in *A Complete Guide to Heraldry* argues that European Heraldry was created using Moorish models, English imitation is possible (1968, 9ff.; Chandler 1996, 304).

The answer to the second question regarding the derivation of the surname More from the Anglo-Saxon *mor* is a rather complicated one. The mere imitation of the phonetic likeness seems dubious in most cases unless punning were involved between the Moor's head and the word *mor*. A careful perusal of the motifs of Heraldry employed by other prominent families of the British Isles found in works such as *Fairbairn's Book of Crests*, or *Fox-Davies' Armorial Families*, or *Elwin's Book of Crests*, uncovers similar crests well-stocked with blackamoors. Would these other More-Moore names have involved punning as well? Rogers is well aware of the Anglo-Saxon word *mor* which means 'damp wasteland,' but he proposes that *mor* is not the root of the surnames he examines. Rogers argues that "since the Romans colonized Britain and were there fully five centuries before the Anglo-Saxons, it is safe to say that Mauros (Moor) as a surname, was deposited in the English language before the Anglo-Saxon, *mor*" (1980, 79-80). Additionally, he reasons, the *mor*-Moor connection falls apart when families with surnames such as Blackmoor and Blackamour, which derive from 'blackamoor,' are found to have Moors' heads in their heraldry as well (1980, 80). But there is another possibility here that Rogers may have overlooked. Reynolds notes that 'Berber' is an indigenous term in North Africa, and that it was not originally synonymous with the Greek and Roman term 'barbarian' (1993, 108). She derives the title from the title for wells and water sources which are so paramount in pastoralists' survival (1993, 108). Could that derivation have been translated from Berber to *mor* in the British Isles? Might the word *mor* have become a *double entendre* in some cases, indicative of a North African who sailed the Atlantic seaway to arrive at the British Isles? The idea is intriguing and may blunt the arguments of those linguists and genealogists who propose that the surnames Moor or More derive from the Anglo Saxon root *mor*. Reynolds ends her discussion of the Berber etymology with this interesting observation: "The ancient Berbers were ethnically related to pastoralists and nomads of Nubia and extending to the Red Sea. There were the first to be called 'Maurusoi' or 'Moors'" (1993, 144). So it is the Red Sea basin, apparently, where the association of water with the name *Moor* is to found in its nascent form.

And there is a literary allusion to Sir Thomas that may cast more light on the More surname. Joseph R. Washington cites the vitriolic, Puritan-Anglican clergyman Peter Heylyn [1599-1662], who in his rather pretentious *Cosmographic: Four Books Containing the Chronographic Histories of the Whole World* uses what today would be construed as a racial slur to vilify the deceased Catholic Thomas More. Heylyn calls him "our Sir Thomas Moor'" (1984, 144). In so doing, Heylyn was referring to a particular passage in More's *Utopia* in which More proposed that just as a man inspects a horse before he purchases it, so should a potential groom peruse his future bride in the buff before tying the marital knot. According to Washington:

> Heylyn read blackness into this passage, tarring More with the flat statement that only in black Africa do men and women 'go naked, til they are married; and then to be clothed only from the waist to the knees.' The sin of nakedness and the mark of blackness were attributed to Sir Thomas More for simply pointing out that if men bought horses only after inspecting them 'in naked carcuse,' why then in 'chusing a wife, should we take one, of whom we see no more than the face and perhaps not that?' (1984, 145)

Was this deliberate misspelling of More as Moor, in fact, based upon mere wit, or upon Heylyn's possible belief that Sir Thomas was descended from ancestors of a darker hue?

Mark Lower in his 1875 edition of *English Surnames* provides additional background on the M-names that are ubiquitous throughout the British Isles and the Continent:

> Moore, Morris. The former may be, and probably is, derived from the topographical expression, as it appears in *Atmore, Amoor*, &c,. q. d. *at the Moor*. With respect the later name, I may observe that is variously spelt Morys, Moris, Morris, Morice, Morrice, Mawrice, &c., and compounded with various initial expressions, De, Mont, Fitz, Clan, &c. Some of the families bearing this name are of Welsh extraction, Mawrrwyce, being the Welsh form of Mavors (Mars), the god of war, anciently given to various chieftains of that country. One of the Welsh family mottoes has reference to this etymology, 'MARTE et mari faventibus.' The other Morrices are supposed to be of *Moorish* blood; their progenitors having come over from Africa, by way of Spain, into various countries of Western Europe at an early period. It is a well-known fact that the particular species of saltation called the morrice-dance, and several branches of magic lore, were introduced into these regions many centuries since by natives of Morocco. The professors of those arts, enriching themselves by their trade, seem in some instances to

have embraced Christianity and to have become founders of eminent families; certain it is that several magnates bearing the names of Morice, Fitz-morice, and Mont-morice, attended William the Conqueror in his descent upon England, and, acquiring lands, settled in this country. The name Montmorris is said to signify 'from the Moorish mountains.' (1875, 55-56)

The most casual glance at the Moors' heads extant in British family armorials pictured in Fairbairn's *Heraldic Crests*, and at continental crests displayed in J. B. Riestap's *Armorial General Illustre*, may convince the most skeptical that the 'moor' root for surnames is widespread and quite diverse in European heraldry. Some examples from Fairbairn's sample are reproduced below:

Scobie's research is helpful here. He notes several British families whose heraldry includes Moor's head insignias:

Among the latter are the Rt. Hon William Ponsoby Moore, Earl of Drogheda;

Moore of Hancot; Moore of Moore Lodge; the Earl of Annesly; and Morrison-Bell of Otterburn. Then, according to *Burke's Peerage*, the bible of British aristocracy, the coat-of-arms of the Marquess of Londonderry consists of 'a Moor wreathed about the temples, arg. and az., holding in his hand a shield of the last, garnished or charged with the sun in splendor, gold.' Bearers of similar coats-of-arms are the Earl of Newburgh; Viscount Valentia, whose family is related to Annesly and whose arms bear a Moorish prince in armour, and Baron Whitburgh. (1993, 346)

And what of third question posed earlier? Was the Moor's head simply placed on the family crest to symbolize a clan's victory over the Saracen during the last Crusade, or to celebrate the expulsion of the Spanish Moors during the *Reconquista* when some British families secretly aided the Spaniards as mercenaries? Doubtless the Moor's head was occasionally used in this manner by families who did not have a color-based surname. But, strangely enough, the Moor's head was also added on rare occasions when indigenous Moors were defeated in Britain itself. Citing page 238 of *Crawford's Peerage*, Simson in *The History of the Gipsies* provides an example of the latter from the year 1460 :

> In the reign of James II, the Barony of Bombie was again recovered by the McLellans. . . it happened that a company of Saracens or Gipsies, from Ireland, infested the county of Galloway, whereupon the king intimated a proclamation, bearing, that whoever should disperse them, and bring in their captain, dead or alive, should have the Barony of Bombie for his reward. It chanced that a brave young gentleman, the laird of Bombie's son, fortunated to kill the person for which the reward was promised, and he brought his head on the point of his sword to the king, and thereupon he was immediately seized in the Barony of Bombie; and to perpetuate the memory of that brave and remarkable action, *he took for his crest a Moor's head*, and 'Think on' for his motto. (1878, 98-99)

In the late nineteenth century Mac Ritchie, unlike many of his contemporaries, does not try to dismiss the incidence of all of these Moors' heads as mere symbols of trophy heads or visual puns. And the majority of those crests with color-based surnames and Moors' heads provide him with leads to explore the hypothesis that an extensive African and Afro-Moorish presence existed in the British Isles during the Middle Ages. Surnames such as More, Moore, Murray, Morris, Morrow etc., initially were used, Mac Ritchie insists, to indicate the existence of what was called *kaulo rat* or 'black blood' of the Romani brand of Gypsy, as noted in the last chapter. He loosely associates these Romani with the swarthy Moors, Picts and Silures, whom, he also insists, arrived in Scotland primarily on the eve of the pre-Christian era (1991, II, 350).

And surnames such as Dow, Douglass, Donn, Glasgow etc. were, Mac Ritchie argues, derived from either the Gaelic *dubh* for 'black' or *glas* meaning 'black' or 'green.' Proposing that traces of the black ancestry of many Britons are evidenced by scores of surnames, Mac Ritchie discusses several British, color-based variants. Some, he argues, refer to complexion either directly or indirectly. He cites the Ruari clan, and the Dougal clan [originally *Dubgaill*, or 'black strangers']. The color-based term *dubh*, he argues, transmutes into surnames which include Duff, Dow, Macduff and more. He also cites more color-based names such as the Donns, Carrs, and Dargs, to say nothing of the Dunns, Browns, Grays, Blacks, and others. The surname Douglas can be derived from *Dubh-glass*, which literally means "Black-Swarthy, according to Mac Ritchie. More color-based names include Murray, Moore, More etc., he goes on (1991, I, 162-63).[3]

Mac Ritchie provides still more surnames which he identifies with marauding gypsy clans of the Scottish Borderlands who referred to themselves as Egyptians (1991, II, 188-89). These surnames include: Gordon, Lindsay, Ruthven, Montgomery, Shaw, Irving, Heron, Fenwich, Allan, Rutherford, Young, Baillie, Fetherstone, Simson, Arington, Kennedy, Stirling, Keith, Wilson, Tait, Graham, Jamieson, Geddes, Robertson, Anderson, Fleckie, Ross, Wallace, Wilkie, Marshall, Miller, Halliday and Gavin (1991, II, 188).

Simson, one of Mac Ritchie's main sources, reveals in *The History of the Gipsies* that the swarthy Gypsies often emulated the names and, allegedly, the beds of some of the noble families, leading to the assumption of the surnames of noble families by Gypsies. These include: Stewart, Gordon, Douglas, Graham, Ruthven, Hamilton, Drummond, Kennedy, Cunningham, Montgomery, Kerr, Campbell, Maxwell, Johnstone, Ogilvie, McDonald, Robertson, Grant, Baillie, Shaw, Burnet, Brown, Keith etc. (1878, 117).

Although many of these surnames were taken by Gypsies from noble Scottish families, others such as Baillie [originally, Bailyow] and Faa [originally Faw] were likely at one time exclusively gypsy self-namings, Simson continues (1878, 117). Documentation for the observation that so-called noble Scottish families were cohabiting with Gypsies on the sly is provided in an amusing anecdote which Simson relates:

> King James V, as he was traveling through part of his dominions, disguised under the character of Gaberlunzieman, or Guid-man of Ballangeigh, prosecuting, as was his custom, his low and vague amours, fell in with a

band of Gipsies, in the midst of their carousals, in a cave, near Wemyss, in Fifeshire. His majesty heartily joined in their revels, but it was not long before a scuffle ensued, wherein the king was very roughly handled, being in danger of his life. (1878, 104-105)

In a footnote, Simson further states that the Gypsies protested that "the King attempted to take liberties with one of their women; and that one of the male Gipsies 'came crack over his head with a bottle'" (1878, 105). Because of this and other indignities visited upon the King, he shortly issued an order in a session of his Privy Council demanding that "if three Gipsies were found together, one of the three was instantly to be seized, and forthwith hanged or shot, by any one of his majesty's subjects that chose to put the order in execution" (1878, 105).

But to continue with this study's examination of the M-word, not only was the Anglo-Saxon *mor* often confused with its darker homonym, but also the O.E. *blac* which meant 'bright,' 'white,' 'pale' was confused with the O.E. *blaec* for 'black.' Ironically, George F. Black, author of *The Surnames of Scotland,* quotes Harrison on the matter:

> 'A great difficulty with the Black names,' says Harrision, 'is the impossibility in many cases of deciding whether the etymon is the O.E. *blaec, blac,* 'black,' or the O.E. *blac* [accented], 'bright,' 'white,' 'pale.' Normally *blaec, blac,* yields 'black,' and 'blac' [accented] should give 'blake' (or 'bloke'); but the forms are inextricably confused, and the present spelling is often no guide to the pronunciation past or present.' (1962, 78)[4]

One cannot help but wonder why the surnames Mor and Black seem so hopelessly mired in ambiguity. Mr. Black, however, appears to let the black cat out of the bag when he reveals that:

> in early Scots Latin character the name [Black] is rendered *Niger*. Hugh Niger appears as a charter witness in Angus in 1217 . . ., and Radulfus Niger, deacon of Lothian, was a charter witness in Fife between 1200-1210. . . . Robertus Niger, burgess of Elgin, witnessed a composition between Simon, bishop of Moray and Freskyn de Moravia, lord of Duffus, in 1248 . . . (1962, 78).

Black also notes that the Black surname appears as Mac Gille dhuibh, or 'son of the black lad,' which is Anglicized to Macilduy and Macildowie (1962, 78). Attempts, often approaching high comedy, to shuffle these etymologies have been quite virulent in the British Isles.

After stating his case that the Moor was clearly defined as a black person in the British Isles from the time of Caesar to well after the Shakespearean era, Mac Ritchie argues that etymology is a necessary key to unlock the ancestral and ethnic origins of various families in the British Isles. He notes that in Scotland, the Gaelic for Negro is *duine dubh*, or black man, while in Ireland the term is *duine gorm*. The term *gor,* or *gwrm*, denotes a brown person in Wales, he goes on (1991, I, 47).

Edwards takes exception to Mac Ritchie's translation of these terms. Edwards notes in his review of Don Luke's article "African Presence in the Early History of the British Isles and Scandinavia" that "in the older language of the Gauls, 'black' (*dubh*) was not used of Africans, who were called 'blue men' (*fir gorma*)" (1987, 405). But this distinction does not logically apply to Mac Ritchie's exegesis, for quite naturally the ultimate African origin of native-born sons living in the various pockets of the British Isles which contained dark-skinned populations would no longer have been at issue. If many had Iberian, Italian, French, Scottish, or Irish ancestry mixed in with their African derivation, who would have bothered to call them *fir gorma* after one or more generations had been birthed on northern soil? Suffice it say that otherwise rational commentators like Edwards often tend to lose objectivity when confronted with evidence such as Mac Ritchie presents.

Fully aware that his hypotheses would not be tremendously popular with many of his readers, Mac Ritchie takes pains to anticipate the howls of his critics. For he proposes that the conventions of Moorish Heraldry, sometimes imitated in the form of the Moors' heads found in the family crests of Britons whose family members aided the Spanish in the *Reconquista*, cannot explain all of the Moors' heads found in the family crests of the British Isles. For many of these heads do not "suggest Granada," but appear to represent indigenous black Britons and ancient ones at that (1991, I, 54-55).

Mac Ritchie argues, then, that the dark-skinned Moors' heads on the crests of the more ancient British families represent dark-skinned inhabitants of Northern Europe and Scotland, some likely the scions of ancient British families; and others, the members of the so-called *Heathenesse* who predated the Moorish conquest of Spain, and who may have been vanquished by the Scots much as the Andalusian Moors were later vanquished by the Spanish (1991, I, 55).

In a further effort to disarm his critics, Mac Ritchie admits that it would have been possible for an individual to bear one these surnames and not to have been directly related to the dark scion of the respective clan. For it was a common practice in Scotland to name children fathered on Scottish plantations after the name of the landowner and not the true father. And in imitation of the Scottish and Irish practice, this kind of ambiguous naming was repeated in America.

Mac Ritchie does, however, concede that it would be an error to assume that all Moors' heads in the heraldry of the British Isles denote the scions of various families, for some, indeed, were depictions of trophy heads used to celebrate the defeat of Saracens and Moors, but that does not rule out a certain affinity and sense of admiration (1991, II, 403-404).

Rogers reinforces this affinity: "Proud white knights thought Negroes such worthy foes they placed them in their family crests, and welcomed those who became Christians as allies and social equals" (1980, 60).

Edwards, otherwise astute in his observations regarding an African presence in the early British Isles, appears not to have examined this passage very carefully when he devalues Mac Ritchie as a credible source. In his mixed review of the 1985 publication *Journal of African Civilizations: The African Presence in Early Europe*, Edwards cautions:

> What is not considered is the use of the Moor's head as a rebus, or punning symbol, in Scotland, on the crests of those called, or related to, people with the name of Moor or Muir, which originates clearly enough in 'moor(land)' or the Gaelic *mor* ('big'). The Campbell clan (Campbell is literally 'wry-mouth') often display a camel on their crests, but one would hardly wish to seek a North African connection for this reason. Further, the Moorish connection is not something to be dismissed, but the presence of the Moor's head on a crest can be explained for different reasons, since Algerine pirates were certainly, from the late sixteenth century, and possibly from the mid fifteenth, attacking northern Europe-- the English Channel, the south coast of Ireland, and the Westmann Islands of Iceland all in the late 1620s to 1630s. (1987, 402)

In light of Mac Ritchie's qualifying statement, Edward's caution seems largely unjustified, for Mac Ritchie expresses a similar reservation. Also, the etymology of *mor* may not only stem from the Indo-European root, but from an Egyptian one as well. In *Black Athena*, Bernal translates the Egyptian *Mr wr* as 'Great Lake' or 'Great Channel' (1991, 119).

In yet another effort to dispel criticism, Mac Ritchie attacks a counter argument which suggests that the appellation 'the black' was cited in early records to indicate not skin color but hair color. Mac Ritchie will not hear of it, asserting that: "dubh means black; without any word of hair . . . . There can be no question about it." For, he goes on, one race categorizes another race not by hair color, but by the color of that race's skin (1991, I, 114).

Mac Ritchie locates more evidence to fend off his critics when he consults the legal records of various hangings of Borderers or so-called Egyptians. One very telling record is dated 8 August 1592. It describes the hanging at Durham of various Egyptians named Simson, Featherstone, Fenwicke, and Lanckaster (*Blackwood's Magazine,* Sept. 1817).

The Acts of the Privy Council records are illuminating to Mac Ritchie as well. He notes that in the Ordinance of 1603, the Privy Council demanded that the "whole race" exit the realm and not return on the penalty of death (1991, I, 252). This race is the so-called gypsy race, noted in the previous chapter, consisting largely of vagabond, defrocked priests, fortune tellers, tinkers, jugglers, sturdy beggars and the like, some of whom were displaced from their previous standings as landed gentry, clergy, minstrels and yeomen farmers by the harsh Tudor laws which dissolved the monasteries and confiscated various properties in the Borderlands of Scotland. In fact, these Borderlands were also known as the disputed territories. These included Northumbria, Annandale, Galloway and Tweeddale. In a heated exchange in the parish of Inch, inhabited by, among others, swarthy Kennedy and Douglas clans, the following exchange between a dark minstrel Walter Kennedy and a Mr. Dunbar is recorded by gypsiologist Simson and serialized in *Blackwood's Magazine* in the early nineteenth century. Mac Ritchie's cites the passage in which Dunbar baits Kennedy:

'Thy skolderit [scortched] skin, hued like ane saffron bag;' 'blackenit is thy blee' ['your complexion is black']; 'blae [blackish], 'barefoot bairn;' 'loun-like Mahoun' [i. e. 'Saracen']; 'Fy! fiendly front!' ['the devil-like visage'] . . . (1991, II, 191-92

Regarding this exchange, Mac Ritchie argues that these slurs indicate that this Irish thief was a Gypsy, descended from a ninth-century Scoto-Egyptian Kennedy (1991, II, 192).

George Mackey of Edinburgh, who raised eyebrows at the turn of the century for comparing the facial type of certain Berbers to the "black Celt" of Scotland, published an article in the *Caledonian Medical Journal* in 1908 entitled "Celtic Tribes in Morocco." In it he proposes, as W. P. Boswell does decades later, that other clan names may be derived from North African Berber titles. Bob Quinn paraphrases Mackey, noting that the more prominent Berber names such as M'Tir, M'Tuga and M'Hill are near matches for Irish clan names such as MacTier, MacDougall and MacGhill. Quinn goes on to note that "The Arabs speak of them as the Bini M'Tir, but the Bini which is Arabic for children is a reduplication of the Sholoh or Gaelic 'M' or 'Mac,' having the same meaning" (1986, 80).

Again, there is no reason to assume that all the Berbers who supplied such names were dark-skinned. Some doubtless were, but many were also at least partially descended from Africans, a proposition which this study is trying to explore, the likelihood of an African and Near Eastern presence in its full pigmentation spectrum in the British Isles. As noted in previous chapters, several nineteenth-century historians other than Mac Ritchie, notably Godfrey Higgins in *Anacalypsis* and *Celtic Druids*, Gerald Massey in *A Book of the Beginnings*, Charles Squire in *Celtic Myth and Legend*, George Gomme in *Folklore as an Historic Science*, and John Rhys in *Celtic Folklore*, call attention to a sizeable African population in the British Isles existing since the Neolithic Age, but Mac Ritchie surpasses them all when he proposes, citing Skene's *Celtic Scotland* as his source, that roughly one-third of transmarine Scotland, including the Hebrides and the Isle of Skye, was inhabited by swarthy clans that often traded with their fairer neighbors prior to the fifteenth century (1991, II, 107).

Mac Ritchie makes the case that before the various gypsy expulsions from the British Isles, the black population was more sizeable than other ethnologists of his day seemed to think. He cites the invading 'black heathen,' or *nigrae gentes*, the *dubh galls*, mentioned earlier, who allegedly swarmed into Scotland when Charles the Great was fighting the Saracens. Arguing that one district of Scotland was invaded by Moors in the fifteenth century, he goes on to note that the Moorish Kings of Alban had done much the same five hundred years earlier. The most illustrious of these kings, he proposes, was Kenneth, also known as Niger, or Dubh. These kings of Alban lorded over "the three black divisions," of Scotland, he argues. But they were preceded by another wave of swarthy inhabitants, called by the Romans "nec falso nomine Pictos," also cited earlier in this study (1991, I, 172-73).

In an attempt to better understand these alleged invaders, Mac Ritchie devotes considerable space to the genealogy of several Scottish surnames. He argues that many of these surnames stem from old Moorish clans. For the most part, these clans appear to have been of Egyptian and North African ancestry, and various members apparently migrated to the British Isles by way of Spain and Ireland. And if his reader cares to object that the Egyptians from whom many invaders claimed descent were not, in the main, black, Mac Ritchie consults the eminent T. H. Huxley, who asserts that:

> although the Egyptian has been much modified by civilization and probably by admixture, he still retains the dark skin, the black, silky, wavy hair, the long skull, the fleshy lips, and broadish alae of the nose which we know distinguished his remote ancestors, and which cause both him and them to approach the Australian and the 'Dasyu' more clearly than they do any other

form of mankind. (1991, I, 6)

In the mid-twentieth century, Cheikh Anta Diop provides additional evidence which indicates that Mac Ritchie was likely on the right track. He notes that the Paleolithic industry existed in the Nile Valley, and that blacks inhabited the Valley from the dawn of humanity until 1300 B.C.E., when Caucasians entered the area under the title of the Peoples of the Sea during the nineteenth Dynasty (1991, 17). Diop cites a genetic table of the races found in the tomb of Ramesses III dating from the twelfth century B.C.E. in which the Egyptian is depicted as a Nubian. He goes on to record the reaction of German scholar Karl Lepsius upon viewing that table: "Where we expected to see an Egyptian, we are presented with an authentic Negro" (1991, 17, 58).

Yet for Mac Ritchie not all the alleged dark-skinned inhabitants of Scotland were of African origin. Some clans, he argues were not Moors at all, but rather swarthy Mongolian descendants of Attila's marauding bands that lingered in Europe and especially in Denmark long after Attila's death in 454 C.E. (1991, II, 406ff.).

By examining various descriptions of a representative sample of the swarthy Scottish clans which Mac Ritchie and later ethnologists focus upon, a fuller understanding of the early history and ethnic diversity of Scotland may be had. Mac Ritchie's observations, coupled with more recent information regarding the genealogy of these clans: The MacAlpins, the Kennedys, the Macduffs, the Douglases, the Campbells, the MacLeods, the Duncans, and the MacRaes, are particularly telling.

The MacAlpins:

The setting is the area surrounding the Firth of Forth in the mid-ninth century C.E. Elizabeth Sutherland quotes *The Scottish Chronicle* in her study *In Search of the Picts* to reveal: "Kenneth, son of Alpin, therefore the first of the Scots, ruled this Pictavia happily for 16 years. Now Pictavia has its name from the Picts, whom Kenneth destroyed" (1994, 236). These Picts, who persistently refused to submit to Christian ways, Sutherland argues, appear to have lived north of the Mouth in the Pictish kingdom called Fidech, which ecompassed Moray and sections of Inverness-shire and Ross (1994, 240-41). Regarding the identity of Alpin himself, Sutherland speculates that although the *Annals of Ulster* do not refer to him, he may have been the only royal Pict left alive to assume the kingship of Dal Riada in 839 C.E., given that large numbers of Pictish and Scottish royals had been slain by the Norsemen. It is known, she goes on, that his son was named Kenneth, who became king of the Scots in 840 C.E. (1994, 237). Skene in *Celtic Scotland* argues that the name Alpin indicates that although the progenitor's father was a lowland Scot, the progenitor of the MacAlpin clan, because of the Pictish law of tanistry, descended maternally from the Picts. As a result, he had a claim the throne of Scone (1886, I, 314ff.).

Drawing upon Skene's observations, Mac Ritchie notes that this clan is very ancient, and he traces its origins to the Siol Alpin, whom he characterizes as former members of the race of Albanach. The scion of this race, he argues, likely stemmed from Kenneth mac Alpin's father, who was the Pictish king from 844-860 C.E. The elder Kenneth, Mac Ritchie proposes, was probably a half-breed Scoto-Pict by a Pictish princess. And his right to the throne, then, would have been derived from his relation to her, according to the martrifocal system of the Picts (1991, I, 81-82).

Mac Ritchie also proposes that numerous descendants of this clan, the Macduffs, Macbeths and the Duncans, would later be called "'blueskins' or "mumpers," [half-breeds] when they devolved into wandering gypsy status during the Tudor period and beyond (1991, I, 82).

Sueno's Stone is a commemorative cross slab dating from the ninth or tenth century. Currently, it rests, encased in glass, at Forres, Moray, and likely pictures Kenneth. But the stone is so eroded that the ethnicity of the leader depicted and that of the decapitated Picts etched beside him cannot be determined with any certainty.

And although Kenneth was likely a half-breed Pict, he, nonetheless, began the dissolution of Pictish hegemony, a bloody process that continued for several generations.

The Kennedys:

There were several prominent Kennedys who made imprints on the history of medieval Scotland. Of the origins of the Kennedy clan, Mac Ritchie, citing Skene again, names the progenitor as Alpin's son, Kynadius, Kinat, or Cinaed. Kynadius, he notes, was the first Scottish king to acquire hegemony over all of the Scottish lands. According to the *Chronicle of Huntington*, Mac Ritchie goes on, the forces of swarthy Kenneth savagely attacked the dark Picts in 844 to secure this hegemony, for these dark-skinned adversaries were often at each others throats (1991, II, 88-89).

Mac Ritchie attempts to explore this genealogical trail of the Kennedy clan into a murkier past. Using Skene and Anderson's *Scottish Nation* for source material, Mac Ritchie traces the Kennedy name to the MacDuff clan.

As a result, he goes on: "The Clan of Kennedy, the son of Alpin, of the stock of swarthy Conally and Tawny Eochaid, were thus the kings of Carrick a thousand years ago" (1991, II, 89). And, coincidentally, the son and successor of this King was one John Kennedy, who slaughtered Gilbert Kennedy of Bargany, [from] a rival clan of the Kings of Carrick (1991, II, 90).

And in the years 971-995 C.E. another descendant of the Kennedy clan emerged. Mac Ritchie again paraphrases Skene:

> Scoto-Pictish Scotland . . . was once partitioned off into various provinces. According to one account, Transmarine Scotland, or Scotland north of the Scythian Valley (the basin of the modern River Forth), was divided into seven provinces, each of which was made up of two districts. These had their respective kings and subkings. So lately as the tenth century three of these provinces were wholly 'black'; and the supreme ruler of these became, for a time, the paramount king of Transmarine Scotland: being known to history as Kenneth, Cin-aed, Kennedy, Niger, Dubh, or The Black, 'of the three black divisions.' (1991, II, 107)

Mac Ritchie goes on to propose that the earlier ancestors of the Kennedy clan were some of the most virulent opponents of the Roman march through Britain (1991, I, 173).

By the time of the Tudors, according to Mac Ritchie's reading of Simson's *History of the Gipsies*, much of the Kennedy remnant joined the ranks of the Tweeddale Gypsies, among which were the Baillies and the Ruthvens. Sadly fallen from their former glory, he goes on, all of these clans lived from hand to mouth in the gypsy Borderlands, namely in the black quarter located in the in the Parish of Inch (1991, II, 191).

The Douglases:

Given that the Douglases are said to comprise one of the ancestral lines of Britain's current royal family, an analysis of that clan's origins is a relevant task, to say the least.

Scobie cites J. A. Ringrose's candidate for the progenitor of the Douglas clan:

> About the year 770 in the reign of Salvathius, King of the Scots, Donald Bane of the Western Isles having invaded Scotland and routed the royal army, a man of rank and figure came seasonably with his followers to the King's assistance. He renewed the battle and obtained a complete victory over the invader. The King being anxious to see the man who had done him

such signal service, he was pointed out to him by his color, or complexion in Gaelic language– *sholto-du-glas*-- 'behold the black or swarthy colored man' from which he obtained the name Sholto the Douglas. (1972, 345)

Using Skene's *Celtic Scotland* and Buchanan's *History of Scotland* for his principal sources, Mac Ritchie argues that the Douglases preceded the Normans, who themselves arrived in Scotland well after William the Conqueror. He notes that the clan of black Douglases of Liddesdale controlled their clan until 1455. Then, after a interfamilial war, the Douglases were overthrown, and a competing branch called the Angus, a surname and title dealt with earlier in this study, took control of their estates. Hence the following saying resulted: "The *red* Douglas had put down the *black*" (1991, I, 204).

Literature preserves the memory of an early member of the Douglas clan in the name of Shakespeare's Douglas in *MacBeth*. And reasoning that *Dubh-glas* signifies 'the black swarthy man,' Mac Ritchie cites a tradition that tells of a battle between the victorious scion of the Douglas clan and the eighth century Norseman Donald the White, fully six-hundred years before Sir James Douglas fought at Bannockburn (1991, I, 206).

Mac Ritchie notes that this descendant, Sir James, who was called The Black Douglas, was reputed to be the most loyal of Robert Bruce's knights, supporting Bruce's fight for Scottish independence. Also noting that the Bruces, the Wallaces, the Stewarts and others who led the cause of Scottish independence were not Scots, but Norman and Flemish late-comers who enlisted the aid of much of the indigenous population, MacRitchie sheds further light on Sir James, noting that he stemmed from a race that was denoted by a surname meaning 'the black man,' and that, according to Godscroft, Sir James retained "a black and swart complexion" (1991, I, 203).

Although Sir James Douglas fought and died battling the Saracens in Spain, ironically enough, he was himself part Moor, Mac Ritchie adds (1991, I, 203). Then too, Sir James' grandson, who was also known as the Black Douglas, met his death at Stirling in 1452 at the hands of King James II' forces. Mac Ritchie further reveals that the latter Black Douglas fought James II to determine whether Scotland would be ruled by the Moorish Douglases or by the Stewarts (1991, I, 208).

His clan lost, and after the estates were dismantled, many members of the Douglas clan, along with those who would not swear allegiance to their new masters, were reduced to birthing a host of wandering Gypsies.

Scotland's James II finally all but annihilated the clan of the black

Douglases and passed harsh laws against others of their kind, but he died shortly thereafter. According to Simson's *History of the Gipsies*, James II's immediate successors put the suppression of the gypsy life-style on the back burner for nearly one hundred years, as noted in the previous chapter. Later, James VI of Scotland enacted more laws not only against so-called Egyptians, but also against any gypsy group which included: "Sorners, strolling-minstrels, mountebanks, jugglers, players at fast-and-loose, fortune-tellers, and nomads of every calling" (Mac Ritchie 1991, II, 369).

The Macduffs [the sons of the Black]:

Mac Ritchie traces the Macduff lineage from the tenth century Kenneth, king of Alban, alias Dubh Niger. It is speculative, but this king may have descended from the ninth century Kenneth Mac Alpin mentioned above. Quoting from Anderson's *Scottish Nation*, Mac Ritchie provides more background on this clan: "Sibbalb, in his *History of Fife*, says, 'that as Niger and Rufus were names of families amongst the Romans, from the color and complexion of men, so it seems Duff was, from the swarthy and black color of those of the tribe' or clan of Macduff" (1991, I, 266). Known, according to Simson's *History of the Gipsies*, for practicing polygamy and morris-dancing, the clan degenerated, birthing what has been called the Fifeshire Gypsies or 'Irreconcilables.' They were so named, Mac Ritchie goes on, because many were averse to mixing their blood with that of their white conquerors (1991, I, 266). Like members of the Duncan and Douglas clans, a member of this clan is also immortalized in Shakespeare's *MacBeth*.

Brief mention of the Campbells, Duncans, the MacLeods, and the MacRaes appears last because, as far as Mac Ritchie is concerned, they descended not only from Pictish Moors, but also from a swarthy remnant of Huns which attacked Scotland beginning in 875 C.E. from bases in Denmark and Ireland prior to settling for a time in the Moray region of the Pictish Moors. Describing the battles waged by the Romans under Marius against the Cimbri, an enormous tribe which Mac Ritchie identifies with the Hun remnant, he then cites the *Cambridge Dictionary* of 1693. A passage alludes to a much later Cimbri occupation of Denmark and the Holstein territories, where they were known as *Cimbrica Chersonesus*, meaning the Peninsula of the Cimbri. Another appellation for them was *Dani, iidem qui Cimbri*, or simply Danes, Mac Ritchie reveals (1991, I, 112-13). Mac Ritchie then states a hypothesis: If the Danes, pirates who invaded the British Isles during the eighth century C.E. and beyond, were dark-skinned like the Black Huns, then these eighth-century Danes may be identical to the

Dani or Cimbri (1991, I, 112-113) Finally, he recalls Skene's observation, gleaned from the *Pictish Chronicles,* which reveals that the Danes, who plundered Scotland and Norway much as the Vikings did, were called *Dubghaill,* or 'Dark Strangers,' and were in constant strife with the Norwegians or *Finngaill.* This competition was resolved in an 877 C.E. battle which the Norwegians won (1991, I, 113). Having been driven out of Ireland, the Danes fled to the northern Scottish territory of the Picts and often became identified with them.

Lest their hue be mistaken, Mac Ritchie, using Skene's *The Chronicles of the Picts and the Scots* as his source, argues that these two sets of Danish and Viking invaders were called *Finn Gennti* [White Gentiles], and *Dubh Gennti* [Black Gentiles]. He goes on to note that hair color is never suggested in the contemporary accounts of the incursions of these "black Danars." For proof, he cites a period account by St. Berchan, who calls the white invaders "the Gentiles of pure color," and argues that logically the black Danars would have not been "pure" but black instead (1991, I, 114).[5]

Referring to the *Annals of St. David's* (*Annals Menvenses*) found in Archbishop Baldwin's *Itinerary,* Mac Ritchie offers more evidence to the skeptical. In these *Annals,* a landing of a group of marauding Danes, clearly denoted as black, destroyed several religious sites in South Wales. One extract regarding certain acts of destruction committed by the Danes in 986 reads in Latin: "986. *Godisric filius Harald cum nigris gentibus vastavit Meneviam* [a Welsh town]" (1991, I, 115). Another devastating attack by the Danars dating from 987 is described along with a tribute demanded by the Danes called "The tribute of the blacke armie" (1991, I, 115).

The origins of the Picts seems less of a problem when accounts such as these are consulted. Clearly, Mac Ritchie's lead should be followed up as new archeological and linguistic data becomes available for corroboration. For Mac Ritchie, the swarthy Picts of the Scottish Lowlands and Highlands appear to have stemmed from several ethnic branches, the earliest being the migrating Silures of South Wales, followed by several waves of Moorish colonists and pillaging bands of Danars, the latter of which were likely direct and/or mixed descendants of the scattered tribes that earlier had followed Attila.

The Campbells:

In *Celtic Scotland,* Skene indicates that O'Duibhn was a synonym for the Campbell clan of Argyll, and he notes their early presence in Lochow, Ardsheodnich, Dunvegan, Glenelg and the Isle of Lewis (1886, III, 330-31).

He goes on to reveal that both the Campbell and MacLeod clans were supposedly associated with one of Ireland's legendary races: "The first group consists of the Clan *Cailin* or Campbells, and the Clan *Leod* or MacLeods . . . are brought from a mythic personage, viz., Fergus Leith Derg, son of Nemedh, who led a colony of Nemedians from Ireland to Scotland" (1886, III, 339). Despite the aura of myth, Skene takes the association quite seriously, and proposes that the Nemedian descendants, who later populated these two clans, colonized Scotland in the thirteenth century c.e. or earlier (1886, III, 339, 359).

Tracing their lineage to Duncan, son of Gilleseaspic, son of Gillacolum, son of Duibne, Skene notes that Duncan M'Duibhn is mentioned in an early Argyll charter. He speculates that in Gaelic their clan title must have been Clan O'Duibne. He goes on to propose that the clan's progenitor was one Gillespic Campbell, who in a 1263 account was awarded the lands of Mentstry and Sawchop by King Alexander the Third (1886, III, 359).

And when Skene goes on to trace the Irish genealogy, the Mor name also surfaces:

> In one of the Irish genealogies his father Dubgal, son of Duncan, who is termed M'Duine in the charter of David II, appears as 'Dubhgal Cambel *a quo*,' that is, from whom the clan is named, and there seems little doubt that it was a personal epithet analogous to that of Cameron, and that from the family formerly called MacDuibhne he took his later name. His son was Calin Mor, and from him the head of the family bears the name of MacCailin More, commonly corrupted as MacCallum Mor. (1886, III, 359)

As is to be expected, Calin [also spelt Cailein or Callum or even Mac Ailein More] was not forgetful of the ways of the old country. MacPhail cites John Major, who notes in the *History of Greater Britain*: "There is also the island of Argadia, belonging to the Earl of Argadia, which we call Argyle, thirty leagues in length. There the people swear by the hand of Callum More, just as in old times the Egyptians used to swear by the health of the Pharaoh" (1994, II, 5).

Mac Ritchie links the origin of at least one line of the Campbells to a black Dane whose travels included a protracted visit to the Mediterranean island of Rhodes. Observations by his source Pennant, tell of Sir Colin, the famous knight of Rhodes, "surnamed from his complexion and from his travels Duibh na Roimh, or Black Colin of Rome." Pennant goes on to reveal that "in a manuscript history of the Campbells, written about 1827," it is revealed "that Righdeirin dubh Loch Oigh (the Black Knights of Loch Awe) was the name then used by the old Highlanders in mentioning the chiefs of

Duin (Campbells)" (1991, I, 117).

Sir Colin's surname was More, and oddly enough, he married a woman by the same appellation, one Helena More, daughter of Sir John Lamont More, who may have been the son of the Earl of Lennox (McPhail 1994, 90). But this genealogical source even baffles Mac Ritchie, who notes that the Campbells were proud to flaunt their yellow hair. He concludes that another race must have intermarried with them to produce such a radical change in hair color.

The McLeods:

Mac Ritchie links the scion of the McLeod clan to a Danish pirate. The members of that clan, he notes, were referred to by the Scots as *cum nigris gentibus,* or the 'black armie' mentioned above. Referring to M. Martin's visit to the Western Islands a century before, Mac Ritchie argues that the McLeod family is descended from Leod, who was the son of the black prince of Man, an island ruled for a time by the Danes. MacRitchie goes on to observe that Olafr Svarti, or Olave the Swarthy of the *Flateyan Manuscripts,* was Leod's father, and that Olave ruled the Isle of Man in the thirteenth century c.e. (1991, I, 116).

With *Armstrong's Gaelic Dictionary* at his side, Mac Ritchie goes on to propose that Olave the Swarthy, was known as "'the black prince of Man,' one of the race of Danes, *dubh galls, nigrae gentes,* or 'black strangers.' Leod is an Old English word signifying 'prince'; the 'son of Healfdane' was 'Leod Scyldinga,' 'Prince of the Scyldings.' *MacLeod,* therefore, is simply Old English for 'the son of the prince'" (1991, I, 190).

Mac Ritchie notes that at one point in his itinerary in *Journey Through The Hebrides* James Boswell records that a boatmen who reminds Boswell of "wild Indians" on "an American river" rows him within sight of "a MacLeod, a robust, black-haired fellow, half naked, and bareheaded, something between a wild Indian and an English tar" (1991, I, 122-23).

Summarizing the importance of both the Campbells and the MacLeods, Skene reveals that before the breakup of tribes into smaller clans, the ancestors of the Campbells and the MacLeods controlled a large portion of Scotland:

> The two great tribes which possessed the greater part of the Highlands were the *Gallgaidheal* or Gael in the west, who had been under the power of the Norwegians, and the great tribe of the Moravians, or Men of Moray, in the Central and Eastern Highlands. To the former belong all the clans descended of the Lords of the Isles, the Campbells and MacLeods probably

representing the older inhabitants of their respective districts; to the latter belong in the main the clans brought in the old Irish genealogies from the kings of Dal Riada of the tribe of Lorn, among whom the old *Moramaers* of Moray appear. (1886, III, 364-65)

The Duncans:

Skene argues that this clan's scion, Duncan, son of Crinan and grandson of Malcolm, king of Scotia, ruled from 1034-1040. Although Skene links this progenitor of the Duncan clan to a Dane, also called Kali Hundason, King of the Scots, who is possibly the Shakespearean Duncan of *MacBeth* fame, Mac Ritchie is skeptical about the proposed linkage. The *Dun* root of the name probably meant dark, although Mac Ritchie does not drive that point home. Kali's mother is alleged to be Ingibiorg, the wife of a famous Black Dane, Earl Thorfinn of the *Orkneyinga Saga*. Mac Ritchie notes that Thorfinn was the wealthiest of the Earls of Orkney who ruled over nine Scottish earldoms, all of the Sudreys, and controlled an extensive *riki* in Ireland (1991, I, 118).

Mac Ritchie goes on to cite a passage from the *Saga of Saint Olave*, in which Earl Thorfinn is described as follows: "Now Thorfinn became a great chieftain, one of the largest men in point of stature, ugly of aspect, black haired, sharp featured, and somewhat tawny, and most martial looking man . . . . " (1991, I, 117). Using historical records from the *Collectanea de Rebus Albanicus*, Mac Ritchie proposes that many years after Thorfinn's victory over Kali Hundason's army, Ingibiorg married Melkolf, King of Scotland, also called Langhals. Dungad, King of Scotland, was their son, who in turn fathered William the Noble (1991, I, 118).

In a footnote, Mac Ritchie recalls that Skene identifies Kali Hundason with Shakespeare's Duncan, and also proposes that Thorfinn and Macbeth were likely allied, or simply two names for a single person. The latter possibility is intriguing to Mac Ritchie who speculates that "if Thorfinn and Macbeth were one, then the memorable duel in the play was between 'the son of a black' (himself either a 'black' or mulatto) and an ugly, black-haired, sharp-featured, and somewhat tawny giant" (1991, I, 118)![6]

The MacRaes:

The home turf of the MacRaes was the Hebrides, also known as the Islands of the Foreigners. Mac Ritchie claims that this archipelago was the haunt of the *ciuthachs*, the Hebrides Gypsies, whom he describes as black savages. He goes on to reveal that these so-called *ciuthachs* were also known as Danes, or black heathen (1991, I, 273). The MacRaes appear to Mac Ritchie to have been among the aboriginal Black Danes of Scotland who were subjugated by the McClellan clan. Dr. Johnson's encounter with the MacRae clan is recorded in Boswell's *Journal of a Tour of the Hebrides*, as cited by Mac Ritchie:

> 'The MacRaes, as we heard afterward in the Hebrides, were originally an indigent and subordinate clan, and having no farms nor stock, were in great numbers servants to the Maclellans, who, in the war of Charles I, took arms at the call of the heroic Montrose, and were, in one of his battles, almost destroyed. The women that were left at home, being thus deprived of their husbands . . . married their servants, and the MacRaes became a considerable race.' (1991, I, 79-80)

Boswell's description of a fireside gathering, also cited by Mac Ritchie, is germane: "There was a great diversity in the faces of the circle around us; some were as black and wild in their appearance as any American savages whatever. One woman was as comely almost as the figure of Sappho, as we see it painted" (1991, I, 81). This description corresponds to those of other Scottish islanders, based upon the observations of Martin who toured the area in the eighteenth century. In *The Western Islands of Scotland*, Martin describes the inhabitants of Skye as "for the most part black;" the natives of Jura as "generally black in complexion;" and those of Arran as "fair or brown in complexion" (1991, I, 122).

Regarding the inhabitants of the Hebrides and neighboring islands, Mac Ritchie, using as his source an Act of the Scottish Privy Council passed thirteen years after James had been proclaimed monarch, reveals that as late as 1635 the Crown drew a distinction between the so-called islanders and his majesty's subjects (1991, II, 133). Up until the eighteenth century many of the islanders lived in wigwams, virtually indistinguishable from those of American Indians, Mac Ritchie explains, citing Simson's *History of the Gipsies* (1991, I, 310). And he goes on to describe the gypsy look that many a MacRae may have sported in earlier times-- long side-locks studded with knotted ribbons, the gipsy kerchief (*couvre-chief*), and long white dresses with scarlet and gold-embroidered sleeves, each decorated with baubles of gold, silver, coral, and gems (1991, I, 310).

As he ponders the ethnicity of many of these dark clans, Mac Ritchie concludes the matter of the Black Danes, arguing that various short, swarthy Welsh, certain diminutive, black Highlanders, and the so-called Black Celts inhabiting lands west of the Shannon River, all still alive in Mac Ritchie's day, are probably the descendants of the black Danars (1991, I, 125).

What is so baffling about reading Mac Ritchie and his sources is that most of this material has been omitted from modern histories of the British Isles. And if Mac Ritchie and his sources are even occasionally on the mark, the living inhabitants of the British Isles, and those of British, Irish, Welsh and Scottish ancestry throughout the world who wish to construct proper genealogies, will inevitably fall prey to this color-based xenophobia exhibited by so many mainstream historians if they also ignore Mac Ritchie's tome. The more one examines the oldest annals extant on the history of the British Isles, the more valid is the charge that a massive cover-up has occurred. The heraldry issue appears to be only the tip of this iceberg. What lies beneath this metaphorical tip is capable of changing irrevocably the heritage of numerous Britons. The verification of this information, if verification is needed, by other historians and ethnologists, may play a small part in reconciling the races in today's Britain. After all, kinship, both then and now, can be a great bond, even if it is a distant kinship. And if Mac Ritchie and his sources are right, then nearly every modern historian who deals with these aspects of British ethnicity is wrong. The hope is that the historical establishment will have the courage to vigorously test Mac Ritchie's hypotheses. But do not hold your breath.

Notes

1. See Fairbairn (1993) for a collection of these crests featuring blackamoors. Burke (1959, 451) notes that the family crest of the Moore family of Broadway and Little Buckland has three Moors' heads in profile. See Rogers (1980, 76) for Sir Thomas More's family crest.

2. See Fairbairn (1993, plates 182, 185, 188, 191-92, 240-41, 264, 267, 281, 299, 303, 311). A simple content analysis of Fairbairn's sample of crests reveals that there are twenty-three Moors' heads or standing Moors of male or female gender. Many are pictured with crowns. From left to right, the Moor's head labeled #4 is found on the crests related to the following surnames: Coker, Livingstone, Main, Moor, Mordaunt, More, Quaderling, Quadring and St. Lo. The female figure labeled #2 is found on crests associated with Christie, Cookes, Faringham, Farneham, Pannell, Peart and Pert. Number 7 is found on the Den crest, while # 4, a crowned Negress in profile, can be found on the Brocas crest. The Moor's head number 6 is on the Andrew, Bugge and Clerke crests; and figure #4 is found on the Amo crest. Figure 6 is found on the crests of the Dauncourt and Morfyn families. Figure 3, a Moor standing over a serpent, is found on the crests of Caster, Clermont, Danand, Gabell, Galliez, Gellie, Gelly, Mackery and Macery families. And finally, the triple Moors'

heads on # 5 is found on the crests of the Big, Bigg, Bigge, Campbell-Miller-Morrison, Haynes, Mason, Monson, Morison, Morrison, Northleigh, Pearson and Pierson families.

3. Shore (1971, 108-09) cites evidence for the existence of "brown people" who lived in England during the period of the Anglo-Saxon. He refers to the "Brun" place-name and notes other place-names which begin with *dun* or *duning*. He goes on to explain that "Dun is an Old English word denoting a color partaking of brown and black, and where it occurs at the beginning of words in such a combination as Duningland, it is possible that it refers to brown people or their children, rather than to the Anglo-Celtic word *dun*, a hill or fortified place."

4. For more versions of the surname Black, see Shore (1971, 111-12).

5. Shore (1971) agrees with Mac Ritchie on the complexion of the "Black Danes" and proposes that some darker members of the German Wend tribe may have joined forces with the Black Vikings, which are mentioned in the Irish *Annals*. That retinue may have also included Welsh. In Wales, the surname Blacmanne-berghe may be a remnant of those warriors. Others who may have merged with the Black Vikings include ancestors in the coastal region of Kent who left the Blachmenestone surname, and ancestors who left the surname of Blachenmanstone on the coast of Dorset. Shore reveals that "As late as the time of the Domesday Survey we meet with records of people apparently named after their dark complexions. In Buckinghamshire, Blacheman, Suartinus, and others are mentioned; in Sussex, one named Blac; in Suffolk, Blakemannus and Suartingus; and others at Lincoln. The invasion of the coast of the British Isles by Vikings of a dark or black complexion rests on historical evidence which is too circumstantial to admit to doubt. In the Irish *Annals* the Black Vikings are called Dubh-Ghenti, or Black Gentiles . . . . In the year 851 the Black Gentiles come came to Athcliath- i. e. Dublin. In 852 we are told that eight ships of the Finn-Ghenti arrived and fought against the Dubh-Ghenti for three days and that the Dubh-Ghenti were victorious. The Black Vikings appear at this time to have had a settlement in or close to Dublin, and during the ninth century were much in evidence on the Irish coast. In 877 a great battle was fought at Lock-Cuan between them and the Fair Gentiles, in which Albann, Chief of the Black Gentiles, fell. He may well have been a chieftain of the Northern Sorbs of the Meckleburg coast."

6. Rhys (1990, 30-31) identifies Macbeth as a Pict. "So both Macbeth and Maelbeth were real names current both in Ireland and in the land of the northern Picts. On page 30 Rhys goes on to trace the etymology of the Macbeth name to the now familiar dog totem: "I should suggest that the Pictish prince was called in full Mael Macbeth 'the tonsured man son of Beth,' and the name Mael Macbeth was shortened sometimes into Maelbeth and sometimes into Macbeth."

Rhys goes on to argue that "this conjecture accounts satisfactorily for the Norse name, Karl Hundason, where *karl* meaning 'a churl or common man,' just renders *mael* as the Irish for a tonsured man or a servant. If I am right in treating Beth as the equivalent of the dog or hound of the Norse Hunda-son, we may be said to be here on track of an ancient totem of the non-Celtic word retained untranslated; when fully translated in Goidelic they appear, according to the view here advocated, Mac Con and Mael Con, Hound's Son and Hound's Slave, respectively. The latter name, Mael

Con, figures more than once in the background of the history of the northern Picts, for their powerful monarch in the time of St. Columba was Brude Mac Maelcon, called by Baeda, *Bridius filius Meilochon*, who, opposed to Aengus, was conquered by him in the year 752." He continues: "This Mac Con, may perhaps be regarded as one of the mythic ancestors or representatives of the non-Celtic race here in question. Maelbeth who did homage to Cnut must have been no other than the Macbeth who became king of Scotland; for St. Berchan gives Macbeth thirty years of power, which, reckoned backwards from the date of Malcolm's accession on 1058, carry us near the time when a mormaer of Murray died in the year 1029. Then Macbeth may have already been in power, so that Maelbeth who did homage to Cnut may be argued to have been Macbeth."

Conclusion

Without a doubt, this study will appear unorthodox to many. But the layering of evidence from the areas of comparative mythology and religion, and other areas such genealogy, phonetics, syntax, blood typology and craniology-- all indicate that a much more profound African and Near Eastern presence in the British Isles during prehistoric and historic time frames should be conceded. That much of the material included in this study is missing from current history texts points to the need for a sweeping revision of the curricula of history courses on all educational levels. Some revision has already begun, thanks to the efforts of pioneers such as Martin Bernal, Ivan van Sertima and a host of others. But this process has only begun, and considerable progress still needs to be made.

Without such revision, a lopsided view of the past, replete with intended or unintended racistic overtones and Aryan overvaluation, will continue to monopolize much of the intellectual menu examined by future students.

The truth of the matter is that the peoples of the Near East, Ethiopia, Egypt, the Sabaean deserts of Arabia, and North Africa long ago amalgamated with the populations of the what are today called the British Isles and profoundly influenced its culture over an enormous span of time.

This study has attempted to serve as a clearing house for African and Near Eastern influences in the British Isles by including numerous theories posed by scholars past and present. It has also spent some time examining the cometary nature of the religious imagery that was imported to the region, imagery that nested with less explicit Christian iconography. In the sixth and twelfth centuries c.e., the British Isles appears to have experienced horrendous meteor showers. The first, which was catastrophic, likely ended the era of Camelot, and the second less potent display spurred on the Crusades and later the frenetic construction of Gothic cathedrals.

The acknowledgment of the cometary base of much religious iconography has begun to resurface in the popular imagination with the release of blockbuster motion pictures such as *Armageddon* and *Deep Impact*, to name a few. What appears to be transpiring in the waning twentieth century is a remarkable return of the repressed. Whether through the medium of fiction or through serious scholarship, a consciousness of the cometary base of much religious imagery appears to be gaining momentum.

This study recommends that educators, currently looking into the murky future of the twenty-first century, muster the courage to finally set the record straight and rewrite the history books. The African and Near Eastern influences in the British Isles have been significant, to say the least. And the information presented in this study may only be the tip of that iceberg.

Selected Bibliography

Aberg, Nils. 1947. *The Occident and the Orient in the Art of the Seventh Century*, Part III. Stockholm: Wahlstrom & Widstrand.

_____. 1943. *The Occident and the Orient in the Art of the Seventh Century, The British Isles.* Stockholm: Wahlstrom & Widstrand.

Adams, W. Y. 1968. *Nubia: Corridor to Africa.* London: Allen Lane & Unwin; Princeton, Princeton University Press.

Addison, C. G. 1875. *The History of the Knights Templars.* New York.

Adolf, Helen. 1947. "New Light on the Oriental Sources for Wolfram's *Parzival* and other Grail Romances." *PMLA*, 62: 2: 306-324.

Aguirre, Manuel. 1990. "Imram Curaig Mailduin." *Etudes Celtique.* Paris: Editions du Centre de las Recherche Scientifique, xxvii: 203-219.

Akurgal, E. 1968. *The Art of Greece: Its Origins in the Mediterranean and the Near East.* New York: Crown Publishers.

Alcock, L. 1971. *Arthur's Britain.* London: Penguin.

Aldred, C. 1971. *The Jewels of the Pharaoh: Egyptian Jewelry of the Dynastic Period.* London: Thames and Hudson.

Ali, Ahmed, and Ali, Ibrahim. 1993. *The Black Celts: An Ancient African Civilization in Ireland and Britain.* Caerdydd, Wales: Punite Publications.

Anati, Emmanuel. 1968. *Rock Art of Central Arabia.* Philby Rykmans-Lippens Expedition in Arabia, I.

Anderson, A. O., and Anderson, M. O., eds. 1961. *Adomnan's Life of Columba.* Edinburgh: Thomas Nelson & Sons.

Arnold, Thomas and Guillaume, Alfred. 1931. *The Legacy of Islam.* Oxford: Oxford University Press.

Ashe, Geoffrey. 1985. *The Discovery of King Arthur.* New York: Doubleday.

Astopovic, I. S. and Terenteva, A. K. 1968. "Fireball Radiants of the 1rst-15th Centuries." *Physics and Dynamics of Meteors.* Reidel: Dordrecht.

Atil, Esin. 1975. *Art of the Arab World.* Washington, D. C.: Smithsonian Institute.

Atiya, Aziz. 1996. "The Copts and Christian Civilization." [www.ftp://pharos.bu.edu/CN/articles/Copts and Christendom.txt.]

Atkinson, Robert, ed. and trans. 1962. *The Passions and the Homilies from Leabhar Breac.* Dublin: The Academy.

_____. 1956. *Stonehenge.* London: Hamish Hamilton.

Atkinson, W. W. 1908. *Reincarnation and the Law of Karma.* Yogi Publishing Society.

Autran, C. 1920. *Pheniciens.* Paris: Paul Guethner.

Badaway, Alexander. 1978. *The Art of the Christian Egyptians from the Late Antique to the Middle Ages.* Cambridge, Mass. & London: The MIT Press.

Baigent, Michael, and Leigh, Richard. 1989. *The Temple and the Lodge.* New York: Arcade Publishing.

_____, _____, and Lincoln, Henry. 1982. *Holy Blood, Holy Grail.* New York: Dell.

Baillie, M. G. L. 1989. "Hekla 3, Just How Big Was It?" *Endeavour* 13.2: 78-81.

_____, and Munro, M. A. R. 1988. "Irish Tree Rings, Santorini and Volcanic Dust Veils." *Nature*, 332, 345-46.

Bailey, Jim. 1994. *Sailing to Paradise: The Discovery of the Americas by 7000 B. C.* New York: Simon and Schuster.

Balabanova, S., Parshe, F., and Pirsig, W. 1992. "First Identification of Drugs in Egyptian Mummies." *Naturwissenshaften*, 79: 358ff.

Barber, Malcolm. 1994. *The New Knighthood: A History of the Order of the*

Temple. London: Cambridge University Press.

Bates, Oric. 1914. *The Eastern Libyans*. New York: MacMillan.

Bauval, Robert, and Gilbert, Adrian. 1994. *The Orion Mystery*. New York:
Random House.

Bayley, Harold. 1988. *The Lost Language of Symbolism*. Secaucus, New Jersey:
Citadel Press.

Beddoe, John. 1885. *The Races of Britain*. Bristol: J. W. Arrowsmith.

Bellamy, H. 1949. *Moons, Myths and Man*. London: Faber and Faber.

Berard, V. 1894. *De l'origine des Cultes Arcadiens: Essai de Methode en
Mythologie Grecque*. Paris: Bibliotheque des Ecoles Francaises d'Athencs et de
Rome.

Bernal, Martin. 1985. "Black Athena: the African and Levantine Roots of Greece."
Journal of African Civilizations: The African Presence in Early Europe, 66-82.
New Brunswick, N. J.: Transaction Press.

____. 1987. *Black Athena: The Afroasiatic Roots of Classical Civilization*. Vol.
1. New Brunswick: Rutgers University Press.

____. 1991 *Black Athena: The Afroasiatic Roots of Classical Civilization, The
Archeological and Documentary Evidence*, Vol. 2. New Brunswick, N.J.:
Rutgers University Press.

Bernard, J. H., and Atkinson, R.. ed. and trans. 1898. *The Irish Liber Hymnorum*.
Vol. 1. London: Henry Bradshaw Society.

Beeson, C. H. 1913. *Isidor-Studien*. Munich.

Birley, Anthony. 1972. *Septimus Severus: The African Emperor*. Garden City,
NJ: Doubleday.

Bjorkman, Judith K. 1973. *Meteors and Meteorites in the Ancient Near East*.
Tempe, Arizona: Center for Meteorite Studies.

Black, George F. 1962. *The Surnames of Scotland*. New York: The New York
Public Library.

Blakely, Allison. 1986. *Russia and the Negro: Blacks in Russian History and
Thought*. Washington: Howard University Press.

Bonwick, James. 1894. *Irish Druids and Old Irish Religions*. London: Dorset
Press

Boswell, James. 1773, 1936. *Journal of a Tour to the Hebrides*. New York:
Literary Guild.

Boswell, Winthrop Palmer. 1972a. *Irish Wizards in the Woods of Ethiopia*.
Master's thesis, Department of History, San Francisco State University.

Boswell, Winthrop Palmer. 1972b. *The Snake in the Grove*. Master's thesis,
Department of History, San Francisco State University.

Bothwell-Gosse, A. 1912. *The Knights Templar*. London.

Boule, Marcellin and Vallois, Henri. 1957. *Fossil Men*. New York: Dryden Press.

Bourgeois, Alain. n. d. *La Grece Antique Devant La Negritude*. Paris: Presence
Africaine.

Bovill, E. W. 1958. *The Golden Trade of the Moors*. London: Oxford University
Press.

Bowen, E. G. 1972 *Britain and the Western Seaways*. London: Thames and
Hudson.

Brace, C. Loriing, Tracer, David P. et al. 1996. "Clines and Clusters Versus 'Race':
A Test in Ancient Egypt and the Case of a Death on the Nile." *Black Athena
Revisited*. Chapel Hill and London: University of North Carolina Press.

Brace, Richard. 1964. *Morocco, Algeria, Tunisia*. Englewood Cliffs, N. J.:
Prentice-Hall.

Brash, R. R. 1879. *The Ogham Inscribed Monuments of the Gaedil*. London:
George Bell & Sons.

Breasted, J. H. 1906-07, 1962. *Ancient Records of Egypt*. New York: Russell &

Russell.

_____. 1912. *Development of Religion and Thought in Ancient Egypt*. New York: Harper & Row.

_____. 1938, 1929-54. *Early Historical Records of Ramesses III*. Chicago: University of Chicago Press.

Briffault, Robert. 1965. *The Troubadors*. Bloomington: Indiana University Press.

Brill, E. J. (1960-1982) *The Encyclopaedia of Islam*. London: Luzac.

Bromwich, Rachel, ed. 1960. *Welsh Triads, Trioedd Ynys Prydein*. Cardiff, Wales.

Brown, Peter, ed. 1980. *The Book of Kells*. London: Thames and Hudson.

Brown, P. L. 1978. *Comets, Meteorites and Men*. Taplinger Press.

Brunson, James. 1985. "The African Presence in the Ancient Mediterranean Isles and Mainland Greece." *Journal of African Civilizations: The African Presence in Early Europe*, 36-65. New Brunswick, N. J.: Transaction Press.

_____, and Rashidi, Runoko. 1993. "The Moors in Antiquity." *Journal of African Civilizations: Golden Age of the Moor*, 27-79. New Brunswick, N. J.: Transaction Press.

Budge, E. A. Wallis. 1895, 1967. *The Book of the Dead: The Papyrus of Ani*. New York: Dover Publications.

_____. Reprinted 1977. *Egyptian Language*. New York: Dover.

_____. 1904. *The Gods of the Egyptians: Studies in Ancient Egyptian Mythology*, 2 vols. London: Methuen.

_____. 1911. *Osiris and the Egyptian Resurrection*.London: Medici Society.

_____. 1932. *The Queen of Sheba and Her Only Son Menyelek*. Oxford, London: Humphrey Milford.

Bulleid, A., and Gray, H. 1911. *The Glastonbury Lake Village*. 2 vols. Glastonbury Antiquarian Society.

Burke, Bernard. 1959. *Burke's Genealogical and Heraldic History of the Landed Gentry*. London: Burke's Peerage Limited.

Burl, Aubrey. 1979. *Prehistoric Avebury*. New Haven and London: Yale University Press.

_____. 1969. *The Gods of the Egyptians*. 2 vols. London and New York: Dover Publishing.

Camden. 1586. *Britannia*. London.

Campbell, Joseph. 1982. "Peripheries of the Indo-European World." *The Celtic Consciousness*, 3-30. New York: George Braziller.

Camps, G. 1961. *Aux Origines de la Berberie*. Arts et Metier.

Cann, Rebecca L., Stoneking, Mark and Wilson, Allan C. 1987. "Mitochondrial DNA and Human Evolution." *Nature*, 325: 31- 36.

Carew, Jan. 1992. "Moorish Culture-bringers, Bearers of Enlightenment." *Journal of African Civilizations: Golden Age of the Moor*, 248-277. New Brunswick, N. J.: Transaction Press.

Castro, Americo. 1971. *The Spaniards: An Introduction to their History*. Berkeley: University of California Press.

Ceram, C. W. 1972. *Gods, Graves, and Scholars*. New York: Bantam.

Chadwick, Henry. 1969, 1987. *The Early Church*. New York: Penguin.

Chandler, Wayne. 1995. "The Jewel and the Lotus: The Ethiopian Presence in the Indus Valley Civilization." *Journal of African Civilizations: African Presence in Early Asia*, 65-80. New Brunswick, N. J.: Transaction Press.

_____. 1985. "The Moor, Light of Europe's Dark Age." *Journal of African Civilizations: The African Presence in Early Europe*, 143-175. New Brunswick, N. J.: Transaction Press.

Charles-Picard, G. 1967. *Hannibal*. Paris: Hachette.

Chatterjee, B. K. and Kumar, G. D. 1965. "Comparative Study of Racial Analysis of the Human Remains of Indus Valley Civilization." Calcutta: Sol Distributors,

W. Neuman.

Chaytor, H. J. 1923. *The Troubadours and England*. Cambridge: Cambridge University Press.

Childe, G. F. 1926. *The Aryans*. London: Kegan Paul.

Childe, V. Gordon. 1956. *Prehistoric Communities of the British Isles*. London and Edinburgh: W. & R. Chambers.

_____. 1935. *The Prehistory of Scotland*. London: Kegan Paul, Trench, Trubner & Co.

Christie-Murray, David. 1976. *A History of Heresy*. Oxford and New York: Oxford University Press.

Clegg, Legrand. 1985 "The First Invaders." *Journal of African Civilizations: The African Presence in Early Europe*, 23-35. New Brunswick, N. J.: Transaction Press.

Clube, Victor and Napier, Bill. 1982. *The Cosmic Serpent: A Catastrophist View of Earth History*. New York: Universe Books.

_____, _____. (1990) *The Cosmic Winter*. Oxford: Basil Blackwell.

Cohane, J. P. 1973. *The Key*. London: Turnstone Books.

Colum, Patrick. 1967. *A Treasury of Irish Folklore*. New York, Crown.

Collinson, M. E. 1986. "Catastrophic Vegetation Changes." *Nature*, 324: 112.

Condit, Ira J. 1969. *Ficus, The Exotic Species*. Division of Agricultural Studies: University of California Press.

Connery, Donald S. 1968. *The Irish*. New York: Simon and Schuster.

Contenau, G. 1949. *La Civilisation Phenicienne*. Paris: Payot Press.

Coon, Carleton S. 1965. *The Living Races of Man*. New York: Alfred A. Knopf.

_____. 1939. *The Races of Europe*. New York: The Macmillan Company.

Cox, George O. 1974. *African Empires and Civilizations*. New York: African Heritage Studies Publishers.

Cross, T. P., Slover, Cross, C. n. d. *Ancient Irish Tales*. London: George C. Harrap.

Crombie, A., trans. 1869. *The Writings of Origen, "De principiis."*

Crow, John A. 1965. *Spain: The Root and the Flower*. Berkeley & Los Angeles: University of California Press.

Crowfoot. J. F. 1911. *The Island of Meroe*. Vol. I. F. L. Griffith, ed. Archeological Survey of Egypt. London: Egypt Exploration Fund.

Curtis, L. P. 1968. *Anglo-Saxons and Celts*. Berkeley: University of California Press.

Daniel, Glyn. 1985. *The Megalith Builers of Western Europe*. Westport: Greenwood Press.

Daniel, Norman. 1975. *The Arabs and Mediaeval Europe*. London: Longman.

Danaher, Kevin. 1982. "Irish Folk Tradition and the Irish Calendar." *The Celtic Consciousness*, 51-67. New York: Robert Braziller.

Dechend, Hertha von and Santillana, Giorgio de. 1977. *Hamlet's Mill: An Essay Investigating the Origins of Human Knowledge and its Transmission through Myth*. Boston: David R. Goldine.

Diop, Cheikh Anta. 1991. *Civilization or Barbarism, An Authentic Anthropology*. New York: Lawrence Hill Books.

_____. 1974. *The African Origin of Civilization, Myth or Reality?* Westport: Lawrence Hill & Company.

Dirkzwager, Arie. 1983. "Velikovskian Catastrophes in the Revelation of St. John." *Catastrophism and Ancient History*, 5: 25-29.

Doresse, Jean. 1959. *Ethiopia*. London: Eleck Books.

Doumas, C. 1982. "The Minoan Eruption of the Santorini Volcano." *Antiquity*, 48: 110-115.

Driss, A. 1966. *Treasures of the Bardo Museum*. Tunis: STD.

DuBois, W. E. B. 1972. *The World and Africa*. New York: International Publishers.

Dunbar, J. H. 1941. *The Rock Pictures of Lower Nubia*. Cairo.

Dunn, Joseph, trans. 1914. *The Ancient Irish Epic Tale: Tain Bo Cuailinge*. London.

Edwards, I., Gadd, C. J., Hammond, N. G. L., and Sollberger, E., eds. 1970-75. *The Cambridge Ancient History*. Vol. VII. Cambridge: Cambridge University Press.

Edwards, J. E. S. 1947. *The Pyramids of Egypt*. New York: Viking Press.

Edwards, Paul and Walvin, James. 1976. "Africans in Britain, 1500-1800." *The African Diaspora*, 172-189. Cambridge: Harvard University Press.

____. 1982. "The Early African Presence in the British Isles." *Essays on the History of Blacks in Britain*, 9-29. Sydney: Avebury.

____. 1987. "Review of the African Presence in Early Europe." *Research in African Literatures*, 18: 402-405.

Ermann, Adolph. 1883. "Aegyptische Lehnworte im Griechischen." *Beitrage zur Kunde de Indogermanischen Sprachen*, 7: 336-38.

____. 1927. *The Literature of the Ancient Egyptians*, trans. A. M. Blackman. London.

Eschenbach, Wolfram von. 1980. *Parzifal*. A. Hatto, trans. New York: Penguin Books.

Ettinghausen, Richard and James, David. 1978. *Arab Painting*. Edinburgh & London: Charles Skilton Ltd.

Evans, Arthur. 1921. *The Palace of Minos*. Vol II. London: Macmillan and Co.

Evans, J. Gwenogvryn, ed. 1910. *Book of Taliesin*. Llanbedrog.

Fairbairn, James. 1968. *Fairbairn's Crests of the Families of Great Britain and Ireland*. Rutland, Vermont: Charles E. Tuttle Co.

____. 1993. *Heraldic Crests: A Pictoral Archive of 4,424 Designs for Artists and Craftspeople*. New York: Dover.

Finch, Charles S. 1995. "Africa and Palestine in Antiquity." *Journal of African Civilizations: The African Presence in Early Asia*, 117-185. New Brunswick, N. J.: Transaction Press.

____. 1985a. "The Evolution of the Caucasoid." *Journal of African Civilizations: The African Presence in Early Europe*, 17-35. New Brunswick, N. J.: Transaction Press.

____. 1985b. "Race and Evolution in Prehistory." *Journal of African Civilizations: The African Presence in Early Europe*, 257- 312. New Brunswick, N. J.: Transaction Press.

Fiore, Silvestro. 1973. "The Western Adventure of Oriental Man: Echoes of Ancient Near Eastern Legends in Medieval Arabic and Celtic Literature." *Studies in Medieval Culture*, 4, 1: 37-43.

Fitzpatrick, H. M. 1933. *The Trees of Ireland-- Native and Introduced*. Vol. 20, no. 48. Dublin: Royal Dublin Society.

Fleure, Herbert John 1922. *The Peoples of Europe*. London: Oxford University Press.

Fox-Davies, Charles A. 1968. *The Art of Heraldry: An Encyclopedia of Armory*. New York: Benjamin Blom, Inc.

Fox, David Scott. 1983. *Saint George: The Saint with Three Faces*. Windsor Forest, Berkshire: The Kensal Press.

Fraser, Angus. 1995. *The Gypsies*. Oxford, UK, and Cambridge, Mass.: Blackwell.

Fraser, Antonia. 1979. *Royal Charles: Charles II and the Restoration*. New York: Alfred A. Knopf.

Frazer, Sir James. 1940. *The Golden Bough*. New York: MacMillan.

____. 1961. *The Golden Bough, Part IV, Adonis, Attis, Osiris*. New York: St.

Martin's Press.

Freeman, David Noel. 1992 *The Anchor Bible Dictionary.* New York: Doubleday.

Ford, Patrick K. trans. 1977. *The Mabinogi and other Medieval Welsh Tales.* Berkeley, Los Angeles and London: Univeristy of California Press.

Frobenius, Leo. 1913, 1968. *The Voice of Africa.* Vol. II. New York & London: Benjamin Blom.

Gardiner, Alan. 1961. *Egypt of the Pharaohs.* Cambridge: Oxford University Press.

Gaster, Moses. 1905. "The Legend of Merlin. " *Folklore,* 6: 407- 427.

____. 1925-1928. "The Legend of the Grail," 895-98. *Studies and Texts.* Vol. 2. London.

Gelb, I. J. 1952. *A Study of Writing.* Chicago: Chicago University Press.

Gerber, Pat. 1992. *The Search for the Stone of Destiny.* Edinburgh: Canongate Press.

Gildas. 1899. *De Excidio Britanniae.* Hugh Williams, ed. London: Cymmrodorion Society.

Ginzberg, Louis. 1925. *Legends of the Jews.* Philadelphia: JPS.

Glendock's Scots Acts. 1579. James VI.

Glick, Thomas. 1979. *Islamic and Christian Spain in the Early Middle Ages.* Princeton, N. J.: Princeton University Press.

Godwin, Malcolm. 1994. *The Holy Grail, Its Origins, Secrets, & Meaning Revealed.* NewYork: Viking Studio Books.

Goldin, F., trans. 1978. *The Song of Roland.* New York: W. W. Norton.

Gomme, George Lawrence. 1908. *Folklore as an Historical Science.* London: Methuen.

Goodrich, Norma Lorre. 1991-92. *Guinevere.* New York: Harper Collins.

____. 1992. *The Holy Grail.* New York: Harper Collins.

____. 1986. *King Arthur.* New York: Harper & Row.

____. 1987. *Merlin.* New York: Harper & Row.

Graves, Robert. 1960. *The Greek Myths.* New York: Penguin Books.

____. 1966. *The White Goddess.* New York: Farrar, Strauss & Giroux.

Greenberg, J. H. 1963. *The Languages of Africa.* The Hague.

Grimal, Pierre, de. 1965. *Larousse World Mythology.* London: G. P. Putnam's Sons.

Grimes, W. F. 1936. "The Megalithic Monuments of Wales." National Museum of Wales reprint from Proceedings of the Prehistoric Society.

Gsell, Stephane. 1921-29. *Histoire Ancienne de l'Afrique du Nord.* Paris.

Hackett, W. E. R, Dawson, G. W. P., and Dawson, C. J. 1956. "The Pattern of the ABO Blood Group Frequencies in Ireland." *Heredity*, 10: 69-84.

Haddon, A. C. 1929. *The Races of Man and their Distribution.* Cambridge: Cambridge University Press.

Hammond, N. G. L., and Scullard, H. H., eds. 1970. *The Oxford Classical Dictionary.* Oxford: The Clarendon Press.

Hancock, Graham. 1992. *The Sign and the Seal: The Quest for the Lost Ark of the Covenant.* New York: Crown.

____, and Bauval, Robert. 1996. *The Message of the Sphinx: A Quest for the Hidden Legacy of Mankind.* New York: Crown.

Hansberry, William L. 1981. *African and the Africans.* Washington, D. C.: Howard University Press.

Harden, D. B. 1956. *Dark-age Britain.* London: Methuen.

____. 1956. "Glass Vessels Found in Britain and Ireland 400-1000." *Dark Age Britain*, 32-167. London: Methuen.

Hare. 1647. *St. Edward's Ghost: or, Anti-Normanisme. Being a A Patheticall Complaint and Motion in the behalfe of our English Nation against her grand (yet neglected) grievance, Normanisme.*

Harris, J. R. 1938. *Isis and Nephthys in Wiltshire and Elsewhere*. Bristol: St. Stephen's Bristol Press.

Harris, Rendell. 1916-1917. "Origin of the Cult of Aphrodite." *John Ryland's Memorial Library Quarterly Bulletin*, Vol. 3.

Hastings, Margaret. 1961. "The Ancestry of Sir Thomas More." *London Guildhall Miscellany*.

Hawkins, Gerald S. 1973. *Beyond Stonehenge*. London: Harper & Row.

Heylyn, Peter. 1666. *Cosmographic: Four Books Containing the Chronographic Histories of the Whole World*. London.

Hibbert, Christopher. 1968. *Charles I*. New York and Evanston: Harper & Row.

_____. 1993. *Cavaliers and Roundheads: The English Civil War 1642-1649*. New York: Maxwell MacMillan International.

Higgins, Godfrey. 1836. *Anacalypsis: An Inquiry into the Origin of Languages, Nations, andReligions*, Vol I. London: Longman.

_____. 1829. *The Celtic Druids, An Attempt to Show that the Druids Were the Priests of Oriental Colonies who Emigrated from India*. London: Rowland and Hunter.

Hillgarth, J. N. 1985. *Visigothic Spain, Byzantium and the Irish*. London: Variorum Reprints.

Hinde, Thomas, ed. 1985. *The Domesday Book: England's Heritage, Then and Now*. New York: Crown.

Holinshed, Rafael. 1577. *The Chronicles of England, Scotland and Irelande*. London: Bishop, Hunne & Harrison.

_____. 1808, 1965. *Holinshed's Chronicles*. 7 vols. New York: Ams Press, Inc.

Holmes, T. Rice. 1936. *Ancient Britain and the Invasion of Julius Caesar*. London: Oxford University Press.

Holscher, W. 1937. "Libyer und Agyter." *Beitrage zur Ethnologie un Geschichte Libyscher Volkershaften nach Altagyptischen Quellen*. Gluckstadt.

Hooke, Beatrix G. E., and Morant, G. M. 1926. "The Present State of Our Knowledge of British Craniology in Late Prehistoric and Historic Times." *Biometrika*, 28: 99-104.

Houston, Drusilla. 1926. *Wonderful Ethiopians of the Ancient Kushite Empire*. Oklahoma City: Universal Publishing Co.

Howe, Stephen. 1998. *Afrocentrism: Mythical Pasts and Imagined Homes*. London: Verso.

Hughes, Kathleen. 1987. *Church and Society in Ireland, A.D. 400-1200*. London: Variorum Reprints.

_____. 1966. *The Church in Early Irish Society*. Ithaca: Cornell University Press.

Hughes, P. L., and Larkin, J. F. 1969. *Tudor Royal Proclamations*. New Haven: Yale University Press.

Hutchinson, R. W. 1968. *Prehistoric Crete*. London: Penguin Books.

Huxley, T. H. n. d. "Map Showing the Distribution of the Chief Modifications of Mankind." *Journal of the Ethnological Society*. 1: 4.

Irwin, Constance. 1963. *Fair Gods and Stone Faces*. New York: St. Martin's Press.

Ivimy, John. 1974. *The Sphinx and the Megaliths*. London: Abacus.

Jackson, John G. 1995. "Krishna and Buddha of India: Black Gods of Asia." *Journal of African Civilizations: The African Presence in Early Asia*, 107-112. New Brunswick, N. J.: Transaction Press.

_____. 1972. *Man, God, and Civilization*. Secaucus, N J: Citadel Press.

Jackson, K. H. 1970. "The Pictish Language." *The Problem of the Picts*, 129-166. Westport: Conn.: Greenwood Press.

Jairazbhoy, R. A. 1985. "Egyptian Civilization in Colchis on the Black Sea." *Journal of African Civilizations: The African Presence in Early Asia*, 59-64.

New Brunswick, N. J.: Transaction Press.

James, David. 1979. *Celtic and Islamic Art*. Art About Ireland.

James, G. G. M. 1954. *Stolen Legacy, the Greeks Were Not The Authors of Greek Philosophy, But the People of North Africa, Commonly Called the Egyptians*. New York: Philosophical Library.

James, Peter. 1991. *Centuries of Darkness*. London: Jonathan Cape.

Jennet, Sean. 1970. *Connacht*. London: Faber & Faber.

Jocelin of Furnes. 1809. *The Life and Acts of St. Patrick*, trans Edmund L. Swift. Dublin: Hibernia Press.

Johnanson, D. and Maitland, E. 1981. *Lucy: The Beginnings of Human Kind*. New York: Simon & Schuster.

Jones, C. W. 1943. *Bedae Opera de Temporibus*. Cambridge, Mass.

Jones, Gwyn. 1984. *A History of the Vikings*. Oxford: Oxford University Press.

____, and Jones, Thomas, trans. 1968. *Mabinogion*. London.

Jones, R. F. 1953. *The Triumph of the English Language*. Stanford: Stanford University Press.

Jordan, Winthrop. 1969. *White Over Black: American Attitudes Toward The Negro, 1550-1812*. Baltimore: Penguin.

Josephus, Flavius. n. d. *Antiquities of the Jews*, ed. H. Stebbling. Philadelphia and New York.

Joyce, James. 1969. *Finnegans Wake*. New York: Viking.

Joyce, P. W. 1920. *Old Celtic Romances*. London: Longmans, Green & Co.

____. 1903. *A Social History of Ireland*. London: Longmans Green.

Jubainville, H. d'Arbois de. 1900. *Cours de Literature Celtique*. Paris: Libraire Thorin.

____. 1884. *Le Cycle Mythologique Irlandais et la Mytholgie Celtique*. Paris.

Kahanne, Henri and Pietrangeli, A. 1965. *The Krater and the Grail: Hermetic Sources of the 'Parzival.'* Urbana, Illinois.: University of Illinois Press.

Keating, Geoffrey. 1908. *The History of Ireland*. 4 vols. London: David Nutt.

Kelly, Allen O., and Dachile, Frank. 1953. *Target Earth: The Role of Large Meteors in Earth Science*. Carlsbad, California: Target Earth.

Kelley, J. Thomas. 1977. *Thorns on the Tudor Rose: Monks, Rogues, Vagabonds and Sturdy Beggars*. Jackson, Miss.: University Press of Mississippi.

Kenney, James F. 1929. *Sources for the Early History of Ireland*. New York: Columbia University Press.

Kenny, Dorothea. 1987. "Cuchulain-- Comet or Meteor?" *Catastrophism and Ancient History*. 9: 15-24.

Keys, D. 1988 "Cloud of Volcanic Dust Blighted North Britain 3000 Years Ago." *Independent*, 16 August.

Kilson, Martin L., Rotberg, Robert I. eds. 1976. *The African Diaspora: Interpretive Essays*. Cambridge, Mass. and London: Harvard University Press.

Klijn, A. F. J. 1977. *Seth in Jewish, Christian and Gnostic Literature*. Leiden.

Knight, Christopher, and Lomas, Robert. 1997. *The Hiram Key: Pharaohs, Freemasons and the Discovery of the Secret Scrolls of Jesus*. Rockport, Mass.: Element.

Krinos, E. L. 1960. *Principles of Meteorites*. Oxford: Pergamon Press.

Krupp, E. C. 1983. *Echoes of Ancient Skies*. New York: Harper & Row.

Laing, Lloyd and Jennifer. 1992. *Art of the Celts*. London: Thames and Hudson.

Lambert, Malcolm. 1977. *Medieval Heresy: Popular Movements from Bogomil to Hus*. New York: Holmes and Meier.

Lane-Poole, Stanley. 1887. *The Moors in Spain*. London: T. Fisher Unwin.

La Paz, Lincoln. 1969. *Topics in Meteorites: Their Recovery, Use, and Abuse from Paleolithic to Present*. Albuquerque: University of New Mexico Press.

Lasater, Alice E. 1974. *Spain to England: A Comparative Study of Arabic,*

European and English Literature of the Middle Ages. Jackson, Miss.:
University Press of Mississippi.

Lattimore, Richmond, trans. 1970. *The Iliad.* Chicago: Phoenix Books.

Lawson, J. 1955. *European Folk Dance.* London: Pitman.

Lea, Henry Charles. 1968. *The Moriscos of Spain: Their Conversion and
Expulsion.* New York: Burt Franklin.

Leahy, G. D. et al. 1985. "Linking Impacts and Plant Extinctions." *Nature*, 318:
318

Leakey, Richard. 1978. *People of the Lake.* Garden City, N.Y.: Anchor/Doubleday.

Lefkowitz, Mary R. and Rogers, Guy MacLean. 1996. "Ancient History, Modern
Myths: Are Ancient Historians Racist?" *Black Athena Revisited*, 3-23. Chapel
Hill and London: University of North Carolina Press.

Lefkowitz, Mary R. 1996. *Not Out of Africa.* New York: Basic Books.

Lewis, C. S. 1973. *The Allegory of Love: A Study in Medieval Tradition.* London:
Oxford University Press.

Lindsay, Jack. 1974. *The Normans and Their World.* New York: St. Martin's Press.
_____. 1976. *The Troubadours and Their World.* London: Frederick Muller Ltd.

List, Robert. 1984. *Dedalus in Harlem: The Joyce-Ellison Connection.*
Washington, DC: University Press of America.

Loomis, Roger Sherman. 1959. *Arthurian Literature in the Middle Ages.* Oxford:
Clarendon.
_____. 1963, 1970. *The Development of Arthurian Romance.* New York: Harper
& Row.
_____. 1956. *Wales and the Arthurian Legend.* Cardiff, Wales.

Lower, Mark Anthony. 1875. *English Surnames: An Essay on Family
Nomenclature, Historical, Etymological, and Humorous.* London: John Russell
Smith.

Lucas, A., Harris, J. 1926. *Ancient Egyptian Materials and Industries.* London:
Edward Arnold Ltd.

Luke, Don. 1985. "African Presence in the Early History of the British Isles and
Scandinavia." *Journal of African Civilizations: The African Presence in Early
Europe*, 223-243. New Brunswick, N. J.: Transaction Press.

Lynch, John. 1848. *Cambrensis Eversus.* Dublin: Celtic Society.

Macalister, R. 1921. *Ireland in Pre-Celtic Times.* London: Maunsel & Roberts Ltd.
_____. 1931. *Tara.* London: Scribners.
_____. 1919. *Temair Breg: A Study of the Remains of theTraditions of Tara.* Vol.
34. Dublin: Proceedings of the Royal Irish Academy.

Macana, Proinsias. 1970. *Celtic Mythology.* London: Hamlyn.

Mac Dougall. 1982. *Racial Myth in English History, Trojans, Teutons, and
Anglo-Saxons.* Hanover and London: University Press of New England.

McEvedy, Colin. 1982. *The Penguin Atlas of Ancient History.* New York:
Penguin Books.

MacKenzie, D. A. 1927. *Footprints of Early Man.* London & Glasgow: Blackie
& Son, Lmt.

MacKenzie, Norman. 1967. *Secret Societies.* New York: Holt, Rinehart & Winston.

Mack, Maynard et. al. 1985. *The Norton Anthology of World Masterpieces.* 5th
ed. New York & London, W. W. Norton & Co.

Mac Ritchie, David. 1881, 1992. *Ancient and Modern Britons: A Retrospect.* 2
vols. Baltimore: Black Classic Press.
_____. 1890. *The Testimony of Tradition.* London: Kegan Paul, Trench, Trubner
& Co.

MacManus, Seamus. 1975. *The Story of the Irish Race.* New York: The Devin-
Adair Co.

Macneill, Maire. 1962. *The Festival of Lughnasa.* London: Oxford Press.

MacPhail, J. R. N., ed. 1916, 1994. *Highland Papers*, 4 vols. Edinburgh: Scottish History Society. Bowie, Maryland: Heritage Press.

Magie, David, ed. 1922. *Sciptores Historiae Augustae*. London: Loeb Classical Library.

Mallory, Sir Thomas. 1906-1961. *Le Morte d'Arthur*. Preface John Rhys. London.

Mann, Nicholas R. 1996. *The Isle of Avalon: Sacred Mysteries of the Arthur and Glastonbury Tor*. St. Paul, Minn.: Llewellyn Publications.

Marechal, Jean R. 1959. "Etat Actuel des Analyses Spectrographiques des Objets Protohistoriques en Cuivre et en Bronze." *Revue des Societes de Haut Normandie Prehistoire-Archeologie*. December 1959.

Marsden, Brian. 1982. *Catalog of Cometary Orbits*. Cambridge: Mass.: Minor Planet Center.

Marius, Richard. 1984. *Thomas More: A Biography*. New York: Alfred A. Knopf.

Markale, Jean. 1976, 1993. *The Celts: Uncovering the Mythic and Historic Origins of Western Culture*. Rochester, Vermont: Inner Traditions International.

____. 1994. *King of the Celts*. Rochester, Vermont: Inner Traditions International.

____. 1981, 1995. *Merlin, Priest of Nature*. Rochester, Vermont: Inner Traditions International.

Martin, Ernst, ed. 1872. *Fergus*. Paris: Halle.

Martin, M. 1981. *Description of the Western Islands of Scotland*. London: Mercat.

Mason, Ellsworth, and Ellmann, Richard. 1959. *The Critical Writings of James Joyce*. New York: Viking.

Massey, Gerald. 1995. *A Book of the Beginnings, Egyptian Origines in the British Isles*. 2 vols. Baltimore: Black Classic Press.

____. 1992 *Ancient Egypt The Light of the World, A Work of Reclamation and Restitution In Twelve Books*. 2 vols. Baltimore: Black Classic Press.

Mattingly, H., trans. 1948. *Tacitus on Britain and Germany*. Hammondsworth: Penguin Books.

Mbiti, John. 1969. *African Religions and Philosophy*. New York: Praeger.

Michell, John. 1977. *Secrets of the Stones: The Story of Astroarcheology*. New York: Penguin Books.

Miller, F. J., trans. 1917 Seneca's *Thyestes*.

Moller, G. 1920-1921. "Die Aegypter unf ihre Lybischen Nachbarn." *Zeitschrift fur Ethnologie*.

Monmouth, Geoffrey. 1966. *The History of the Kings of Britain*. Lewis Thorpe, trans. Baltimore: Penguin.

____. 1973. *Vitae Merlini*. Basil Clarke. ed. Cardiff.

Monroe, James T. 1974. *Hispano-Arabic Poetry*. Berkeley: University of California Press.

Montelius, O. 1903. "Die Alteren Kulturperioden im Orient und in Europa," Vol. I. *Die Methode*. Stockholm.

Mooney, H. E. 1961. *A Glossary of Ethiopian Plant Names*. Dublin: Dublin Institute for Advanced Studies.

Morant, G. M. 1925. "A First Study of the Craniology of England and Scotland." *Biometrika*, 18: 56-98.

____. 1925. "A study of Egyptian Craniology from Prehistoric to Roman Times." *Biometika*, 17: 1-15.

More, Sir Thomas. 1529. *A Dyaloge of Syr Thomas More*. London.

Morris Jones, John. 1918. "Taliesin." *Y Cymmrodor*. London.

____. 1899. "Pre-Aryan Syntax in Insular Celtic." Reprinted as Appendix in Rhys, John. 1969. *The Welsh People*. London: Haskell House.

Mourant, A. E. 1983. *Blood Relations, Blood Groups in Anthropology*. London: Oxford University Press.

____, and Watkin, I. Morgan. 1952. "Blood Groups, Anthropology and Language in Wales and the Western Counties." *Heredity*, 6: 12-36.

Munster, Thomas. 1960. *Kreta Hat Andere Sterne*. Munich.

Murtagh, J. 1949. *The Copts*. Le Scribe Egyptian.

Nasr, Seyyed Hossein. 1978. *An Introduction to Islamic Cosmological Doctrines*. Boulder, Colo.: Shambhala.

Niel, Fernand. 1955. *Albigeios et Cathares*. Paris.

Nitze, W. M., and Paris, Gaston, eds. 1971, 1886. *Joseph of Arimathie (Le Roman de L'Histoire dou Graal)*. Biblioteque Nationale. MS 20047

Norwood, Frederick Abbott. 1969. *Stangers and Exiles: A History of Religious Beliefs*. New York: Abington Press.

Nykl, A. R. 1946. *Hispano-Arabic Poetry, and its Relations with the Old Provencal Troubadours*. Baltimore: J. F. Furst Co.

O'Curry, Eugene. 1873. *Manners and Customs of the Ancient Irish*. London: Williams and Norgate.

_____. 1861. *Manuscript Materials of Irish History*. Dublin: James Duffy.

O'Donovan, John, ed. 1860. *Annals of Ireland: Three Fragments*, ed. Donald McFirbis. Dublin.

O'Farrell, Patrick. 1971. *Ireland's English Question*. New York: Shocken Books.

O'Keefe, G., ed. 1913. *Buile Suibne, The Adventures of Suibne Geilt*. London.

Oldenbourg, Zoe. 1961. *Massacre at Montsegur: A History of the Albigensian Crusade*. Peter Green, trans. New York: Pantheon Books.

Oldfather, C. H., trans. 1961. *Diodorus of Sicily*. Cambridge and London: W. Heinemann and Harvard University Press.

O'Rahilly, Cecile, trans. 1967: *The Book of Leinster*. Dublin: Irish Texts Society.

O'Rahilly, Thomas. 1957. *Early Irish History and Mythology*. Dublin: Dublin Institute for Advanced Studies.

Ovid. 43 B.C.- A.D. 17. 1985. *Metamorphoses. The Norton Anthology of World Masterpieces*, Vol I. New York and London: W. W. Norton and Co.

Oxenstierna, Eric. 1965. *The Norsemen*. Greenwich, Conn.: New York Graphic Society Publishers.

Pagels, Elaine. 1981. *The Gnostic Gospels*. New York: Vintage Books.

Pankhurst, Richard. 1965. *Travelers in Ethiopia*. London: Oxford Press.

Partner, Peter. 1990. *The Knights Templars and their Myth*. Rochester, Vermont: Destiny Books.

Pausanias. 1966. *Description of Greece* W. H. S. Jones, trans. London: Heinemann.

Payne, Robert. 1963 *The Splendor of France*. New York: Harper & Row.

Pellegrino, Charles. 1991. *Unearthing Atlantis*. New York: Random House.

Pender, Seamus. 1951. *Analecta Hibernica*. Dublin: Stationery Office.

Petrides, Pierre. 1966. "Sur L'Epigraphie Ethiopienne de Langue Grecque." Addis Ababa: Institute of Ethiopian Studies.

Pettinato, G. 1978. "L'atlante Geografico ne Vicino Oriente Antico Attestate ad Ebla ed ad Abu Salabikh." *Orientalia* 47: 50-73.

Picard, Gilbert Charles. n. d. *Catalogue du Musee Alaoui*. Tunis: Institute des Hautes Etudes.

_____. 1967. *Hannibal*. Paris: Hachette.

Pimienta-Bey, Jose V. 1993. "Moorish Spain: Academic Source and Foundation for the Rise and Success of Western European Universities in the Middle Ages." *Journal of African Civilizations: Golden Age of the Moor*, 182-247. New Brunswick, N. J.: Transaction Press.

Pindar. *Pythian Odes*, X.

Pliny (Gaius Plinius Secundus C.E. 23-79). 1938-62 *Natural History*. Loeb Classic Library, trans. London.

Plutarch. 1970. *De Iside et Osiride.* J. Gwyn Griffiths, trans. Cardiff: University of Wales Press.

Poe, Richard. 1997. *Black Spark, White Fire.* Rocklin, Calif.: Prima Publishing.

Pokorny, J. 1959-69. *Indogermanisches Etymologisches Worterbook.* 2 vols. Bern and Munich: Franke.

Potvin, Charles, ed. 1866-71. *Perceval le Gallois.* Mons.

Powledge, Tabitha M., and Rose Mark. 1996. "The Great DNA Hunt." *Archeology*, September: 37-44.

Preston, William. 1981. "Black History Supplement." *The Glory of the Black Race.* Vincent J. Cornell, trans. (Reproduction of Medieval Arabic text.) Los Angeles: Preston Publishing Co.

Procopius. n .d. *De Bello Vandalico.* H. B. Dewing, trans. Cambridge: Harvard University Press.

Pytheas of Massilia (c. 350 BC) 1952-1959. "Fragments Preserved in Various Greek and Latin Authors, Collected. Mette, H. J., ed. *Pytheas von Massilia.* Berlin: Stichtenoth, D. *Pytheas von Marseille.* Weimar.

Quinn, Bob. 1986. *Atlantean.* London, New York: Quartet Books.

Radford, C. A. 1956. "Imported Pottery Found in Tintangel, Cornwall." *Dark Age Britain,* 59-70. London: Methuen.

Ranelagh, E. L. 1979. *The Past We Share, The Near Eastern Ancestry of Western Folk Literature.* London, Melbourne and New York: Quartet Books.

Rashidi, Runoko. 1985. "Blacks in Early Britain." *The African Presence in Early Europe,* 251-260. New Brunswick, N. J.: Transaction Publishers.

____. 1995. "Africans in Early Asian Civilization: An Overview. " *Journal of African Civilizations: The African Presence in Early Asia,* 21-57. New Brunswick, N. J.: Transaction Publishers.

Rawlinson, Henry, and Rawlinson, George. 1858. *History of Herodotus* Vol. I. London: John Murray.

Redd, Danita R. 1985. "Black Madonnas of Europe: Diffusion of the African Isis." *Journal of African Civilizations: The African Presence in Early Europe,* 106-133. New Brunswick, N. J.: Transaction Publishers.

Read, Jan. 1975. *The Moors in Spain and Portugal.* Totowa, N. J.: Rowan and Littlefield.

Reid, R. W., and Morant, G. M. 1928 "A Study of Short Scottish Cist Crania." *Biometrika,* 20: 379-388.

Renan, Ernest. 1887-95 *Histoire du Peuple d'Israel.* Paris.

Renfrew, Colin. 1973. *Before Civilization: The Radiocarbon Revolution and Prehistoric Europe.* New York: Alfred A. Knopf.

Renouf, P. Le P. 1887 *On Some Religious Texts of the Early Egyptian Period.* 10 vols.

Reynolds, Dana. 1993. "The African Heritage and Ethnohistory of the Moors." *Journal of African Civilizations: Golden Age of the Moor,* 93-150. New Brunswick, N. J.: Transaction Publishers.

Reynolds, E. E. 1965. *The Life and Death of Thomas More.* London: Burns & Oates.

Rietstap, J. B. 1884, 1887, 1950. *Riestap's Amorial General Illustre.* Lyon: Sauvegarde Historique.

Rhys, John. 1941. *Celtic Folklore, Welsh and Manx.* Oxford: The Clarenden Press.

____. 1890, 1990. "Traces of a Non-Aryan Element in the Celtic Family." *The Rhind Lectures in Archeology,* 3-38. Facsimile Reprint. Llanerch Enterprises.

____. 1969. *The Welsh People.* London: Haskell House.

Ritchie, Anna. 1993. *Picts, An Introduction to the Life of the Picts and Carved Stones in the Care of Historic Scotland.* Edinburgh: HMSO.

Robinson, John J. 1991. *Dungeon, Fire and Sword: The Knights Templars and the Crusades.* New York: M. Evans and Co.

Rodd, Francis R. 1926. "The Origin of theTuareg. " *The Geographical Journal,* 67: 26-53. London: The Royal Geographical Society.

Rodinson, Maxime. 1967. *Magie, Medecine et Possession a Gondar.* Paris: Mouton et Co.

Rogers, J. A. 1952, 1980. *Nature Knows No Color-Line.* St. Petersburg, Florida: Helga M. Rogers.

____. 1941-1944, 1967. *Sex and Race.* 3 vols. St. Petersburg, Florida: Helga M. Rogers.

____. 1972. *World's Great Men of Color,* 2 vols. New York: MacMillan.

Rolleston, T. W. Reprinted 1995. *Celtic Myths and Legends.* London: Senate.

Runciman, S. 1952-54. *A History of the Crusades.* 4 vols. London: Cambridge.

Rutherford, Ward. 1978. *The Druids and their Heritage.* London & New York: Gordon & Cremomesi.

Sandars, N. K. 1978. *The Peoples of the Sea, Warriors of the Ancient Mediterranean.* London: Thames and Hudson.

Savage, Anne, trans. 1983. *The Anglo-Saxon Chronicles.* New York: Dorset Press.

Schliemann, Henrich. 1967. *Tiryns.* New York: Benjamin Blom.

Scobie, Edward. 1985. "African Women in Early Europe." *Journal of African Civilizations: The African Presence in Early Europe,* 203-222. New Brunswick, N. J.: Transaction Publishers.

____. 1972 *Black Britannia, A History of Blacks in Britain.* Chicago: Johnson Publishing Co.

____. 1993. "The Moors and Portugal's Global Expansion." *Journal of African Civilizations: Golden Age of the Moor,* 331-359. New Brunswick, N. J.: Transaction Publishers.

Selincourt, de, trans. 1954. *Herodotus: The Histories.* London: Penguin.

Sergei, Giuseppe. 1901. *The Mediterranean Race: A Study of the Origin of European Peoples.* London.

Sewar, Desmond. 1979. *Eleanor of Aquitaine.* New York: Times Books.

Shearman, J. F. 1882. *St. Patrick or Loca Patriciana.* Dublin: M. H. Gill.

Sherrat, Andrew , ed. 1980 *The Cambridge Encyclopedia of Archeology.* New York: Crown Publishers, Inc.

Shove, D. Justin. 1950. "Visions in North-west Europe (A.D. 400- 600) and Dated Auroral Displays." *The Journal of the British Archeological Association,* xiii, 42ff.

Simson, Walter. 1878. *History of the Gipsies with Specimens of the Gipsie Language.* New York: James Miller.

Sjoo, Monica, and Mor, Barbara. 1987. *The Great Cosmic Mother.* New York: Harper & Row.

Skeat, W. W., ed. 1865. *Lancelot of the Laik.* London: EETS.

Skene, William F. 1886. *Celtic Scotland: A History of Ancient Alban.* 2 vols. Edinburgh: David Douglas.

Smith, G. Eliot. 1923. *The Ancient Egyptians and the Origin of Civilization.* New York: Harper Brothers.

Snowden, Frank M. 1983. *Before Color Prejudice.* Cambridge: Harvard University Press.

____. 1970. *Blacks in Antiquity, Ethiopians in Greco-Roman Experience.* Cambridge: Harvard University Press.

Sommer, H. O., ed. 1908-1916. *Prose Lancelot. Vulgate Version of the Athurian Romances.* Washington, DC.

Soucek, Priscilla P. 1988. *Content and Context of Visual Arts in the Islamic*

World. London: The Pennsylvania State University Press.

Spanuth, Jurgen. 1979. *Atlantis of the North*. New York: Van Nostrand Reinhold Company.

Squier, G. 1975. *The Serpent Symbol, and the Worship of the Reciprocal Principles of Nature*. New York: George P. Putnam. (Millwood, NY: Kraus Reprint.)

Squire, Charles. 1975 *Celtic Myth and Legend*. Newcastle: New Castle Publishing Co.

____. 1994. *The Mythology of Ancient Britain and Ireland*. New York: Gramercy Publishing Co.

Stephanos, Robert C. 1983. "'As Above, So Below,' Eathquakes, Volcanoes, and Straight-line Phenomena." *Catastrophism and Ancient History*, 5, 1, 31-54.

Stoddard, Lothrop. 1924. *Racial Realities in Europe*. New York: Charles Scribner's Sons.

Stoessiger, Brenda N. 1927. "'A Study of the Badarian Crania Recently Excavated by the British School of Archeology in Egypt." *Biometrika*, 11: 110-149.

Stokes, Whitley, ed. and trans. 1905. *The Martyrology of Oengus the Culdee*. London: Henry Bradshaw Society.

____. 1862. *Three Irish Glossaries*. London: Williams & Norgate.

____. ed. and trans. 1887. *The Tripartite Life of Patrick*. London: Eyre & Spottiswoode.

Sturlusson, Snorri. 1967. *Heimskringla: History of the Kings of Norway*. Trans Lee M. Hollander. Austin: University of Texas Press.

Sutherland, Elizabeth. 1994. *In Search of the Picts: A Celtic Dark Nation*. London: Constable.

Swanwich, Anna. 1890. *The Dramas of Aeschylus*. London: George Bell.

Swire, Otta F. 1966. *The Outer Hebrides and their Legends*. Edinburgh: Oliver & Boyd.

Talbott, Stephen, ed. 1976. *Velikovsky Reconsidered*. New York: Warner Books.

Te Velde, H. 1977. *Seth, God of Confusion*. 3 vols. Leiden: E. J. Brill.

Thomas, C. 1959. "Imported Pottery in Dark-age Western Britain." *Medieval Archeology*. 3: 89-111.

Tierney, J, Wright, L, and Springen, K.. 1988. "The Search for Adam and Eve." *Newsweek*, 11 January.

Todd, J. H., ed. and trans. 1848. *The Irish Version of the Historic Britonum of Nennius*. Dublin: Irish Archeological Society.

____. 1864. *St. Patrick, Apostle of the Irish*. Dublin: Hodges Smith & Co.

Tolstoy, Nikolai. 1985. *The Quest for Merlin*. Boston: Little, Brown & Co.

Tomkins, Peter. 1976. *The Secret of the Mexican Pyramids*. New York: Harper & Row.

Tribbe, Frank C. 1989. "Was Glastonbury a Stepping Stone?" *Glastonbury Treasures*. Santa Barbara, Calif.: Stonehenge Viewpoint.

Tritle, Lawrence A. 1996. "Black Athena: Vision or Dream of Greek Origins." *Black Athena Revisited*, 303-330. Chapel Hill and London: University of North Carolina Press.

Tuckman, Barbara A. 1956, 1983-84. *Bible and Sword*. New York: Ballantine Books.

Turberville, A. S. 1964. *Medieval Heresy & The Inquistion*. London: Archon Books.

Ullendorf, Edward. 1955. *The Semitic Languages of Ethiopia*. London: Taylor's Foreign Press.

Ussiskhin, David. 1982. *The Conquest of Lachish by Sennacheriib*. Tel Aviv:

The Institute of Archeology.

Vallancey, Charles, ed. 1781. *Collectanea de Rebus Hibernicis*. 2 vols. Dublin: Antiquarian Society.

Van Dam, Raymond, trans. 1988. *Gregory of Tours: Glory of the Confessors*. Liverpool: Liverpool University Press.

Van Sertima, Ivan. 1985. "The African Presence in Early Europe, the Definitional Problem." *Journal of African Civilizations: The African Presence in Early Europe*, 134-143. New Brunswick, N. J.: Transaction Publishers.

_____. 1989. "Introduction." *Journal of African Civilizations: Egypt Revisited*, 3-8. New Brunswick, N. J.: Transaction Publishers.

Velikovsky, Immanuel. 1977a. *Peoples of the Sea*. Garden City, New York: Doubleday & Company, Inc.

_____. 1977b. *Worlds in Collision*. New York: Simon & Schuster.

Verstegen. 1673. *A Restitution of Decayed Intelligence in Antiquities Concerning the Most Noble and Renowned English Nation*.

Vesey-Fitzgerald, Brian. 1973. *Gypsies of Britain: An Introduction to their History*. London: David & Charles.

Villaneuve, Joachim de. 1833. *Phoenician Ireland*.

Waddell, L. A. 1924. *The Phoenician Origins of the Britons, Scots and Anglo-Saxons*. London.

Wagner, Heinrich. 1982. "Near Eastern and African Connections with the Celtic World." *The Celtic Consciousness*, 51-67. Robert O'Driscoll, ed. New York: Robert Braziller.

Wainwright, G. A. 1930. "The Relationship of Amun to Zeus and His Connection with Meteorites." *Journal of Egyptian Archeology*, 5. 16: 35-38.

Walsh, John R. and Bradley, Thomas. 1991. *A History of the Irish Church, 400-700 A.D.* Dublin: The Columba Press.

Walvin, James. 1982. *Black and White: The Negro and English Society 1555-1945*. New York: Penguin.

Warmington, B. H. 1960. *Carthage*. New York: Praeger.

_____. 1954. *The North African Provinces from Diocletian to the Vandal Conquest*. Cambridge: Cambridge University Press.

Washington, Joseph R. 1984. *Anti-Blackness in English Religion, 1500-1800*. New York: The Edwin Mellen Press.

Watkin, I. Morgan. 1956. "ABO Blood Groups and Racial Characteristics in Rural Wales." *Heredity*, 10: 161-193.

_____. 1967 "Human Genetics in Worcesterhire and the Shakespeare Country." *Heredity*, 22: 349-358.

Watt, W. M. 1972. *The Influence of Islam on Medieval Europe*. Edinburgh: Edinburgh University Press.

Weigall, Arthur. 1925. *A History of the Pharaohs, The First Eleven Dynasties*. London: Thornton Butterworth.

Weitzmann, Kurt. 1971. *Studies in Classical and Byzantine Manuscipt Illumination*. Chicago: University of Chicago Press.

Wellard, James. 1967. *Lost Worlds of Africa*. New York: Dutton.

West, M. L. 1966. *Hesiod's Theogony*. Oxford: Clarendon Press.

_____. 1983. *The Orphic Poems*. Oxford: Clarendon Press.

Weston, Jessie L., trans. 1901. *Morien*. London: Long Acre.

Wheeler, R. E. 1935. *Prehistoric and Roman Wales*. London: Oxford University Press.

Whiston, William, trans. 1981. *Josephus: Complete Works*. Grand Rapids: Kregel Publications.

Williams, John ab Ithel, ed. 1961, 1979. *Annals of Wales, Annales Cambriae*.

Cardiff: Wales.

Wilthum, W. 1953. *Glacialgeologische Untersuchungen in den Alpen*. Vienna.

Winkler, Louis. 1985a. "An Earth Canopy after Cometary Capture." *Stonehenge Viewpoint*, 65: 37-39. Santa Barbara, Calif.: Donald Cyr.

_____. 1985b. "Astronomical and Meteorological Implications of an Earth Canopy." *Stonehenge Viewpoint*, 64: 3-7. Santa Barbara, Calif.: Donald Cyr.

_____. 1979. "Comets, Almanacs, and the Dead." *Griffith Observer*, V. 43, 8: 2-9.

Winters, C. A. 1981. "African Influence on Indian Agriculture." *Journal of African Civilizations*, 3.

Woo, T. L. 1931. "A Study of Seventy-one Ninth Dynasty Egyptian Skulls from Sedment." *Biometrika*, 21-22: 65-93.

Wunderlich, Hans Georg. 1974. *The Secret of Crete*. New York: Macmillan Publishing Company.

Zimmer, Heinrich. 1948, 1956, 1968. *The King and the Corpse*. Princeton: Bolligen Series XI.

Index

418